B1095.

Canadian Business and Society

ETHICS, RESPONSIBILITIES, & SUSTAINABILITY

Fourth Edition

ROBERT W. SEXTY

Professor Emeritus, Faculty of Business Administration
Memorial University of Newfoundland

Canadian Business and Society

Ethics, Responsibilities, & Sustainability

Fourth Edition

ISBN-13: 978-1-25-908754-7

ISBN-10: 1-25-908754-9

1 2 3 4 5 6 7 8 9 0 TCP 1 9 8 7

Printed and bound in Canada.

Care has been taken to trace ownership of copyright material contained in this text; however, the publisher will welcome any information that enables them to rectify any reference or credit for subsequent editions.

Portfolio and Program Manager: *Karen Fozard*
Group Product Manager: *Kim Brewster*
Senior Marketing Manager: *Cathie Lefebvre*
Product Developer: *Daphne Scriabin*
Senior Product Team Associate: *Stephanie Giles*
Supervising Editor: *Jessica Barnoski*
Photo/Permissions Editor: *Alison Lloyd Baker*
Copy Editor: *Margaret Henderson*
Plant Production Coordinator: *Michelle Saddler*
Manufacturing Production Coordinator: *Sheryl MacAdam*
Cover Design: *Jennifer Stimson*
Cover Image: © *Dennis Flynn*
Interior Design: *Michelle Losier*
Compositor: *MPS Limited*
Page Layout: *SPi Global*
Printer: *Transcontinental Printing Group*

Dedication

To Suzanne, who has travelled with me through five books including many editions—and to more than 60 countries on seven continents!

About the Author

Dr. Robert Sexty was a Professor of Business Administration at the Faculty of Business Administration at Memorial University of Newfoundland for 39 years, and was awarded a *Professor Emeritus* title in 2008. He holds bachelor, masters, and doctoral degrees in Business Administration from the University of Alberta, Queen's University, and the University of Colorado, respectively. Sabbatical years have been spent at the Harvard Business School, Boston, and the University of Auckland, New Zealand. He was awarded one of the "2001–2002 Leaders in Management Education Awards" sponsored by the *National Post* and PricewaterhouseCoopers.

At Memorial, Robert Sexty taught Business Policy (Strategic Management), Introduction to Business, and Business and Society (Business Ethics) courses at the undergraduate and graduate levels. He developed, and has taught, the strategy and business and society courses in Athabasca University's Electronic MBA Program. He has taught numerous management development seminars and workshops on many management topics, including strategic management and the ethics of business.

Robert Sexty is the author of *Issues in Canadian Business*, the fourth edition of which was published in 1998 as *Canadian Business in the New Stakeholder Economy*. He is also the co-author of *Exploring Strategic Management*, published in 1989, and *Contemporary Management in Canada*, published in 1992, 1995, and 1998. A fourth book, *Canadian Business and Society: Understanding the Social and Ethical Challenges*, was published in January 1995.

Robert Sexty is a past President of the Administrative Sciences Association of Canada, and is a member of, and active in, many academic and professional associations. He consults in the area of strategic planning and management for business, government, and non-profit organizations, and acts as a facilitator in sessions for management groups and boards of directors. He has served on the Boards of Directors of the Egg Farmers of Canada, East Coast Trail Association, and Anglican Homes Inc.

Brief Contents

PART I: INTRODUCTION TO BUSINESS AND SOCIETY — 1

CHAPTER 1: *The Relationship between Business and Society* — 1
CHAPTER 2: *Ethics and Capitalism* — 22

PART II: BUSINESS STAKEHOLDERS AND ISSUES — 42

CHAPTER 3: *Identifying Stakeholders and Issues* — 42
CHAPTER 4: *Stakeholder and Issue Analysis* — 64

PART III: ETHICAL AND SOCIAL RESPONSIBILITIES — 86

CHAPTER 5: *Ethics of Business: The Theoretical Basis* — 86
CHAPTER 6: *Ethics of Business: Management and Leadership* — 106
CHAPTER 7: *Corporate Social Responsibility: The Concept* — 129
CHAPTER 8: *Corporate Social Responsibility: In Practice* — 152
CHAPTER 9: *Measuring, Reporting, and Communicating CSR* — 173

PART IV: INFLUENCING CANADIAN BUSINESS — 191

CHAPTER 10: *Regulating Business' Ethics and Responsibilities* — 191
CHAPTER 11: *Responsible Ownership and Governance* — 211
CHAPTER 12: *Ethics and Responsibilities in the Workplace and Marketplace* — 233
CHAPTER 13: *Civil Society Stakeholders* — 257

PART V: THE ENVIRONMENT, GLOBALIZATION, AND CHANGING CAPITALISM — 278

CHAPTER 14: *The Environment and Business Responsibilities* — 278
CHAPTER 15: *Globalization and Business Responsibilities* — 304
CHAPTER 16: *The Socialization of Capitalism* — 325

Ethics, Responsibilities, and Sustainability Cases — 348
Endnotes — EN-1
Glossary — GL-1
Index — IN-1

Contents

Preface xiv

PART I: *Introduction to Business and Society* 1

CHAPTER 1: *The Relationship between Business and Society* 1

1.1 The Complexity of Business and Society 3
1.2 Integrity in Business 4
1.3 Main Approaches to Ethical Thinking 6
1.4 The Canadian Business System 7
1.5 The Corporation and the Business System 9
1.6 Society's Permission for Business 10
1.7 Society's Attitudes toward Business 11
  Factors Influencing Attitudes toward Business 11
  Social Media 13
1.8 The People Who Run Canadian Business 14
  Owners 14
  Boards of Directors 14
  Managers 15
1.9 Business and Academic Integrity 16
1.10 Integration of Business and Society 17

Summary 18
Key Terms 18
Critical Thinking and Discussion Questions 19
Cases 19
  CASE 1.1—The Pillaging of Pensions 19
  CASE 1.2—Detecting Plagiarism and Academic Integrity 20

CHAPTER 2: *Ethics and Capitalism* 22

2.1 Introduction to the Fundamentals of Capitalism 23
2.2 The Right of Private Property 24
  The Fundamental 24
  Ethical Implications 24
2.3 Individualism and Economic Freedom 26
  The Fundamental 26
  Ethical Implications 27
2.4 Equality of Opportunity 27
  The Fundamental 27
  Ethical Implications 27
2.5 Competition 29
  The Fundamental 29
  Ethical Implications 29
2.6 Profits 30
  The Fundamental 30
  Ethical Implications 30

2.7 The Work Ethic — 31
The Fundamental — 31
Ethical Implications — 31
2.8 Consumer Sovereignty — 32
The Fundamental — 32
Ethical Implications — 32
2.9 The Role of Government — 33
The Fundamental — 33
Ethical Implications — 33
2.10 Canadian and Other Forms of Capitalism — 34
2.11 The Ethics of Capitalism — 35
The Challenges — 35
Capitalism as an Ethical System — 37

Summary — 38
Key Terms — 38
Critical Thinking and Discussion Questions — 39
Cases — 39

CASE 2.1—Campus Boycotts: Who Makes the Call? — 39
CASE 2.2—Zapping Sales and Taxes — 40

PART II: *Business Stakeholders and Issues* — 42

CHAPTER 3: *Identifying Stakeholders and Issues* — 42

3.1 The Stakeholder Concept and Business — 43
3.2 Identifying Stakeholders — 44
3.3 The Dynamics of Stakeholder Influence — 51
Categorizing Stakeholders — 52
Differing Goals and Power — 52
3.4 The Manager: A Special Stakeholder — 52
3.5 Arguing the Stakeholder Concept — 54
The Argument Against the Stakeholder Concept — 54
The Argument For the Stakeholder Concept — 54
3.6 Issues Relating to Ethics, Responsibilities, and Sustainability — 55
3.7 Issue Life Cycles — 56
3.8 Crisis Management — 57

Summary — 60
Key Terms — 60
Critical Thinking and Discussion Questions — 61
Cases — 61

CASE 3.1—"Boondocking" at Walmart — 61
CASE 3.2—Accepting a Job in the Payday Loan Industry — 62

CHAPTER 4: *Stakeholder and Issue Analysis* — 64

4.1 Basic Stakeholder Analysis — 65
4.2 Freeman's Stakeholder Management Capability — 66
4.3 Stakeholder Matrix Mapping — 67
4.4 The Diagnostic Typology of Organizational Stakeholders — 70
4.5 Stakeholder Identification and Salience — 72
4.6 Stakeholder Influence Strategies — 75
4.7 Stakeholder Collaboration — 77

4.8 Issue Analysis 79
The Issues Management Process 79
Issue Salience Analysis 81

Summary 82
Key Terms 82
Critical Thinking and Discussion Questions 83
Cases 83

CASE 4.1—CSR and the Closure of a Neighbourhood Supermarket 83
CASE 4.2—The Economics and Ethics of Textbook Pricing 84

PART III: *Ethical and Social Responsibilities* 86

CHAPTER 5: *Ethics of Business: The Theoretical Basis* 86

5.1 Introducing the Ethics of Business 87
5.2 Assessment of Ethical Implications in Business Decisions 88
5.3 Influences on Ethical Behaviour 89
Influences of Individuals 89
Corporate or Organizational Influences 89
Economic Efficiency Influences 90
Government and the Legal System Influences 90
Societal Influences 90
5.4 The Theoretical Basis for Ethical Conduct 92
Self-Interest Ethic (Ethical Egoism) 92
Personal Virtues Ethic 94
Ethic of Caring 95
Utilitarian Ethic 95
Universal Rules Ethic 96
Individual Rights Ethic 96
Ethic of Justice 97
5.5 Moral Reasoning 98
Kohlberg's Stages of Moral Development 100
5.6 Ethics in Business: Some Challenges 101

Summary 103
Key Terms 103
Critical Thinking and Discussion Questions 103
Cases 104

CASE 5.1—Working Overtime 104
CASE 5.2—Ethical Responsibility on Mount Everest 104

CHAPTER 6: *Ethics of Business: Management and Leadership* 106

6.1 Ethical Leadership Forms 107
6.2 Statement of Values 108
6.3 Codes of Conduct and Codes of Ethics 109
Content 112
Criticisms 113
6.4 Ethics Training 113
Checklists and Tests 113
Understanding Conflicts of Interest 114
6.5 Ethics Audits, Managers, and Committees 116
6.6 Ethics Reporting Systems and Whistleblowing 117

6.7 Ethics—Who Is Responsible? 119
Board of Directors Responsibility 119
Management Responsibility 119
6.8 Ethics Programs: Approaches 121
Classification of Programs 121
Compliance-based versus Values-based Programs 121
6.9 Ethics Programs: Evaluation and Benefits 122
6.10 Why Ethical Leadership and Programs Fail 124

Summary 125
Key Terms 126
Critical Thinking and Discussion Questions 126
Cases 127

CASE 6.1—Citizen's Arrest: The Law and Ethics 127
CASE 6.2—Heidi Heise, Sub Samaritan 127

CHAPTER 7: *Corporate Social Responsibility: The Concept* 129

7.1 Describing Corporate Social Responsibility 130
The Importance of Corporate Social Responsibility 131
7.2 The Corporate Social Responsibility Debate 132
The Case for Involvement 132
The Counterargument to the Case for Involvement 134
Critiquing CSR 135
7.3 Social Responsibility Theories 136
The Amoral View 136
The Personal View 137
The Social View 137
7.4 The Pyramid of Corporate Social Responsibility 139
7.5 Contemporary CSR Concepts 141
Corporate Sustainability 141
Reputation Management 142
Social Impact Management 142
Triple Bottom Line (TBL) 143
7.6 Views on Corporate and Business Citizenship 144
The Inappropriate View 145
The Limited, Equivalent, and Extended Views 145
Approach to Corporate Citizenship 146
The Business View 146
7.7 The VBA Model: An Integration of CSR Concepts 147

Summary 149
Key Terms 150
Critical Thinking and Discussion Questions 150
Cases 150

CASE 7.1—Would You Like to Donate ...? 150
CASE 7.2—The TD Grade One Book Giveaway 151

CHAPTER 8: *Corporate Social Responsibility: In Practice* 152

8.1 Responses to Corporate Social Responsibility 153
8.2 Corporate Philanthropy 156
Donations 156
Arguments For and Against Corporate Giving 156

		Making Corporate Giving Decisions	157
		Trends and Concerns in Corporate Giving	158
	8.3	Corporate Voluntarism	160
		Organizations Supported and Forms of Support	160
		Corporate Policies Regarding Voluntarism	161
	8.4	Corporate Sponsorship	162
		Charity or Marketing?	163
	8.5	Social Venture Philanthropy	164
	8.6	Social Enterprise and Social Entrepreneurship	165
	8.7	Small Business and CSR	166
	8.8	The Community Investment Concept	168
	Summary		170
	Key Terms		170
	Critical Thinking and Discussion Questions		171
	Cases		171
		CASE 8.1—Responsible Alcohol Consumption	171
		CASE 8.2—Having to Give at the Office	172

CHAPTER 9: *Measuring, Reporting, and Communicating CSR* — 173

	9.1	Measuring and Reporting CSR	174
	9.2	Corporate Reputation and CSR	176
	9.3	Stakeholders Expect CSR Accountability	177
	9.4	CSR and Profitability	178
	9.5	Social Auditing and Reporting Criteria	179
	9.6	Evaluating Canadian CSR Reporting	181
		Questioning the Rankings and What Makes a Good Report	182
	9.7	Communicating CSR and Sustainability Results	183
	9.8	Business Schools and Sustainability Reporting	184
	9.9	The Future of CSR and Social Reporting	185
	Summary		187
	Key Terms		188
	Critical Thinking and Discussion Questions		188
	Cases		188
		CASE 9.1—Philanthropy and Academic Freedom	188
		CASE 9.2—Ethics of Oil	189

PART IV: *Influencing Canadian Business* — 191

CHAPTER 10: *Regulating Business' Ethics and Responsibilities* — 191

	10.1	Types of Regulation	192
	10.2	Government Regulation of Business	194
	10.3	Government Attempts at Dealing with Corruption	196
	10.4	Government Involvement in Corporate Social Responsibility	198
	10.5	The Ethics of Business and Involvement in Politics	199
	10.6	The Ethics of Business Lobbying	200
	10.7	Ethics and Responsibilities of Taxation	202
		Corporate Taxation	202
		Small Business Taxation	203
		Individual Taxation	204
	10.8	Corporate Public Affairs Departments	204
	10.9	Business Regulating Itself	206

Summary 207
Key Terms 208
Critical Thinking and Discussion Questions 208
Cases 209

CASE 10.1—Regulating Tips 209
CASE 10.2—The Ethics of Asbestos 210

CHAPTER 11: *Responsible Ownership and Governance* 211

11.1 The Ownership of Canadian Business 212
11.2 Ethical and Responsibility Issues of Ownership 214
11.3 Responsible Investing 216
11.4 Protecting Owners and Investors 219
11.5 Corporate Governance and the Board of Directors 221
Board Structure and Membership 222
Board Diversity 223
Executive and Director Compensation 224
Disclosure and Transparency 225
Evaluation 226
11.6 Ownership, Governance, and CSR 227

Summary 229
Key Terms 230
Critical Thinking and Discussion Questions 230
Cases 230

CASE 11.1—Aunt Mabel's Experience with Ownership 230
CASE 11.2—What Shareholder Democracy? 231

CHAPTER 12: *Ethics and Responsibilities in the Workplace and Marketplace* 233

12.1 The Corporation's Key Stakeholder Relationships 234
12.2 Employees in the Workplace 234
The Work Ethic 235
Employee Loyalty 236
Managing Employment Diversity 237
Influence of Feminist Ethics on Business Ethics and CSR 238
Workplace Privacy 239
Employees and CSR 240
12.3 Consumers and Consumption 240
Defining Consumer Sovereignty 240
Consumers and the Marketplace 241
Consumers and CSR 243
12.4 Competitors and Competition 245
Competition: Ethics and Responsibilities 245
Government Influence to Encourage Competition 245
12.5 Suppliers and the Supply Chain 247
12.6 The Supply Chain 249
Sustainability Purchasing 251
Fair Trade 251

Summary 253
Key Terms 254
Critical Thinking and Discussion Questions 254

Cases 254

CASE 12.1—Loblaw's Treatment of Its Suppliers 254

CASE 12.2—Sodium and Ethics 255

CHAPTER 13: *Civil Society Stakeholders* 257

13.1 The Non-Governmental Organization (NGO) Stakeholder 258
13.2 The Case For and Against NGOs 261
13.3 Strategies for Relationships with NGOs 261
13.4 Partnership Relationships with NGOs 262
13.5 The Media Stakeholder 264
The Influence of Popular Media 265
13.6 The Interaction Between Business and the Media 266
13.7 Media Ownership 267
13.8 The Media and CSR 268
13.9 Policy Development Institutions (Think Tanks) 269
13.10 Religious Institutions 270
13.11 Educational Institutions 272

Summary 274
Key Terms 275
Critical Thinking and Discussion Questions 275
Cases 276

CASE 13.1— A Union Strikes and a Small Business Is Challenged 276

CASE 13.2—SLAPPing Greenpeace Canada 277

PART V: *The Environment, Globalization, and Changing Capitalism* 278

CHAPTER 14: *The Environment and Business Responsibilities* 278

14.1 Business, Its Stakeholders, and the Natural Environment 280
14.2 Defining the Environmental Ethic and Sustainable Development 281
14.3 Environmental Concerns in Business and Society 282
14.4 Government's Influence 284
14.5 Environmental NGO Influence 285
14.6 Market-Driven Environmentalism 286
14.7 Managing Responses to Environmental Concerns 288
14.8 The "Greening" of Business Functions 290
Financial Management 290
Marketing 291
Human Resources 292
Operations 293
14.9 Measuring and Reporting on Environmental Sustainability 295
14.10 Dissenting Views on the Environment 297
14.11 The Environment: Corporate Opportunities and Challenges 299

Summary 299
Key Terms 300
Critical Thinking and Discussion Questions 301
Cases 301

CASE 14.1— A Dog's "Eco-pawprint" 301

CASE 14.2—Is Dr. Seuss Misleading Children? 302

CHAPTER 15: *Globalization and Business Responsibilities* — 304

15.1 Global Business Responsibilities — 305
15.2 Defining Globalization and the Implications for Business — 306
15.3 Globalization and International Non-governmental Organizations (INGOs) — 308
15.4 Institutions of Globalization — 309
15.5 Globalization and Canadian Business and Society — 310
15.6 Standards of Conduct and Accountability for Global Business — 313
15.7 Special Challenges of Global Business — 314
15.8 The Acceptance of Global Capitalism — 318

Summary — 321
Key Terms — 322
Critical Thinking and Discussion Questions — 322
Cases — 322

CASE 15.1—The Ethics of Bioprospecting — 322
CASE 15.2—Food Retailing in India: Revolution or Evolution? — 323

CHAPTER 16: *The Socialization of Capitalism* — 325

16.1 Socialization of Capitalism and the Fourth Sector — 327
16.2 Socialization of Capitalism Through Corporate Sustainability Strategy — 328
16.3 Socialization of Capitalism and New Corporate Structures — 331
Social Enterprise — 331
For-benefit and B Corporations — 332
Social Enterprise/Non-profit Sustainability Matrix — 333
16.4 Socialization of Capitalism Concepts and Expressions — 334
Social Licence — 334
Social Innovation — 335
Social Impact Investing — 336
The Shared Economy — 336
Philanthrocapitalism — 337
Social Capital — 338
Sustainable Capitalism — 339
Corporate Social Integration — 340
16.5 Socialization of Capitalism and Business School Programs — 341
Teaching Sustainability in Business Schools — 341
Students and Sustainability — 343
Concluding Comment — 344

Summary — 345
Key Terms — 345
Critical Thinking and Discussion Questions — 346
Cases — 346

CASE 16.1—Stadiums, Taxpayers, and Sports Millionaires — 346
CASE 16.2—A University's Centre for Corporate Sustainability — 347

Ethics, Responsibilities, and Sustainability Cases — 348

Energy Drinks at Prairie Pharmacy — 348
Gabriel Resources Ltd. and the Rosia Montana Saga — 350
Corporate Social Responsibility to Food Banks — 352
Caterpillar Shuts Down Its Canadian Locomotive Plant — 353
500 Birds On a Pond — 356

Alberta Energy Company and the Ethics of Operation Kabriole 358
Crisis at Maple Leaf Foods Inc. 361
Just Dump It in the Lake 362
Professor Murray's Ethical Dilemmas 364
Fortis and the Chalillo Dam: Balancing Economic Development and Environmental Impact 366

Endnotes EN-1
Glossary GL-1
Index IN-1

Preface

The Philosophy of the Book

Ethics is all the rage throughout society these days; the ethics of business is no exception. Today, integrity is important to business performance and acceptance by society. Society expects business' adherence to moral standards such as honesty, fairness, and justice. This book provides a broad overview of the Canadian business system and society's expectations of it.

The book's title emphasizes "business and society" in addition to three key words: ethics, responsibilities, and sustainability. The ethics of business refers to the rules, standards, codes, values, or principles that provide guidance for morally appropriate behaviour in managerial decision-making relating to the operation of businesses and business's relationship with society. Business is accepted by society as long as it recognizes the responsibilities in its operations and considers the needs and desires of society. The result has been increasing obligations with business agreeing to do more. Sustainability represents a management approach that integrates economic, ethical, and environmental responsibilities into all management systems.

The corporation—the main business institution—accepts the necessity for integrity in business and recognizes the accompanying responsibilities. Throughout the book, the term *corporation* is used to represent business enterprises. The formal and legal entity of the corporation does not supply all the goods and services to society, but it is by far the principal business institution.

The ethics and responsibilities of business in society are connected to the concept of *stakeholders,* individuals or organizations that influence the corporation and/or that are influenced by the corporation. This concept will be described fully in the book and is key to the connection to or linkage between business and society.

Fourth Edition Changes

There have been revisions to all chapters with the most substantial being Chapters 3, 4, 10, 11, and 16. Chapter 3 now covers the identification of stakeholders and issues while Chapter 4 covers stakeholder and issue analysis. Chapter 10 has been renamed to reflect a more focused discussion of regulation, "Regulating Business' Ethics and Responsibilities." The emphasis is less on government regulation with additional discussion of market and self-regulation. In Chapter 11 the discussion of ownership types has been reduced and replaced with topics reflecting the influence of owners for social and environmental responsibilities. The chapter's title has been changed to "Responsible Ownership and Governance" to indicate the role of owners in social responsibility. Chapter 16 has been revised to focus on new concepts emerging in business and society. The new title is "The Socialization of Capitalism" which is the process through which the business system conforms to the expectations of society resulting in desired socially responsible outcomes.

New topics and the enhancement of existing ones include: social media (Chapter 1); income and gender inequality (Chapter 2); animals as stakeholders (Chapter 3); issue salience analysis (Chapter 4); robots and ethics (Chapter 5); ethical leadership forms (Chapter 6); government ethical framework policy and ethics and taxation (Chapter 10); management information circulars (Chapter 11); and the fourth sector, sharing economy, for-benefit and B-corporations, and sustainable capitalism (Chapter 16). Other changes are identified in the the following overview of the book's contents.

Overview of the Book's Contents

The topics covered in the book represent a consensus on the current subjects making up the business and society field. Business and the corporation operate within various societal environments,[1] and these environments provide a basis for the book's organization.

- **Business Environment**—The description of the business environment is given in Chapters 1, 2, and 16. Chapter 1, "The Relationship between Business and Society," provides an overview to the book and describes the concept of *business and society.* Other topics covered in this chapter include an outline of the Canadian business system, the role of the corporation, the stakeholders responsible for operating corporations, a brief introduction to ethical thinking, and society's acceptance of business. Chapter 2, "Ethics and Capitalism," describes the fundamentals of capitalism upon which the Canadian business system is based. It is important to understand these fundamentals, as the ethical implications associated with them reappear throughout the book. Finally, Chapter 16, focuses on new developments in the relationship between business and society.

- **Stakeholder Environment**—Chapters 3, 4, 11, 12, and 13 focus on stakeholders and their relationships with business and the corporation. Chapter 3, "Identifying Stakeholders and Issues," gives a detailed list of a corporation's stakeholders and the rationale for the stakeholder concept. The following chapter, "Stakeholder and Issue Analysis," advances the discussion of stakeholders by presenting approaches to the corporation's interrelationships with stakeholders. Although stakeholders are referred to throughout the textbook, some are studied in more detail. Owners and directors in Chapter 11, "Responsible Ownership and Governance"; employees, consumers, competitors, and suppliers in Chapter 12, "Ethics and Responsibilities in the Workplace and Marketplace"; and non-governmental organizations, media, think tanks, religious organizations and education institutions in Chapter 13, "Civil Society Stakeholders."

- **Ethical Environment**—The ethical environment is addressed in two chapters: Chapter 5, "Ethics of Business: The Theoretical Basis," and Chapter 6, "Ethics of Business: Management and Leadership." The former chapter outlines several theoretical ethical principles that will assist in understanding and analyzing moral dilemmas and integrity issues confronting business and the corporation. The latter chapter takes a pragmatic approach to outlining the managerial techniques or methodologies of ethics programs in corporations.

- **Social Environment**—Similar to the approach taken with the ethical environment, the social environment is discussed from theoretical and practical perspectives. Chapter 7, "Corporate Social Responsibility: The Concept," describes the various theories of social responsibility that can be used when analyzing issues and cases throughout the book. In Chapter 8, "Corporate Social Responsibility: In Practice," the approaches taken by corporations to implement their social responsibilities are outlined.

- **Regulatory Environment**—Business and the corporation are accountable to stakeholders as they are influenced by them in various ways. In effect, this is a form of regulation of the corporation. Chapter 9, "Measuring, Reporting, and Communicating CSR," identifies auditing processes used by corporations in reporting how they respond to their economic, stakeholder, ethical, and social environments. Chapter 10, "Regulating Business' Ethics and Responsibilities," identifies the range of regulation—from government legislation and policies through to self-regulation performed by industry associations and the corporation itself. Corporate governance is, in effect, the regulation or oversight of the corporation's activities provided by the board of directors. Corporate governance has been reformed in recent years, with emphasis placed on the corporation's ethics and responsibilities.

- **Ecological Environment**—The natural or ecological environment is considered in Chapter 14, "The Environment and Business Responsibilities." Ecology is a major issue involving many responsibilities and thus is discussed as a separate chapter.

- **International Environment**—The international environment, also referred to as *globalization*, involves many ethical issues and responsibilities. Chapter 15, "Globalization and Business Responsibilities," outlines how globalization is impacting almost every business and identifies how corporations are responding.

The business and society field can be described through the primary frameworks that are identified and discussed in an article by Schwartz and Carroll as:

- Corporate society responsibility
- Business ethics
- Stakeholder management
- Sustainability
- Corporate citizenship[2]

The contents are also consistent with the new domain statement for the Academy of Management's Social Issues in Management Division which "studies the social issues, institutions, interactions, and impacts of management." In particular, the Division addresses: individual and organizational ethics; organizational and systemic governance; and stakeholder behaviours, relationships, and systems.[3]

The frameworks are covered throughout the book and, with the environments described above, provide a comprehensive and contemporary view of the ethics, responsibilities, and sustainability of business.

Features and Benefits of the Book

- **A unique approach.** Each chapter offers unique materials or extensive descriptions of various topics as they relate to the ethics, responsibilities, and sustainability of business. Ethics refers to the fairness and integrity with which business functions in society; responsibilities refers to the increasing obligations that business is agreeing to undertake in society; and sustainability represents a management approach that integrates economic, ethical, and environmental responsibilities into all management systems.

- **A building approach.** The sequence of the chapters and the concepts covered enable students to learn about business and society incrementally. Thus, concepts relating to capitalism and the economic responsibilities of the corporation are introduced early, followed by the stakeholder concept. This body of knowledge is key to understanding the subsequent chapters. Similarly, theoretical material is followed by managerial practice in the social and ethical environments and becomes the basis for understanding the discussions in parts IV and V.

- **A focus on Canadian content.** The material in the book emphasizes Canadian content; it is an indigenous manuscript rather than a conversion of an American or European text.

- **Business and managerial perspectives.** The book is written from the perspective of business and managers, as they have to cope with social, ethical, and environmental responsibilities while also having to meet economic responsibilities. The materials are not intended to make judgments about business behaviour, but instead to increase the understanding of businesspersons and managers of their influence on society and of society's influence on business. Both good and undesirable examples of business behaviour are presented.

- **Non-profit sector included.** Non-profit organizations also play a role in business and society. This sector is represented by stakeholders such as non-governmental organizations, educational institutions, religious groups, and charities. These stakeholders are important in social responsibility initiatives described throughout the book but particularly in Chapters 7, 8, and 9. Most of Chapter 13, "Civil Society Stakeholders," is devoted to non-profit stakeholders. Chapter 16 includes a discussion of the interaction between business and the non-profit sector.

- **A student perspective.** Efforts have been made to present materials, vignettes, example inserts, and cases to which students can relate. Students are the future business leaders and managers and must understand the dynamic relationship between business and society and the ethics and responsibilities involved. More emphasis has been put on the ethics, responsibilities, and sustainability of students, in business programs, and at educational institutions.

- **"Learn more" boxes.** Readers who want to know more about certain topics are directed to "Go to Connect" where applicable.

Chapter 1
- Adam Smith
- Corporate wrongdoing in Canada
- Academic integrity

Chapter 2
- The right to intellectual property
- Inequality and why it is an issue for business
- Business fundamentals and the story of The Little Red Hen

Chapter 3
- Saint Homobonus
- Assessing information about stakeholders
- Identifying and engaging stakeholders

Chapter 4
- The principles of stakeholder management
- Matrix mapping
- Influence strategies

Chapter 5
- Ayn Rand
- Ethics cowboy style
- Your ethics

Chapter 6
- Giving voice to values

- A guide to practical ethics
- Business ethics by joining a blog

Chapter 7
- Sustainability
- *Corporate Knights*
- CSR jobs

Chapter 8
- Most socially responsible corporations in Canada
- Canadian corporate volunteerism
- CSR and small business

Chapter 9
- Trusting business
- Evaluating sustainability reports
- CSR in Canadian business

Chapter 10
- Your view of government regulation
- Lobbying government
- Canadian taxation policies

Chapter 11
- What shareholders are demanding of corporations
- Shareholder democracy
- Investment scams and frauds

Chapter 12

- Privacy in the workplace
- Ethical products and services
- Sustainability in supply chains

Chapter 13

- Digital protest movements
- "Watch" sites
- The efforts of OpenMedia.ca to keep the Internet affordable

Chapter 14

- The "tragedy of the commons"

- Calculating your carbon footprint
- An environmental folk song

Chapter 15

- The International Principles for Responsible Investment
- Transparency International
- Global corporate corruption

Chapter 16

- Types of capitalism
- Canadian social enterprises
- The sharing economy

Encouraging Critical Thinking

Critical thinking is a higher-order intellectual, purposeful thought and action process. It integrates inquiry, reflection, and deliberation to facilitate more thorough and meaningful learning. This book enables students to accomplish this in several ways: by introducing new ideas and concepts, linking ideas to illustrations, addressing issues from different perspectives, and exposing readers to new sources of information. The concepts, theories, and illustrations allow students to use their skills to clarify facts, assess information, formulate and defend their own intellectual positions, and develop appropriate courses of action. The pedagogical approaches listed below encourage student critical thinking. The Instructor's Manual provides teachers with additional materials that will enhance this process.

Pedagogy: User Approach

- **Learning Outcomes.** At the beginning of each chapter, numbered Learning Outcomes are listed. These tie in with the numbered section headings in each chapter.

LEARNING OUTCOMES

After studying this chapter, you will be able to:

LO 4.1   Explain stakeholder analysis in an organization.

LO 4.2   Describe stakeholder management capability.

LO 4.3   Understand stakeholder matrix mapping.

LO 4.4   Discuss the diagnostic typology of organizational stakeholders.

- **In-depth examples.** Instead of inserting numerous but short one- or two-sentence examples in the text, this book takes a different approach. Lengthier boxed inserts allow for more discussion of the examples. The two types of boxes are Everyday Ethics and Responsibility for Ethics.

- **Everyday Ethics** boxes provide examples not only of best practices, but also of inappropriate or questionable practices. More than 20 new Everyday Ethics boxes have been included and all the remaining ones updated. Instructors are provided with additional information to facilitate classroom discussion in the Instructor's Manual and online.

EVERYDAY ETHICS 5.3

The Ethics of Robots

A robot is defined as an engineered machine that senses, thinks and acts. More autonomous robots are being created and a challenge exists relating to how robots face ethical decisions, that is, how can they be designed to make moral judgments. Robots are presently used in manufacturing, the military, and automated aircraft, trains, and motor vehicles. From a consumer perspective, driverless cars and robo financial advisors are being designed. There will be increasing use of robots in the areas of research, entertainment, medicine and personal care.

- **Responsibility for Ethics** boxes refer to or describe individuals, organizations, practices, or concepts that affect or influence the behaviour of business leaders, managers, or corporations. Most describe the roles or influence of stakeholders. Thirteen new Responsibility for Ethics boxes have been included and the remaining ones updated.

RESPONSIBILITY FOR ETHICS 11.10

Best Corporate Governance Practices

Each year *The Globe and Mail* identifies the best corporate boards in Canada. The criteria used in assessing th Boards of Directors included:

- Board Composition—the percent of independent directors, board diversity, in particular, the number (women, and the approach to evaluation of directors.

- **Opening vignettes.** All vignettes are original and based on Canadian materials and examples. Each chapter begins with a real-world situation that introduces the chapter content. All require an individual to respond to an issue or dilemma. Five new vignettes are included in this edition and several others have been revised.

What would you do if... ?

George Lafontaine had always been an enthusiastic Volkswagen (VW) customer. As a young man, he drove a Beetle, then as he got older he purchased a Golf, then a Jetta, and most recently a Passat. It was time for George to purchase a new car, but he was hesitating at buying another Volkswagen. He had heard some disturbing news about VW's use of software manipulation devices to avoid regulated emissions standards. At first it was believed to be an isolated incident, the result of a few rogue employees. But, investigations by the media and others found that this was not the case. In fact, some believed that unethical behaviours were common in the auto industry.

- **"Your Advice to . . ." boxes.** These boxes have been placed before each chapter summary and relate back to the chapter's opening vignette.

Your advice to George...

George likely feels that he has been let down by the corporation and he likely has doubts about CSR. The issue is whether or not VW's reputation has been damaged so severely that he may not trust the corporation. He has not been personally harmed financially, but the environment is suffering because of VW's deliberate unethical behaviour. The challenge for George is how he can assess and believe the CSR claims of VW and for that matter, the claims of any automobile corporation. Unfortunately, some corporations become so focused on a goal, in this case to become the world's largest car manufacturer, that they are willing to ignore their own CSR policies.

- **End-of-chapter cases.** Cases relevant to the chapter content can be found in the end-of-chapter material. The cases are of two types: (1) descriptive of an issue in business and society to which management must respond and can be used as a basis for discussion; and (2) decision making in that the student faces a dilemma that must be addressed. Fourteen new cases are included in this edition, and many others have been altered and updated.

Cases

8.1 RESPONSIBLE ALCOHOL CONSUMPTION

Twelve producers of beer, wine and spirits have formed an industry association, Producers' Commitments, dedicated to the reduction of harmful drinking. The five key areas to be addressed are: reducing underage drinking; strengthening and expanding marketing codes of practice; providing consumer information and responsible product innovation; reducing drinking and driving; and enlisting the support of retailers to reduce harmful drinking. They also support the World Health Organization's (WHO) *Global Strategy to Reduce Harmful Use of Alcohol*. Two members of the association are Diageo plc and Molson Coors.

- **"Learn more" boxes.** Boxed features directing readers who want to know more about certain chapter topics to "Go to Connect" are included where applicable.

connect   Want to learn more about **what shareholders are demanding of corporations?**

- **Critical Thinking and Discussion Questions.** Every chapter ends with a set of questions that challenge the students to apply the concepts they have learned in each chapter. Some questions require students to think on their own to understand and evaluate concepts and, in some instances, to apply them appropriately. Other questions are designed to generate discussion and the articulation of different points of view.

Critical Thinking and Discussion Questions

1. Is the work ethic concept relevant in today's workplace?
2. Why should employees be loyal to the corporation? How does the corporation express its loyalty to employees?
3. What does the corporation gain from workplace diversity?
4. To what extent does the consumer sovereignty concept apply in today's marketplace?
5. Are consumers adequately protected in the marketplace?
6. What are the pros and cons when competition results in the failure of a business?

- **Ethics, Responsibilities, and Sustainability Cases.** Longer cases are included that allow for more in-depth discussion of issues and dilemmas relating to the ethics, responsibilities and sustainability of business. The cases are of two types: (1) descriptive of an issue in business and society to which management must respond and can be used as a basis for discussion of the issue; and (2) decision making in that the student faces a dilemma that must be addressed. Two new cases are provided.

Energy Drinks at Prairie Pharmacy[1]

Victor Lukasik has just taken over the operation of the family drug store, Prairie Pharmacy. The pharmacy was started by his grandfather and carried on by his father, who now is semi-retired working as a relief or part-time pharmacist. The pharmacy was located in a Western Canada community of about 5,200 that was also served by a large retail drugstore chain. Despite the competition, Prairie Pharmacy continued to prosper because the loyalty of long-time customers and its personalized service. The pharmacy had started as a prescription filling outlet and sold a few over the counter mediations. Over the years, the pharmacy had grown and now sold a large variety of over-the-counter medications, snack food, candies and soft drinks, cosmetics, greeting cards, magazines, and personal care products. It had a Canada Post franchise outlet.

The book's contents have been developed and designed to make the study of Canadian business and society attractive and challenging. The capitalist business system exists in Canada and the ethics, responsibilities, and sustainability of business must be studied in this context. Ethical challenges do exist, and corporations should be held accountable for the responsibilities they have to Canadians. Increasingly, Canadian business is moving toward corporate sustainability strategies. It is hoped this book will increase students' understanding of Canadian business and society.

MARKET LEADING TECHNOLOGY

connect

Learn without Limits

McGraw-Hill Connect® is an award-winning digital teaching and learning platform that gives students the means to better connect with their coursework, with their instructors, and with the important concepts that they will need to know for success now and in the future. With Connect, instructors can take advantage of McGraw-Hill Education's trusted content to seamlessly deliver assignments, quizzes and tests online. McGraw-Hill Connect is the only learning platform that continually adapts to each student, delivering precisely what they need, when they need it, so class time is more engaging and effective. Connect makes teaching and learning personal, easy, and proven.

Connect Key Features:

SmartBook®

As the first and only adaptive reading experience, SmartBook is changing the way students read and learn. SmartBook creates a personalized reading experience by highlighting the most important concepts a student needs to learn at that moment in time. As a student engages with SmartBook, the reading experience continuously adapts by highlighting content based on what each student knows and doesn't know. This ensures that he or she is focused on the content needed to close specific knowledge gaps, while it simultaneously promotes long-term learning.

Connect Insight®

Connect Insight is Connect's new one-of-a-kind visual analytics dashboard—now available for both instructors and students—that provides at-a-glance information regarding student performance, which is immediately actionable. By presenting assignment, assessment, and topical performance results together with a time metric that is easily visible for aggregate or individual results, Connect Insight gives the user the ability to take a just-in-time approach to teaching and learning, which was never before available. Connect Insight presents data that empowers students and helps instructors improve class performance in a way that is efficient and effective.

Simple Assignment Management

With Connect, creating assignments is easier than ever, so instructors can spend more time teaching and less time managing.

- Assign SmartBook learning modules.
- Instructors can edit existing questions and create their own questions.
- Draw from a variety of text specific questions, resources, and test bank material to assign online.
- Streamline lesson planning, student progress reporting, and assignment grading to make classroom management more efficient than ever.

Smart Grading

When it comes to studying, time is precious. Connect helps students learn more efficiently by providing feedback and practice material when they need it, where they need it.

- Automatically score assignments, giving students immediate feedback on their work and comparisons with correct answers.
- Access and review each response; manually change grades or leave comments for students to review.
- Track individual student performance—by question, assignment or in relation to the class overall—with detailed grade reports.
- Reinforce classroom concepts with practice tests and instant quizzes.

Integrate grade reports easily with Learning Management Systems including Blackboard, D2L, and Moodle.

Instructor Library

The Connect Instructor Library is a repository for additional resources to improve student engagement in and out of the class. It provides all the critical resources instructors need to build their course.

- Access Instructor resources.
- View assignments and resources created for past sections.
- Post your own resources for students to use.

INSTRUCTOR RESOURCES

- **Instructor's Manual:** Includes comments on each chapter's opening vignette, material by section with the objective for each section, additional notes/materials/suggestions for instructors, responses to discussion questions, analysis of cases, additional resources such as references to case studies relevant for each chapter, video resources, and assignments/ questions.

  The IM also provides additional information on the **Everyday Ethics** and **Responsibility for Ethics** boxes. The boxes are considered a key aspect of the text. Rather than give hundreds of one-line examples, the examples/illustrations in the boxes give more detailed information, and are constructed so that instructors can use them for discussion purposes or assignments. Features found throughout the boxes include:

- Discussion questions
- Additional information
- Suggested assignments for students
- Updated information
- Internet links and related sites

- Computerized Test Bank: Our ground-up, comprehensive Computerized Test Bank is flexible and easy-to-use. Instructors can create tests from book-specific items, including a wide range of question types (true/false, multiple-choice, essay questions), and add their own questions. Multiple versions of the test can be created, and any test can be exported for use with WebCT, BlackBoard, or any other course management system.
- **PowerPoint^{TM} Presentation Slides:** These visually stimulating slides provide an overview using illustrations, definitions, and examples, focusing on the primary concepts in each chapter.

eBook

Connect reinvents the textbook learning experience for the modern student. Every Connect subject area is seamlessly integrated with Connect eBooks, which are designed to keep students focused on the concepts key to their success.

- Provide students with a Connect eBook, allowing for anytime, anywhere access to the textbook.
- Merge media, animation, and assessments with the text's narrative to engage students and improve learning and retention.
- Pinpoint and connect key concepts in a snap using the powerful eBook search engine.
- Manage notes, highlights, and bookmarks in one place for simple, comprehensive review.

SUPERIOR LEARNING SOLUTIONS AND SUPPORT

The McGraw-Hill Education team is ready to help instructors assess and integrate any of our products, technology, and services into your course for optimal teaching and learning performance. Whether it's helping your students improve their grades, or putting your entire course online, the McGraw-Hill Education team is here to help you do it. Contact your Learning Solutions Consultant today to learn how to maximize all of McGraw-Hill Education's resources.

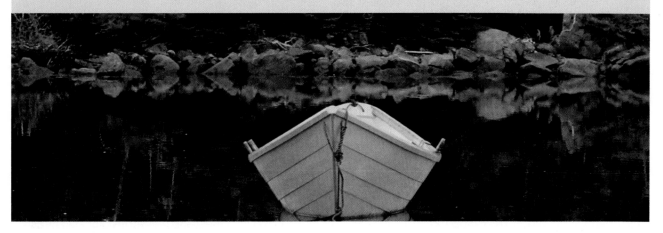

Used with the permission of Dennis Flynn

CHAPTER 1

The Relationship between Business and Society

LEARNING OUTCOMES

After studying this chapter, you will be able to:

LO 1.1 Describe the complexity of the interrelationships between business and society.

LO 1.2 Define the terminology relating to the integrity of business.

LO 1.3 Differentiate between the three main approaches to ethical thinking.

LO 1.4 Provide a brief description of the Canadian business system.

LO 1.5 Explain the role of the corporation as the main economic institution in the business system.

LO 1.6 Recognize that business operates with the consent of society.

LO 1.7 Summarize factors that influence society's attitudes toward business that lead to criticisms of the system.

LO 1.8 Identify the three stakeholders mainly responsible for the operation of Canadian businesses.

LO 1.9 Understand the relationship between business and academic integrity.

LO 1.10 Describe the integration of business and society.

What would you do if...?

Angela Clegg was in the second month of her business program. She was enjoying the courses and interacting with her student colleagues. She was having a good time and felt that she had made a correct decision to enter the program.

When Angela announced that she was taking business, many of her friends questioned the wisdom of her choice by pointing out various business misdeeds. They said that the financial crisis in 2008–09, and the economic downturn that followed, was caused by the greed and mismanagement of bankers, particularly in the United States and Europe. Her friends pointed out that insult had been added to injury when taxpayers, through their governments, had to bail out some banks and automobile companies. Several other examples presented to her involved financial advisers who destroyed people's life savings with fraudulent Ponzi schemes; massive recalls of automobiles, especially Toyotas and VWs; environmental damage of the Alberta oil sands; excessive executive compensation schemes; and numerous plant closures throwing thousands out of work. Lastly, her friends said there are no ethics in business and that "business ethics" is an oxymoron.

These arguments did not discourage Angela. She was aware of ethics in business and society and of social responsibility from the extensive coverage they were receiving in the media. The media frequently carried stories about business ethics and social responsibility. Many corporations even took out advertisements in newspapers, including Angela's campus newspaper, describing the contributions they were making to the community. Also, Angela had participated in the Junior Achievement program in high school and enjoyed developing and operating a small venture.

During a student society meeting, Angela heard about an interesting proposal—"The First Year Pledge of Social Justice, Economic Strength, and Environmental Responsibility":

> I pledge that during my years in higher education I will explore and take into account the social, economic, and environmental consequences of my behaviour and that of my institution. I will learn about issues of environmentalism, social justice, and economic strength, and will try to promote a sustainable and just society both at my institution and in the wider world.

The pledge was developed in the United States but seemed applicable to Canadian business students. The purpose of the pledge was to increase awareness of social responsibility among students through teaching and by encouraging them to undertake social initiatives while in school. Examples given of such initiatives included counselling entrepreneurs on ethics, organizing recycling projects on campus, assisting Aboriginal business enterprises, and developing financial literacy programs for teens and seniors. It was argued that a business program would be given added meaning through participating in these initiatives rather than merely relying on the completion of courses.

Angela had some questions about the pledge proposal. Would it make any difference? In particular, would her friends view her goals to succeed in business any differently? Would anyone recognize or respect the pledge? What would be expected of her?

What is your advice to Angela?

Sources: North Carolina Campus Compact, *Digest*, April 2009, http://org.elon.edu/nccc/news/ResourcesApril09.html; and "Combining First-Year Engagement and Civic Engagement," *Inside Higher Ed*, January 28, 2008, http://www.insidehighered.com/news/2008/01/28/engage.

Ethical implications are present in all facets of life, and business and society is no exception. For this reason, students of business should learn about ethics in the relationship between business and society. This chapter gives some background on the setting for understanding the complexity of the relationship. The factors influencing morality in Canadian business are identified. The role of the corporation is outlined, as it is the principal institution in the business system along with the three main stakeholders in the governance and management of the corporation—owners, boards of directors, and managers. Society has expectations of business, and various factors influence society's attitudes toward business. The possible connection between academic integrity and the ethics of business is also discussed.

LO 1.1   The Complexity of Business and Society

Canadian business and society is a fascinating topic. It involves studying the history and background of the Canadian business system in addition to examining the contemporary issues confronting business. It is very important to obtain all the viewpoints that contribute, or should contribute, to what business' role will be in society. Canadian society comprises many institutions and groups that interact, including governments, labour unions, minority groups, environmentalists, consumers, the communications media, business organizations, and a variety of interest groups or non-governmental organizations. All have an important role to play, and all, in some way, influence business decision making. This book emphasizes several things about the Canadian business system, with certain goals in particular:

1. To increase awareness of the system by describing Canadian capitalism, the stakeholders involved, and society's attitudes toward business;
2. To identify business' response to its role in society by examining who owns and runs business corporations, how business has incorporated ethics and responsibilities into its operations, and how business manages its role;
3. To learn how business corporations have responded to many challenges in their environment; and
4. To address the above from the perspective of the manager or owner of a corporation to emphasize the dynamic nature of the environment in which they manage.

Rather than focusing on what is right or wrong beyond any doubt, the emphasis in this text is on the appropriate analysis of problems and issues using information from a variety of sources, including the conflicting and maybe erroneous perceptions of various parties as to the motives, strategies, and tactics of others. Since we are dealing with so many individuals and organizations, perceptions of business vary—from the very negative attitudes held by some political parties and non-governmental organizations to the very positive attitudes held by business-oriented groups.

The issues that arise as a result of these differing perceptions and points of view are not easily resolved. Solutions are not always straightforward or simple, and tend to be less than optimum for all involved. Trade-offs are a factor, and what is an appropriate solution for one group is not as appropriate for another. An optimum solution is still sought, but it is certainly realized that each group in society will not benefit to the maximum.

A shift has occurred in what society believes business responsibilities should be, and at the same time many corporations are recognizing that they must respond to this belief if they are to survive and continue to be profitable. As a result, corporations are considering the following in their relationship to society:

- Business corporations should meet humanity's needs without harming future generations.
- Social responsibility or corporate sustainability reports published should move beyond the public relations exercises they may have been in the past.
- Increasing numbers of stakeholders are demanding corporations account for more than economic responsibilities.
- Progressive and innovative responses to social, ethical, and environmental responsibilities constitute a valuable intangible asset.
- Executives must have the skills and competencies to manage these additional responsibilities successfully.
- Responses to these responsibilities will determine the corporations that will survive.[1]

One attempt at measuring the responsiveness of corporations is the *Corporate Knights* Magazine's annual ranking of the best corporations in Canada described in Everyday Ethics 1.1.

EVERYDAY ETHICS 1.1

Canada's Best Corporate Citizens

Annually, *Corporate Knights* Magazine identifies the 50 best corporate citizens in Canada. In 2015, the five top-ranking corporations were Tim Hortons, Vancouver City Savings Credit Union, Mountain Equipment Co-op, Teck Resources Limited, and Telus Corp.

Corporations are evaluated on twelve key performance indicators covering resource, employee and financial management.

- Energy consumption
- Direct/indirect GHG emissions
- Water withdrawal
- Waste produced
- Taxes paid
- Percentage of women on board of directors and in management positions
- Executive compensation tied to clean capitalism
- CEO compensation as a multiple of average worker wages
- Employee safety performance
- Innovation capacity measured by R&D expenditure
- Employee turnover
- Pension fund status

Source: For indicator details refer to "2015 Best 50 Methodology," *Corporate Knights*, Summer 2015, accessed January 2, 2016, http://www.corporateknights.com/magazines/2015-best-50-issue/2015-best-50-methodology-14306256.

Most business academics and practitioners would agree that the business system is progressing in the right direction. However, other stakeholders would suggest that business is changing too slowly or not at all. The next section, "Integrity in Business," discusses the appropriateness of the business relationship to society.

LO 1.2   Integrity in Business

In the business environment, **integrity** refers to the appropriateness of a corporation's behaviour and its adherence to moral guidelines acceptable to society such as honesty, fairness, and justice. Integrity is the same as acting ethically, but without the negative connotation, the moralizing tone, or the sense of naiveté. According to De George, "Acting with integrity means both acting in accordance with one's highest self-accepted norms of behaviour and imposing on oneself the norms demanded by ethics and morality."[2] Managing with integrity means that business leaders behave in a manner consistent with their own highest values and norms of behaviour, which are self-imposed but at the same time not arbitrary or self-serving. De George states behaviour need not be perfect either: "The imperative to act with integrity cannot insist on moral perfection. It can and does demand taking ethical considerations seriously."[3] Throughout this book, how business enterprises accomplish integrity is discussed and evaluated.

Some fundamental points are to be made about integrity in business. Ethics exist throughout society and are not unique to business. When referring to *business ethics,* what is meant is the ethics that apply to business. It does not mean there is a special kind of ethics peculiar to business and not applicable elsewhere in life. Thus, the phrase "ethics of business" is used in this book unless referring to another work or spokesperson.

Key terminologies relating to integrity in business are listed in Table 1.1. Many definitions for these terms exist; the table provides the basics to assist in understanding their usage prior to reading about them in more detail in the chapters identified within square brackets.

In this book, some assumptions are made about the integrity of business:

- Ethics apply to business in the same manner as they do in any other institution in society, for example public administration, politics, religious organizations, the professions, and the legal, health, and educational systems. There are no ethics unique to business; it is only the issues and settings that are different.
- The appropriateness of behaviour is examined in terms of the ethical implications of addressing issues or decisions and of the distribution of harms and benefits to the relevant stakeholders.
- Integrity results in the **responsible corporation**, a business undertaking that responds to social, ethical, and environmental responsibilities in addition to its economic obligations. Everyday Ethics 1.2 illustrates how Canadian National Railway Company describes its efforts as a responsible corporation.

TABLE 1.1 **Key Terminology Relating to Integrity in Business**

Ethics of business: The rules, standards, codes, or principles that provide guidance for morally appropriate behaviour in managerial decision making relating to the operation of the business enterprise's and business' relationship with society. [Chapters 5 and 6] It is broadly defined to include corporate social responsibility (CSR), corporate sustainability (CS), triple bottom line, corporate citizenship, corporate governance, accountability, and environmental stewardship. [Chapters 7, 8, 9, 11, 14]

Stakeholder: An individual or group who can influence and/or is influenced by the achievement of an organization's purpose. [Chapters 3 and 4]

Corporate social responsibility (CSR): The way a corporation achieves a balance among its economic, social, and environmental responsibilities in its operations so as to address stakeholder expectations. [Chapter 7]

Corporate sustainability (CS): Corporate activities demonstrating the inclusion of social and environmental as well as economic responsibilities in business operations as they impact all stakeholders to ensure the long-term survival of the corporation. The term *sustainability* was first used in the context of environmental sustainability, but corporate sustainability has the wider meaning and includes economic, ethical, and social responsibilities as well. The difference from CSR is that the responsibilities are completely integrated to the structure, policies, and operations of the corporation. [Chapters 7, 16]

Triple bottom line: The triple-E bottom line (3E) is the evaluation of a corporation's performance according to a summary of the economic, social or ethical, and environmental value the corporation adds or destroys. A variation is the triple-P bottom line (3P), which is an evaluation of the corporation's performance according to people, planet, and profits. [Chapter 7]

Corporate citizenship: A corporation demonstrating that it takes into account its role in and complete impact on society and the environment as well as its economic influence. [Chapter 7]

EVERYDAY ETHICS 1.2

Delivering Responsibly at Canadian National Railway Company (CN)

CN's 2014 Sustainability Report used the theme of "Delivering Responsibly" as a key dimension for what the company stands for. This dimension is involved in what it does every day: "moving customer goods safely and efficiently, ensuring environmental stewardship, attracting and developing the best railroaders, adhering to the highest ethical standards and building safer, stronger communities."

CN's sustainability strategy covers:

"Governance: We are committed to the highest standards of ethical business conduct.

Environment: We conduct our operations in a manner that protects the natural environment.

People: We are focused on providing a safe, supportive work environment that values diversity, respect, integrity and pride.

Safety: We are committed to safeguarding employees, assets, customers and the communities in which we operate at all times.

Community: We contribute to communities through our impact on economic development, outreach in communities and community investment programs, including the numerous safety initiatives that we support."

Source: "Delivering Goods Safely and Responsibly," Canadian National Railway Company, accessed April 28, 2016, https://www.cn.ca/en/delivering-responsibly. Used with Permission of CN.

These assumptions do not mean that business is not involved in wrongdoing or in inappropriate behaviour, as will be pointed out throughout the book. The responses to the issues created relating to the ethics of business and society are usually complex, with implications for many stakeholders. Sometimes the actions, solutions, or outcomes are unsatisfactory to society, in which case business may be required to change its behaviour or may voluntarily change its behaviour.

In order to assess the integrity of business and corporations, a brief overview of some approaches to ethical thinking are presented.

LO 1.3   Main Approaches to Ethical Thinking

Not everyone understands or interprets ethics in the same way, and thus disagreement exists as to the appropriate behaviour by business in society. Many decisions involving ethics are made automatically without thinking, based on individual value standards and judgments and not ethical principles. Unfortunately, automatic decisions cannot be relied upon. Different countries, cultures, and religions may define right and wrong differently. More complexity results in situations where no option is clearly right, giving rise to dilemmas where effort is required to sort out right versus wrong. For some dilemmas, the choice might be between what some would consider two wrongs. Sometimes, because of the challenges presented, it is preferable to have different views of what is right or wrong.

Throughout history, ethicists have described various theories and principles to help understand the ethics of decision making. The difficulty is that numerous theories exist and some even have multiple interpretations. This section describes the three dominant approaches to normative theories of ethics: deontological, teleological, and virtue ethics.

In **deontological ethics**, or rule-based theories of ethics, actions are ethical if done for the sake of what is good without regard for the consequences of the act. Decisions are based upon duty and adherence to universal principles. In other words, individuals have a duty to do the right thing even if the consequences of another action are preferable. It is most important to act in a way in which one would like to see others act in the same or similar circumstances. A variation of deontology is broadened to the societal level, where individuals are born with natural rights possessed equally. But it is difficult to determine the rights to possess. Another variation is based on the principles of justice used to meet a "veil of ignorance" test. That is to say, a rule is just if everyone agrees to it is made ignorant of their position in society, thereby eliminating personal bias and guaranteeing fairness. A universal rule would result that could be used in similar circumstances and treating everyone with respect.

Teleological ethics, or consequential theories of ethics, focus on the outcomes or results of actions. A well-known variation is utilitarianism, which is based on utility or usefulness. The approach looks to the end results and individuals make decisions based on the consequences of the action. The decision is believed to be good if the end result is good. A decision is to result in the greatest good or happiness for the greatest number, and allows for bad consequences or harms. This approach is used every day by individuals and in business to view the relative outcomes; that is, the distribution of harms and benefits. Thus, moral character depends upon the practical matter relating to the extent to which actions benefit or harm those involved.

The third approach is **virtue ethics**, which emphasizes the character or identity of the individual and focuses upon *being* rather than *doing*. Morality is based on the development of good character traits or virtues and assumes that a good person will perform ethically. There are dozens of desirable traits; nine were listed by Aristotle—wisdom, prudence, justice, fortitude, courage, liberality, magnificence, magnanimity, and temperance. Virtue ethics acknowledges that absolute rules are unlikely to apply in all situations. Dozens of possible virtues exist, and the approach does not focus on which sorts of actions are morally permitted and which ones are not. An illustration is provided by responses to the question, "What virtues make a good businessperson or leader?" Possible answers include foresight, courage, commitment, compassion, respectfulness, and honesty. Table 1.2 compares the three approaches, all of which are applicable to the ethics of business as any other facet of life and society. In Chapter 5, these and other approaches to assessing ethical implications will be described.

This brief introduction to theoretical approaches to understanding ethics can be used to assess the behaviour of Canadian business, corporations, and managers. Ethical dilemmas often exist where the choice is between what those involved consider two right responses—or, put in the negative, two wrong responses. Different approaches can result in two responses where benefits are bestowed on some stakeholders and harms to others. Thus, no matter which choice is made, some stakeholders will consider it "wrong."

TABLE 1.2 **Comparison of Approaches to Ethical Thinking**

Deontological or Rule-Based Theories *[Rule-Based Theories.]*	Teleological or Consequential Theories *[consequential Theories.]*	Virtue Ethics
Description:	**Description:**	**Description:**
• Focus on moral obligations, duties, and rights	• Focus on goals, outcomes, or results *[3]*	• Based on character of individual
• Rules should guide decision making and behaviour	• Emphasizes maximum benefit and minimum harm	• If individual has good traits or virtues, decisions will be good or ethical
• More individualistic focus, as individuals should be treated with respect and dignity	• Considers all stakeholders impacted	• Virtuous characteristics come into play when resolving ethical dilemmas
Limitation: *[avoid responsibility as they are.]*	**Limitation:**	**Limitation:**
• Allows individuals to avoid responsibility as they are following rules or orders *[following rules or orders]*	• Difficult to calculate benefits and harms and apply weights to each	• Disagreement over what are virtues; that is, how a virtue is defined
Example: Categorical Imperative	**Example: Utilitarianism**	**Ethicists:**
• Respect for individuals, treating them as ends, not as means to ends	• Greatest good for the greatest number	• Plato
• Test: Would you do the same thing in similar circumstances?	• Aims to produce the most net utility; that is, benefits versus harms	• Aristotle
Ethicists:	• Provides a group or societal perspective	• Revived recently by several ethicists including Robert Solomon
• Immanuel Kant	**Ethicists:**	
• John Locke	• John Stuart Mill	
• John Rawls	• Jeremy Bentham	

LO 1.4   The Canadian Business System

Every country has an **economic system** defined as an arrangement using land, labour, and capital to produce, distribute, and exchange goods and services to meet the needs and wants of people in society. The objective of an economic system is to use a society's resources to meet the society's needs. The Canadian business system produces, markets, distributes, and exchanges goods and services to satisfy society's needs and wants. The majority of goods and services demanded by Canadians are provided by a private-sector economic system or capitalism. Most Canadians feel it is desirable to allow individual businesspersons and corporations—rather than some centralized government agency—to provide the goods and services they require. Business institutions have a history in Canada of more than 450 years, and their role in our economic and social development has been substantial. But, it is a role in a continuous state of change.

Terminology is a problem in discussing a business enterprise system. The following list provides definitions of some frequently mentioned terms:

• **Capitalism**—An economic system that allows for private ownership of the means of production (land, labour, and capital) and assumes that economic decision making is in the hands of individuals or enterprises who make decisions expecting to earn a profit. An early advocate of capitalism was Adam Smith, whose views are still influential as described in Responsibility for Ethics 1.1.

- **Free enterprise system**—An economic system characterized by ownership of private property by individuals and enterprises, the profit motive, a competitive market system, and a limited involvement by government. Also referred to as the *private enterprise system.*
- **Laissez-faire capitalism**—An economic system operating with absolute minimum interference by the government in the affairs of business. Government involvement is strictly limited to providing essential services such as police and fire protection. Laissez-faire stems from a French term that means "allow to do."
- **Responsible enterprise system**—An economic system operating as a free enterprise system but incorporating the element of accountability. This definition implies that business enterprises are responsible to society for their actions and are answerable or accountable for being the cause, agent, or source of something.
- **Stakeholder capitalism**—An economic system in which corporations accept broader obligations beyond financial ones for shareholders. Corporations are expected to balance the interests of shareholders with those of other stakeholders in the business system, for example employees, suppliers, customers, and the community at large. In stakeholder capitalism, corporations are expected to behave with greater social responsibility and be sensitive to the ethical consequences of their actions.
- **Clean capitalism**—*Corporate Knights* magazine uses this term to associate capitalism with social responsibility. The magazine defines clean capitalism as "an economic system that incorporates the social, economic and ecological costs (and benefits) into our marketplace activities and the prices we pay."[4]

RESPONSIBILITY FOR ETHICS 1.1

Adam Smith, the "Father of Capitalism"

Adam Smith, 1723–90, was a Scottish philosopher and economist whose ideas have had a major impact on capitalist economic systems worldwide. He wrote extensively, but two books have been the most influential: *The Theory of Moral Sentiments*, published in 1759, and *An Inquiry into the Nature and Causes of the Wealth of Nations,* published in 1776.

Smith proposed a different view of morality than was prevalent at the time. One view was that moral principles could rationally identify right versus wrong, while the other view believed that governments and the laws they created established a standard of morality. Smith believed that people were born with a moral sense, or conscience, that told them what was right or wrong. For Smith, morality was a product of nature, not of reason. In any event, Smith believed that economic man and moral man had to co-exist.

The "invisible hand" concept was originated by Smith. He believed that well-functioning, competitive markets efficiently distributed society's scarce resources without the guiding hand of government or economic planners. Pursuit of individual self-interest through consumption and the achievement of profits resulted in economic growth that benefited everyone.

Smith's writings continue to influence morality in capitalist economies, even though they are still being challenged by some in society.

connect   Want to learn more about **Adam Smith?**

Our economic system has changed over time from a relatively "free" system with limited government involvement to one where government involvement became more intensive during most of the twentieth century. Although government involvement has declined recently, business is now expected to account to other stakeholders in society. Even with these changes, the economic system of Canada is still based on such fundamentals as individualism and economic freedom, the right to private property, the importance of competition, and the profit motive. Thus, the economic system is not laissez-faire, but is a capitalist system. The principal advantage of this business system is that it decentralizes decision making from a central authority to many individual enterprises. The system also provides freedom of choice to workers, consumers, and entrepreneurs. High productivity and a high standard of living have resulted.

However, problems have occurred with the system throughout the history of business in Canada. Business provided appalling working conditions for labour in the nineteenth century and has sold unsafe products to consumers. Monopolistic behaviour has been evident in the operation of some business corporations, as witnessed by price fixing and supplier discrimination. Other problems include stock manipulation, misleading advertising, misrepresentation of financial information, and regional disparity. Business is blamed by some for failing to solve many social problems, for example inadequate housing, workplace discrimination against women and minorities, and the impact of business operations on the environment

Although capitalism is the economic system that provides most of the goods and services in society, two other sectors are involved: public and non-profit. The public or government sector is responsible for providing many services in society including the infrastructure that business uses. Government-owned corporations provide some transportation, insurance, pensions, and health and education systems. The non-profit sector, also known as the third sector or plural sector, is a part of the economic system. Examples of organizations in this sector are charities, cooperatives, and non-profit social enterprises.

The result is a business system that has changed over time, and today is quite different from 50 to 75 years ago. It is important to appreciate the fundamentals upon which the system is based, and how the system has changed to accommodate the demands of society. Chapter 2 examines in more detail how the business system works.

LO 1.5 The Corporation and the Business System

The Canadian business system comprises business enterprises varying from sole or single proprietorships to partnerships and incorporated entities. A business can be established and operated by an individual under very few legal requirements. Any individual may operate a business provided he or she is capable of entering into a binding agreement, that the business activity is lawful, and that the individual respects the general legal principles governing persons, property, and obligations. For larger undertakings, or where two or more persons wish to share in ownership, a partnership is formed. In proprietorships or partnerships, the business is identified only with the person or persons involved. The owners take all responsibility for success or failure, receive all profits and assume all losses, and can be held directly responsible for business wrongdoing. Today, most business enterprises are incorporated and so holding the owners, or shareholders, responsible is more complicated. Business enterprises are referred to as corporations in this book, but it is recognized that not all enterprises are incorporated, and that most businesses in Canada are small- and medium-sized enterprises.

The corporate form of business enterprise is quite unique. When a business incorporates, a separate legal entity is created. This entity is an "artificial being": invisible, intangible, existing only in contemplation of law, and with limited liability for owners. There are two doctrines of incorporation that represent two distinct views of the relationship of the corporation to society.

The privilege of incorporation was traditionally viewed as a concession granted by the sovereign. The first corporations were granted by British sovereigns to nobility, allowing them to explore, colonize, or commercially exploit some geographical area. It is often suggested that the Hudson's Bay Company, with a charter granted in 1617, was one of the first corporations formed in this manner. The "concession" doctrine held that incorporation was conferred by public act and could not be generated merely by private agreements among several persons to associate together for business purposes. The concession was not followed to the letter, especially as monarchies lost their power to legislatures. There were obvious dangers to individual or group freedoms in the concession approach as the sovereign, and then the state, had the authority to grant the privilege of existence to a corporation. An alternative doctrine of incorporation evolved, and the relationship between business and society has changed.

The second doctrine of incorporation is based on the right to "freedom of association." The association of individuals coming together for some purpose is fundamental to forming a corporation. The argument is that it takes more than a formal agreement among incorporators, between the state and the corporation, and between the state and the shareholders to create and maintain a corporation. The entity, a "going concern," is given life by real people and exhibits collective behaviour unique to it and governed by rules of its own making. Thus, the corporation can be thought of as a "state within a state" and is the most highly developed and useful means of voluntary cooperation as it provides an easy way for people to join and leave. Therefore, incorporation is a right, not a privilege as it is in the "concession" doctrine.

These two doctrines, and others, underlie the statutes that determine how to incorporate a business activity, and who may do so. With the freedom of association doctrine, the privilege of incorporation is freely available with a minimum of special conditions and limitations being imposed by government. Legislative safeguards have been interposed at critical junctures where experience indicates difficulties may arise. These safeguards exist to protect investors and creditors, and to create and preserve the atmosphere of public confidence necessary for the legitimacy of the business system. In the past few decades, additional obligations have been placed on the modern corporation to function for the benefit of the broader society in addition to the benefit of investors, creditors, employees, and customers.

The modern corporation is not the state-created entity of the concession doctrine, nor the uncontrolled free association of owners. But it is more appropriately described by the freedom of association doctrine—and this requires greater responsibility and accountability to society. Incorporation doctrines are one approach to viewing the relationship to society, but contemporary views include the business' legitimacy in society and whether or not business has a social license to undertake operations in society.

LO 1.6   Society's Permission for Business

The business system and corporations do not function in isolation to society and must receive some form of permission to operate. Two concepts that illustrate this relationship are legitimacy and social licence.

The attitudes toward business and the criticisms of it present challenges to its legitimacy as an economic system. **Legitimacy** is the belief in the rightness of an institution, in this case the appropriateness of our business system to supply the goods and services wanted by Canadian society. Society must believe in the business system, which involves trust and confidence and the perception that the system operates in the public interest.

The legitimacy of business is questioned by some in society who are suspicious of materialism and excessive consumption. They argue that there are nobler goals than the pursuit of wealth or material things in society. The hypocritical attitudes business has taken toward government lead society to question the legitimacy of the system. Businesses ask for government assistance in a great variety of ways—through tax concessions, grants, and tariff protection, for example—and have requested that the free enterprise system be rescued from particular difficulties in such areas as the automobile, textile, aircraft, and fishing industries. Although businesspersons speak highly of the free enterprise system and competition, many are reluctant to live in an unregulated competitive environment. Lastly, many in society simply do not understand how business works and are concerned by the poor examples set by some businesspeople.

The legitimacy of business is increasingly being shaped by a broader sense of values that includes the treatment of employees, respect for the environment, commitment to product safety and public health, perceived openness and honesty, enlightened recognition of all stakeholder interests, and overall contribution to community, society, and the quality of life. The conclusion is that, to be legitimate, the business enterprise system must respond to the changing values and expectations in society.

Two observations are important from the discussion of society's attitudes toward business: (1) the attitudes—in particular the criticisms—must be monitored by management; and (2) where justified and feasible, management should take actions to counter the negative views of business.

Social licence is the privilege of operating in society with minimal formalized restrictions—that is, legislation, regulation, or market requirements—based on maintaining public trust by doing what is acceptable to stakeholders in the business and society relationship. It has emerged as a concept to explain the relationship between business and society and is mentioned in several contexts, all attempting to explain the relationship between business and society in a general sense, between businesses or corporations and society within an industry, and between a corporation and society related to a particular project. The concept is sometimes referred to as a social licence to operate, which is particularly relevant to the latter relationship.[5]

A social licence must be earned and maintained—it is non-permanent because society's beliefs, perceptions, and opinions change, as do the influential stakeholders. There must be an acceptance and approval of the project by stakeholders, which is accomplished when the corporation establishes its legitimacy and credibility and ultimately gains their trust.

A key point to make is that a general or project social licence is not granted by a government, but instead by the acceptance received from the stakeholders involved. A social licence is one approach to describing the relationship between business and society.

LO 1.7   Society's Attitudes toward Business

Occasionally, Canadians are surveyed about their attitudes toward business. A Hewlett-Packard (Canada) Co. survey of 1,506 Canadians found that 90 percent said the more socially and environmentally responsible they believe a corporation is, the more likely they are to purchase its goods and services.[6] Another survey commissioned by Canadian Business for Social Responsibility (CBSR), a coalition of Canadian companies, found that "three-quarters of 141 companies surveyed feel their companies are engaged in corporate social responsibility." In a survey of 1,000 consumers, only "5 per cent perceive Canadian business as being 'completely' involved in corporate social responsibility, and only 16 per cent felt business is 'somewhat' involved."[7]

Factors Influencing Attitudes toward Business

Many factors influence these attitudes toward Canadian business. The following list discusses some of the more commonly identified factors that can lead to positive or negative attitudes.

Standard of living—A prominent argument used in justifying or supporting the business enterprise system is the standard of living that it provides. As living standards increase, it is more likely society will view business in a positive manner.

Decentralized decision making—Another factor of the business system considered desirable is the decentralized decision-making process involved. Millions of businesses make decisions independently of one another, ensuring that a wide variety of goods and services are available. This choice is viewed favourably by consumers.

Allocation of resources—Some argue that the efficient allocation of resources is more likely to occur with a business system, as allocation is based on the price and availability of resources. However, critics of the business system challenge the efficiency claim. They argue that enterprises control prices, for example in oligopolistic industries, or that business enterprises control the availability of resources, creating artificial scarcities.

Self-interest—In a business enterprise system, the individual can behave in his or her own self-interest. Self-interest acts as a motivator and provides the drive for profit that encourages individuals to get things done. In a competitive business enterprise system, consumers choose among businesses that provide basically the same goods and services. Everyone working in his or her own self-interest provides a stimulus to the operation of the economy, even though it is referred to by some as greed. Positive self-interest is intended to produce intelligent and informed pursuit of wealth. However, some claim that self-interest sometimes becomes cruel and malicious—and, at other times, dumb and hysterical—and that this is appropriately referred to as greed. Self-interest appeals to many as a motivating force, but to others it is a source of negative attitudes toward the business system.

Inequities in society—Some critics of the business enterprise system claim that a system based on a capitalistic market leads to inequities. Supporters of the system say that inequities are inevitable and necessary in a dynamic economy to provide incentive and prevent the regimentation of equality. A problem arises when particular groups in society are discriminated against economically to an extent that cannot be tolerated

Business cycle—Business cycles are natural in a market system, and probably are more accentuated in a business enterprise system than in a centralized economy. With periods of prosperity followed by recessions, the business enterprise system is vulnerable to criticisms because of the hardships imposed upon particular individuals and types of businesses at various times. The instability created by business cycles is resented by society.

Business wrongdoing—Corporate misdeeds also influence society's attitudes. Some of the most common examples of corporate wrongdoing are in the financial area, and include misleading financial statements, insider trading, stock manipulation, bid rigging, embezzlement, and bankruptcy fraud. Members of society were particularly annoyed at bank and corporate bailouts in 2008–09, when governments loaned or gave corporations billions of dollars and executives still received high salaries. Some other recent criticism of business has related to workplace health and safety violations, bribery in international markets, weak or absent food safety practices, pollution of the environment, the plundering of natural resources, and excessively high profits and executive compensation. Everyday Ethics 1.3 gives examples of corporate wrongdoing.

EVERYDAY ETHICS 1.3

Examples of Business Wrongdoing

The following are examples of business wrongdoing.

- Volkswagen AG: In September 2015, it was disclosed that VW had rigged the emissions tests on vehicles with diesel engines. Environmental emissions testing agencies did not notice the deception, which was revealed by West Virginia University and an ENGO. The VW CEO was fired.

- SNC-Lavalin: Since 2012, SNC-Lavalin has faced corruption scandals including fraud, bribery, and money laundering in Algeria, Bangladesh, Libya, and Montreal. Former managers face criminal charges relating to corruption of Libyan officials. The perpetrators and SNC-Lavalin's CEO were fired as a result.

- Ponzi Schemes: These schemes promise high returns to investors. Instead of investors being paid from earnings, they are paid from the contributions made by new investors. A key to the success of the scheme is to continuously attract ever-increasing numbers of new investors to pay the previous ones. The schemes eventually collapse as the inflow of money cannot be sustained. They occur regularly.

- Montreal, Maine and Atlantic Railway derailment: An inappropriately secured train of tank cars containing crude oil derailed in Lac-Mégantic, Quebec killing 47 people, forced 2,000 from their homes and destroyed much of the town's downtown core.

- Algo Centre Mall, Elliot Lake, Ontario: On June 23, 2012, a part of the mall collapsed killing two and injuring twenty persons. An inquiry found that decades of incompetence, neglect, greed, and dishonesty by a succession of owners, engineers, and municipal officials lead to the collapse. The mall has been demolished.

 connect   Want to learn more about **corporate wrong doing in Canada?**

Globalization—Business is being increasingly conducted on a worldwide or global scale. This trend applies to large as well as small businesses, and has led to several challenges. Increased competition comes from foreign producers, job loss occurs as production is outsourced to other countries, and businesses must respond to the demands of customers in other nations. Corporations operating globally are faced with ethical, social, and environmental issues relevant to local areas. As an example, Canadian mining corporations have had to respond to complaints about pollution and poor working conditions in their international operations. Chapter 15 will discuss the implications and challenges of globalization.

Unemployment—Employment is associated with a country's economic performance, business cycles, and productivity. How well the country's major industries are performing and the levels of consumer spending determine employment levels. Unemployment occurs when business lays off or fails to hire employees as business activity declines. Declining productivity of Canadian business may result in goods and services being provided from other countries.

Innovation—The business enterprise system is designed to constantly seek innovation. A large portion of technological development has been the result of the efforts of business enterprises. Some people criticize continuous and accelerating technology and social change while conceding that technology has improved their material well-being. A problem associated with rapid technological change is alienation, particularly alienation in the workplace.

Popular media—The popular media influence society's views of business. Books, magazines, newspapers, television, film documentaries, movies, and the Internet describe the activities of business and the implications for society. Some of the portrayals are positive, but many are negative and receive a lot of attention—for example, Michael Moore's documentaries *Roger & Me, The Big One,* and *Capitalism: A Love Story.* The extent to which the popular media influence attitudes toward business is not known for certain. As an example, the documentary *The Corporation* is very critical of business and presents a one-sided view of issues. The media as a stakeholder will be discussed further in Chapter 13.

Government—Government is always involved in business and the relationship between business and society. Governments often identify what is unacceptable corporate behaviour and their influence is always changing, at times increasing while at other times declining. Government influence is described throughout the book, and particularly in Chapter 10.

Social Media

Social media has had a dynamic influence on the relationship between business and society. One definition of **social media** is the various forms of interaction or communication enabled by technology-based tools, most of which are Internet based. The interaction is made possible through networking tools such as Facebook, Twitter, YouTube, and LinkedIn, the use of webcasts, blogs, and Internet forums, and the existence of websites. These tools allow individuals and organizations to create, share, and exchange information in the form of written materials, and pictures and videos through virtual communication networks.

Social media has several characteristics that enable it to influence business in ways that is different from other media. Exchanges of information are instant, often interactive, cover all topics, and require minimum knowledge of the technology involved. The costs to participants are low or even free allowing large numbers to publish and receive information. Participation in social media can be for personal use, that is, at home, or used in the workplace.

Social media has created new connections between business and society, in particular with employees, customers, suppliers, and non-governmental organizations. Social media can build, or destroy, a corporation's reputation. Many issues have resulted that present challenges.

Social media has enabled society to hold business more accountable. Unethical practices are more likely disclosed and sooner. Bloggers are free to make comments about the corporation that may or may not be accurate, placing the corporation in a difficult position to respond or counter untruths. Fake blogs might exist that portray corporations negatively. Some social media experts state that corporations have lost control over how they communicate, while bloggers are free to say what they want. From a positive perspective, corporations can view participation on social media as a way to interact with stakeholders and as a source of feedback on their performance.

Several issues exist in the human resources area. A prominent issue is how much time employees should spend on social media during working hours. Contributing to a social media site is a time waster and the acceptable level of monitoring employees' use is not easy to determine as their right to privacy should be respected. Another problem is what action should be taken when employees make negative comments about the corporation. Employers could, if they wanted, scan social media for employee involvement and comments and the possibility for discipline or even termination exists. Also, employers could scan social media for information when evaluating potential employees for positions. Applicants might be disqualified based on inaccurate information that appeared on a social media site.

Marketing and advertising practices also give rise to some issues. Corporations may distort endorsements by misrepresenting credentials, affiliations and expertise, or by placing fake stories. Some marketers may inappropriately collect data on consumers or use social media as a source of email addresses for spamming purposes and profile creation. Responsibility for Ethics 1.2 describes how Google online advertising service violated Canadian law. On the other hand, social media can be used to engage customers more directly including providing them with more information.

The security of computer systems is an issue, especially when corporate websites are hacked and confidential employee, customer or supplier information disclosed. Any activities involving the harassment or cyberbullying by posting misleading or incorrect information about competitors are inappropriate.

It is recommended that corporations develop written policies that prevent or resolve the issues arising from social media. The corporation's expectations for social media should be clearly outlined. Employees must understand that they are responsible for what they contribute to social media both personally or behalf of their employer. The legal and reputational consequences of their actions should be considered.

The use of social media by corporations is a matter of balancing harms versus benefits, that is, a utilitarian ethic perspective. The identification of the rights of various stakeholders is necessary, for example the rights of privacy for consumers and employees. Involvement in the social media should be guided by virtues such as honesty, trust, openness, respect, and fairness. From a management perspective, managing and controlling the social media is challenging.

At any time, one or a combination of the above factors influences attitudes. Even though the factors can be listed, it is unlikely consensus will occur on which factors are the most influential. Nevertheless, society's attitudes toward business change through time and business persons must always be aware of these changes. Monitoring attitudes toward business is important as it operates as the consent or permission of society.

RESPONSIBILITY FOR ETHICS 1.2

Google's Online Advertising Service and Privacy

The Office of the Privacy Commissioner of Canada was established to act as a guardian of privacy in Canada and enforces legislation protecting personal information, the *Privacy Act* and the *Personal Information Protection and Electronic Documents Act* (PIPEDA). In 2014 an individual complained that after searching on Google for devices for a medical condition follow up advertisements appeared while searching any topic. This was the result of Google's AdSense service that tracked the sites surfed while the individual searched for devices to solve that was considered a sensitive personal medical condition.

The Office investigated the complaint and confirmed that online behavioural advertising (OBA) was taking place. These particular advertisements were counter to the Office's OBA guidelines, which state that advertisers should avoid collecting sensitive personal information for the purpose of delivering tailored advertisements. Initially Google claimed that the practice occurred because of a technical issue with the keyword advertising system. After more investigation, Google found that the practice occurred because of a weakness in their "re-marketing" advertising system, which allowed an advertiser to target advertisements to recent visitors to their site. The company agreed to take remedial measures to bring it in compliance with the PIPEDA.

Source: News Release: "Google Ads Sparked by Web Surfing on Health Sites Violate Privacy Rights, Investigation Finds," Office of the Privacy Commissioner of Canada, January 15, 2014, accessed January 2, 2016, https://www.priv.gc.ca/media/nr-c/2014/nr-c_140115_e.asp; and "Report of Findings: Use of Sensitive Health Information for Targeting of Google Ads Raises Privacy Concerns," Office of the Privacy Commissioner of Canada, January 14, 2014, accessed January 2, 2016, https://www.priv.gc.ca/cf-dc/2014/2014_001_0114_e.asp.

LO 1.8 · The People Who Run Canadian Business

Three stakeholders are primarily responsible for the operation of Canadian business: owners, boards of directors, and managers. Each has some influence on the morality of the business system, overseeing the corporation's ethical behaviour, and responsibilities to society.

Owners

A variety of owners exist, categorized as direct and indirect. Direct individual owners are shareholders or investors and entrepreneurs. Also, sometimes employees participate in ownership through stock-purchase and grant programs, and customers and producers participate in ownership through cooperatives. There are other direct owners, including corporations that own shares in other corporations, venture capitalists that finance growing businesses by purchasing shares, and governments that use corporations to deliver some goods and services to citizens.

A growing form of ownership is the indirect category, which occurs when consumers invest in mutual funds, or when employees contribute to pension plans. The managers of these funds have become much more active recently and are influencing corporate decisions frequently now.

Through direct and indirect ownership possibilities, most Canadians participate in the ownership of business, a fact that is often overlooked. The influence of these owners varies and will be discussed in Chapter 11.

Boards of Directors

Owners are represented by a board of directors, which, according to section 97(1) of the *Canada Business Corporations Act*, "shall manage the business and affairs of a corporation"—a process referred to as corporate governance. The board members are elected by shareholders—that is, the direct owners—and thus are concerned with the shareholders' primary objective, return on investment, though in recent years there has been increasing interest in corporate social responsibility. The board's main tasks are to:

- Select, evaluate, and terminate employment of top management, including planning executive succession.
- Provide shareholders with financial statements and an external auditor's report on the financial affairs of the corporation presented in an annual corporate report.
- Direct and evaluate strategic planning, including formulating plans, keeping management accountable for implementation, and assessing performance.
- Represent shareholders by participating in any major decisions impacting the corporation's operations relating to ownership, investments, acquisitions, divestments, takeovers, or insolvency.
- Fulfill the fiduciary and legal requirements as outlined in the *Canada Business Corporations Act*.

Recently, many boards have been active in overseeing the ethics of the corporation and its social and environmental responsibility. The role of the board will be examined in Chapter 11.

Managers

Managers require a variety of skills to oversee the operations of corporations in today's dynamic business environment. Managers must know how to direct the corporation's affairs in an increasingly competitive environment and how to cope with large-scale change in their corporations. Technological developments and the globalization of business present additional challenges. In addition, managing relationships with stakeholders has become increasingly important, and knowledge of the ethics of business and social and environmental responsibility is necessary.

Everyday Ethics 1.4 describes one corporation's social responsibility policy and the committee established to implement it. The policy applies to all employees, including managers, and to the Board of Directors. In Chapters 7 and 8 other examples will be presented that describe the roles and responsibilities of managers in implementing morally acceptable behaviour and social responsibility in their corporations.

EVERYDAY ETHICS 1.4

Corporate Social Responsibility at Agrium® Inc.

Agrium® is committed to working with stakeholders to enhance economic, environmental and social sustainability. In support of this commitment, within our sphere of influence, we will:

1. Conduct our business with integrity, and in an open, honest, and ethical manner.
2. Engage local stakeholders in our planning and operations through timely, transparent and collaborative dialogue.
3. Promote business practices that respect the value of human life and that minimize environmental impacts.
4. Respect the diverse cultures and perspectives of all people.
5. Not knowingly take part in human rights abuse, or be complicit in any activity that solicits or encourages human rights abuse.
6. Support the communities in which we operate through financial and/or non-financial contributions.

The Policy is overseen by a CSR Committee which is comprised of the members of the Executive Leadership Team (ELT); Senior Director, Sustainability & Stakeholder Relations; Manager, Corporate Social Responsibility; and Chief Officer, Compliance.. The Committee provides guidance in issues such as Sustainability, Human Rights, including Indigenous Rights, Stakeholder Engagement, and Community Outreach and Investment.

This policy applies to all employees of Agrium, all subsidiaries and affiliates, its Board of Directors and to those authorized to speak on behalf of the Company.

Source: Corporate Social Responsibility (CSR) Policy, Agrium® Inc., accessed January 2, 2016, http://www.agrium.com/system/files/corporate-social-responsibility-csr-policy.pdf.

It has been argued that integrity is now at the top of the list of essential qualities of a good CEO. The operation of a business is about managing relationships with others, and the development of trust and credibility with stakeholders is necessary. Transparency is more important, and keeping hidden agendas or covering up information is more difficult. Relationships with others require a commitment to teamwork and partnerships, and managers must have the ability to build and sustain relationships. Finally, it must be remembered that managers are members of society and their behaviour is likely to reflect the standards of morality existing in society.[8]

All three of these stakeholders—owners, boards of directors, and managers—are more aware than ever of the ethics of business and the resulting implications. This awareness also includes monitoring society's attitudes toward business.

LO 1.9   Business and Academic Integrity

This chapter has introduced the integrity of business, but the integrity of *future* business entrepreneurs, managers, and employees must also be examined while they are in academic programs. A *Maclean's* article provides some statistics that are of concern for the future integrity of business:

- 53 percent of students admit to cheating in written assignments.
- 56 percent of business students admit to cheating.
- 44 percent of professors said they didn't report students caught cheating.[9]

At issue is whether the lack of academic integrity will have an influence on business integrity. College and university business programs are facing demands from society and the business community to better prepare their graduates to identify and address ethical implications in business. In business schools, ethics had been largely neglected until recently, and had emphasized functional areas, some which have focused on the financial rather than the social responsibilities of business. Corporate corruption practices have increased awareness of ethical practice in business, and graduates who will be managers and businesspersons need a moral compass and sensitivity to acting consistently. In other words, graduates must be prepared to face the reality of moral dilemmas.

The focus must be not only on graduates and their future behaviour but also on the practices internal to business schools. Numerous ethical issues arise during the educational experience within the business school. These issues involve not only students, but also faculty members. The business school itself must become aware of and address moral dilemmas in the teaching and administrative processes. Processes must be put in place to detect moral deviation and to develop remedies. Many behaviours by students—for example, cheating on examinations, allowing others to cheat, plagiarism, false sources, signing attendance sheets for others, vandalizing school property, and failing to contribute appropriately to group work—have ethical implications; a list of ethical issues facing students is given in Table 1.3. Likewise, the behaviours of faculty members—for example, letting students get away with cheating, improper approaches to grading and examinations, favouritism and bias, one-sided presentation of concepts and theoretical materials, excessive workload, talking about students, and inappropriate relationships with students—have ethical implications.

TABLE 1.3	Ethical Issues for Students

Students are no different from any other group in society, and provide numerous examples of questionable behaviour or academic offences. Examples of such behaviour include:

- Plagiarism or copying without giving proper credit or acknowledgment from any printed or electronic source; in other words, theft of intellectual property.
- Copying from another student's paper or exam, or allowing another student to copy one's own.
- Cheating on examinations or any other tests, assignments, and projects, including copying from another student's work.
- Bringing unauthorized materials or electronic devices into the classroom or examination room.
- Having communications or discussions with others during an examination, including through electronic means.
- Turning in the same work for two or more different courses, or turning in the work of others as one's own.

- Giving false reasons for not attending class or handing in an assignment.
- Taking an examination for another student.
- Changing answers after a test or assignment has been graded and asking that it be graded again.
- Engaging in disrespectful and disruptive behaviour in class.
- Harassing others.
- Stealing or defacing the property of the school or others.
- Posting unfair, false or exaggerated comments on RateYourProfessor.

connect Want to learn more about **academic integrity**?

LO 1.10 Integration of Business and Society

An article by Porter and Kramer made a good case for business and society needing each other. Business needs a healthy society in which education and health-care systems exist. There should be equal opportunity in the workforce and safe products for consumers. Carefully developed government policies increase the efficiency of business. This creates demand for products and services, and corporations pursuing profits at the expense of society are naive.

On the other hand, society needs successful companies. Business is needed to create jobs, wealth, and innovations that improve the standard of living for society. If business is weakened by governments and non-governmental organizations jobs disappear, competitiveness is lost, wages stagnate, and wealth declines.

In the past, too much focus has been placed on friction between society and business with not enough attention given to the interaction and integration between the two. There must be a shared value in which business and society both benefit. Illustrations of the benefits are provided throughout the book, although some of the frictions are described also. The direction of the ethics and responsibilities of business is toward reducing the frictions and increasing the benefits.[10]

This brief summary of Porter and Kramer's research provides an appropriate conclusion to this chapter on the relationship between business and society.

Your advice to Angela . . .

Students of business face a similar situation to that confronting Angela. On the surface, pledges and oaths of this type appear to have little influence. But, they do remind students of business about their responsibility to society. Whether or not Angela can defend her choice depends upon the circumstances in which she finds herself. Today, most business students are interested in economic, social, and environmental sustainability. In a course focusing on business and society, an understanding of the ethics of business and the responsibilities involved prepares students to answer questions like those posed in the opening vignette.

Summary

- The relationship between business and society is complex. To understand the relationship it is necessary to be knowledgeable of the business system and of capitalism in particular. There should also be an appreciation of the efforts being made by business to be responsive to society's expectations of its social and its economic responsibilities. (LO 1.1)
- Business integrity is the appropriateness of a corporation's behaviour and its adherence to moral guidelines acceptable to society such as honesty, fairness, and justice. The concepts used to describe the integrity of business are ethics of business, corporate social responsibility, corporate sustainability, the triple bottom line, and corporate citizenship. The integrity of business is no different from that of individuals or other institutions in society. (LO 1.2)
- The three main approaches to ethical thinking are deontological, teleological, and virtue ethics. (LO 1.3)
- The Canadian business system is referred to by various terms, but usually as a form of capitalism. The business system does have some defects, but it is constantly changing to reflect society's demands upon it. (LO 1.4)
- Several forms of business enterprise exist, but the most common is the incorporated enterprise referred to as the corporation. At one time, it was a privilege to form a corporation; that is, the monarch or government granted the right to incorporate. Today the corporation is viewed more as a free association of individuals who can incorporate as long as they are engaged in a legal activity. Thus, the modern corporation is accountable not only to the government, but also to society in general. (LO 1.5)
- Society allows business to function as a system to provide goods and services. Two concepts that help to understand this consent are legitimacy and social licence. (LO 1.6)
- Society's attitudes toward business vary over time, and its views are influenced by several factors. Corporate wrongdoing receives a lot of attention and creates negative views of business. (LO 1.7)
- Owners, boards of directors, and managers are the three most important stakeholders in the actual operation of the corporation. Each has a distinct role, and all influence the integrity of the corporation. (LO 1.8)
- Students and business academic programs are also challenged by issues of integrity. In particular, the behaviour of students has ethical implications, and they are no different than other stakeholders. (LO 1.9)
- Business needs society and society needs business. (LO 1.10)

Key Terms

Integrity	Economic system
Ethics of business	Capitalism
Stakeholder	Free enterprise system
Corporate social responsibility (CSR)	Laissez-faire capitalism
Corporate sustainability (CS)	Responsible enterprise system
Triple bottom line	Stakeholder capitalism
Corporate citizenship	Clean capitalism
Responsible corporation	Legitimacy
Deontological ethics	Social licence
Teleological ethics	Social media
Virtue ethics	

Critical Thinking and Discussion Questions

1. Do most Canadians understand the workings of the Canadian business system or capitalism? Do you? Give reasons to support your answer.

2. Do you agree with the position that the frequency of wrongdoing by business is about the same as for individuals or any other institutions in society?

3. Why do people disagree on what is morally appropriate behaviour? Which approach to ethical thinking do you practise?

4. How would you describe the Canadian business system?

5. Which two factors influence the integrity of Canadian business the most?

6. Should corporations be formed only with the permission of society as represented by government, or should they be allowed to form freely without much government oversight?

7. What is the connection between the type of approach to incorporation and society's expectations of the corporation?

8. Why should the members of the board of directors have any interest in the relationship between business and society?

9. What most influences your attitude toward business?

10. Should businesspersons be concerned about how they and business are portrayed in the popular media and social media?

11. What are the ethical challenges you confront as a student?

Cases

1.1 THE PILLAGING OF PENSIONS

Most Canadians expect employers to provide pensions as one benefit of the employment contract. The expectations include not only coverage but also adequate funds to maintain a desired retirement lifestyle and security for the longevity of the pension. Government officials and financial industry spokespersons are warning of a crisis in the pension system, especially pensions in the private or business sector. Some claim that the crisis in pensions will have a negative impact on overall economic efficiency.

The two most common types of pension plans are defined benefit and defined contribution. The defined benefit type is the most common, but this type is experiencing a major problem: there are insufficient assets to support the payment of pension obligations to retired employees. The deficits in the plans have resulted from lower interest rates reducing earnings, stricter standards imposed by government regulations, and higher costs or payouts.

Defined benefit plans guarantee a retirement payment based on income level and years of service. The risk of return and longevity is assumed by the employer; that is, the employer is responsible for deficits in the plan. Business employers have begun to collapse defined benefit plans or restrict new entrants, and have usually replaced them with defined contribution plans. In this type of plan, employees and employer make contributions in registered retirement savings plan (RRSP)–type accumulation accounts, with employees allocating the funds among investment alternatives. The risk of return and longevity is transferred to individuals, something with which Adam Smith would most likely agree. The difficulty is that individuals are less able to bear the risk of failures and they are less knowledgeable of investment opportunities and dangers. Also, there is a possibility they will pay financial advisers too much to guide them in the investment process.

The process of switching from defined benefits to defined contributions has begun. IBM Canada stopped offering defined benefit plans to new employees in 1995. Some plans are reducing payments to retirees, and in some cases plans are unable to pay any pensions. When companies go bankrupt, pension plans are sometimes threatened. When the St. Anne Nackawic Pulp Company in New Brunswick ceased operations, younger employees were expected to lose pension benefits and older workers and retirees would experience cuts. Nortel retirees are uncertain of their pensions after the bankruptcy and dissolution of the company. A 2012 study of 45 publicly traded corporations with defined benefit plans found that their plans were underfunded by $18.8 billion.

While some employee pension plans are experiencing difficulties, others are flourishing. Some CEOs are negotiating and getting huge pensions while employees are having theirs reduced. Most politicians in Canada have pension plans that have superior benefits to those allowed to other citizens.

Questions

1. How is the integrity of business illustrated, or not illustrated, with pension plans?
2. Which approach to ethical thinking would aid decision making regarding this issue?
3. How do the difficulties and changes being experienced by pension plans influence society's attitudes toward business?
4. What responsibility do corporations have to provide pension plans?
5. What responsibility do employees have to manage their own pension plans?

Sources: Lana Payne, "Grasping a True Pension Solution," *The Telegram* (St. John's, NL), August 13, 2012, A19; "Paying Pensions to a Greying Nation," *National Post,* December 22, 2011, A17; David Milstead, "Corporate Canada's Pension Hole," *The Globe and Mail,* October 11, 2012, B15; and Jack M. Mintz, "Tackle the Pension Crisis Now," *National Post,* April 19, 2012, FP11.

1.2 DETECTING PLAGIARISM AND ACADEMIC INTEGRITY

Students and faculty at colleges and universities are concerned about cheating in the academic environment. The reasons given for cheating include high expectations, pressures to succeed, students feeling they were unfairly treated in some way, and the belief that "everyone is doing it." There are many forms of cheating, but one that is receiving a lot of attention is plagiarism.

Studies indicate that about one in three students admit to plagiarizing at some time in their academic program. About 5 percent admit to purchasing an essay online and handing it in as their own. Business, engineering, journalism, and education students were found to be the most likely to plagiarize. There is no definitive reason why business students are the worst offenders, but there is speculation they have a "bottom-line" mentality toward getting things accomplished.

One approach to combat this problem is for educational institutions to use plagiarism detecting services such as Turnitin.com and Plagiarism.org. Essays are submitted directly by students or by faculty members. These services identify copied materials and issue a report to the instructor.

In some schools, the use of the detection systems has not been opposed by students or faculty. It is considered normal practice and is compared to the use of metal detectors at airports. The argument is made that it ensures the integrity of a degree and reduces the possibility of someone obtaining a degree by improper means. The point is made that detection also takes other forms, for example paid invigilators at examinations. Use of detection systems ensures everyone plays by the same rules and serves as a deterrent to improper behaviour. Faculty time is saved and the detection process is simplified, reducing the need for faculty to play police.

In other schools, the detection systems are criticized for several reasons. Students are often given no alternative but to submit their papers. Students resent the assumption of guilt and the impression that students are being hunted down for violations. Some argue that it is an infringement of their copyright, but legal experts refute this claim. The fact that private companies are making a profit at detection is considered inappropriate. The reliability of the systems is questioned, as they detect only about 50 percent of the actual plagiarism. Overall, an antagonistic atmosphere is created that does little to resolve the underlying causes of plagiarism.

Questions

1. Academic integrity involves students, faculty members, and post-secondary institutions. Who is served by the use of detection systems?
2. What responsibility should professors take to detect plagiarism?
3. When should disciplinary action be taken against a student?
4. What should be done about the problem of plagiarism other than using detection systems?
5. Is cheating in school through plagiarism a predictor of cheating in business careers?
6. Which approach to ethical thinking would increase understanding of behaviour regarding plagiarism?

Sources: Léo Charbonneau, "The Cheat Checker," *University Affairs*, April 2004, 16–20; Sarah Schmidt, "Professors Using In-class Exams and Essays to Fight Plagiarists," *National Post*, March 31, 2004, A1; and Heather Sokoloff, "One in Three Students Plagiarize," *National Post*, August 30, 2003, A1.

Used with the permission of Dennis Flynn

CHAPTER 2

Ethics and Capitalism

LEARNING OUTCOMES

After studying this chapter, you will be able to:

LO 2.1 Enumerate and discuss the eight fundamentals of a capitalist business system.

LO 2.2 Define the right of private property and identify ethical implications associated with it.

LO 2.3 Explain individualism and economic freedom and the related ethical implications.

LO 2.4 Define equality of opportunity and elaborate upon the ethical implications for business.

LO 2.5 Describe the competition fundamental and link ethical implications to it.

LO 2.6 Understand profits and the associated ethical implications.

LO 2.7 Link the work ethic to ethical implications.

LO 2.8 Define consumer sovereignty and understand related ethical implications.

LO 2.9 Explain the role of government in a capitalist business system and what the ethical implications are in this system.

LO 2.10 Define Canadian capitalism and recognize that capitalism exists in different forms around the world.

LO 2.11 Recognize the challenges to presenting the case for the ethics of capitalism.

What would you do if...?

Stephen Jacovich was encouraged by one of his Business School professors to read the business media, in particular, the Report on Business section and magazine of *The Globe and Mail*, the Financial Post section and magazine of the *National Post*, and *Canadian Business* magazine. These were available in online editions easily accessed and viewed from his PC or tablet.

Many interesting topics were covered, but in the past two years, one topic in particular drew his attention: income inequality. The following are examples of the stories he read:

Income Inequity Grows Even More
(*The Globe and Mail*, June 16, 2014)

The Upside of Income Inequality
(*Canadian Business*, August 2015)

Help Businesses to Reduce Inequality
(*National Post*, August 11, 2015)

Stephen was overwhelmed with information as illustrated when his search of "income inequality in Canada" on Google produced 70,400 results. There were numerous definitions but most identified it as how evenly or unevenly household or individual income was distributed in society. Quite often the focus is on the gap between the rich (one to five percent of the population) and everyone else. Some researchers claim income inequality has been growing rapidly for 30 years according to any major statistical measure used. President Obama in one of his "State of the Union Addresses" considered inequality a threat to capitalism and the World Economic Forum stated that it was a top issue facing the global economy.

Stephen's research also showed him that the business community has an interest in the issue as indicated by publications from The Conference Board of Canada, the Fraser Institute, and the TD Bank. There is a consensus among business organizations that capitalism is the best economic system at creating opportunity and a higher standard of living. There is also the view that if the issue is not addressed social unrest could occur and/or oppressive taxes imposed by governments to solve the problem. Economic growth would be diminished as poor people purchase less and business was not fully using the skills and capacities of workers. Inequality raised the questions of fairness and social justice, and it was unfair to punish those who have bad luck and some simply did not have opportunities. More equality would lower poverty and could be achieved by providing good jobs, child benefits, affordable housing, and child care.

He also discovered that government policies do address the issue. Social spending transfers income to lower incomes and investments are made in education and training. Minimum wages alleviate the problems, and changes to the taxation system would help, in particular taxing the rich. As business has the most to gain, it could also invest in employees by paying a fair wage and investing in their operations to improve productivity and increase innovation.

The more he read, the more Stephen recognized not everyone considered income inequality to be an issue. The interpretation of the inequality data varied and there are points of view that income inequality is not as serious as claimed. It is not necessarily a bad consequence of the capitalist system as it was a driver of prosperity. Inequality was an incentive for people to seek out income improving opportunities. In a capitalist system, inequality was simply part of the economic progress and despite income inequality, there has been extraordinary increases in living standards.

The volume of information and the diversity of views on the issue from a Canadian perspective alone were daunting. He wondered how he could get a grip on the issue. Was it a major issue in society? Did the issue threaten capitalism? How did or might the issue impact him? He started to read again.

What is your advice to Stephen?

LO 2.1   Introduction to the Fundamentals of Capitalism

The purpose of this chapter is to describe capitalism in Canada through the commonly accepted fundamentals of this economic system. This provides the context in which business operates and identifies the ethical implications of a capitalist system.

The assumption made is that the Canadian economic system has been, and still is, largely composed of business enterprises operating in a market system. The majority of goods and services wanted by Canadians are provided by the market system, which coordinates and organizes economic activity (see Everyday Ethics 2.1). Most Canadians accept that an economic responsibility of business is to make a profit in providing goods and services. It is argued that this private system is less cumbersome and less costly to run than a centralized, government-operated system, and that it is more responsive to society's needs because it allows individuals and business corporations to be more innovative.

EVERYDAY ETHICS 2.1

How Business Works for You

Think about the following goods and services you encounter on a typical day as a student. The cereal, fruit, and milk you eat for breakfast. The vehicle you use to get to classes. The music you listen to and the technology you use to listen to it. The coffee you purchase. The textbook you use in a course. The laptop computer you carry all day. The pens, pencils, and paper you use. The pizza you have for lunch. The video game you play to relax. The social media sites in which you participate. The cell phone or smartphone you use constantly in addition to iPads and other tablets. The aspirin you take for a headache. The newspaper, magazine, or comic book you read during break. The clothing you wear. The fried chicken you eat for dinner at home. The television programs or movies you watch in the evening. The bed you sleep in at night.

Business enterprises are responsible for providing most of these goods and services. Most are provided without a problem, but sometimes there are issues about this responsibility that relate to the fundamentals of capitalism. This is how the business system works for you.

The theory of capitalism can be described by examining some of the fundamental elements of such a system. In reality, it is more difficult to explain how the business system works. The ideal operation of the system is not expected, and much of the theory of the classical capitalist system is based on the philosophical underpinnings of the American system and may never have been applicable in Canada. These fundamental elements exist in different forms in various countries, and they are important to examine as they provide a basis for explaining some of the ethics and responsibilities of business that exist today.

In this chapter, eight fundamentals are described and some ethical implications of each are identified. The fundamentals are: the right of private property; equality of opportunity; competition; individualism and economic freedom; profits; the work ethic; consumer sovereignty; and the role of government. Capitalism requires a strong system of ethical behaviour; without it, the government and the justice system will intervene. The business system's approach to addressing economic, social, and ethical challenges is influenced by the form of capitalism in practice. The issues confronting managers today are assessed in the context of these fundamentals.[1]

LO 2.2   The Right of Private Property

The Fundamental

The right to ownership of property by individuals and enterprises is fundamental to the business system. The **right of private property** is the legal right to own and use economic goods, for example land and buildings. Property is not owned by the state, and individuals may own property and use it as they see fit. Individuals are allowed to accumulate property and other forms of capital and wealth without restriction. This accumulation of privately owned property allows individuals to control their own destiny and not have decisions affecting them made by others. Other rationales for the right to private property are that the pride taken in ownership results in better care of property; the ownership of private property gives a sense of security and a feeling of satisfaction from participation in society; and private ownership develops respect for the property of others.

Ethical Implications

Individuals and enterprises have been allowed to accumulate capital wealth, but there is an uneven distribution of wealth among members of society. This has led to demands for a more equitable distribution, usually achieved by government actions or abridgements to the right of private property. The government has "eminent domain" over property and can expropriate after payment of a fair price. Governments have even nationalized corporations and whole industries in some countries.

Taxation is one method of redistributing wealth. Despite this taxation, business retains some advantages because corporations are allowed to consolidate financial statements, to average taxable income over several years, to depreciate fixed assets, and to receive tax concessions. The government controls property through zoning regulations and restrictions on foreign ownership of property in some provinces. Most of the natural resources of Canada are still owned by the federal or provincial governments. Also, in the modern knowledge economy, the protection of another type of property—intellectual—is becoming increasingly important. **Intellectual property** is an umbrella term for patents, copyrights, trademarks, industrial designs, integrated circuit topographies, and plant breeders' rights.

connect   Want to learn more about **the right to intellectual property**?

In theory, property rights guarantee an individual's security and freedom. Today, membership rights, such as those offered by labour unions, cooperatives, trade associations, and professional societies, are for some a preferred basis for security and freedom. This leads to the discussion of the desirability of having property in private hands versus held by governments or some form of collective. An example of the issues involved with property rights in the aboriginal culture are described in Everyday Ethics 2.2 and it is felt that the lack of these rights is attributing to aboriginal economic inequality.

EVERYDAY ETHICS 2.2

First Nations and Property Rights

Most First Nations peoples are denied individual property rights, one of the basic freedoms of individuals and a fundamental of business. However, granting property rights on Aboriginal lands has been discussed as a way to encourage economic prosperity. Currently the lands are owned by the federal government in trust for Aboriginal peoples living on them. This is a collective arrangement leading to an absence of a sense of ownership and belonging fostering dependence on the federal and Aboriginal governments (band councils). An example of the consequence of collective ownership is that some Aboriginal peoples neglect their homes, allowing them to become uninhabitable.

It is proposed that full property rights be granted to individual Aboriginal peoples to buy, sell, mortgage, lease, and develop property. A benefit of this approach is that it creates an ownership culture leading to more productive use of the land. Privately owned property provides collateral for mortgages and capital for business enterprises. Overall, this will create wealth on Aboriginal lands, lead to increased economic activity, and improve living conditions. In other words, Aboriginal peoples would have control over their economic destiny.

There are difficulties with granting individual property rights. The concept of individual property rights is contrary to the traditional way of life of Aboriginal peoples and their attachment to land in general. There would be some difficulties in allocating property among present band members, and whether or not members who had left but previously resided on the reserve had a right to some property. There is fear that a class system based on property may emerge. Another issue is whether or not individuals could sell their acquired property to non-native peoples. Some chiefs oppose the individual property rights as it will limit their power over the bands.

Property rights in some form do exist on a few First Peoples nations and various possibilities are being considered. A land tenure system has to reflect a nation's culture and traditions by maintaining a sense of community and collective interest. The federal government is considering allowing property rights on native lands, but it is feared that the proposed approach will not be in the best interests of all First Nations.

Sources: Richard Truscott, "Property Rights Are the Key to Indian Posperity," Canadian Taxpayers Federation, accessed August 20, 2012, http://taxpayer.com/commentary/property-rights-are-key-indian-prosperity; Christopher Alcantara, "Individual Property Rights on Canadian Indian Reserves: The Historical Emergence and Jurisprudence of Certificates of Possession," available at http://www2.brandonu.ca/library/cjns/23.2/cjnsv23no2_pg391–424.pdf; Tom Flanagan, Christopher Alcantara, and Andre Le Dressay, *Beyond the Indian Act: Restoring Aboriginal Property Rights*, Montreal: McGill-Queen's University Press, 2010; and Tom Flanagan and Christopher Alcantara, "Individual Property Rights on Canadian Indian Reserves," Fraser Institute, 2002, available at http://www.fraserinstitute.org/publicationdisplay.aspx?id=12290&terms=property+rights+indian.

LO 2.3   Individualism and Economic Freedom

The Fundamental

Individualism is the view that the individual, and not society or a collective, is the paramount decision maker in society and assumes that the individual is inherently decent and rational. Individuals should have the privilege of determining their own course of action; that is, of behaving in their own self-interest with the minimum of authority being exercised over them. The privilege of determining for oneself what actions to take encourages individual initiative and self-interest.

Individualism is linked to freedom, and this has provided a connection between the business system in Canada and a democratic form of government. In general terms, freedoms are identified as the capability to have and control property, freedom of association, freedom of information, and freedom of movement. **Economic freedoms** exist when the business system operates with few restrictions on its activities. Examples of economic freedom include the freedom of individuals to enter business; to locate anywhere; to enter contracts; to choose among competing goods and services; to choose an occupation; to access consumer and output markets; and to develop their own economic ends, and the means to attain these ends by choosing and utilizing resources as they see fit. This approach encourages entrepreneurial talent and innovation.

Individualism and economic freedoms were based on the division of labour, or specialization. Individuals did things that naturally contributed to the production of the goods and services required by society. Likewise, each corporation performed some functions in the production system, but several corporations were involved in the realization of the final product. The production system was based on specialization and was fragmented, but the idea was that if attention were paid to the parts of the system, the whole would take care of itself. Responsibility for Ethics 2.1 gives another description of economic freedoms.

RESPONSIBILITY FOR ETHICS 2.1

Economic Freedoms

Conservative-oriented research organizations have developed indices of economic freedoms. Two examples are The Heritage Foundation and The Fraser Institute (in conjunction with several other institutes). How individuals view these economic freedoms has an effect on their ethical behaviour.

The following is a list of some factors that are considered when identifying and measuring economic freedoms:

- Property rights—Rule of law that protects property rights.
- Taxation—All taxes are considered harmful to economic activity.
- Government intervention—Economic freedom improves with less government.
- Regulation—Regulations should be straight forward, efficient, and at a minimum.
- International exchange—No restrictions should be on the movement of goods, services, or money between nations.
- Foreign investment—Few, if any, limits should exist on the extent of foreign investment.
- Money and inflation—Government maintains a tight monetary policy where the supply of currency does not exceed the demand.
- Wage and price controls—A free economy allows corporations to set the prices on the goods and services they require and to establish the wages they pay workers.
- Corruption—Corruption in the economy, as represented by a black market, should not exist.

For each of these factors, grading scales have been developed. After scoring the factors, a total score is ascertained by country and countries ranked. In recent years, Canada has been one of the top 10 countries on these economic freedom indices. Detailed descriptions of these freedoms are available at: current Index to Economic Freedom,

The Heritage Foundation website at http://www.heritage.org/index/, and the most recent Economic Freedom of the World Annual Report, The Fraser Institute website http://www.freetheworld.com/release.html. Different freedoms are used in each index.

Ethical Implications

Many in society consider the emphasis on individuals inappropriate and believe that communitarianism is more important in society as individuals seek to join and identify with some type of community organization. Status is achieved by working with others rather than by struggling alone. Unions and cooperatives are examples of such organizations, as are the recent developments in industrial democracy and social enterprise.

It is argued that a systematic societal approach is preferable to the atomistic thinking of individualism. The whole society is viewed, rather than its parts, and understanding the interrelationships among the parts is favoured over a highly specialized, subdivided view of society.

The issue arises as to the extent individuals are responsible for their economic well-being versus governments or some form of collective organization. Governments operate many social programs for various members of society, and individualism and economic freedom become less important than social well-being, distribution of income, health, and education. Although most of the economic freedoms mentioned in the previous section exist to some extent, there have been abridgements to these freedoms. All business enterprises now require some form of licensing prior to commencing business, and if an enterprise wishes to incorporate, it must be registered with the government. Also, the freedoms of employees are restricted by the corporations that employ them (dress codes, required purchase of firm's products) and by membership in unions (compulsory membership, allocation of work).

Recently, economic freedoms have been defined by various research organizations and national economies have been evaluated according to the extent that the freedoms exist. Ethical implications are present as the issue arises about the desirability of individual versus collective action, and about the extent to which economic freedoms should exist.

LO 2.4 Equality of Opportunity

The Fundamental

Equality of opportunity is the assumption that all individuals or groups have an even chance at responding to some condition in society. Many of those involved in Canadian business in the nineteenth and twentieth centuries were attracted to Canada because there was less influence exerted by nobility, landed gentry, or a rigid class system in North America than in Europe. There was less established wealth, and the "frontier" environment allowed individuals the opportunity to create their own wealth no matter what their background. This type of environment was appropriate for business: everyone was more likely to start the economic challenge of establishing and operating a corporation on about the same terms, and to have about an equal chance of succeeding. The opportunity existed to make one's own way by establishing a new business with minimum government intervention, and it was possible to pull up stakes and move to another part of the frontier.

Ethical Implications

In reality, equality of opportunity is challenging to achieve in a capitalist system. It is a societal issue because lack of equality of opportunity leads to economic or income inequality, which often is blamed on business. Many examples stem from income distribution, for example wages that are stagnant while profits increase, the gap between the poor and the rich (among individuals within an organization or a country and among countries), and male versus female income disparity. Gender equality is discussed in Responsibility for Ethics 2.2 particularly as it relates to economic income.

RESPONSIBILITY FOR ETHICS 2.2

Business' Responsibility for Gender Equality

Gender equality means that women and men have equal means and opportunities for realizing their full human rights and responsibilities. There are many bases for inequality including economic, racial, health, education, and political. In Canada, women enjoy the same health and educational levels as men, but economic participation is not optimal. Thus, business corporations must be concerned about women having the means and opportunities to participate in corporate economic endeavours and decision making. Gender equality is an issue for business because the inequalities are quickly disclosed, for example, by social media.

Some statistics highlight the issues for business. Women's income is only about 60 percent of that of men. Women are concentrated in lower-level and -income occupations, and too many are in contingent jobs, that is, are part time and seasonal. Access to the highest paying jobs is often denied, for example, women comprise only five percent of skilled labourers, ten percent of fire and police staff, and twenty percent of senior management positions. On the World Economic Forum's Global Gender Gap Index, Canada ranks 19th out of 142 countries and on the economic participation and opportunity component ranks 17th. The McKinsey Global Institute completed a study that identified the potential growth in the world's GDP if gender economic equality was achieved. It developed a Gender Parity Score to measure the distance each country has advanced towards gender parity (that is, 1.00) Canada's score was 0.75, behind Norway, Belgium, Sweden, New Zealand, and Denmark. There is room for improvement.

There is a strong business case for improving gender equality: economic and social conditions are improved and productivity and economic growth enhanced. Countries with higher gender equality maximize competitiveness and economic potential. Studies have shown that better corporate performance, governance, and profits occur with higher gender equality. The pool of prospective employee talent is increased for business. Moreover, as women dominate the consumer base, their improved economic well-being creates product demand.

There are several initiatives that business can undertake to foster gender equality. Human resources policies that would facilitate gender equality include: increase access to education and training; ensure hiring and recruitment practices are not discriminatory; provide affordable child care; develop policies relating to employment maternity and paternity leave; provide for the same opportunity for a job regardless of gender; and allow flexible work arrangements and job sharing. Corporations can provide mentorship with successful female managers serving as role models, and develop practices and policies to provide equal opportunities for rising to positions of leadership. To increase representation in decision-making positions on boards of directors and in senior management, voluntary targets or quotas, and disclosure requirements could be used. Assistance could be provided to women wishing to become entrepreneurs and support given to female-operated businesses in the corporation's supply chain.

Sources: "Closing the Gender Gap: Act Now," Organization for Economic Cooperation and Development (OECD), accessed November 5, 2015, http://www.oecd.org/social/inequality.htm and http://www.oecd.org/gender/closingthegap.htm; "Gender Equality: A Smart Proposition for Business," The Millennium Challenge Corporation (MCC), accessed November 5, 2015, https://www.mcc.gov/resources/story/story-kin-apr-2015-gender-equality-a-smart-business-proposition; "The Global Gender Gap Index 2014," World Economic Forum, accessed November 5, 2015, http://reports.weforum.org/global-gender-gap-report-2014/part-1/; *The Power of Parity: How Advancing Women's Equality Can Add $12 Trillion to Global Growth,*" McKinsey Global Institute, September 2015; "Gender Inequality," Centre for Social Justice, accessed November 5, 2015, http://www.socialjustice.org/index.php?page=gender-inequality; and "Gender Equality in Canada Going Nowhere Fast: Study," Canadian Centre for Policy Alternatives, accessed November 5, 2015, https://www.policyalternatives.ca/projects/making-women-count.

In place of equality of opportunity has come the call for equality of results, such as the desire for an adequate income, quality health care, good education, and retirement security. In other words, a more egalitarian society and a move away from opportunity, individualism, and personal freedom toward social, economic, and cultural levelling has been sought. Equality was redefined to be an equality of result, with all persons in society having nearly equal incomes, status, and power. The new equality was to be achieved through government involvement. The result has been a conflict between the motivational incentive provided by a competitive system and a system advocating equal reward to all despite the extent of effort or contribution.

Inequality is inevitable with a capitalistic system and has ethical implications. As economic growth occurs, the wealth created is not distributed equally and a debate centres on the relationship between growth and equality. Does faster growth necessarily cause greater inequality? Or, does greater inequality cause faster growth? If growth results in everyone being better off, most people are satisfied. But if the rich get richer and the poor get poorer, a problem arises in that social instability might occur. Another outcome might be demands for an engineered egalitarian society attempted through government initiatives such as affirmative action in employment and education, hiring quotas, and pay equity.

connect   Want to learn more about **inequality and why it is an issue for business?**

As it is not possible to achieve equality of opportunities or results, an alternative is to think in terms of increasing equity or fairness in the business system. This approach would have the corporation striving to achieve greater perceived fairness in the distribution of economic wealth and in its treatment of stakeholder interests. Equity would involve fairness in the opening up of economic opportunity, fairness in the way stakeholders are treated by the corporation, and fairness in the way the economic pie is divided. Examples of inequities would be sudden and drastic layoffs, large drops in living standards, excessively high executive salaries, and fortunes for some while the bargaining power of others is reduced. Although it is difficult to define what is fair, it is easier to achieve equity than equality.

LO 2.5   Competition

The Fundamental

Competition is the condition in a market system in which many rival sellers seek to provide goods and services to many buyers. It is believed that competition is natural and desirable: it ensures that corporations provide the goods and services desired by society. The survival of the corporation is at stake as it exists in rivalry with others to provide goods and services to consumers who usually have alternative sources of supply. No one corporation or seller can influence the market by its behaviour—a multitude of sellers ensures competition, thus preventing concentration of economic power. The advantages of competition are that it ensures goods and services are provided at lowest costs; reduces waste and inefficiency and holds profits to a minimum; widens the choice of goods and services available to consumers; and regulates prices. Competition is the invisible hand that is responsible for the orderly operation of the market. Society rewards the most competitive firms, and only the fittest survive.

Ethical Implications

The circumstances described in the previous paragraph represent perfect competition—which seldom exists today. The pricing system is sometimes controlled or influenced by business or government actions. An **oligopoly**, where the few sellers in an industry behave similarly, exists in many industries, and even monopolies exist in others. Some business enterprises have become very large and have diversified into many industries. Government regulates prices in some industries such as utilities, and in oligopolies there is a tendency for price leadership by one of the larger enterprises. Some industries, such as real estate and insurance, tend to charge identical commissions or establish premiums from rate books available to all enterprises in the industry. The professions have suggested price ranges for their services. Governments control or influence prices through direct control over wages and profits (as during the Second World War, or the period from 1975 to 1978), taxation, direct regulation, provincial barriers to trade, and tariffs.

No longer is it possible for corporations to easily enter some industries, as barriers to entry exist in the form of the size of plant necessary to achieve economies of scale, the domination of the market by one or a few corporations through advertising, or the inability to obtain the necessary technology. The ideal situation of perfect competition no longer exists, if it ever did. The invisible hand of a free market is now sometimes replaced by the visible hand of government.

The nature of competition in an industry influences behaviour between the corporation and various other stakeholders, including other corporations in the industry, consumers, and suppliers. There are ethical implications of competitive behaviour, and governments in developed economies have attempted to influence this behaviour to protect various stakeholder interests. Everyday Ethics 2.3 gives an example of the ethical consequences occurring when competition exists in an industry.

EVERYDAY ETHICS 2.3

Competition, Espionage, and Ethics

The competitive environment in an industry can result in some questionable ethical behaviour. One example occurs when an employee is hired from an employer by another who is a competitor. This is a fairly regular occurrence in any industry.

Canadian National Railway Co. (CNR) and Canadian Pacific Railway Ltd. (CPR) operate different systems which are partially overlapping. There is aggressive competition between them and each is seeking to attract the customers of the other. Attempts are made to acquire information on each other's customers and CNR accuses CPR of hiring their managers for that purpose.

CPR has hired two managers from CNR, which alleges that the two managers downloaded confidential customer information that was made available to CPR. As a result, CNR took legal action against CPR. CPR says that CNR is attempting to smear its reputation and that no employment contracts were broken.

The competitive nature of the rail transport industry has highlighted the tensions between the corporations leading to legal issues that will be resolved in court. CNR wants the court to issue an order preventing the solicitation of business from its customers and is suing for $2 million in damages. The matter will be resolved in court.

But, there are ethical issues in this type of industrial espionage for the corporations and the two employees involved.

Source: Eric Atkins, "Railways' Corporate Espionage Case Returns to the Courtroom," *The Globe and Mail*, October 26, 2015, B1, B7; Ben Dummett and David George-Cosh, "Canadian Railroad Rivals Set to Square Off in Trade Secret Court Case," *The Wall Street Journal*, October 5, 2015, accessed November 10, 2015, http://www.wsj.com/articles/canadian-railroad-rivals-set-to-square-off-in-trade-secret-court-case-1444088188; and "CN Rail Sues Rival CP over Alleged Corporate Spying," CBC Business, September 22, 2015, accessed November 10, 2015, http://www.cbc.ca/news/business/cn-rail-sues-rival-cp-over-alleged-corporate-spying-1.3238881.

LO 2.6 | Profits

The Fundamental

Profits are the excess of revenues over expenses and are closely associated with competition. The pursuit of profits spurs people into action and provides the drive and desire to do things. Corporations compete for profits, yet competition ensures that if excessive profits are made, others will be attracted to the industry. Profits are not only a regulator of efficiency, but also a measure of effectiveness. They can be retained in the business as a source of funds, and provide both an incentive to develop new products and technology and a reward for risk taking.

Ethical Implications

Many in society view profits with disdain, and some even consider them immoral. Many consider earning a profit to be appropriate, but some consider attempting to maximize profits through reducing competition to be inappropriate. As corporations have become larger and fewer in number in some industries, and more prices are government- or self-regulated, the role of profits as envisioned in classical theory has altered. Profits do not act as a "regulator" for many reasons. The introduction of taxation, especially income taxation, and the rates of inflation redistribute profits. The barriers to entry existing in many industries and the need for increasing size to achieve efficiency may have led to profits higher than normal under perfect competition. Competition not only is reflected by the number of corporations operating in an industry, but also is impacted by the services offered, advertising, brand loyalty, and image or reputation. Profits are controversial, as illustrated in Everyday Ethics 2.4.

EVERYDAY ETHICS 2.4

Banking Industry Profits—Reasonable or Excessive?

The year 2014 was a good one for corporations in the banking industry. The following list gives an indication of the industry's profitability, referred to as net income or net earnings, in 2014:

- Royal Bank of Canada - $9 billion
- Toronto-Dominion Bank - $7.8 billion
- Bank of Nova Scotia - $6.6 billion
- Bank of Montreal - $4.3 billion
- Canadian Imperial Bank of Commerce - $3.2 billion

Note that the word *profits* was not used by the corporations in the presentation of these financial data. Are these profits reasonable at a time when consumers are paying high service fees? Should the excessive profits be taxed by the government? Should the pricing practices in the industry be investigated? These questions raise issues with ethical implications for the banking corporations, consumers, and government.

LO 2.7   The Work Ethic

The Fundamental

The **work ethic** is a code of values, or a body of moral principles, claiming that work is desirable, it is a natural activity, and it is good in and of itself. It has been assumed that work is the purpose of one's life and that unemployment is only a temporary misfortune. Individuals in society are assumed to be willing to support themselves and the members of their family. Work in itself is worthy, admirable, and both personally and socially valuable. The Protestant ethic reinforced the work ethic by claiming that hard work, diligence, thrift, and "busyness" were desirable for religious reasons; that is, work served as an earthly expression of God's will.

Ethical Implications

It is argued that individuals' attitudes toward work have changed as a result of government programs and society's expectations. Government programs now support the less fortunate, and the effects of unemployment have been reduced by Employment Insurance payments. These programs may not have a socially desirable impact, as sometimes labour markets are distorted—actually causing unemployment. Individuals now expect that more will be done for them, usually by governments but also by business enterprises by way of working conditions, fringe benefits, and salaries—as illustrated, for example, in Responsibility for Ethics 2.3. The tendency toward government handouts and a somewhat more paternal attitude by employers has resulted in less need to work hard—or, as some argue, to work at all. The traditional form of the work ethic encouraged thrift and saving. In modern society, the desire to consume is a driving force, and individuals work hard to acquire material possessions. The resulting consumption ethic relates to the next fundamental, consumer sovereignty.

RESPONSIBILITY FOR ETHICS 2.3

Work Ethic of the Millennials

If you were born between 1981 and 2000, you are a "Millennial." Millennials, also known as Generation Y or the Net Generation, have entered, or are now entering the workforce. Some describe them as spoiled, narcissistic layabouts who spend too much time with social networking; they spend a lot of time and effort downloading audio and video materials, often illegally; and they have a tendency to plagiarize. They are considered to be overly self-confident, disrespectful and indifferent of authority, and treat work as a way to personal fulfillment. Managers say that they are difficult to manage, requiring precise direction and more feedback, particularly praise. They have unrealistic career expectations and often hop from one job to another seeking advancement. Unreasonable demands are put on employers as Millennials think work should be not only fulfilling but also fun, with flexible hours, good salaries, and ample vacations. They grew up in good times and believe that they are entitled to a particular lifestyle and workplace environment.

Not everyone holds this view of the Millennials' work ethic and instead see them as computer-literate multi-taskers who are good at online collaboration, making them natural team players. Some say they are smarter, quicker, and more tolerant of diversity. They provide fresh perspectives and ideas, and have lots of energy. They care about society's problems, respect the environment, believe in justice, value innovation, and insist on integrity. Also, the economic downturn has imposed some reality to their work ethic as obtaining jobs and job hopping has become more difficult.

Sources: "Managing the Facebookers," *The Economist*, January 3, 2009, 10; "Generation Y Goes to Work," *The Economist*, January 3, 2009, 47–48; Don Tapscott, *Grown Up Digital: How the New Generation Is Changing Your World* (New York: McGraw-Hill, 2009); Josh Rubin, "Wooing the Millennial Worker," *The Globe and Mail*, June 7, 2013, B12; and Rebecca Walberg, "Business Needs New Millennial Strategy," *National Post*, Aril 3, 2013, SR2.

LO 2.8   Consumer Sovereignty

The Fundamental

Consumer sovereignty is the assumption existing in an economy that consumers have and exercise power over producers through the decisions they make in purchasing the goods and services provided by corporations. It is assumed that consumption is the end purpose of production. Consumers, by "voting" for a product when they purchase it, dictate the types, styles, and quality of goods and services provided by business. It is the consumers' evaluation and acceptance or rejection that determines the success of a business. It is clear that the producer is servant to the consumer and is to obey the instruction of the consumer, who commands and directs. Consumer sovereignty is a fundamental part of any competitive system, and generally the more competitive the market the stronger the power of the consumer.

Ethical Implications

Consumers often face challenges in exercising their sovereignty. Sometimes consumers are not aware of all alternatives available to them and sometimes they are not capable of understanding the technical complexities of many goods and services. With some goods and services there is less choice, or no choice, available to the consumer. Giant corporations are said to mould consumers' tastes and preferences through persuasive advertising. It is argued that producers have the power to ignore some consumer wishes, something necessary for mass production. On the other hand, it is suggested that there are too many products, or brands, with too little difference. Trivial product differentiation and artificial product obsolescence have encouraged this proliferation of products.

Canadian governments have passed legislation relating to consumer matters that has imposed many regulations, standards, and approvals prior to the introduction of a product. Governments influence or regulate in the "public interest," which frequently is more in the "producer interest." Monopolistic institutions are tolerated or created by the government, such as agricultural marketing organizations or professional associations. Tariffs and quotas on imported goods create contrived scarcities, increasing the prices paid by consumers. It is doubtful that consumers have much influence on the market compared to the impact of organizations of large corporations, government agencies, organized labour, or minority producer groups such as farmers. Responsibility for Ethics 2.4 illustrates how even one consumer can change the way a corporation conducts its business.

RESPONSIBILITY FOR ETHICS 2.4

One Consumer Influences Facebook

Harley Finkelstein was concerned about the personal details being collected about his 14-year-old sister when she used Facebook. Harley and Jordon Plener, both law student interns at the Canadian Internet Policy and Public Interest Clinic (CIPPIC) at the University of Ottawa, decided to investigate the issue. Their research eventually led to a complaint being filed with the Privacy Commissioner of Canada under the *Personal Information Protection and Electronic Documents Act* (PIPEDA).

The Privacy Commissioner determined that many of the complaints identified were well founded, including the following:

- The sharing of information with third-party developers
- A lack of distinction between account deactivation, where personal data are held in storage, versus deletion, where data are actually erased
- The inadequate protection of the privacy of non-users who are invited to join the site
- The treatment of the accounts of deceased users

Facebook responded to the complaints by altering its policies. It agreed to retrofit its application platform to prevent the use of information unless express consent is given. It agreed to make clear to users the option of deleting versus deactivating their account. More information would be provided in Facebook's terms of use statement, and wording included in its privacy policy to explain what will happen in the event of a user's death.

The changes applied to Facebook's estimated 2 million users in Canada and, more importantly, to its more than a quarter of a billion users around the world.

Sources: Office of the Privacy Commissioner of Canada, Elizabeth Denham, "Report of Findings into the Complaint Filed by the Canadian Internet Policy and Public Interest Clinic (CIPPIC) Against Facebook Inc. under the *Personal Information Protection and Electronic Documents Act*," July 16, 2009, accessed November 7, 2015, http://www.priv.gc.ca/cf-dc/2009/2009_008_0716_e.cfm#sect1; Office of the Privacy Commissioner of Canada, News Release, "Facebook Agrees to Address Privacy Commissioner's Concerns," August 27, 2009, accessed November 7, 2015, http://www.priv.gc.ca/media/nr-c/2009/nr-c_090827_e.cfm; and Matt Hartley, "How a Kid Sister Changed Facebook," *National Post*, August 28, 2009, A1, A2.

LO 2.9   The Role of Government

The Fundamental

Government's role is to be kept to a minimum and is frequently expressed as a laissez-faire approach: "leave us alone." Although minimum government involvement is advocated, government is to provide for such things as national security, internal law and order, and a system of currency and measures. Government also provides the mechanisms for individuals to associate with others for a common, lawful purpose by evolving a body of law relating to contracts between individuals, which provide a basis for individual behaviour and expectations with respect to contractual arrangements. Government intervention in the business system for other than these types of activities is considered to lessen efficiency as the movement of resources is restricted and market pricing is interfered with.

Ethical Implications

Instead of the modest intended role of government, the government now is an influential stakeholder in the business system. Government involvement in the economy has always been greater in Canada than in the United States. Government was involved in building or financing transportation facilities very early in Canadian history. The National Policy of the 1880s and through the twentieth century, involving the imposition of tariffs to protect domestic manufacturers, has been a major intervention in the economy. Governments are now extensively involved in the economy through subsidies, taxation, tariffs, regulations and legislation, loans and grants programs, and ownership. Government is not only a monitor of business activity, but also an active participant in the system.

connect   Want to learn more about **business fundamentals and the story of The Little Red Hen?**

Governments restrict capital movements and natural resource sales, impose product standards, and in some cases even prevent businesses from shutting down plants when they want. Legislation governs how employees are treated and regulates the types of contracts that can be made with customers. Competition legislation makes some types of trade practices illegal and attempts to prevent monopolization. Governments also influence a corporation's approach to ethics and responsibilities, a topic examined in Chapter 10.

These eight fundamentals are not isolated from but rather linked to one another and become the basis for the capitalist market system. Private property is the basis of individualism and economic freedom; competition regulates profits; profits motivate individuals and reinforce the work ethic; the work ethic is rewarded by profits and the accumulation of property; individualism is critical for competition and consistent with the work ethic; and consumer sovereignty is related to economic freedom, competition, and profits. The fundamentals are the basis of capitalism, but capitalism takes different forms around the world and at different times.

LO 2.10   Canadian and Other Forms of Capitalism

Capitalism is an economic system that allows for private ownership of the means of production (land, labour, and capital) and assumes that economic decision making is in the hands of individuals or enterprises that make decisions expecting to earn a profit. Canadian capitalism satisfies this definition to some degree, but not all means of production are privately owned, not all economic decision making is in the hands of individuals, and many economic decisions are made where profit is not the motive.

Canada does not have a pure free-enterprise system, but instead a complex, "patched up" one. This patched system is the best that can be expected given human limitations; that is, no system can be perfect if it is to operate democratically. Moreover, the system is an integrated and complex one, making the separation of fundamental elements difficult. Government involvement has increased as the underlying assumptions of capitalism have become less valid in practice. Some would argue that laissez-faire capitalism was a myth in the first place and never really operational.

While capitalism takes one form in Canada, different forms or versions are in existence around the world. Also, the form of capitalism within a country can change. Canadian managers and entrepreneurs must recognize this phenomenon.

The following list outlines some of the more common forms of capitalism.[2]

Consumer capitalism—This form of capitalism is also referred to as *liberal market capitalism* and is practised in the United States, Britain, Canada, and Australia. Government involvement in the economic system is limited, there are open borders, and a profit mentality exists. Consumers have considerable influence over the market and producers respond to their wishes. Potential problems with this form are income inequity, low savings rate, and weak central governments.

Producer capitalism—This form emphasizes production, employment, and statist policies; that is, the concentration of economic controls and planning in the hands of a centralized government. As practised in Germany, it is referred to as a *social market economy* and is a regulated capitalist market with generous social welfare. Input is sought from other stakeholders, particularly employees or labour, a practice referred to as *co-determination*. Other forms of producer capitalism are practised in France, Japan, and Mexico. Potential problems with this form are that the social safety nets fray, innovation is slowed, and consumer dissatisfaction often occurs.

Family capitalism—Also referred to as *crony* and *Confucian capitalism*, this form is found in eastern Asian countries such as Taiwan, Malaysia, Thailand, and Indonesia. In some economies, extended clans dominate business activities and control capital flows. In many countries, the clans or families are created by Chinese descendants scattered throughout the region. In Japan, the form is based on the implicit belief in social balance and harmony or domestic peace. An emotional attachment is formed with groups, family, households, working teams, and nature, with an embracing of belongingness. This view differs from the Western beliefs in objectivity, equal treatment, and the "level playing field." Under this form, outsiders are not considered equal, modern corporate organizations are less likely to be formed, and money markets are restricted.

Frontier capitalism—Russia and China are examples of frontier capitalism, suggesting that capitalism is in its beginning stages. The fundamentals of business are being introduced as the government pursues for-profit business activities and an entrepreneurial class sprouts. The fundamentals are in various stages of being made operational. The role of government changes with the need to develop commercial law and regulation. The rule of law is not clearly established, and criminal activity often fills the void. Barriers to trade with other economies have to be removed. Mechanisms and institutions have to be developed that will facilitate a transition to consumer or producer capitalism.

In addition, other phrases are often used: *employee capitalism*, when workers own shares in the corporation; *democratic capitalism*, when shareholders have the right to vote on major initiatives; and *people's capitalism*, when ownership of corporations is widely distributed. Recently, the phrase *stakeholder capitalism* has even been used to describe some forms of producer capitalism, such as that practised in Germany.

Various forms of capitalism are advocated as a result of changes in society's view of business. Three examples currently receiving attention are conscious capitalism, creative capitalism, and state capitalism.

Conscious capitalism is the reorientation of business from a single focus on profits to emphasizing integrity, higher standards of corporate behaviour, and inclusion of all stakeholders. A higher social purpose is pursued and assumes that the fundamentals of business must change if society is to thrive. Business must have a stakeholder orientation where conscious leadership should involve and consult those influenced. The culture of business must embody values, principles, and practices incorporating social responsibilities.[3]

Creative capitalism is a new form of capitalism that places the resolution of social needs as a primary goal of economic activity rather than as secondary consequence of economic activity and performance. It was described initially by Bill Gates of Microsoft, who was concerned by the inequities between the world's rich and poor peoples. He asserts that non-creative capitalism does not have to concern itself directly with the well-being of people. It took for granted its benefits to all, through its mechanisms of social Darwinism, competition, and evolutionary success of the fittest. Creative capitalism would discover new, innovative ways to solve the problems of the poorest by combining self-interest (or individualism) and caring for others.[4] An alternative form has emerged from the 2008 financial crisis and resulting recession.

A different type of capitalism being sought by some involves a greater role of government directly in the business system through the ownership of corporations. **State capitalism** is "an economic system in which governments manipulate market outcomes for political and social purposes." The financial crisis and economic downturn of 2009 shook the fundamentals of free markets, spurring countries to take control of property and financial resources within a country. The stimulus packages offered by governments included expenditures of goods and services and refinancing corporations, in particular in the banking and automobile industries, in which governments became a part owner. Many economists fear that government involvement in business for political or economic purposes will not result in the most efficient use of resources.[5]

The discussion of capitalist fundamentals and the differing forms of capitalism explains the lack of clarity surrounding the description given to the economic systems operating in particular countries. Students of business should appreciate that different forms of capitalism exist in different economies and that the form changes over time in the same economy. All this complicates the relationship between business and society.

LO 2.11   The Ethics of Capitalism

The ethics of capitalism are often questioned by members of society. As an economic system capitalism faces many challenges that lead to this doubt. On the other hand, many defend capitalism as a moral system.

The Challenges

Capitalism is a controversial economic system: many stakeholders advocate the benefits of the system, and many oppose or are critical of it. This has been the case with the financial crises, economic downturns, and occurrences of corporate crime. The following discussion examines some of the challenges.

Greed—Humans act in their own self-interest to some extent; that is, they desire to improve their situation. **Greed** is an excessive and selfish form of self-interest where individuals desire more of something than what is needed or fair. Of course, what is needed and fair is open to interpretation. Self-interest is harmful if channelled improperly through deceit, corruption, force, fraud, and theft; an example is given in Everyday Ethics 2.5. Some say capitalism is only about greed, but this is unfair as it is also about creativity, innovation, and entrepreneurship, which provide society with employment and goods and services.

EVERYDAY ETHICS 2.5

Gordon Gekko's "Greed Is Good"

Michael Douglas played Gordon Gekko, a ruthless businessman who symbolized greed and corruption, in the 1987 movie *Wall Street*. In the movie, Gekko made an often-quoted reference to greed:

> *The point is, ladies and gentleman, that greed—for lack of a better word—is good. Greed is right. Greed works. Greed clarifies, cuts through, and captures the essence of the evolutionary spirit. Greed, in all of its forms—greed for life, for money, for love, knowledge—has marked the upward surge of mankind.*

In 2009, a sequel to the film came out with Michael Douglas again playing Gekko. In *Wall Street: Money Never Sleeps,* Gekko is back in business after being in jail for 20 years for insider trading—this time, though, he has a seemingly different view of morality.

Sources: "'Greed is Good,' Again," *The Telegram* (St. John's, NL), April 29, 2009, B4; "Recession Won't make Gekko Blush in Sequel," *National Post*, April 30, 2009, A1; and Terence Corcoran, "In Hollywood, War and Wall St. are Both Hell," *National Post*, March 23, 2010, FP15.

Mistrust—Trust is important in all relationships, including between business and society. It should not be taken for granted or assumed to exist. It is dynamic and involves reputation and integrity. After corporate failures when people have lost jobs and investments, there is likely to be less trust of business. The 2015 Edelman Trust Barometer found that 47 percent of Canadians trusted business (down from 62 percent the previous year). This result compared to 47 percent who trusted the media (down from 58 percent), 49 percent who trusted government (down from 51 percent), and 67 percent who trusted NGOs (same as previous year).[6] Business must build trust with internal stakeholders, such as employees and lenders, and with external stakeholders, such as consumers, governments, and non-governmental organizations.

Economic downturns—Economic cycles are a feature of capitalism. Because capitalism is based on a market system, there will be swings between prosperous times and recessions or even depressions. An example is the 2008 collapse of financial institutions in the United States and Europe. Several investment banks failed, followed by many banks in other parts of the world, resulting in a credit squeeze and fall in value of financial assets. This was attributed to the lack of government regulation and oversight plus business practices such as the focus on share value and incentive-based executive compensation. But markets are dynamic and correct themselves eventually.

Business failures—Another aspect of capitalism is failure that disposes of weak corporations and shifts resources to new or stronger ones. Thus, bankruptcy laws need to work well to transfer resources efficiently from less-productive to more-productive uses. Governments could become involved and bail out or prop up these corporations. This involvement is expensive, and the selection of which corporations to support is complicated. Nevertheless, those who have lost jobs and investments do pay a price for failure.

Corporate crime and wrongdoing—Crime and wrongdoing exists in all societal institutions. As mentioned in Chapter 1, corporate crime and wrongdoing come in many forms and often receive considerable publicity and damages the reputations of businesses.

There are other challenges including the stagnant incomes of many Canadians at a time of higher and higher CEO salaries. Various forms of inequality exist particularly of income. It is claimed that capitalism lacks a caring view of weaker members of society. Damage to the environment is a challenge that business will have to address more urgently in the future. Lastly, a fundamental of capitalism is the reliance on a market system that seldom works perfectly.

Capitalism as an Ethical System

Given these challenges, many in society wonder whether capitalism operates with *any* ethics, while others argue that capitalism does not prevent the pursuit of what is good for society. Advocates of capitalism argue that it is a system that produces wealth, promotes prosperity, and provides greater human well-being than any other economic system. Capitalism allows creative and productive forces to operate that, in turn, create value in the form of superior goods and services resulting in a better quality of life. In a capitalist system, business must plan to be successful, which involves an empathy towards others or stakeholders. Cooperation is encouraged despite the existence of a market system based on competition.

For those arguing that capitalism is moral or ethical system, some features are significant. Capitalism respects freedoms including the right of individuals to set their own objectives and to pursue happiness as they perceive it to be. In other words, capitalism allows and encourages the virtues necessary for human life by safeguarding the freedom of an independent mind and the sanctity of the individual. Advocates believe that government would be less successful at respecting the freedoms of individuals.

The advocates of capitalism state that signs of an ethically minded business culture exist. Business has to respond to consumers demanding products consistent with their moral values and to society in general, for example, insisting on respect for the environment. Business is expected to address social issues and is increasingly accountable because of the Internet, in particular, social media. Business' efforts in responding to these demands is considered to be a virtue.[7]

At the level of the corporation, an assumption exists that moral individuals operate the business system and that they are in the majority. For capitalism to operate effectively, a strong system of moral behaviour and integrity is necessary. Aspects of this include the need to be honest and truthful, to operate by the rules of society and government, to keep one's word, to be responsible for actions, and to treat others as you would like them to treat you, including with compassion and forgiveness. Most corporations behave ethically because if they behave inconsistently with the values of society and its stakeholders their behaviour would be corrected in various ways. For example, employees would leave, customers would be lost, and governments would legislate appropriate behaviour. Integrity in business makes sense, and many contend that a more ethically minded business culture is emerging. Many demonstrations of this culture will be examined throughout this book.

The fundamentals of capitalism are to be viewed in light of ethically minded corporate developments such as social responsibility, business ethics, corporate citizenship, and stakeholder management. More importantly, how these fundamentals are interpreted in society influences the values held by businesspersons and managers. If capitalism is to be accepted as the economic system in society, businesspersons and managers must somehow take into account the ethical implications resulting from the workings of the fundamentals.

Other models or forms of capitalism are being proposed that take into account the ethics and responsibilities of business. But all incorporate the fundamentals in some way. Various stakeholders of the business system are impacted by how the fundamentals are interrupted or applied. It should be noted that many business organizations, businesspersons, and corporations are advocating greater responsibility and sensitivity to society and stakeholders. The following chapters will provide illustrations of these business initiatives, and Chapter 16 will describe new forms of capitalism that are being proposed.

The fundamentals were described as together they form the basis of Canadian capitalism. These elements give rise to many social or ethical issues that present challenges for Canadian businesspersons and managers. Therefore, the fundamentals discussed will provide a basis for an understanding of economic, social, or ethical responsibilities and of the relationships between business and its various stakeholders.

Your advice to Stephen ...

There are always some stakeholders in society who believe that there should be improvements to how capitalism works; that is, how it harms or benefits various stakeholders. You might support organizations concerned about the issue, for example, food banks, homelessness centres, and religious institutions, and organizations such as Oxfam and the United Way. The programs proposed by political parties and local politicians could be reviewed and supported if appropriate. It is not inconsistent for a business student or business person to have a social conscience.

Summary

- Most goods and services needed by Canadians are supplied by business enterprises operating in a capitalist system. Many ethical implications arise as a result. Eight fundamental elements of Canadian capitalism were identified: the right of private property; equality of opportunity; competition; individualism and economic freedom; profits; the work ethic; consumer sovereignty; and the role of government. The elements represent values that must be held to some extent by a society in order for capitalism to operate effectively as an economic system. (LO 2.1)
- The right of private property facilitates the operation of business, but some in society resent a few acquiring large amounts. (LO 2.2)
- For capitalism to be acceptable to most Canadians, it must allow for equality of opportunity to share in economic well-being even though the results are not the same for everyone. (LO 2.3)
- To ensure that capitalism is regulated in the best interests of stakeholders, competitive rivalry must exist between sellers of goods and services to provide buyers with choice. The difficulty is that even in Canada's form of capitalism competitive markets do not exist. (LO 2.4)
- Individualism encourages people to participate in a capitalistic system, because they are free to make economic decisions in providing goods and services in a marketplace. Some Canadians resent the focus on individuals and believe the economy should be directed more by governments. (LO 2.5)
- In theory, when profits become too high in an industry, more businesses are attracted to that industry. Due to market imperfections, such as barriers of entry, this sometimes does not occur. (LO 2.6)
- How employees and employers view the work ethic influences the ethics and responsibilities of a corporation. (LO 2.7)
- The goods and services produced by capitalism should be determined by consumers as they make purchase decisions. Unfortunately, consumer choice is restricted by various business practices and some government regulations. (LO 2.8)
- Government has a role in a capitalistic system, but its involvement should be only to protect the interests of stakeholders unable to defend themselves and to provide the infrastructure for the market system to operate effectively. (LO 2.9)
- Capitalism exists in several forms around the world. The functioning of capitalism faces changes, but does operate most of the time with moral standards. New forms of capitalism are always being proposed to make business more responsive to society's needs. (LO 2.10)
- The ethics of capitalism involve several challenges, but an argument can be made that it is a moral system. (LO 2.11)

Key Terms

Right of private property	Profits
Intellectual property	Work ethic
Individualism	Consumer sovereignty
Economic freedoms	Conscious capitalism
Equality of opportunity	Creative capitalism
Competition	State capitalism
Oligopoly	Greed

Critical Thinking and Discussion Questions

1. Identify the intellectual property you use in your studies. Have you always respected the rights of the owners of this type of private property?

2. Should equality of opportunity equal equality of results? What are the implications for business because of the inequalities that result from capitalism?

3. Why doesn't competition exist in some industries, and what are the ethical implications?

4. Assess the amount of economic freedom that exists in Canada today. How does this freedom, or lack thereof, influence Canadian businesses?

5. What is the connection between competition and profits?

6. Do you believe that employees no longer possess a genuine work ethic?

7. In Canadian business, is the consumer sovereign?

8. Is government's role in the Canadian business system increasing or decreasing?

9. What individual and societal values are involved with each of the fundamentals? Values are defined as core beliefs or desires that guide or motivate attitudes and actions.

10. Does capitalism or the free market system erode moral character?

11. Is ethical capitalism possible?

Cases

2.1 CAMPUS BOYCOTTS: WHO MAKES THE CALL?

In March 2013, Local 7004 of the Newfoundland and Labrador Public and Private Employees (NAPE) went on strike against the Labatt Brewery Company in St. John's, Newfoundland. Labatt is owned by Anheuser-Busch InBev (AB InBev), a multinational corporation and the world's largest brewer with over 200 beer brands. In 2012, it had revenue of about $40 billion and profits of over $7 billion. The union claimed that Labatt was seeking concessions including the introduction of two-tiered wages, a reduction in health and dental benefits, and requiring workers to contribute to the pension plan and share the costs of benefit programs. The average Labatt employee salary was $81,000 versus the provincial average of $48,000. In June 2013, NAPE called for a boycott of Labatt products.

The Memorial University of Newfoundland Student Union (MUNSU) decided to join the boycott by discontinuing the sale of Labatt products in the bar it operated, The Breezeway, which had lost $120,000 in 2012 and was budgeted to lose money in 2013. MUNSU also owed the City of St. John's $360,000 in back taxes on The Breezeway after losing a property taxation court case. MUNSU considered The Breezeway as a service to its 13,000 undergraduate student members enabling them to purchase reasonably priced beer and socialize in a safe place as well as providing employment for 40 students.

The MUNSU had supported workers in previous strikes at the public transit system and the local airport. In a Membership Advisory, Candace Simms, MUNSU Director of External Affairs, explained the move. She stated that "MUNSU recognizes the importance of acting now to ensure current and future workplace equality" as "Students expect a fair and equitable workplace, free of two-tiered benefits that hurt younger employees ... " MUNSU thought it inappropriate to require its Breezeway employees to sell Labatt products. MUNSU stated that it had a responsibility to support the boycott as doing so was in the best interests of its members. The Advisory concluded by "encouraging all members to get informed and to support the actions being taken by NAPE 7004 to safeguard workers' rights and advocate for equality for young workers."

Noah Davis-Power, a third-year student, objected to MUNSU's boycott. Firstly, he felt that MUNSU should not impose a boycott and instead leave it to students to make their own decision with regard to purchasing Labatt products. Also, as a consequence of the boycott, Labatt had stopped supporting various university student groups. According to Davis-Power, this support involved tens of thousands of dollars and he wondered from where the replacement money would come. Lastly, without the Labatt products, The Breezeway would lose even more money. Overall, he believed that MUNSU should stay out of labour disputes. Many students were critical of Davis-Power's positions although some supported him.

MUNSU countered that sales had not declined in in The Breezeway and that many members supported the decision. Labatt used replacement workers to produce beer and claimed that it had not lost sales during the strike and boycott. The strike was eventually ended in February 2014 when the company and union reached an agreement. Labatt products returned to The Breezeway.

Questions

1. How is the equality of opportunity fundamental applicable to the issues in this case?
2. How is the consumer sovereignty fundamental applicable to the issues in this case?
3. How is the role of government fundamental applicable to the issues in this case?
4. What consideration should be given to the following assertions mentioned in the case?

   - that Labatt Breweries of Canada belongs to a foreign multinational corporation
   - that the corporation is seeking concessions
   - that Labatt employees earn much more than the average
   - that The Breezeway is viewed as a service to students and loses money

5. Is MUNSU's decision to boycott Labatt beer justified?
6. Is Noah Davis-Power's position appropriate?

Source: "Boycott of Labatt Products," Membership Advisory June 2013, MUNSU; Laura Howells, "MUNSU's Labatt Boycott Source of Controversy This Summer," *The Muse*, August 29, 2013, 3; and Noah Davis-Power, "Labatt Boycott Costing MUN Students" (Letter to the Editor), *The Telegram* (St. John's, NL), A6; and Josh Dehaas, "Memorial University Student Blasts Beer Boycott: Student Union Says It's Standing Up for Young Workers" *Maclean's,* Online edition, July 25, 2013, accessed July 12, 2016, http://www.mcleans.ca/general/memorial-university-student-blasts-beer-boycott/.

2.2 ZAPPING SALES AND TAXES

Julia Hoben had graduated from a college business program with a major in accounting. She designed her program so that it enabled her to obtain a Chartered Professional Accountant (CPA) designation within two years. She was employed as an accountant with a regional school board and she was enjoying the work.

Recently, her uncle asked if she was interested in doing some accounting for his restaurant. Julia first thought about this as moonlighting, of which her employer might not approve. She checked her employer's policy hand-book and did not find any mention of moonlighting.

Julia had learned in a Human Resources course about moonlighting and the issues involved. Moonlighting, or outside employment, is defined as paid work in which an employee engages outside of the normal working hours of his or her primary job. The most common reason for engaging in such activity is to earn extra money to pay expenses, reduce debt, or save. Individuals also do it to gain experience, improve their skills, start small businesses, and simply because they enjoy it.

Employers are concerned about the possible interference with job performance and conflicts of interest. Moonlighting may result in employees being stressed or fatigued, reducing productivity. It could involve the inappropriate use of company resources, for example communications, computers, and copying facilities. Conflicts of interest can arise, especially if the work being performed is the same and in the same industry. Conflicts also occur when personal interests resulting from moonlighting clash with the interests of the employer who expects employee loyalty. As a result, employers often require that employees disclose outside employment. From a societal perspective, moonlighting is perceived as taking jobs that could be filled by unemployed persons, and governments are concerned about tax evasion.

Her uncle assured her that he needed Julia's services for a maximum of three hours a week and would pay her an hourly rate. Julia would not be performing bookkeeping tasks, because her aunt looked after that aspect. Her uncle wanted Julia to look after the various tax filings for the provincial government and the Canadian Revenue Agency (CRA) as the filings would be considered more reliable if prepared by someone with a professional accounting designation. Julia concluded that there was no conflict between working for a school board and in the restaurant industry, and agreed to the offer. She did not feel it necessary to inform her employer.

During the first months, Julia experienced several complications in this part-time employment. Her first concern was prompted when her uncle paid her in cash for the first two weeks of work. At first, Julia did not think much about this, but upon further reflection she acknowledged that cash payments to employees or suppliers in the restaurant industry was a possible approach to avoiding taxes.

Things got more complicated in the following weeks. The restaurant used a POS (point of sale) computerized system to record sales according to whether they were credit card or cash, and summarized sales by menu items and waiter. Julia reviewed the reports from this system in preparing taxation returns. She noticed that daily cash versus credit sales fluctuated greatly and more than would be expected. Also, she found two POS reports for the same day with differing totals.

Julia had read newspaper articles about tax avoidance in the restaurant industry. In fact, CRA had conducted an extensive investigation into tax fraud in the industry. One practice involved the use of "zapper" computer software to delete specific data, for example cash sales or employee hours. This practice was difficult to detect because a stand-alone software application was used that was contained on a CD or memory stick.

This situation placed Julia in a difficult position. First of all, family was involved and it would harm family relationships if she reported the practice to the taxation agencies, or if she even mentioned it to her uncle. Besides the personal dilemma, there was also a professional one. As a member of Chartered Professions Accountants she had to follow its ethical principles and rules of conduct. She was not allowed to provide services that could be unlawful, to present financial information that was misleading, or to be associated with any reports or statements she knows are false.

These principles and rules seemed very clear to Julia. Her conscience would not allow her to sign a taxation return when she suspected fraud. Julia felt very alone as she was not sure with whom she could discuss this matter, and more importantly, what she should do.

Questions

1. What ethical issues are involved?
2. What fundamentals of capitalism are involved?
3. Why should individuals and businesses pay taxes?
4. What should Julia do?

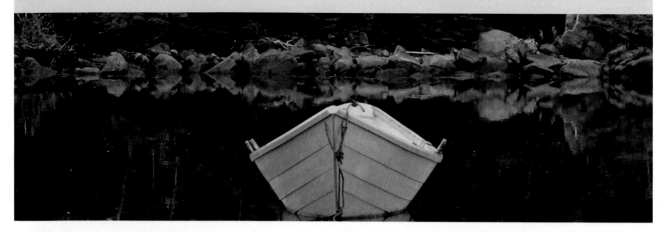

Used with the permission of Dennis Flynn

CHAPTER 3

Identifying Stakeholders and Issues

LEARNING OUTCOMES

After studying this chapter, you will be able to:

LO 3.1   Recognize business as one institution in society and understand that its activities are influenced by other institutions and individuals referred to as stakeholders.

LO 3.2   Identify the corporation's stakeholders generally and the stakeholders relating to particular issues confronting the corporation.

LO 3.3   Understand the dynamic nature of stakeholder influence and that stakeholders have different goals and influence.

LO 3.4   Recognize the role of managers in relation to stakeholders.

LO 3.5   Formulate arguments supporting and opposing the stakeholder concept.

LO 3.6   Define an issue and describe issues management.

LO 3.7   Describe an issue life cycle.

LO 3.8   Learn the importance of managing issues that become crises.

What would you do if...?

Tom Carroll operated a small construction business building new homes and renovating older ones. He had been in business for 20 years and had a good reputation for quality work completed on time. His company employed six workers year-round, but the number increased to about 20 between May and October when outside construction was viable. He operated his business "by the book" and attempted to be fair in dealings with employees and customers. In addition, he made a point of dealing with the Canada Revenue Agency fairly and did not avoid or evade taxes. He believed that this was not the case with many of his competitors.

Tom felt that some of his competitors were simply greedy. In chatting with them about evading taxes, they said that they were unlikely to get caught and customers did not care. Furthermore, they felt that it was necessary sometimes to survive and that entrepreneurs deserved the extra compensation for working hard and long hours. Although they believed that evading large amounts in taxes was a crime, evading small amounts was okay. There was a common feeling that small business pays too much tax, the government wastes money, and large businesses get more tax breaks than small businesses.

The two main areas where the contractors evaded paying taxes were paying workers off the books and hiding income. The downsides of paying off the books were the always-present chance of being caught, the inability to declare the labour costs as an expense, the liability in the event of worker injury, and the risk of worker disclosure. Income was more likely to be hidden when the business was struggling financially, the owner had close control of operations, the business's objectives were short-term, and workers were paid off the books. Hiding income was facilitated by customers paying cash, sometimes in exchange for a lower price.

Hearing all this got Tom to thinking. There were certainly opportunities to evade taxes with slight chances of being caught. It was clear that his competitors were benefiting from the evasion practices while he paid all his taxes. He asked his wife about it, and she said he should not follow the same practice. Despite this, he started considering the possibility.

What is your advice to Tom?

This chapter introduces three topics that enable managers to assess the overall business environment—that is, to understand the economic, ethical, and environmental circumstances in which a corporation finds itself. The first topic describes the stakeholder concept, lists the corporation's stakeholders, and examines the pros and cons of the concept. The second topic is the identification of the issues confronting the corporation. Another topic will be the managing of crises. The three topics are closely related, as issues always involve stakeholders, and issues sometimes become crises. The identification of the corporation's relevant and salient stakeholders along with the issues is one approach to scanning the environment and will assist in understanding the corporation's circumstances.

LO 3.1   The Stakeholder Concept and Business

The business enterprise system impacts the lives of all citizens. In Canada, and in other democracies with private enterprise systems, business operates in a pluralistic social system where a variety of groups and institutions use power or influence to represent the interests of particular groups of citizens. The business corporation is one of many institutions in a pluralistic society, but its influence is widespread.

A **pluralistic society** is one where influence or power is decentralized by dispersing it among a variety of institutions. No one institution is completely independent of others, but each institution does possess some autonomy to pursue its own interests. With power diffused in this way, society is somewhat protected from the dominance of one group or one institution. Business is subject to the influence of other institutions in society and must respond to the various participants in society. In this book, these participants are referred to as stakeholders.

A stakeholder is an individual, or group, who can influence and/or is influenced by the achievement of an organization's purpose.[1] Stakeholders may also be referred to as claimants, influencers, publics, or constituencies. Although all these terms have their merits, the term "stakeholder" is preferable as it provides the most general identification of the parties to which business is responsible or accountable.

It is important for managers to identify the complete array of stakeholders for two reasons: (1) to obtain resources, business has to recognize the groups that control scarce resources; and (2) to maintain the legitimacy of business as an institution in society, the support of other groups is required. Freeman argues that the use of the word "stakeholder" and the stakeholder concept is important for the following reason:

> By using "stakeholder," managers and theorists alike will come to see these groups as having a "stake." "Stakeholder" connotes "legitimacy," and while managers may not think that certain groups are "legitimate" in the sense that their demands on the firm are inappropriate, they had better give "legitimacy" to these groups in terms of their ability to affect the direction of the firm. Hence, "legitimacy" can be understood in a managerial sense implying that it is "legitimate to spend time and resources" on stakeholders, regardless of the appropriateness of their demand.[2]

Freeman points out that managers must seek out stakeholders and argues that if "you want to manage effectively, then you must take your stakeholders into account in a systematic fashion."[3] Furthermore, the corporation should undertake on its own to identify and to satisfy key stakeholders before a solution is imposed, often by government or the courts. It is important that corporations develop managers with the expertise to deal with stakeholders.

All stakeholders have expectations, such as reasonably priced and good-quality products, adequate wage levels, good working conditions, and a clean, safe environment. Business must understand the preferences and expectations of the various stakeholder groups. Managers cannot look only inward to the needs of owners; in order to be successful, managers must behave in a manner compatible with the beliefs and values of their stakeholders.

The complexity of business is often due to changing relationships between a corporation and its stakeholders. It should be remembered that the relationships are two-way. Corporations must understand how their activities influence stakeholders and also how stakeholders can influence their activities. Another approach to viewing these relationships is in terms of ethics and responsibilities. The corporation must consider the ethical implications of its behaviour toward stakeholders as must stakeholders toward the corporation. Corporations have responsibilities to stakeholders, depending on the situation and issue. Likewise, stakeholders must consider their responsibilities to the corporation depending on the circumstances of the relationship.

LO 3.2   Identifying Stakeholders

The first step for business is to identify the stakeholders that influence the corporation and/or that are influenced by the corporation. The following is a generic listing (that is, a list that applies to most corporations) of a corporation's stakeholders. This list is not intended to be in any particular order of importance.

Owners

Owners of the corporation, usually referred to as shareholders, are those individuals or groups who have invested in the form of equity, or shares. Shareholders can number in the hundreds of thousands for large corporations, or be a single individual in the case of an unincorporated business. Large institutions, such as trust or pension funds, may hold shares in corporations, as may a government. A corporation may be a shareholder in one or several other corporations. The influence shareholders have on business varies. One generalization is based on the number of shareholders: where there are thousands of investors, each holding a small number of shares, the individual shareholder's influence is usually minimal. But, where ownership is concentrated in the hands of a few shareholders, they usually exert significant influence over the corporation. In recent years mutual and pension funds, which in the past did not exercise their influence despite substantial holdings, have become more active in influencing major corporate decisions. Owners are stakeholders fundamental to the corporation and will be discussed in detail in Chapter 11.

Directors

Directors are elected by shareholders to represent their interests. They vary in number but are usually fewer than 20, and comprise a board that meets to decide on issues confronting the corporation. Directors can be from inside or from outside the corporation, in which case they are usually executives, managers, or owners of other corporations. The purpose of a board of directors is to determine the corporation's strategic direction, monitor and review the corporation's performance, and hire and fire the top executives. In theory, the ultimate responsibility for the corporation rests with the directors, but in reality, their influence varies. If the board comprises mainly insiders—that is, management—its influence on the corporation is substantial. Often boards comprising outsiders are mainly token bodies that rubber-stamp management's decisions. However, the board of directors has the potential to be a very powerful body. The influence of directors will be examined in Chapter 11.

It should be noted that small, unincorporated business enterprises do not have directors. In these enterprises the owners are also the operators and/or managers, and no board of directors exists. However, even small enterprises can be incorporated, and the owner/manager often is the principal shareholder and serves on the small board of directors, which operates on an informal basis.

Employees

Employees are individuals who work for the corporation and are categorized in several different ways. Managers are employees involved in supervising tasks at low, middle, and top levels in the corporation. Workers may be thought of as blue- versus white-collar. Blue-collar workers are involved in manufacturing, production, or servicing tasks, while white-collar workers are office employees. A corporation employs several professional groups, such as engineers, lawyers, and accountants. Employees may be hired on a part-time or full-time basis, with part-time employment becoming more prevalent recently. Labour unions often represent some employees, especially blue-collar workers. One issue relating to unions is dealing with the corporate trend to seek wage and benefit concessions from employees during a period of economic downturn.

Retired employees, either managers or workers, have a stake in the corporation where company pension plans exist. Recently, more attention has been focused on the employment of disadvantaged groups, including women, minorities, and persons with exceptionalities. Employees are considered among the most obvious and, perhaps, most important stakeholders. They have considerable influence for the simple reason that they are critical for the operation of the corporation. The ethics and responsibilities relating to employees will be discussed in Chapter 12.

Customers or Consumers

A corporation's customers may be members of the public, usually referred to as consumers; other corporations, referred to as industrial (or business-to-business) customers; or governments or government agencies. Customers are the source of revenue for the corporation and should be treated carefully. However, where a corporation is a monopoly, or where there is a lack of competition in the market, customers can be taken for granted. It is argued that the needs of individual consumers are ignored by large corporations that, through persuasive promotional practices, manipulate consumers. Instead of consumers influencing production decisions, producers influence or determine what consumers will purchase. Today, consumers are influencing the ethics of corporations, as described in Responsibility for Ethics 3.1. The ethics and responsibilities relating to consumers will be discussed in Chapter 12.

RESPONSIBILITY FOR ETHICS 3.1

Ethical Consumers

Consumers are influencing corporations to offer goods and services that they consider to be "ethical" or "socially responsible." Also, many businesses have taken the initiative and are responding to these "ethical" consumers. Consumers can also exert influence on corporations through boycotts.

- *Whole Foods Market*—This Austin, Texas, company claims to be the world's leading natural and organic food supermarket, with 341 stores throughout North America and the United Kingdom, including ten in the Vancouver and Toronto areas. It is publicly traded on the NASDAQ as WFM.
- *Fair Trade products*—This involves the identification of products such as coffee, cocoa, sugar, and flowers that have been produced under conditions where human rights, good working conditions, and the environment are respected.

Boycott [handwritten]

- *Product Red brand*—Corporations are allowed to license this brand, with a percentage of the profits going to The Global Fund to provide sustainable funding for programs to fight AIDS, tuberculosis, and malaria in developing countries.
- *Boycott*—Organized boycotts of products or particular corporations are increasing in number. These efforts have been made easier and more successful because of the Internet.

Lenders and Creditors

Different types of individuals or groups lend corporations money. Some lend for long terms by purchasing bonds or debentures, while others advance funds for short periods, as with trade creditors. The lenders may be individuals or other corporations, usually financial intermediaries that exist to lend money. This stakeholder has substantial influence: if the lender is not paid as agreed upon in the contract, the corporation's assets can often be seized. Mortgagees, lenders, and creditors have a prior claim on the assets of a corporation if it ceases operations or goes bankrupt.

Suppliers

Suppliers are usually other corporations that provide raw materials, component parts, or finished materials used in the manufacture or provision of the corporation's goods and services. The influence of suppliers varies. If a supplier is the only source of a particular material or component, then more of the corporation's attention must be devoted to this supplier. If the material component is available from several suppliers, the corporation has alternative sources and is not dependent upon a sole source. Sometimes, a corporation may, for a variety of reasons, own its supplier. The ethics and responsibilities relating to suppliers and supply chains will be discussed in Chapter 12.

Service Professionals

Service professionals are individuals who are not employees of the corporation but provide services on a fee-for-service basis. Included in this type of stakeholder are lawyers, accountants, engineers, and management consultants. Their influence is in the form of the advice they provide the corporation. It is in their own interest to see that the advice is reliable, as they are then more likely to be rehired. Corporations rely on service professionals as it is often too expensive to employ such expertise on a permanent basis.

A key professional in business is the accountant. Corporations must present financial and non-financial information according to certain standards to that stakeholders, in particular owners and lenders, can have confidence in the data. The Chartered Professional Accountants of Canada insure that this is done and the organization is described in Responsibility for Ethics 3.2.

RESPONSIBILITY FOR ETHICS 3.2

Chartered Professional Accountants of Canada

The Chartered Professional Accountants of Canada (CPA Canada) is the national organization with provincial branches representing 200,000 accounting professionals. CPA Canada ensures that highly qualified professionals will demonstrate a commitment to providing the highest standards of accounting, ethics, and best business practices. It funds the development of Canadian accounting and assurance standards, and the work of the independent standard-setting boards and oversight councils. This is important to ensure the financial and non-financial information in the private and public sectors is reliable, comparable, transparent, and credible.

CPA Canada is also involved with setting of ethics standards and its Code of Ethics is in alignment with the Code of Ethics for Professional Accountants issued by the International Ethics Standards Board for Accountants (IESBA). This Code is 179 pages in length and is derived from five fundamental principles of ethics:

- The behaviour of accountants must be such as not to damage the reputation of the profession.
- Professional services will be performed with integrity and due care.
- Accountants will maintain their professional skills and competence.
- The confidentiality of information must be maintained.
- Objectivity must be practised and not compromised by bias, conflict of interest, and undue influence of others.

Source: The Chartered Professional Accountants of Canada (CPA Canada), accessed December 2, 2015, https://www.cpacanada.ca/; Chartered Professional Accountants of British Columbia (CPABC), accessed December 2, 2015, https://www.bccpa.ca/; and the CPABC Code, June 2015, accessed December 2, 2015, https://www.bccpa.ca/CpaBc/media/CPABC/Members/Regulatory/Governing%20Documents/CPABC-Code-of-Professional-Conduct-FINAL-(June-23-2015).pdf.

Dealers, Distributors, and Franchisees

In some types of business, many other corporations distribute a firm's product to customers along a distribution or supply chain. A good example is the automobile industry, where hundreds of dealers form a distribution system. Wholesalers are also this type of stakeholder. Some corporations allow others to sell their product or service through a franchising system. The arrangement under which distributors or franchisees operate varies, but can be complex, especially in the case of franchising. The extent and complexity of these arrangements determine the influence a corporation has over the distributors or franchisees. But this influence is not one-sided, as the corporation depends on these types of businesses to get its products to the customers. If the corporation in question is a dealer, distributor, or franchise, the operations of the business will be impacted substantially by the agreement under which it operates.

Business Organizations

Corporations join together to form hundreds of organizations to represent their interests. An example of such an organization representing large business corporations is the Business Council of Canada, a group comprising the executives of Canada's largest 150 corporations. Chambers of Commerce or Boards of Trade exist in thousands of communities, and a national coordinating organization operates as the Canadian Chamber of Commerce. There are organizations representing small businesses, including the Canadian Federation of Independent Business and the Association of Chinese Canadian Entrepreneurs. Trade associations represent corporations operating within particular industries, for example the Forest Products Association of Canada or the Canadian Manufacturers & Exporters. Business also forms self-regulating agencies such as the Advertising Standards Council, which monitors advertising practices. In some areas, or industries, corporations are represented by employer associations usually dealing with industrial relations matters.

The impact of these types of organizations varies, but by uniting to speak as one they are bound to have more influence than by acting individually. Often it is difficult to obtain consensus within these groups, as not all businesspersons think the same way. The effectiveness of voluntary, self-regulating agencies has been questioned.

Competitors

Competitors are those firms that sell the same products. However, competitors should be viewed more broadly. Corporations producing substitute products should be identified and monitored. Not only should existing competitors be considered, but potential future competitors should be identified. With rapid technological advances, new products and services are constantly being researched and developed. Competitors should not be restricted to those from the domestic environment: those from foreign countries should also be considered. The ethics and responsibilities relating to competitors will be discussed in Chapter 12.

Joint-Venture Participants

Joint-venture participants are partners cooperating in a particular enterprise or project. Usually, written agreements outline the relationships between the corporation and its partners. Several other terms are also used to describe this cooperation, including alliances, consortia, networks, and partnerships. The word "strategic" is often used in conjunction with these terms, for example strategic alliances, cooperative strategies, and strategic partnerships.

Non-Governmental Organizations (NGOs)

Principal to do good.

A **non-governmental organization (NGO)** is any group outside of the public and private sectors that holds shared values or attitudes about an issue confronting society. Such organizations, previously known as interest groups, operate on a non-profit basis with volunteer members or networks, with many having paid employees. They are numerous, but their impact on the corporation varies. Examples of groups currently having considerable impact on the corporation are environmental, women's, and neighbourhood (community) groups. Chapter 13 will examine this stakeholder in detail.

Society at Large

This stakeholder represents the general public; that is, the views of society. The views of this stakeholder can be difficult to determine, making it difficult to ascertain this stakeholder's influence. In opinion surveys, members of society will express concern for energy conservation but continue to purchase high-gasoline-consumption vehicles or choose to live long distances from where they work. Communities in which businesses are located fall into this category, but their views are often made explicit to the corporation.

Educational Institutions

Schools colleges universities

Schools, colleges, and universities educate not only employees but also the general public. Business relies on these institutions to provide it with educated and skilled employees. These institutions also educate the public about economic systems and the role of business in society. Universities, in particular, are relied upon to perform basic research that is often applied to industrial situations. Educational institutions, although mainly government funded, are now seeking financial and other support from business, giving rise to the issue of commercialization involving corporate advertising on campus, research funding, and naming buildings after major donors. The student is also a stakeholder of the corporation in several ways including as a consumer of goods, as employees with part-time jobs while in school, and as potential employees in the future. The topic of educational institutions as stakeholders is discussed in Chapter 13.

Religious Groups

Churches often speak out on issues related to business. Religious leaders occasionally speak of concerns with capitalism and the dangers of the free market and profits.[4] Businesspersons are individually influenced by the values and beliefs upheld by religious groups. The influence of this stakeholder will be described in Chapter 13. There is even a patron saint of business, described in Responsibility for Ethics 3.3, who was an early practitioner of corporate social responsibility.

RESPONSIBILITY FOR ETHICS 3.3

The Patron Saint of Business

The patron saint most closely related to business is Homobonus, who was a successful merchant and tailor, and is acknowledged for his good works in the community. Saint Homobonus (meaning "good man") is listed as the patron to merchants, cloth workers, tailors, and shoemakers. In addition, he is also recognized as the patron saint of businesspeople, the only saint recognized as such.

Homobonus Tucingo was born sometime during the first half of the twelfth century in Cremona, Italy, the son of a wealthy tailor and merchant. He never attended school but his father taught him the trade and how to conduct business diligently and honestly. He successfully operated the business after his father's death, and viewed it as an employment given him by God and as a means of serving both his family and the wider society of which he was a member.

He is described as an industrious and thrifty businessman, yet exhibiting boundless charity. His business prospered in spite of his generous charity to the poor. There is a claim that the more he gave away, the more prosperous he became. He died on November 13, 1197, and was canonized in 1199. It was unusual to canonize a layman, especially one in business, and to do it within two years after his death. An invocation or prayer to Saint Homobonus is:

St. Homobonus, you merited the favour of both God and man by being a doer of the Word, and not just a hearer. You have shown us that it is possible to live a Christian life in the world, for you, yourself were a prosperous businessman—yet you loved God with all your heart, and you loved your neighbour as yourself. We bring to you our petition [specifically mention here] and ask you to intercede before the Father on our behalf.

Source: Robert W. Sexty, "Recognizing Saintly Business: Lessons from Saint Homobonus," *New Academy Review,* Autumn 2003, Vol. 2, No. 3, 55–56.

connect   Want to learn more about **Saint Homobonus**?

Charities

Charitable organizations receive some of their funding from corporations, and in return the business donors expect careful stewardship of the funding. In addition, some corporations have a direct involvement in charitable activities. Charities are a part of the non-profit sector and some operate commercial enterprises.

Service, Fraternal, Cultural, and Ethnic Associations

Employees of business corporations join numerous service, fraternal, cultural, and ethnic associations, such as Rotary and Lions Clubs, Parents for French, and the Association of Ukrainian Businessmen. These memberships often involve volunteerism through the donation of employee time and efforts, and association with such organizations is often viewed as a source of business contacts. Responsibility for Ethics 3.4 is an example of a service organization attempting to influence the behaviour of its members.

RESPONSIBILITY FOR ETHICS 3.4

Rotary's Guiding Principles

Business networks and social organizations are involved in activities for the betterment of the communities in which they exist. Pledges, codes, and principles of these organizations impact the behaviour of members, most of whom are businesspersons. An example is Rotary International's Guiding Principles, part of which is highlighted below:

The Four-Way Test

The test, which has been translated into more than 100 languages, asks the following questions:

Of the things we think, say or do

1. Is it the TRUTH?
2. Is it FAIR to all concerned?
3. Will it build GOODWILL and BETTER FRIENDSHIPS?
4. Will it be BENEFICIAL to all concerned?

Source: "Guiding Principles," Rotary International, accessed December 3, 2015, http://www.rotary.org/en/AboutUs/RotaryInternational/ GuidingPrinciples/Pages/ridefault.aspx.

The Media

The media cover events associated with business. Managers are interviewed and quoted on a corporation's plans or business issues. Media publicity about the practices of a particular corporation or the quality of its products or services can have a substantial positive or negative impact on a corporation's sales. On some occasions, the corporation attempts to influence media coverage through media releases and public relations initiatives. Chapter 13 will discuss this stakeholder further. The impact of social media was discussed in Chapter 1.

Government

It is important to recognize that government is not a monolith. Instead, government has several dimensions. In Canada, there are three levels of government: local, provincial/-territorial, and federal. Governments are formed by politicians and staffed by civil servants. Business must consider the impact of both of these groups within each level. Governments are organized by departments, and the influence of these departments on business varies by industry and by corporation. Governments have agencies that impact business operations, including regulatory bodies such as the Canadian Transport Commission, the Canadian Radio-television and Telecommunications Commission, and provincial public utility boards. Governments own many business enterprises, wholly or in part, and many government-owned financial institutions lend money to business corporations. Even foreign governments may have an impact by influencing sales in other countries.

Two other institutions are associated with governments: political parties and the legal system. Political parties play a role in business, and business supports these parties financially. The legal system is established and maintained by governments, and court decisions impact business corporations. Government is an influential stakeholder in the business system including its role in promoting corporate social responsibility as discussed in Chapter 10.

There is some controversy about whether or not the environment and animals should be identified as stakeholders. Some stakeholder theorists argue that the environment should be a stakeholder. Their main point is that this would give the natural environment prominence—or make it a priority—with management and stakeholders. Others disagree, saying that stakeholders must have a voice; that is, the capability to speak for themselves. The natural environment is unable to do this, but its well-being is certainly the concern of others. Furthermore, the environment does not meet the definition of a stakeholder upon which the theory is based. In this book, the natural environment is considered and taken into account and is described in Chapter 14, but not as a stakeholder.

In society, the treatment of animals varies: one view is that they have rights and a moral status in themselves and views continue to the opposite thought that there is no need to give them any status. Animals are not commonly portrayed as stakeholders of the corporation. There is an academic field that studies animal ethics, but there have been limited connections made to the ethics of business. Animals as stakeholders is described in Everyday Ethics 3.1.

EVERYDAY ETHICS 3.1

Animals as Stakeholders

Animals have a prominent presence in society and can be categorized into several groups, each with issues relating to the treatment or welfare of animals. The most obvious group is the use of animals as pets or companions. The pet industry is huge and ranges from the provision of the medical care to marketers of pet food supplies. Exotic animals such as snakes and monkeys are illegally traded in the world. Animal shelters exist in every community to care for abandoned and abused pets.

Business and governments use animals in the development and testing of life-saving pharmaceuticals and other drugs. Consumers are concerned about the treatment of these animals and NGOs have been formed to protect them. Animals are admired in the wild through tourism and they also provide entertainment in zoos and circuses. The exploitation of wild animals is a concern, for example, killing them for ivory, for hides for clothing, or just for sport.

The harvesting of animals for human food raises issues. Wild animal species may be become extinct or seriously reduced in numbers. The raising of animals in farms for food is opposed by many consumers and NGOs. In many economies, animals still perform work related tasks such transportation and hauling or a source of power in agricultural cultivation.

There are different views towards the moral status of animals. One view is that animals should be treated so that the maximum welfare is achieved for the animal. Another view is that animals have the right to be treated respectfully and should not be harmed. A virtue view proposes that animals be treated with compassion and kindness.

Now that the stakeholders of the corporation have been identified, the following sections discuss other aspects of the relationships between corporations and stakeholders.

connect   Want to learn more about **assessing information about stakeholders?**

LO 3.3   The Dynamics of Stakeholder Influence

Traditionally, the principal stakeholders or power groups were identified as owners, government, and labour (employees). This list is too simplistic: many others have a stake, and the enlarged view illustrated in the previous section is becoming more widely accepted. In effect, these stakeholders act as a system of checks and balances and business cannot act alone without considering the possible actions, and impacts, of groups other than government and labour.

All of these groups, or stakeholders, influence business decision making in a pluralistic society. However, this list is not exhaustive or definitive. It is not possible to list all stakeholders, and they vary by industry and corporation. A corporation's stakeholders may be defined differently for several reasons.

Each of the above stakeholder categories can be broken down further in a manner appropriate to a particular corporation. There are differing perceptions of stakeholders, and their power—or stake—varies depending upon one's point of view. One corporation may consider the influence of stakeholder groups not considered "legitimate" by another corporation, as the two have vastly different values—for example terrorist groups, which some corporations must take into account. The perceived relevance of stakeholders also varies with level of management and functional area. Middle managers conceptualize a different set of stakeholders as being more influential than do chief executives.

When identifying stakeholders it is important to know the corporation's relevant stakeholders, in particular those that have a moral claim. Some stakeholders have a limited or non-evident moral claim on the corporation. This varies with industries and corporations and over time. These factors add to the dynamics of stakeholder influence. An example of the stakeholders identified by one corporation is given in Everday Ethics 3.2.

EVERYDAY ETHICS 3.2

Catalyst Paper's Stakeholders

Corporations often identify their stakeholders in CSR or Sustainability reports in different ways and illustration is provided by Catalyst Paper Corporation. Catalyst Paper manufactures a broad range of high-quality paper products and is one of the largest producers of mechanical printing paper. It is recognized for its sustainable business practices.

In its 2015 Sustainability Report, *The Steps We Take*, Catalyst identified the following key stakeholder groups:

- Employees, retirees, communities
- Investors
- Non-governmental organizations
- Suppliers and business partners
- Indigenous groups
- Governments
- Customers

For each group stakeholder, the Report included the objectives and outcomes relating to the interactions, or engagement, with them in 2015.

Source: *The Steps We Take*, Catalyst Sustainability Report 2015, page18, Catalyst Paper Corporation, accessed May 12, 2016, http://www.catalystpaper.com/investors/sustainability-reports,

Categorizing Stakeholders

No attempt has been made here to categorize the stakeholders as other writers do. Frederick, Davis, and Post[5] categorize the corporation's interactions with society as primary or secondary. Primary interactions are with employees (unions), shareholders, creditors, suppliers, customers, competitors, and wholesalers or retailers, while secondary interactions are with local communities, governments, social activist groups, media, business support groups, and the general public. The difficulty with such a categorization is that stakeholders' involvement and influence shift over time and vary among corporations. It is difficult to ascertain who should be on each list; for example, government is listed as secondary, whereas in Canada it is primary in regulated or protected industries.

Stakeholders are sometimes categorized as being external versus internal to the corporation. Mintzberg's external influencers are owners, associates, employee associations, the public, and directors, while internal influencers are the chief executive officers, line managers, operators, analysts of the technostructure, support staff, and ideology. This categorization serves Mintzberg well for conceptualizing power in and around organizations, but is not sufficiently detailed to identify all stakeholder groups in society. Problems also occur in identifying influencers as internal or external. Mintzberg considers owners to be external, but it might be argued that they are internal; directors might be considered to fit in between the two categories.[6]

Phillips identifies two types of stakeholders, making a useful distinction. Normative stakeholders are those to whom the organization has an obligation and stakeholders from whom the corporation has voluntarily accepted benefits. Examples are financiers, employees, consumers, suppliers, and the local community. In contrast, derivative stakeholders are those from whom the corporation has not accepted benefits, but they hold power over the corporation and may exert either a beneficial or harmful influence. Two examples are NGOs and competitors.[7]

Differing Goals and Power

Conflict may exist among stakeholders. The goals of the various groups differ and may or may not be compatible with those of the corporation. This is natural, as all are in effect sharing from one pot and benefits to one most likely represent losses to another. Corporation managers must be aware of this fact and, if necessary, negotiate an accommodation. The interaction between the corporation and stakeholders is very much a balancing act. If priority is given to profits for shareholders at the expense of benefits to employees or consumers, then these stakeholders will react. They may reduce the quantity or quality of their contribution (effort or purchases) until they receive what they perceive as a return commensurate with their contribution. Ultimately, such action can jeopardize returns on capital to shareholders.

It should be recognized that some stakeholders have more power or influence than others. There may be a shifting of power among the groups at various times, or coalitions may form to counterbalance a powerful group exerting too much influence. Business management may even attempt to co-opt an interest group's or regulatory agency's influence. When some stakeholders become too influential, other stakeholders may somehow counterbalance the power. An example is provided by a corporation's actions to exert control over its suppliers or purchasers: government may impose competition legislation or other laws to counter such restrictive trade practices. It is also argued that there is a managerial elite, comprising managers of larger businesses plus politicians and senior civil servants, that controls business within a nation, resulting in most important business decisions being made by a few. Hopefully, if such elite control is the case, other stakeholders will point this out (media) or initiate action (non-governmental organizations).

Just because a stakeholder is out of the limelight does not mean it is not exerting influence on business. Some stakeholders are just more evident than others; for example, the demands of unions, employees, and shareholders are usually known, while the demands of others are emerging. Also, the influence of stakeholders varies over time. Consumer interest groups were influential in the 1960s and 1970s but declined in the 1980s as government and public support was reduced. The reverse was the case with environmental interest groups. It is the task of managers to identify the most influential stakeholders; that is, those groups that make a difference to the well-being of the corporation.

LO 3.4   The Manager: A Special Stakeholder

The managers of Canadian business enterprises are also stakeholders, of course: they can be employees, and may be shareholders as well. The uniqueness of managers is that they are in charge of enterprises; that is, they are very influential in dealing with other stakeholders. Managers, and chief executive officers (CEOs) in particular, determine the corporation's social responsibility initiatives where the stakeholders supported are recognized as influencing the corporation.

Managers are responsible for carefully identifying and analyzing the stakeholders influencing the enterprise and the stakeholders influenced by the enterprise. They are also responsible for responding to stakeholders. This managerial responsibility might be outlined as follows:

- Identify stakeholders influenced by, or having an influence on, the corporation.
- Understand how the corporation currently views the stakeholders.
- Examine how each stakeholder will or might influence the corporation.
- Assess opportunities or threats, and the magnitude of their influence on the stakeholder.
- Rank stakeholders by influence.
- Prepare programs or policies detailing how to deal or cope with stakeholders.

A controversial issue is the level of compensation managers, in particular CEOs, should receive for their efforts. Everyday Ethics 3.3 lists the compensation of Canada's highest paid CEOs. High CEO compensation raises several ethical implications:

- Some executive compensation packages are so large they can affect the returns of shareholders, including employee pension plans.
- Compensation often increases when the performance of the corporation declines.
- Employees feel unfairly treated when layoffs occur while the CEO's salary increases.
- Often the compensation packages are not disclosed or properly accounted for.
- Stock options are exercised before performance is achieved, and sometimes at share prices beyond the market price.
- Pension plans for executives are much more generous than for other employees, some of whom may not even have a pension plan.
- The highly paid executives are able to hire the best expert tax accountants to avoid paying taxes.

A related aspect is the practice of tying executive compensation to environmental, social, and governance performance targets, known as *sustainable pay*. Few Canadian corporations have implemented this practice and the ones that have use past performance instead of pre-determined performance goals. Sustainable pay should be implemented as it protects and creates long-term shareholder value. Where sustainable performance measures are used, they are primarily directed at compliance, risk mitigation, and value protection rather than value creation.[8]

EVERYDAY ETHICS 3.3

Executive Compensation and Ethical Implications

A report by the Canadian Centre for Policy Alternatives (CCPA) found that the five highest-paid Canadian chief executives in 2014 were:

- John Chen, BlackBerry Ltd., $89.7 million
- Donald Walker, Magna International Inc., $23.4 million
- Gerald Schwartz, Onex Corporation, $21.1 million
- Hunter Harrison, Canadian Pacific Railway Ltd., $17.6 million
- Mark Thierer, Catamaran Corp., $16.3 million

These figures represent total compensation including salary, bonus, shares, and options.

It is argued that chief executive officers (CEOs) of Canadian corporations are earning a disproportionate share of the wealth. According to a study by the CCPA, the average compensation of the 100 best-paid CEOs was $8.96 million in 2014, while the average wage and salary earnings of Canadians was $48,636. CEOs made 184 times more than the average Canadian worker. Canadians working at the minimum wage would earn $22,010. The study found that the 100 highest-paid corporate executives earn an average Canadian's annual salary by 12:18 pm on the first working day of the year.

Several initiatives are proposed to counter the trend toward high compensation packages, including placing restrictions on the exercising of options, limiting severance benefits, delaying payment of bonuses until performance is clear, requiring shareholder approval of preferential pensions, and implementing the complete disclosure of all costs associated with compensation. Some governments, including those in the United States and United Kingdom, are regulating executive compensation in industries to which they have provided financial support. A simple approach would be to tax the compensation of highly paid executives at a higher rate.

Source: Hugh Mackenzie, *Staying Power: CEO Pay in Canada*, Canadian Centre for Policy Alternatives, Ottawa, ON. January 2016, ISBN 978-1-77125-254-6.

The next chapter will outline various ways managers can analyze relationships with stakeholders and their influence on the corporation and vice versa.

LO 3.5 Arguing the Stakeholder Concept

The Argument Against the Stakeholder Concept

Although the stakeholder concept has been widely accepted, some opposition does exist. The case against the concept can be summarized by four main points: problems of categorization, challenges in meeting expectations, dilution of top management focus, and the impracticality of shared governance.

Opponents argue that the list of stakeholders is extensive and diverse and the stakeholders often have contrary objectives. Furthermore, there is no agreement on the priority or importance of the stakeholders. In fact, it has been pointed out that there is not even agreement on the number of stakeholders.

Meeting the expectations of all stakeholders maybe an impossible challenge. There is no clear statement of stakeholder expectations except for shareholders. Determining the "share" each stakeholder should claim (or be entitled to claim) is difficult. There are complex trade-offs among the stakeholders, making it impossible to operate for the benefit of all.

To meet the objectives of the corporation, managers need a clear, unequivocal corporate purpose. The "social market" as represented by the communist and socialist economic systems has failed for the most part. The social goals of many stakeholders divert management attention from the measurable results necessary to judge corporate performance.

The corporation's governance structure does not accommodate multiple stakeholders, and efforts to do so have failed. It is challenging to have competing and conflicting interests attempting to govern the corporation. The corporation as it functions today is designed to confer advantages to one set of stakeholders, the shareholders.[9]

The Argument For the Stakeholder Concept

Advocates of the stakeholder concept argue that the opponents do not understand the basis for the concept. They argue that an appreciation for stakeholders is fundamental to understanding how to make money. Recognition of stakeholder interests does not promote equity, and certainly not equality. Responding to stakeholders is simply good business, as they are often capable of adversely impacting the performance of the corporation.

It is necessary not only to recognize the interests of all stakeholders but also to promote the loyalty of other individuals and groups. Shareholders are a principal stakeholder, but ignoring others—for example, employees, customers, and lenders—can have substantial economic consequences. Even interest groups or NGOs can prevent the corporation from accomplishing its goals. Stakeholder thinking identifies the full range of individuals and groups from whom loyalty is needed (or, in some cases, is not needed).

The purpose of the corporation in today's society is a complex combination of desires and expectations. The stakeholder concept is a systematic approach to recognizing these expectations and deciding whether to respond. Through an assessment of each stakeholder, the value of each to the corporation can be ascertained to suit the stakeholder and to suit the corporation's purpose.[10]

A topic related to the stakeholder concept is the process of issues management, which involves the identification of issues that confront business or the corporation as well as the development of appropriate responses. The following section describes issues and their management.

connect Want to learn more about **identifying and engaging stakeholders?**

LO 3.6 Issues Relating to Ethics, Responsibilities, and Sustainability

Issues arise from the relationships between business corporations and their stakeholders. In the context of business and society, an **issue** is a point in question or a matter that is in dispute where different views are held of what is or what ought to be corporate performance–based management or stakeholder expectations. Everyday Ethics 3.4 identifies some issues in selected industries.

EVERYDAY ETHICS 3.4

Main Issues in Selected Canadian Industries

	Industry				
	Automotive	Telecommunications	Mining	Banking	Pharmaceutical
Main Issues	Green manufacturing	Restrictions on competition	Community relations	Executive compensation	Product safety
	Emissions	Complicated contracts	Health and safety	International financial crisis	Pricing
	Union wage concessions	Health and safety risk of using devices	Corruption in developing countries	Government regulation	Marketing practices
	Electric and robot cars	Construction of cell phone towers	Waste and discharges	Credit card charges	Competition from generics
	Production overcapacity	Higher fees than in other countries	Environmental legacy	Service charges	Responding to pandemics
	Shift to smaller cars less profitable				

Wartick and Mahon expanded the definition of a corporate issue by identifying the following:

a. a controversial inconsistency based on one or more expectation gaps,

b. involving management perceptions of changing legitimacy and other stakeholder perceptions of changing cost/benefit positions,

c. that occur with or between views of what is and/or what ought to be corporate performance or stakeholder perceptions of corporate performance, and

d. imply an actual or anticipated resolution that creates significant, identifiable present or future impact on the organization.[11]

These definitions will assist in identifying economic, ethical, social, and environmental issues important to the study of business's relationship to society. They are the first step in establishing an issues management process.

Issues management is a systematic process by which the corporation can identify, evaluate, and respond to those economic, social, and environmental issues that may impact significantly upon it.[12] The definition suggests that corporations can manage the issues confronting them. The term "issues management" is considered a misnomer, as no corporation can manage or influence events to attain a desired outcome on a particular issue in all situations at all times. Issues management does not mean the corporation can create social change, or can control or manipulate society. Instead, the term refers to the process by which the corporation responds to economic, social, and environmental issues.

One purpose of issues management is to minimize surprises relating to events or trends in society by serving as an early warning system. Also, it prompts managers to be more systematic in coping with issues and stakeholder concerns by using foresight to anticipate change, and by participating in the resolution of existing issues. Issues management attempts to fill a void by providing a framework for assessing matters confronting the corporation that otherwise may be overlooked. It also provides the mechanism for coordinating and integrating management of issues that might confront several departments or units throughout the corporation.

There are several benefits to practising issues management: corporations are more likely to maintain a competitive advantage over rivals; corporate behaviour is more likely to be consistent with societal expectations; and the corporation is less likely to make a serious social or ethical mistake. Issues management enables the corporation to detect issues earlier and develop appropriate responses much sooner, sometimes even when the issues are emerging. The corporation's vulnerability is reduced and its credibility enhanced.

Like any other management methodology or technique, issues management does not just happen and appropriate conditions must exist for success. Top management must support it and be involved. There must be broad participation at the operating and staff levels. The approach must adapt to the culture and the management dynamics of the corporation. The issues management approach should be implemented gradually, making sure that it is supported by operating units. It is important to stress output (position papers, ideas, and interpretation of data) over process (the techniques and mechanisms used for issues identification, issues evaluation, and response development). Decisions must be made, and analysis cannot go on forever.[13]

LO 3.7   Issue Life Cycles

One aspect of issues management is monitoring for issue life cycles. Issues can be viewed in two dimensions, over time and by degree of awareness. In Figure 3.1, the degrees of awareness at various stages of the cycle are identified as none or little, increasing, prominent, peak, and declining. Issues are often present that receive little or no attention (T1). It is also possible for an issue not to be evident at all. Managers should be aware of these possibilities, particularly when facing the early stages of a new issue or the re-emergence of an old issue. The public and media may not be aware of the issue and the government most likely inactive. But, NGOs and those stakeholders directly impacted by the issue may be.

According to Coates, Coates, Jarratt, and Heinz,[14] early identification, in period T1, of an emerging issue having *any* of six characteristics is important. These characteristics are as follows:

1. The terms of the debate cannot yet be clearly defined.
2. One of the actors (stakeholders) will define the emerging issue and make it a current issue.
3. It deals with matters of conflicting values and interest.
4. It is not a problem that expert knowledge will automatically be able to resolve.
5. It is stated in value-laden terms.
6. Trade-offs are possible.

FIGURE 3.1   *Issue Life Cycle*

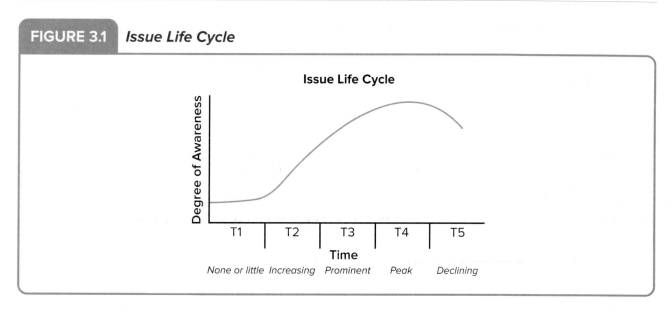

This list indicates that an emerging issue may not be easy to resolve in the short term.

In period T2 the awareness of the issue increases—for example, as the issue receives some media attention. It is unlikely that all corporations have formulated a response by this time. NGOs and other stakeholders will have become more active and seeking attention. Government is most likely reactive at this stage. The urgency of the issues are unlikely to be clear at this point.

In period T3, the issue is very prominent and cannot be ignored. Responses or solutions are widely discussed, and most corporations have taken a stance. The government becomes active and all stakeholders influenced recognize the importance and implications of the issue.

The issue peaks at T4 And corporations will be defensive. The issue may become a crisis at the time. NGOs would be seeking settlements or other solutions. Government would be proactive and may be proposing legislation to address the issue. The decline or maybe dormant stage (T5) should not necessarily be viewed with relief, because issue awareness may not decline, as indicated in Figure 3.1. The issue may re-emerge and awareness increase, or awareness may remain constant. The challenge for managers is to be sensitive to the degrees of issue awareness of society or a significant number of stakeholders.

LO 3.8   Crisis Management

Sometimes an issue will become a crisis for management. Crises could arise from issues such as industrial accidents, product failure or tampering, product recalls, product safety, technology failure, hostile takeovers, malicious rumours or media leaks, natural disasters, environmental problems, labour disputes, acts of terrorism, fraud or embezzlement, and violations of government regulations. These crises involve many stakeholders depending upon the incident. Issues that become crises can be addressed through approaches to crisis management.

Many discussions of crisis management make reference to Fink's "anatomy of a crisis."[15] A **crisis** is defined as a turning point, a crucial time, and a situation that has reached a critical point. Fink states that a crisis is an unstable time but the outcome may not necessarily be bad, and that there can be positive outcomes. He defines **crisis management** as an approach involving planning and removing much of the risk and uncertainty, allowing the corporation to achieve more control over events.[16] Everyday Ethics 3.5 describes an example of a crisis and the responses from various stakeholders.

Fink proposed that there were four stages to any crisis: prodromal, acute, chronic, and resolution, which are shown diagrammatically in Figure 3.2. The prodromal, or pre-crisis, stage is one where the corporation receives some warning or some symptoms appear, even if subtle. This stage represents a turning point that, if recognized, should not be ignored because an anticipated crisis is much easier to manage at this stage. Situations exist where management, even if aware of a crisis, may not be able to do anything in advance.

EVERYDAY ETHICS 3.5

The Outbreak of Escherichia Coli O157.H7 at XL Foods Inc.

XL Foods operates one of the three largest beef processing plants in Canada at Brooks, Alberta. On September 4, 2012, a U.S. food safety agency found evidence of the bacterium *Escherichia Coli (E. coli)* in beef crossing the border. It was not until later in the day that Canada's food safety agency, the Canadian Food Inspection Agency (CFIA), found the same *E. coli*. The CFIA continued to investigate the incident but believed that a recall was not necessary because harmful products had not reached Canadian consumers. The CFIA allowed the plant to continue operating but recalled some products on September 16. On September 27, the plant was closed.

Many issues surfaced as a result of this incident. The company, the government through the Minister of Agriculture, and the CFIA were all slow in providing information, and it was often incomplete. XL Foods took responsibility for the outbreak, but offered no apology. Only brief messages were provided on the company's telephone system or website, and managers made only brief statements. The government assured consumers that the Canadian food safety system was protecting Canadians. The CFIA allowed the plant to operate for two days before closing it. Eventually, about 1,800 products were recalled from 33 retail chains.

There are serious consequences for many stakeholders. It was confirmed that an estimated 18 consumers became sick from the XL Foods products. The cattle industry was concerned about its future, because consumers may purchase less beef and there may be damage to international markets. Many questioned Canada's food safety system and the way the CFIA operated. Some believed that too much reliance was placed on industry self-regulation because it was disclosed that XL Foods had not followed its own *E. coli* protocols. Employees became very concerned as layoffs occurred and the union called for a public inquiry.

Many stakeholders questioned whether the crisis in food safety was handled properly.

Source: Adapted from Canadian Food Inspection Agency, "Timeline of Events: CFIA Investigation into XL Foods Inc. (*E. coli* O157:H7)," archive accessed July 28, 2016, http://www.inspection.gc.ca/food/consumer-centre/food-safety-investigations/xl-foods/timeline/eng/1349149063487/1349149874246.

FIGURE 3.2   *Fink's Anatomy of a Crisis*

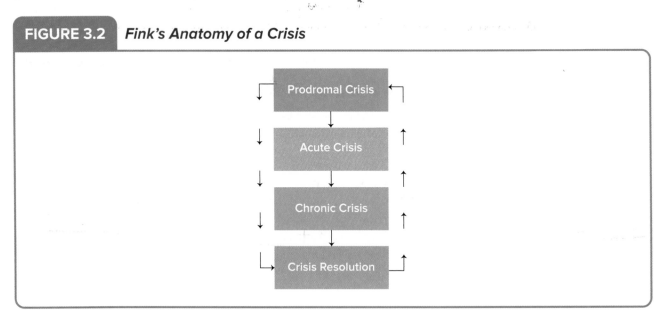

Source: Based on description in Chapter 3 of Steven Fink, *Crisis Management: Planning for the Inevitable* (New York: AMACOM, 1986), 20–28.

The acute crisis stage is the point at which the crisis has occurred and the damage has resulted. At this stage it is easier to control the response if the corporation is prepared; but there are often rapid developments that may be hard to control. The cleanup or post-mortem phase is referred to as the chronic crisis stage. This is a stage for recovery, investigations, audits, and self-analysis, as well as for further development of crisis management approaches. It is a stage that can linger for some time. The final stage is crisis resolution, when the corporation has recovered from the damage of a crisis.

Fink points out that all four stages may not be present, they may overlap, and their duration and intensity varies. Ideally, he says, the prodromal stage should be followed immediately by resolution, as shown by the arrows on the left side of the figure. The arrows on the right side indicate a learning process is possible so that previous stages of future crises can be dealt with more effectively.[17]

Fink's four stage framework is representative of the many models of crisis that exist. For example, Pearson and Mitroff's model had five stages: signal of detection, preparation/prevention, containment/damage limitation, recovery, and learning.[18] Augustine extended his framework to six stages including a final one "profiting from the crisis."[19]

Most corporations will experience crises to some degree and it is important to be prepared and, if possible, proactively invest in approaches to deal with a crisis. Managers should identify aspects of the corporation's operations where a crisis is mostly likely to occur. For example, a food manufacturer should anticipate a crisis involving food contamination, and a railway can plan for derailments that will inevitably occur. Managers and employees must organize responses and practice the procedures to follow. Crisis incidents should be monitored and analyzed and lessons learnt from them.

Crisis management always includes a discussion on communications. All the relevant or key stakeholders must be identified and contacted including the media, social media, and those stakeholders affected including governments. Internal stakeholders such as employees should be fully informed of the situation. Transparency is stressed, where the corporation tells everything it knows, what it does not know, and what it would like to know. There should be answers to all questions and the media should be provided with accurate and timely information. It is important to be honest, disclose all facts, and demonstrate concern.

A key ingredient is honesty. Telling the truth is viewed as the only policy as it is the ethical and practical thing to do. Incomplete information to guard against possible legal actions should be avoided. The correct facts should be stated clearly without media spin. Above all, there should be empathy for those stakeholders harmed. The spokesperson should be carefully selected and possess effective communication skills. Arm's length advisers should be engaged to objectively assess the corporation's communications approach.[20]

Most likely an apology is necessary. The apology should be timely, most likely soon after the incident, and not limited by possible legal consequences. An apology will contribute to rebuilding trust in and the reputation of the corporation. An apology must be sincere, include assuming responsibility, and not placing blame on others. Most corporations recover from a crisis if the response is properly managed.[21]

The use of the stakeholder concept and issue and crisis management provide good frameworks for examining the economic, ethical, and environmental responsibilities of the corporation. The following chapter will discuss the approaches to influencing or engaging stakeholders, and the approaches or tactics that stakeholders use to influence the corporation. Issues are associated with stakeholders and approaches to analyzing issues will be described.

Your advice to Tom . . .

What Tom is facing is a common dilemma that involves numerous rationalizations: taxes are too high and he pays too much, it is necessary to survive in a competitive business, and everyone is doing it. Several stakeholders influence Tom. Many of his competitors are doing it, so the government collects less tax revenue, which in turn places a larger burden on those who do pay taxes. Some customers are attracted by a lower price and will not care even though they may be liable for accidents on their property—and employees who are not covered by workers' compensation schemes have little recourse if injured. Tom would be wise to consult another person!

Summary

- This chapter defines and identifies the stakeholders in the business system and describes the management of issues that arise in the system. A stakeholder is an individual, or group, that has some share, interest, or "stake" in the business system and the activities of corporations. (LO 3.1) *Share, interest & stake"*
- Nineteen types of stakeholders are listed and described, but several things should be remembered about the list:

  - The list is not necessarily complete but it includes the most commonly acknowledged stakeholders and comprises generic or general labels. The stakeholder names or participants have to be customized for each corporation. (LO 3.2) *commonly acknowledged stakeholders*
  - Although some stakeholders—for example, employees, shareholders, and customers—are important to all corporations, the dynamic nature of the relationships between business and stakeholders means that the importance of other stakeholders will vary by corporation and over time. Because of this variability, the list is not categorized in any way so the reader is less likely to predetermine the influence of particular stakeholders. (LO 3.3)

  - Each stakeholder has different goals and expectations of the corporation. Sometimes conflict exists among stakeholders and/or the interests of stakeholders. Overseeing the various stakeholder interests is an important aspect of the modern manager's job. Stakeholders, and their influence, are referred to constantly throughout this book, as is the influence managers have over stakeholders. (LO 3.3)

- Managers perform a key role in the relationship between the corporation and stakeholders. Manager or CEO compensation is an issue and it proposed that executive compensation should be tied to ethical, social, and environment criteria. (LO 3.4)
- Despite the widespread use of the stakeholder concept in business organizations, it is not universally accepted as legitimate. However, today most managers believe that the stakeholder concept is a systematic approach to understanding and responding to various influences in the corporation's environment. (LO 3.5)
- The identification and management of economic, ethical, and environmental issues that may confront the corporation is described. Issues always involve stakeholders, and their appropriate identification and management is important. (LO 3.6)
- Understanding issue life cycles is important to identifying issues and to implementing a response. (LO 3.7)
- Some issues lead to crises and the response must be timely and comprehensive. Crises in business have been described and crisis management frameworks developed that enable the corporation to take appropriate actions in such situations. (LO 3.8)

issues lead to crises response must be timely and comprehensive

enables the corporation to take appropriate actions in such situations

Key Terms

Pluralistic society

Owners

Non-governmental organization (NGO)

Issue

Issues management

Crisis

Crisis management

Critical Thinking and Discussion Questions

1. List the stakeholders that have influence and/or are influenced in the opening vignette of this chapter. What are the economic, social, and ethical issues involved? *employees, shareholders, customers*

2. How can all stakeholders be satisfied? Should a corporation be accountable to stakeholders, or take into account stakeholders? *importance of stakeholders will vary by corporation and over time. each stakeholder has diffrent goals and expectations*

3. Why can different stakeholders have more influence at one time and less at another time?

4. Access the websites of three large corporations and list the members of the board of directors by occupation. What are your conclusions about the type of people who serve on boards?

5. Discuss the influence that business corporations and businesspersons have on your educational institution.

6. Monitor the media's coverage of Canadian business in newspapers or on radio and television. Identify whether the coverage is positive or negative. *problems of categorization, challenges in meeting expectations, list is extensive and diverse*

7. Why do some businesspeople still oppose the stakeholder concept despite its widespread adoption?

8. Identify the three main issues confronting business in Canada today.

9. Where in their life cycle are the following business and society issues?

   – Consumption of bottled water
   – Climate change
   – Obesity
   – Excessive executive compensation
   – Global outsourcing
   – Privatization of health care

NDP. Jagmeet Singh.
Progressive Conservative Party Doug Ford.

Cases

3.1 "BOONDOCKING" AT WALMART

Ted McAfee owns the Blue Spruce RV Park on the outskirts of Prince George, B.C.—and he has a problem. Business has declined substantially in recent years as recreational vehicle (RV) owners are parking (or camping) in Walmart store parking lots for free.

The RV owners are allowed by the stores to park for free, but no facilities are provided such as electricity, fresh water, or waste water disposal. In RV slang this practice is known as "boondocking." The practice is also made possible as many of the RVs are self-contained with their own electrical systems and with water supplies for several days.

Parking in the Walmart lots has become more appealing to owners as the prices at RV parks have risen and the cost of gasoline increased. The lots provide a safe location as they are lighted all night and monitored by security cameras. Also, the stores are a convenient source for supplies and services such as pharmacies.

The Walmart stores have an RV-friendly policy although it is not an official one. A Rand McNally atlas sold at Walmart gives directions to every store, and RV owners can purchase a store locator from the RV website rvtravel.com.

In Prince George and many other communities, the practice of staying overnight in a store parking lot is not allowed by local city regulations. Prince George city authorities had Walmart put up signs informing RV owners of the regulations. But it is difficult to enforce the regulations, especially as Walmart does not care about the practice. In addition, there is a threat from RV owners who are organized, and in the U.S. communities that enforced the local regulations were boycotted.

Meanwhile, Ted McAfee and other park owners are losing business and may close down.

Questions

1. List the stakeholders involved and their influence. Identify any fundamentals of business or capitalism involved.
2. What are the issues for Walmart and stakeholders?
3. What can or should RV park operators like Ted McAfee do?

Sources: Based on Eric Moskowitz, "On the Road: A Paved, Well-lighted Campsite," *BusinessWeek*, October 11, 2004, 18; Chris Wattie, "In Newfoundland, Camping is Yet Again Controversial," *National Post*, September 21, 2004, A1, A9; and Jonathan Woodward, "The World of the RV: A Wal-Mart Atlas and Freeloading in B.C.," *The Globe and Mail*, July 19, 2005, A1, A6.

3.2 ACCEPTING A JOB IN THE PAYDAY LOAN INDUSTRY

Matthew Simmons was agonizing about whether or not to accept a management job in the payday loan industry. Matthew had graduated from a college business program and had received three job offers, the best of which in terms of salary was as a management trainee with a payday loan company.

Payday loans are small, unsecured loans against the customer's next paycheque. This type of lending began in the mid-1990s and today has about two million customers in Canada. There are more than 1.7 million storefronts and online platforms, some of which are open seven days a week, 24 hours a day. It is estimated that the industry does about $2 billion a year in business.

The operation of these stores has become an informal banking system for a segment of the population. The loans are made and covered by a postdated cheque cashed on the next payday. The average loan is about $280 and made for 10 days. The service offered is convenient, but high interest rates are charged and fees are levied. It is even alleged by some consumer advocates that the payday loan business is illegal and a form of loan-sharking. The industry responds that their lending practices are better than the alternatives available to some in society who would have to resort to using pawnshops or unscrupulous lenders.

The payday loan industry is responding to a consumer need for short-term, unsecured loans. The chartered banks and credit unions are unwilling and/or unable to provide the service. In fact, it is argued that the banks have encouraged the industry by closing so many branches. The banks say they have overdraft and credit card loans available. Some critics have determined that the payday loan stores are increasingly being set up near banks.

Some consider the industry to be a scam against poor and financially illiterate consumers that traps many into a never-ending spiral of debt. Industry observers counter that there is a business case for the payday loans. First of all, there is a huge demand, suggesting a need. Flexibility is provided to consumers in managing their financial affairs and other services are provided, such as cheque cashing and money transfer. The loans may be used to pay off other loans with even higher interest rates, such as those on some credit cards. The high interest rates and fees are justified as there is a high default rate, and there are high administrative costs involved with small loans. The industry is mostly unregulated as there are jurisdictional complications, with the federal government being responsible for interest rates and the provinces for consumer protection.

An industry association, the Canadian Payday Loan Association (CPLA), is attempting to clean up the industry's reputation and supports regulation by government. Its mandate is "to work with governments toward a national regulatory framework that will allow for a viable industry and protect consumers." Of the 1,771,400 retail outlets in Canada, about 957,760 are CPLA members. The members must adhere to a "Code of Best Business Practices" that covers such things as rollovers (businesses are not allowed to grant another loan to pay off a previous one), collection practices, privacy protection, advertising, and responding to consumer complaints.

From a career perspective, the payday loan industry appeared promising to Matthew. The company was expanding rapidly by adding locations in smaller communities and adding financial services such as insurance, mortgage referrals, foreign exchange, and tax preparation. Matthew's offer stated that he would start with a six-week training course followed by an intern period in a branch under the supervision of a manager. There was a good possibility of being a branch manager in less than a year and a division manager a few years afterwards.

Questions

1. What fundamentals of capitalism are relevant to this case?
2. Which stakeholders benefit from the payday loan industry, and which ones are harmed?
3. What are the economic, social, and ethical implications or issues in the industry?
4. Should Matthew take the job?

Sources: This case was prepared from public sources to provide material for classroom discussion, and it is not intended to illustrate either effective or ineffective response to a business and society managerial situation. Statistics on number of outlets obtained from the Canadian Payday Loan Association, accessed November 20, 2015, http://www.cpla-acps.ca/english/home.php.

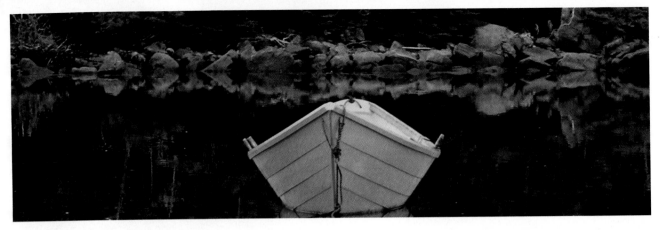

Used with the permission of Dennis Flynn

CHAPTER 4

Stakeholder and Issue Analysis

LEARNING OUTCOMES

After studying this chapter, you will be able to:

LO 4.1 Explain stakeholder analysis in an organization.

LO 4.2 Describe stakeholder management capability.

LO 4.3 Understand stakeholder matrix mapping.

LO 4.4 Discuss the diagnostic typology of organizational stakeholders.

LO 4.5 Apply the stakeholder identification and salience typology.

LO 4.6 Explain the application of stakeholder influence strategies.

LO 4.7 Identify the use of stakeholder collaboration approaches.

LO 4.8 Learn about two approaches to issue analysis.

What would you do if...?

Carol Duggan had recently been promoted to manager of The Coffeepot, one of several coffee shops owned by her boss, who had delegated responsibility for day-to-day management of the shop to her. It was a new shop and in addition to serving coffee and other beverages offered a light food menu including sandwiches and desserts.

Carol was interested in the shop doing well, because in addition to her salary she was to receive bonuses based on the shop's financial performance. Things were going quite well but she was always on the lookout for ways to increase business. Since she had become manager, she observed that some customers occupied tables and lounges for extended periods of time. She felt that many customers viewed the shop as a way to get out of the house or as a place to get away from other distractions.

Internet connections were provided free through a Wi-Fi service, and many customers sat for hours surfing the net. The shop also offered students a discount on purchases to encourage their patronage. Post-secondary students would purchase a coffee and then do their studying or assignments with books and computers spread out at the tables.

At the same time, she noticed that other customers could not find a table or a place to sit. Some students did give up their tables, but others did not. Several customers complained to Carol about the monopolization of tables by students. As a result, she decided to monitor the offenders and began to maintain a record of their behaviour. She found that some were staying three to four hours three or four nights a week despite the signs posted at the counter and on the walls requesting that table occupancy be limited to one hour.

The next step was to decide what to do. Carol faced a dilemma involving balancing profitability with a social service to the community. She was reluctant to address the offending individuals verbally, as this might lead to a confrontation or embarrassment. Instead, she slipped a small orange-coloured note to offending customers that stated "Your time is up. Please make this table available for other customers. Thanks." This action was taken only when the shop was busy and customers were seeking tables.

The reaction was immediate. Customers went online (some from within the shop!) on Facebook and Twitter to share their thoughts about this new practice with hundreds of contacts. Within 24 hours, various student leaders were proposing a boycott of The Coffeepot. A writing group announced that it would no longer meet there. Some students claimed that they paid for their food and drinks and were entitled to stay as long as they wanted. Others stated that they realized that the shop was a business and had to make profits. The incident became a feature story in the local media. Responses to Carol and the shop owner were split about 50/50 between negative and supportive.

What is your advice to Carol?

This chapter reviews the analysis of stakeholders and issues. The approaches to stakeholder analysis range from the basic listing and mapping to more complicated concepts such as stakeholder collaboration and social capital. The phrase *stakeholder management* is used for some approaches because this represents how managers perceive stakeholders; that is, as individuals or groups that could be "managed," suggesting that stakeholders could be controlled or even manipulated. Recently, stakeholder-theory academics and researchers have developed other approaches to understanding stakeholders, particularly those with a moral claim. Today, many enlightened corporations are using these approaches to enhance their understanding of stakeholder relations, referred to as **stakeholder engagement**—any efforts by a corporation to understand and involve relevant individuals, groups, or organizations by considering their moral concerns in strategic and operational initiatives.

Issue analysis is a logical accompanying process to stakeholder analysis. Two approaches to issues analysis will be described in the last section.

LO 4.1 Basic Stakeholder Analysis

All corporations should involve themselves in stakeholder management, even at a preliminary level. If nothing else, corporations should identify and attempt to understand the stakeholders that influence and are influenced by the corporation. At the least, the corporation should prepare a stakeholder map of its stakeholders.

The corporation can increase its understanding of these stakeholders by answering the following questions, which will capture the essential information needed for effective stakeholder management:

1. Who are our stakeholders?
2. What are their stakes?
3. What opportunities and challenges are presented to our firm?
4. What responsibilities (economic, legal, ethical, and philanthropic) does our firm have to all its stakeholders?
5. What strategies or actions should our firm take to best deal with stakeholder challenges and opportunities?[1]

A similar approach is to complete a stakeholder analysis worksheet for each stakeholder, like the one in Table 4.1. Note that two parts exist in the lower portion of the worksheet, for stakeholders that influence the organization and for those that are influenced by the organization. Some stakeholders are one or the other, while others may be both.

TABLE 4.1	Stakeholder Analysis Worksheet

Definition

Stakeholder—An individual or group who can influence, or is influenced by, the operations (or activities) of an organization.

Stakeholder Identification

Stakeholder _____

Sub-categories _____

Stakeholder Analysis

Influences the organization _____

How? _____

Organization's response _____

How satisfactory is the response? _____

Influenced by the organization _____

How? _____

Stakeholder's response _____

How successful is this influence? _____

Basic stakeholder analysis may include a map or diagram of the stakeholders arrayed around the corporation. Such diagrams are of value in appreciating the extent of stakeholders influencing the corporation and that are influenced. Lines connecting the stakeholders to the corporation can include arrows to indicate the direction of influence. The thickness or colour of the lines can also be indications of influence. The main value of such diagrams is to gain an appreciation for the number of stakeholders and an understanding of real and possible influences. This is the beginning of an analysis, as the nature of the influence—the direction and extent of the influence—would have to be ascertained.

LO 4.2   Freeman's Stakeholder Management Capability

According to Freeman,[2] the process an organization uses to manage relationships with its stakeholder groups involves three levels: (1) identifying the organization's stakeholders and their perceived stakes according to the rational perspective; (2) determining the organizational processes used to manage relationships with stakeholders and fitting these processes with the stakeholder map of the organization; and (3) understanding the set of transactions or bargains between the organization and its stakeholders and deciding whether these negotiations fit the map and the processes. Thus, Freeman defines **stakeholder management capability** as the ability of managers to identify stakeholders and their influence, to develop the organizational practices to understand stakeholders, and to undertake direct contact with stakeholders.[3]

The rational level, the first level, involves preparing a stakeholder map that identifies specific stakeholders. For example, the stakeholder map should include the names of non-governmental organizations (NGOs) influencing the corporation, or the government agencies with which the corporation is involved. A problem arises in that membership among groups may overlap; for example, someone can be an employee but also a shareholder through stock purchase plans. There also may be networks or coalitions among stakeholders, and these should be indicated somehow. An attempt must be made to ascertain the "stake" of each group and the power it has, keeping in mind that different perceptions of stake and power exist.[4]

The second level, process, identifies the procedures used to assess stakeholders. Freeman mentions some possible procedures—including portfolio analysis, which he believes applies to some stakeholders but is too financially oriented, and strategic management, which applies if stakeholder questions are included in each component.[5] In some corporations, specific managers are responsible for stakeholder relations and examples are presented in Responsibility for Ethics 4.1.

RESPONSIBILITY FOR ETHICS 4.1

Jobs in Stakeholder Relations

The following is a sample of stakeholder relations job opportunities. The posting of these jobs indicates the importance corporations are placing on stakeholder relations. Note that these listings are not the complete job descriptions.

- Manager, Stakeholder & Aboriginal Relations, Suncor Energy Services, Calgary, AB. Position responsibilities include: community liaison with individuals, organizations, and associations; ensuring compliance to Suncor stakeholder and Aboriginal relations policies; bringing the external stakeholder voice into the organization; and supports cross company initiatives to support Aboriginal employment, procurement, consultation, community development, land and environmental issues, and training.

- Supervisor, Stakeholder Relations & Outreach, The Ontario College of Trades, Toronto. Among the responsibilities of the position are: lead and develop a comprehensive stakeholder relations and outreach strategy; oversee stakeholder and outreach activities; coordinate stakeholder partnerships and meetings; and maintain a reliable database of stakeholder contacts.

- Associate Manager/Manager, Stakeholder Relations, Gilead Sciences, Inc., Mississauga, ON. The responsibilities of this manager include: plans, establishes, and maintains stakeholder relationships; creates and implement strategic plans for engagement with stakeholders; works to understand the diverse nature of stakeholder groups; and coordination of key stakeholder relations projects.

- Coordinator, Stakeholder Engagement, United Way of Saskatoon and Area. The Coordinator will be involved with activities such as: coordinating existing engagement initiatives and activities; and developing and leading new engagement opportunities and initiatives for various stakeholders.

- Senior Advisor - Stakeholder Relations and Planning, Export Development Corporation, Ottawa, ON. Responsibilities of this position include: building long-term relationships with a set of stakeholders; develops relations and builds trust with key external stakeholders; and identifies external trends and issues in the government and stakeholder community.

Source: Compiled from Careerjet, Workopolis, and Simply Hired websites, accessed December 17, 2015.

Finally, the "transactional" level deals with the actual interaction with stakeholders. It is important to employ managers with the appropriate value set to deal with particular stakeholders if the relationship is to be an effective one. An obvious example is dealing with the media. Some executives are not comfortable dealing with the media, and such contact should be assigned to someone with skills in that area.[6]

Freeman's work is the basis upon which other approaches to understanding stakeholders were formulated.

connect   Want to learn more about **the principles of stakeholder management?**

LO 4.3   Stakeholder Matrix Mapping

The identification of stakeholders is an important first step, but the interpretation of the relationships between the organization and the stakeholders is important. Stakeholder theory has progressed substantially in recent years, and several methodologies or models now exist that can be used to understand or interpret the influence stakeholders have on the organization and/or the influence the organization has on the stakeholders.

Matrix mapping is a technique of categorizing an organization's stakeholders by their influence according to two variables, and usually involves plotting them on a two-by-two matrix. Managers need such a methodology for assessing the importance or power of stakeholders to achieve their demands and whether they have the means or resources to influence. Through a mapping process, management can ascertain the likely impact of stakeholder demands on the corporation's strategies and identify appropriate courses of action to counter or influence these demands.

The matrix in Figure 4.1 illustrates one methodology in which stakeholders are categorized according to their position on a particular issue or proposal and their importance. On the vertical axis, the stakeholders are identified and assessed on whether they oppose the corporation on the issue or support it. A numerical value of 0 to -5 is assigned to those stakeholders opposing, and a value of 0 to $+5$ is assigned to those supporting. The importance of stakeholders is measured on a horizontal axis and varies from least, at a value of 0, to most, at a value of 10. After the two values are agreed upon, the location of the stakeholder is plotted on the matrix.

FIGURE 4.1   *The Position/Importance Stakeholder Matrix*

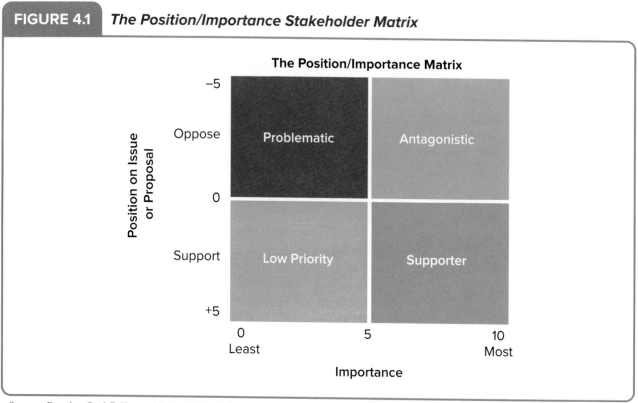

Sources: Based on Paul C. Nutt and Robert W. Backoff, *Strategic Management of Public and Third Sector Organizations: A Handbook for Leaders* (San Francisco: Jossey-Bass Publishers, 1992), 191; and John M. Bryson, *Strategic Planning for Public and Nonprofit Organizations: A Guide to Strengthening and Sustaining Organizational Achievement,* revised edition (San Francisco: Jossey-Bass Publishers, 1995), 284.

Four categories of stakeholders result from this analysis:

- *Problematic stakeholders*—those who would oppose the organization's course of action and are relatively unimportant to the organization.
- *Antagonistic stakeholders*—those who would oppose or be hostile to the organization's course of action and are very important to the organization.
- *Low priority stakeholders*—those who support the organization's course of action and are relatively unimportant to the organization.
- *Supporter stakeholders*—those who would support the organization's course of action and are important to the organization.[7]

An example of stakeholder categorization is given in Responsibility for Ethics 4.2 relating to the issue of a large retailer entering a small community.

RESPONSIBILITY FOR ETHICS 4.2

Stakeholders and Large Retail Development

An ethical issue arises when large retailers such as Walmart or Canadian Tire enter smaller communities and compete against local, small businesses. From the perspective of the large retailer, the stakeholders involved with the issue are plotted on a position/importance matrix.

Stakeholders:

- Existing competitors (EC), including small businesses
- Municipal government (MG), mostly likely supporter; considers development desirable
- Consumers (CO), most likely supporter as prices lower and selection increases
- Chamber of Commerce (CC), supporter but some members may oppose
- Residents (RE) in area of the development
- NGOs (NG), especially environmental ones, would oppose
- Possible employees (PO) in development view as opportunity
- Employees (EE) of existing retailers
- Media (ME) would outline both positions

After all stakeholders are identified, the large retailer can develop strategies to influence some stakeholders and to counter the influence of other stakeholders.

After the categorization is completed, managers can develop tactics or strategies to most appropriately deal with each stakeholder. The following are examples:

- *Strategies for problematic stakeholders*—Target moderate stakeholders with educational programs, adjust corporate plans to accommodate stakeholders, and prepare defensive plans if coalitions of stakeholders form.
- *Strategies for antagonistic stakeholders*—Identify potential coalitions and take defensive action, prepare for undermining of supporters, anticipate nature of objections and develop counter-arguments, engage selected stakeholders in bargaining, and determine plan changes to gain support.
- *Strategies for low priority stakeholders*—Provide educational programs and promote involvement with supporters.

- *Strategies for supporter stakeholders*—Provide information to reinforce position, and ask supporters to influence indifferent stakeholders.[8]

This stakeholder matrix mapping uses two variables relating to position and importance. Other matrices could use variables such as power/dynamism, or power/interest. Regardless of the variables used, the importance of the technique is a systematic analysis of stakeholders and their influence.

connect Want to learn more about **matrix mapping**?

LO 4.4 The Diagnostic Typology of Organizational Stakeholders

One methodology for assessing and managing stakeholders is outlined by Savage, Nix, Whitehead, and Blair[9] and appears to be based on Freeman's generic stakeholder strategies.[10] The authors claim that a stakeholder's significance or influence depends on the situation and the issues involved, and as a result managers must use the appropriate methods to deal with various stakeholders. Two assessments are considered critical: the assessments of stakeholders' potential to threaten the organization, and of their potential to cooperate with it.

Diagnosing the potential for threat involves ascertaining the stakeholder's power to disrupt the organization's accomplishment of its objectives. Diagnosing the potential for cooperation allows the organization to move beyond defensive and offensive strategies against a threat to a situation in which cooperation with stakeholders allows the organization to accomplish its objectives.

The stakeholder's potential for threat or cooperation becomes the basis for categorizing, on a matrix, the types of stakeholders. Figure 4.2 indicates that stakeholders can be classified into four types—supportive, marginal, non-supportive, and mixed blessing—and that different strategies exist for responding to each type. The following is a brief description of each stakeholder type and corresponding strategy.

- *Type 1: Supportive stakeholder and strategy*—This is the ideal stakeholder, providing support by being a low threat and high on potential for cooperation. Examples are boards of directors, managers, employees, parent companies, and possibly suppliers and service providers. The strategy for managing this type of stakeholder is to encourage the cooperative potential and not ignore them or take them for granted.

- *Type 2: The marginal stakeholder and strategy*—These stakeholders are neither highly threatening nor especially cooperative. They potentially have a stake, but it varies by issue or is limited to particular issues. Examples are consumer groups, shareholders, and professional associations for employees. The strategy for managing stakeholders of this type is to monitor them closely while recognizing that their interests are narrow and issue-specific.

- *Type 3: The non-supportive stakeholder and strategy*—These stakeholders have a high threat potential, but low cooperation potential. Because of this, they are the most challenging to manage. Examples for, say, a manufacturing firm are competing firms, employee unions, government, and perhaps the media. The strategy to follow with this type of stakeholder is defensive, attempting to reduce the organization's dependence on the stakeholder.

- *Type 4: The mixed blessing stakeholder and strategy*—These stakeholders play a major role in the organization as their threat and cooperation potential are high. Examples are employees who are in short supply, important clients, and organizations with complementary products or services. The two arrows in Figure 4.2 represent the two possibilities for such stakeholders: to become supportive or non-supportive. The strategy to deal with this type of stakeholder is collaboration of some sort, for example joint ventures, alliances, or mergers.

FIGURE 4.2 *Diagnostic Typology of Organizational Stakeholders*

Source: Grant T. Savage et al. "Strategies for Assessing and Managing Organizational Stakeholders," *Academy of Management Executive*, 5(2) (1991): 65. This work is protected by copyright and it is being used with the permission of Access Copyright. Any alteration of its content or further copying in any form whatsoever is strictly prohibited.

Savage et al. outline a stakeholder management process based on this typology. The first step is to identify the key organizational stakeholders by considering factors such as relative power, the specific context and history of the relationship, and specific issues that may be salient. Next, managers diagnose stakeholders according to critical dimensions of potential for threat or cooperation. Following this step, appropriate strategies are formulated to enhance or change current relationships with the key stakeholders. Finally, the strategies must be effectively implemented, including the possibility of transforming the stakeholder relationship from a less favourable to a more favourable one if appropriate. Strategies should attempt to satisfy the needs of marginal stakeholders minimally and to satisfy the needs of supportive and mixed blessing stakeholders maximally. Savage et al. recommend that managers develop objectives for the organization's relationship with current and possible stakeholders as part of an ongoing strategic management process. Responsibility for Ethics 4.3 analyzes the issue of bank automated teller machine (ATM) fees using this typology.

RESPONSIBILITY FOR ETHICS 4.3

Bank ATM Fees, Stakeholders, and Strategies

The issue of fees charged by banks for ATM services has been contentious. Critics said the banks were not being responsible in that consumers were being charged high fees for withdrawing their money. The following is an analysis of this issue, the stakeholders involved, and possible strategies from the perspective of one Canadian bank.

Stakeholder Type 4—Mixed Blessing/Collaborate Strategy

- Government: non-interventionist, but could make election issue
- Minister of Finance: has power to regulate, but prefers not
- Competing banks: have same fee structure, but one may decide to go for lower or no fee
- Media: balanced reporting of issue, but do give voice to critics; also cover banks' views on issue

Stakeholder Type 1—Supportive/Involve Strategy

- Canadian Bankers Association: preparing case in support of existing fee structure
- University finance professors: view fees as "user pay"; research indicates fees reasonable
- Shareholders: keep informed and more concerned with dividends
- White-label ATM providers: may be concerned with future revenue and connections with banks

Stakeholder Type 2—Marginal/Monitor Strategy

- Consumers: 75 percent are not charged for service (i.e., use their own bank); no concern
- Consumer groups: given 75 percent of consumers do not view as issue, unlikely to do anything
- Credit unions: some do not charge customers fees; may decide to promote this feature

Stakeholder Type 3—Non-supportive/Defend Strategy

- New Democratic Party (NDP) raised the issue
- House of Commons Finance Committee: may force government to take action
- Consumers: 25 percent who are charged feel disadvantaged and overcharged
- Some media, for example *Toronto Star*, very critical of banks
- Society at large: general mistrust and dislike of banks due to high profits and poor service

Sources: Based on Steven Case, "Flaherty to Talk Fees with Banks," *The Globe and Mail*, December 12, 2006, B2; Sinclair Stewart and Steven Case, "On Fees: Banks to Give Flaherty a 'Win,'" *The Globe and Mail*, February 22, 2007, B1, B10; and Paul Vieira, "Politics Runs Deep in ATM Attack," *National Post*, February 27, 2007, FP1.

LO 4.5 Stakeholder Identification and Salience

Despite the popularity of the stakeholder concept, little consensus exists on who (or what) the stakeholders of the firm are and to whom (or what) managers pay attention. Mitchell, Agle, and Wood[11] developed a theory of stakeholder identification and salience based upon stakeholder possession of one or more of three attributes: power, legitimacy, and urgency. **Salience** is the degree to which managers give priority to competing stakeholder claims.

The authors provide an extensive review of stakeholder theory, develop a typology of stakeholders, formulate propositions concerning their salience to managers, and discuss research and management implications. Only the stakeholder attributes and the typology will be reviewed here.

Mitchell, Agle, and Wood define the three attributes as follows:

- **Power** is exercising a relationship among social actors in which one social actor, A, can get another social actor, B, to do something that B would not otherwise do. Power can be based upon force or threat, incentives, or symbolic influences.
- **Legitimacy** is a generalized perception or assumption that the actions of an entity are desirable, proper, or appropriate within some socially constructed system of norms, values, beliefs, and definition that is based on the individual, the organization, or society.
- **Urgency** is the degree to which the stakeholder's claim or relationship calls for immediate attention, and exists when a claim or relationship is of a time-sensitive nature and when that claim or relationship is important or critical to the stakeholder.[12]

Additional features make the stakeholder attributes dynamic: the attributes are variable—that is, they do not exist in a steady state; the attributes are socially constructed—not objective; and the consciousness and wilful exercise of the attributes may or may not be present.

It is assumed that managers who wish to achieve a particular end will pay attention to the various classes of stakeholders, and that managers' perceptions dictate stakeholder salience. In addition, the various classes of stakeholders might be identified based upon the possession of one, two, or all three of the attributes power, legitimacy, and urgency. The stakeholder classes resulting from possessing the attributes are illustrated in Figure 4.3. The authors group the stakeholders into the following classes: (a) those with one attribute are latent or warrant low salience (areas 1, 2, and 3); (b) those with two attributes are expectant or moderately salient (areas 4, 5, and 6); and (c) those with three attributes are definitive or highly salient (area 7). Individuals or entities possessing none of the attributes are non- or potential stakeholders (area 8). Table 4.2 provides examples of each type of stakeholder.

FIGURE 4.3 *Stakeholder Typology: One, Two, or Three Attributes Present*

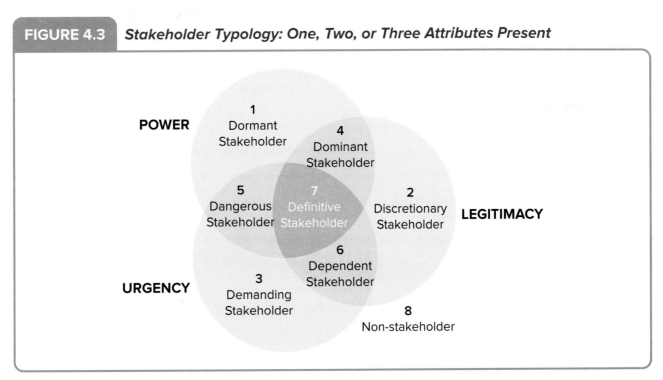

Source: Ronald K. Mitchell, Bradley R. Agle, and Donna J. Wood, "Toward a Theory of Stakeholder Identification and Salience: Defining the Principle of Who and What Really Counts," *Academy of Management Review*, Vol.22, No.4 (1997): 874. This work is protected by copyright and it is being used with the permission of Access Copyright. Any alteration of its content or further copying in any form whatsoever is strictly prohibited.

TABLE 4.2 **Definitions and Examples of Stakeholder Types**

Latent Stakeholders

- Managers may not recognize the existence of these stakeholders or may not give them any attention. There are three types:

  - Dormant—Possess power and should receive attention, as in the case of a fired or laid-off employee speaking out against the firm or filing wrongful dismissal suit (area 1).
  - Discretionary—Possess legitimacy, as would the recipients of discretionary corporate social responsibility (area 2).
  - Demanding—Possess urgency, as with a lone picketer opposing actions of the corporation who gets passing attention as he/she is troublesome but not dangerous (area 3).

Expectant Stakeholders

- Expectant stakeholders possess two attributes, are more salient, and require more attention from management. There are three types:

  - Dominant—Have legitimate claims and have power to act upon the claims (area 4). An example is shareholders and creditors who expect to receive management's attention.

— Dangerous—Possess power and urgency attributes but lack legitimacy; will be coercive and possibly violent thus making the stakeholder dangerous (area 5). This is illustrated when employees are involved in wildcat strikes or sabotage, or by interest group terrorism or blockages.

— Dependent—Stakeholders who lack power but have urgent legitimate claims and often depend on others for power (area 6). Examples are local residents of the environment who depend on a dominant stakeholder, often the government.

Definitive

• Management must address the claims of stakeholders immediately and give priority as they possess all three attributes (area 7). An example is shareholders voting to replace management.

Non-stakeholder

• Non- or Potential Stakeholders—Individuals or entities possessing none of the attributes.

Source: Compiled based on Ronald K. Mitchell, Bradley R. Agle, and Donna J. Wood, "Toward a Theory of Stakeholder Identification and Salience: Defining the Principle of Who and What Really Counts." *Academy of Management Review*, Vol. 22, No.4 (1997): 299-304

RESPONSIBILITY FOR ETHICS 4.4

PETA's Milk Campaign and the Three Salience Attributes

Many businesses are confronted by the activities of People for the Ethical Treatment of Animals (PETA), an animal rights NGO. One of PETA's campaigns is to discourage the consumption of milk and, if possible, ban it. PETA's criticisms of milk include the following: it is produced on factory farms by inhumanely treated animals, it is an inefficient food source placing demand on the environment, and it is linked to various health problems such as allergies, constipation, obesity, heart disease, and cancer. PETA's ultimate goal is to convert people to vegetarianism.

This campaign concerns the dairy industry. The following is an example of how PETA, as a stakeholder in the dairy industry, can be evaluated according to the three salience attributes.

	Attribute		
Stakeholder	**Power**	**Legitimacy**	**Urgency**
PETA's "Milk Sucks" campaign	Through the media and the Internet there is some influence on consumers. To date, it appears that PETA lacks power to change the minds of many consumers. It uses celebrities to support its position.	PETA quotes medical studies and health researchers on the dangers of consuming milk. All this evidence can be countered by other scientists and health organizations.	The campaign should be monitored but other immediate action is not necessary. The industry would continue its advertising messages on the benefits of milk.
	Conclusion: Low	**Conclusion: Low**	**Conclusion: Medium**

Although the salience is relatively low when the attributes are considered together, the campaign cannot be ignored. Thus, there is some salience based on urgency, and PETA is therefore a "demanding" stakeholder.

The authors acknowledge that the typology they have developed may require refinement, further development, and testing. Its advantage not only is that stakeholders are identified, but also that their salience is assessed and the dynamic nature of stakeholder relationships emphasized. By acquiring a missing attribute or attributes, or by losing an existing attribute, the salience of the stakeholder changes. Managers must be aware of such changes and adjust their responses.

The typology presented incorporates the three attributes of power, legitimacy, and urgency that previously had been used in developing various stakeholder theories. It enables managers to perform a systematic categorization of stakeholder–management relationships, and allows them to deal with multiple stakeholder influences. The result is a more dynamic and comprehensive theory that will assist managers to more effectively deal with the corporation's stakeholders. The salience of one stakeholder is described in Responsibility for Ethics 4.4.

LO 4.6 Stakeholder Influence Strategies

Frooman[13] takes another approach to understanding the relationship between the corporation and its stakeholders. He states that in developing responses to stakeholders, three general questions must be answered: who are they (that is, what are their attributes), what do they want, and how are they going to try to get it? He suggests that the first two questions have been addressed by researchers while the third has been neglected.

Frooman was interested in determining how stakeholders try to act to influence the organization's decision making and behaviour. In his research, he sought to answer two questions: What are the different types of influence strategies? and What are the determinants of the choice of influence strategy?

He chose resource dependence theory as a framework for answering these questions, as organizations are usually dependent on stakeholders for some of their resources. **Resource dependence** exists when a stakeholder is supplying a resource and can exert some form of control over it. For example, this control could be based on the amount of the resource controlled, the non-substitutability of the resource, or the essentiality of the resource.

Types of resource control and the types of influence pathways determine the influence strategies available to stakeholders. There are two general means of control over an organization: withholding strategies and usage strategies. **Withholding strategies** are those where the stakeholder discontinues providing a resource to an organization with the intention of changing a certain behaviour. **Usage strategies** are those in which the stakeholder continues to supply a resource but specifies how it will be used—that is, it attaches conditions to the use of the resource. Both strategies could be credible threats to an organization.[14]

A second source of power or influence involves the resource dependence that arises from relationships between stakeholders. An **influence pathway** occurs where withholding and usage strategies could be performed by an ally of the stakeholder with whom the organization has a resource dependence. Direct strategies are those in which the stakeholder itself manipulates the flow of resources by withholding or through usage conditions. Indirect strategies are those where the stakeholder works through an ally by having the ally manipulate the flow of resources by withholding or through usage conditions. Indirect strategies require substantial communication and cooperation between stakeholders and are difficult to sustain.[15]

The influence strategies available to stakeholders were summarized by Frooman in a typology of influence strategies such as the one presented in Table 4.3. The table generated is based upon two questions: Is the stakeholder dependent on the corporation? and Is the corporation dependent on the stakeholder? In the four cell possibilities created, the resource dependence is identified and the applicable influence strategies specified. The influence strategies chosen will be determined by who is dependent upon whom and by how much.

Of the four cells, indirect/usage represents no difficulties for the firm, but the other three do. Indirect/withholding exists where the stakeholder, for example an NGO, encourages a customer of the corporation to withhold its business unless the corporation supplied goods in a particular form or condition. The corporation has no influence over the NGO, but the customer has influence over the corporation. British Columbia timber producers faced this situation when environmental groups convinced European customers to boycott original-growth timber resources. The direct/withholding cell is illustrated by a consumer boycott, and if successful, the stakeholder has the power. The fourth cell, direct/usage, is more complicated. An example is KFC restaurants directing suppliers to provide chickens that were produced under specified humane conditions. These types of influence strategies have become more common and are more challenging for managers.

Managers can gain an understanding of stakeholders and their influence by utilizing this typology. If managers can forecast the influence strategies to be used, they can counter the influence strategy likely to occur. Instead of formulating their own strategies to influence stakeholders, it may be more appropriate for managers first to anticipate and understand the possible influence strategies available to stakeholders. Responsibility for Ethics 4.5 illustrates the use of influence strategies in the Canadian mining industry.

TABLE 4.3	Typology of Influence Strategies		
		Is the stakeholder dependent on the corporation?	
		No	**Yes**
Is the corporation dependent on the stakeholder?	**No**	Indirect/withholding (low interdependence)	Indirect/usage (firm power)
	Yes	Direct/withholding (stakeholder power)	Direct/usage (high interdependence)

Source: Jeff Frooman, "Stakeholder Influence Strategies," *Academy of Management Review*, Vol. 24, No. 2(1999):200. This work is protected by copyright and it is being used with the permission of Access Copyright. Any alteration of its content or further copying in any form is strictly prohibited.

 Want to learn more about **influence strategies**?

RESPONSIBILITY FOR ETHICS 4.5

Stakeholders and Their Influence in the Canadian Mining Industry

This is a typology of influence strategy for corporations operating in the Canadian mining industry in general. Particular corporations and issues would result in a different allocation of stakeholders.

		Is the stakeholder dependent on the corporation?	
		No	**Yes**
Is the corporation dependent on the stakeholder?	**No**	*Low Interdependence* Stakeholders: • Environmental NGOs • Aboriginal groups • Religious organizations • Educational institutions	*Firm Power* Stakeholders: • Suppliers • Employees • Service professionals • Charities
		↓ *Indirect/Withholding Influence Strategy*	↓ *Indirect/Usage Influence Strategy*

		Is the stakeholder dependent on the corporation?	
		No	**Yes**
Is the corporation dependent on the stakeholder?	**Yes**	*Stakeholder Power* Stakeholders: • Government regulators • Customers • Media • Local communities • Activist shareholders	*High Interdependence* Stakeholders: • Owners/investors • Business organizations • Local communities • Suppliers • Competitors
		↓ *Direct/Withholding Influence Strategy*	↓ *Indirect/Usage Influence Strategy*

Note: The allocation of stakeholders could be challenged. It could be argued that environmental NGOs and Aboriginal groups currently have power over companies. Local communities are in two categories, as operations may depend on whether it was a single-industry community. The influence of suppliers and competitors would depend on the nature of the market.

LO 4.7   Stakeholder Collaboration

Recent research and consulting efforts focus on changing the relationship between the corporation and its stakeholders from "management" to "collaboration." Stakeholder management emphasized mechanisms of how an organization identified, monitored, and responded to its stakeholders. The mechanisms included issue analysis, consultation, strategic communication, and formal contacts. The impression was created that managers could direct and control the interactions with stakeholders, and that the main purpose was to buffer the organization from negative or challenging stakeholder activities. In the corporation, the responsibility for stakeholder management was assigned to functional departments rather than being a top-management task.

The recent approach focuses on building stakeholder relationships that are reciprocal, evolving, and mutually defined, and that are a source of opportunity and competitive advantage. **Collaboration** is a meta-capability to establish and maintain relationships that allows the organization to tap into a powerful source of creative energy, a large pool of innovative ideas, and a wider network.[16] The goal is to increase the organization's environmental stability and to enhance control over changing circumstances. The approach would be more integrated and company-wide, with responsibility for stakeholder collaboration assigned to a senior executive.[17] Stakeholder collaboration is also referred to as stakeholder engagement in the academic literature and in corporate reports. A summary of the approach is given in Table 4.4.

Svendsen provides a framework or guide for organizations that wish to develop collaborative stakeholder relationships. The framework, identified as FOSTERing stakeholder relationships, involves six steps:

Creating a foundation—The beginning stage involves relationship building in a strategic mode by incorporating it into corporate missions, values, and ethics guidelines.

Organizational alignment—The organization's internal systems and structures need to be aligned—that is, put in a state of readiness—to support the development of collaborative relationships including dialogue with stakeholders to obtain a clear understanding of their comments and perceptions.

Strategy development—A strategy is necessary to forge new stakeholder relationships.

Trust building—Trust is essential for stable social relationships as it promotes cooperation and understanding.

Evaluation—The effectiveness of the relationship-building effort must be assessed and improvements identified.

Repeat the process—The process is repeated to further improve social performance.[18]

TABLE 4.4	Characteristics of Old and New Approaches to Corporate–Stakeholder Relations
Stakeholder Management	**Stakeholder Collaboration**
Fragmented among various departments	Integrated management approach
Focus on managing relationships	Focus on building relationships
Emphasis on buffering the organization	Emphasis on creating opportunities and mutual benefits
Linked to short-term business goals	Linked to long-term business goals
Idiosyncratic implementation dependent on division interests and personal style of manager	Coherent approach driven by business goals, mission, values, and corporate strategies

Source: Reprinted with permission of the publisher. From *The Stakeholder Strategy*, copyrighted 1998 by Ann Svendsen, Berrett-Koehler Publishers, Inc., San Francisco, CA. All rights reserved. www.bkconnection.com

Svendsen outlines the various tasks necessary at each stage, describes the tools and methodologies to be used, and identifies results to be expected. Stakeholder collaboration moves beyond the stakeholder management approach to a new level of stakeholder analysis and understanding. Many corporations consider stakeholder relations an important management function. Everyday Ethics 4.1 describes the approaches to stakeholder collaboration or engagement at one corporation.

EVERYDAY ETHICS 4.1

Stakeholder Engagement at Celestica Inc.

Celestica Inc. provides technological solutions so that its customers can manage their supply chains more effectively. The solutions provided are in the areas of design and engineering, joint design and manufacturing, manufacturing services, precision machining, supply chain services, logistics and fulfillment, and after-market services. The company was included in *Corporate Knights* 2016 Best 50 Corporate Citizens listing.

Celestica has an extensive program of stakeholder engagement. The table below lists the stakeholders and the main engagement approaches.

Stakeholder	Engagement Approaches
Employees	Town hall meetings, internal communications, leadership meetings, employee surveys, sustainable workplace program, open-door policy, sustainability report, annual risk assessment
Customers	Teleconferences, voluntary reporting, surveys, audits, scorecards, collaboration projects

Stakeholder	Engagement Approaches
Academia	Working group meetings, surveys, research projects
Consortia (joint-venture participants or partners)	Meetings, working groups, seminars, webinars
Government	Local government regulations
Investors	Investor surveys
Non-governmental Organizations (NGOs)	Face-to-face meetings, teleconferences, on-site tours, collaboration projects
Suppliers	Emails, teleconferences, questionnaires, facility tours

More information on the company's stakeholder engagement is provided on pages 18–20 of its *2015 Sustainability Report*. In addition to listing stakeholders and engagement approaches it also identifies the topics dealt with for each stakeholder and the actions taken.

Source: Based on Celestica Inc. accessed July 4, 2016, https://www.celestica.com/home; and the *2015 Sustainability Report*, accessed July 4, 2016, https://www.celestica.com/uploadedFiles/Site/About_Us/Sustainability/Sustainability_Overview/2015%20Sustainability%20Report%20Final.pdf.

LO 4.8   Issue Analysis

The academic and practitioner literature has been giving more attention to issue analysis. This is a logical development as the stakeholder concept and analysis complement each other. This section presents two approaches to issue analysis: the issues management process and issue salience analysis.

The Issues Management Process

The following discussion is an outline of a typical issues management process, broken into six steps: identification, analysis, ranking, response formulation, implementation, and monitoring and evaluating. The description is a general one and is based on the steps outlined by Carroll and Bryson.[19] There may be variations in the overall process used, and different methodologies or techniques may be used in the steps. This description is meant to serve as a general description of the issues management process.

1. *Identification of issues*—This step involves the formulation of issues in many ways, including social forecasting, futures research, environmental scanning, and public issues scanning.

2. *Analysis of issues*—In this step issues are described and evaluated, usually in writing, so that a consensus is achieved among managers. All stakeholders who are influenced and/or can influence the issue should be identified. Everyday Ethics 4.2 identifies a major issue confronting the telecommunications industry and the relevant stakeholders.

3. *Ranking or prioritizing of issues*—The purpose of this step is to establish the importance of the issues identified, which should be possible after the description of each issue has been agreed to in Step 2.

4. *Formulating issue response*—The choices available to the corporation are identified and evaluated. It is important to identify all response alternatives that may be pursued to address the issue.

5. *Implementing issue response*—At this stage, specific plans are formulated to implement the response selected. A work plan is developed to ensure the implementation of the response.

6. *Monitoring and evaluating issue response*—The status of the issue and the response is reviewed on a regular basis.

EVERYDAY ETHICS 4.2

Stakeholders and Cell Phone Towers

In order to provide cell phone service to larger geographic areas or to improve reception quality, a telecommunications corporation must erect towers. If the tower height is more than 15 metres, the corporation must consult with residents. However, if the tower is less than 15 metres, the corporation is allowed to erect the tower without consulting residents or even informing them. The industry is erecting towers 14.9 metres high in many cities without consultation.

The issue: How can telecommunications corporations erect needed cell phone towers in a socially responsible manner?

The stakeholders:

- Cell phone users: Consumers who have cell phones demand good service, and are unhappy when reception is not available or of poor quality. They put pressure on the corporations for better service.
- Community residents: People living near the cell phone towers are concerned about the effect they will have on property values and the health hazards associated with the radio frequency fields they give off.
- The federal government: Industry Canada regulates the erection of towers and has final say as to where they are placed.
- Local governments: Municipal governments receive complaints from residents, but have limited, if any, power to control the erection of the towers.
- Competitors: All telecommunications corporations are confronted by the issue.
- Health professionals: Health risks have been studied extensively and are believed to be low, although some European studies have found a risk. However, many persons living near the towers are not convinced that a risk does not exist.
- Churches: Towers are placed on church properties or structures as a source of revenue; neighbours often are annoyed.
- Shareholders: Most are concerned about profitability and dividends and thus want cell phone revenues to increase.
- Media: National and local media have given extensive coverage to the issue, making more people aware of it.

This process ensures that the most salient or critical issues are addressed. The remaining issues are not dropped, but are maintained in a list of issues that is reformulated on a regular basis.

Managers must identify and recognize all the relevant stakeholders for their corporation and also those that have influence on particular issues relating to the corporation's operations. From a managerial perspective, the next consideration is how to influence the stakeholders. Issues can be dealt with in a variety of ways, for example lobbying to influence the government, improving media relations, improving ethics programs, and consulting or engaging stakeholder groups such as NGOs. Some issues appear suddenly and require immediate and comprehensive responses; crisis management is required in these situations.

Issue Salience Analysis

The degree to which managers give priority to competing stakeholders was examined by Mitchell, Agle, and Wood and a stream of research has been based upon this article.[20] Very little has been written about issue salience, the degree to which managers give priority to competing issues. One exception is the paper by Bundy and Buchholtz.[21] The conceptual model and hypotheses proposed is complex and as the authors point out research is needed to prove or disapprove their hypotheses.

A more modest alternate is presented in Figure 4.4. The approach is to analyze the importance of issues to the corporation's stakeholders and the corporation's management. The attempt is to rank the issues by importance instead of the stakeholders. For any issue, one or several stakeholders may be influenced or in a situation where the corporation can be influence them. The results of this salience or importance analysis are plotted on a two-dimension grid by "Importance to stakeholders involved with the issue" and the "Importance to the corporation's business."

FIGURE 4.4   *Issue Salience Matrix*

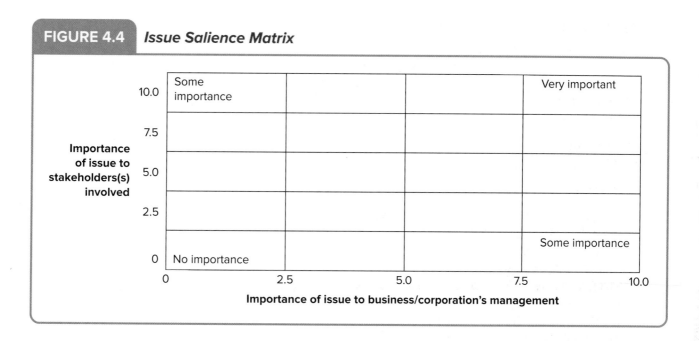

The importance of issues to stakeholders would be measured by surveys, media monitoring, NGO activities, government regulation or other action. The importance of issues to the corporation would be measured by internal interviews, employee feedback, management discussions, and Board attention.

After the issues are plotted, they are ranked in decreasing order to importance. The priority issues for management would tend to be located in the upper right-hand corner. The next priority would be issues located in the upper left and lower right corners. Their influence on operations and the ease or difficulty of addressing the issues would be deciding factors for rating. Issues in the lower left corner are of little importance to stakeholders or management.

This approach was illustrated in the Air Canada's 2014 Corporate Sustainability Report.[22] The issues considered important to Air Canada's business were identified through internal interviews and workshops and those considered important to stakeholders were determined from surveys of customers, employees, and suppliers. The issues identified as being highly important to the corporation and stakeholders included safety, regulatory compliance, ethical business practices and policies, customer engagement, and fleet management. Issues considered of lesser importance included noise and air emissions, sustainable procurement practices, water management, and diversity. Air Canada's matrix was colour-coded to indicate the stakeholders associated with each issue.

Various approaches to stakeholder and issue analysis have been presented leading to the most comprehensive and inclusive approaches. A corporation establishes many relationship networks with stakeholders through analysis, communications, consultation, participation, collaboration, and partnership. Stakeholder engagement is an integral aspect of corporate social responsibility or corporate sustainability. It involves creating value for all stakeholders and an honest, open, and respectful engagement of stakeholders vital to corporate strategy. Stakeholder analysis is increasingly being performed in conjunction with issue analysis. This increases the understanding of stakeholders and related issues for the corporation and management.

Your advice to Carol ...

Stakeholder relations or engagement exists in all types of business and not just in large corporations, as this vignette illustrates. Large corporations often have a manager or even a department devoted to stakeholder relations. In smaller business, stakeholder relations are looked after by operational managers already responsible for other business functions. Carol must be sensitive not only to who the coffee shop's stakeholders are, but also to the influence that these stakeholders have on her and the influence she might have on them. For example, Millennials may expect different amenities from a coffee shop than senior citizens would. It is important for Carol, like all managers, to think through the consequences of a decision for various stakeholders before acting.

Summary

- The appropriate identification of stakeholders is very important to business corporations as one approach to understanding the environment in which they operate. Identification should be only the first step, as managers must analyze the nature of the relationships between the corporation and its stakeholders. (LO 4.1)
- Freeman's stakeholder management capability provides a good starting point for understanding stakeholder relationships. Although he stresses the importance of proper identification of stakeholders, he also appreciates that appropriate organizational arrangements must be in place to understand the relationships and ultimately to interact with stakeholders. (LO 4.2)
- The various stakeholder matrix mapping methodologies give managers a practical approach to assessing the influence of stakeholders. Matrices can be based on a variety of dimensions and designed to suit the corporation's purpose in stakeholder understanding. The variables illustrated were position on an issue and importance of the issue to the stakeholder. (LO 4.3)
- The diagnostic typology of organizational stakeholders attempts to understand stakeholder influence by assessing the potential threat or potential for cooperation. (LO 4.4)
- The salience stakeholder typology increases the complexity of analysis by using three attributes to assess stakeholder importance: power, legitimacy, and urgency. (LO 4.5)
- Frooman's influence strategies provide another perspective on understanding stakeholders. He argues that managers should appreciate that stakeholders can influence one another and the corporation in direct and indirect ways and by withholding or specifying usage conditions. Understanding influence strategies further enhances managers' understanding of stakeholder actions. (LO 4.6)
- The most sophisticated approach to understanding stakeholders is through collaboration or engagement. Collaboration changes the approach from managing stakeholders to dialoguing with them. (LO 4.7)
- Issue analysis has a logical connection to stakeholder analysis. Examining stakeholders and issues together increases management understanding of the environment in which the corporation operates. (LO 4.8)

Key Terms

Stakeholder engagement	Urgency
Issue analysis	Resource dependence
Stakeholder management capability	Withholding strategies
Matrix mapping	Usage strategies
Salience	Influence pathway
Power	Collaboration
Legitimacy	

Critical Thinking and Discussion Questions

1. Complete the stakeholder analysis worksheet for three stakeholders of a local business, or for your business program at a university or college.

2. How do corporations develop "stakeholder management capability"?

3. Write a job description for a "manager of stakeholder relations."

4. Why should corporations develop "stakeholder management capability"?

5. How does stakeholder matrix mapping help managers?

6. Can stakeholders be managed? If yes, why should they? If no, what can management do to influence stakeholders?

7. Some stakeholders are more important, or salient, than others. How do the concepts of power, legitimacy, and urgency assist managers in assessing stakeholder salience?

8. Explain how stakeholder influence strategies impact the corporation.

9. What are the benefits for management of performing both stakeholder and issue analyses?

10. Freeman identified three levels of "stakeholder management capability": identification, organization processes for understanding stakeholders, and establishing relations. Which of these levels are illustrated by the following:

   - Stakeholder analysis worksheet
   - A stakeholder manager position
   - Stakeholder matrix mapping
   - The stakeholder typology based on salience
   - Stakeholder influence strategies
   - Stakeholder collaboration

Cases

4.1 CSR AND THE CLOSURE OF A NEIGHBOURHOOD SUPERMARKET

On January 14, 2012, Loblaw Inc. closed its SaveEasy supermarket in the Churchill Square shopping centre in St. John's, NL. There had been a supermarket on the site for 55 years, originally operated by a local business but later acquired by Loblaw Inc. The Churchill Park residential area was developed after World War II and included a small-scale mixed retail square and open spaces.

The Square was located on the edge of the Memorial University of Newfoundland campus, which had about 20,000 students, faculty, and staff. By 2012, there was a predominance of retired persons living in apartment buildings and individual homes in and around the Square. The SaveEasy supermarket closure left a gap in the retail makeup of the Square. As one resident pointed out, the Square had a lot to offer including medical and dental offices, restaurants, clothing stores, and a pharmacy, post office, bank, hairdresser, coffee shop, pub, sports outfitter, and dry cleaner—but now no food store.

Most of the students did not own cars and many retirees either did not own cars or were unable to drive. As the nearest supermarkets were now a distance of about two kilometres away, both these groups were inconvenienced by the closure of the neighbourhood supermarket. The closure was consistent with the trend in food stores. The Churchill Square SaveEasy was a small-scale supermarket that, when built, replaced smaller local grocery stores. Recently, the model for supermarket stores used by Loblaw and other food retailers was to centralized, full-service stores as they followed the big-box store trend. Loblaw's centralization of its stores resulted in the closure of several other stores in St. John's.

Residents objected to the closure and contacted Loblaw. The information they received was that the store was not very profitable and the building was deteriorating, requiring expensive repairs. The Deputy Mayor expressed concern over the closure of SaveEasy grocery store in Churchill Square and asked that the Mayor write Loblaw expressing concern. In addition, the Deputy Mayor suggested that Council meet with Loblaw on the matter. A petition with hundreds of signatures was tabled at a City Council meeting, which read:

> We the undersigned deplore the closure of SaveEasy in Churchill Square. We urge City Council not to approve any other kinds of uses of the location. A food store is absolutely essential to the neighbourhood, particularly for seniors and students.

A copy of the petition was forwarded to Loblaw. These initiatives had no impact.

Many residents and students felt that Loblaw was not being a good corporate citizen and referred to a quotation from the corporation's 2014 Corporate Responsibility Report: "We strive to be an exemplary corporate citizen..." The report described Loblaw's CSR commitment that included respecting the environment, sourcing with integrity, making a difference in communities, reflecting the nation's diversity, and being a good place to work. In 2015, Loblaw was one of *Maclean's* magazine's Top 50 Socially Responsible Corporations. Those opposing the closure felt that Loblaw was focusing more on its bottom line than on good corporate citizenship.

As the months passed, another issue arose relating to the closure: Loblaw would not allow another grocery store to rent or purchase the building, in effect keeping competition out. Considerable discussion took place in the local media about Loblaw's unwillingness to give up the space, creating what was referred to as "economic black holes." Some people argued that City Council should have a vacant building policy requiring the owners to allow the structure to be occupied if some business were willing to rent or acquire the space. It was pointed out that Loblaw was not breaking any laws and was paying the taxes on the building. Others pointed out that Loblaw could not be expected to help its competitors. Meanwhile, the vacant store was a constant reminder of the inconvenience imposed on several stakeholders.

Questions

1. Who were the stakeholders and what was their influence?
2. Is it socially responsible to prevent the former store from being rented or sold to another business?
3. Should City Council take any action in this situation?
4. Was Loblaw being socially responsible? Does it have a moral obligation to keep the store open?

Sources: John Furlong, "Assigning Blame for Lost Jobs Helps No One," CBC News, January 1, 2012, accessed February 5, 2013, http://www.cbc.ca/news/canada/newfoundland-labrador/story/2011/12/30/nl-john-furlong-supermarket-fishery-101.html; Morgan Murray, "Not in the Market," The Scope, February 29, 2012, accessed February 5, 2013, http://thescope.ca/storefront/not-in-the-market; John Gushue, "St. John's, Old Superarkets and Economic Black Holes," CBC News, May 27, 2012, accessed February 5, 2013, http://www.cbc.ca/news/canada/newfoundland-labrador/story/2012/05/25/nl-john-gushue-dominion-vacant-527.html; Susan Flanagan, "All I Want for Christmas is A Supermarket," *The Telegram* (St. John's, NL), December 11, 2012, accessed February 5, 2013, http://www.thetelegram.com/Arts%20-%20Life/2012-12-11/article-3137642/All-I-want-for-Christmas-is-a-supermarket/1; and Susan Flanagan, "Place-Holder Policies," *The Telegram* (St. John's, NL), January 22, 2013, B1; City of St. John's Council Minutes for January 9, 2012 and May 14, 2012; and Loblaw Inc., "Responsibility," http://www.loblaw.ca/English/responsibility/default.aspx.

4.2 THE ECONOMICS AND ETHICS OF TEXTBOOK PRICING

Several students were gathered around the section of the College Bookstore where business textbooks were shelved. Martin Tremayne heard comments about the outrageous and unethical prices being charged for the required books and that the cruel publishers were profiteering at the mercy of students. Martin decided to delay the purchase the Business Ethics book he had come to get.

Later over a coffee, Martin reflected about the incident. He had enough money with him to purchase the book but didn't want do so in front of his angry colleagues. Martin was having a good time at college. He was in a co-operative program and the work terms that paid most of his expenses. He lived at home, but had car payments and maintenance expenses. He had taken a couple of trips to the Caribbean while at college and attended several concerts in Toronto and New York. Overall, he has enjoyed his time at college.

Martin decided to find out about the textbook publishing industry and what caused the high prices. The industry was unusual in that textbooks were selected by professors who did not have to purchase them, that is, students were captive consumers in that they are required to purchase the book. The publishers market to professors and most selected the best textbook to meet the requirements for the course and seldom considered the price. According to studies, the cost of textbooks had increased about four times faster than the Consumer Price Index resulting in many universities and colleges becoming concerned about possible overpricing. On average, students spent between $500 and $1,000 per semester on textbooks and other course materials.

The publishers claimed that textbook publishing was competitive and that they were not profiteering. To ensure quality, textbooks were subject to an extensive reviewing process often involving 30 reviews. Textbooks were published on high quality paper, unlike trade publications, and involved sophisticated design with colour, graphs, indices, and photos. Publishers developed a large selection of books, not all of which were successful and some lose money. In addition, publishers had to provide instructor's manuals, lecture slides, test banks, and online platforms for each book. The publishers received 80 per cent of the retail price with the bookstores receiving the remainder.

Universities had responded in several ways. They suggested that professors change textbooks and editions only when absolutely necessary so that there was a second-hand market for the books. Some encouraged professors to assign books from the Open Textbook Library or Project Gutenberg where books were available for free online. The books were written by academics and were adequate for some courses. The use of other Internet materials was encouraged but quality control was a problem. Other universities started renting textbooks, most book stores purchased textbooks for resale, and sometimes several copies were put on reserve in the library. Some textbooks were published as digital copies which somewhat cost less, but these editions had expiration dates, cannot be copied and printing is limited. Students may have e-readers, but some still preferred the paper edition.

Students complained that new editions were published forcing them to buy new books despite minor changes, and often professors sometimes only used a small portion of the book. With increasing tuition fees and living expenses, students were accumulating increasing amounts of debt. The more money spent on textbooks meant less for food, transport, health, and leisure.

Martin wondered whether to go back and purchase the textbook or investigate other ways to obtain it.

Questions

1. What fundamentals of capitalism are relevant to this case?
2. Who are the stakeholders and what are the issues along the supply chain for textbooks?
3. Are textbooks too expensive? Is money spent on textbooks a legitimate expense in the educational system?

Sources: Christopher Ragan, "Why Textbooks Are so Expensive," *The Globe and Mail,* September 9, 2014, B2; "Why Are Textbooks so Expensive?," Campus Store, McMaster University, accessed November 7, 2014, https://campusstore.mcmaster.ca; "Textbook Prices that Break the Bank," CBC Radio, September 21, 2014 accessed November 7, 2014, http://cbc/ca; "Reducing Textbook Costs," Campus Bookstore, University of Windsor accessed November 7, 2014, http://uwindsor.ca/bookstore, Project Gutenberg at https://www.gutenberg.org/; and the Open Textbook Library at http://open.umn.edu/opentextbooks.

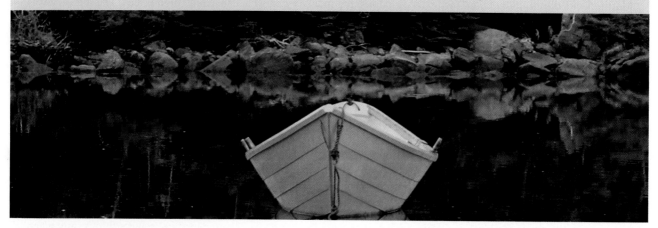

Used with the permission of Dennis Flynn

CHAPTER 5

Ethics of Business: The Theoretical Basis

LEARNING OUTCOMES

After studying this chapter, you will be able to:

LO 5.1 Define the ethics of business.

LO 5.2 Understand the different approaches managers and businesspersons take to assessing the ethical implications of their decisions.

LO 5.3 Identify the influences on ethical behaviour and define ethical relativism.

LO 5.4 Describe the seven common theoretical bases for ethical conduct.

LO 5.5 Outline a sequence of moral reasoning.

LO 5.6 Appreciate the challenges of ethics in business.

What would you do if...?

Jonathan Devereaux graduated with his Bachelor of Commerce but could not find the type of job he wanted and that matched his qualifications. He was competing for jobs not only with other recent graduates, but also with people who had been recently laid off because of the economic downturn. He had school loans that had to be repaid—and, because he no longer lived at home, he had living expenses to cover. After two months of rejections, Jonathan was getting desperate and somehow had to earn a living. He decided to apply for jobs for which he was overqualified in order to improve his financial situation until he could get his desired job.

He applied for several positions, but was turned down because he was considered too qualified. Jonathan decided to overcome this hurdle by customizing—or "stripping"—his résumé. When applying for some jobs, he omitted his degree. When applying for others, he deleted information about academic awards received in high school and university. He altered his résumé to reflect the skills he thought were relevant to each specific job. He found this ironic as he had been enhancing his résumé in an attempt to impress potential employers. His conscience bothered him and it presented him with a dilemma, but he felt that he had no other alternative. One job he applied for was to work as a cook in a fast food outlet.

Rosemary Lynch was the manager of the fast-food outlet to which Jonathan had applied. She found him to be very personable and enthusiastic. She glanced over his résumé quickly and did not notice anything unusual. Few skills were necessary to be a cook in the fast-food outlet and she thought he could be trained very quickly. She was about to call to offer him the job when one of the staff approached and asked to have a word with her. The staff member said that she had seen Jonathan around the university and thought that he had graduated last year. This information presented Rosemary with a dilemma and caused her to rethink the job offer.

What is your advice to Jonathan and Rosemary?

Business ethics: Isn't that an oxymoron? Many stakeholders in society believe that business simply has no ethics. This position is unfair, and most likely reflects a lack of understanding of business—and of ethics. Ethics are involved in all aspects of human interaction and ethical implications exist in religious institutions, government, policing organizations, family life, and union organizations. As illustrated above, students are also confronted by ethical issues. It is no different for business enterprises, and so the phrase "ethics of business" is used instead of "business ethics."

This chapter presents materials that will enable you to better understand the ethical implications of business so that you will be better able to respond to this "oxymoron" argument. The phrase *ethics of business* is defined, and the influence on moral behaviour is identified. The most common ethical principles are described, and moral reasoning is explained.

LO 5.1 Introducing the Ethics of Business

Ethics has always been a concern for society and its various institutions. Business corporations and their managers are no different, despite the view held by many that businesspersons are somehow less ethical than others. To some extent this has been the result of the traditional view of the free enterprise system, alleging that profits are the only motivating force for business, business activity requires and rewards deception, business evades the law, businesspersons and managers manipulate others, and business activity leads to materialism.

At times, business ethics became a focus for discussion in society and among managers, as in the latter half of the 1980s and the first years of the twenty-first century. The ethics of business is constantly in the media, especially after the financial crisis and economic downturn since 2008.

Many definitions of business ethics exist. The definitions include terms such as moral principles, morality of human actions, standards of conduct, rights and wrongs, truth, honesty and fairness, values, customs, the Golden Rule, and philosophy. One researcher, Philip Lewis, developed a definition that synthesizes what he found to be the four most mentioned concepts in existing definitions: "**Business ethics** is the rules, standards, codes or principles which provide guidelines for morally right behaviour and truthfulness in specific situations." Lewis and others argue that business ethics is difficult to define as it apparently means different things to different managers.

In this book, the preference is to use the term "ethics of business," which in Chapter 1 was defined as the rules, standards, codes, or principles that provide guidance for morally appropriate behaviour in managerial decision making relating to the operation of the corporation and business's relationship with society.

LO 5.2   Assessment of Ethical Implications in Business Decisions

Figure 5.1 illustrates how managers consider the ethical implications of business decisions or actions. Three levels of assessing ethical implications are identified: awareness, assessment based upon influences, and assessment based upon ethical principles.

FIGURE 5.1   *Levels of Ethical Assessment*

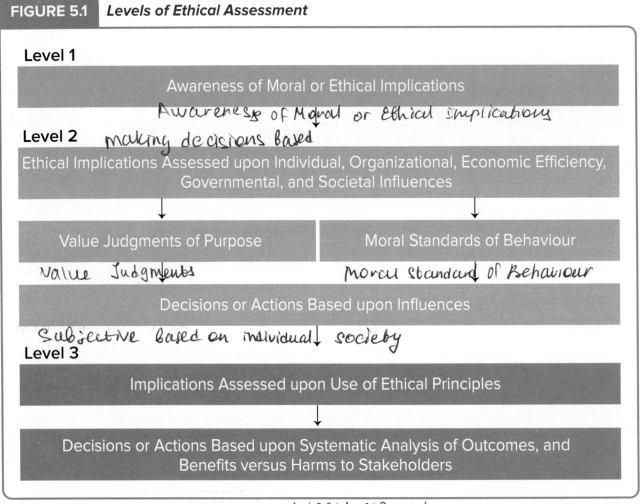

Level 1 assumes an awareness of moral or ethical implications of business decisions or actions. This may not be the case, as some managers behave in an amoral manner. Managers with an amoral approach to ethics disregard all moral responsibilities when making decisions. In order to assess ethical implications there must be an awareness of ethics.

The ethical implications of business decisions or actions can be assessed by individual and/or societal influences that are described as value judgments of purpose and moral standards of behaviour. **Value judgments** are subjective evaluations of what is considered important and are based on how managers intuitively feel about the goodness or rightness of various goals.[2] **Moral standards** are defined as the means by which individuals judge their actions and the actions of others based upon accepted behaviour in society.[3] Both types of influences can vary by culture, country, and time. Level 2 is the one most commonly used by managers, and most individuals.

Level 3 represents a more systematic analysis or assessment of ethical implications. The assessment is based on the use of fundamental ethical principles to evaluate the outcomes from decisions or corporate actions. A conscious effort is made to identify and analyze the distribution of benefits and harms to all stakeholders affected.

Levels 2 and 3 are described in the following sections.

LO 5.3   Influences on Ethical Behaviour

No definitive factor can explain ethical behaviour, but many influences can provide an understanding of behaviour. These influences become the bases for an individual's value judgments and moral standards that determine behaviour. For many individuals, value judgments and moral standards are used in making a Level 2 ethical-related decision. The action resulting is certainly better than a Level 1 assessment, and may not be inappropriate or even wrong. Furthermore, the assessment is not as comprehensive as it might have been if a Level 3 assessment were used.

The influences on ethical behaviour are summarized in five categories: influences of individuals, corporate or organizational influences, economic efficiency influences, government and the legal system influences, and societal influences.

Influences of Individuals

Managers often make ethical decisions based on the morals they acquire while growing up. The family or home environment is a major influence, making the personal convictions of individual managers a source of ethical standards. For some managers, religious upbringing and contact with religious organizations as an adult provide a basis for assessing and analyzing ethical decisions. The moral standards set by other businesspersons may become the basis on which an individual manager considers ethical issues. The educational process that a manager is exposed to may become a reference point. Ethical matters in general are examined in schools, and some managers may be influenced by university-level education in ethics or philosophy.

Corporate or Organizational Influences

The culture of a corporation or organization influences how a manager behaves. In other words, the behaviour of superiors and colleagues sets the tone or standard by which ethical decisions are made. Many corporations develop mission, vision, and values statements that identify the values that are held by the organization and reflected in the corporate culture. As described in Chapter 8, many corporations and organizations have codes of conduct and ethics. Corporate social responsibility objectives emphasize values or moral considerations to be considered when operating in society.

Many business or industry organizations encourage members to act ethically. One of the most widely known is the Better Business Bureau (BBB), described in Responsibility for Ethics 5.1. Business employs professionals such as lawyers, architects, engineers, and doctors. Ethical codes or guidelines have been developed by their respective professional associations and must be adhered to by their members. In some associations the codes are rigorously enforced, and expulsion from the profession is possible.

RESPONSIBILITY FOR ETHICS 5.1

The Better Business Bureau's (BBB) Ethical Marketplace

Vision: An ethical marketplace where buyers and sellers can trust each other.

Mission: BBB's mission is to be the leader in advancing marketplace trust. BBB accomplishes this mission by:

- Creating a community of trustworthy businesses
- Setting standards for marketplace trust
- Encouraging and supporting best practices
- Celebrating marketplace role models, and
- Denouncing substandard marketplace behaviour

One BBB value is integrity by being honest and ethical in all business activities. Another is trust, and its standards for trust include the following: advertise honestly, tell the truth, be transparent, honour promises, be responsive, safeguard privacy, and embody integrity.

Sources: Reprinted with permission of the Council of Better Business Bureaus, Inc. Copyright 2016. Council of Better Business Bureaus, Inc., 3033 Wilson Blvd.,6th Floor, Arlington, VA 22201, www.bbb.org.

Economic Efficiency Influences

The capitalist economic system was discussed in Chapter 2 and the implications for the ethics of business were identified.

Some managers assess the moral implications of a decision by its economic consequences, and a moral justification is based on the workings of a market system. They believe it is necessary to maximize output as it is in society's interests to provide the essentials of food, clothing, and shelter. Adam Smith's *Wealth of Nations*[4] is held up as the foundation for this focus on economic efficiency whereby managers and corporations may appear to take selfish actions and be motivated by personal gains in business dealings. Self-interested actions in the marketplace are justified as they contribute to the efficient operation of the economy, which in turn results in prosperity and the optimum use of society's resources. Profits are maximized but are subject to market and legal constraints, and the role of the state is minimized.

The corporation's success is measured by its economic efficiency and competitive effectiveness, which leads to social betterment. Society benefits, or the public good is increased, when there is an improved use of scarce resources. This does not mean cutting corners and producing poor-quality products or providing unsafe working conditions for employees. But it does involve the substitution of capital for labour and making use of the economies of scale, scope, and experience. Abuses will be avoided if effective markets exist, and economic efficiency differs from self-interest in that business must operate within market constraints.

There are some difficulties with economic efficiency influences. Often non-competitive markets exist resulting in market domination and excessive profits. Economic efficiency leads to some stakeholders not participating fully, and inequalities will result. Those who oppose capitalism and those who advocate for alleviation of the perceived abuses of business frequently criticize this influence.

Government and the Legal System Influences

In order to maintain fair competition, fair treatment of stakeholders, and a set of laws governing business transactions, there has to be a central authority that has the power to enforce basic rules of conduct. In a democratic society, this authority is the government that enacts legislation and regulations; that is, a code of laws. Government legislation does influence business decisions. The *Competition Act* makes some questionable market practices illegal and thus discourages some managers from becoming involved in such practices. Government regulations require the disclosure of information to protect the interests of stakeholders—for example, when selling shares to the public, a corporation must clearly state certain information about its finances and operations.

The legal system makes certain behaviour illegal, and most managers are sensitive to behaving within the law. Many laws at one time were moral standards and became laws because practice showed it was necessary to control some behaviours. Businesspersons often argue that it is better to self-regulate or to self-police than to encourage legislation or regulations. This is one of the main arguments for corporations to practise social responsibility.

The minimal moral standard for some managers and corporations is to take actions that do not violate the law—that is, "It's legal so it's okay." This approach to ascertain what is right has some drawbacks. Morality is more than just what is legal versus illegal, and laws cannot cover everything. Laws or government regulations can be arbitrary and designed to further the interests of particular individuals or organizations in society. Nevertheless, for many in business the law does represent the minimal moral standards. Chapter 10 examines the ethics implications of government's regulation of the business system.

Societal Influences

Members of society form social relationships with those of similar interests, customs, beliefs, or values. These relationships can be based on the views of a particular community—for example, a town's reaction to a plant closure. Views of appropriate ethical behaviour may be influenced by a dominant culture, political views, and economic status. Some stakeholders of business represent societal views including volunteer, charitable, religious, service, fraternal, cultural, and ethnic organizations. The cultural traditions of a country or an ethnic group influence how managers view society and business practices especially for Canadian managers operating in a foreign country.

One test of ethical behaviour is whether the manager can defend the decision if it becomes known through the media. The numerous activist or advocacy groups in society known as NGOs (non-governmental organizations) can have an impact on business decisions. An example is the pressure NGOs applied to Talisman Energy for its alleged role in Sudanese genocide, eventually causing the company to divest its petroleum interests in that country.

ethical relativism —

Together these influences on ethical standards affect the decisions of managers and how they view moral dilemmas. But, by themselves, these influences do not ensure any type of standardized or uniform behaviour. These influences result in individual value judgments and moral standards that affect the assessment of ethical implications by managers.

Most of these influences are not based on any theoretical basis of ethical assessment. As a result, the degree of assessment of ethical implications is most likely not complete or thorough. Proper and acceptable decisions may be made, but to perform a more systematic assessment of business decisions or actions managers should consider a Level 3 analysis, as described in the following section.

The reliance on a variety of influences illustrates **ethical relativism,** the belief that ethical answers depend on the situation and no universal standards or rules exist to guide or evaluate morality. In other words, ethics is relative and people set their own standards for judging their behaviour. One example of ethical relativism occurs when consideration is given only to one's self-interest and values with the assumption that different people have different beliefs. Another example is cultural relativism, where various societies have different customs and belief systems. What is considered morally appropriate in one society may not be so in another, and outsiders should be careful about condemning behaviours within a society. There are problems with ethical relativism. It is considered a lazy way to approach ethics as it lacks a rigorous analysis of the circumstances and consequences. Also, it contradicts everyday behaviour where individuals seek differing views and opinions. On the other hand, it is dangerous when individuals become moral absolutists, believing that they alone know what is acceptable in society.

Table 5.1 distinguishes among value judgments and moral standards as discussed in this section, and ethical principles as described in the next section. The principles described offer some guidance for managers when confronted with decisions that have ethical implications. These principles by no means describe the only approaches to making such decisions.

TABLE 5.1	Distinguishing among Values, Morals, and Ethics	
Value Judgments	**Moral Standards**	**Ethical Principles**
Managers use value judgments when they must decide what is right or wrong	Managers turn to moral standards of behaviour in decision making	Managers can examine standards of behaviour and choice of goals by using the fundamental logic of ethical principles of analysis
Subjective evaluations of what managers think is important; based upon a manager's own values	Represent the expectations of society and the means by which managers judge their actions	Ethics is the study of what is good or right in human beings
The way managers intuitively feel about right or wrong	Vary with individuals and by culture, country, organization, and time	Ethics is a way of thinking about morality in a logical and systematic manner
Can be thought of as priorities or preferences and are variable	Are subjective gauges of conduct, and are the way managers bring intuitive feelings about right or good into decision making	Do not differ between people and remain the same
Used along with moral standards when confronted with a complex managerial dilemma	Are not objective, consistent, or timeless, as are ethical principles	Are the foundation of moral philosophy
		Are the fundamental rules by which moral standards and value judgments can be examined

Source: Summarized from Larue Tone Hosmer, "Strategic Planning as if Ethics Mattered," *Strategic Management Journal,* Vol. 15 (1994): 22–24.

Managers can examine standards of behaviour and choice of goals by using the fundamental logic of ethical principles of analysis.

LO 5.4 The Theoretical Basis for Ethical Conduct

Businesspersons do incorporate morality into decision making, but it is commonly based on value judgments and moral standards. Formal ethics principles exist, but they are often described in very theoretical, abstract, and complex language. The same principle is sometimes broken down into several categories that can be confusing for individuals without ethics education. Many businesspersons simply do not know how to apply ethics principles to business circumstances.

Hosmer claims that it is no longer necessary to recognize all the distinctions in ethical theories for them to be useful.[5] Moral problems should be defined as resulting in harms to some and benefits to others. This introduces more realism in the business context—for example, it takes into account the effects of competition. Some management actions have to be taken despite the harms to some stakeholders in order to maintain or enlarge the benefits to other stakeholders.

To enable businesspersons to apply ethical principles, the seven most cited principles of ethical analysis are described in more detail: self-interest, personal virtues, caring, utilitarian benefits, universal rules, individual rights, and justice. These ethical principles are applied the same way in any context. Ethical principles are not subjective measures that vary with cultural, social, and economic conditions. Instead, they are objective statements that transcend countries, religions, cultures, and times.

Self-Interest Ethic (Ethical Egoism)

Ethical egoism
do what is right for you

The **self-interest ethic** means that individuals or corporations set their own standards for judging the ethical implications of their actions; that is, only the individual's values and standards are the basis for actions. Most individuals are influenced by their own interests and have a tendency to do what is right for them. Self-interest is always present and cannot be ignored, even though many moralists have a low opinion of it as a basis of behaviour. Self-interest is extended to organizations, and in particular to corporations, that are criticized for profit maximization.

There are problems associated with the self-interest ethic. Carried to the extreme, self-interest is not desirable as an ethic. It is considered an easy way out and implies laziness because the person is relying on his or her own beliefs without a more complicated analysis. In the short term self-interest is viewed as selfish behaviour even though the long-term results of a self-interested action may be beneficial. Individuals relying on this ethic may become absolutists who consider only what they think is right and fail to take into consideration the interests of others. Few in society practise extreme self-interest or egoism.

Yet, many observers fail to recognize that some degree of self-interest can be reconciled with morality and does include the consideration of others. Maitland claims that many people confuse self-interest with selfishness, self-absorption, disregard for the rights and interests of others, money-making, greed, materialism, hedonism, and profit maximization.[6] He argues that many people do not distinguish between morally acceptable and unacceptable expressions of self-interest.

Kaler admits that the line between self-interest and concern for others is blurred, but has attempted to make the distinction through the gradations of self-interest and morality presented in Figure 5.2. At the two extremes are complete altruism and egoism. The goals of altruists are to account for and be sensitive to the interests of others to the point where their own interests are sacrificed or neglected (ultra-moral). Egoism, or extreme self-interest, is excessive interest in oneself, ignoring completely the interests of others.[7]

In between these extremes are degrees or gradations of self-interest. In Figure 5.2, the shaded area represents the blurred distinction between the appropriate consideration of others and consideration only of oneself. Quasi-egoism and complete egoism could be considered unacceptable approaches to morality. However, the gradations above the box could be considered acceptable.

Many people find no fault with reasonable, measured, and proportionate self-interest, and it is acceptable for an individual to be appropriately self-concerned as long as the interests of others are considered. Maitland argues that it is in an individual's interests to not be too self-concerned. An appropriate gradation of self-interest draws the egoist into relations with others who are required to assist or enable the accomplishment of his or her self-interest. Thus, the enlightened egoist will be attentive to the needs of others, and self-interest provides an incentive to restrain one's self-interest. Maitland counters the various attacks on self-interest and argues that it is not the same as money-making, greed, and hedonism. Maximization of profits is acceptable in society as long as the interests of all relevant stakeholders have been considered and the corporation stays within the rules of operation provided in society through government.[8] An advocate of self-interest was Ayn Rand, who provides an explanation of the relationship between self-interest and ethics in Responsibility for Ethics 5.2.

FIGURE 5.2 *Kaler's Gradations of Self-Interest and Morality*

Ultra-moral
(self-sacrificial altruism)
↑
Extraordinarily Moral
(altruism without self-sacrifice)
↑
Ordinarily Moral
(equal self-interest to others)
↑
Quasi-moral
(disproportionate but not dominant self-interest)
↑
Dividing line between moral and non-moral
↓
Quasi-egoism
(self-interest dominant but not total)
↓
Egoism
(totally self-interested)

Source: Adapted from John Kaler, "Reasons to Be Ethical: Self-Interest and Ethical Business." *Journal of Business Ethics*," Volume 27 (2000):163. With kind permission of Springer Science and Business Media.

RESPONSIBILITY FOR ETHICS 5.2

Ayn Rand's Views on Ethics and Self-Interest

Ayn Rand (1902–82) was a philosopher whose writings have influenced many including the advocates of capitalism; she still has a substantial following. Rand developed a theory of objectivism that involved the concepts of reality of nature, reason, self-interest, and capitalism. She described her philosophy in the best-selling novels and films *The Fountainhead* (1943) and *Atlas Shrugged* (1957), in plays and short stories, and also in nonfiction writings.

She believed that rationality was an individual's basic virtue and rested on three fundamental values: reason, purpose, and self-esteem. For individuals, reason was the judge of values and the only guide to action, and the proper standard for ethics was man's survival.

Self-interest was to be discovered and achieved in individuals through a rational process instead of by a random means. The individual was an end in him- or herself but was not the means to the ends of others. Individuals were to behave in their own rational self-interest, not sacrificing themselves to others—this did not mean a right to sacrifice others in the pursuit of their self-interest. An individual's pursuit of rational self-interest and happiness was the highest moral purpose in life.

Sources: The Ayn Rand Institute, accessed June 28, 2012, http://www.aynrand.org/site/PageServer?pagename=index; and The Ayn Rand Institute Canada, http://aynrandinstitute.ca.

 connect   Want to learn more about **Ayn Rand**?

The self-interest ethic has been described in some detail because it is so pervasive in society (despite denials), it is often cited by critics of business as the only ethic businesspersons use, and it is widely misunderstood.

Personal Virtues Ethic

The application of self-interest, especially in the short term, may not result in the fair and courteous treatment of others. The lack of forceful interference is not enough even if the long-term result is good. The **personal virtues ethic** means that an individual's or corporation's behaviour is based upon being a good person or corporate citizen with attitudes and character traits such as courage, honesty, wisdom, temperance, courage, fidelity, integrity, and generosity. People should act in ways to convey a sense of honour, pride, and self-worth. Virtues are acquired or developed through learning and practise, and will become habits.

The moral decisions made are not necessarily based on being kind and compassionate, and are not necessarily concerned about rights or benefits. Instead, the decision maker is concerned about the virtuous basis for his or her own actions. An individual should ask, "Does this action represent the kind of person I am or want to be, or present the desired corporate image or reputation?" An illustration of undesirable virtues is given in Everyday Ethics 5.1. In this example, the lack of virtue traits can harm a person's reputation and be expensive.

EVERYDAY ETHICS 5.1

Business and Lance Armstrong's Virtues

Lance Armstrong was considered an outstanding athlete and had won the Tour de France cycling race seven times before retiring in 2011. He was a high-profile athlete and had sponsorships from sports shoe and apparel company Nike, brewer Anheuser-Busch, and bicycle manufacturer Trek. In 1996 he was diagnosed with testicular cancer and was admired for his fight to overcome it. The Lance Armstrong Foundation was established in 1997 to support cancer research, and Livestrong formed in 2003 to provide services and other support to cancer patients. There were various accusations during Armstrong's career that he used illegal, performance-enhancing drugs, a practice known as doping. He denied the accusations and was very critical of his accusers. Investigations were started but did not find evidence to support the accusations.

The release of a United States Anti-Doping Agency (USADA) report in October 2012 changed things. The comprehensive report was hundreds of pages long and contained eyewitness testimony from teammates, email correspondence, financial records, and laboratory analyses. The report accused Armstrong of running "the most sophisticated, professionalized and successful doping program that sport has ever seen." The doping included administration of testosterone, cortisone, human growth hormone, and blood booster erythropoietin (EPO). Armstrong was accused of having deep character flaws that included lying, bullying, cheating, and attacking people. As a result of the report, he was stripped of his seven Tour de France titles and barred for life from participating in Olympic sports. He later resigned from the board of Livestrong.

In January 2013, Armstrong confessed that he used drugs in interviews on the Oprah Winfrey Network. A common reaction to the interviews was that Armstrong did little to redeem himself, failed to convey a genuine sense of remorse, and lacked credibility. In a later media interview, he claimed that he was the fall guy for the cycling doping culture where cheating was common. Moreover, he claimed that doping existed in other endurance sports. It was felt that he did little to repair his tarnished reputation.

Armstrong still had admirers, as evidenced by support for Livestrong, an organization supporting cancer survivors that still exists. After the USADA report, 16,000 donations averaging $97 were received, twice the usual number. On the other hand, his sponsors either cancelled or did not renew their sponsorship contracts, worth millions of dollars. Armstrong is no longer associated with Livestrong. Some believe that Armstrong has suffered rough justice as others in the cycling sport used drugs but he was singled out for punishment.

Sources: USADA, "Report on proceedings under the World Anti-Doping Code and the USADA Protocol: Reasoned decision of the United States Anti-Doping Agency on disqualification and ineligibility," accessed February 20, 2013, http://d3epuodzu3wuis.cloudfront.net/ReasonedDecision.pdf; Mark Gollom, "Did Lance Armstrong Redeem or Incriminate Himself? Armstrong Did a Poor Job of Rehabilitating His Image, Experts Say," CBC News, January 18, 2013, accessed January 20, 2013, http://www.cbc.ca/news/canada/story/2013/01/18/f-lance-armstrong-apology-reaction.html; NBC News, "Lance Armstrong Steps Down from Livestrong, Loses Nike, Bud Contracts," accessed January 20, 2013, http://www.nbcnews.com/business/lance-armstrong-steps-down-livestrong-loses-nike-bud-contracts-1C6512991; Nick Hoult, "Lance Armstrong Says He is 'Fall Guy' for Cycling's Problems," The Telegraph, accessed January 20, 2013, http://www.telegraph.co.uk/sport/othersports/cycling/lancearmstrong/9838064/Lance-Armstrong-says-he-is-fall-guy-for-cyclings-problems.html; and "Times Topics: Lance Armstrong," The New York Times, February 7, 2013, accessed February 20, 2013, http://topics.nytimes.com/top/reference/timestopics/people/a/lance_armstrong/index.html.

Managers and corporations must be honest, open, and truthful, and should be proud of their actions. Standards of behaviour toward others reflect fair and courteous treatment of one another—or, in the case of business, the treatment of its stakeholders. Managers should ask themselves how they would feel if the bases and details of a moral action became known. Managers should ask, "Would I feel comfortable explaining to a national television audience why a particular decision was made?" The disclosure audience can be colleagues, friends, partners, family, or the public. The application of this principle in this manner is referred to as the "TV test" or "light of day test" by some ethicists (e.g., Pagano[9]). The personal virtues of managers and businesspersons do provide a basis for deciding what is the right thing to do in business.

Ethic of Caring

Managers should consider what is truly good for society. Honesty, truthfulness, and temperance are not enough, and there has to be some degree of caring, compassion, and kindness toward others. The **ethic of caring** gives attention to specific individuals or stakeholders harmed or disadvantaged and their particular circumstances. There should be some sense of responsibility for reducing the harm or suffering of others, and solutions are designed to respond to the needs of particular individuals or stakeholders. Decision makers will be concerned with equity, or what is appropriate in the circumstances. Exceptions to universal application are fine when they will relieve suffering and harm. Stated another way, this ethic assumes there should be a sense of responsibility to reduce actual harm to or suffering of particular stakeholders.

Managers and corporations should act toward others in a way they would expect others to act toward them. The moral decision should be examined from the perspective of other parties or stakeholders involved or affected to try to determine what response the other stakeholders see as the most ethical. This principle is referred to as the Golden Rule: "Do unto others as you would have them do unto you." Managers would take actions that would be caring and work toward building a sense of community. In the corporation, this would include developing people, recognizing effort, considering family responsibilities, responding to a community problem, and accommodating disadvantaged groups.

The advantage of this ethic is that it is responsive to immediate suffering or harm. It allows for flexibility, enabling the manager to respond quickly to changing circumstances, and precedents are not a concern. There are downsides to the use of this ethic in decision making. The consideration of individual stakeholder problems might result in losing sight of the bigger picture and thus unintentionally harming some other stakeholder. Quite often the caring actions rely on subjective criteria or gut responses that limit the understanding of all the factors involved. If used to the extreme, this ethic can result in decisions that appear subjective and arbitrary.

In business organizations, the ethic of caring is exemplified by developing employees, responding to family or community problems, and participating in affirmative programs for disadvantaged groups—an example of which is given in Everyday Ethics 5.2.

EVERYDAY ETHICS 5.2

Rogers Communications Cares about the Community

Rogers aims to create positive social and economic impacts through community investment, while also aligning giving to causes that are important to stakeholders and Rogers employees. Rogers follows the benchmarks of corporate citizenship established by Imagine Canada, with the target to commit at least one percent of its net earnings before taxes to charities and nonprofit organizations. Rogers Corporate Donations and Sponsorship Policy ensures that all donations are aligned with their community investment strategy in order to have a greater impact. Rogers employees get involved too – Rogers Employee Volunteer Program and Volunteer Policy allow employees to take one paid day off per year to volunteer at the charity of their choice.

Source: Used with permission of Rogers Communications Inc. All rights reserved.

Utilitarian Ethic

The **utilitarian ethic** focuses on the distribution of benefits and harms to all stakeholders with the view to maximizing benefits. One approach to this ethic is that managers and corporations should make moral decisions that do "the greatest good for the greatest number." When managers make decisions, they should consider whether the harm in an action is outweighed by the good—that is, a cost–benefit analysis is conducted. If the action maximizes benefits, then it is the optimum course to take among alternatives that provide fewer benefits. Ethicists have described many variations of the utilitarian ethic, but this description is the most appropriate for business. It is particularly appropriate when managers are attempting to understand the impact of an action on society and its various stakeholders. Some ethicists prefer the utilitarian ethic instead of relying on government legislation and policies as those associated with government, such as politicians and civil servants, also have their self-interests.

As with other ethical theories, there are difficulties. The utilitarian ethic does not account for what is just. Also, there is a question of what is maximized to result in the community's happiness. There is no accepted means to accurately measure some costs and benefits, and even if there were, there is a risk of miscalculating them. Finally, there is no method for distributing the costs or benefits. Despite these difficulties, managers often make a moral decision based on what they perceive to be the greatest good for the greatest number.

Universal Rules Ethic

The determination of the net social benefit is good in theory, but it is difficult to apply, especially in business situations. It is challenging to distribute benefits and allocate harms fairly, as it is not possible to eliminate the self-interest of the person who decides. The **universal rules ethic** ensures that managers or corporations have the same moral obligations in morally similar situations. Managers should behave in such a way that the action they take under the circumstances can be an appropriate decision or rule of behaviour for others in a similar situation. One way to express this principle is, "What individuals believe is right for themselves, they should believe is right for all others." Persons should be treated as an end in themselves, worthy of dignity and respect and never as a means to one's own ends. An advantage of the ethic is that it eliminates self-interest.

The ethic indicates there should be rules and morals in society that should be fair to everyone, that they should universally apply, and that they should apply over time. This principle is also referred to as *categorical imperative ethics*—that is, it is complete in itself without reference to any other ends. This means that a manager acts only if he or she were willing to have the decision become a universal law.

There are drawbacks to this approach to moral decision making. It is questionable whether it is possible to always work to universal rules, as exceptions usually exist. The ethic provides no scale between actions that are considered to be morally right or wrong.

Individual Rights Ethic

Given human nature, it is difficult—if not impossible—to eliminate self-interest. The **individual rights ethic** relies on a list of agreed-upon rights for everyone that will be upheld by everyone and that becomes the basis for deciding what is right, just, or fair. Examples of such rights are guarantees against arbitrary actions of government, the reinforcement of freedom of speech and religion, security against seizure of property, access to due process, and protection of privacy. Governments identify rights in constitutions, and the United Nations has published a *Universal Declaration of Human Rights*. The advantage of this ethic is that there is no need to determine the greatest good or to establish a universal duty.

Attention to rights is important in assessing behaviour. First of all, it is necessary is ask if the rights of all have been respected as a right is a justified claim on others. Rights depend on standards and their acceptance by individuals and society in general. Some rights are more concrete than others, for example, some rights are guaranteed by legislation. Responsibility for Ethics 5.3 identifies where the legal rights of Canadians are explicitly stated in law. Other rights are moral in nature and are standards that most in society acknowledge but they are not necessarily codified in law. Even legally guaranteed rights are disputed in court cases and moral rights result in different interpretations in society.

RESPONSIBILITY FOR ETHICS 5.3

Rights and Responsibilities of Canadians

The legal rights of Canadians are based on the unwritten constitution of Great Britain, legislation by Canadian governments, English common law, the *Canadian Charter of Rights and Freedoms*, and the Constitution of Canada. These rights include the following:

- Freedom of conscience and religion

- Freedom of expression, including freedom of speech and of the press
- Freedom of peaceful assembly
- Freedom of association
- Mobility rights; that is, the choice of where to live within Canada and whether to enter and leave the country
- Aboriginal peoples' rights
- Official language rights and minority language educational rights
- Multiculturalism as a fundamental characteristic of Canadian heritage and identity.

With rights come responsibilities, including the following:

- Obeying the law
- Respecting the rights and freedoms of others
- Taking responsibility for oneself and one's family
- Serving on a jury
- Participating in democracy, for example by voting in elections
- Helping others in the community
- Protecting and enjoying heritage and environment

Source: "Rights and Responsibilities of Citizenship," Citizenship and Immigration Canada accessed July 3, 2012, http://www.cic.gc.ca/english/resources/publications/discover/section-04.asp.

Problems exist in determining and agreeing upon the list of rights. Often rights are in conflict with one another, or there is a conflict between the holders of those rights, creating dilemmas that are not easily resolved. As a result, some rights might need to be limited. Rights should not be the sole determinant in ethical decision making. They are not absolute and overemphasis on one right may result in injustice. Moreover, there is not a universally recognized list of rights and the use of a particular right must be defended or justified. In business, stakeholders have various rights, some of which are supported by laws. Employees have a right to privacy, and shareholders to disclosure of information that will affect their investments.

Ethic of Justice

The **ethic of justice** considers that moral decisions are based on the primacy of a single value: justice which will result in an outcome that is fair. It is preferred by those who view ethical dilemmas as involving a conflict among rights that can be resolved by the impartial application of some general principle. Thus, the fairness of the process is important, but so is the equitable (but not necessarily equal) distribution of results. Each stakeholder has rights relating to the distribution of benefits or harms from an action or decision. In the equitable treatment of stakeholders, precedents should be avoided. There is a need to ensure that no stakeholders are left out, and an implicit social contract exists in society that the poor, uneducated, and unemployed should not be made worse off, in particular by any actions of business.

Ethicists have identified several forms of justice.

- *Procedural*—This involves the impartial application of rules or procedures.
- *Compensatory*—Stakeholders are compensated appropriately for wrongs that are suffered.
- *Retributive*—This form is concerned that punishment should fit the offence but will be just and fair.
- *Distributive*—There is concern for how all stakeholders are treated. Benefits and harms are distributed in a way that is just and fair. This form of justice is often applicable in business situations.

The advantage to using this ethic is that it attempts to look at a dilemma logically and impartially. This ethic is appealing, as all are perceived to have an equal right to equitable treatment. Only when rights differ in some way relevant to the situation are there justifiable grounds for different treatment. Reasons of inequality might include: worked harder than others, accomplished more or performed better, contributed more to group or society, seniority, or a prior agreement about how the distribution should be made.

A disadvantage is that it is difficult to decide, outside of the law, who has the moral authority to reward or punish whom. Ensuring that benefits are distributed fairly to everyone is challenging, and there may be arbitrariness in deciding which rules to apply. Persons relying on this ethic may unintentionally ride roughshod over some stakeholders in favour of some abstract ideal. The immediate interests of particular stakeholders may be overlooked, and the ethic is perceived as being impersonal, inflexible, cold, and uncaring. Persons who prefer this ethic may tolerate harms to some stakeholders in the name of justice or some right. Discriminatory behaviour is acceptable as long as the relative inputs of those affected are considered.

With this ethic, managers should act to ensure a more equitable distribution of benefits so that all individuals get what they deserve and what is just and fair. But markets are unjust in the distribution of resources, resulting in poverty, some poorly educated citizens, and unemployment. Justice is reflected in the following business practices: the development of outstanding goods and services, employee skill and competency development, the use of teams, and fair and honest treatment of all stakeholders. Responsibility for Ethics 5.4 is an example of how one industry attempts to resolve customer grievances in a just manner.

RESPONSIBILITY FOR ETHICS 5.4

CAMVAP: The Canadian Motor Vehicle Arbitration Plan

The Canadian automobile industry was concerned about the increasing number of customers who were frustrated by not having an accessible way to resolve disputes involving new-car warranties. In 1994, the industry created the Canadian Motor Vehicle Arbitration Plan (CAMVAP), which provides consumers with recourse to justice without going to court.

CAMVAP is an arbitration program for resolving disputes with an automobile manufacturer. In a dispute, the consumer and the manufacturer agree to accept the decision of an impartial person, or arbitrator, who hears both sides of the case, considers the evidence, and makes a final decision binding on both parties. Fifteen manufacturers participate in the plan and CAMVAP claims several advantages including "fair, fast, free, friendly, and final."

Source: Based on the Canadian Motor Vehicle Arbitration Plan, http://www.camvap.ca/.

The seven principles represent a wide range of ethical philosophy. The assessment of the appropriateness of behaviour would vary substantially among these principles. This is one reason why there is such a deviance of views regarding whether particular actions are correct. Managers and corporations can use these principles to become better informed of the consequences of their decisions.

 Want to learn more about **ethics "cowboy" style?**

LO 5.5   Moral Reasoning

Moral reasoning is a systematic approach to thinking or reasoning through the implications of a moral problem or issue. In general terms, an approach to moral decision making includes the following steps, although variations to the sequence do exist:

- Define the moral issue or decision
- Gather all relevant information
- Identify the stakeholders involved
- Develop possible alternative solutions
- Consider the applicable value judgments, moral standards, and ethical principles
- Identify the distribution of harms and benefits to the stakeholders by each alternative with each ethical principle used
- Determine any practical constraints that might apply
- Decide on the action or decision to be taken that can be supported, explained, and defended if necessary

Hosmer argues that one or more of the ethical principles should be used to analyze a moral dilemma. For each principle the distribution of harms and benefits to the relevant stakeholders is identified. Because the principles represent a wide range of perspectives, and no one principle is necessarily consistent with the others, the conclusions reached through the use of each principle will vary. By using a range of perspectives, managers can increase their understanding of the various ethical implications of their decisions. It is unlikely that any single ethical principle can ensure a satisfactory analysis to every business decision or to a complex decision. The use of several principles provides a broad-based range of options to the manager, and identification of harms and benefits to stakeholders enables the manager to better understand the consequences of an ethical decision.

According to Hosmer, managers confuse ethics, morals, and values. Whereas ethics remain the same and do not differ among people, cultures, or countries, morals and values do. Decisions involving moral considerations are often based upon moral standards of society and value judgments held by individuals. It is important that managers use ethics principles as the basis of analysis and do not rely solely on morals and values. The moral standards and value judgments are partly determined by the influences mentioned above.[10]

Many managers rely solely on moral standards and value judgments, but this approach may not provide a sufficient analysis of the situation or result in the most satisfactory course of action. The ethical principles offer a form of analysis that systematically allocates the benefits and harms in a manner that recognizes the interests and rights of each stakeholder. This is more likely to result in an accommodation of stakeholders that will lead to more confidence and trust in the corporation.

Table 5.2 summarizes the approaches managers might take to consider the ethical implications of business decisions. Approach 1 is to ignore the ethical implications and not consider them, an approach increasingly considered unacceptable in today's society. Approach 2 represents Level 2 of ethical assessment, where value judgments and moral standards are considered. Depending upon the values and morals identified, this approach might be acceptable and result in a satisfactory consideration of ethical implications. Approach 3 involves the systematic evaluation of business decisions through the use of ethical principles. This approach would most likely result in a more satisfactory decision, because the distribution of harms and benefits among stakeholders is analyzed from different ethical perspectives and is viewed as being the most appropriate method.

TABLE 5.2 Approaches to Considering the Ethical Implications in Business Decisions

Approach 1	Approach 2	Approach 3	Approach 4
Amoral	May be appropriate	Most appropriate	Inappropriate
Identify decision alternatives	Identify decision alternatives	Identify decision alternatives	Identify decision alternatives
Ignore ethical implications	Evaluate alternatives with value judgments and moral standards	Evaluate alternatives in terms of ethical principles	Make decision and implement
Make decision	Make decision	Make decision	Search for value judgments, moral standards, and ethical principles to justify decision
Implement decision	Implement decision	Implement decision	Rationalization

In approaches 2 and 3, consideration of ethical implications is performed prior to making the decision. Approach 4 is thought to be inappropriate as the decision is made without any consideration of ethics but value judgments, moral standards, and ethical principles are searched for after the fact as justification of the decision. Such an approach would not be considered acceptable given today's sensitivity to social responsibility and ethics.

Kohlberg's Stages of Moral Development

How managers assess ethical issues and challenges varies greatly; one explanation is provided in this reading. Another commonly referred-to theory of moral reasoning was developed by Kohlberg and speculates that individuals have identifiable cognitive skill levels that they use in resolving moral dilemmas.[11] These skills are developed over time as a result of educational experience and the socialization processes in maturing from childhood to adulthood. Table 5.3 summarizes Kohlberg's six stages of moral development in three levels. He has also proposed a seventh stage, "Beyond morality and justice," which is not described.[12]

TABLE 5.3 Kohlberg's Stages of Moral Development
Pre-conventional Level   *Pre-conventional level*
At this level, individuals are focused on themselves and awareness of others is virtually non-existent. What is right is determined by self-interest.
Stage 1—Punishment and obedience orientation. There is obedience to rules and authority and concern for possible punishment if caught. Good or bad is decided in terms of the power to determine the rules. Authority is exercised and fear used as an influencer.
Stage 2—Individual instrumental purpose and exchange orientation. The individual focuses on what he or she will get out of an exchange; that is, the reward involved or "what is in it for me." What is right is defined in terms of whether something serves one's own needs. The situation is evaluated on the basis of fairness to one's self or self-satisfaction.
Conventional Level   *conventional level*
The individual is more aware of others at this level, and is group- or organization-focused. Individuals take into account the expectations and overall welfare of society and therefore are responding to notions of fairness and justice as outlined in laws, rules, and codes.
Stage 3—Mutual interpersonal expectations, relationships, and conformity orientation. Individuals are concerned with being a good person. The well being of, and fairness to, others is considered. Group norms are followed and loyalty and belonging are important.
Stage 4—Law and order orientation. Laws are viewed as promoting societal welfare and thus observed. What is right is determined by a sense of duty to society.
Post-conventional Level   *Post-conventional level*
Involves universal and humankind orientation. Concepts of rights and justice are considered when determining what is right. There is an increased capacity to consciously use principled judgment; that is, ethical principles. Rules and laws are questioned as the only basis for making moral decisions.
Stage 5—Social contract orientation. Laws and morals may be in conflict, and another basis more appropriate for determining what is considered right is necessary. Societal standards apply that are established through consensus.
Stage 6—Universal ethical principles orientation. Ethical principles are chosen as a basis for what is considered right regardless of society's views. Decisions are based upon one's conscience, and logical ethical principles are used.

Sources: Based on Lawrence Kohlberg, "Stage and Sequence: The Cognitive Development Approach to Socialization," in *Handbook of Socialization Theory and Research*, D.A. Goslin, ed. (Chicago: Rand McNally, 1969), 347–480; Lawrence Kohlberg, "The Claim of Moral Adequacy of a Highest Stage of Moral Judgment," *The Journal of Philosophy*, Vol. LXX (1973), 630–646; and Lawrence Kohlberg, *Essays on Moral Development Vol. 1: The Philosophy of Moral Development* (New York: Harper and Row, 1981).

Kohlberg's work has been criticized on theoretical and methodological grounds but is often described in relation to the ethics of business. It is another approach to explaining how managers behave morally, and it is believed that most managers use stages 3 and 4. The stages of moral development suggest that managers learn through experience and training to consider the ethical implications of decisions differently over time and in different situations.

How can managers and businesspersons be moved toward Approach 3 identified in Table 5.2, and the Post-conventional Level in Table 5.3? Several things can be suggested in general terms. Managers should be encouraged to view situations from various points of view or from the perspectives of relevant stakeholders. They should be introduced to moral reasoning processes and engage in logical thinking or a reasoned argument. In addition, they should be exposed to moral controversy, through training or by example. Resource persons more experienced in moral reasoning should be available to advise managers and businesspeople.

LO 5.6   Ethics in Business: Some Challenges

Everyone is confronted by moral dilemmas and faced with difficult moral decisions, whether in one's personal life, the workplace, or management. Ethical breaches can never be eliminated, and it is idealistic or naive to think otherwise. But there should be some approach to keeping wrongs or harms to a minimum. Most individuals and organizations strive toward increasing the likelihood of "getting it right" through some systematic and thoughtful approach to resolve ethical dilemmas. Thus, there are challenges to ethics in business including simplistic approaches, myths, and lack of awareness.

Quite often the expression "just do the right thing" is proposed as a guide or standard for determining acceptable moral behaviour. This is not satisfactory because it is too open-ended and leads to many interpretations. What is "right" is in the eyes of the beholder and can have many meanings. Accountability is not achieved with this approach because no standard exists to measure or judge against. Instead, accountability is achieved by organizational processes and structures that will be examined in Chapter 6.

Treviño and Brown identified several myths pertaining to business ethics, three of which are applicable to this chapter. The first myth is *It's easy to be ethical*. Ethical decisions and theories are complex even when discussed in applied situations. They state that moral awareness—that is, ethical recognition and ethical sensitivity—is necessary as a first step in moral reasoning. Usually ethical decision making is a complex, multi-stage process, and the organizational context creates additional pressures and complexity. Another myth is *Unethical behaviour in business is simply the result of "bad apples."* The first reaction is to look for a culprit who can be punished and removed. Most people are followers when it comes to ethics, and they engage in unethical conduct when directed by a boss. Ethics can be taught and the behaviour of adults influenced. Finally, it is a myth that *People are less ethical than they used to be*. Ethical behaviour today is not that different than in the past. The tendency is to remember recent unethical behaviour or events and forget those of the past.[13]

Another challenge relates to an individual's perception of his or her own morality. Most people believe that they behave ethically toward others, but self-perception often falls short. People are not objective in self-assessment; there are sources of unintended, unethical decision making that are an unconscious, implicit bias of which they are unaware. Banaji, Bazerman, and Chugh identified four biases: prejudice, favouritism, overclaiming credit, and conflict of interest.[14]

Implicit prejudice is a bias that emerges from unconscious beliefs such as stereotyping. Associations are made that may not always be valid. In-group favouritism is a bias that favours a group to which a person belongs or is associated. Such groups can be based on friendship, sharing a nationality, religion, social class, race, or educational affiliation. Extra credit is given for group membership leading to discrimination against from outside the group. Overclaiming credit is a bias that favours one's self. Many people hold positive views of themselves and believe that they are entitled to more than they deserve. Finally, conflict of interest is a bias that favours those who benefit the individual. Such conflicts lead honest, ethical persons to make decisions that are neither sound nor ethical.

Developments in society lead to new ethical challenges. Technological advances are demanding as new situations or circumstances occur, for example, the use of robots in business and society as discussed in Everyday Ethics 5.3. Another responsibility for managers is to be knowledgeable of ethics and their application in new settings.

EVERYDAY ETHICS 5.3

The Ethics of Robots

A robot is defined as an engineered machine that senses, thinks and acts. More autonomous robots are being created and a challenge exists relating to how robots face ethical decisions, that is, how can they be designed to make moral judgments. Robots are presently used in manufacturing, the military, and automated aircraft, trains, and motor vehicles. From a consumer perspective, driverless cars and robo financial advisors are being designed. There will be increasing use of robots in the areas of research, entertainment, medicine and personal care.

Many issues relate to safety and errors. As an example, research is being undertaken to ascertain how a robot would make a decision between colliding with other cars and striking a pedestrian. Other issues involve the relationship between laws and robots. Laws must be designed that enable robots to be accountable for their actions and to insure their judgments will benefit the most. Ethicists, government, and engineers will need to cooperate in formulating appropriate laws. A third area of issues involves the social and economic impact of robots. In particular, economic disruption occurs as humans are replaced by robots leading to societal changes.

As robots acquire ability to act independently, society will have to decide whether or not robots should be allowed to make ethical and social responsibility decisions. To address this concern, roboethics is a new field of study and research that deals with the social, ethical, and legal implications of robotics technology. The field will attempt to create of an integrity framework that can be included in the design of robots.

Sources: Tim Johnson, "I, Robot Need Ethical Guidance," *University Affairs*, June-July 2015, 13-16; Patrick Lin et al, "Robot Ethics: Mapping the Issues for a Mechanized World," *Artificial Intelligence*, 175, (2011), 942-949; and Peter M. Asaro, "What Should We Want From a Robot Ethic," *International Review of Information Ethics*, Vol. 6, (12/2006), 9-16.

 Want to learn more about **your ethics**?

This chapter identifies why business morality is complex and challenging. Managers can rely on intuitive approaches based on value judgments and moral standards to identify what they consider proper. This is not a reliable approach, as it may not consider the distribution of harms and benefits among all stakeholders. A more systematic approach is necessary, as frequently dilemmas exist and it is not possible to avoid harms. Ethics principles are relied upon to provide a more thorough approach.

Naturally, conflicts occur among the corporation's economic, legal, and social responsibilities. As discussed in Chapter 2, the market-based business system involves certain fundamentals, the application of which involves ethical implications. In addition, the corporation has legal responsibilities that must be obeyed, but the application of government requirements does not address all economic and ethical responsibilities. Chapters 7, 8, and 9 examine the ethical responsibilities—social and environmental—of business in its relationship to society. The next chapter describes how the ethics of business can be managed within the corporation.

Your advice to Jonathan and Rosemary ...

Several issues and stakeholders are involved in this situation. For Jonathan, it appears that self-interest is the primary motivator, but the personal virtues ethic also is evident. When considering other stakeholders, the utilitarian and universal rules ethics come into play. What about the consequences for other applicants who have the appropriate qualifications? What are the implications for employers? How do Jonathan's fellow employees feel about his being hired? If Jonathan thinks about the ethics of this situation at all, he is bound to be faced with a dilemma—but a different one from that facing Rosemary.

Summary

- The topic of business ethics has been "in" for the past decade and has been discussed extensively in the literature, the media, and the classroom as well as on the Internet. Ethical behaviour as it relates to a variety of contexts has been examined, for example as it relates to public administration and government, the environment, multinational corporations, banking, competitiveness, and industrial relations. An extensive examination of ethical behaviour has occurred not only as it relates to business and the corporation but also as it impacts the various interrelationships among business, society, and stakeholders. (LO 5.1)

- The operations of any business involve the potential that decisions will have ethical implications for managers and stakeholders. The preferred phrase *ethics of business* is defined as the rules, standards, codes, or principles that provide guidance for morally appropriate behaviour in managerial decision making relating to the operation of the corporation and business' relationship with society. (LO 5.1)

- The three levels of ethical assessment are (1) awareness of moral or ethical implications; (2) ethical implications assessed upon individual, organizational, economic efficiency, governmental, and societal influences, described as value judgments and moral standards; and (3) implications assessed upon use of ethical principles. (LO 5.2)

- The multitude of influences on ethical behaviour range from educational and religious backgrounds to professional organizations and governments. These influences lead to ethical relativism, the belief that ethical answers depend on the situation and that no universal standards or rules guide or evaluate morality. (LO 5.3)

- Seven theoretical bases, or ethics, for understanding ethical conduct are described: self-interest, personal virtues, caring, utilitarian, universal rules, individual rights, and justice. (LO 5.4)

- The process of moral reasoning is described. In particular, Kohlberg's theory of the stages of moral development is outlined in regard to its application to the ethics of business. The pre-conventional, conventional, and post-conventional levels and the six stages illustrate the attitude that managers may have toward assessing the implications of ethics in the business environment. (LO 5.5)

- The consideration of the ethical implications of the responsibilities of business is prevalent in what corporations do. The theoretical basis for ethics has been outlined and sets the stage for further examination of the ethics and responsibilities of business. But, there are several challenges to ethical behaviour in corporations. (LO 5.6)

Key Terms

Business ethics

Value judgments

Moral standards

Ethical relativism

Self-interest ethic

Personal virtues ethic

Ethic of caring

Utilitarian ethic

Universal rules ethic

Individual rights ethic

Ethic of justice

Moral reasoning

Critical Thinking and Discussion Questions

1. Why should managers consider ethical relativism when doing business in a foreign country?
2. How is an ethical principle different from a moral standard?
3. Why can the self-interest ethic not be avoided when studying the ethics of business?
4. Which personal virtues are most important in the operation of a corporation?

5. Under what circumstances would a manager or a corporation use the ethic of caring in assessing the ethical implications of a decision?

6. What is attractive about the utilitarian ethic when analyzing business decisions?

7. How do corporate managers apply the universal rules ethic?

8. What are the rights of a corporation?

9. In what situations would it be appropriate to use the economic efficiency ethic in assessing ethical implications?

10. Is the ethic of justice applicable to capitalism?

11. Why is a system of moral reasoning important for managers?

Cases

5.1 WORKING OVERTIME

It was 9:05 p.m. and Tyler Simms was facing a dilemma. He was at the office working late, again, completing a report that his boss asked him to have ready for the next morning. She had received the draft report ten days earlier but waited until 4:33 p.m. that afternoon to return it for revision. Tyler felt that there was no excuse for the rushed revision because there had been plenty of time for his boss to give the feedback necessary to prepare the final draft. Tyler was becoming increasingly annoyed at having to work overtime under these circumstances. She had done this to him six times in the last month, and the practice was disrupting his family life. Other than for this annoyance, he liked his job, it paid well, and there were career opportunities. His dilemma was what he could do about this situation without risking his career.

The telephone rang. It was his wife, who was experiencing a problem of her own. She had been helping their six-year-old daughter with a school project and was missing some supplies to complete it. It was getting late and she did not think she could get to any stores in time. Furthermore, she would have to get their one-year-old twin boys out of bed to go to the store with her. She said that she needed poster board, coloured markers, and tape. Given where his office was located, Tyler did not think he had time to get to a store stocking these supplies. He knew that the supplies were in the stationery cabinet in the outer office, to which he had access. He also knew that there was an explicit company policy not to use stationery for personal reasons. While on the phone, he wondered whether he should mention to his wife the existence of the supplies in his office. He also pondered whether he should immediately leave and go to a store to buy supplies. If he did, there was a risk of not completing the report. Thus, a second dilemma emerged.

Questions

1. What are the issues involved with these dilemmas?

2. Who are the stakeholders?

3. What ethical principles could be applied to this situation?

4. What should Tyler do? Justify your choice using ethical reasoning.

5.2 ETHICAL RESPONSIBILITY ON MOUNT EVEREST

Many mountain climbers dream of scaling the highest mountain on Earth. It is a dangerous venture and some of them die in pursuit of this dream every year, including a 33-year-old Canadian woman in May 2012. The following describes one situation involving the ethics and responsibilities of climbers toward one another.

In May 2006, several climbing parties passed by David Sharp, 34, who was near death at 28,000 feet on Mount Everest. He later died alone, without companionship in his final hours. He was one of 11 who perished during the 2006 climbing season and one of more than 200 who have died attempting to climb the mountain.

One climber to leave Sharp was Mark Inglis, 47, a New Zealander who was climbing the mountain on artificial legs. He and his party stopped to consider Sharp's situation. He was in poor condition and near death, but was given oxygen. Rescue was not feasible as helicopters cannot operate at that altitude. The lives of Inglis's party would likely have been endangered trying to move Sharp to a base camp.

It was disclosed that Sharp's group was loosely organized without a leader. The members of the group appeared to be functioning independently according to an expedition outfitter. The outfitter said that Sharp's group did not have sufficient oxygen and climbed without a Sherpa guide.

Discussion of the incident was extensive. One position presented was that climbers do not endanger themselves to save another. Furthermore, looking after another climber may jeopardize one's own chance at climbing the mountain. Sir Edmund Hillary, who, with his Sherpa Tenzing Norgay, became the first to reach the summit of Mount Everest, said that human life is more important than conquering mountains. Others suggested that the incident was an example of a lack of sense of responsibility and caring for one another.

Questions

1. What ethical principles are involved in this situation?
2. Why blame Inglis?
3. Who is responsible?
4. Should the climbing of Mount Everest be regulated?

Sources: Thomas Ball, "Amputee Defends Decision to Let Climber Die on Everest," *National Post,* May 23, 2006, A2; Oliver Moore, "Left to Die at 28,000 Feet," *The Globe and Mail,* May 25, 2006, A1, A9; Paul Chapman, "Saving Life More Important than Peak," *National Post,* May 25, 2006, A2; and "No Heroes in Thin Air," *National Post,* May 26, 2006, A16.

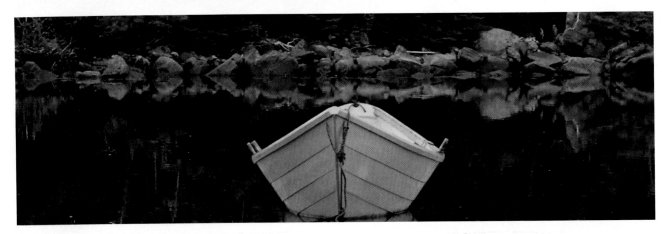

Used with the permission of Dennis Flynn

CHAPTER 6

Ethics of Business: Management and Leadership

LEARNING OUTCOMES

After studying this chapter, you will be able to:

LO 6.1 Recognize appropriate ethical leadership

LO 6.2 Define and describe the pros and cons of a statement of values.

LO 6.3 Make the distinction between codes of conduct and codes of ethics.

LO 6.4 Appreciate the purpose of ethics training in an organization.

LO 6.5 Define an ethics audit and explain the role of ethics officers and ethics committees

LO 6.6 Understand how ethics reporting systems work and define whistleblowing.

LO 6.7 Know who is responsible for managing the ethics of business.

LO 6.8 Identify the approaches to ethics programs.

LO 6.9 Evaluate ethics programs and list their benefits.

LO 6.10 Recognize that ethical misbehaviour may occur despite management efforts and the implementation of ethics programs.

What would you do if...?

Paul O'Doherty is the ethics officer for a medium-sized petroleum company; in this role he is responsible for the company's comprehensive ethics program. The program includes a code of business conduct that outlines the values to guide behaviour, identifies conflicts of interest, specifies appropriate and inappropriate practices, and provides an approach to reporting violations or suspected wrongdoing. One aspect of the reporting system is an employee hotline to which employees can contribute in written form, including by email, or orally by telephone or in person. Participants must identify themselves and all communications go directly to Paul, who reports directly to the corporate secretary and legal counsel. The identity of the employee is not disclosed and confidentiality is maintained except in rare cases where legal action occurs.

Paul is a member of the Ethics Practitioners' Association of Canada (EPAC). According to EPAC, the skills of an ethics officer include "facilitating constructive dialogue on ethics-related issues, analyzing ethics issues and problems, and providing coherent, realistic solutions to ethical issues." Paul finds his job to be rewarding and his work has enabled the company to keep abreast of developments in the ethics area. The company has received awards for its ethics program, and is recognized as a leader in corporate ethics.

Recently, Paul has experienced a problem with the hotline component of the ethics program. An employee has been making numerous complaints to the hotline, almost weekly. The complaints cover many aspects of the employee's department: a supervisor is giving unfair treatment, co-workers are stealing office supplies, management is exercising favouritism in assigning holidays, a fellow employee is moonlighting, and co-workers are providing a poor quality of service to customers. All of the complaints have been investigated according to the procedures outlined in the corporation's reporting guidelines. The investigations have been costly, both monetarily and in time. None of the complaints have been determined to be justified, and many lack credibility. Paul has reluctantly concluded that the employee is a whiner or troublemaker, but he cannot state this to others. It also appears that the employee's reporting practices have been damaging to department morale. Paul's challenge now is to decide what should be done about the situation.

What is your advice to Paul?

Source: Information on the skills of an ethics officer was obtained from Ethics Practitioners' Association of Canada (EPAC), "Competency profile of ethics practitioners," accessed October 21, 2012, http://www.epac-apec.ca/competency-profile-ethics-practitioners.

Business has responded to the increased concern surrounding ethics and its social and environmental responsibilities. Various initiatives have been taken to institutionalize ethics; that is, to implement policies or programs that increase the awareness of ethics in the organization. Every organization has an ethics program, whether it knows it or not. In organizations there is a set of factors both implicit and explicit that communicate corporate values, define parameters of decision making, establish general rules for behaviour, and provide mechanisms for analysis. In order to implement policies or programs, the leadership of the corporation must support ethical behaviour by all corporate stakeholders including the CEO.

LO 6.1 Ethical Leadership Forms

Leadership styles have been extensively researched, but the styles applicable to ethics of business have not, according to Christensen et al. They reviewed research on leadership and identified possible styles or forms applicable to the ethics of business and corporate social responsibility. These forms are: ethical, responsible, and servant leadership.[1]

Leaders using an ethical form of leadership communicate ethical standards and encourage ethical conduct. They also provide a model of ethical behaviour and set an example for others in the corporation. Unethical behaviour is opposed and is dealt with promptly and appropriately. Decisions are made that consider the needs of different stakeholders, and encouragement is given to supporting worthy community activities including through volunteerism. The operations of the corporation reflect support for socially responsible activities, for example, designing safe products, treating employees fairly, and reducing pollution and other threats to the environment.

The concept of responsible leadership has two different orientations, a narrow one focused on financial performance and an extended one with a stakeholder view. The latter is consistent with corporate social responsibility where the corporation is not run to only make profits, but thinks of profits as an outcome likely to result from managing a purposeful and responsible business. Business is considered as a means, not an end, in addressing social problems and serving stakeholders in need. With this form of leadership, a manager might base actions on religious or spirituality beliefs.

A third form is servant leadership, which emphasizes concern for others, and combines the motivation to lead with the need to serve others. Characteristics of this form include: empowering and developing of people, acting authentically, showing of humility, and providing direction. Managers practising this form act as stewards who work for the good of the whole while creating value for relevant stakeholders. Focus is on all stakeholders and a wider set of goals than only profits. Social responsibility or sustainability is more likely included with the focus on disenfranchised stakeholders or maybe the environment. Most importantly the response of servant leadership is greater engagement with stakeholders, for example, including greater commitment, job satisfaction, and empowerment by employees. Survival of the corporation is important but so is responsibility to the community and meeting the needs of stakeholders.

The third form of leadership would include the design and implementation of some type of corporate ethics program and there are several components that managers or entrepreneurs can use. **Corporate ethics programs** comprise some combination of the following: a statement of values, code of conduct and/or ethics, ethics training, ethics audits and consulting services, ethics officers and committees, and ethics reporting systems.

Many initiatives can be taken, and several of these are described in this chapter. In the beginning sections, the explicit aspects of ethics programs are outlined. Toward the end of the chapter, the more implicit aspects of programs are described, including those responsible for providing leadership. The approaches of ethics programs are categorized and their evaluation discussed. Several components might comprise an ethics program, whether on a formal or informal basis. No model or standard program has emerged, and programs vary by business enterprise.

LO 6.2   Statement of Values

A **statement of values** contains a description of the beliefs, principles, and basic assumptions about what is desirable or worth striving for in an organization. Many corporations have articulated their values in such statements, also referred to as creeds and statements of philosophy. A statement of values also becomes the basis for a code of ethics. An example is provided in Everyday Ethics 6.1.

Most business enterprises are concerned to some extent about ethical behaviour, integrity, employee health and safety, the environment, quality, and service. Such concerns are a part of corporate life today. A study of 15 Canadian multinational corporations found the top ten corporate values to be integrity, honesty, justice, equality, objectivity (impartiality), loyalty, devotion, respect, prudence, and tolerance.[2]

EVERYDAY ETHICS 6.1

Values at Cameco Corporation

Cameco, which produces 18 percent of the world's uranium, has identified the following values that will guide its behaviour:

"Safety and Environment—The safety of people and protection of the environment are the foundations of our work. All of us share in the responsibility of continually improving the safety of our workplace and the quality of our environment.

People—We value the contribution of every employee and we treat people fairly by demonstrating our respect for individual dignity, creativity and cultural diversity. By being open and honest we achieve the strong relationships we seek.

Integrity—Through personal and professional integrity, we lead by example, earn trust, honour our commitments and conduct our business ethically.

Excellence—We pursue excellence in all that we do. Through leadership, collaboration and innovation, we strive to achieve our full potential and inspire others to reach theirs."

There is no uniformity in content or format in these statements. Kooten found that a value statement may contain any combination of components, such as:

- the key interests to be satisfied and balanced; for example, the public or community interest, owners, employers, and suppliers;
- an emphasis on quality and/or excellence in relation to product and service, employees, and technology;
- efficiency as indicated by low cost, high productivity, and value for money or investment;
- the atmosphere or climate of enterprise; for example, a good place to work, an emphasis on teamwork, managers' support of staff, and development of employees;
- the observance of codes of conduct to enhance integrity and to ensure fairness in all dealings.[3]

By using a statement of values, managers are recognizing that individual and corporate actions are caused, in part, by the values that the individuals and the corporation have in common. Values need to be shared by everyone, at least to some degree, so that the values are reinforced and widely accepted. It is important that everyone in the corporation is able to identify the shared values and describe their rationale.

The values the organization wishes to operate with in the future are not necessarily the values implicit at the present. It is important to identify the organizational values desired, to compare them to individual values, and to ascertain how they can be reinforced. Value statements should be developed with the involvement, over time, of as many employees as possible. Although the production of a statement is the desired end result, the process used to accomplish that end is an important learning process.

What happens in practice is often quite different. The statements usually express the beliefs of the chief executive or top-level management and little, if any, effort is made to communicate or explain the values. In other cases, value statements, creeds, or philosophies are designed to improve the public image of the corporation and are only cited in advertisements, press releases, and newsletters. As a result, they are not taken seriously. A related problem is that no effort is made to instill the values throughout the corporation. In effect, the values are not shared and do not become a part of daily life—the ideals expressed are not reflected in reality, the meaning of the values is unclear, and employees and others do not understand the process.

Despite these problems, it is argued that management should be value-driven; that is, all plans, decisions, actions, and rewards are governed by a value focus. Thus, values have influence on organizational objectives, corporate plans, individual accountability, standards of performance, and reward systems.[4] This type of thinking is necessary if values are to influence corporate operations. Values must be identified, defined, prioritized, and then communicated throughout the enterprise, including corporate training programs and employee meetings. Whether the desired values are being practised should be measured within the organization and with customers or clients. In particular, current management practices must be monitored to ascertain the extent to which values are supported and incorporated into decision making, which may necessitate modifying leadership styles and management systems. Finally, values must be reinforced, including through a reward system.

connect   Want to learn about **giving voice to values**?

LO 6.3   Codes of Conduct and Codes of Ethics

A **code of conduct** explicitly states what appropriate behaviour is by identifying what is acceptable and unacceptable. A **code of ethics** is a statement of principles or values that guide behaviour by describing the general value system within which a corporation attempts to operate in a given environment. A distinction should be made between a code of ethics and a code of conduct even though academics and practitioners often do not do so; these differences are described in Table 6.1. As there is little consistency in the contents of the codes in practice, the following discussion refers to codes generally. Codes are referred to by a variety of titles, including "Standards of Practice," "Code of Behaviour," and "Standards of Professional Conduct," and can be 20 or more pages in length. Corporations often develop codes that are a mix of conduct behaviour and ethics guides.

TABLE 6.1	Distinction between Codes of Conduct and Codes of Ethics	
Codes of Conduct	**Codes of Ethics**	
Enforced by an external power and authority; convey rules that tell people what they must or must not do. Members of organizations must obey or face penalties for failing to do so.	Codes of ethics suggest guidelines to follow and empower individuals to act according to their consciences. Penalties are not imposed and writers emphasize the qualities they think members should have.	
Key characteristics:	Key characteristics:	
• Imposed by others • What must be done or what must not be done • Rules	• Self-imposed • Who we are • What we stand for • Guidelines or guiding principles	

[Handwritten annotations: "must obey face penalties"; "external power authority"; "tell people what they must or must not do."; "Self-imposed"; "who we are"; "what we stand for"; "Guidelines guiding principles"]

Codes have been developed at different levels in the business system, and they all contribute to the managing of ethics:

- *Corporate or business enterprise*—Individual corporations prepare codes for their own use (see Everyday Ethics 6.2).

- *Professional organizations*—Professions such as lawyers, accountants, and architects have been early users of codes and are influenced by them when employed by business enterprises.

- *Industry and sector*—Industry associations formulate codes that enterprises in the industry or sector may voluntarily follow. Also referred to as *voluntary codes*, sometimes these codes are developed in conjunction with government agencies. As an example, see Everyday Ethics 6.3, which outlines the principles that must be followed in order to become a Certified Financial Planner (CFP®).

- *Single issue*—Non-governmental organizations (NGOs) or business associations develop codes applicable to a particular issue, for example sweatshop labour in developing countries.

- *Codes from national and international bodies*—International NGOs or agencies such as the United Nations or the Organisation for Economic Co-operation and Development (OECD) prepare codes.

EVERYDAY ETHICS 6.2

Manulife Financial's Code of Business Conduct and Ethics

"The Manulife Financial Code of Business Conduct and Ethics (the "Code") reaffirms the Company's commitment to ethical conduct and its practice of complying with all applicable laws and avoiding potential or actual conflicts of interest. We should all be thoroughly familiar with its provisions and conduct ourselves according to both the letter and the spirit of the Code. With a long tradition of uncompromising dedication to the highest standards of business conduct, Manulife enjoys a reputation of unquestioned integrity and honesty. This reputation is among our most valuable assets and we must protect it."

[Handwritten annotations: "unquestioned integrity"; "Reputation is honesty among our most valuable asset"]

The Code is organized into the following sections:

I. Why Ethics Matter—Outlines the purpose of the code and how it is applied.

II. Living Manulife Financial's Values—Lists corporate values, which guide operations.

III. Ethics in the Workplace—Articulates workplace principles, fairness, professionalism, and safety.

IV. Ethics in Your Business Relationships—Includes fairness and honesty toward customers, compliance with laws, gifts to government officials, lobbying and campaign finance issues, and handling of media inquiries.

V. Conflicts of Interest—Identifies possible conflicts and indicates how to avoid them.

VI. Handling Information—Discusses appropriate information disclosure to ensure privacy of stakeholders, including that of employees, policyholders, and investors.

VII. Ethics and the Law—Stresses the need to be knowledgeable of appropriate laws and the duty to report inappropriate behaviour.

VIII. A Final Word—Reinforces the importance of employee conduct and good judgment as it impacts Manulife's reputation.

IX. Disclosure Policy—Helps to ensure Manulife makes required disclosures clearly, completely, and in a timely manner.

Each of the sections is described in more detail. A sample *Code of Business Conduct and Ethics Certification and Conflict of Interest Disclosure Statement* is included.

Source: Compiled from Manulife, "Code of Business Conduct and Ethics" accessed January 28, 2016, http://www.manulife.com/public/files/201/1/CodeofBusinessConductandEthics.pdf#page=7.

EVERYDAY ETHICS 6.3

FPSC® *Code of Ethics—Synopsis of the Principles*

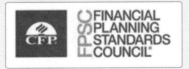

Financial Planning Standards Council (FPSC®) continually strives to ensure all standards for CERTIFIED FINANCIAL PLANNER® professionals and FPSC Level 1® Certificants in Financial Planning are relevant and rigorous. It is critical that standards evolve with the needs of the public and the profession, to ensure the public is well served.

The FPSC® Code of Ethics, as found in the *Standards of Professional Responsibility for CFP® Professionals and FPSC Level 1® Certificants in Financial Planning,* outlines the eight principles guiding the conduct of CFP professionals and FPSC Level 1 certificants.

The following [is] a synopsis of the Principles embodied in the FPSC Code of Ethics to which all CFP professionals and FPSC Level 1 certificants must adhere.

- *Principle 1: Client First*—A CFP professional shall always place the client's interests first.
- *Principle 2: Integrity*—A CFP professional shall always act with integrity.
- *Principle 3: Objectivity*—A CFP professional shall be objective when providing advice and/or services to clients.
- *Principle 4: Competence*—A CFP professional shall develop and maintain the abilities, skills and knowledge necessary to competently provide advice and/or services to clients.
- *Principle 5: Fairness*—A CFP professional shall be fair and open in all professional relationships.
- *Principle 6: Confidentiality*—A CFP professional shall maintain confidentiality of all client information.
- *Principle 7: Diligence*—A CFP professional shall act diligently when providing advice and/or services to clients.
- *Principle 8: Professionalism*—A CFP professional shall act in a manner that reflects positively upon the profession.

Source: Reprinted from the *Standards of Professional Responsibility for CFP® Professionals and FPSC Level 1® Certificants in Financial Planning.* The most up-to-date version of this document can be found at fpsc.ca. Used with permission of FPSC.

Codes are the most common approach to institutionalizing ethical behaviour, and aid in understanding relationships with stakeholders. They can improve customer confidence in the quality of a product or the level of service, and also help ensure ethical and fair treatment of customers. The reputation of the business enterprise or organization that develops codes is improved and attracts high-calibre employees and customers. Codes simplify the detection of unethical behaviour in competitors and employees by standardizing norms of behaviour. Lastly, codes provide for self-regulation, which is preferable to external control.

Overall, codes increase awareness, discourage ethical apathy, facilitate ethical decision making, and make it easier to refuse an unethical request. The content of codes varies, but Table 6.2 identifies commonly found items.

TABLE 6.2	Content of Codes of Conduct and Codes of Ethics
A general statement of ethics, values, or philosophies	
Criteria for decision making and compliance with laws	
Responsibility toward employees, including items such as health and safety, non-discrimination, and privacy	
Conflicts of interest, their identification, and how to handle them	
Protection of corporate assets, including accurate accounting, security or property, and insider information	
Appropriate business practices, including honesty, fairness, obeying the law, and information disclosure	
Appropriate conduct on behalf of the corporation; for example, relationships with customers, suppliers, competitors, creditors, and government	
Responsibilities to society at large, including contribution to political parties, responses to media, treatment of communities, and concern for environmental protection	
Implementation procedures, including familiarity with the code, reporting of violations, refusing unethical requests, and seeking help on ethical matters	
Specification of enforcement/compliance procedures and the penalties for inappropriate or illegal behaviour.	

Content

The content of codes has evolved over time and through five generations. The *first generation* focused on conflict of interest, involving the protection of company interests from employees, and was concerned with the shareholder interest and mostly excluded the public interest. Commercial conduct was emphasized in the *second generation,* including such things as bribery of foreign officials and arranging for kickbacks. It was argued that ethical practices protected the corporation's interest and reputation, as there was a relationship between ethical behaviour and profitability. The *third generation* focused on employee rights and the motivation of the workforce along with relationships with customers and suppliers. Ethical consumerism emerged with renewed mention of the importance of satisfying the customer. During this generation of codes, the exploitation of child labour also emerged. A wider responsibility was assumed in the *fourth generation* of codes, with attention to the protection of the environment and respect for communities in which corporations operated. Corporations wished to reduce legal liabilities as well as maintain their image. Finally, the *fifth generation* extended coverage to international concerns, for example countries whose governments ignored human rights, the rule of law, and labour conditions in developing countries.[5]

The development and implementation of codes has not been a static process. Corporations have been challenged by societal demands to address different social responsibilities. As a result, codes have become more challenging not only to develop but also to implement.

Criticisms

[handwritten: Criticisms Criticisms. code is not specific enough]

Some critics claim that codes of ethics or conduct are at best a minimal but unenforceable standard and at worst a hollow pretence. An implication of this claim is that most corporations and professions operate at an ethical level above that specified in the codes. It is for only the less scrupulous that the codes are intended, but the guidelines may not be very effective with this group. It is, therefore, difficult to enforce the codes and, even if they are enforced, the penalties may be insignificant. Those following a code may also be placed in a disadvantageous position because those who don't adhere to the code are not restricted in their actions. As a result, convincing everyone to comply is not easy. In corporations, codes are sometimes pointed to with pride but ignored in practice. Frequently, the codes are idealistic or written in meaningless generalities.

Sometimes, codes of ethics are developed merely to control competitive conduct among business corporations or individuals. They specify conduct that is considered unprofessional, such as pricing practices in some industries. In these cases the code of conduct is really designed to reduce competition, and this kind of self-regulation is sometimes a stop-gap measure of questionable intent designed merely to prevent government legislation and serve as a response to public criticism.

Nevertheless, the use of codes and their reasons for existing are no longer issues for many corporations. Codes are important devices for communicating and controlling employees' behaviour within the corporation, and the behaviour of corporations and industries in society. Codes can be made more effective through improving their content, increasing commitment to the codes, and creating mechanisms that encourage employees to embrace the codes and live by them on a daily basis.

LO 6.4   Ethics Training

Ethics training involves teaching employees about the values and policies on ethics they should follow in their decision making. The teaching sessions involve an orientation on values or ethics and related policies and deal with reputation and legal risks. A code of ethics or statement of values may be used in this teaching process, in addition to handbooks or policy statements. Such teaching can be done by managers or outside consultants and addressed to all levels of employees, but more emphasis has been placed on management levels.

Larger corporations have developed online exercises to increase awareness of ethical implications. Employees complete such exercises at their computers, with appropriate responses presented or a scoring of the employee's ethical awareness given. Such training programs are established not only to develop employee awareness of ethics in business but also to draw attention to the ethical issues to which an employee may be exposed.

Training involves giving participants practical checklists and tests to evaluate their actions. Training usually also includes a description of conflict of interest, something that inevitably arises in a discussion of ethics.

Checklists and Tests

Lists of questions, moral standards, and tests have been developed to assist managers in making ethical decisions. Writing in the *Harvard Business Review*, Nash argues that plainly worded questions, such as the following, should be used by managers when examining the ethics of a business decision:

1. Have you defined the problem accurately?
2. How would you define the problem if you stood on the other side of the fence?
3. How did this situation occur in the first place?
4. To whom and to what do you give your loyalty as a person and as a member of the corporation?
5. What is your intention in making this decision?
6. How does this intention compare with the probable results?
7. Whom could your decision or action injure?
8. Can you discuss the problem with the affected parties before you make your decision?
9. Are you confident that your position will be as valid over a long period of time as it seems now?
10. Could you disclose without qualm your decision or action to your boss, your CEO, the board of directors, your family, society as a whole?

11. What is the symbolic potential of your action if understood? If misunderstood?
12. Under what conditions would you allow exceptions to your stand?[6]

Nash refers to this approach as the "good puppy" theory, as it allows corporate morality to be defined and explored halfway between the rigorous moral analogy of the corporation being the "good person" and the purely amoral definition of good. According to Nash,

> Moral capacity is perceived as present, but its potential is limited. A moral evaluation of the good puppy is possible but exists largely on concrete terms: we do not need to identify the puppy's intentions as utilitarian to understand and agree that its "ethical" fulfillment of the social contract consists of not soiling the carpet or biting the baby.[7]

A second example is the Pagano model, which uses six clear questions that serve as several tests of the ethics of a particular action. Pagano identifies six tests that he feels provide useful insights into the ethics of a business' actions. The tests are as follows:

1. *Is it legal?*—This is a core starting point.
2. *The benefit–cost test*—This test employs the utilitarian perspective of the greatest good for the greatest number.
3. *The categorical imperative*—Do you want this action to be a universal standard? This test takes the view that if it's good for the goose, it's good for the gander.
4. *The light of day test*—What if your actions appeared on TV? Would you be proud?
5. *Do unto others*—This test uses the Golden Rule. Do you want the same to happen to you?
6. *The ventilation test*—Get a second opinion from a wise friend with no investment in the outcome.[8]

The author feels that this approach has the advantages of being compact and simple. Note that most of the questions represent the principles discussed in Chapter 5.

Understanding Conflicts of Interest

A conflict of interest occurs when there is a clash between the interests of an individual—that is, a manager or employee—and the organization that employs the individual. A **conflict of interest** is a situation in which an individual has a private or personal interest that is sufficient to appear to influence the objective exercise of that individual's duties.[9] The personal interest usually involves a financial gain or a promised future promotion or gift obtained by the individual or his or her immediate family. "Duties" refers to the responsibilities the individual was hired to perform in good faith and loyalty. Common conflicts are listed in Table 6.3.

TABLE 6.3 Common Conflicts of Interest
Self-dealing—Exists where a manager or employee takes an action in an official capacity that involves dealing with oneself in a private capacity and that confers a benefit to oneself. Today this extends to one's spouse, family members, and business partners.
Accepting gifts or benefits—Involves the acceptance of some benefit.
Influence peddling—The practice of soliciting some form of benefit; for example, asking for a kickback or gift from a supplier if a purchase is made.
Using employer's property—The inappropriate use of an employer's property; for example, taking office supplies for home use.
Using confidential information—The use for personal or private purposes of confidential information obtained from some other source, for example customers or suppliers, to gain some benefit.
Outside employment or moonlighting—The work or activity in which an employee engages outside normal working hours for additional remuneration.

Post-employment—Subsequent or future employment where information or contacts obtained during employment results in some benefit.

Personal conduct—The situation where an employee's behaviour in private life may reflect adversely on the employer.

Sources: Kenneth Kernaghan and John W. Langford, "Conflict of Interest," Chapter 6 in *The Responsible Public Servant* (Halifax: The Institute for Research on Public Policy and The Institute of Public Administration of Canada, 1990), 133–155; and Michael McDonald, "Ethics and Conflict of Interest," The W. Maurice Young Centre of Applied Ethics, University of British Columbia.

Several complications exist in defining a manager's or employee's involvement in a conflict of interest. There are many variations of conflict of interest, from "influence peddling" to the improper use of company property. Interpretation of conflict of interest varies from one organization to another, from one department to another, and from one individual to another. Some conflicts of interest are defined in laws or regulations, but it is not possible to prohibit all possible business arrangements. Finally, it is difficult to distinguish among the types of conflict of interest.

The following are brief explanations of the three types of conflict:

- *Real*—A situation in which a manager or employee has knowledge of a private economic interest, or any kind of private or personal gain, that is sufficient to influence the exercise of his or her duties and responsibilities. Conflict occurs when there is an existence of a private interest, when it is known to the employee, and when there is a connection with the employer's duties or responsibilities that is sufficient to influence the exercise of those duties or responsibilities.
- *Apparent*—A situation where a conflict of interest can be deduced from appearances; exists when there is a reasonable apprehension that a well-informed person could make the connection.
- *Potential*—A situation that may develop into an actual conflict; exists when an employee can foresee that he or she has a private interest that may be sufficient to influence a duty or responsibility.[10]

Managers or employees must be aware of and concerned about all types and categories of conflict, and many corporations have statements describing potential conflicts. They must be familiar with any conflict of interest rules that exist, and also be able to recognize unidentified potential conflicts. Managers and employees must be continuously sensitive to conflicts of interest, as their reputation and the corporation's is at stake. Responsibility for Ethics 6.1 is an example of a corporation's conflict of interest policy.

RESPONSIBILITY FOR ETHICS 6.1

Husky Energy Inc.'s Conflict of Interest Policy

Husky Energy Inc.'s Code of Conduct includes a substantial section on conflict of interest. In general it states that all employees and directors are to avoid all situations in which their personal interests conflict with their duties or the interests of the company. The conflict of interest definition states that it arises when an employee (including family members and acquaintances) will benefit at the expense of Husky or will interfere with the employee's objectivity or effectiveness on the job.

Examples of conflict of interest include outside employment, use of Husky's resources for outside work, activities that reflect negatively on Husky's reputation, and holding a financial interest in a company doing business with Husky. Guidelines are listed for the implementation of the policy and detailed descriptions of possible violations are provided. Potential conflicts of interest must be immediately disclosed to the employee's supervisor. New employees must disclose any potential conflict of interest prior to accepting employment. If a violation of the policy is considered serious, disciplinary action will be taken, including possible termination of employment.

Source: Summarized from Husky Energy Inc., "Code of Business Conduct," Conflict of Interest Section, pages 4-6, http://www.huskyenergy.com/downloads/abouthusky/coporategovernance/CodeofBusinessConductPolicy101.pdf. © 2002-2013 Husky Energy Inc.

LO 6.5   Ethics Audits, Managers, and Committees

An **ethics audit** is a systematic effort to discover actual or potential unethical behaviour in an organization. It is designed not only to uncover unethical behaviour, but also to identify existing opportunities for unethical behaviour. There is a preventive as well as a remedial purpose. Audits are particularly useful when used in conjunction with a code of ethics, as the code can be the basis for comparison to establish how well or poorly the organization is doing. Regular audits foster ethical practice.

In recent years, several ethics audits or ethics accountability measures have been developed. These will be discussed in Chapter 9.

Consultants knowledgeable in the area of ethics advise management on how to put "integrity" into enterprise culture. Ethics audits or surveys can be conducted by consultants to ascertain compliance to ethical standards, and consultants may be involved in training and code development. The consultants are usually persons external to the organization who have some education and experience in ethics management. The Ethics Practitioners' Association of Canada (described in Responsibility for Ethics 6.2) is attempting to improve the quality of ethics advice.

Some corporations have gone beyond implementing codes, training, audits, and the use of consultants and established ethics officers, indicating that ethical issues are being treated seriously. An **ethics officer** is an independent manager, reporting to the board of directors or CEO, who reviews complaints or information from anyone in the organization or any stakeholder, studies the situation, and recommends action if necessary. Sometimes this role is performed by an ombudsperson or advocate, who also must be independent to ensure the trust of stakeholders. Such officers can alert the organization to ethical problems or issues before they become public knowledge, allowing time to prepare a defence or to take remedial actions.

In larger corporations, the position of chief ethics officer is responsible for the ethics program. Increasingly, the title of compliance officer is appearing in the executive ranks of corporations. This person makes sure that all legal requirements are followed, in particular those originating in government legislation and regulation. This position might also include responsibility for other aspects of an ethics program. In Canada, the corporate secretary quite often performs this role.

An **ethics committee** is a group comprising directors, managers, or staff formed to monitor ethical standards and behaviour. The formation of such a committee, sometimes referred to as a business conduct committee, injects ethics at the highest level in the organization, and is a signal to all stakeholders of the company's commitment to ethical practice. This type of committee is involved in developing an ethics program and may monitor management and employee behaviour for ethical issues.

Ethics committees comprising management, employees, and outside stakeholders can also exist within the organization. Present practice appears to be that ethics committees are top-management focused. Such committees may also be called corporate ethics and responsibility committees, or advisory boards or councils, which usually comprise a variety of stakeholders.

RESPONSIBILITY FOR ETHICS 6.2

Ethics Practitioners' Association of Canada

The Ethics Practitioners' Association of Canada was formed in 1996 "to maintain a community of individuals promoting ethical behaviour in organizations in Canada." Its members include ethics and values officers, compliance and CSR officers, consultants, educators, students, and others interested in applied ethics for any type of organization. Membership comes from all sectors: government, business, voluntary, and academic. The Association has developed ethical standards for its members, a competency profile that describes functions a practitioner in the field of organizational ethics carries out, and a list of skills that such a practitioner should possess. Its activities are designed to encourage members to operate in an exemplary ethical and social manner locally and internationally.

Source: Based on Ethics Practitioners' Association of Canada website, accessed January 28, 2016, http://epac-apec.ca/who-we-are/overview/.

LO 6.6 Ethics Reporting Systems and Whistleblowing

Corporations have established reporting systems so that they can become aware of issues and concerns relating to corporate ethical conduct or irregularities. The reporting systems are known by various names, the most common being "hotlines." Codes of ethics or conduct usually contain sections outlining the reporting system, and outside service providers are hired to process the reports. An example of one corporation's compliance and reporting system is outlined in Everyday Ethics 6.4. Corporations believe that such systems alert them to problems before they become public and allow time for remedial action. The system also reinforces the importance of the corporation's code of ethics or business conduct. The systems are a secure forum to report problems and enable individuals to be anonymous without fear of retaliation.

The practice of reporting alleged wrongdoing, code violations, and irregularities in corporate operations is commonly referred to as whistleblowing. **Whistleblowing** is an act of voluntary disclosure of inappropriate behaviour or decisions to persons in positions of authority in the organization. The term may have originated from the practice of English police officers blowing whistles to get someone's attention, or from the use of whistles by sports referees. The most frequent form of whistleblowing occurs in the workplace where employees, managers, or directors are concerned about some matter. Whistleblowers are also referred to as do-gooders, bell-ringers, lighthouse keepers, people's witnesses, snitches, rats, tattletales, and squealers.

Several issues relating to whistleblowing have ethical implications for whistleblowers and managers:

- The whistleblower is faced with the choices of silence, quitting, and disclosing when he or she becomes aware of the inappropriate behaviour. All these choices can be uncomfortable and involve risk.
- The range of concerns may go from clearly illegal, to maybe illegal, to an issue of morality, all of which may be difficult to define.
- The whistleblower is faced with several moral obligations to self and to professional, corporate, or industry codes. There most likely is an obligation to an employer due to a legal duty, loyalty, or confidentiality agreement. There may be an obligation to society at large.

EVERYDAY ETHICS 6.4

Compliance and Reporting at Barrick Gold Corporation

Corporate codes of ethics or conduct usually include a mechanism to identify issues arising from the codes, and to prevent and identify violations. This enables employees to seek guidance on these matters and allows the corporation to act prior to them becoming problems.

Barrick Gold has an extensive "Compliance and Reporting" section in its Code of Business Conduct and Ethics, which includes the following topics:

- That employees and directors have a duty to report suspected code violations to the appropriate management level is clearly established.
- "Formal reporting channels" are identified.
- The matters that must be reported through the "formal reporting channels" are specified; for example alleged misstatement of financial statements, or known or suspected fraud.
- A compliance hotline is available and is operated by an outside service provider.
- The process for handling reports of alleged issue or concern is outlined.
- A statement is made about the confidentiality of any reports and there will be no retaliatory action against the individual raising the concern.

Source: Based on "Code of Business Conduct and Ethics," Barrick Gold Corporation, accessed January 28, 2016, http://www.barrick.com/files/governance/Barrick-Code-of-Business-Conduct-and-Ethics.pdf.

- The whistleblower faces a credibility issue: Will he/she be believed? Will the disclosure be taken seriously? Is the matter important enough? Will the matter be addressed at all?
- Concern also exists about the perception of others toward the whistleblower: noble, honourable, ethical hero, or snitch, mole, traitor?
- When to tell and who to tell are often problems. The whistleblower must decide how far to let the concern continue before disclosure and then has the challenge of deciding whom to tell, particularly in organizations without reporting systems.
- The whistleblower must be concerned about his/her self-interest. There are costs and risks, consequences for personal and professional lives, and the possibility of retaliation to consider.
- Anonymity encourages reporting, but it might result in trivial claims that are a nuisance and unfounded.
- There is an issue of whether or not whistleblowers should be rewarded by government, regulatory organizations, or industry associations. Rewards encourage reporting but might result in perverse incentives such as reporting to government agencies instead of the corporation. Also, there is an issue of whether it should be necessary to pay whistleblowers to do the right thing when they should be doing it anyway.

Although this discussion has focused on workplace stakeholders—employees, managers, and directors—other stakeholders may be whistleblowers. Suppliers and consumers may disclose inappropriate corporate practices to the corporation's reporting system, the legal system, government regulators, or the general public. The media often are whistleblowers, as are non-governmental organizations (NGOs). The movie industry also has used whistleblowing in a business setting as a plot device (see Everyday Ethics 6.5).

EVERYDAY ETHICS 6.5

Whistleblowing in the Movies

The ethics of business is the topic of many popular movies. The following is a list of some movies with a focus on whistleblowing:

The Informant! (2009)—The story of a corporate executive who blows the whistle on price fixing in the large agri-business corporation where he works.

Michael Clayton (2007)—A ruthless corporate "fixer" faces a crisis of conscience when he is asked to work on behalf of a chemical company that knowingly contaminated an entire Wisconsin community and aims to cover it up.

Boiler Room (2000)—The story of a stockbroker operation using aggressive selling techniques to the disadvantage of clients. An employee discloses the abuses.

Erin Brockovich (2000)—A small law firm discovers that a chemical company is polluting and discloses the cover-up.

The Insider (1999)—Detailed account of an employee who discloses the misleading practices in the tobacco industry.

A Civil Action (1998)—Story of the disclosure of industrial pollution contaminating drinking water in New England.

The Rainmaker (1997)—Disclosure of the insurance industry's denial of health care payments to a dying client.

Silkwood (1983)—An employee tries to disclose that she and others have been exposed to radiation in the workplace. Based on a real story and widely considered the best movie on whistleblowing.

In addition to corporate disclosure or reporting policies, several government whistleblowing regulations impact on a corporation's reporting system. All are designed to facilitate regulation and enforcement in particular areas and may require employees to disclose corporate practices.

- *Canadian federal and provincial/territorial governments*—Whistleblowing provisions exist in many regulatory areas including environmental protection, health and safety, competition, and industrial relations. There is no comprehensive whistleblowing legislation except in New Brunswick. The federal government has passed regulations relating to whistleblowing within the public service including in the Competition Bureau.[11]

- *Canadian Securities Industry*—The Investment Industry Regulatory Organization of Canada and the Mutual Fund Dealers Association have whistleblower programs. In December 2015, the Ontario Securities Commission proposed a whistleblower program that would reward informants up to $5 million when penalties for wrongdoing exceed $10 million.[12]

- *United States government*—U.S. legislation impacts Canadian corporations with operations in that country. There is extensive legislation requiring disclosure and protecting whistleblowers, and the *Whistleblower Protection Act* applies to federal government employees. The *Sarbanes-Oxley Act* of 2002 contained several whistleblowing provisions, including prohibition against employment discrimination and the acceptance of social responsibility complaints.[13]

An ethics reporting system is challenging to administer and involves risks for the corporation and the discloser, but recently it has become an important component of a corporate ethics program.

LO 6.7   Ethics—Who Is Responsible?

A simple answer to the question "Who is responsible for ethics?" is "Everyone." But in a corporation it is argued that the responsibility for recognizing the importance of ethical behaviour in business and doing something about it has to start at the top—that is, with the board of directors.

Board of Directors Responsibility

Researcher Steven Bavaria claims that directors have been remiss in this area, especially the docile outside directors who have the independence to monitor ethical behaviour.[14] Gillies states that directors have two tasks in relation to ethics: to collectively identify values that determine acceptable behaviour in the firm, and to put in place a process that ensures values are reflected in action. Merely acting on the basis of one's own values is not sufficient, and it is necessary to deliberately consider the implications of unethical behaviour. Not all directors agree with this position, and the arguments for and against it reflect the general discussion of whether or not business has any social responsibility.[15]

The reasons given for the board's responsibility for ethical or moral behaviour include the point that it is simply good management to develop an appropriate culture that is sensitive to ethics issues. In addition, the board itself is involved in ethical questions such as conflicts of interest, compensation schemes, management buyouts, the rights of minority shareholders, and changes in management. Finally, it is easier to make decisions if the fundamental principles or values of the corporation are known and can serve as a reference point. In the past, and maybe the present, directors often were not aware that ethics were involved in a decision. They must be aware that values change over time and that their own values may not have altered. Because directors are the ultimate decision makers in corporations, they must demand that decisions made by management and all employees be based on ethical standards acceptable to society. Chapter 11 will also discuss the role of the board of directors in a corporation's social responsibility program.

Management Responsibility

The success of any ethics program depends on the commitment of top management. Managers must announce the program, champion its development and implementation, and always aspire to lead in an ethical manner. They must provide moral leadership as opposed to immoral or amoral leadership. Table 6.4 distinguishes the three models of moral management and leadership.

TABLE 6.4   Management and Leadership Models

Immoral	Amoral	Moral
A posture or approach that is devoid of ethical principles and actively opposed to what is moral	A posture or approach that is without ethics, but not actively immoral	Conform to high standards of ethical behaviour or professional standards
Management's motives are selfish and it cares only about the individual's or the organization's gains	Two types: intentionally or unintentionally amoral	Aspire to succeed only within confines of ethical principles; for example fairness, justice, and due process
Management to some degree knows right from wrong and chooses to do wrong	Intentionally amoral leaders do not consider ethics, as they believe business activity lies outside of moral judgments; neither moral nor immoral, as different rules apply to business	Concerned with letter and spirit of the law
May be motivated by greed and profitability, and organizational (or personal) success is the goal to be achieved at any price	Unintentionally amoral leaders are morally careless, unaware of or inattentive to impact of their decisions on others	Prefer standards that are higher than the minimum set by the law
Do not care about claims or expectations of others	They lack ethical perception, sensitivity, or awareness	Assume leadership when ethical dilemmas arise
The law is regarded as a barrier to be overcome and will circumvent if it will achieve their ends	May be well-intentioned but unaware of harms from their actions	Make ethics a driving force of the organization
Do not make good corporate citizens	"Ethical gears in neutral"	
	Use letter of the law instead of spirit	
	Cannot make good corporate citizens	

Source: © Greenleaf Publishing. First published in *Perspectives on Corporate Citizenship* by Jorg Andriof and Malcolm McIntosh (2002). Reproduced by kind permission of Greenleaf Publishing

Carroll, in an article that summarized his views on moral leadership, identified seven attributes of a moral leader: having a passion to "do right," being morally proactive, considering stakeholder inclusiveness, having a strong ethical character, being obsessed with fairness, practising principled decision making, and integrating ethics wisdom with management wisdom.[16]

Inside the organization, managers are responsible for developing and supporting a variety of policies and procedures to ensure the ethical implications of decision making are considered. An ethics manual should be available, maybe even online. A values statement and codes would be included. Such a manual would include policies regarding such things as whistleblowing protection, guidelines for offering or accepting gifts, and the privacy of employee records. Codes of conduct or ethics would be supported through training, the appointment of an ethics ombudsperson, the establishment of an ethics hotline, and regular consultation with employees. Corporate publications or newsletters would feature articles on ethics, and consideration of ethics would be integrated into corporate planning, recruitment, and performance appraisals.

Managers not only must be supportive of ethics programs within the organization, but also must advocate for ethical approaches to management with external stakeholders. Executive speech making provides an example. Speeches should inform certain stakeholders that the business enterprise and its management are concerned about ethics and are responding to society's interest in the matter. It is not always clear to which stakeholders the speeches are directed, but they most likely address society at large, NGOs, business groups, students, and possibly even shareholders.

The next section outlines approaches to ethics programs.

LO 6.8   Ethics Programs: Approaches

From the materials presented, corporations can design a variety of programs to provide ethics leadership in an organization. The resulting programs are classified as formal, monological, and dialogical,[17] and as being compliance-based versus values-based.

Classification of Programs

A *formal approach* is based on organizational norms that are written as a code of conduct. This approach focuses on unacceptable practices or behaviour and emphasizes compliance and penalties. Usually the approach is top-down, as codes are imposed from top management. The advantages of such programs are that they provide clear guidance for decision making and that their fulfillment is measurable. The rights ethical principle is likely to be used in this approach. The disadvantages are that employees may resist the necessary coercion and indoctrination.[18]

The *monological approach* allows organizational members, for example managers and employees, to determine for themselves what is right or wrong. Codes of values, philosophies, and ethics would facilitate this approach. Organizational members are encouraged to reflect on the appropriateness of their behaviour by considering their own values, the circumstances of the incident or issue, and the alternative choices for resolution. This approach focuses on argument and reflection but leaves room to act upon specific circumstances. The justice ethic is the principle most likely to be used. On the other hand, performance is difficult to measure and the possibility exists that it will lead to differences in behaviour.[19]

The *dialogical approach* emphasizes communication before decisions are made and implemented. The stakeholders influenced or that can influence are consulted and an appeal is made for input. The approach is similar to that advocated in the collaborative view of stakeholder relations, and the values and opinions of all stakeholders involved are included. It seeks inclusive solutions and attention is given to the social dynamic side of ethical issues, usually based on the ethic of caring. The monitoring of these programs is more challenging, as it is based on the process and not on outcomes. There is a danger of ethical relativism, which may lead to differences in behaviour by the stakeholders involved.

The formal approach is the most commonly used and the dialogical approach the least common. Larger organizations most likely use a combination of approaches, especially formal and monological. Nijhof, Fisscher, and Looise state that it is challenging to combine the approaches, and suggest that it might be more appropriate to use different approaches in different circumstances.[20] Although conscientious programs have been discussed, it is possible that corporations will have informal, unwritten programs that are implemented implicitly instead of explicitly and without a structured, deliberate approach.

Compliance-based versus Values-based Programs

Increasingly in the literature and in practice a distinction is made between compliance-based versus values-based approaches to managing the ethics of business. Table 6.5 summarizes the differences between the two approaches.

The compliance-based approach focuses on adherence to legal and regulatory requirements and to corporate policies. Clear rules guide ethics and the rules are clearly communicated, limiting an individual's discretion. These rules are enforced and sanctions are imposed for violating them. In contrast, the values-based approach is defined by organizational values and ethical standards, which are to be applied to decision making. This approach increases awareness of ethical issues through dialogue, training, and fostering an ethical corporate climate. It is the preferred approach, as many people do not like rules that cannot cover all the circumstances that are encountered.

The trend is to incorporate both approaches, because it is recognized that one alone cannot yield results. It is necessary to recognize compliance to rules or policies on the one hand, but also the positive effects of values on the other. A compliance-based approach has reduced misconduct, but a values-based approach is a more powerful influence on attitudes and behaviour. Combining the two approaches is referred to as **integrity management**. The codes of many corporations now follow this approach.[21]

TABLE 6.5   Compliance-based versus Values-based Approaches

Compliance-based	Values-based
Rules, laws, policies	Values, ethics, guiding principles
Conformity with externally imposed standards	Self-governance to chosen standards; self-imposed
Prevent criminal misconduct	Enable responsible conduct
Lawyer-driven	Management-driven
Educational approach: policies and rules, legalistic	Educational approach: policies and rules, but also guidelines and awareness through leadership
Employee discretion: limited	Employee discretion: increased
Control: auditing, penalties	Control: accountability, organizational systems, and decision processes
Code of Conduct:	Code of Ethics:
• Specific • Prescriptions/directives • Uniformity • Enforceable statements of specific behaviour	• General • Values/principles • Judgment • "Empowering" and "aspirational"

connect   Want to learn about **a guide to practical ethics**?

LO 6.9   Ethics Programs: Evaluation and Benefits

The components of a corporate ethics program have been outlined. Just because a corporation is not involved in the components mentioned does not mean that it does not have an ethics program, according to Max Clarkson, the founding Director of the Centre for Corporate Social Performance and Ethics. He argued that all corporations have programs, but that some of them were implicit. The implicit ethics programs were implemented through such things as the organization's culture, reward systems, valued behaviour, promotion policies, management example, general practice, and performance measures.[22]

Clarkson identified criteria for evaluating the effectiveness of an ethics program: visibility, ownership, fit, and balance. The components of an ethics program were clearly evident in statements such as codes, which should be widely distributed and communicated in a variety of formats. There was evidence of a commitment to the ethics program, as demonstrated by awareness and usage of the initiatives, and by their integration into the organizational culture. Initiatives should be appropriate to the circumstances of the corporation; that is, programs should be complementary with the type of business or industry. Lastly, there should be a balance in the programs among rules, redress, and principles, or a balance between "imposed control" and "self-control." Clarkson also identified criteria for evaluation of the program's implementation. Such criteria were the extent of resource commitment to the program, the CEO's involvement, the extent of communication about the program, and the training and education carried out.[23]

Business ethics is identified as an "in" topic, yet it has been discussed seriously for four decades. Much of the earlier material on ethics is still applicable. An article by Laczniak contains some ethical propositions that are still appropriate and can serve as criteria for justifying the formulation and implementation of ethics programs.

- Ethical conflicts and choices are inherent in business decision making.

- Proper ethical behaviour exists on a plane above the law. The law merely specifies the lowest common denominator of acceptable behaviour.

- There is no single satisfactory standard of ethical action agreeable to everyone that a manager can use to make specific operational decisions.

- Managers should be familiar with a wide variety of ethical standards.

- The discussion of business cases or of situations having ethical implications can make managers more ethically sensitive.

- There are diverse and sometimes conflicting determinants of ethical action. These stem primarily from the individual, the organization, professional norms, and the values of society.

- Individual values are the final standard, although not necessarily the determining reason for ethical behaviour.

- Consensus regarding what constitutes proper ethical behaviour in a decision-making situation diminishes as the level of analysis proceeds from abstract to specific.

- The moral tone of an organization is set by top management.

- The lower the organizational level of a manager, the greater the perceived pressure to act unethically.

- Individual managers perceive themselves as more ethical than their colleagues.

- Effective codes of ethics should contain meaningful and clearly stated provisions, along with enforced sanctions for noncompliance.

- Employees must have a non-punitive, fail-safe mechanism for reporting ethical abuses in the organization.

- Every organization should appoint a top-level manager or director to be responsible for acting as an ethical advocate in the organization.[24]

The propositions summarize many of the components described in this chapter. They also indicate that, within the corporation, directors and managers are all responsible for ethical behaviour, with top management assuming leadership. Despite being compiled more than two decades ago, these propositions provide practical guidance to the institutionalization of ethical behaviour in corporations.

It is not known how many business enterprises have formally organized programs, but there is no doubt that many are consciously attempting to increase awareness of ethical behaviour even though it may be done in an informal manner. Some benefits of programs to manage ethics are listed below.

- Many improvements in business practices and benefits to society have occurred as a result of attention paid to ethics in the past. Some practices are no longer considered acceptable, for example misleading advertising, child labour, and price fixing.

- Turbulent times have increased the awareness of ethics, and business leaders need a moral compass and to be sensitive to acting consistently.

- Ethics programs align corporate behaviour, especially that of managers and employees, with the principal ethical values preferred by the leaders of the business enterprise.

- Employees are prepared to face the reality of moral dilemmas; that is, to be sensitive to what might be considered good or bad.

- A focus on ethics sensitizes managers and employees to the legal requirements in a moral dilemma.

- Criminal acts are more likely to be avoided, as such behaviour is likely to be detected earlier and violations caught within the organization.

- Awareness of ethics helps managers to integrate values with quality management practices and strategic management.

- The implications or influence of management decisions on various stakeholders is more likely recognized.

- A more favourable public image is created for the business organization.[25]

The components of an ethics program can be evaluated by their focus. Some components are values-based, providing guidelines to influence behaviour with fewer specific rules or directions.

A concluding note to this chapter is supplied by Treviño and Brown. They argued it is a myth that "ethics can be managed through formal ethics codes and programs." Compliance-based approaches including codes alone cannot address ethical behaviour and values-based approaches are also needed. It is necessary to reinforce an ethical culture every day. Another myth focuses on leadership: "Ethical leadership is mostly about leader integrity." Managers must lead others to behave ethically, not just be ethical themselves. Not all leaders are capable of this. Four types of executive ethical leadership were identified:

- hypocritical leader = strong moral manager and weak moral person

- unethical leader = weak moral manager and weak moral person

- ethical leader = strong moral manager and strong moral person

- ethically silent leader = weak moral manager and either a weak or strong moral person

Unfortunately, not all corporations are led by ethical leaders. The authors concluded their article by indicating what executives can do to provide ethical leadership. Their guidelines for effective ethics management are:

"First: Understand the Existing Ethical Culture

Second: Communicate the Importance of Ethical Standards

Third: Focus on the Reward System

Fourth: Promote Ethical Leadership Throughout the Firm."[26]

LO 6.10   Why Ethical Leadership and Programs Fail

There are frequent examples in the media of executives, managers, or corporations engaging in unethical behaviours such as accounting fraud, bribery, insider trading, price fixing, and Ponzi schemes. Sometimes these behaviours are portrayed as being a modern phenomenon, but in reality ethical mistakes have occurred throughout history, they are inevitable, and they come in waves or cycles. It is important to increase understanding of why unethical decisions are made by business managers and corporations even though the unethical behaviour occurs in other professions and institutions in society.

The issues of unethical leadership and failed ethics programs are not easy to explain. Conduct that is illegal, like the behaviours mentioned above, is relatively easy to condemn because laws or regulations are violated. Other conduct may be unethical or immoral but not illegal, in which case right versus wrong is often difficult to ascertain. Also, the literature on this topic presents contradictory findings and conclusions are often difficult.[27] The following discussion provides some explanations or answers from the literature.

Managers are morally imperfect—With well-designed systems and policies such as the organization's culture, governance system, and ethical programs plus the existence of government regulations to influence behaviour, it could be assumed that unethical behaviour is unlikely. But some individuals are morally imperfect and will take advantage when systems and regulations fail, and at the same time there is a good possibility of not being caught. Managers with moral commitment are less likely to be unethical. Note that personality screening for unethical predispositions is not an exact science and is unlikely to prevent bad behaviour.

Self-interest—Managers may do something wrong simply because they will benefit and they will get away with it. Self-interest also influences managers not to be unethical because of the possibility of being caught and the fear of punishment.

Rationalization and self-delusion—If managers observe others getting away with inappropriate behaviour, they are more likely to become involved in similar activities. When others are cheating and getting away with it, individuals feel that it is only fair that they should also. This is a form of rationalization and may even be self-delusion.

Threat of formal sanctions—When managers perceive that the threat of legal action and the imposition of sanctions are high, they may avoid unethical conduct. Unethical conduct is more likely when the sanctions are not imposed quickly, not highly likely to occur, and not punitive. Some research has found that the threat of formal sanctions or punishment does not deter unethical behaviour.

Threat of informal sanctions—An informal sanction such as social disapproval by colleagues, family, or society in general may be sufficient to discourage unethical behaviour.

Tolerance to risk-taking behaviour—Those managers who accept high risk taking are more likely to be involved in unethical behaviour.

Pressure in particular situations—Managers may be willing or forced to compromise their personal values when pressured to do so by superiors or a particular situation or requirement. Thus, bad behaviour may be exhibited by an otherwise good manager. An example of a situational pressure may be investor expectations to achieve returns, which may result in illegal activities such as price fixing, overcharging customers, or inappropriately polluting the environment.

Despite designing and implementing comprehensive ethics programs and an active role by management in emphasizing ethical behaviour, misbehaviour will still occur. When misbehaviour does occur, an issue arises relating to how much responsibility management, particularly top management, should assume for the misdeeds. The issue is complicated in large corporations when top management does not even know about the misbehaviour, and by the fact that he or she could not reasonably be expected to be aware of the circumstances.

Real, Potential, apparent

connect   Want to learn more about **business ethics by joining a blog?**

Your advice to Paul ...

You are faced with a dilemma in advising Paul, because he faces difficulties no matter what he does. One possibility is to do nothing. This choice potentially harms co-workers, the supervisor involved, and perhaps customers and suppliers. Asking the violator to stop would be a sensitive matter; it may not be Paul's place to do it, and involving the supervisor and the human resources department involves confidentiality. The final possibility is to seek to change the policy or process. No clear alternative exists to the current approach to the hotline, and even if there were, the same difficulties would likely be present.

Summary

- As emphasized in Chapter 5, increasing sensitivity to the ethical implications of managerial actions in general is a start. In addition, corporations must take deliberate actions to reinforce the importance by considering ethical implications in decision making. Key to this is the appropriate form of ethical leadership. (LO 6.1)

- The components of a corporation's ethics program to accomplish this are described in the chapter. The initial stage should be a statement of values or the equivalent that states in general terms the behaviours expected. These values become the foundation for the corporation's ethics program. (LO 6.2)

- A code of ethics reflects the values of an organization. A distinction should be made from a code of conduct, which focuses on compliance to rules or regulations instead of values. The contents of codes are outlined and drawbacks are presented. (LO 6.3)

- Today, corporations are not leaving an understanding of morality to chance and are engaged in a variety of training for everyone in the organization. (LO 6.4)

- Ethics audits are becoming more common as an approach to assessing the ethical implications of a corporation's practices. Usually such audits are conducted by outside consultants, who can also provide a range of advice about ethics programs. In larger corporations, there is a trend toward an ethics officer of some type being responsible for all aspects of compliance and morality in the organization. Ethics committees in many corporations facilitate the implementation of ethics programs. (LO 6.5)

- Ethics reporting systems are being established. Closely associated with such systems is the practice of whistleblowing. Several complicated issues are associated with whistleblowing and whistleblowers. Managers must carefully monitor the practice to make sure its benefits outweigh the drawbacks. (LO 6.6)

- Someone must take responsibility for the development and implementation of ethics programs. The board of directors and top management must signal their commitment to any program if it is to be successful. A "moral" leadership model is necessary to achieve this. (LO 6.7)

- Approaches to ethics programs are described. The formal approach is most common; the dialogical the least. Most corporations have programs that are a combination of these approaches. Also, the components of programs can be identified as being compliance-based versus values-based. (LO 6.8)

- Ethics programs should be evaluated on a regular basis and the benefits clearly identified. The programs can be justified on several bases ranging from economics to doing the right thing. The components of an ethics program are either compliance-based, following rules and requiring conformance, or values-based, emphasizing values as a way to influence behaviour. In most corporations today, a combination of these approaches is used and referred to as integrity management. (LO 6.9)

- There are several explanations for why ethical leadership and programs fail despite the best efforts and intentions of the corporation and its managers. (LO 6.10)

Key Terms

Corporate ethics programs

Statement of values

Code of conduct

Code of ethics

Conflict of interest

Ethics audit

Ethics officer

Ethics committee

Whistleblowing

Integrity management

Critical Thinking and Discussion Questions

1. What values do you think corporations and their managers should observe in business? Which ones do you think they really follow?
2. How would the stakeholders of a corporation be influenced by codes of ethics or conduct?
3. What are the drawbacks to codes of ethics or conduct?
4. Is it possible or feasible to train managers in ethics?
5. Why is it becoming necessary to have one manager to coordinate corporate ethics programs?
6. What are the benefits of ethics reporting systems?
7. What are the positive aspects of whistleblowing? What are some downsides?
8. How are governments involved in whistleblowing?
9. Why should responsibility for ethics programs rest with top management?
10. Should ethics programs rely on compliance-based or integrity-based approaches?
11. What is the justification for corporate ethics programs?
12. In your experiences in the workplace or educational institution, have you been provided with appropriate ethical leadership?

Cases

6.1 CITIZEN'S ARREST: THE LAW AND ETHICS

David Chen was very frustrated by the theft of goods from his store, particularly one individual's repeated stealing. David operated the Lucky Moose convenience store in Toronto's Chinatown, and the thievery not only was annoying but also impacted on profits. This was a problem for most retailers and is referred to as shoplifting.

It is estimated that shoplifting costs Canadian retailers about $3.5 billion a year. About 90 percent of small independent retailers like David reported being victims of crime, and lost about $1,000 a month. Shoplifting was done by individuals and by organized crime groups posing as customers. Employees may also steal from their employers.

After noticing the theft on a surveillance system, David decided to pursue the individual and located him about an hour later. David and two employees caught him, tied him up, and threw him in their van. After returning to the store David called police.

The shoplifter was charged, but so was David—with assault and forcible confinement. In court, the shoplifter stated that he feared for his life when arrested by David. The *Criminal Code* states that a property owner ". . . may arrest without warrant a person whom he finds committing a criminal offence on or in relation to that property." In David's case, it was alleged that the arrest was not made within a reasonable time.

The situation received extensive media coverage, especially on radio talk shows, and David became known as the "vigilante grocer." Public opinion was that David should be considered a hero for capturing the shoplifter, and not punished with a criminal record. Local Members of Parliament agreed, and even Prime Minister Harper visited David at his store and expressed agreement with David's actions.

Questions

1. What are the ethical issues involved?
2. Did David do the right thing in arresting the shoplifter?
3. What rights do business owners have to protect their property?
4. What are the dangers of taking the law into your own hands, that is, becoming a vigilante?

Sources: Library of Parliament Research Publication, "Legislative Summary of Bill C-26: The *Citizen's Arrest and Self-Defence Act*," accessed May 3, 2012, http://www.parl.gc.ca/About/Parliament/LegislativeSummaries/bills_ls.asp?Language=E&ls=c26&Parl=41&Ses=1&source=library_prb; CBC Documentaries, "Fact Sheet: Shoplifting," accessed July 13, 2012, http://www.cbc.ca/documentaries/doczone/2009/shoplifting/factsheet.html; "Taking the Law into Our Own Hands," *National Post*, April 26, 2012, A14; and "Trial Begins for Shopkeeper David Chen, Charged in Citizen's Arrest Case," CP24 Canadian Press Online, October 6, 2010.

6.2 HEIDI HEISE, SUB SAMARITAN

On June 3, 2010, a fire broke out in Heidi Heise's Dartmouth, N.S., apartment building. Several tenants had to find other accommodations, but fortunately Heidi's apartment was not damaged and she did not have to move out. Two of her neighbours were affected and, feeling sorry for them, Heidi offered them the use of her apartment while they looked for other accommodations.

Heidi had worked at three Subway fast-food restaurants during the previous three years, most recently including ten months full time at one outlet. After the fire the neighbours to whom she had lent her apartment came to the restaurant to thank her. Because they were hungry and had no money, Heidi prepared two six-inch subs for them. As an employee working over her lunch period she was entitled to one free 12-inch sub, but decided to forgo it and gave it away. Store policy required that she record her consumption of the sub, but she forgot to do this.

A restaurant manager observed Heidi giving away the subs on a surveillance camera a few days later and fired her. Heidi was not impressed to have been fired for helping someone in need. She also believed that she had been a good employee: she had never receiving warnings or punishments related to her job. Several people intervened on Heidi's behalf, including her direct supervisor, but the general manager insisted on the firing. One of the neighbours and the apartment building manager also appealed to Subway in favour of Heidi.

A representative of Atlantic Subway Ltd. commented that the incident was unfortunate. Subway Restaurants Canada issued a statement saying that it was concerned, but personnel matters were the responsibility of the franchise owner. Calls by the media to Subway were not answered, but the incident received nationwide coverage. Reader comments to a Halifax *Chronicle Herald* story stated the following opinions:

- Subway had missed an opportunity to recognize an employee doing a good or right thing.
- The incident may have a negative impact on the morale of other employees.
- Subway should be boycotted.

About a week later, Heidi was offered a job by Subway competitor Quiznos, which also decided to donate $2 from the sale of subs to the victims of the fire.

Questions

1. What are the issues involved in this incident?
2. What ethical theories can be applied to analyze this incident?
3. Was Subway justified in firing Heidi?
4. As a manager, how would you have handled this incident? What aspects of an ethics program would have assisted you?

Sources: "Subway Worker Fired for Feeding Fire Victims," Cnews, canoe.ca, June 11, 2010, accessed February 23, 2012, http://cnews.canoe.ca/CNEWS/Canada/2010/06/ 11/14355351.html?cid=rssnewscanada; *CTV News,* June 10, 2010, http://www.ctv.ca/CTVNews/TopStories/20100610/ns-subway-firing-100610, accessed February 23, 2012; "Fired Subway Worker Doesn't Want to Work There Anymore," *CTV News,* June 11, 2010, accessed August 12, 2016, http://www.ctvnews.ca/fired-subway-worker-doesn-t-want-to-work-there-anymore-1.521608; "Nova Scotia Quiznos Offers Job to Submarine Samaritan Fired by Rival Chain," *National Post,* June 12, 2010, A12; Roger Taylor, "Fired Sandwich Artist Back on Job with Competitor," *The ChronicleHerald.ca,* June 12, 2010, accessed June 21, 2010, http://thechronicleherald.ca/Business/1186991.html; and Mark Harden, "Quiznos Franchisee Rescues Canada's Hoagie Hero," *Denver Business Journal,* June 15, 2010, accessed August 12, 2016, http://www.bizjournals.com/denver/blog/broadway_17th/2010/06/quiznos_franchisee_helps_out_canadas_hoagie_hero.html.

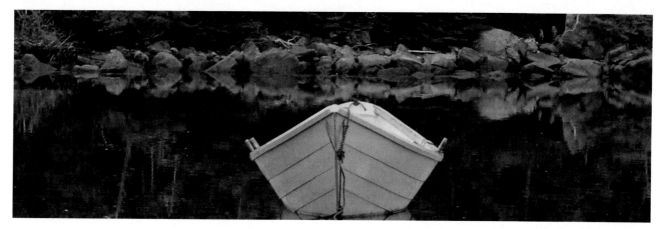

Used with the permission of Dennis Flynn

CHAPTER 7

Corporate Social Responsibility: The Concept

LEARNING OUTCOMES

After studying this chapter, you will be able to:

LO 7.1 Describe corporate social responsibility (CSR).

LO 7.2 Debate the pros and cons of corporate social responsibility in Canadian business.

LO 7.3 Appreciate the various foundations of social responsibility theories.

LO 7.4 Explain Carroll's pyramid of corporate social responsibility.

LO 7.5 Define the four contemporary CSR concepts: corporate sustainability, reputation management, social impact management, and triple bottom line (TBL).

LO 7.6 Describe corporate and business citizenship.

LO 7.7 Explain the complexity of corporate social responsibility by understanding a unifying CSR framework.

What would you do if...?

George Lafontaine had always been an enthusiastic Volkswagen (VW) customer. As a young man, he drove a Beetle, then as he got older he purchased a Golf, then a Jetta, and most recently a Passat. It was time for George to purchase a new car, but he was hesitating at buying another Volkswagen. He had heard some disturbing news about VW's use of software manipulation devices to avoid regulated emissions standards. At first it was believed to be an isolated incident, the result of a few rogue employees. But, investigations by the media and others found that this was not the case. In fact, some believed that unethical behaviours were common in the auto industry.

George decided to research the Volkswagen website for information on ethics and social responsibility. He found a comprehensive code of ethics that included phrases like:

- we act responsibly, for the benefit of our customers, shareholders, and employees

- we consider compliance with ... laws, and internal rules to be the basis for sustainable and successful economic activities

- we stand for respectable, honest actions...

In addition, he found detailed corporate social responsibility guidelines. Two of these guidelines related to the environment and product safety. The corporation claimed it was responsible to the environment by producing clean cars which would throughout their life cycle minimize their impact on the environment. Responsibility for their products would be designed to protect the health and safety of the customer.

Overall, the guidelines stated that VW viewed itself as a corporate citizen who took responsibility to society seriously. The VW corporation supported numerous CSR projects around the world related to the arts, sciences, education, health promotion, sports, and nature conservation as well as local infrastructure development. In Canada, for example, VW employees volunteered at Camp Oochigeas, a camp for children with cancer.

On November 30, 2015, VW placed advertisements in Canadian daily newspapers apologizing for their mistake and stating "...we won't rest until we earn back your trust and restore our integrity."

George was undecided about purchasing another VW product and disillusioned about CSR.

What advice would you give George?

Source: Adapted from *Volkswagen Sustainability Report*, accessed January 6, 2016, http://www.volkswagenag.com/content/vwcorp/content/en/sustainability_and_responsibility.html;Corporate Responsibility, accessed January 6, 2016, http://en.volkswagen.com/en/company/responsibility/corporate-responsibility.html; and "Volkswagen is Giving Back at Camp Oochigeas," accessed January 6, 2016, http://www.vw.ca/en/corporate/vw-cares.html.

This chapter defines social responsibility, reviews the case for business social involvement, reviews the arguments against involvement, and describes recent theories and approaches to corporate social responsibility including corporate citizenship.

LO 7.1   Describing Corporate Social Responsibility

Corporate social responsibility (CSR) has had many definitions to date; one is the way a corporation achieves a balance among its economic, social, and environmental responsibilities in its operations so as to address shareholder and other stakeholder expectations. CSR is known by many names, including corporate responsibility, corporate accountability, corporate ethics, corporate citizenship, sustainability, stewardship, and the triple-E bottom line (economical, ethical, and environmental). CSR is a general management concern; that is, it is important to all aspects of business, and it is integrated into a corporation's operations through its values, culture, decision making, strategy, and reporting mechanisms.

A definition receiving some attention is the one developed by the International Organization for Standardization (ISO). This standards-setting organization already has formulated standards for risk, quality, environmental, and energy management. Its ISO 26000 standard defined social responsibility as the responsibility of an organization for the impacts of its decisions and activities on society and the environment, through transparent and ethical behaviour that:

- contributes to sustainable development, including health and the welfare of society;
- takes into account the expectations of stakeholders;
- is in compliance with applicable law and consistent with international norms of behaviour; and
- is integrated throughout the organization and practised in its relationships.[1]

Rather than use a precise definition, researchers have identified the elements or topics that might be included. Buchholz identified five key elements found in most, if not all, definitions:

- Corporations have responsibilities that go beyond the production of goods and services at a profit.
- These responsibilities involve helping to solve important social problems, especially those they have helped create.
- Corporations have a broader constituency than shareholders alone.
- Corporations have impacts that go beyond simple marketplace transactions.
- Corporations serve a wider range of human values than can be captured by a sole focus on economic values.[2]

In another example of this approach, Dahlsrud examined 37 definitions through content analysis and found that five dimensions of CSR existed:

- Environmental: the natural environment
- Social: the relationship between business and society
- Economic: socio-economic and financial aspects
- Stakeholder: stakeholders and stakeholder groups
- Voluntariness: actions not prescribed by law

He concluded that existing definitions were largely congruent and that "the confusion is not so much about how CSR is defined, as about how CSR is socially constructed in a specific context."[3]

According to Wood, the "basic idea of corporate social responsibility is that business and society are interwoven rather than distinct entities" and that expectations are placed on business due to its three roles: as an institution in society, as a particular corporation or organization in society, and as individual managers who are moral actors within the corporation. These roles result in three levels of analysis—institutional, organizational, and individual—and can be expressed in terms of three principles of corporate social responsibility: legitimacy, public responsibility, and managerial discretion.[4]

The principle of *legitimacy* refers to society's granting of legitimacy and power to business, and business' appropriate use of that power and the possibility of losing that power. Corporate social responsibility defines the institutional relationship between business and society that is expected of any corporation. Society has the right to grant this power, to impose a balance of power among its institutions, and to define their legitimate functions. The focus is on business' obligations as a social institution, and society takes away power or imposes some sort of sanction on business if expectations are not met.

The principle of *public responsibility* means that business is responsible for outcomes related to its areas of involvement with society. The level of application is organizational—that is, the corporation—and confines business' responsibility to those problems related to a firm's activities and interests. This principle includes the view that corporations are responsible for solving the problems they create. The nature of social responsibility will vary from corporation to corporation as each corporation impacts society's resources in different ways or creates different problems. The principle involves emphasizing each corporation's relationship to its specific social, ethical, and political environment.

Last, the principle of *managerial discretion* refers to managers as moral actors who are obliged to exercise such discretion as is available to them to achieve socially responsible outcomes. Discretion is involved because the actions of managers are not totally prescribed by corporate procedures. The level of application is the individual who has the choices, opportunities, and personal responsibility to achieve the corporation's social responsibility.[5] Table 7.1 summarizes the three principles.

The many elements of corporate social responsibility have been introduced so that the concept's complexity is appreciated. A later section of this chapter will present a unified framework of corporate social responsibility as it relates to business and society.

The Importance of Corporate Social Responsibility

CSR is important because the business system is the mechanism selected by society to produce and distribute goods and services. Originally, people felt that a business enterprise had fulfilled its social responsibility by surviving and realizing the maximum profit possible. The resources of society could be used by the corporation to make profits as long as the corporation complied with the few rules imposed by governments to check abusive practices. The market system provided the regulation necessary to police the system, and profits provided incentive and ensured efficiency. The work ethic and self-interest were the guiding principles of the system. By making a profit, corporations contributed to a growing, healthy economic system that provided employment and adequate incomes for all. In other words, corporate social responsibility was to operate profitably, and the corporation could not survive without profits, much less play a social role.

Important to know

TABLE 7.1 Wood's Principles of Corporate Social Responsibility

Principle of Legitimacy	Principle of Public Responsibility	Principle of Managerial Discretion
• External focus on expectations of society • Society grants the right to business to operate • Adherence to social norms of society	• Beyond general expectations of society, that is, at the corporation level • Determined by uniqueness for circumstances of the corporation	• Involves individual choice or managerial discretion • Individual decision makers or managers determine • Relates to latitude of action possible by management
• Pressures particularly strong on some corporations, e.g. large ones or consumer products	• Resource dependence determines • Involves managing relationships with immediate environment	• Focuses on range of strategic options available to management

Source: Compiled from Christine Shropshire and Amy J. Hillman, "A Longitudinal Study of Significant Change in Stakeholder Management," *Business & Society*, Volume 46, Number 1, March 2007, 68–74.

More recently, there has been a belief that business exists for more than profits (or economic goals), with the public expecting something else from business. As a result, the original concept of social responsibility involving the maximization of profits has been modified. Although profits are to be made, social goals are also to receive attention. Society depends on business to achieve social as well as economic goals—that is, social responsibilities are placed on business.

The issue of social responsibility cannot be easily resolved. To illustrate, consider the following questions: How should corporate performance in society be judged apart from traditional economic standards? Are there goals and measures that individuals inside and outside the corporation can use for guidance? Given the relationship between the corporation and its social environment, what is the scope of managerial responsibility? To what extent should the corporation involve itself in social concerns? How do corporations typically respond to social involvement issues? Is there a common process that will enhance the corporation's understanding of corporate social performance?

It must be appreciated that corporate social responsibility and a corporation's social performance are two of many factors in an extremely complex business environment in which the corporate manager is called upon to operate the business. Various stakeholders are constantly seeking a different role for business in society. Government continues to influence the business system and to change the forms and manner of this influence. Technological change is occurring at a very rapid pace. The media advise citizens quickly of events in the business world, allowing for quick public reaction.

The discussion of definitions and meanings of corporate social responsibility could be extensive, but the purpose here is to provide an introduction to and appreciation for social responsibility. Further understanding of the concept, its origins, and its interpretations is achieved by summarizing some of the debate surrounding social responsibility.

LO 7.2   The Corporate Social Responsibility Debate

The discussion of the appropriateness and meaning of social responsibility continues. This debate is treated in two ways in this chapter: through a listing of the arguments for and against social responsibility, and through a summary of the theories used to represent the variety of views toward social responsibility.

The Case for Involvement

Many arguments support the involvement of business in society; that is, they support the social responsibility or social responsiveness of business.

Business must realize that society is a "system" of which corporations are a part, and that the system is interdependent. Therefore, if business institutions interact with others in society, the need for social involvement along with increasing interdependence brings the need to participate in the complex system that exists in society. There are many mutual involvements among individuals, groups, and organizations in society, or among subsectors of society. Business is vulnerable to the actions or events that occur in other subsectors. As a result business should operate in such a way as to fulfill society's needs or expectations. It should do so for a very pragmatic reason: it is believed in some quarters that business functions by the consent of society and therefore must be sure to satisfy the needs of society. In other words, the existence of the business system depends on its acceptance by society. If business is to prevent criticisms or mutinous behaviour, it must be receptive to what is happening in society and respond in some way.

Corporations must be concerned with the public image and the goodwill generated by responsible social actions. A social responsibility role should be undertaken in order to prevent some public criticism and discourage further government involvement or regulation. This is a defensive approach designed to offset possible government action against those in the business system who use their power irresponsibly. Preventing is better than curing. It is better to take a proactive stance than a reactive one.

Social responsibility is in the shareholder's interest; that is, corporate virtue is good for profits, especially in the long term. A poor social responsibility role on the part of the corporation means poor management to some investors. They view failure to perform in society's interests in much the same way as they view the corporation's failure to perform in financial matters. Similarly, investors and consumers are showing increasing interest in and support for responsible business. Most top corporate managers consider social responsibility or corporate sustainability very importance in their approach to management as illustrated in Everyday Ethics 7.1.

EVERYDAY ETHICS 7.1

Managers' Views of Corporate Social Responsibility

These quotations were obtained from recent corporate social responsibility or sustainability reports. The terms *corporate social responsibility* and *corporate sustainability* are interchangeable.

- At TransAlta, we believe it makes good business sense to share our sustainability story. First, because we have a great story to tell, and second, because like many other companies that participate in the energy industry, our sustainability and business strategies are essentially one and the same.

  Dawn Farrell, President and CEO

- Ultimately, we look at Corporate Social Responsibility (CSR) not as a facet of our business, but as a reflection of the way we conduct our business and an expression of our core values of integrity, responsibility, collaboration and innovation.

  Russ Girling, President and CEO, TransCanada

- At Catalyst, our sustainability program is built upon three traditional pillars of performance improvement: Economic, social and environmental. Our commitment is to be transparent with our successes and our setbacks. Our fundamental belief is that integrating sustainability into our overall strategic framework is the cornerstone of success.

  Joe Nemeth, President & Chief Executive Officer

- Sustainability continues to be a key focus for Celestica as we strongly believe it is an area in which we are well-positioned to lead change in our industry, drive value for our customers and improve the communities in which we live and work.

  Craig Muhlhauser, President and Chief Executive Officer

- The Company's performance in the realm of corporate social responsibility (CSR) is central to our overall business strategy. This is why we have continued to invest in the implementation of industry-leading practices with respect to working conditions, community support, environmental footprint, and responsibly-made product offerings.

  Glenn J. Chamandy. President and Chief Executive Officer, Gildan Activewear

Business must realize that social problems can become opportunities, or can lead to profits, lower costs, and reduced risks. Expenditures on pollution abatement may result in the retrieval of materials that were formerly disposed of as waste, or may allow for equipment to operate more efficiently, thereby generating more profits on future operations. Also with regard to social responsibility matters, business should take a long-run as opposed to a short-run view. Profits may increase in the long run as a result of actions taken at the present time. Judging the benefits of social responsibility becomes a simple matter of ascertaining whether it is in the corporation's longest-term self-interest to be conscious of social responsibility matters by reducing risk. Finally, some corporations have built their competitive advantage on social responsibility initiatives or strategies that set them apart from competitors.

Business should be given an opportunity to solve some social problems. The logic behind this argument is that business can solve problems as well as government can and that it certainly cannot do any worse than government has in the past. Business possesses the expertise, in its managers and executives, to develop plans to overcome social problems. As government is reducing its efforts to address some social problems, business needs to fill the gap. Businesspersons are also concerned citizens and humans; it is not appropriate for them to ignore social matters.

The Counterargument to the Case for Involvement

Although several arguments can be made for social involvement by business corporations, there also are many arguments *against* business social involvement.

Profit maximization is the primary purpose of business, and to have any other purpose is not socially responsible (as argued in Responsibility for Ethics 7.1). To have anything other than a profit-maximizing goal is to sabotage the market mechanism and distort the allocation of resources. Generally, then, it is contrary to the basic function of business to become involved in social matters. It should not be forgotten that business is an economic institution, not a social one, and its only responsibility is to manage efficiently within the law. The corporation would be irresponsible if it did not pursue profits and operate in the efficient market.

Business corporations are responsible to the shareholders and, in effect, have no authority to operate in the social area. When a corporation becomes involved in social matters, there is a question of legitimacy. Even if corporations are sufficiently competent and powerful to bring about social changes in matters considered beyond the range of their immediate involvement, there is a real question as to whether such endeavours are appropriate. Managers should let shareholders decide whether or not they wish to become involved in social issues.

RESPONSIBILITY FOR ETHICS 7.1

Milton Friedman

Milton Friedman, a Nobel Prize winner in economics, is often quoted as saying the only social responsibility of business is to make profits. Here is the quotation often used by proponents of a free economy:

> The view has been gaining widespread acceptance that corporate officials and labor leaders have a "social responsibility" that goes beyond serving the interest of their stockholders or their members. This view shows a fundamental misconception of the character and nature of a free economy. In such an economy, there is one and only one social responsibility of business—to use its resources and engage in activities designed to increase its profits so long as it stays within the rules of the game, which is to say, engages in open and free competition, without deception or fraud. Similarly, the "social responsibility" of labor leaders is to serve the interests of the members of their unions.

Source: Based on Milton Friedman, *Capitalism and Freedom: A Leading Economist's View of the Proper Role of Competitive Capitalism* (Chicago: The University of Chicago Press, 1962), 133. Used with permission The University of Chicago Press.

Social policy is the jurisdiction of governments, not business. Business lacks training in social issues, and lacks social skills necessary to carry out social programs. In other words, business is not competent to undertake social responsibility tasks. Furthermore, social responsibility is viewed by some as another excuse to let big business increase its power. The increase in power comes as a result of business becoming involved in social as well as economic matters. Imposing business values on social issues may lead to inappropriate domination: business already has sufficient power, and it would be inappropriate to extend that power to other matters.

Business involvement in social matters increases costs—not only costs to the organization, but also possibly even social costs—instead of decreasing them. This in turn may lead to business failures. There is no acknowledged source of reliable guidance or policy for business in social responsibility questions, and it is not easy to make the choice between responsible and selfish action in social issues. Social responsibility is an elusive concept for which few standards are available to evaluate and control the actions of corporations.

As institutions in society, business corporations cannot be held accountable for their actions in a way sufficient to satisfy demands for social involvement. Institutions involved in social matters should be accountable to society for that involvement. At the present time, few mechanisms are available to ensure that business corporations are accountable for their social actions.

It is particularly difficult to argue for CSR when events occur that are not clearly inappropriate or wrong even though the corporation has an elaborate and professional social responsibility or sustainability program. Recent examples are SNC-Lavalin, which was involved in bribery of foreign officials, and Volkswagen, when it deceived regulators about vehicle emissions. The reasons for these events is similar to why ethical managers fail as discussed in Chapter 6. Managers are not morally perfect and self-interest overtakes decision making. Pressure to perform may lead managers to take short cuts and violate clearly stated CSR policies. Another criticism is that some corporations may have CSR programs for appearances or because it has become the current trend when the culture of the organization and its managers are not committed to them.

There is divided support in the business community for social involvement and, as a result, there is unlikely to be a very satisfactory treatment of social issues by business.

Critiquing CSR

Explanations and critiques of corporate social responsibility appear regularly in the media and academic literature (some examples are provided in Responsibility for Ethics 7.2). Many of these discussions are repetitious, but one that added to the analysis of the concept was a special section in *The Economist*, "The Good Company: A Survey of Corporate Responsibility."[6] The thesis of the section was that the corporate social responsibility movement dominates most management thinking, and that this is unfortunate because it is not necessary if the functioning of capitalism is understood. Furthermore, CSR is practised in many different ways, creating confusion regarding what it really means.

The article argues that there is no need to impose CSR on corporations, because they are acting in a responsible manner already. The point is made that capitalism has been the driving force behind unparalleled economic and social progress, but unfortunately it is still suspected, feared, and deplored. Two reasons are given for this fear of capitalism: the idea that profit is inconsistent with the public or social good, and the belief that in their pursuit of private gain corporations are placing crippling burdens on society and the environment. *The Economist*'s article does not consider either of these reasons to be appropriate.[7]

The Economist article says that enlightened self-interest and ethical conduct work well together. But, two values must be understood in relation to the proper good of the corporation, and without these two values business is not possible. The first value is ordinary decency—that is, being just, honest, and fair. The second value involves distributive justice, where the benefits within the corporation are aligned to the contribution made in adhering to the aims of the corporation—for example, pay is linked to performance and promotion to merit. With regard to stakeholders, corporations should take them into account without being accountable to them.[8]

This critique generated substantial response, including several letters to the editor in subsequent issues—the majority of which disagreed with the thesis of the survey. An invited contributor to *The Economist* responded with a countering view. Ian Davis, worldwide managing director of McKinsey & Company, stated that business leaders should not fear greater advocacy of the contract between business and society and that the role of business is changing.[9] *Corporate Knights* did an analysis of the survey, pointing out that the complete separation of government and society from the private sector was no longer a reasonable assumption to hold.[10] Most commentators thought that to be successful the modern corporation must consider the interests of stakeholders in addition to shareholders.

RESPONSIBILITY FOR ETHICS 7.2

Critical Comments on CSR

 Despite widespread acceptance of corporate social responsibility, there are those who are critical of it. The following quotations from the business press illustrate the criticism.

 "Business ethics has become not so much about honesty and fair dealing as about the additional burdens companies should be taking on in the name of infinitely expansive corporate social responsibility and getting out in front of environmental issues."—Peter Foster, "Trading Honesty for 'Social Responsibility'," *National Post*, April 17, 2009, FP11.

 "When corporations take on a social role, often at the urging of elected officials themselves, it relieves governments of their responsibilities to mediate social demands. It removes policy-making from its proper forum. Put plainly, CSR is undemocratic."—Konrad Yakabuski, "The Kindness of Corporations," *Report on Business Magazine*, July/August 2008, 68.

 "Under the label of Corporate Social Responsibility, firms are to take on a non-wealth-producing agenda of goals: profits will be lowered to safeguard labour rights, human health, civil liberties, environmental quality, sexual equality, and social justice. The fact that the corporation already plays its most effective role in these areas by profit maximization is little understood by CSR advocates."—Steve Forbes, "Welcome to Market Socialism," *National Post*, January 15, 2005, FP11.

 "Corporate Social Responsibility is a proposition with which it is allegedly impossible to argue. If you question its multiplying meanings or its murky metrics, you are accused of espousing 'irresponsibility,' of wanting to outlaw philanthropy and trash the environment, of being a blinkered ideologue who believes employees, suppliers and local communities should be treated with contempt. This is all, to put it bluntly, baloney."—Peter Foster, "The Bottomless Pit of CSR Policies," *National Post*, March 2, 2005, FP23.

The Economist published a follow-up report in January 2008, "Just good business: A special report on corporate social responsibility."[11] An accompanying editorial was entitled "Ethical Capitalism: How Good Should Your Business Be?"[12] The tone of the second report was somewhat different from the first one. The first report questioned the legitimacy of CSR, while the second report focused on how CSR was being accomplished. An observation from the second report was that CSR has gained considerable momentum and, rather than being a sideshow, is now seen as mainstream. Few corporations are doing it well and it has some limitations. The report concluded that CSR is just good business.

The arguments for and against CSR have been made. Various forms of CSR are widely practised and knowledge of the concept is essential for effective management in today's environment. The following section also addresses this debate but from a different perspective, summarizing the varying corporate social responsibility theories that exist. The existence of these theories helps explain why so many interpretations are associated with the concept.

LO 7.3   Social Responsibility Theories

Klonoski[13] sets out to address a fundamental question: "Does business and the corporation have a social nature, or not?" The answer given by any stakeholder can be associated with a theory of corporate social responsibility, and these theories fall into three categories: amoral, personal, and social.

The Amoral View

This category represents a traditional view of business and the role of the corporation; that is, the corporation is seen as a "highly individualized rights bearing economic entity designed for profit making and legitimatized by the laws governing incorporated businesses."[14] Free market defenders and legal recognition theorists are among those holding this view, including some who believe there is no such thing as corporate social responsibility. Over the years many theories have advocated this view of social responsibility; these are listed in Table 7.2. The amoral view is still held by some in the business community.

TABLE 7.2	Examples of Amoral-View Theories of Social Responsibility

Fundamentalism—The corporation has no or very little social responsibility.

Legal recognition—The corporation is an autonomous entity and not the creation of society.

Individual agreement—Corporations can be socially responsible, but only within the limits of a prior contractual agreement with shareholders.

Traditional shareholders model—Beyond individual agreements, corporations are not ethically required to be socially responsible; they are responsible only to monies and to maximize profits (as so famously stated by Milton Friedman).

Source: Summarized from Richard J. Klonoski, "Foundational Considerations in the Corporate Social Responsibility Debate," *Business Horizons* (July/August 1991): 9–18. With permission from Elsevier.

The "amoral" view should be carefully defined and not confused with an "immoral" view. Amoral refers to an activity without a moral quality; that is, something that is neither moral nor immoral: moral standards, restraints, or principles do not exist. This is quite different from immoral, which denotes activities that are not moral and do not conform to usually accepted or established patterns of conduct. Amoral means lacking in morals, good or bad, while immoral connotes evil or licentious behaviour. Although in some contexts being amoral is considered as reprehensible as being immoral, that is not the position taken by most advocates of the theories listed in this category.

The Personal View

This view discusses the nature of the corporation in ascertaining whether it can be held accountable. The question involved is whether corporations are "moral agents" or "full-fledged" moral persons. Corporations are viewed as collectives that act as individuals; they exist as legal persons and can be held responsible for their actions. This question has been extensively discussed in the literature.

Those arguing that corporations are persons claim that corporations are responsible for their actions in a way comparable to the actions taken by natural persons or individuals. Therefore, the corporation can be morally blamed in a way that is identical or very similar to natural persons. A strong counterargument in the literature claims that corporations are not persons. Supporters of this view argue that it is not possible to impose moral sanctions or punishments on corporations as corporations. It is possible to blame or punish the people who work for or manage the corporation, but not the corporation itself. Some punishments, such as fines, are in effect paid by shareholders or passed on as costs to consumers.

The debate over whether the corporation can be seen as a moral person does not provide an answer as to whether the corporation is a social institution. Those who claim the corporation is a person believe that it is socially responsible for its impact on society, and that it can be held morally accountable for its actions in the social sphere. Those who do not consider the corporation to be a person say that claims against the corporation by society need a different basis than that provided by the moral person or agency theory. The "personal" view represents a middle position between the amoral and social views.

The personal view leaves the debate unresolved. However, the arguments favouring the treatment of corporations as persons lead to the next theoretical view of corporate social responsibility: the social view.

The Social View

This view holds that the activities of corporations occur within an interpersonal and, most likely, social context. The corporation is considered a social institution in society, with social responsibilities. The social nature of business can rest in many different theories, some of which are listed in Table 7.3. The extent of corporate social responsibility depends on the theoretical foundation used to support the view.

TABLE 7.3 **Examples of Social-View Theories of Social Responsibility**

Social contract—An implicit social agreement exists between business and society that determines the social nature of the corporation, identifies its duties and rights, and is considered to be an evolving document.

Ideological/Historical—Society evolves and history gives rise to new social needs, societal demands, and changes in social values to which business is expected to contribute.

Stakeholder—There is a social responsibility function of the interrelationships developed by the corporation with groups that have a stake. This approach was also referred to as "constituency theory." This theory is one of the main underpinnings of this book.

Legal creator—The corporation is a creature of law, existing only in contemplation of law, and is thus made by society for the common good of society.

Social permission—Society can legitimately demand the corporation do certain kinds of activities and, if the corporation is harming the public good, can restrict or eliminate its activities.

Corporate citizenship—With the charter, the corporation becomes a legal entity with standing as a citizen similar to that of the individual and has duties as well as rights and privileges.

Social impact—Business has the power to change society and must consider social responsibilities.

Social interpenetration—Business is so intertwined with society that it cannot avoid social responsibilities.

Moral gratitude/reciprocity—As business operates within a social system, it should be socially responsible out of "gratitude" or have a moral responsibility to "reciprocate." Corporations benefit from and thus owe society.

Utilitarian—It is to the benefit of society or for the greatest good for the greatest number of people that corporations are socially responsible; social responsibility is in business' best interest.

Virtue-based—This view focuses on the development of good or morally virtuous people instead of principles or contracts. A morally responsible business is one in which good people make decisions based on generally developed moral character, self-discipline, moderation, hard work, courage, creativity, good humour, and intelligence.

Source: Summarized from Richard J. Klonoski, "Foundational Considerations in the Corporate Social Responsibility Debate," *Business Horizons* (July/August 1991): 9–18. With permission from Elsevier.

It is argued that the corporation should be considered a social institution, as it exists because individuals come together to achieve some objective related to the provision of goods and services. Today, corporations exist because society implicitly sanctions them to operate in that form. Many in society believe that corporations now operate within the "social" view of corporate social responsibility despite the continuing claims of those who argue the "amoral" view, with its incomplete vision of the corporation operating as a private institution with a solely economic purpose.

Many theories and frameworks have been presented to describe corporate social responsibility. Some of them overlap and some parallel the arguments for and against corporate social involvement. The existence of numerous theories supporting corporate social responsibility makes it difficult to find a comprehensive and precise definition, as mentioned in the previous section about describing social responsibility.

Despite the numerous views of corporate social responsibility, many business-supported organizations advocate it; some of these are listed in Responsibility for Ethics 7.3. The literature contains numerous models of social responsibility, and one has been selected for presentation. Carroll's pyramid of corporate social responsibility is a practical framework for managers that incorporates economic, legal, social, and ethical responsibilities.

RESPONSIBILITY FOR ETHICS 7.3

Business-supported Organizations Working on CSR

Several organizations are promoting CSR with support from Canadian businesses:

Network for Business Sustainability (NBS)—The non-profit NBS network of international academic experts and business leaders was established in 2005 with its main office located at the Ivey Business School (Western University) in London, Ontario. It produces resources on important sustainability issues with the goal of shaping management practice and research. It connects with thousands of researchers and professionals worldwide who are interested in corporate social responsibility (CSR) and who believe in the value of research-based practice and practice-based research. NBS uses its academic and industry funding to commission research on the business community's top sustainability challenges

Canadian Business for Social Responsibility—Founded in 1995, CBSR is a business-led, non-profit CSR consultancy and peer-to-peer learning organization that provides its members with candid counsel and customized advisory services as they formulate powerful business decisions that improve performance and contribute to a better world.

Conference Board of Canada—The Conference Board of Canada is an independent source of insights for business leaders. CSR is considered relevant to business, a key determinant of a corporation's relationship to the world. It conducts and publishes research, and disseminates knowledge to its members by conducting and publishing research and sponsoring conferences and seminars.

Corporate Knights—Founded in 2002, Corporate Knights Inc. is an independent, Canadian-based media company that publishes the world's largest-circulation magazine with an explicit focus on corporate responsibility.

Canadian Centre for Ethics and Corporate Policy (EthicsCentre.ca)—EthicsCentre.ca is a registered charity and independent ethics centre formed to champion the application of ethical values in the decision-making process of business and other organizations.

Canadian Centre for Ethics in Public Affairs—CCEPA facilitates critical thinking, public discussion, and research into current ethical challenges in society. It promotes the public good through research into and dissemination of knowledge of ethical issues, which helps generate new insights, provide greater awareness, and heal misunderstandings.

Imagine Canada—Imagine Canada is a non-profit organization that helps charities and non-profit organizations fulfill their missions, champions corporate citizenship, and helps businesses partner in the community. It accomplishes this through research, developing public policy, promoting public awareness, and encouraging businesses to become better corporate citizens.

LO 7.4   The Pyramid of Corporate Social Responsibility

One way to view corporate social responsibility is through Carroll's[15] pyramid, which he claims presents the concept such that social responsibility will be accepted by a conscientious businessperson. There are four kinds of social responsibility—economic, legal, ethical, and philanthropic—which can be depicted in a pyramid, as presented in Figure 7.1. Carroll contends that all of these responsibilities have always existed to some degree, but ethical and philanthropic responsibilities have become significant only in recent years.

FIGURE 7.1 *Carroll's Pyramid of Corporate Social Responsibility*

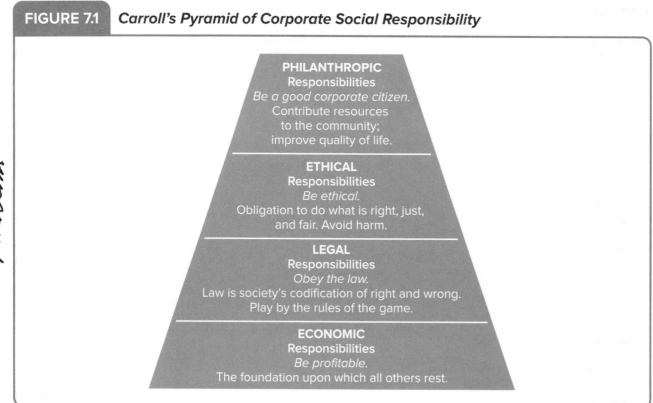

Source: Archie Carroll, "The Pyramid of Corporate Social Responsibility," p. 42 in *Business Horizons*, July/August 1991. Copyright Elsevier & Kelley School of Business, Indiana University.

Economic responsibilities relate to business' provision of goods and services of value to society. Profits result from this activity and are necessary for any other responsibilities to be carried out. It is assumed that corporations will be as profitable as possible, maintain a strong competitive position, and maintain a high level of operating efficiency. These are responsibilities that the corporation "must do" and the key stakeholders are shareholders, creditors, and consumers.

Society expects business to conform to laws and regulations formulated by governments that act as the ground rules under which business must operate. Corporations are expected to pursue profits within the framework of the law, which establishes what are considered fair operations. Society expects that all goods and services and relationships with stakeholders will meet at least minimal legal requirements.

Ethical responsibilities include those activities that are not expected or prohibited by society as economic or legal responsibilities. Standards, norms, or expectations that reflect concern for select stakeholder input are fair, just, or in keeping with their moral rights. Ethics or values may be reflected in laws or regulations, but ethical responsibilities are seen as embracing the emerging values and norms that society expects of business even if not currently required by law. These responsibilities can be thought of as things the corporation "should do." These responsibilities are more difficult for business to deal with as they are often ill-defined or under continual public debate. Ethical responsibilities also involve the fundamental ethical principles of moral philosophy, such as justice, human rights, and utilitarianism. The changing or emerging ethical responsibilities are constantly pushing legal responsibilities to broaden or expand, while at the same time expecting business' ethical behaviour to go beyond mere compliance with laws and regulations.

Philanthropic responsibilities involve being a good corporate citizen and include active participation in acts or programs to promote human welfare or goodwill. Examples are contributions to the arts, charities, and education. Such responsibilities are not expected in an ethical or moral sense, making philanthropy more discretionary or voluntary on the part of business even though society may have such expectations of business. Few in society expect corporations to have these responsibilities, and they can be thought of as things corporations "might do."

Carroll views the pyramid as a basic building-block structure, with economic performance as the foundation. At the same time, business is expected to obey the law, behave ethically, and be a good corporate citizen. Although the responsibilities are portrayed as separate elements, in practice they are not mutually exclusive; however, the separation aids managers to appreciate the different obligations that are in a constant but dynamic tension with one another. For example, there are particular tensions between economic and ethical responsibilities. In summary, Carroll views the total social responsibility of business as involving the simultaneous fulfillment of the four responsibilities—which, stated in pragmatic terms, means that the corporation should strive to make a profit, obey the law, be ethical, and be a good corporate citizen.[16]

Carroll's pyramid represents one of the earliest attempts to integrate the economic and social responsibilities of the corporation. Evidence is accumulating that supports consideration of economic (tangible) and social (intangible) responsibilities:

- Economic (profits) and social responsibilities (ethics) are not mutually exclusive.
- Research shows that economic and social responsibilities are often inseparable.
- Corporations that consider social responsibilities seriously tend to outperform solely profit-seeking corporations.

Resistance to this convergence of economic and social responsibilities does occur. Managers who incorporate social responsibilities into decision making are sometimes labelled as "do-gooders" who are ignoring profits. There are segments of society that suggest there is nothing good about business and that it cannot be ethical or concerned about social issues. It is argued that business should stay out of social responsibilities, as it is often difficult to judge what is right or wrong and managers are not prepared to make such decisions.

An outcome of this shift toward integrating economic, social, and environmental responsibilities has been the emergence of new concepts, several of which are discussed in the following section.

LO 7.5   Contemporary CSR Concepts

Corporate social responsibility is the terminology still widely used to represent business' social responsibilities. However, other terms have appeared that incorporate the consideration of economic responsibilities as well, including corporate sustainability, reputation management, social impact management, triple bottom line (TBL), and corporate citizenship. The first four terms will be briefly described here; corporate citizenship is a more prominent term and will be discussed in detail in the following section.

Corporate Sustainability

As with the definition of CSR, academics, consultants, and practitioners have formulated many definitions of corporate sustainability, some of which are similar to those for CSR. **Corporate sustainability (CS)** refers to corporate activities demonstrating the inclusion of social and environmental as well as economic responsibilities in business operations as they impact all stakeholders. Marrewijk identified five levels of CS that are similar to how CSR could be viewed:

- *Compliance-driven CS*—Involves following government regulations and responding to charity and stewardship considerations considered appropriate by society.
- *Profit-driven CS*—Consideration is given to the social, ethical, and environmental aspects of business operations provided they contribute to the financial bottom line.
- *Caring CS*—Initiatives go beyond legal compliance and profit considerations where economic, social, and environmental concerns are balanced, as it is the right thing to do.
- *Synergistic CS*—Well-balanced and functional solutions are sought that create value in the economic, social, and environmental areas, as it is a winning approach for all stakeholders.
- *Holistic CS*—Corporate sustainability is fully integrated and embedded in every aspect of the corporation's activities, as this is important to the quality and continuation of life on this planet.[17]

Corporate sustainability has been recognized by the financial markets because it creates long-term shareholder value by embracing opportunities and managing risks as the result of economic, social, and environmental developments. This idea is illustrated in Responsibility for Ethics 7.4.

connect   Want to learn more about **sustainability?**

RESPONSIBILITY FOR ETHICS 7.4

The Dow Jones Sustainability Indexes

Dow Jones states that corporate sustainability is important to long-term shareholder value, which is achieved by embracing opportunities and management risks from economic, social, and environmental developments. Launched in 1999, the Dow Jones Sustainability Indexes (DJSI) are offered cooperatively by RobecoSAM and S&P Dow Jones Indices. The indices track the financial performance of the leading sustainability-driven companies worldwide in in terms of economic, environmental, and social criteria. The indices serve as benchmarks for investors who integrate sustainability considerations into their portfolios, and provide an effective engagement platform for companies who want to adopt sustainable best practices

Each year, over 3,000 publicly traded companies are invited to participate in RobecoSAM's Corporate Sustainability Assessment. Of these, the largest 2,500 global companies by market capitalization are eligible for inclusion in the flagship DJSI World. In 2016, there were 17 members from Canada including Bombardier Inc., Barrick Gold Corp., and Gildan Activewear. The corporations included in the indices vary from year to year.

Source: Adapted from Dow Jones Sustainability Indices accessed January 4, 2016, http://www.sustainability-indices.com/about-us/dow-jones-sustainability-indices.jsp.

Reputation Management

Reputation management is any effort to enhance the corporation's image and good name. In the past, the focus of these efforts was on media and public relations and, to some extent, crisis management. Today, reputation management is being extended to relations with all stakeholders. Many managers believe that reputation management enhances financial performance, improves competitive positions, and increases public approval of corporate activities, and studies support this view.[18]

A successful process to implement reputation management involves several stages: the identification of a desired perception of the corporation, the recognition of the significance of image with all stakeholders, an awareness of the influence of interactions with stakeholders on the corporation's reputation, and continuous efforts at maintaining relationships with stakeholders.

Reputations take a long time to establish and can be destroyed quickly. As a result, a reputation can be an asset but at times a liability. Managers must understand all the factors that encompass a reputation and be aware of the measures used to differentiate a good reputation from a bad one. Examples are provided by surveys appearing in the media, including the "Canada's Most Respected Corporations" survey in *The Globe and Mail*, sponsored by KPMG and conducted by Ipsos-Reid; the "Canada's Best Managed Companies" survey in the *National Post*, sponsored by Deloitte, CIBC, and the Queen's School of Business; and the "Best Corporate Citizens in Canada" survey by *Corporate Knights: The Magazine for Clean Capitalism*. The purpose in describing these surveys is to establish that public measures assessing a corporation's reputation are available. It also establishes the importance of reputation and the need for managers to consciously monitor it.

 Want to learn more about *Corporate Knights*?

Social Impact Management

One of the main advocates of social impact management is the Aspen Institute. The Institute defines **social impact management** as "the field of inquiry at the intersection of business needs and wider societal concerns that reflects and respects the complex interdependency between the two."[19] This is very much a "business and society" approach, stressing the need for contemporary business to recognize and understand this interdependency if business and the society in which it operates wish to thrive. The Institute argues that this understanding is becoming increasingly important as corporations take on a bigger role and society increases pressure for corporations to address more essential social and environmental concerns.

The approach stresses the intersection of traditional business concerns (i.e., for financial or economic matters) and society's concerns for the consequences of the impact of the corporation (i.e., the social impact of business). Thus, social impact management is two-directional: society's influence on corporations, and the corporations' influence on the social and environmental concerns of society.

The Institute believes that "social impact management, as a way of thinking about business activities, explicitly considers and evaluates three aspects of a business:

1. Purpose: What is the purpose—in both societal and business terms—of a business or business activity?

2. Social Context: Are the legitimate rights and responsibilities of multiple stakeholders considered? Is a proposed strategy evaluated not only in terms of predicted business outcomes, but also in terms of its broader impacts—for example, on quality of life, the wider economy of a region, and security and safety?

3. Metrics: How is performance and profitability measured? What is being counted and what is not being counted? Are impacts and results measured across both short- and long-term time frames?"[20]

Triple Bottom Line (TBL)

The **triple-E (economic, ethical, and environmental) bottom line** evaluates a corporation's performance according to a summary of the economic, social, and environmental value the corporation adds or destroys. A variation of the term is the triple-P bottom line: people, planet, profit. The narrowest meaning of the term is a framework for measuring and reporting corporate performance against economic, social, and environmental indicators. Recently, a broader meaning has been attributed to the term in that the concept is used to capture a whole set of values, issues, and processes that corporations must address in order to minimize any harm resulting from their value-adding or destroying activities. This includes clarifying the corporation's purpose and taking into consideration all stakeholders. The triple bottom line approach is often the basis for corporate reporting of economic, ethical, and environmental responsibilities. Everyday Ethics 7.2 is an example of TBL at Novex Couriers.

EVERYDAY ETHICS 7.2

Triple Bottom Line at Novex Delivery Solutions

Novex Couriers, a B.C.-owned and -operated company, is one of the largest local same-day couriers in the Lower Mainland and has operated for over 30 years. Novex has a strategic plan to become a truly sustainable organization based on a triple bottom line approach. This plan focuses environment leadership, social and community leadership, and ethical business practices.

Novex understands that the nature of its business contributes to the growing environmental problem and accepts its responsibility by "going green." It uses a variety of emission-reducing vehicles including hybrids, natural gas, and biodiesel, all choices that minimize the company's carbon footprint. Waste-reduction and paper-conservation programs, energy-reduction initiatives, and environmental-awareness campaigns have been implemented. Its environmental management system is ISO 14001 certified, the first local courier company in Canada to obtain such credentials. Also, it is the first Carbon Neutral courier service in North America.

Novex engages with internal and external stakeholders. It is engaging its employees by supporting a diversity program, rewarding employees for their personal and organizational performance, and offering a training benefits program. In the community, the company and its employees support and assist in fundraising for a variety of social causes and community events including Big Brothers of Vancouver, Juvenile Diabetes, United Way, Breast Cancer Research, Boys and Girls Clubs of Vancouver, and the Canadian Cancer Society.

Novex voluntarily reports our social, environmental and economic impacts of our operations through an approach called SEE-IT (Social-Environmental-Economic Integration Toolkit). SEE-IT enables all stakeholders, including employees, clients, suppliers, and the public, to monitor the progress and status of the company's TBL initiatives. The company views SEE-IT as not only a presentation of results but also a way of communication and education about sustainability.

Source: Novex Couriers, "Sustainability," at http:www.novex.c/sustainability and http://www.novex.ca/see-it-how- novex-manages accessed on January 3, 2016. Used with permission of Novex Couriers.

The triple bottom line approach has been criticized as being of limited value and even misleading. Norman and MacDonald argue that conceptually and practically the approach is not helping the discussion of CSR. According to these scholars, the claims made are difficult to assess and amount to misleading rhetoric. The authors claim that the use of the triple bottom line may be providing a smokescreen behind which corporations can avoid ethical and environmental responsibilities and reporting.[21]

LO 7.6   Views on Corporate and Business Citizenship

Corporate citizenship has recently become a commonly used term to describe the role of business in society. The term appears in the academic literature and business media and is used by corporations to describe their activities. Consulting firms promote their version of corporate citizenship and sell services to assist corporations in establishing and describing their citizenship activities. University research centres have been established on the topic, numerous books describe the concept, and there is a *Journal of Corporate Citizenship*.

Despite the common usage of the term, definitions vary. **Corporate citizenship** occurs when a corporation demonstrates that it takes into account its complete impact on society and the environment as well as its economic influence. It concerns the economic, ethical or social, and environmental responsibilities to all stakeholders involved, with consideration given to inputs from various stakeholders and the practices of corporations to develop relationships with stakeholders.

Many justifications for corporate citizenship exist, with one of the most frequently referenced being the "Business Case for Corporate Citizenship" that was posted on the World Economic Forum website.[22] According to this report, good corporate citizenship can provide business benefits in eight areas:

- *Reputation management*—A corporate reputation is built and maintained by fulfilling the expectations of multiple stakeholders.
- *Risk profile and risk management*—Risk is reduced when corporations understand stakeholder concerns.
- *Employee recruitment, motivation, and retention*—Obtaining and keeping employees is made easier for companies known as good corporate citizens.
- *Investor relations and access to capital*—Many investors are interested in non-financial as well as financial performance, and there is a proven link between good corporate citizenship and good financial performance.
- *Learning and innovation*—Corporate citizenship objectives can encourage creativity and innovation.
- *Competitiveness and market positioning*—Increasingly, consumers are inquiring about the corporate citizenship performance of companies and tend to be loyal to those with a good record.
- *Operational efficiency*—A focus on corporate citizenship can lead to direct improvements to the bottom line.
- *Licence to operate*—Companies with a good record of corporate citizenship are given greater leeway when problems occur and are less subject to unfair criticism.

This list illustrates the broad scope of activities and stakeholders that are impacted by corporate citizenship practices, including on a global scale. The report concluded that increasing corporate citizenship was an integral part of good business management. Everyday Ethics 7.3 is an example of how one corporation defines citizenship.

EVERYDAY ETHICS 7.3

Corporate Citizenship at Imperial Oil

Many corporations are utilizing the concept of corporate citizenship to outline their relationship with society. Imperial Oil's "Corporate Citizenship Report" contains information such as:

- a statement of commitment to sustainable development by balancing economic growth, social development, and environmental protection;
- a review of safety management and practices;

- a listing of environmental performance;
- a summary of the economic contribution to the Canadian economy;
- details of community initiatives including community investment, stakeholder engagement, and Aboriginal relations;
- a statement on the approach to governance;
- an evaluation of their corporate citizenship performance using independent indexes.

Source: Adapted from Imperial Oil Limited, "2014 Corporate Citizenship Report," accessed January 4, 2016, http://www.imperialoil.ca/Canada-English/Files/Imperial_CCR_Report_2014.pdf.

The quantity and diversity of the literature on corporate citizenship makes it difficult to concisely review. The following discussion attempts to organize the views that are held regarding corporate citizenship (inappropriate; limited, equivalent, extended; and business). The final section argues that a more appropriate term is *business citizenship*.

The Inappropriate View

Many have posed the questions, "Can the corporation be a citizen?" and "Is a corporate citizen the same as an individual citizen?" The nature of citizenship has its roots in political theory, philosophy, law, sociology, and psychology and is a complex phenomenon that has been discussed and debated for centuries. Individual citizenship involves the relationship of the person to the state, the rights and duties of citizens, and the national and cultural identity involved.[23]

Any attempt to extend the individual's role as a citizen to that of a corporation is thought by many to be completely inappropriate. A corporation is not an individual citizen, as it does not possess the attributes or characteristics of a person. Any attempt to project the qualities of a person to the corporation is false and meaningless. Given the prominence of corporate citizenship in the academic and practitioner spheres, this view is not widely held, although it does have its advocates.

The Limited, Equivalent, and Extended Views

Matten and Crane[24] described three views of corporate citizenship: limited, equivalent, and extended. These views will form the categories of how corporate citizenship is considered. These three views are summarized in Table 7.4, which is followed by an explanation of why "corporate" citizenship would be more appropriately viewed as "business" citizenship.

TABLE 7.4	Three Views of Corporate Citizenship	
Limited	**Equivalent**	**Extended**
Corporate giving or philanthropic responsibility was the focus	Citizenship is defined as what society expects are responsibilities of business	Citizenship is defined as a set of individual, social, civil, and political rights
Reasoning is that something should be given back to the community	Emphasis on sustainability, the stewardship role of business, and the stakeholder approach	Social rights provide the individual with the freedom to participate in society, for example the right to education
Considered to be enlightened self-interest	Considered to be rebranding or re-launching existing ideas and concepts of business–society relations	Civil rights provide freedom from abuses and interference by third parties, for example the right to own property
		Political rights extend beyond the protection of the individual and involve the individual's participation in society, for example the rights to hold office and to vote

Source: Compiled based on Dirk Matten and Andrew Crane, "Corporate Citizenship: Towards an Extended Theoretical Conceptualization," *Academy of Management Review* 30, No. 1 (2005): 168–170. Permission conveyed through Copyright Clearance Center, Inc.

Approach to Corporate Citizenship

Building on the "extended" view that citizenship is based on the shared understanding of basic social, civil, and political rights, a different way of considering corporate citizenship emerges. However, it is questionable whether social and political rights can be regarded as rights of the corporation. Instead, the corporations could be viewed as powerful actors that have a responsibility to respect individual rights.

Globalization has shifted responsibility for protecting citizenship rights away from governments, as seen by the activism of non-governmental organizations (NGOs). Instead of seeking from governments a solution to corporate misdeeds, NGOs pressure corporations directly or indirectly through stakeholders such as consumers and the media. The result is that many social changes are taking place beyond the power and influence of the nation-state. The absence of government initiatives has caused a gap in providing these rights, and corporations are increasingly filling this gap as they are principal actors in society and drivers of globalization.

Matten and Crane[25] cited some examples of change that have resulted as governments ceased to be the only guarantor of citizenship. There are areas where governments cease to administer citizenship rights, and corporations may step in or their role may become more pronounced, as illustrated in privatization and welfare reform. Another occurs where governments have not yet administered citizenship, for example in the regulation of sweatshop working conditions. Lastly, there are areas where the administration of citizenship rights may be beyond the nation-state or government, for example the creation of transnational institutions and global codes of conduct.

In this context, corporate citizenship is described as the role the corporation plays in administering citizenship rights for individuals, moving away from considering the corporation a citizen toward a view where the corporation administers some rights. Corporations would take on this role for altruistic, enlightened self-interest and pure self-interest motivations. This extended role of the corporation is represented in the following diagram:

Social role of the corporation in administering citizenship rights

↓

Social rights: The corporation as a *provider*

+

Civil rights: The corporation as an *enabler*

+

Political rights: The corporation as a *channel*[26]

This view describes the role of the corporation as being involved with administering citizenship rights for individuals rather than as a "citizen" as such. Matten and Crane's summary argument is that:

> We have identified citizenship as an arena where two parties are involved: (1) the state (originally) as the party administering rights of citizenship and (2) the private citizen as the receiver of those rights. We have then argued that corporations have become major actors in this arena. Our extended conceptualization locates CC [corporate citizenship] in the administration of citizenship rights, which, in the liberal view, is clearly an aspect of citizenship. Of course, this does not mean that corporations "are" citizens or that they "have" citizenship, but they are certainly active in citizenship behaviors.[27]

Corporate citizenship is considered at a different level; that is, not at the same level as for a private citizen. This view of corporate citizenship implies that corporations have replaced some of the functions of government as they administer citizenship. Corporations enter this different level on a discretionary or voluntary basis and accountability becomes an issue. The adequacy of such accountability will be discussed later.

The Business View

Wood and Logsdon[28] argue that the term "business citizenship" may better incorporate the broader perspective on business rights and duties, stakeholder relationships, and responses to the opportunities and challenges that accompany the global socio-economy of the twenty-first century. **Business citizenship** includes the responsibilities of corporate citizenship on a local and national basis and extends it to a global or universal scope.

The authors explain the status of citizenship for individuals and then compare this reasoning to the business organization or the corporation. Thus, the individual as citizen is local, community, and national in scope and the relationship of the individual is with the state and involves rights and duties. Today, the individual as citizen is global or universal in scope and concerned with common humanity, interdependence, and universalism, which are less grounded on fixed rules or laws.

Further, the corporation as citizen can be considered as either a "corporate" citizen or a "business" citizen. As a corporate citizen, corporations are a responsible player in local environments, involved with volunteerism, charity, and rights and duties in and for the community. Today, thinking in terms of being a corporate citizen associated with corporate–community relations may be too narrow to represent the depth and variety of business–society relationships. Thus, a "business citizen" would be responsible not only for local actions—that is, concerned with organizations' rights and societies within and across national and/or cultural borders—but also for global or universal actions. Wood and Logsdon provide the rationale for moving from individual citizenship to corporate citizenship by outlining the similarities and differences, and then moving the corporate citizen on a local, community, and national scope to the global or universal scope.[29]

The following quotation summarizes Wood and Logsdon's argument for using "business" instead of "corporate" citizenship:

> *"Business citizenship," . . ., provides an overarching rationale for corporate social performance, for the study of ethics in business, for stakeholder theory and issues management, for business-government relations and for concerns over major social, political and human issues such as labour rights and environmental protection. Business citizenship can be one of the conceptual balance beams of the long-standing paradox of self-interest and other interest, of individual versus collective outcomes.[30]*

This presentation has provided background on the views of corporate and business citizenship in the literature and in practice. Currently, the more widely accepted term is *corporate citizenship*, but the use of business citizenship is considered more appropriate as it avoids the problematic discussion of whether or not the corporation is a citizen. It is also more inclusive as it incorporates the complete business system, including the global nature of business.

LO 7.7 The VBA Model: An Integration of CSR Concepts

Schwartz and Carroll developed a model of the business and society field that integrated and unified five frameworks in common usage by academics and managers: corporate social responsibility (CSR), business ethics (BE), stakeholder management (SM), sustainability (SUS), and corporate citizenship (CC). They named their framework the VBA model and believed that it would reduce the confusion resulting from the existence of the various frameworks. Three core concepts were identified as being common, to some degree, in all frameworks: value, balance, and accountability.[31]

The generation of value to business and society was found to be a fundamental element of all the frameworks. Value results "when business meets society's needs by producing goods and services in an efficient manner while avoiding unnecessary negative externalities."[32] A degree of balance occurs when some effort is made in "addressing and appropriately responding to potentially conflicting stakeholder interests and/or moral standards."[33] Other similar concepts are respect, weigh, trade-off, and satisfy. Accountability is present in all frameworks, meaning that while attempting to fulfill its economic, legal, and ethical responsibilities, business "must acknowledge responsibility for [its] actions and decisions and take steps to rectify failure and prevent them from happening again in the future."[34] The authors note that the three core concepts receive different emphasis in the frameworks, but they are present to some degree.

The VBA model integrating the frameworks is represented by the equation:

Value + Balance + Accountability = Proper Role of Business in Society

Schwartz and Carroll set forth the following normative proposition relating to their VBA model:

> *All organizations and individuals operating within a business context have a responsibility (CSR) as good corporate citizens (CC) to (a) contribute to sustainable societal value (SUS), and (b) appropriately balance stakeholder interests (SM), including shareholders or owners and/or moral standards (BE), while (c) demonstrating sufficient accountability.[35]*

The integration of the five frameworks and three core concepts in the VBA model is portrayed in Figure 7.2. The authors argue that by focusing on three core elements of the five frameworks, the VBA model integrates the shareholder theory and emphasizes the importance of others in managerial decision making while maintaining relevance for managers and ensuring a long-term global prospective.

FIGURE 7.2   *The VBA Model: Five Business and Society Frameworks and Their Three Core Concepts*

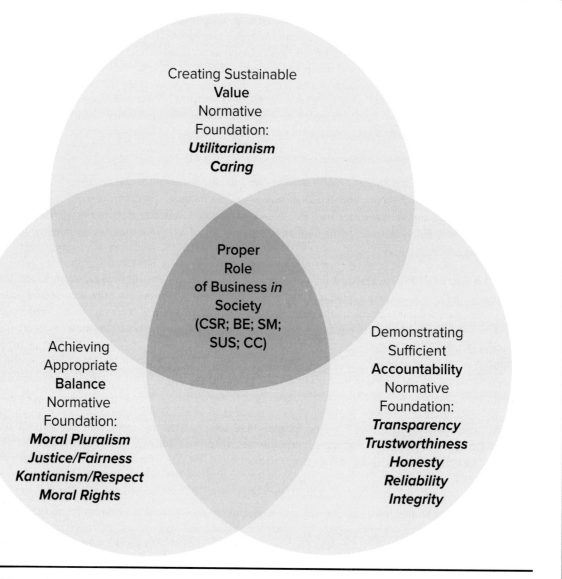

Creating Sustainable **Value** Normative Foundation: *Utilitarianism* *Caring*

Proper Role of Business *in* Society (CSR; BE; SM; SUS; CC)

Achieving Appropriate **Balance** Normative Foundation: *Moral Pluralism* *Justice/Fairness* *Kantianism/Respect* *Moral Rights*

Demonstrating Sufficient **Accountability** Normative Foundation: *Transparency* *Trustworthiness* *Honesty* *Reliability* *Integrity*

Note: VBA = value, balance, accountability; CSR = corporate social responsibility; BE = business ethics; SM = stakeholder management; SUS = sustainability; CC = corporate citizenship.

Source: Mark S. Schwartz and Archie B. Carroll, "Integrating and Unifying Competing and Complementary Frameworks: The Search For a Common Core in the Business and Society Field," *Business and Society*, Volume 47, Number 2, June 2008, 175. Permission conveyed through Copyright Clearance Center, Inc.

The VBA model clarifies the relationships among the various frameworks of corporate social responsibility presented in this chapter. In doing so, the confusion over the terminology should be reduced. The theoretical basis for social responsibility has been outlined, and the following chapters will discuss approaches used by corporations to implement or apply it and the methodologies used to evaluate it.

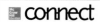 Want to learn about **CSR jobs**?

Your advice to George. . .

George likely feels that he has been let down by the corporation and he likely has doubts about CSR. The issue is whether or not VW's reputation has been damaged so severely that he may not trust the corporation. He has not been personally harmed financially, but the environment is suffering because of VW's deliberate unethical behaviour. The challenge for George is how he can assess and believe the CSR claims of VW and for that matter, the claims of any automobile corporation. Unfortunately, some corporations become so focused on a goal, in this case to become the world's largest car manufacturer, that they are willing to ignore their own CSR policies.

Summary

- Rather than provide one definition of social responsibility, the chapter identifies the elements found in the majority of definitions. Corporate social responsibility is a reflection of the fact that business and society are interwoven and can be expressed in terms of three principles: legitimacy, public responsibility, and managerial discretion. The principle of legitimacy refers to society's granting of legitimacy and authority to business, along with business' appropriate use of that power; the principle of public responsibility means business is responsible for outcomes related to its areas of involvement with society; and the principle of managerial discretion refers to managers as moral actors who are obligated to exercise such discretion as is available to them to achieve socially responsible outcomes. (LO 7.1)

- The debate as to whether social responsibility is an appropriate concept is summarized in arguments for and against corporate social involvement. Arguments for and against corporate social involvement are provided and supported with quotes from recent CSR reports and Milton Friedman. (LO 7.2)

- These arguments are reflected in Klonoski's summary of social responsibility theories, categorized according to three alternative views of the corporation as amoral, personal, and social. The arguments and theories are presented not to provide a definitive answer to the question of corporate social responsibility but to review the background to the debate. In fact, the debate has not been resolved to date, as evidenced by the critique of CSR in a leading business magazine. (LO 7.3)

- A pyramid of corporate social responsibilities is presented, based on economic, legal, ethical, and philanthropic responsibilities. A hierarchy of responsibilities exists; economic and legal obligations are primary and basic. In recent years, the ethical and philanthropic responsibilities have received more attention. (LO 7.4)

- Social responsibility has evolved and today other terminology is being used to describe the concept, including *corporate sustainability, reputation management, social impact management, triple bottom line*, and *corporate citizenship*. Definitions are provided so that a distinction can be made among the terms. (LO 7.5)

- Corporate citizenship is another term used interchangeably with CSR. It is an inclusive term to capture the economic, social, and environmental responsibilities of the corporation and relies on stakeholder theory. As with CSR various interpretations are given to the term, and it is argued that the term *business citizenship* would be even more inclusive as it is global or universal in scope. (LO 7.6)

- The VBA model is an attempt at unifying and integrating the various frameworks within CSR around three core concepts: value, balance, and accountability. This model reduces the confusion resulting from the various terminology used in the business and society and CSR field. (LO 7.7)

Key Terms

Corporate social responsibility (CSR)

Corporate sustainability (CS)

Reputation management

Social impact management

Triple-E (economic, ethical, and environmental) bottom line

Corporate citizenship

Business citizenship

Critical Thinking and Discussion Questions

1. Why should corporations and their management be concerned with corporate social responsibility?

2. Distinguish among Wood's three principles of corporate responsibility: legitimacy, public responsibility, and managerial discretion.

3. Why do some corporations and their management oppose corporate social responsibility?

4. Is there any legitimacy to the argument put forth by Milton Friedman and *The Economist*'s article on corporate social responsibility?

5. Social responsibility is interpreted in many ways. State your understanding of corporate social responsibility.

6. List the ten stakeholders you think have the greatest influence on a corporation's social responsibility.

7. Can the corporation have a conscience?

8. Do you agree that "economic responsibilities" are a component of corporate social responsibility?

9. What does a corporation have to do to have a "good" reputation?

10. Is the corporation a "citizen" of society?

Cases

7.1 WOULD YOU LIKE TO DONATE ...?

Suzanne Valentine had been noticing an increasing number of businesses asking their customers to donate to charities when they make a purchase, a practice known as checkout charity or point of sale fundraising. One example was the Shoppers Drug Mart "SHOPPERS LOVE. YOU" campaign, which encourages customers to purchase a leaf for $1, a butterfly for $5, an apple for $10 or a bird for $100. All proceeds go directly to the women's health organizations chosen by each Associate-owner, best reflecting local community needs. Over the past five years, $57 million has been contributed to local, regional and national women's health initiatives.

Many other corporations have similar programs including Indigo, Loblaw, Walmart, and McDonald's. Even Governor General David Johnston's "My Giving Moment" encourages participating in such programs.

Suzanne was directly affected by this type of corporate social responsibility fundraising. She worked part-time as a cashier at her neighbourhood grocery store where the owner established a donation scheme, "Pennies for Pets." The owner was a strong supporter of animal causes and the donations were to support the local animal shelter. All cashiers were instructed to ask customers if they wanted to donate $1 or $2 to the shelter.

Suzanne followed instructions but she had several reservations about the scheme. She felt awkward asking customers for the donation, particularly those who looked like they could not afford it. Some customers might be intimidated by the request and she did not believe that they should be put on the spot to say yes or no. Some customers may not wish to support this particular charity. As well, she was not convinced that the particular shelter deserved funding, as there had been some articles in the media about its poor management and treatment of animals. Lastly, she was not sure how much of the money collected was forwarded to the charity, and whether or not the owner matched the customer donations.

Questions

1. What are the ethical implications in this example of corporate social responsibility?
2. What information should the company provide to Suzanne and its customers?
3. Carroll has identified four corporate social responsibilities: economic, legal, ethical, and philanthropic. Which responsibilities are involved in "Pennies for Pets" or similar fundraising schemes?
4. How should Suzanne resolve her personal ethical dilemma?

Sources: Shoppers Drug Mart Inc., "Growing Women's Health," accessed July 19, 2016, http://www.shoppersloveyou.ca/events/growing-womens-health-1026; and The Governor General of Canada, His Excellency the Right Honourable David Johnston, accessed July 19, 2016, http://www.gg.ca/document.aspx?id=15397.

7.2 THE TD GRADE ONE BOOK GIVEAWAY

The TD Bank Group (TD) supports several initiatives to encourage literacy and reading in Canada. TD believes that literacy is a key skill for the future. In 2000, TD established the Grade One Book Giveaway program after consulting ministries of education, school boards, and library organizations. The program is organized by the Canadian Children's Book Centre (CCBC), a not-for-profit organization dedicated "to the encouraging, promoting and supporting reading, writing and illustrating of Canadian books for young readers." CCBC focuses on books published in Canada and it is committed "to raising awareness and the quality and variety of Canadian books for young readers."

The program is the largest free-book program to school aged children in Canada. About 500,000 Grade 1 English and French students receive the book compliments of TD. They can keep the book and take it home to read with their parents and caregivers. The book distribution is supported by an author/illustrator reading tour across Canada. The books' printing and distribution costs are paid for by the bank and their logo appears on the front cover. Inside there is short letter from TD's CEO.

There has been some opposition to the program. In 2013, some school boards claimed that the books are corporate advertising and should not be distributed in the classroom. The boards claimed that it forces students to be exposed to advertising. As a result, the free book was not distributed in the classrooms that year but was made available at local public libraries in the area.

Defenders of the program state that the book has nothing to do with banking. Many Grade 1 students do not even know the letters T and D and the logo means nothing. The defenders suggest that the school boards have lost sight of their mission, that is, literacy. They state that there are all kinds of issues in the educational system and this is not one worthy of discussion.

Questions

1. Will the program promote a love of reading and a passion for books?
2. In whose best interests are the books being distributed?
3. Is TD being purely altruistic?
4. Are there other corporate programs there this issue exists?

Sources: TD Grade One Book Giveaway at https://tdreads.com/home/td-supported-initiatives/td-grade-one-book-giveaway/ accessed January 12, 2016; Canadian Children's Book Centre accessed January 12, 2016, http://www.bookcentre.ca/about; and Tristan Hopper, "School Spurn Free Books over Bank Logo: Keep Eye on The Prize, and The Prize is Children's Literacy," *National Post*, November 13, 2013, A1.

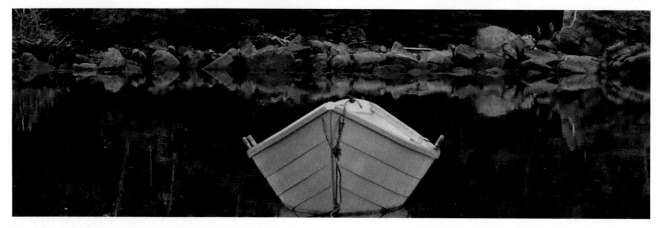

Used with the permission of Dennis Flynn

CHAPTER 8

Corporate Social Responsibility: In Practice

LEARNING OUTCOMES

After studying this chapter, you will be able to:

LO 8.1 Identify the different responses to corporate social responsibility.

LO 8.2 Define corporate philanthropy and describe the forms it takes.

LO 8.3 Define corporate voluntarism and describe the implications for employees, employers, and the community.

LO 8.4 Define corporate sponsorship and identify trends in this approach to CSR.

LO 8.5 Define social venture philanthropy and understand this approach to CSR.

LO 8.6 Explain what a social enterprise is and what social entrepreneurship means.

LO 8.7 Appreciate the challenges confronting small businesses in practising CSR.

LO 8.8 Understand the community investment approach to CSR.

What would you do if...?

Walter Zuberek once read a quote from Warren Buffett: "Giving money away is easy. Giving money away well is fiendishly difficult." He was learning just what Buffett meant.

Walter has just stepped down as CEO of York and Smith Limited after being associated with the company for 50 years. Walter came to Canada from Europe in the 1950s and went to work as an engineer for a small construction company known as York Construction. Over the years, the company expanded and acquired a building materials company from the Smith family, which led to the name change to York and Smith. Walter started as a site foreman, but steadily rose in the company as the owners recognized his managerial abilities. In the mid-1960s, the owners decided to sell the business and Walter was able to purchase it with financial assistance from a venture capitalist.

York and Smith grew into a $200 million a year business that manufactured and distributed building products for North American construction markets. The company served four construction market sectors: residential (both new construction and renovations), non-residential, agricultural and industrial storage, and infrastructure. The company believed in operating in a socially and ethically responsible manner and in providing the broadest possible opportunity for personal and professional development for its employees. The company also believed in giving back to the community and supported hospital and university capital fund campaigns, literacy programs, sports programs for the disabled, and school lunch programs.

Walter's two sons now run the business, but Walter provides some oversight as chair of the board of directors. Because he is not as closely associated with the day-to-day operations, Walter has time to pay more attention to things that are of interest to him. He considers himself fortunate to have worked for York and Smith and to have been able to acquire the business. He is grateful for the opportunities provided in Canada, and appreciates the support he has received from various stakeholders over the years.

York and Smith Limited is experiencing good financial returns, with some discretionary funds available for social responsibility endeavours. Walter himself has accumulated a small fortune and wonders what to do with the money beyond leaving some to family members. He thought maybe it was appropriate to give something back to society.

Now that Walter is retired, a reassessment of the company's social contributions would be a good job for him, and at the same time he could investigate what he could do with his fortune. He wants to make sure the company's—and his—contributions to society are used in the most effective and efficient manner. This is a challenge, as Charity Intelligence Canada points out. There are issues about which charities to select, how the charities will spend the donation, and what the charities will achieve. Alternatively, Walter could set up a new charity for a cause that he and his family support.

What is your advice to Walter?

This chapter describes the various forms or approaches to practising or implementing corporate social responsibility (CSR) or corporate sustainability (CS) in corporations. Corporate social responsibility and the related concepts described in Chapter 7 have resulted in a range of activities. Large corporations have CSR or equivalent departments, with staff trained in the area that oversees the implementation of CSR initiatives. Corporate websites often contain details of all CSR activities. Professional associations provide advice to corporations, as do various newsletters. In addition, numerous consultant services are available to assist with CSR activities.

Corporations have moved from expressing CSR through corporate philanthropy in the form of donations to other approaches involving some form of direct community involvement or investment. Corporate giving, or donations, is the most traditional approach and is still practised. Many corporations now view writing a cheque to be insufficient or inappropriate to demonstrate their commitment to the community.

Corporations are now involved in voluntarism programs and corporate sponsorship in addition to donations. Recently, as corporations seek more effective approaches to contributing to the community, two forms of CSR have emerged: social venture philanthropy and social enterprise. Today, many corporations are involved in more than one of these approaches to CSR, with corporate philanthropy being the most common. In addition, the final section of this chapter will discuss CSR in small business as a separate topic. It should be noted that the corporation's CSR toward the environment is not dealt with in this chapter but is the focus in Chapter 14.

LO 8.1   Responses to Corporate Social Responsibility

Despite the widespread acceptance and practise of CSR, business enterprises are responding to it in different ways. Table 8.1 identifies business responses to CSR, beginning with high acceptance and declining to little or none.

The businesses most committed to CSR are social enterprises, which will be defined in a later section. Such businesses practise the *social paradigm*, which can be described as "Doing well by doing good." This means that the corporation will undertake socially desirable activities that will result in its doing well economically. There appear to be an increasing number of businesses responding to CSR in this manner. This approach is the highest level of CSR acceptance.

TABLE 8.1   Responses to CSR

Response	Explanation	Acceptance of CSR
Social enterprise—social return	Organizations that operate with a social mission without the intention of operating to make profits with all earnings committed to social causes or projects. Example: Habitat for Humanity, Goodwill	High
Social enterprise—mixed return	Organizations that operate with a social mission but with the intention of making a profit. "Doing well by doing good" (social paradigm). A portion of profits are committed to social causes or projects with the remainder reinvested or returned to owners. Examples: Whole Foods Market Inc. and Value Village	High
CSR recognition or embracers	CSR and sustainability placed high on corporate agenda. Often are larger corporations and traded on stock exchanges. Corporate giving and citizenship are involved. Publish "social reports" of their initiatives. "Doing good by doing well" (economic paradigm).	Above average
Cautious CSR adaptors	Recognize CSR and sustainability but focus on savings from environmental projects, energy cost reductions, material efficiency, and risk reduction.	Some recognition
Tokenism or greenwashing	Corporations are not serious about CSR, but believe they should respond. Might be forced into initiatives by non-governmental organizations (NGOs), the media, or competitors. NGOs allege many multinational corporations are responding this way.	Low commitment
Amoral	Corporations, and their managers, simply ignore CSR, intentionally or unintentionally. Difficult to identify and measure numbers.	Very little, by chance, or legal requirement
Anti-CSR	As CSR is widely accepted and practised, it is unlikely that these corporations will identify themselves as being anti-CSR. Difficult to identify numbers.	Very little, most likely as required by law
Unknown	Businesses about which not much is known regarding CSR initiatives, including small business enterprises and privately held companies. There is a modest literature on CSR in these types of enterprises.	Low, but not documented

Many businesses are recognizing CSR as an essential aspect of management. Usually, these businesses audit their activities and report them to relevant stakeholders. This response is based on the *economic paradigm*, which can be described as "Doing good by doing well." This means that the corporation will do well economically and then undertake to do good socially.

The tokenism response is the one alleged by some non-governmental organizations (NGOs) when they evaluate CSR programs. An example is the report published by Christian Aid, an agency of churches in the United Kingdom and Ireland, entitled *Behind the Mask: The Real Face of Corporate Social Responsibility*. This report challenges the effectiveness of CSR efforts by multinational companies. It claims to have revealed the true face of CSR—a false image and public relations. The following quotation is an illustration of the argument:

In simple terms, companies make loud, public commitments to principles of ethical behaviour and undertake "good works" in the communities in which they operate. It sounds and looks like a modern version of selfless philanthropy and no doubt in many individual cases is motivated by a genuine wish to help and has led to some benefits. What's different is that companies frequently use such initiatives to defend operations or ways of working which come in for public criticism.[1]

An amoral response is illustrated by several views of CSR. Managers believe that a corporation has no or very little social responsibility, or that the corporation is an autonomous entity and not the creation of society. Others believe that the corporation is socially responsible only within the limits of a prior contractual agreement with shareholders. Finally, the traditional shareholder model argues that corporations are not ethically required to be socially responsible and their only responsibility is to maximize profits. This view is closely related to the fourth response, anti-CSR. Since CSR is a widely accepted conventional wisdom, those opposing it are unlikely to be vocal.

Lastly, the CSR response "unknown" has not been widely studied. Two examples are privately held corporations and small businesses. Small business will be discussed later in the chapter.

Not responding to society's demands for CSR can be risky. Several of these risks are listed in Table 8.2, emphasizing the need for corporations to plan their CSR initiatives.

When corporations are involved with CSR in some manner, there is a need to establish a planning process if the effort is to be most effective. To start with, there must be commitment from top management, including the board of directors. Without this commitment, any CSR efforts are unlikely to be as successful as they might be. Small as well as large businesses can plan for CSR although there is media coverage of large corporation activities. CSR also involves many stakeholders both internal and external to the corporation that should be involved in the process. The following sections describe some of the CSR approaches that are being undertaken by businesses.

TABLE 8.2	Risks of Not Practising CSR

The risks associated with not practising CSR include:

Damaged reputation

- Negative media coverage
- Consumer boycotts
- Lost sales and revenues
- Labour disruptions
- Blockages, attacks against assets
- Decrease in share value
- More onerous financing or insurance terms

Increased spending to remedy past damage for core activities

- Increased shareholder activism
- Failure to attract and retain quality employees
- Civil lawsuits, including class-action initiatives
- Criminal and regulatory prosecution

Suspended operating permits

- Liability for the conduct of subsidiaries and arm's-length affiliates, for example suppliers
- Increased and onerous government regulation

Source: Compiled from the December 2003 issue of Canadian Business for Social Responsibility's *Good Company Newsletter*, and other sources.

 Want to learn more about **the most socially responsible corporations in Canada?**

LO 8.2   Corporate Philanthropy

Corporate philanthropy is the effort of business to contribute to society socially and is manifested by donations of money or goods and services in kind; voluntarism, where corporate employees work for social causes; and sponsorship of events that contribute to society. Also referred to as corporate giving, philanthropy takes many forms. Three of these forms are discussed here: corporate giving, or the making of donations; support for employee voluntarism; and sponsorship of social events and causes.

Donations

Canadian business corporations donate to a variety of causes and organizations, including health and welfare agencies, educational institutions, community services, service clubs, civic projects, arts and culture groups, athletic organizations, and environmental groups. Some corporations spread contributions across a variety of causes, while others are more focused in their giving. In addition to the donation of money, corporate giving or philanthropy can involve the donation of goods and services. Imagine Canada gives some idea of the magnitude of corporate giving; more than $2.3 billion was given in charitable donations by corporations that claimed it on their tax returns.[2] The industries that gave the most were finance and insurance, and manufacturing. The majority of the support went to three non-profit sectors: sports and recreation; grant making, fundraising, and voluntarism; and arts and culture.

Most Canadians believe corporations have a responsibility to provide support to charities and non-profit organizations, as illustrated in Everyday Ethics 8.1. This section provides arguments for and against corporate giving, examines how the decision to donate is made, and indicates trends in corporate giving.

EVERYDAY ETHICS 8.1

Corporate Donations: Cameco Corporation

Cameco is one of the largest uranium producers, accounting for 18 percent of world production from its mines in Canada and the United States. Its target is to donate 1 percent of after-tax net earnings. The corporation supports dozens of community projects, large and small, and believes that it makes a difference. Although Cameco's community investment takes several forms, the list below identifies the focuses on its donations to the community.

- *Youth*—Supports youth projects from preschool to high school.
- *Education and Literacy*—Provides support because education and literacy benefit society.
- *Health and Wellness*—Supports projects that improve access to health services.
- *Community Development*—Helps to build sustainable communities by contributing to their prosperity and quality of life.

Source: Adapted from "Community," Cameco Corporation, accessed January 4, 2016, https://www.cameco.com/community. Used with permission.

Arguments For and Against Corporate Giving

The arguments for and against corporate giving are similar to those for social responsibility. Corporate giving is a widely used and acceptable approach to express social responsibility to the community and to show that business is not just concerned with society as a market for its goods and services. The act of corporate giving promotes an image of good citizenship and creates goodwill. This is important for the acceptance of business by society either in terms of legitimacy or a social licence to operate. Most businesspersons recognize that the volunteer sector provides some services very efficiently, and that even business enterprises benefit from such services—as, for example, when employees belong to Alcoholics Anonymous.

Corporations receive significant benefits from a corporate community investment program in terms of employee commitment, corporate reputation, marketing visibility, and relationships with customers, suppliers, neighbours, and governments. It is argued that a corporation's success is tightly linked with economic health and social conditions in the community in which it operates, and thus a corporation should invest in the organizations that underpin community vitality.

Not everyone accepts the argument that business should be involved with corporate giving. It is argued that the funds given actually belong to shareholders, and it is presumptuous first for management to make the decision to give the funds, and then to choose particular recipients. Some claim that business corporations should not become involved with social welfare because that is the job of governments. Support for social causes could give business even more power in society at a time when many feel that it already has too much. By supporting any cause or charitable organization the corporation might become accountable for the actions taken by the charity, or adverse publicity could damage the corporation's image or reputation. Usually there are no guidelines, no standards to measure against, and no evaluation process for making decisions and monitoring corporate giving. The benefits of corporate giving are seldom measurable or directly related to the corporation.

Despite the arguments against corporate giving, most businesses, including small ones, are involved with corporate giving in some way.

Making Corporate Giving Decisions

In earlier times, corporate giving decisions were made by individual executives who often were members of the family at the helm of a corporation—the Eatons, Woodwards, Burtons, Molsons, and Labatts. This is still the case today as many wealthy individuals contribute large amounts to society.

On the other hand, many large corporations make donation decisions by committee consensus where the process is more complicated. In the most formalized processes, decisions relating to corporate giving are made in head offices by chief executives and boards of directors with assistance from a committee. The first decision relates to the donations budget. Budgets are set as a percentage of expected pre-tax profit, increased an arbitrary amount from the previous year, set in relation to industry norms or in comparison to peers, or set upon a formula based on number of employees. Assistance is available from several organizations, including the ones listed in Responsibility for Ethics 8.1. These organizations provide advice to individual executives and corporations including evaluations of a charity's efficiency and use of funds.

Some corporations carefully establish the objectives for giving so that some guidelines are available to ascertain how much money is given and to whom. Criteria for evaluating requests are formulated and used by in-house staff or consultants in making decisions. Some givers perform cost–benefit analyses of the grant, while others require that social performance programs be proactive. Grants given in one year are evaluated prior to another grant being made. Some corporate givers, such as Imperial Oil Ltd. and John Labatt Ltd., have managers to supervise the process. Despite the formalization suggested above, the single most important influence in the decision-making process is still often the chair of the board or the chief executive officer (CEO).

RESPONSIBILITY FOR ETHICS 8.1

Organizations Assisting in Corporate Philanthropy

Organizations outside the corporation that provide advice on corporate giving or donations include:

Imagine Canada (formerly the Canadian Centre for Philanthropy)—Established in 1980, the Centre's mission is to promote the generous application of charitable time and funds, and to strengthen the philanthropic community of Canada through research and training. The Centre initiated the IMAGINE program, a Canada-wide corporate and individual awareness program, to increase support for charitable non-profit organizations.

MoneySense—Each year this magazine and website evaluates the 100 largest charities in Canada on efficiency and where the money is spent.

Charity Intelligence Canada—This organization provides advice to donors and helps them identify which charities should receive money, how the donations are spent, and what the charities achieve.

Better Business Bureau (BBB) Canada—Corporations wishing to donate can check out charities to ascertain whether they comply with the BBB's Wise Giving Alliance *Charitable Accountability Standards*. Information provided about the charity includes how it is governed, how the money is spent, the truthfulness of their representatives, and their willingness to disclose information to the public.

Either through formal or ad hoc processes, decisions are made to fund—or to reject—requests. A request is typically rejected when policy excludes a particular type of project or charity; there are not enough funds; a donation has already been made to an organization with parallel services; the organization is located outside the corporation's community; there is no Canada Revenue Agency registration number; there are inadequate financial statements; no new approaches are being accepted; the size of the request is too large; or the corporation receives too many requests.

Another form of rejection is the decision to cease giving to a particular organization. Such a decision may have serious consequences, including the failure of the organization. Many causes are rejected because they are somehow controversial. For example, many corporations are reluctant to support Planned Parenthood organizations because of possible backlash from pro-life groups. There is without doubt a tendency to seek out "safe" causes on the part of those who make the donating decision.

Trends and Concerns in Corporate Giving

A number of trends and concerns have occurred that have affected corporate giving. Large requests from institutions such as universities and hospitals have resulted in a higher portion of the donation budget being committed to five-year programs. This doesn't leave much opportunity to fund new causes or groups.

Business corporations in Canada are supporting a wide variety of charities, and this support has become much more important as government grants have declined. For those corporations that donate on a regular basis, philanthropy is a responsibility, a part of the cost of doing business. For other corporations, it is a frill. Some corporations support charities while they are experiencing good financial performance but in economic downturns or recessions reduce or stop corporate giving. It appears that some corporations are willing to give, but are becoming more selective and will have to be convinced to part with their money.

Some businesses or their owners choose to set up charitable foundations to handle corporate philanthropy. A **charitable foundation** is defined as a corporation or trust that is constituted and operated exclusively for charitable purposes. They are established by families of successful entrepreneurs, corporations, communities, special interest groups such as schools and hospitals, and governments. There are about 3,000 grant-making foundations in Canada that donate about $1.3 billion to a wide variety of causes including education, health, environment, community development, and arts and culture (see the examples provided in Everyday Ethics 8.2).

Some of the strongest supporters of charitable organizations in Canada produce products that are not considered socially desirable by some—for example, tobacco, beer, and liquor. At issue is whether a group should be associated with the consumption of these products. Society might even find such support unacceptable. For example, in 1987 the federal government proposed legislation to prohibit the advertising and promotion of tobacco products. Yet corporations in the tobacco industry have been innovative and imaginative in their support of the arts. Groups that received support from the tobacco industry may find it difficult to obtain other sources of funding.

The trend to "marketing" and "business" orientations in supporting charities has raised concern. Marketing can be viewed as being "too commercial," as products or services are being directly promoted. Also, conditions can be placed on support, which is considered a threat to artistic or administrative freedom. Support may be given to activities and events where a marketing tie-in is possible, while other activities are neglected.

Some corporate giving is conditional on non-profit organizations becoming more efficient. The argument is that since corporations are tightening their belts, charitable organizations must also become more efficient. Included in this request for efficiency are demands that organizations share resources, avoid duplication, and reduce administrative costs. Charities must develop strategic plans, information and control systems, and generally improve their administrative systems.

Thus, pressure is on charities to produce returns, to be more accountable, and to ensure high visibility for their corporate supporters. Managers of charities argue that this restricts their activities and might prevent them from achieving their objectives. Corporations are also focusing their support on particular programs, projects, or events and are reluctant to provide support for basic operating expenses, placing even more pressure on the charitable organizations.

Another trend is toward **cause-related marketing**, where the purchase of a particular product results in a donation being made by the corporation to a non-profit organization's program. For example, the purchase of a particular brand of frozen vegetables results in a contribution to a food bank, or the purchase of a cake mix helps to fund a health cause. There are several criticisms of this approach, as it pushes philanthropy past even the marketing aspect of sponsorship.

EVERYDAY ETHICS 8.2

Philanthropy through Charitable Foundations

Philanthropic Foundations Canada (PFC) is a national membership organization for Canada's independent grant-making foundations and is a registered charity. There are about 10,000 public and private foundations in Canada that give away about $4.5 billion per year. Examples of foundations established by businesspersons are:

- The J.W. McConnell Family Foundation (various businesses including newspapers):

  The Foundation is a private family foundation funding programs to foster a more inclusive, sustainable, and resilient society The Foundation's purpose is to enhance Canada's ability to address complex social, environmental and economic challenges.

- The Birks Family Foundation (jewellery retailing):

  The mission of the Birks Family Foundation is to contribute to a higher standard of living and quality of life for all Canadians. It funds Canadian universities through capital campaigns and other special projects; hospitals, health services, long-term care institutions and specialized health organizations; social service agencies; and arts organizations that promote the development and understanding of Canadian culture.

- Donner Canadian Foundation (petroleum):

  The Donner Canadian Foundation funds public policy research and supports environmental, international development, and social service projects. Every year, the Donner Book Prize honours the best book on Canadian public policy.

Sources: Compiled from Philanthropic Foundations Canada, http://www.pfc.ca/; The J.W. McConnell Family Foundation, http://www.mcconnellfoundation.ca/en/about; The Birks Family Foundation, http://www.birksfamilyfoundation.ca/Index.htm; and the Donner Canadian Foundation, http://www.donnerfoundation.org/. All accessed January 4, 2016.

Cause-related marketing is considered another way of making a profit, and there are fears that it will replace philanthropy by reducing the amount of no-strings corporate giving. The selection of causes is problematic. Safe, non-controversial causes are selected that will sell, and some companies base their selection of charities on opinion polls conducted to ascertain the most popular causes.

This approach to corporate giving is likely to continue as government funding declines, making commercial tie-ins inviting to managers of non-profit organizations. For business, it makes their product stand out, and if they can associate with the correct "hot" causes sales performance improves. Target audiences are chosen and promotional strategies are selected, making corporate giving "like selling soap suds," according to some critics. These critics question whether self-interested charitable investment or strategic giving is not becoming self-serving commercial activity.

Overall, these trends or concerns have given rise to **strategic giving**, an attempt to rationalize the shareholder interest with corporate philanthropy where the corporation benefits directly from the funds given. Some believe it is really shareholders' money that is being given away. To avoid complaints from shareholders, management should act in enlightened self-interest as a counterargument to the profit maximization position of shareholders. Thus, strategic giving is donating with an eye to the corporation's eventual best interests.[3]

Strategic giving leads corporations to make contributions within their own areas of interest. For example, funding of educational programs would be considered appropriate, as would support for a park facility that could be used by employees and their families. This enlightened self-interest, however, may not lead to support for women's shelters or housing for the poor, where the benefits to the corporation are not as evident. Although strategic giving is a way of justifying philanthropy consistent with shareholder interests, it would require managers to walk an ethical tightrope when rationalizing their proposals for support of particular charities.

LO 8.3   Corporate Voluntarism

Corporate voluntarism is the time and talent employees commit to community organizations with support and/or consent from employers who recognize the value of such efforts to society. Corporations view voluntarism as giving something back to the community and society beyond monetary donations. In addition to employees, corporations now support the voluntary activities of retirees. An example of voluntarism is given in Everyday Ethics 8.3.

EVERYDAY ETHICS 8.3

Volunteerism at TELUS Corporation

As a part of its commitment to corporate citizenship, TELUS has encouraged employees and retirees to donate their time to personal causes and community volunteer work for ten years. In fact, "since its inception in 2006, TELUS Days of Giving has racked up over 337,000 hours of making our communities both here and abroad a better place. Team members, retirees, family and friends have made up over 112,000 passionate participants who 'give where they live'." Volunteerism activities have resulted in:

- 715 bags of waste collected from river valleys, parks, and fields
- 10,179 meals prepared or served to the homeless and those in need
- 40,239 pounds of food sorted at food banks
- 6,822 trees and plants planted in parks and gardens
- 12,670 Kits for Kids school supplies assembled for students in inner city schools
- 5,834 Comfort Kits and charity relief kits assembled for the homeless and others in need
- 131,295 breast cancer ribbons tied for the Canadian Breast Cancer Foundation
- 69 cans of paint used to refresh local communities
- 42,574 books sorted for local book drives

Source: TELUS Corporation, "Sustainability Report 2015." TELUS Corporation, accessed July 27, 2016, https://sustainability.telus.com/en/community-investment/celebrating-a-decade-of-giving/. Used with permission.

The principle of voluntarism is well established in society, and there is a continuing need to recruit and motivate members of society to support the many voluntary organizations. Employee voluntarism has become more important for two reasons: the decline of the professional volunteer of the past, the homemaker who did not work outside the home; and the increasing need for volunteers to serve. The former point results from more women working, and the latter refers to the increasing load on volunteers during cutbacks in government support and greater demand from an aging population.

There are benefits to employers, employees, and, of course, the non-profit organizations involved. But there also can be drawbacks, especially for employers and employees. Many of these benefits and drawbacks for the parties are summarized in Table 8.3.

The general benefits for employers include the creation of a better community environment, and opportunities for employee team building and corporate image building. For employees, general benefits are that the personal involvement improves the quality of life in the community; that contacts are made with community members, especially helpful to new employees in an area; and that an educational and broadening experience is received.

Organizations Supported and Forms of Support

A majority of corporations support voluntary activities and encourage employees to become involved in the community. Voluntary activities that are encouraged involve organizations such as the United Way, professional associations, business and trade associations, the Chamber of Commerce, service clubs, Junior Achievement, and community athletic groups. Several voluntary activities are usually excluded from employer support, for example working for trade unions (not in collective agreement), political parties, religious groups, and special interest advocacy groups.

TABLE 8.3   Employee Voluntarism: Advantages and Disadvantages

ADVANTAGES

- Benefits employee morale by enhancing professional skill development, providing a learning experience, and providing a personal experience
- Good for the community
- Good for the organizations supported
- Improves the corporation's local and national image or profile
- Good for the overall environment in which employees, customers, and the corporation must operate
- Can contribute to corporate team building, employee involvement initiatives, and employee retention
- Sets a good example
- Helps employees integrate with the community, provides a source of contacts or a network, and encourages a sense of community commitment

DISADVANTAGES

- Possible employee resentment at perceived coercion to participate
- Possible distractions from the job, corporate objectives
- Cost in dollars and time
- Implication of picking "winners" or "losers" from among community organizations; that is, deciding which to support
- Possibility of controversy over objectives of some voluntary organization reflecting adversely on the corporation
- Some employees may overcommit themselves, impacting upon job performance
- A controversy involving the efforts of an employee volunteer may reflect unfavourably on the corporation

Sources: Based on Peter M. Brophey, "Corporate Voluntarism: Putting Something Back," *Canadian Business Review* (Spring 1987); Julie Traves, "What Goes Around . . . Corporate Volunteering Boosts the Bottom Line," *Canadian Business,* January 31–February 13, 2005, 67–68; and Shirley Won, "Doing Good Helps You Do Well at Work," *The Globe and Mail,* January 19, 2005, C1.

The forms of support given to voluntary activities include providing facilities, allowing time off or schedule adjustments, assisting with personal expenses incurred while undertaking voluntary activities, extending special recognition to employees exhibiting outstanding performances, and issuing letters of thanks. Many corporations do not consider support and recognition for volunteer work to be an element in the regular performance review process. However, many corporate recruiters consider voluntary experience when assessing a candidate for employment.

Corporate Policies Regarding Voluntarism

Many corporations do not allow employee voluntarism to just exist without some policies formulated to serve as guidelines in the activity. Some corporate actions that would encourage involvement in the Volunteering section of their policies:

- Provide information for new employees on available volunteer organizations and opportunities.
- Provide recognition or awards to employees who volunteer in order to spur additional employee involvement.
- Encourage employees to volunteer via corporate-sponsored loaned executive and paid leave programs (a recent practice in this area is described in Everyday Ethics 8.4).
- Supporte programs for retirees.
- Establish formal programs and designating someone to give administrative support.

EVERYDAY ETHICS 8.4

Corporate Service Corps

A recent form of voluntarism is "corporate service corps" set up by some corporations where employees donate their time to working on development projects in various countries. The IBM Corporate Service Corps was launched in 2008 as a corporate version of the Peace Corps and has involved 2,400 employees in projects. It is viewed as a form of training for global employees in addition to providing assistance in developing countries. IBM cooperates with various non-governmental organizations (NGOs) to place its volunteers, and placements are usually for only a few weeks. Other corporations with similar programs include Novartis Pharmaceuticals Corporation, Dow Corning Corporation, and FedEx.

A Canadian initiative is "Leave for Change" operated by the Uniterra Program, a joint effort of the Centre for International Studies and Cooperation (CECI) and the World University Service of Canada (WUSC) and financially supported by the Canadian International Development Agency (CIDA). It is a corporate volunteering initiative that enables employees to spend a period on assignment in a developing country. Employers support the programs by investing in their human resources and because it demonstrates their social responsibility. Benefits are afforded to communities, employees, and the corporation. Communities receive pro bono help in solving problems confronting them economically, socially, and environmentally. Having the volunteers work in the communities increases international understanding. Benefits for the employee volunteers include gaining leadership training, experience in emerging countries, an opportunity to develop new knowledge and skills, and possibly increased job satisfaction. Corporations obtain insights into potential markets, and their employees obtain new skills and knowledge of developing countries.

It is questioned whether these volunteer placements of only a few weeks can accomplish much. Communities may be overwhelmed by enthusiastic volunteers promoting North American approaches to local problems. Projects may fail, creating ill will and not solving the problems of the communities.

Sources: Adapted from IBM, "Corporate Service Corps," accessed January 4, 2016, http://www.ibm.com/ibm/responsibility/corporateservicecorps/programdetails.html; and Uniterra, Leave for Change®, accessed January 4, 2016, http://uniterra.ca/en/partnership/leave-for-change.

Policies on voluntarism are of three types: encouraging, enabling, and promoting. Encouraging policy statements set the tone or position of the corporation relating to employee voluntarism, and are positive statements about the value of volunteer activities. Enabling policies provide guidelines to managers and employees regarding the implementation of the positive policy. They often set the boundaries and establish procedures relating to voluntarism; for example, the policy relating to a leave of absence to work for a voluntary organization. Overall, enabling policies facilitate the participation of employees in voluntary activity. The third policy category promotes participation in voluntary activity. These promoting policies recognize and reward employee achievement in voluntary activities. Taken together, these types of policies encourage employee voluntarism in Canada.

Employee voluntarism is most successful where top management, especially the chief executive officer, indicate it is a worthy and commendable activity. Top management support is vital for the corporate volunteer program to succeed. Employee voluntarism has endured even through the difficulties created by the economic downturns and will continue to be a significant way in which corporations contribute to the communities where they operate.

connect   Want to learn more about **Canadian corporate volunteerism?**

LO 8.4   Corporate Sponsorship

Corporate sponsorship is defined as "a partnership, which has been established for mutual benefit between a business sponsor and an event or a non-profit."[4] A distinction should be made between corporate donations and sponsorship. A donation is a gift that goes one way, from a corporation to a charity, while a sponsorship, whether a single event or a series of events, confers benefits on both parties.

Sponsorship covers a wide range of sport, cultural, and educational events. There are also examples of extending corporate sponsorship programs to such social concerns as literacy, race relations, drug abuse, and environmental issues. Sponsorship provides a definite link between business and social issues.

Charity or Marketing?

Some acknowledge that corporate sponsorship has little to do with charity, donations, or philanthropy but instead is a business or marketing arrangement. Yet companies often mention sponsorships in "Involvement in or Contribution to the Community" sections of their annual or social reports. The trend toward sponsorships has been found to be attractive for a variety of reasons, including:

- favourable media exposure or publicity;
- opportunity to entertain clients;
- building a company/product presence;
- reaching select market segments; and
- business-to-business networking.[5]

Sponsorship is one way to increase corporate awareness, as broad exposure of a name or logo increases recognition and may result in a purchase decision. It is considered a positive and low-cost image-building approach and allows targeting; that is, the sponsorship can be directed at specific audiences or potential customers. An example is given in Everyday Ethics 8.5 which illustrates the diversity of sponsorship programs of one corporation.

The corporate sponsor looks for a charitable situation that both satisfies the company's marketing ambitions and coincides with the needs of the charity group. There must be some common ground so that both parties benefit. To accomplish this, the sponsorship agreement should define clearly the role and needs of each partner. For the corporation, the sponsorship must fit into the marketing scheme, while the charity's integrity must not be threatened. A well-defined plan is necessary to avoid failure and disagreements. Many now consider corporate sponsorship to be a form of advertising.

EVERYDAY ETHICS 8.5

Sponsorship at Air Canada

Air Canada has extensive sponsorship programs as a part of its community involvement. The programs operate nationally, regionally, and locally. Air Canada states that these programs are undertaken for commercial reasons, but also so that the corporation can play a cultural role in the communities it serves, assist in areas such as health care and economic development, and enrich lives in areas of entertainment and sports. The following are a few examples of the sponsorship programs:

Arts—support for numerous orchestras and ballets, museums and cultural events.

Canadian film—promotion of National Canadian Film Day and Air Canada enRoute® Film Festival™, and Canadian content on aircraft entertainment systems.

Nurturing Canadian talent—development of Canadian student and emerging filmmakers; in-flight magazine featuring work from Canadian writers, photographers, and illustrators; listing of the best new Canadian restaurants; and co-sponsoring a literary prize and publishing the work of winners by established and developing Canadian writers.

Sports—sponsor of Canada's Olympic Team since 2006 and a sponsor of Canada's Paralympic Team since 2007; commercial sponsorships with Canada's National Hockey League Teams and the Toronto Raptors basketball team, the Toronto Marlies and St. John's IceCaps of the American Hockey League.

Source: "2014 Corporate Sustainability Report," Air Canada, accessed January 4, 2016, at http://www.aircanada.com/en/about/documents/csr_2014_report_en.pdf?r=Friday, 21-Aug-15 19:48:31. Used with permission of Air Canada.

Sponsorship is now so common that it has lost its novelty, and thus its capability to attract attention. The public may be cynical about cause-related sponsorships, or simply may not understand the linkage. Many question the appropriateness of the support given by alcohol companies to the arts and sports. The government might question whether some sponsorship violates advertising regulations.

Corporations may find it difficult to keep their hands off the event after the initial agreement is reached, and the relationship may turn sour. The return from a sponsorship is seldom precisely known, and it might be difficult to withdraw support without attracting attention. For example, the sponsorship of the Canadian equestrian team became awkward for some corporate sponsors when the sport experienced problems with drugs and dishonesty. But the withdrawal of support becomes a problem, as without corporate sponsorship many programs fail.

New approaches are being used by business to address social ills beyond giving money, social venture philanthropy, and social enterprises. Both assume that it is appropriate for business to solve social problems such as jobs in communities, training programs, and housing. The purpose of these approaches is to give the underprivileged the tools to create new opportunities by creating their own wealth instead of it being transferred to them.

LO 8.5　Social Venture Philanthropy

Social venture philanthropy is the investment of human and financial resources by corporations in non-profit community development agencies to generate a social return instead of only a financial one. This approach is also known as social venturing, the new philanthropy, and high-engagement philanthropy. Sometimes it is used interchangeably with social enterprise, but there is a distinction that is explained in the next section.

Social venture philanthropy applies venture capital management practices to social responsibility. Investments are made, but a social return is expected rather than a financial one. There is a high engagement with the non-profit agency that provides leadership, bold ideas to address social problems, and strong teams with an active board involvement. Whereas venture capitalists plan an exit strategy, the social venture capitalist focuses on long-term funding and sustainability of the recipient.

Several examples of social venture philanthropy organizations exist in Canada, including Social Venture Partners (described in Everyday Ethics 8.6), B.C. Technology Social Venture Partners, Social Capital Partners, the Tides Foundation, and the Enterprising Non-Profits Program Vancouver.[6]

EVERYDAY ETHICS 8.6

Social Venture Philanthropy and Social Venture Partners Calgary

Social Venture Partners Calgary's mission is to stimulate positive social change in Calgary. It is a partnership among generous individuals, businesspersons, and others, and needy not-for-profits to create a new model of giving. Social Venture Partners Calgary combines the time, expertise, financial, and physical resources of its partners and turns them into a powerful tool of positive change for cash-strapped, advice-ready, and resource-constrained not-for-profits. These organizations get not only the commitment of money and resources over a number of years, but also the professional advice that leads to more successful outcomes. Examples of the investments made include the following:

The Calgary Youth Justice Society—Support to this organization contributes to the success of Youth Justice Committees by providing fundamental support through public awareness, resources, training, and guidance.

Connections Counselling and Consulting Foundation—This grant recipient empowers individuals by providing ongoing education, programs, and advocacy; ongoing family support to parents with an intellectual disability and their children; and counselling to persons with an intellectual disability.

EvenStart for Children Foundation—The organization gives "at-risk" children who are economically disadvantaged the educational, therapeutic, nutritional, and nurturing support necessary to gain an "even start" in their lives.

Source: Based on Social Ventures Partners Calgary, accessed January 5, 2016, http://www.svpcalgary.org/.

LO 8.6 Social Enterprise and Social Entrepreneurship

A **social enterprise** is a model of business operation where some or all profits are deliberately used to further social aims. There are two types: non-profit enterprises that contribute all profits to social initiatives, for example the St. John's Bakery described in Everyday Ethics 8.7, and for-profit enterprises that divide profits between social initiatives and shareholders, such as The Body Shop. Social enterprises are dynamic business operations capable of improving the well-being of citizens while making money, but are distinct from charities and from private-sector companies that practise social responsibility. Although the idea has received attention recently, it has existed for some time, for example in the co-operatives of the 1800s. Social enterprises take various forms including community enterprises, credit unions, commercial operations of charities, employee-owned businesses, co-operatives, development trusts, housing associations, and companies operating under "fair trade" principles.

Although social enterprises take various forms, there are some common characteristics. They have an enterprise orientation; that is, they are involved in the production of goods or provision of services to a market with the intention that revenues will exceed costs. They have social aims, such as providing employment, training, and investment funding. There is a commitment of local capacity building, and they are accountable to their members and community stakeholders. They are autonomous organizations with governance and ownership structures based on participation by stakeholder groups such as users and local community groups or shareholders. Profits are distributed to stakeholders or used for the benefit of the community.[7]

Social entrepreneurship involves the activities undertaken to enhance social wealth in some innovative way. A **social entrepreneur** is an innovative, visionary leader of a non-profit or for-profit business with real-world problem-solving creativity and a high awareness for ethical, social, and environmental considerations. Social entrepreneurs seek out innovative approaches to social issues in the community and use business skills to achieve social objectives. They also have the ability to meet community needs while being financially self-sufficient and paying attention to market forces. Successful social entrepreneurs do not believe that capitalism and profits are societal evils, but instead believe that business enterprises can be operated to enhance social aims.

Several centres focus on social enterprises and entrepreneurship; these are usually associated with universities, and sometimes are in association with regular entrepreneurial studies. In Canada, colleges and universities offer programs or courses that focus on social entrepreneurship, and many business graduates are seeking employment in social enterprises where they apply their business and managerial skills.[8] In order to gain experience in social entrepreneurship and social enterprises, university and college students can participate in Enactus groups or teams as described in Responsibility for Ethics 8.2.

EVERYDAY ETHICS 8.7

St. John's Bakery

The St. John's Bakery in Toronto is operated by the St. John's Mission "to provide our customers with outstanding artisan breads and sweets" and "to be and to build an inclusive community through the gifts and the needs that each of us brings." Its mission notes "…it is more than our breads. It is about connecting with people, about building community. We draw people in with our bread. We believe our bread builds community."

The bakery sells a variety of organic breads and sweets to consumers, retailers, cafés and restaurants, farmers' markets, and wholesale customers. It is sponsored by the St. John the Compassionate Mission, a non-profit organization of the Carpatho-Russian Orthodox diocese, with support from other orthodox churches in the Greater Toronto Area. It employs people on Ontario Works, people with disabilities, people new to Canada, persons suffering addictions or mental illness, single parents, and those struggling with poverty.

Sources: Adapted from St. John's Bakery, accessed January 4, 2016, http://stjohnsbakery.com; and St. John the Compassionate Mission, accessed January 4, 2016, http://stjohnsmission.org.

RESPONSIBILITY FOR ETHICS 8.2

Enactus

Enactus, formerly Students in Free Enterprise (SIFE), is a student-run organization whose purpose is to create community empowerment projects with the assistance of academics and business leaders. Each project can be considered a social enterprise that uses the power of entrepreneurial spirit and skill to transform lives and shape a better, more sustainable world.

It is an international non-profit organization with groups around the world, including about 60 teams at Canadian universities and colleges involving 2,344 students and 260 projects. Student participation in Enactus provides an opportunity for students to develop talents and skills necessary for leadership roles in business. The values encouraged are imagination, courage, determination, partnership, accountability, and curiosity.

Source: Adapted from Enactus website accessed January 6, 2016, http://enactus.org/ and http://enactus.org/country/canada/.

LO 8.7   Small Business and CSR

Many small business enterprises are involved with CSR but it has a lower profile. A survey of 500 small Canadian businesses found that over 90 percent felt it was their duty to give back to the community. About 75 percent found that CSR attracted like-minded employees, that customers expected CSR initiatives, and that the environment should be considered in decision making. Over 85 percent believed that the ability to contribute to the community is one of the rewards of business ownership.[9]

There are challenges to implementing CSR in small businesses. Entrepreneurs do not have time to devote to it as they are confronting the daily demands of their business. The expenses associated with obtaining the resources necessary, including consultants and employee time, may be beyond the means of a small business.[10] There is likely a lack of knowledge of CSR planning and monitoring methodologies, as resources relevant to small businesses are not readily available.[11]

TABLE 8.4   Differences in CSR in Large Corporations versus Small Businesses

Large Corporations	Small Businesses
• Accountable to a large number of stakeholders	• Accountable to fewer stakeholders
• Responsible to society at large	• Responsible to local communities
• Concerned with brand image and reputation	• Concerned about retaining business
• Shareholder pressure; ethical investing	• Pressure from lenders
• Based on corporate values	• Based on owner values
• Formal planning for CSR	• Unlikely to be formal planning
• Emphasis on standards and indices	• Emphasis on intuition and ad hoc processes
• Involvement of CSR professionals	• No dedicated personnel
• Prominent campaign; for example, cause-related marketing	• Small scale activities; for example, sponsoring local sports teams
• Awareness through CSR reporting, publicity	• Often unrecognized as CSR activities

Source: Compiled and adapted from Heledd Jenkins, "A Critique of Conventional CSR Theory: An SME Perspective," *Journal of General Management*, Vol. 29, No 4, Summer 2004, Table 3: Divergence in CSR Theory for Large and Small Organizations, page 51.

The understanding of CSR that does exist is strongly influenced by the personal values of the entrepreneur. Small businesses must confront most of the social and ethical issues experienced by large business. But some issues are associated more with small business: entrepreneurs are more likely to participate in the underground economy, misleading advertising and financial reporting, improper gift giving and receiving, and tax evasion. In addition, human resource abuses are more common as entrepreneurs ignore or are unaware of workplace regulations. Entrepreneurs are sometimes accused of nepotism in the hiring and promotion of family members instead of employees.[12] Research has found differences between CSR practice in large versus small businesses; the findings are summarized in Table 8.4.[13]

The Network for Business Sustainability has developed a guide for small business involvement with local communities. A community comprises individuals or groups by issues, interactions, geography, or a sense of identity, and includes residents, community associations, sports leagues, online networks, parent–teacher associations, environmental activists, and religious groups. Examples of typical community concerns could be the hiring or laying off of local people, problems created such as pollution, and the construction of facilities. Working with community groups improves management decision making, creates legitimacy or social licence, and makes recruitment easier.[14] Table 8.5 outlines the three strategies for working with communities. Small business owners must carefully identify the relevant community groups, prioritize them, and then pick the best engagement strategy.

TABLE 8.5	Three Strategies for Working with Communities		
	Investment	Involvement	Integration
Company perspective	"Giving Back"	"Building Bridges"	"Changing Society"
Description	The company provides information or resources to the community	The company uses community input to shape its actions	The company and the community jointly manage projects
Communication	One-way	Two-way	Two-way
Number of partners	Many	Many	Few
Interaction	Occasional	Repeated	Frequent
Information/ knowledge	Goes from company to community	Goes from community to company	Is jointly generated
Control over process	Company	Company	Company and community
Tools and techniques	Advertisements; information kiosks; press releases; newsletters; door-to-door visits; information sessions; charitable donations; employee volunteering	Surveys; studies; interviews; consultative committees; interactive websites; public hearings; neutral forums	Strategic local or regional partnerships; sector discussion groups; joint brainstorming; conflict resolution; work groups

Source: Network for Business Sustainability, *Working with Community Groups: A Guide for Small Business*, November 5, 2012. Available at http://nbs.net/wp-content/uploads/SME-Resource-Community-Engagement.pdf. Used with the permission of Network for Business Sustainability

connect   Want to learn more about **CSR and small business?**

EVERYDAY ETHICS 8.8

Citigrow Inc. and Urban Food

David Gingera, founder and president of Citigrow Inc., wanted to create a socially responsible business that would solve food problems through growing food in cities. He started Citigrow in Winnipeg in 2014 and connects property owners, gardeners, and food buyers, especially restaurants. The result is urban farms or urban agriculture, the process of growing food within the cities where it will be consumed. The approach produces fresh vegetables locally.

Property owners agree to utilize their available space to grow vegetables on small lots or "micro-farms." Citigrow coordinates the production, markets the vegetables, and pays the property owner a royalty. In July 2015, Citigrow won the AirMiles 2015 Small Business Achievement Award for social responsibility. Gingera believes urban agriculture is the best way to grow better food, at lower costs and in a way that is better for the environment.

Source: Adapted from "2015 Small Business Achievement Awards," *Canadian Business* (Profit Guide Section), March 2015; Citigrow, accessed January 5, 2016, http://www.citigrow.ca/; Geoff Kirbyson, "Green Machine: Winnipeg Company Builds Urban Gardens, Pays Royalties on Produce Sold," *Winnipeg Free Press*, 09/4/2014, accessed January 5, 2016, http://www.winnipegfreepress.com/local/green-machine-273890731.html; "CitiGrow Brings Farm to Table a Small Plot Closer," PegCity Grub, accessed January 5, 2016, http://www.pegcitygrub.com/tag/citigrow/.

Although this guide is based on 200 studies of small business involvement in communities, it can be used by larger corporations at a local level, for example when building a plant in a community. Other assistance with CSR is available for entrepreneurs from industry associations, for example accessing the Canadian Federation of Independent Business, completing self-assessment checklists available on the Internet, cooperating with local non-profit organizations, and referring to the limited literature.[15] Although not receiving the attention for their CSR practices that large corporations do, most small businesses and their owners do contribute to local communities. Small business entrepreneurs make donations to local charities, sponsor area sports teams and cultural activities, and volunteer in community organizations. An example of a small business practising CSR is given in Everyday Ethics 8.8.

LO 8.8   The Community Investment Concept

Community investment (CI) has become another approach to describing a corporation's CSR activities. It is defined as the efforts of a corporation to help develop a community and create economic opportunities through a variety of means from donations to direct involvement in commercial undertakings. According to Business for Social Responsibility, "corporate community investment bridges traditional areas of philanthropy and volunteerism with commercial-community relationships in sourcing, workforce, financial investments, site selection, and the development and delivery of products and services."[16] The purpose of community investment is to develop CSR strategies in relation to corporate community–related issues and to link economic responsibilities with the social needs of the community.

In 2015 The Conference Board of Canada conducted the first national survey of corporate community investment activity and produced a report on its findings, *Canadian Corporate Community Investment: Emerging Trends and Impact Measurement.*[17] The survey found that the most common elements of CI programs were: donations to organizations, sponsorship or marketing activities, contribution of in-kind resources, employee gift-matching/donations programs, and employee volunteer programs. The most commonly selected investment areas were: community, social, environmental, education and health. The choice of investment was most influenced by a fit with corporate values. Other influences were the ability to engage employees with project partners, the anticipated positive impact on corporate reputation, the ability to effect meaningful change, and the connection between the program and the corporation's products and services. Senior leadership engagement was found to be very important to the success of any CI program. Several factors motivated senior leadership to support a CI program. The most important factor was the alignment with overall corporate strategy. Other factors included the enhancement of the corporation's reputation, the ability to engage employees, and a personal association with a program. Two-thirds of corporations communicate their CI program impacts publicly, often through a formal report.

RESPONSIBILITY FOR ETHICS 8.3

Imagine Canada's Caring Company Program

Imagine Canada describes a Caring Company as one that is a good corporate citizen, drives social innovation, and invests money, ideas, and time in communities. It considers the Caring Company Program to be Canada's leading corporate citizenship initiative, and about 90 businesses are members. Membership assures stakeholders that the company is committed to investing in the community.

Commitments necessary to join include:

- Donate one percent of pre-tax profits to the community;
- Champion and sustain and least one community investment project; and,
- Publicly report their community investment activities.

Large or small corporations can become members once they agree to the principles of corporate citizenship and the benchmarks for community investment established by Imagine Canada.

Source: Adapted from Imagine Canada, "Caring Company Program," accessed January 6, 2016, http://www.imaginecanada.ca/our-programs/caring-company-program.

A multitude of awards and recognition are designated for effective CSR or corporate sustainability programs. Examples of such awards are the *Corporate Knights'* Best 50 Corporate Citizens in Canada, the *Maclean's* Top 50 Socially Responsible Corporations in Canada, and the Global 100 Most Sustainable Corporations in the World. The receipt of such awards is displayed on the corporation's website and in CSR or sustainability reports, and are mentioned in this book. Imagine Canada recognizes the best CSR programs with its Caring Company Program, described in Responsibility for Ethics 8.3.

Despite all the evidence of community investment/CSR initiatives, there is concern that it will receive less attention during an economic downturn. An article in *The Guardian* examined the possibility that CSR might be less of a priority with corporations as turbulent economic conditions refocus attention to the bottom line.[18] The advocates of sustainability or CSR feared that it may not receive as much attention by management and boards of directors, and that it would not be viewed seriously. Examples were given where corporations did not mention CSR in their annual strategy statements to the financial market. Evidence to the contrary comes from consultants who claim that CSR has been temporarily derailed before and re-emerged in a revised form. It is pointed out that commitment to CSR in times of economic turndown is even more important for corporations as it differentiates them from competitors. Furthermore, CSR has moved into the mainstream because of climate change, financial scandals, and alleged human rights and environmental abuses. Corporations will continue commitment to CSR as they want to avoid government regulation being demanded by NGOs while others argue that regulation is necessary—a voluntary approach does not work. Even with the doubts, the approaches discussed in this chapter illustrate an increasing belief that business should be investing in CSR or sustainability with the goal of a social return, and that business-type practices will be used in its implementation.

Your advice to Walter...

There are thousands of charities in Canada, and selecting which among them to support is a challenging task. For businesspersons with considerable funds they wish to give back to society, it is an even greater challenge. Walter might consider the Giving Pledge, but this is not appropriate to everyone. If Walter is thinking of giving to a charity, Charity Intelligence Canada might be of help. It evaluates charities on various criteria and recommends a list of the most efficient and effective. Walter does have access to some resources to address his challenge.

Summary

- A spectrum of corporate social responsibility and corporate sustainability approaches are described: corporate giving or donations, voluntarism, sponsorship, social venture philanthropy, and social enterprise. Most corporations practise one or more of these approaches as they seek the most effective way to practise CSR. (LO 8.1)

- There are arguments for and against corporate donations; in particular, the issue of whether such activity is in the best interests of the corporation and its shareholders has not been resolved. Once the corporation decides to become involved in corporate giving, another challenge emerges—how to manage the process. A decision-making process involving committees or foundations should be established if the corporation wants to be consistent and perceived to be treating all requests fairly. Although something positive can be gained from donations, there is the possibility of negative outcomes when requests are rejected. Rejections must be handled as professionally as successful requests. Philanthropic decision making is even more challenging given the increasing demands for corporate support and the limited amount of funds available. In addition, there is a trend toward tying giving to economic gains, an issue that re-emerges throughout the chapter. (LO 8.2)

- Voluntarism is receiving more attention as an approach to corporate philanthropy. Employees and retirees of corporations make contributions to charitable organizations, often with the encouragement of managers. Many corporations have well-defined policies relating to employee volunteer activities to avoid conflicts with work obligations or to protect the reputation of the corporation. Although voluntarism is usually encouraged, it is not without challenges for management. (LO 8.3)

- Sponsorship has grown as a form of philanthropy. Discussion continues as to whether such an activity is in support of a charity or an aspect of marketing. Corporations are pressured for greater return on donation funds, and tying support to sponsorship of projects or events appears to result. The discussion of sponsorship is a logical lead-in to the examination of the trend toward corporations seeking to satisfy economic as well as social objectives with corporate philanthropic initiatives. Corporate management is demanding more efficiency and accountability from non-profit charities, and receivers of support from corporations in "sin industries" are being challenged for accepting it. (LO 8.4)

- Social venture philanthropy is a newer approach to CSR where donors believe their funds should be invested rather than merely handed over as a cheque. The approach also involves more engagement with the recipient organization to encourage the use of entrepreneurial and managerial approaches. (LO 8.5)

- Social enterprises can be viewed as two types. One type is as a commercial enterprise operated by a non-profit organization with the goal of making profits that are devoted completely to social purposes. Another type is a for-profit organization, which distributes its earnings to social causes and to shareholders. Both types are committed to contributing to the alleviation of social problems in society. The for-benefit corporation is another approach to the social enterprise that has emerged recently. (LO 8.6)

- Small businesses are involved in CSR but receive less recognition than large corporations. CSR decisions are driven by the entrepreneur and focus on local community social issues. (LO 8.7)

- Some corporations prefer to implement CSR using the community investment concept. This concept is a comprehensive approach to CSR in the corporation's local, national, or international areas of operation. (LO 8.8)

Key Terms

Corporate philanthropy

Charitable foundation

Cause-related marketing

Strategic giving

Corporate voluntarism

Corporate sponsorship

Social venture philanthropy

Social enterprise

Social entrepreneurship

Social entrepreneur

Community investment

Critical Thinking and Discussion Questions

1. What is the strongest argument for business participating in corporate giving? What is the strongest argument for business not participating in corporate giving?

2. Why should corporations develop formal plans for implementing CSR?

3. How is the position that all corporate profits belong to the shareholders countered?

4. List guidelines that corporations might follow in developing and implementing a corporate giving program.

5. Why do some argue that corporate giving is now nothing more than corporate marketing or advertising?

6. Should a charity accept donations from tobacco, alcohol, or beer companies?

7. What are the drawbacks to corporate voluntarism?

8. What criteria should be used in selecting a charity for a corporate voluntary program?

9. What are the positive features of sponsorship programs? What are the drawbacks?

10. Should business be involved in social venture philanthropy? Is business better than government at addressing social ills?

11. From a business perspective, what are the positive features of social enterprises?

12. Why should small businesses become involved with CSR?

13. Should corporations be thinking of CSR as an investment?

Cases

8.1 RESPONSIBLE ALCOHOL CONSUMPTION

Twelve producers of beer, wine and spirits have formed an industry association, Producers' Commitments, dedicated to the reduction of harmful drinking. The five key areas to be addressed are: reducing underage drinking; strengthening and expanding marketing codes of practice; providing consumer information and responsible product innovation; reducing drinking and driving; and enlisting the support of retailers to reduce harmful drinking. They also support the World Health Organization's (WHO) *Global Strategy to Reduce Harmful Use of Alcohol*. Two members of the association are Diageo plc and Molson Coors.

Diageo is the producer of beer and spirits including such brands as Smirnoff, Johnnie Walker, Captain Morgan, Barleys, Tanqueray, and Guinness. There are six main priorities to Diageo's Sustainability & Responsibility Strategy with the first one being "Alcohol in society." The company states that it wants to contribute to the World Health Organization's goal of reducing alcohol-related harm. It plans to do this by communicating about alcohol responsibly and tackling misuse through effective programs and policies. It will work with industry to promote responsible marketing, to provide appropriate consumer information, and to implement programs to address alcohol misuse.

Molson Coors Brewing Company states that one measure of success is to have their products consumed in the right way. Their brands include Carling, Coors, Black Horse, Black Ice, Becks, and Corona. The company is concerned about excessive consumption and in particular underage drinking. They have several programs targeting alcohol abuse including: Responsible Entertaining and Serving; Binge Drinking; Drinking and Driving; Underage Drinking; Drinking and Risky Activities; Drinking and Health; Drinking and Pregnancy; and Responsible Consumption.

Questions

1. Are beer, wine, and spirits producers good corporate citizens?

2. Is excessive consumption of alcohol a serious societal problem? Who are the stakeholders and what are the issues involved?

3. Are the CSR initiatives of Diageo and Molson Coors motivated only by economic self-interest?

4. What else the industry do about this social issue?

Source: Beer, Wine, Spirits Producers' Commitments, accessed January 15, 2016, http://www.producerscommitments.org/; "Our Sustainability & Responsibility Strategy," Diageo plc, accessed January 15, 2016, http://www.diageo.com/en-row/csr/sustainability/Pages/default.aspx; and "Responsible Consumption," Molson Coors Brewing Company, accessed January 15, 2016, http://www.molsoncoors.com/en/responsibility/what-matters-to-us/alcohol-responsibility.

8.2 HAVING TO GIVE AT THE OFFICE

Roxanne Kampf was an accounts payable clerk for a large corporation. She enjoyed the job and was generally happy with her workplace. Her employer had an extensive corporate giving program and supported employee voluntarism, in which she participated. For example, Roxanne volunteered to participate in the cleanup of a park near the office. It was an enjoyable activity and involved social interaction with many colleagues. Overall, she was pleased to be working for a corporation that was socially responsible.

Roxanne had reservations about the corporate giving program—in particular, about the annual United Way campaign. Firstly, she did not agree with the purposes of some of the charities covered by United Way. Secondly, she preferred to contribute directly to the charities she supported and whose aims she endorsed. Lastly, she felt pressure from supervisors and peers to contribute. This last reservation caused Roxanne some anxiety.

She had been reading in the newspaper about workplace charity drives. A poll of readers of *The Globe and Mail* found that 51 percent liked to support charity drives, 36 percent preferred to make their donations privately, and 13 percent felt pressured to contribute. Obviously Roxanne was not alone in her concern.

Roxanne felt very uneasy about her direct supervisor heading up the campaign in her department. Although the actual canvassing was done by peers, she still felt pressure and anxiety. She was not sure how to say no or what excuse to make. She wondered if anyone would believe a statement that she had already used up her "charitable budget." Also, she was not sure how others would feel when she stated that she should be able to give to the charities she preferred and in private. Even more troublesome was her concern about how saying no would impact her career.

The campaign made her very uncomfortable and she was even feeling guilty. Fun campaign activities were organized in the office and it was obvious to all when she did not attend. Also, the office had a goal to raise $5,000 and she was not contributing as expected of team members. Roxanne faced a dilemma and did not know what to do.

Questions

1. What are the pros and cons of workplace charity drives? What are the issues involved?

2. Does Roxanne have an ethical dilemma? State what it is.

3. What ethical principles (from Chapter 5) might she use to analyze the dilemma?

4. What should Roxanne do?

Sources: Marjorie Polycarpe, "Re-examining Workplace Giving Programs," Inside Corporate Philanthropy (December 31, 2003); Tara Weiss, "Giving at the Office Without Going Broke," *Forbes*, June 22, 2006, accessed August 16, 2016, http://www.forbes.com/2006/06/22/business-basics-donation-cs_tw_0622officegifts.html; David Aston, "'Tis the Season to be Inundated," *The Globe and Mail*, November 14, 2007, C1–C2; and Jennifer Myers, "Giving Spirit Untarnished by Recession," *The Globe and Mail*, November 28, 2009, B17.

Used with the permission of Dennis Flynn

CHAPTER 9

Measuring, Reporting, and Communicating CSR

LEARNING OUTCOMES

After studying this chapter, you will be able to:

LO 9.1 Understand the background to measuring and reporting CSR performance.

LO 9.2 Define corporate reputation and understand its relationship to corporate social responsibility.

LO 9.3 Identify the stakeholders who influence CSR reporting.

LO 9.4 Describe the relationship between CSR and corporate profitability.

LO 9.5 Enumerate and discuss the types of criteria used in social auditing.

LO 9.6 Recognize the surveys that evaluate Canadian CSR reporting.

LO 9.7 Outline how CSR and sustainability results are communicated to stakeholders.

LO 9.8 Explain the role of business schools in CSR reporting.

LO 9.9 Discuss the future of CSR and CSR reporting.

What would you do if...?

Clare O'Neill was confused. She had been introduced to the ethics of business and corporate social responsibility (CSR) in a university business course. She had become very interested in business and in particular how corporations were responding to social and environmental issues. Her instructor had used various corporate websites and had reviewed several corporate responsibility or sustainability reports in class, and also had recommended that students who were interested in the topic should subscribe to *Corporate Knights*—described as "the magazine for clean capitalism."

Clare's confusion began when she received the Spring 2015 issue, which featured a list titled "The 2015 Best 50 Corporate Citizens in Canada." The list contained some prominent corporations that she recognized as socially and environmentally responsible, such as Mountain Equipment Co-op, Vancouver

City Savings Credit Union, and Desjardins Group. But also on the list were several industries that Clare did not feel were the most responsible, and she did not understand why they were represented. Popular media coverage was not always positive, and a series of documentaries she viewed at the college had been particularly critical.

The industries and corporations that Clare found doubtful included the following:

- *Chemicals*—Agrium Inc. Clare felt this industry extensively polluted the environment, and produced chemicals used in the mass production of food and home/beauty products with potentially negative impacts.

- *Petroleum*—Encana Corp., Enbridge Inc., Suncor Energy Inc., Husky Energy Inc., Talisman Energy Inc., and Nexen Inc. Clare viewed the petroleum industry as being irresponsible toward the environment, especially the operations in the Alberta oil sands. Recent reports had confirmed a significant increase in pollution in Alberta due to the oil sands developments.

- *Mining*—Cameco Corp., Barrick Gold Corp., Yamana Gold, Kinross Gold Corp., and Teck Resources Ltd. Claire knew that Cameco was in the uranium business, which supplied the nuclear energy industry. She believed many mine properties were polluters and harmed the environment and local communities, especially when operating in developing countries.

- *Forestry*—Domtar Corp., Catalyst Paper Corp., and Cascades Inc. In Clare's view, forestry corporations were not doing enough reforestation nor making sufficient efforts to prevent harm to the environment. They also had closed many plants and laid off thousands of workers, many of whom had inadequate pensions.

Clare looked up the CSR reports for the corporations mentioned, and found that indeed they were involved with many significant socially responsible programs. She still viewed the industries as problematic in their responsibility to society. Also, she wondered if the corporations were reporting only good news and overlooking less favourable situations.

Clare wondered if she should cancel her subscription to the magazine. She also thought about writing a letter to the editor. She considered the possibility that she had misunderstood the CSR and corporate citizenship concepts. She was disappointed and confused.

What is your advice to Clare?

This chapter reviews how CSR and sustainability performance is measured, reported, and communicated in Canada by:

- Establishing the existence of this reporting and examining why it is taking place.
- Evaluating the quality of the reporting in terms of the reliability of the information.
- Reviewing the verification or assurance mechanisms used to enhance the credibility of the reporting.
- Identifying the efforts made by corporations to communicate the reports to stakeholders.[1]

Two other sections examine related topics: CSR education in business courses, and the future of corporate social responsibility and CSR reporting.

The terms CSR and sustainability are used interchangeably in this chapter.

LO 9.1   Measuring and Reporting CSR

The first step in the measurement of CSR or sustainability performance involves some type of auditing. **Social auditing** is a systematic assessment that identifies, measures, evaluates, reports, and monitors the effects an enterprise has on society that are not covered in the traditional financial reports. The purpose of social auditing is to provide information to management and to various stakeholders about the impact of the enterprise on society, and to provide a basis of accountability for the social consequences of corporate activities. Such audits can be used to assess existing performance, to evaluate the performance of managers in relation to social objectives, to provide an information base for planning, and to serve as a measure for assessing future performance.

There are many social auditing approaches. The main ones are:

- *Inventory*—a listing of social activities without any evaluation.

- *Program management*—a statement describing particular programs or initiatives, including an indication of the resources committed.

- *Process*—a more elaborate approach incorporating the inventory and program management approaches. It includes an assessment of how each social program came into being, a statement of each program's objectives and the rationales behind each activity, and a description of what has been accomplished.

- *Cost or outlay*—a social–economic operating statement that tabulates the expenditures an enterprise makes on social objectives less the negative costs for social objectives not addressed. The approach is to measure the total social impact, positive and negative.

- *Social responsibility accounting*—a system of accounting that tabulates social costs and benefits with the objective of the best social return for the social investment made.

- *Social indicators*—an audit of the community is conducted using social indicators to provide data on the most pressing needs. Corporate social performances are compared or related to community or social indicators.

Corporations have moved beyond the social auditing approaches listed above. The following is a representation of the trend to the more sophisticated social auditing necessary for sustainability reporting:

- *Social objective setting*—In addition to economic objectives, corporations are establishing social and environmental objectives and reporting on their accomplishments in corporate annual reports.

- *Triple bottom line reporting*—Corporations prepare and publicize reports outlining economic, social, and environmental criteria and the extent to which they have been satisfied. Examples of such bottom lines are economic, ethical, and environmental, and people, planet, and prosperity.

- *Social reports*—Quite often the objectives and triple bottom line criteria are presented in comprehensive social reports prepared by the corporations themselves.

- *Sustainable guidelines*—Comprehensive sets of economic, social, and environmental criteria and performance indicators are being developed by organizations independent of corporations such as business research institutes, consultants, and non-governmental organizations (NGOs). These criteria and indicators are also referred to as guidelines or benchmarks and are being used in the preparation of social reports.

- *Externally verified social reports*—The corporations are using outside, independent organizations not only to develop the guidelines, but also to verify the corporation's performance relating to the guidelines. This independent verification is a major turning point in social reporting, or sustainability reporting. Although this practice is not widespread, it is gaining acceptance.

- *Consultation with stakeholders*—Some corporations are consulting stakeholders on the preparation of CSR or sustainability reports. Such consultation obtains the views of relevant stakeholders and is another approach to evaluating the corporation's CSR program.

The results of this auditing process become the basis for social reporting. **Corporate social responsibility (CSR) reporting** is a management function that documents the corporation's economic, ethical/social, and environmental responsibilities and initiatives, and communicates this information to relevant stakeholders. It is also known as *sustainability reporting*.

Managers and businesspersons must now be familiar with this trend and its implications. Traditionally they worried about financial audits, but now many corporations are performing audits or developing reporting mechanisms that measure how well the corporation is achieving its social responsibilities as well as its economic responsibilities. The formats and organization of these reports differ among corporations, with some being innovative and creative. Several of these reports are referenced in this chapter.

Three reasons why reporting is necessary are to maintain the corporation's reputation, to meet the demands of stakeholders, and to sustain corporate profitability.

LO 9.2 Corporate Reputation and CSR

Corporate reputation is "a perceptual representation of a corporation's past actions and future prospects that describes the corporation's overall appeal to all of its key constituents [stakeholders] when compared with other leading rivals."[2] It is often associated with corporate image, especially as promoted through public relations. The problem is that a corporate image has a temporary effect and is not an enduring solution to the relationship between business and society. Today corporate reputation is related more to the "character" of the corporation and involves corporate credibility, trust, and responsibility.

Corporate reputation is an asset, though an intangible one. It is difficult to measure, although surveys attempt it[3] (see Everyday Ethics 9.1 for examples). Reputation is measured by being able to do the right thing, and through CSR reporting corporations hope to convince stakeholders that they are indeed behaving this way.

A distinction should be made between CSR and corporate reputation. CSR involves the way in which a corporation interacts with its stakeholders (as discussed in Chapters 4 and 8), whereas corporate reputation focuses on the perceptions that stakeholders have about the corporation as a result of the interactions. Thus, stakeholders' impressions are most often formed by a corporation's CSR performance. The drivers of corporate reputation include customer service, ethical conduct, community involvement, employee relations, quality of products and services, innovativeness, and environmental stewardship.[4]

A connection exists not only between corporate reputation and stakeholders but also to issues management and strategy.[5] Stakeholders determine the issues that affect reputation, and managers must address stakeholders and the issues that concern them. Because reputation is good for business, responsibility for it lies with all managers, starting with the chief executive officer (CEO). A corporate reputation builds trust with stakeholders, might enable the corporation to command higher prices, attracts qualified people, and minimizes the risk of damage from a crisis. Corporate reputation rather than image has become a key to a successful corporate strategy.

EVERYDAY ETHICS 9.1

CSR and Reputation and Trust of Canadian Business

Two studies provide information on reputation and trust of Canadian business, The Conference Board of Canada benchmark report on reputation management and the Edelman Trust Barometer Canada,. The following are some findings.

The Conference Board of Canada report found that the three greatest reputational risks were product and service quality and safety, environmental impact, and mishandling of an incident or crisis. Canadian corporations had a greater interest in reputation because of the growing importance of intangible assets (for example, brand or intellectual property), the increasing complexity of supply chains, the growth and influence of social media, and higher stakeholder expectations. Corporations are managing reputation by preparing for crises, engaging stakeholders, and managing issues. Employees played a key role in reputation management and corporate reputation was influenced by the reputation of the industry, competitors, and suppliers.

Edelman, a public relations firm, annually surveys the trust that the public has in various institutions, including business. In its 2015 survey, the trust in business declined to 47 percent from 62 percent in the previous year. The trust in the CEO as a spokesperson has declined for several years and in 2015 was 28 percent. The trust in NGOs remained the same at 62 percent, government declined to 49 percent and the media to 47 percent. Other findings applicable to business were: trust in family-owned business was much greater than in big business and government-owned corporations. Trust in the energy, chemicals, automobile, and health industries declined. The main determinants of trust involved the corporation's integrity, engagement with stakeholders, quality of products and services, approach to social responsibility, and performance of operations. The survey concluded that distrust in business drives the demand for government regulation.

Sources "2015 Edelman Trust Barometer: Canadian Results Canada" accessed January 13, 2016, http://www.slideshare.net/fullscreen/EdelmanInsights/2015-edelman-trust-barometer-canadian-findings/7; and "Public Affairs Reputation Management: Benchmarking Report," The Conference Board of Canada, September 2015, accessed January 13, 2016, http://www.conferenceboard.ca/e-library/abstract.aspx?did=7348.

Want to learn more about trusting business?

Researchers have found a relationship between corporate reputation and social responsibility, particularly when the corporation experiences a crisis or event that damages its image or reputation. A study by Minor and Morgan found that corporations with higher CSR ratings are more successful at overcoming setbacks.[6] Another study found that CSR created a layer of protection, and corporations known for social responsibility experienced less decline in stock prices when a crisis occurred.[7] Other researchers examined the influence that socially responsible images or reputations have on consumers. A commitment to ethics statements such as a values statement or code of ethics creates a reputation of responsibility that legitimizes a corporation in the eyes of consumers. They also found that consumers expect financially successful corporations to contribute to society. A corporation's reputation decreases consumer perception of purchase risk and increases consumer loyalty.[8]

Corporate reputations are hard to build and easy to lose. Corporate social responsibility or sustainability can help build a corporation's reputation—and can help preserve it when an ethical crisis occurs.

LO 9.3 Stakeholders Expect CSR Accountability

Several stakeholders are expecting—or even demanding—corporations to be accountable for their economic, social, and environmental responsibilities. The following is a list of the most influential stakeholders.

- *Shareholders and financial institutions*—Institutional investors and individual shareholders interested in ethical or social investing require additional information on CSR. Financial indexes have been formulated to guide investors, for example the Jantzi Social Index[9] in Canada and the Dow Jones Sustainability Index[10] in the United States. Responsibility for Ethics 9.1 describes the Jantzi Social Index.

- *Employees*—Informing employees of the corporation's CSR initiatives results in intangible benefits such as increasing employee satisfaction and reducing turnover. In a recent survey, about 80 percent of employees agreed with the statement that the more socially responsible their employer was the more motivated and loyal the employees became.[11]

- *Consumers*—Consumers are concerned about aspects of the goods and services they purchase including, for example, such things as the conditions under which they were produced, genetic modifications, environmental harm, and treatment of employees.

RESPONSIBILITY FOR ETHICS 9.1

The Jantzi Social Index

The Jantzi Social Index (JSI) is a socially screened, common stock index modelled on the S&P/TSX 60 of 60 corporations that have passed a set of broadly based environmental, social, and governance rating criteria. Criteria have been developed to evaluate issue areas such as Aboriginal relations, community involvement, corporate governance, employee and customer relations, environment, and human rights. Some indicators may exclude corporations with significant involvement in the production of nuclear power; the manufacture of tobacco products; and weapons-related contracting.

The index measures how a market for the selected corporations has changed over time. A benchmark is also established against which the success of the process is measured. Thus, the JSI provides a process against which institutional investors—for example, pension and mutual funds—can measure the performance of their socially screened stock portfolios. Also, the Jantzi–Sustainalytics Canadian Social Investment Database provides a comprehensive analysis of approximately 300 companies and income trusts, including all constituents of the S&P/TSX Composite Index.

Source: Adapted from Sustainalytics, Jantzi, accessed January 11, 2016, http://www.sustainalytics.com/JSI.

- *Society at large*—Local communities are interested in social and environmental issues confronting them. Corporate reporting is now addressing this by presenting materials by facility and community. Even students are seeking more information on corporate reporting, either for personal use or for use in classroom discussions or assignments.

- *Service professionals*—The professional accounting associations are recommending more elaborate CSR and sustainability reporting. An example is the Canadian Institute of Chartered Accountants' efforts encouraging corporations to enhance sustainability disclosure in the Management Discussion and Analysis (MD&A) filing. Other professions also encourage increased disclosure.

- *Non-governmental organizations*—NGOs are constantly seeking information on corporations. In many cases, it is questionable how they use the information. For this reason, CSR reporting should be scrutinized and verified prior to release. This stakeholder will be discussed more in Chapter 13.

- *Charities*—CSR reporting informs the public of the corporation's philanthropic efforts. In addition, many social reports identify the corporation's giving policies, including areas of interest, and provide application information.

- *Media*—Journalists are constantly seeking story ideas or information to complete a story. The availability of CSR reports, especially online, is one quick source for them.

- *Government*—Numerous government acts and regulations require disclosure. On the other hand, governments are also interested in corporate self-disclosure because it avoids the need for legislation. Chapter 10 examines the association between ethics and government's role in society and its involvement with business.

Although this is not a complete list, it does indicate that many stakeholders are demanding or expecting increasing amounts of CSR or sustainability disclosure—one good reason why corporations should be serious about considering this type of disclosure.

LO 9.4   CSR and Profitability

It is generally accepted that the blind pursuit of maximum profits would be socially irresponsible. It is also believed that most enterprises have multiple objectives, some of which are social in nature. If these statements are accurate, it is interesting to speculate about the relationship between the extent of socially responsible actions of an enterprise and its level of profitability.

The relationship between profitability and CSR has been extensively studied, with mixed conclusions that can be summarized as follows:

- Expenditures on social responsibility initiatives do not contribute to profits.
- Expenditures on social responsibility initiatives do contribute to profits.
- Expenditures on social responsibility initiatives might contribute to profits.

A study by Laffer, Coors, and Winegarden found that CSR is not positively correlated with business profitability. Furthermore, the authors found some evidence that CSR activities lead to decreased profitability.[12] Another study found that up to some point, increased expenditures in social responsibility are associated with higher profits but further increases are associated with lower profit levels.[13]

An example of a study supporting the position that a positive relationship exists between CSR and profitability was a mega-analysis of 52 previous studies on the impact of CSR on profits by Orlitzky et al. Their findings confirmed that social responsibility and, to a lesser extent, environmental responsibility do have a measurable positive impact on profits. They concluded that their analysis established a greater degree of certainty with respect to the corporate social responsibility and corporate financial performance relationship than was assumed to exist by many business academics.[14]

On the other hand, a study by Margolis and Walsh expressed doubt about research methodologies used in examining the relationship. They examined the 30-year quest for an empirical relationship between a corporation's social initiatives and its financial performance—127 studies were analyzed, almost half of which pointed to a positive relationship between CSR and financial results. The other half reported a negative relationship, a non-significant relationship, or a mixed relationship. The authors argue that a definite link between CSR and profits may be more illusory than the research results suggest. Serious questions are raised about methodological difficulties, including problems with the sample used, concerns about reliability and validity of the measures used, and influence of moderating conditions.[15]

The research and debate on the relationship will continue, most likely without a definitive conclusion, for some time. However, the Network for Business Sustainability (NBS) has taken another view of the CSR and profitability relationship. It points out that 63 percent of the studies on CSR and profitability have found a positive relationship, 15 percent a negative one, and 22 percent a mixed or neutral one. NBS suggests calculating the return of investment of CSR by thinking in terms of creating value. Corporations have financial management systems and financial metrics or measures, but few metrics relating to CSR or sustainability. Initiatives can result in positive impacts, and the social and environmental benefits fall into one of three categories:

- *Firm processes*—The value created can be identified by readily available measures. The costs and savings of an energy conservation program can be measured, most likely with savings exceeding costs.

- *Firm outcomes*—The value created is less obvious and as a result may not be measured—but it should be. An example is provided by a conservation program that may improve employee satisfaction and increase productivity.

- *External outcomes*—The value created is in the more positive perceptions of external stakeholders, such as consumers who may view the corporation more favourably and increase their loyalty, thus increasing sales of the corporation's products.

Some of this value may have been overlooked in the past. NBS has identified three categories of metrics that business should use to capture this value. Financial metrics are the easiest to measure; for example, stock price or return on investment. Valuing CSR at this stage is relatively easy. The second metric is operational, which measures the direct bottom-line impacts of CSR activities and represents the direct costs and revenues associated with an activity. Lastly, strategic metrics are those that result in the corporation improving its strategic position. The metrics are less tangible but are value created from improved employee motivation, the creation of a culture of innovation, and greater brand loyalty.[16]

Now that reasons have been given for CSR reporting, the criteria used in evaluating such reports are discussed.

LO 9.5   Social Auditing and Reporting Criteria

The contents of corporate social reports reflect the criteria used in social audits. Several surveys or guidelines are examined to provide illustrations of the criteria used to assess the ethics of business and identify socially responsible initiatives.

Canadian Business for Social Responsibility (CBSR) is a business-supported, non-profit CSR consultancy that assists Canadian businesses in their social reporting. Responsibility for Ethics 9.2 gives more information on the organization.

RESPONSIBILITY FOR ETHICS 9.2

Canadian Business for Social Responsibility

Canadian Business for Social Responsibility (CBSR) is a non-profit member organization with a mission to accelerate and scale corporate social and environmental sustainability in Canada. It brings together stakeholders to collectively tackle key issues to influence progressive public policy towards addressing social, environmental, and economic challenges.

CBSR operates as a network and key resource in Canada for small and large corporations, researchers, opinion leaders and the media with a mandate to advance corporate responsibility and sustainability. CBSR's values are:

C – Collaborate, creative, connected

B – Bold ideas, business-led, blended value

S – Social innovation, systems, sustainability

R – Restorative, responsible, regenerative

One project is to develop the "Transformational CSR Framework and Approach" that provides a road map for corporations to transform from their present business models toward a sustainability one.

Source: Adapted from "About Us," Canadian Business for Social Responsibility, accessed January 12, 2016, http://www.cbsr.ca/about-us.

Other resources on CSR are available to Canadian businesspersons and managers. The Conference Board of Canada has a "Corporate Responsibility Assessment Tool" to help members better understand how to effectively manage and integrate CSR.[17] The Canadian Centre for Ethics and Corporate Policy operates EthicsCentre.ca, an independent ethics centre promoting an ethical orientation to Canadian organizations. It operates as a registered charity governed by volunteers and supported by corporations and individuals; it sponsors speaker events for members and publishes a newsletter, *Management Ethics*.[18] Finally, The Accountability Project is an initiative to improve CSR and sustainability reporting among business leaders and managers.[19]

Everyday Ethics 9.2 describes one corporation's approach to CSR reporting.

EVERYDAY ETHICS 9.2

Corporate Responsibility Reporting at RBC

Royal Bank of Canada (RBC) uses a comprehensive approach to sustainability reporting that includes the following components:

- A 52-page corporate responsibility report and public accountability statement
- A Global Reporting Initiative (GRI) report of RBC's performance
- A listing of investments in the community and their impact
- A pool of capital RBC invests in businesses that tackle social and environmental challenges
- A statement of RBC's commitment to the environment, including the RBC Blue Water Project
- Listing of awards and recognition
- Social finance initiative in support of social enterprises
- Policies and programs covering: Corporate Integrity, RBC's Economic Impact, RBC in the Marketplace, Working at RBC

Sources: Adapted from RBC, "Community and sustainability," http://www.rbc.com/community-sustainability/index.html accessed January 8, 2016.

An example of an international undertaking to establish reporting criteria is the **Global Reporting Initiative (GRI)**, a non-profit organization that works toward a sustainable global economy by providing guidance in sustainability reporting. Its vision is "to create a future where sustainability is integral to every organization's decision making process." Its mission is to "make sustainability reporting standard practice" which "will enable all companies and organizations to report their economic, environmental, social and governance performance and impacts."[20]

Among GRI's principles are those intended to define report content: materiality, stakeholder inclusiveness, sustainability context, and completeness, and those intended to define report quality: balance, comparability, accuracy, timeliness, reliability, and clarity. Corporations using the GRI *Sustainability Reporting Guidelines* are expected to include the following standard disclosures:

- General Standard Disclosures
  - Strategy and Analysis
  - Organizational Profile
  - Identified Material Aspects and Benchmarks
    - Stakeholder Engagement
    - Report Profile
  - Governance
  - Ethics and Integrity
- Economic
- Environmental

- Social
  - Labour Practices and Decent Work
  - Human Rights
  - Society
  - Product Responsibility[21]

The standard disclosures vary by industry.

The organization states that GRI reports can be used for three purposes, among others: (1) benchmarking and assessing sustainability performance with respect to laws, norms, codes, performance standards, and voluntary initiatives; (2) understanding how the organization influences and is influenced by expectations about sustainable development; and (3) comparing performance within an organization and between different organizations over time.

The GRI indicators are continually being enhanced and a fourth version (G4) of the *Sustainability Reporting Guidelines* is now available. Many corporations, including Canadian ones, utilize the *Guidelines* in their CSR reporting. According to GRI, 93 percent of the world's 250 corporations report on their sustainability performance.

There are numerous other guidelines and indicators, some of which are listed in Responsibility for Ethics 9.3. These and other indicators will be discussed in Chapter 11, "Responsible Ownership and Governance," Chapter 14, "The Environment and Business Responsibilities," and Chapter 15, "Globalization and Business Responsibilities."

RESPONSIBILITY FOR ETHICS 9.3

Global Corporate Reporting Guidelines

Several international comprehensive indicators exist in addition to the ones mentioned in the text. Some examples include the following:

- *OECD Guidelines for Multinational Enterprises*—recommendations to multinational corporations operating in or from an adhering country.
- *UN Global Compact*—an initiative to bring together UN agencies, labour, and civil society to support universal environmental and social principles.
- *Caux Round Table Principles for Business*—an international network of principled business leaders working to promote a moral capitalism.
- *International Code of Ethics for Canadian Business*—a statement of the beliefs, values, and principles Canadian corporations should follow in global business operations.
- *ISO 26000 CSR Standard*—The International Organization for Standardization (ISO) has developed a guidance standard for corporate social responsibility that relates to CSR reporting. The 14000 standards apply to the environment.

LO 9.6   Evaluating Canadian CSR Reporting

CSR and sustainability reports cover the corporation's economic, social, and environmental responsibility initiatives as identified in the auditing process. At this time in Canada, CSR reporting is voluntary. Several surveys evaluate the reporting of Canadian corporations and are listed in Responsibility for Ethics 9.4. The assessment criteria vary among the surveys, but all refer to those identified in the previous section.

RESPONSIBILITY FOR ETHICS 9.4

Surveys of Canadian Social Responsibility and Sustainability Reporting

- Corporate Knights m*agazine's "Best 50 Corporate Citizens in Canada"*—The corporations are selected on several environmental, social, and governance indicators found in the public domain. Refer to Everyday Ethics 1.1 for performance indicators used.

- Maclean's *magazine's "Top 50 Socially Responsible Corporations"—Maclean's,* in cooperation with Sustainalytics, selects the corporations on the basis of several social, environmental, and governance indicators. Indicators used relate to environmental initiatives, impact of local communities, treatment of employees, and supply-chain management. All corporations selected must demonstrate strong disclosure such as by a social responsibility or sustainability report.

Sources: Adapted from "2015 Best 50 Corporate Citizens," *Corporate Knights,* Summer 2015 Issue accessed June 15, 2015, http://www.corporateknights.com/magazines/2015-best-50-issue/; and; "Top 50 Socially Responsible Corporations," *Maclean's,* June 15, 2015, 42-48.

Questioning the Rankings and What Makes a Good Report

Dozens of codes and standards rank or evaluate corporations on every aspect of CSR. Corporations are confronted with lengthy forms and are required to meet various compliance practices. An issue that exists involves whether or not the standards and codes are valid measures of the numerous aspects of CSR. The information supplied by management may be manipulated to the corporation's advantage. Some corporations ignore all requests as there are too many, and too much work is needed to complete the surveys.[22]

Chatterji and Levine make several recommendations for improving the process:

- The codes or standards should be more transparent.
- The measures should be better explained and the source of weightings justified.
- Efforts should be made to reduce compliance costs by better designed forms and measures.
- The data used should be improved, with less reliance on information being supplied by management and more being sought from stakeholders.
- Financial performance measurement uses sophisticated methodology which should be incorporated into the measurement of social indicators.[23]

As indicated in Responsibility for Ethics 9.4, CSR reports are analyzed by several stakeholders. The analysis has identified best practices that corporations should consider when preparing a CSR report. These include:

- Identify the stakeholders to the target audience.
- Describe trends, risks, challenges, and opportunities facing the industry and the corporation. Give an outlook for the future.
- Identify issues, indicating which are priorities so the report has a focus.
- Identify major stakeholders and the approaches used to engage them. Report negative feedback as well as positive.
- Describe the reporting guidelines or standards used; for example, the Global Reporting Initiative. Consider having an external auditor verify the measures.
- Include objectives for the future and report on objective accomplishments from previous years.
- Use visuals such as photographs, illustrations, and graphs to effectively enhance appearance and readability.
- Identify the managers responsible for CSR in the corporation.[24]

Another aspect of CSR reporting is understanding how the report should be communicated to stakeholders.

 Want to learn more about **evaluating sustainability reports?**

LO 9.7 Communicating CSR and Sustainability Results

The reports themselves are a form of communication that will enhance reputation, but the production of a report in itself is not sufficient. Efforts must be made to communicate it to stakeholders.

Within the corporation, various communications activities will inform employees: articles in newsletters, information on the employee intranet, agenda items at regular meetings, and corporate reputation committees. The integration of reporting with any performance measures is key so that employees are reminded constantly of CSR reporting.[25]

Communication with other stakeholders can be with the complete CSR report, or with brochures or mini-reports that mention only the highlights. These summaries can be inserted in customer invoices or billings, or other correspondence. Corporate websites should include electronic versions of the report that are easily accessed. Reporting is being segmented by audience to match messages with stakeholders, for example reports by facility site or community. Also, reporting should be communicated to those who are ready for it, or who are demanding it.

Managers should be aware that newspaper and magazine articles and television news programs are important sources of information for many stakeholders. Corporations must "manage the message," being honest in all communications and informing stakeholders how the corporation has promptly responded to issues or crises. Word of mouth should not be forgotten, as it is a form of communication among some stakeholders. Stakeholders who are influencers or opinion leaders should be identified and communications designed specially to reach them. Finally, communicating CSR and sustainability information is a continuous process, as is the practice of CSR.

In a corporation, one manager or department should be made responsible for the reporting process. Responsibility for Ethics 9.5 describes who this person might be. Throughout this book, numerous Responsibility for Ethics and Everyday Ethics inserts have been obtained from corporate sustainability or social responsibility reports. An emphasis on CSR auditing, reporting, and communication will be part of the education received by future entrepreneurs and managers. Business programs are initiating changes to incorporate the ethics and responsibilities of business topics into their programs.

RESPONSIBILITY FOR ETHICS 9.5

Corporate Responsibility Officer (CRO)

Some managers should be responsible for preparing and communicating CSR or sustainability reports; it is a function unto itself that requires managerial leadership. The manager responsible for this is now being referred to as the corporate responsibility officer (CRO), a title being advocated by a membership-based organization by the same name.

Today, various management positions are responsible for this function, including chief compliance officer, chief ethics officer, director or VP of corporate social responsibility, general counsel, corporate secretary, and executive vice-president for human resources or investor relations. The new position consolidates such activities as compliance management, corporate communications and public relations, environmental sustainability, government relations and lobbying, investor relations, socially responsible investing, and workforce diversity.

CRO members receive information on current trends, success stories, best practices, methodologies, and navigational tools. Membership includes subscriptions to *CRO Magazine* and *Business Ethics Magazine* as well as newsletters, access to TheCRO.com website, and information on conferences.

Source: Adapted from CR. © SharedXpertise. All Rights Reserved. License #CR12533.

 Want to learn more about **CSR in Canadian business?**

LO 9.8 Business Schools and Sustainability Reporting

Business schools are facing demands from society and the business community to better prepare their graduates to identify and address ethical implications in business. Ethics and social responsibility have received attention in business schools only recently, as the emphasis has been on functional areas—many of which have focused on financial rather than social responsibilities. Corporate corruption practices have increased awareness of ethical practice in business, and graduates who will be managers and businesspersons need a moral compass and sensitivity to acting consistently. In other words, graduates must be prepared to face the reality of moral dilemmas.

Corporations are increasingly using accountability audits to develop social responsibility reports for various stakeholders. Although very few business schools publish CSR reports on themselves, they are being held accountable for the integration of ethics of business and social responsibility topics into courses and programs.

The Association to Advance Collegiate Schools of Business (AACSB) is a global, nonprofit membership organization of educational institutions, businesses, and other entities devoted to the advancement of management education. AACSB assists business schools with the continuous improvement of their business programs and schools, including in the area of business ethics and social responsibility. Meeting AACSB's standards and other requirements is the business school is to receive accreditation.

AACSB does not require stand-alone courses in the ethics of business, assuming that the treatment of ethics is infused into other courses. Some controversy in the business and society academic community exists regarding this standard, with many arguing for stand-alone courses in addition to infusion. Responsibility for Ethics 9.6 describes some AACSB requirements relating to ethics and social responsibility of business schools. The performance on the core values specified must be acted and reported upon regularly for the school to retain is accreditation.

RESPONSIBILITY FOR ETHICS 9.6

Ethics and Social Responsibility in Business Schools

Part 1 of The Association to Advance Collegiate Schools of Business' Eligibility Procedures and Accreditation Standards for Business Accreditation describes its core values and guiding principles, which a business school must demonstrate that it will pursue with an ongoing commitment. Core Values and Guiding Principles are:

A. Core Value: Ethical Behavior.

Guiding Principle: The school must encourage and support ethical behavior by students, faculty, administrators, and professional staff.

B. Core Value: Collegiate environment.

Guiding Principle: The school must demonstrate a commitment to address, engage, and respond to current and emerging corporate social responsibility issues (e.g., diversity, sustainable development, environmental sustainability, and globalization of economic activity across cultures) through its policies, procedures, curricula, research, and/or outreach activities. The basis for judging whether or not the values and principles are adhered to is provided along with guidance to the documentation required.

C. Core Value: Commitment to corporate and social responsibility

Guiding Principle: The school must demonstrate a commitment to address, engage, and respond to current and emerging corporate social responsibility issues (e.g., diversity, sustainable development, environmental sustainability, and globalization of economic activity across cultures) through its policies, procedures, curricula, research, and/or outreach activities.

Source: Adapted from "Eligibility Procedures and Accreditation Standards for Business Accreditation," *The Association to Advance Collegiate Schools of Business*, pages 5-6, accessed August 16, 2016, http://www.aacsb.edu/~/media/AACSB/Docs/Accreditation/Standards/2013-bus-standards-update.ashx.

The performance of business schools are also ranked according to their record in business sustainability. *Corporate Knights: The Magazine for Clean Capitalism,* annually prepares the "Better World MBA Ranking." The schools are assessed on three indicators: curriculum involving the courses in sustainability offered; institutes and centres affiliated with the school; and faculty research in particular publications.

Corporate Knights researched 121 MBA and 40 schools were ranked as leaders. Canadian schools included were: Schulich School of Business, York University; Desautels Faculty of Management, McGill University; Haskayne School of Business, University of Calgary; John Molson School of Business, Concordia University; Sobey School of Business, Saint Mary's University; Ecole des sciences de la gestion, Université de Québec à Montréal; Alberta School of Business, University of Alberta; and Rowe School of Business, Dalhousie University.[26]

Finally, a comprehensive ethics program for a business school will create a more favourable public image—within universities, the business community, and society. An ethics program will enable business schools to align their behaviour more closely with that demanded by society. Given the trends in society and in the field of business and management education, business schools need to prepare themselves for possible demands relating to the ethics of business and the implications of ethics on the business programs and schools as well.

LO 9.9   The Future of CSR and Social Reporting

To understand the form CSR reporting will take, it is necessary to speculate on the future of CSR itself. The following are two views of what might happen with CSR.

In a report for VanCity Credit Union, Strandberg interviewed 47 CSR thought leaders about the future and a variety of views emerged. It is agreed that CSR is an aspect of the paradigm shift from industrial to sustainability capitalism. The progress on CSR has been slow, but it appears to be moving into the mainstream of business.[27]

Some of the interviewees felt corporations will lose interest in CSR and it will not move beyond a token baseline. Others thought CSR would develop quickly, especially if driven by high-profile wrongdoing. Continuous improvement would occur in CSR but it would be inconsistent across industry sectors. It was felt by some that CSR was part of a search for a new social contract between business and society. Despite the differences in views of the social impact and degree of corporate commitment, the majority agreed that in five to ten years,

> *CSR will nonetheless become increasingly mainstream within business, even if not with the public consciousness. CSR tools, resources, language—all will become more aligned with business norms and systems. CSR standards—to greater or lesser effect—will be part of business basics and not an add-on.*[28]

Strandberg identified a continuum of CSR possibilities, from "CSR Lite" to "Deep CSR"; these are presented in Table 9.1.

Some other main findings by Strandberg are that:

- The role of stakeholders will become more important and consultation will become a core competency for managers. The relationship with NGOs will become more challenging and CSR will extend along the corporation's supply chain. Ethical consumers will be more powerful, and employees and investors will place more demands on the corporation.
- The top CSR issues will be the environment, reduction of poverty, governance, and accountability.
- There will be a new focus on CSR measurement and reporting with increased standardization.
- Governments may impose mandatory reporting.
- Corporations will be expected to play a greater role in social change.[29]

Overall, most participants in the study agreed that "CSR progress will be slow over the next ten years, but will become increasingly mainstreamed by business."[30] This observation is for the most part still applicable and the only finding that has not occurred is the imposition of mandatory reporting.

In another study, White developed three scenarios of the future of CSR: fade, integrate, or transform. Each of these is described briefly.

- *Fad-and-fade scenario*—Awareness and practise of CSR will decline significantly. This is the result of external trends or events beyond the control of the corporation. Government regulation emerges, replacing the self-regulatory purpose of CSR. The failure to address social, ethical, and governance challenges is also blamed.

TABLE 9.1   Continuum of Future Commitment to CSR

Possible Future CSR	Corporate Commitment
CSR Lite	Superficial and marginal, may be required by law Concerned mainly about responsiveness to complaints May use indicators such as GRI and think they are in compliance
CSR Compliant	Voluntarily take on environmental and social obligations to maintain licence to operate Keep abreast of emerging standards and norms of CSR
CSR Strategic	Become compliant with standards and then create niches in areas more strategic to the corporation May use CSR as key to survival by providing goods and services acceptable to society
CSR Integrated	Believe the need to take social and environmental impacts and opportunities into account. Comprehensive CSR policies and operationalizing CSR principles through rigorous standards and objectives
Deep CSR	Business model where mission is to improve social or environmental conditions Move to addressing trade-offs between different elements of triple bottom line

Source: Based on Coro Strandberg, *The Future of Corporate Social Responsibility* (Vancouver: VanCity Credit Union, September 2002), 6. Available at http://corostrandberg.com/wp-content/uploads/2002/12/future-of-csr.pdf.

- *Embed-and-integrate scenario*—CSR is accepted and the case for it no longer has to be made. Continuous enhancement of CSR approaches and practices occurs, and managers demonstrate a strong sense of moral and ethical commitment.

- *Transition-and-transformation*—Incremental changes to CSR are insufficient and stakeholders demand a redesign of the corporation. This will alter the nature and purpose of the corporation and broaden its social function. There is a challenge to the prevailing wisdom relating to the rights and obligations of the corporation. This became necessary as the public lost confidence in the corporation.[31]

Implications for reporting and communication exist depending what the future holds for CSR. Assuming that CSR becomes "CSR integrated" or "deep CSR," as argued by Strandberg, or that it follows the "embed-and-integrate" or "transition-and-transformation" scenarios proposed by White, the following are considerations:

1. A multiplicity of standards or guidelines exist, and at this time there does not appear to be any convergence around one.

2. The willingness of corporations to make the extensive disclosures necessary and the reliability of information provided are issues.

3. The process of independent verification has not become routine or formalized.

Management must continue to consciously reinforce the CSR measuring, reporting, and communicating process within corporations. Acceptance of CSR reporting has been relatively slow, with only a small number of publicly listed corporations—usually in consumer products and resource industries—making the effort. It is clear that CSR initiatives must be sincere and benefit society, and this is not achieved by merely reporting token actions or approaching it as a public relations tactic.

Your advice to Clare . . .

This chapter identified some of the difficulties with CSR reports that would help explain Clare's confusion. You advise her to check out the methodology used when she is looking at any of the rankings or lists of the "best" corporations; the criteria that were considered in selecting the corporations will be identified and should explain how a particular corporation made the list. Some criteria or measures are better than others. Clare also should keep in mind that corporations often "self-report," which may not be reliable. Furthermore, with any set of criteria, a corporation's good attributes may outweigh its (real or alleged) bad attributes.

Summary

- Corporate reporting of social responsibility and sustainability has become a management function in many organizations. Social auditing is performed and the results become the basis for social reporting. Today, economic, ethical, and environmental standards or measures are being developed and used by corporations. The ultimate in social reporting is to evaluate the corporation's performance on these standards and to have the results externally verified. (LO 9.1)

- An important reason for social reporting is to sustain the corporation's reputation; that is, the stakeholders' perceived views of the corporation. There are connections among reputation, the corporation's stakeholders, the management of the issues they raise, and the approach to strategic management. Today, corporate reputation rather than image has become important to a successful corporate strategy. (LO 9.2)

- Today, CSR reporting is expected or demanded by several stakeholders, in particular shareholders, employees, consumers, society at large, service professionals, NGOs, charities, the media, and government. So many stakeholders are interested in the corporation's social and environmental initiatives that reporting cannot be ignored by management. (LO 9.3)

- The relationship between CSR and profitability has been extensively studied. A majority of studies have found a positive relationship, but the research approaches and techniques used are being questioned. (LO 9.4)

- Several organizations are establishing criteria to be used in social auditing, which in turn determine the contents of CSR reports. Organizations assisting managers in this area include Canadian Business for Social Responsibility, the Conference Board of Canada, the Accountability Project, and the Global Reporting Initiative. The latter is the most prominent, and its indicators are utilized by many corporations in their CSR reports. (LO 9.5)

- The CSR reports produced by Canadian corporations are evaluated by newspapers, magazines, consulting firms, and professional organizations. This evaluation provides best-practice examples for corporations beginning to develop CSR reports. (LO 9.6)

- The act of producing the CSR report is a good learning exercise for the corporation, but it is necessary to communicate the results to stakeholders in various formats and delivery modes. (LO 9.7)

- Few business schools produce a CSR report on themselves. But they are being evaluated in terms of how they are integrating corporate social responsibility and the ethics of business into programs, courses, faculty activities, and student initiatives. (LO 9.8)

- The future of CSR and reporting is not certain. It is thought that it will become a required management function with a minimum baseline standard being established. What happens to CSR will determine the changes in social measuring, reporting, and communicating approaches. (LO 9.9)

Key Terms

Social auditing

Corporate social responsibility (CSR) reporting (sustainability reporting)

Corporate reputation

Global Reporting Initiative (GRI)

Critical Thinking and Discussion Questions

1. Why should CSR measuring or auditing be externally verified?
2. What are the interrelationships among stakeholders, issues management, social responsibility, and corporate reputation?
3. Why are shareholders interested in social auditing and CSR reporting?
4. Why will the debate about the relationship between CSR and profitability not be resolved soon?
5. Why is transparency important in CSR reporting?
6. Why would a corporation use GRI's *Sustainability Reporting Guidelines* in its CSR reporting?
7. What kind of influence do the surveys of Canadian business' social responsibility and sustainability have on management?
8. What advice would you give to a manager responsible for preparing and communicating a CSR report?
9. What influence will business schools have on social auditing and reporting?
10. What is the future of CSR and corporate social reporting?

Cases

9.1 PHILANTHROPY AND ACADEMIC FREEDOM

A fundamental principle of any university or college is the concept of academic freedom. The Canadian Association of University Teachers (CAUT) defines academic freedom as "the right to teach, learn, study and publish free of orthodoxy or threat of reprisal and discrimination." It allows academics to criticize the university and comment on issues that affect their academic activities. Academic freedom applies in many areas, but a particular issue of concern in recent years has occurred when a businessperson donates funds to the university for a certain purpose, for example the funding of a building, research, scholarships, or research centres. Often the donor's name is associated in some way with the area funded. Many business schools or programs are named after prominent businesspersons who have provided funding.

These collaborations between universities and businesspersons are usually welcomed, because universities are insufficiently funded by governments. The CAUT has developed *Guiding Principles for University Collaborations*, which require the protection of academic freedom, university autonomy, and academic integrity in all activities; a commitment of free and open exchange of ideas and research results; the disclosure of real, potential, or perceived conflicts of interest; and the assurance of transparency. The Association of Universities and Colleges of Canada (AUCC) has also recently issued a "Statement of Academic Freedom" that included "ensuring that funding and other partnerships do not interfere with autonomy in deciding what is studied and how."

An example of the issues related to business funding was illustrated by a project to establish an international law studies program at York University. Jim Balsillie, co-founder of Research in Motion (RIM), established an independent, non-partisan think tank on international governance, the Centre for International Governance Innovation (CIGI), to support research activities at Canadian universities. The Balsillie School of International Affairs had been established by a partnership among CIGI, Wilfrid Laurier University, and the University of Waterloo. In early 2012, he proposed establishing an international law studies program at York that included 10 research chairs and 20 graduate scholarships. He planned to donate $30 million, which would be matched by the province.

Faculty, particularly those in the law school, opposed the plan even though York's administration had supported the proposal. The faculty argued that the proposal had too many strings attached, including rights over hiring, renewal and termination of faculty, influence over curriculum and research, and veto over the program's budget. CAUT opposed the program, but it was accused of spreading misleading information about the program.

Questions

1. What are the issues involved in business philanthropy to universities?

2. Who are the stakeholders influencing these issues and/or those influenced by them?

3. What role does business have in funding universities and colleges? How will the York incident influence business support for universities?

Sources: "Academic freedom," November 2011, Canadian Association of University Teachers (CAUT), accessed August 16, 2016, http://www.caut.ca/issues-and-campaigns/academic-freedom; "Guiding Principles," April 2012, (CAUT), accessed August 16, 2016, http://www.caut.ca/about-us/caut-policy/lists/other-guidelines-principles/guiding-principles-for-university-collaborations-(april-2012); Media Release, "Canada's Universities Adopt New Statement on Academic Freedom," October 25, 2011, Association of Universities and Colleges of Canada, accessed August 16, 2016, http://www.univcan.ca/media-room/media-releases/statement-on-academic-freedom/; "About CIGI," Centre for International Governance Innovation, accessed August 16, 2016, http://www.cigionline.org/about; Tristin Hopper, "York U Rejects RIM Founder's $60M deal," *National Post* online edition, April 3, 2012, p. A2; Joseph Brean, "The Academy vs. Jim Balsillie," *National Post* online edition, April 4, 2012, pp. A1, A6; and "Professors Happy to Keep Balsillie's Hand Off York," *National Post* online edition, April 5, 2012, p. A13.

9.2 ETHICS OF OIL

The phrase "ethical oil" has been popularized through the publication of Ezra Levant's book *Ethical Oil: The Case for Canada's Oil Sands* and is frequently used by politicians, including Prime Minister Stephen Harper and his federal minister of the environment.

Those who use the phrase argue that the oil sands petroleum has been unfairly demonized and they wish to downplay the negatives. They claim that petroleum from the oil sands is "ethical" compared to that from some other sources. Oil purchased from dictatorships and kleptocracies has been problematic because in those countries human rights, worker welfare, and social programs may be ignored. Corruption also has occurred in situations where leaders siphon off wealth for themselves and their friends. Saudi Arabia, Venezuela, Iran, and Libya have been mentioned as examples.

It also has been pointed out that oil produced in Canada must meet higher environmental standards than that produced in many countries. Alberta oil could be considered a morally superior resource because Canada has a democratically elected government, is concerned with peace, and maintains social programs for its citizens. Supporters claim that "ethical oil" is comparable to fair trade products such as coffee and certified non-conflict diamonds.

Critics state that it is inappropriate to use the phrase because ethics involves rules, standards, codes, or principles that provide guidance for morally appropriate behaviour in decision making. Others believe that the ethical question is really whether consumers should be consuming oil at all. In contrast to "ethical oil," environmental NGOs and some U.S. and European Union politicians have labelled petroleum from the oil sands as "dirty oil."

Critics claim that oil from the Alberta sands should be considered unethical or dirty oil because it is an unsustainable product, produces high emissions per barrel, lacks environmental monitoring, threatens wildlife (with the use of tailings pools), pollutes lakes, soils, and groundwater, has health consequences for local residents, and causes deforestation. Some U.S. politicians and government agencies have proposed that petroleum from the Alberta oil sands be banned, but California has been the only jurisdiction to impose restrictions to March 2011. European Union agencies have considered sanctions against oil sands production. The delay of the Keystone XL pipeline was linked to the branding of Alberta oil sands; this $7.0 billion project would carry oil sands bitumen across the Midwestern states, including Nebraska, to surplus refining capacity on the U.S. Gulf Coast.

According to some, the use of the phrases "ethical oil" and "dirty oil" is merely a rhetorical device or a way to spin the issue to get people to think of the positives or forget the negatives associated with oil sands production. Environmental NGOs argue that comparisons among oil producers are distractions and do nothing to make oil from any source a better product.

Questions

1. Is there such a thing as "ethical oil"?
2. Who are the stakeholders involved in the discussion of this issue?
3. How does the use of terms like "ethical oil" and "dirty oil" contribute to the discussion of the issue? Are they merely a rhetorical device or method for spin intended to distract?
4. Does using the term "ethical oil" change how stakeholders view oil from the oil sands?
5. What are the implications for CSR measuring, reporting, and communicating?

Sources: Ezra Levant, *Ethical Oil: The Case for Canada's Oil Sands* (Toronto: McClelland & Stewart, 2010); Ethical Oil, accessed August 16, 2016, http://www.ethicaloil.org; Garnet Barlow, "Spinning Alberta's Oil Sands Disaster," *National Post,* January 15, 2011, FP19; Adam McDowell, "Alberta Tar Sands Praised as 'Ethical Oil,'" *National Post* online edition, September 22, 2010; "Ethical Oil: A Debate," Small Dead Animal, accessed August 16, 2016, http://www.smalldeadanimals.com/archives/015431.html; "Rant: Ethical Oil . . . Really?" Rantrave, accessed August 16, 2016, http://religion.rantrave.com/Rant/Ethical-Oil-Really.aspx; Andrew Nikiforuk, "The Fallacy of 'Ethical Oil,'" The Tyee, accessed August 16, 2016, http://thetyee.ca/Opinion/2010/09/22/EthicalOilFallacy; Steven Chase, "Peter Kent's Plan to Clean Up the Oil Sands' Dirty Reputation," *The Globe and Mail*, January 7, 2011, A8–A9; and Jane Taber, "Meet the Prime Minister's Oil-Sands Muse," *The Globe and Mail*, January 15, 2011, A12.

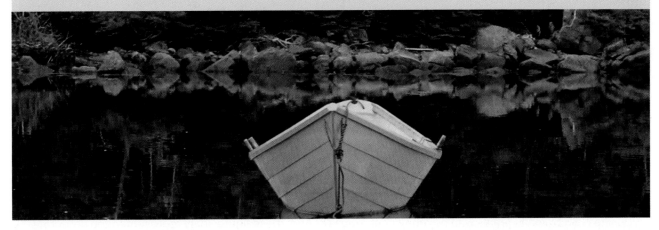

Used with the permission of Dennis Flynn

CHAPTER 10

Regulating Business' Ethics and Responsibilities

LEARNING OUTCOMES

After studying this chapter, you will be able to:

LO 10.1 Understand that there are different types of regulation to enhance corporate ethics and responsibilities.

LO 10.2 Describe the extent of government's involvement in business regulation.

LO 10.3 Learn about government's concern for business corruption and its attempt to prevent it.

LO 10.4 Describe government initiatives to encourage corporate social responsibility and accountability.

LO 10.5 Acknowledge the involvement of business in politics and identify the related ethics and responsibilities.

LO 10.6 Define lobbying and understand its influence.

LO 10.7 Identify the ethics and responsibilities associated with taxation.

LO 10.8 Explain the role of corporate public affairs departments, and define corporate agenda and corporate welfare

LO 10.9 Realize that to some extent business regulates itself.

What would you do if...?

Luke Boychuk was in the kitchen reading the newspaper as his mother prepared dinner. He had graduated from a business program at the local college but was still living at home as he attempted to pay off his student loans. He said to his mother, "Here's another story about the federal government assistance to business. I really resent those big companies not paying back all their loans when I have no choice but to pay back my student loans with interest. They are nothing but corporate welfare bums."

Luke's annoyance was prompted by a story he had recently seen in the newspaper, detailing how between 1982 and 2012 the federal Department of Industry made loans totalling $7.4 billion that were intended to be repaid. However, only $2.1 billion had been repaid to taxpayers. Furthermore, only $9 million had been collected in interest by the department on all the loans made. In addition, the government had given business $6 billion in grants with no repayment required. And, these figures only represented the corporate welfare dispersed by one federal government department and did not included assistance received from provincial and municipal governments.

Defenders of the government programs to business argued that employment has been created, although exact figures were not known. Also, these programs redirect or stimulate economic growth and development not otherwise likely to occur. Some starting businesses needed help to obtain financing as private lenders were not willing to provide. This was particularly the case in high technology industries. On the other hand, the Canada Student Loans Program requires students to start paying interest immediately upon graduation, and to start repaying their loans six months after graduation.

Luke's mother, a chartered public accountant, stopped her dinner preparations and turned to him. "But aren't you some kind of a welfare bum? The government paid the interest on your loans while you were in school. Besides, while you were a student, you were eligible for the GST/HST tax credit, could deduct tuition and education expenses, and, when you moved, you could also deduct those expenses. Now you can deduct the interest paid on your loans. I don't recall you paying any income tax while you were in college. Today, students get an even better deal as they receive tax credits for transit passes and textbooks, and don't pay income tax on any scholarship, fellowship, or bursary income."

This information took Luke by surprise as he realized that individuals as well as corporations receive subsidies from the government. He thought he should reconsider the appropriateness of government programs to assist business.

What is your advice to Luke?

Sources: "Canada Student Loans Program," Employment and Social Development Canada (HRSDC), http://www.esdc.gc.ca/en/student_loans/government.page; "Students and Income Tax," Canada Revenue Agency, http://www.cra-arc.gc.ca/E/pub/tg/p105/p105-e.html; "Technology Partnerships Canada," Industrial Technologies Office, Government of Canada, https://ito.ic.gc.ca/eic/site/ito-oti.nsf/eng/h_00839.htmlhttps://ito.ic.gc.ca/eic/site/ito-oti.nsf/eng/h_00839.html; and Mark Milke, "Corporate Welfare Bums at Industry Canada," Fraser Alert, Fraser Institute, September 2012.

There are a variety of ways that the corporation's behaviour is regulated so that it is aware of ethical issues and recognizes and fulfills its responsibilities to stakeholders. This is accomplished through a range of regulation from government imposed to that provided by market forces. In between corporations and industry practice self-regulation, that is, not relying on government or the marketplace. This chapter discusses how business' ethics and responsibilities are influenced by these types of regulation.

Following sections will describe examples of government attempting to influence business' ethical behaviour and how business influences government regulation. A final section describes the role of self-regulation.

LO 10.1   Types of Regulation

When considering the regulation of business, most think immediately of government regulation. This section lists types of regulation that influence corporations based on market forces, government, and self-regulation.

If a rigorous and competitive market exists, there is less need for government-imposed laws or regulations as the corporation is influenced or regulated by market forces. This could also be referred to as a laissez-faire approach, where government does not interfere with business. The market disciplines would include competitive rivalry among firms with entry to the market possible and substitutes available. Various stakeholders are involved in influencing the corporation and in effect regulate its behaviours. An example is consumers who can take action to force the corporation to behave in particular ways by refusing to purchase goods or services, or through organized action such as a boycott or applying pressure through social media. Abuses are possible, but are corrected by the market or stakeholder pressures. No economies rely on market forces exclusively.

Another scenario is that government extensively regulates an economy, the industries that make it up, and operations of organizations that supply goods and services. Government most likely owns all or much of the economy organizations. It is argued that government regulation is necessary because society cannot trust business to regulate itself. Only a few socialist countries rely almost totally on government regulation, for example, Cuba and North Korea.

What is more likely to happen is that government will regulate parts of the economy that it believes to be the most important. Standards are developed, applied, and enforced by government or its agents, and the standards apply to everyone. Government provides a countervailing power to business by reflecting society's concerns. On the other hand, government regulation is criticized for being oppressive, ineffectual, confused, conflictual, costly, rigid, weakly enforced, and amenable to capture by those it is regulating.

RESPONSIBILITY FOR ETHICS 10.1

The Chemistry Industry's Responsible Care® Ethic and Principles for Sustainability

Launched in 1985 by the Chemistry Industry Association of Canada (CIAC), Responsible Care® is a UN-recognized sustainability initiative that has been adopted in more than 60 countries around the world.

Commitment to Responsible Care inspires CIAC member-companies to continuously improve their health, safety, and environmental performance while delivering products essential to everyday life.

The Responsible Care® Ethic and Principles for Sustainability

We are committed to doing the right thing, and being seen to do the right thing.

We dedicate ourselves, our technology and our business practices to sustainability—the betterment of society, the environment and the economy. The principles of Responsible Care® are key to our business success, and compel us to:

- work for the improvement of people's lives and the environment, while striving to do no harm;
- be accountable and responsive to the public, especially our local communities, who have the right to understand the risks and benefits of what we do;
- take preventative action to protect health and the environment;
- innovate for safer products and processes that conserve resources and provide enhanced value;
- engage with our business partners to ensure the stewardship and security of our products, services and raw materials throughout their life cycles
- understand and meet expectations for social responsibility
- work with all stakeholders for public policy and standards that enhance sustainability, act to advance legal requirements and meet or exceed their letter and spirit
- promote awareness of Responsible Care®, and inspire others to commit to these principles

Source: Reprinted with permission from the Chemistry Industry Association of Canada, http://www.canadianchemistry.ca/responsible_care/index.php/en/our-commitment.

In Canada, government with few exceptions regulates the distribution and sale of alcohol beverages. The labour collective bargaining process is almost totally regulated directly by government with few aspects delegated to other types of regulation. Governments also are the principal regulators in competition policy, bankruptcy laws, and intellectual property. Governments are always introducing new regulations. In recent years they have regulated online transactions, tattoo artists, organic foods, and ingredients in pet food.

Self-regulation is that imposed by the corporation or industry and not by the government or market forces. Businesspersons advocating this type of regulation claim that it is faster, cheaper, and more efficient and effective than government regulation. It is more likely to be accepted because it is voluntarily developed and adapted. It improves the relationship between business and consumers, and allows government to focus on other priorities. An example of industry self-regulation is the Chemistry Industry Association of Canada's Responsible Care® Ethic described in Responsibility for Ethics 10.1.

Self-regulation is criticized because it impairs business competition and innovation due to self-serving restraint by industry participants. It may result in lower standards than those imposed by government, and it is ineffective whenever competition and other laws forbid compulsory membership necessary to ensure the worst offenders are involved. Its administration presents challenges, including the lack of adequate penalties for those who violate the regulations; insufficient financing, publicity, and promotion; and lack of public or consumer representation.

In most forms of capitalism operating in democracies, a mixture of regulation provides a balance among market, government regulation and self-regulation. The types of regulation discussed will clarify that regulation is not solely a government initiative. Also, regulation varies substantially among industries and even within industries.

What is being sought is a balance between private (business) and public (government), two extremes on the spectrum. The private sector provides for innovation, investment, and risk taking that promotes growth and employment. On the other hand, government provides the institutions, rules, safety nets, education, research, and infrastructure to empower the private sector. There are two possibilities in the relationship: where business directly controls more of the economy than the public sector and where the government controls the economy through a variety of methods. The balance shifts back and forth with different consequences for business and society stakeholders.

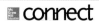 Want to learn about **your view of government regulation?**

LO 10.2   Government Regulation of Business

The influence and involvement of government in the business system is substantial and there are implications of ethics and responsibilities of business. The scope of government in society includes:

- Government is the architect of economic growth, which is accomplished by expenditures, taxation and policies.
- Government is a major purchaser of goods and services provided by business.
- Government is a major promotor and subsidizer of business.
- Government is a provider of financial capital through loans and grants.
- Government is a rescuer of failed business corporations.
- Government is the owner of business enterprises.

In addition to the above, there are four other areas where the government has a major influence on business' ethics and responsibilities: by prescribing legal rules of conduct, by protecting the interests of business, by protecting the interests of various stakeholders, and by using regulation to manage large areas of business activity.

The government provides the framework legislation enabling businesses to operate. This legislation includes laws relating to competition policy, anti-dumping, bankruptcy, incorporation, intellectual and industrial property, contractual agreements and property rights. These laws provide the "rules of the game"; that is, the conditions under which business will operate.

Government is the protector of business interest, for example, the protection provided by tariff and non-tariff barriers that exist to shield Canadian industry from foreign competition. Since 1879, Canadian manufacturing has been protected by tariffs and other barriers such as quotas and regulations. Industries receiving substantial protection in the past have been textiles and shoes, furniture, and appliances. It is argued that this has caused some Canadian industries to be less efficient than they might have been. Freer trade is reducing the influence of these protective measures. Protective measures also exist between provinces, and many businesspersons believe that these barriers are a greater impediment to free trade within Canada than between Canada and other countries.

Government is the protector of various interests in society against business exploitation and redistributes resources to meet social ends. Governments have legislated to protect the interests of those with low incomes (for example, rent control), minorities facing discrimination, and the environment. Consumers have been protected by extensive legislation as they are often unable to represent themselves or make their voice heard. Corporations are involved in collecting taxes for governments, for example the retail sales tax and the payroll deduction of personal income tax. They also pay taxes on profits, but the total amount they contribute is substantially less than that raised by personal income taxation.

Government directly manages, through regulation, large areas of private business activity. In theory, the regulation of the economy and the business enterprise system should be done by the forces or influences of the marketplace. But in practice this is not the way it works, and a mechanism is required to control monopoly and oligopoly powers, to control the transfer of income from consumers to producers, and to increase efficiency in production. Regulatory organizations do a variety of things, including establishing prices and levels of service, mediating between corporations, advising governments on policy, controlling expenditures, administering acts or regulations (such as licensing), and operating as quasi-judicial bodies. A good example of the complications in regulations is provided the discussion of the taxi industry in Responsibility for Ethics 10.2.

Various governments regulate the operation of business enterprises through commissions, tribunals, agencies, and boards. The following are examples of industries regulated by government-sponsored regulatory agencies: petroleum, insurance, pipelines, some agricultural products including dairy and poultry, utilities (electric, telephone), transportation (trucking, rail, airline, bus, taxi), communications (radio, television), and securities. Government, in one form or another, directly regulates about one-third of the economy through more than 600 organizations. Examples of such regulatory organizations are the Canadian Radio-television and Telecommunications Commission, the Canadian Transportation Commission, the National Energy Board, and public utilities boards in most provinces.

Regulation impacts every business enterprise, and every Canadian, but there are two trends reducing regulation by government, deregulation and privatization. The implication of these trends is shift from government regulation to market and self-regulation.

Deregulation is the reduction of government influence or impact over the economy allowing for a freer and more efficient marketplace. The reason given for deregulation is that fewer and simpler regulations will lead to a more competitive business environment, resulting in higher productivity, more efficiency, and lower prices. Those opposing deregulation argue that it results in reduced environmental quality standards, greater financial uncertainty as occurred in 2008, and market control by monopolies.

RESPONSIBILITY FOR ETHICS 10.2

Regulating the Taxi Industry

The taxi industry is one of the most regulated in Canada. Municipal governments impose numerous requirements on the industry including: driver qualifications, vehicle conditions, driver and passenger insurance, and conditions on where they can operate. Licenses or permits are restricted and in some cities can cost tens of thousands of dollars. All the rules limit competition, reduce the supply of taxis, and force up prices creating in what could be viewed as a cartel. None of this is good for the consumer.

The industry's regulations were challenged with the entry of ride-sharing apps by Uber and others. The ride-sharing taxis proved popular by providing better service at lower prices. The regulated taxis objected to the ride-sharing companies as they were taking business and did not have to adhere to the expensive regulations. Municipal governments are struggling to develop regulations that will allow the ride-sharing taxis to operate. Even Uber agrees that it should be subject to some regulation relating to safety and insurance.

In the meantime, some stakeholders are benefiting from the changes technology as enabled in the taxi industry while others are harmed.

Privatization, one manifestation of lessened government involvement, is discussed as it has substantial implications for business corporations. **Privatization** is the "strengthening of the market at the expense of the state."[1] After reviewing several definitions of privatization, Goodrich concluded that they had four things in common: privatization is defined as the provision of public service by the private sector; there are degrees of privatization, complete or partial; there are many techniques or forms of privatization (for example, divestiture, contracting out); and different terms are used that have overlapping meanings (for example, "contract public agencies," "contracting out service delivery").[2]

The privatization trend provides numerous opportunities for business. Private-sector businesses can provide services formerly delivered by government in several ways, namely participation in conventional markets where buyers and sellers compete for projects or contracts to perform work; monopoly franchises where the private company provides services at specified standards; management contracts; and acquiring ownership of the corporation. The challenges for entrepreneurs and managers are to make sure they are aware of the possibilities by monitoring government initiatives.

The following two sections discuss government's efforts at dealing with major ethical and responsibilities issues relating to corruption and its direct efforts to influence on the social responsibility in some industries.

LO 10.3 Government Attempts at Dealing with Corruption

The approach to dealing with corporations and executives who had engaged in wrongdoing or corruption was not easy for government. Corporate crimes were difficult to detect and prosecute. There is disincentive for a corporation to report corruption or co-operate with authorities. The government can take the corporation to court or negotiate a guilty plea if charged with wrongdoing. A guilty conviction or plea would preclude the corporation from doing business with government customers. An alternative was for the government to not address the issue although they may want to discourage corrupt behaviour. This alternative may not be possible once the corruption is public knowledge and pressure could come from organizations such as Transparency International, media coverage, and social media discussions.

Corruption of Canadian public officials was covered by the *Criminal Code of Canada* and it was not until 1999 the *Corruption of Foreign Public Officials Act* (CFPOA) was passed covering foreign officials.[3] These laws were to discourage Canadian corporations from engaging in corrupt acts at home or abroad. The CFPOA covered bribery of public officials, the possession of proceeds derived from bribery of public officials, and money laundering. CFPOA investigations were often not disclosed by the government or the corporations. The first prison sentence for charges under the Act was in 2014.

In 2012, the Government of Canada introduced its Integrity Framework to deal with the lack of action on this issue. The Framework "was established to protect the integrity of procurement and real property transactions managed by the department by ensuring that these transactions are carried out free from the influence of corruption, collusion and fraud and that the Government of Canada does not inadvertently support suppliers involved in such illegal activities." Its purpose was to safeguard public funds, to promote conduction of business in a fair, open, transparent, accountable, and cost-efficient manner, and to encourage businesses to engage in ethical conduct. The offences covered include: fraud under Federal Government legislation; money laundering; involvement with criminal organizations; tax evasion; bribery; secret commissions; forgery; and falsification of books or documents.[4]

Corporations wishing to do business with the Government must certify that they and any affiliates have not been charged with any of the offences anywhere in the world in the past ten years. If they have been charged, they are disbarred from doing business with the Government for ten years. Exceptions will be made if no other corporation is able to supply the goods, an emergency exists, or national security is involved.

Even with these exceptions, the Canadian framework is stricter than requirements in the United States, the European Union, and many other countries and was considered an overreaction to the corruption issue. In the United States and other countries, corporations may be prosecuted but legal action can be deferred or suspended. This is done where corporations agree to undertake remedial actions.

Business claimed that this pragmatic approach is not available in Canada and that the consequences are serious. Disbarment might be considered a restraint of trade and lawsuits may result under the World Trade Organization and NAFTA. Disbarment of a corporation may result in a loss of Canadian jobs, reduced foreign investment, and higher prices from reduced competition. It is argued that the Canadian Government's rule-based integrity framework should be more flexible and take into consideration that the corporation is taking remedial actions.

The Government was lobbied to revise the Framework by the industry associations including Canadian Manufacturers and Exporters, Canadian Council of Chief Executives, Information Technology Association, and the Canadian Chamber of Commerce. These initiatives resulted in the revision of the Framework announced in July 2015 with a name change to the Integrity Regime. The ten year ineligibility can be reduced to five years if the corporation cooperated with legal authorities or addressed the causes of the misconduct. The actions of affiliates would no longer automatically result in ten year ineligibility. The Government would have the ability to suspend a supplier for up to 18 months if the supplier is charged or admitted guilt to a listed offence. The Government also announced that would continue to consult anti-corruption experts and industry. Administrative agreements would be allowed which were agreements between the supplier and Government that reduced the risks of contracting with a particular supplier. It was not specified how these agreements would work.[5]

Canadian business leaders were still unhappy with the policy and critics claimed that the Government had caved into to business interests. The Integrity Regime was still harsh compared to legislation in Europe and the United States under the *Foreign Corrupt Practices Act* enacted in 1977. Also, there was no presumption of innocence until proven guilty and the five year disbarment was still too long. The revised Framework still did not have provision for a type of negotiated settlement, referred to as "deferred prosecution agreement." Such agreements might include the corporation acknowledging wrongdoing, dismissing employees involved, paying of penalties, implementation of compliance measures, declarations that the corporation will avoid wrongdoing the future, and undertaking anti-corruption policies. This type of agreement saves the corporation and employees from more negative consequences, but still addresses the issue. Charges are stayed, that is, no action is taken, and the corporation can be recharged in the future if it does not comply with the agreement and if it did, the charges are dropped.

Industry associations pointed out that a deferred prosecution agreement alternative would act as an incentive for corporations to disclose ethics breaches and co-operate with authorities. The Integrity Regime did not make the distinction between punishment and deterrence of misconduct. Deferred prosecution agreements would allow the corporation to take corrective actions, for example, firing employees guilty of misconduct and the implementation policies and ethics programs that would help prevent corruption in the future. Everyday Ethics 10.1 describes the impact of the Integrity Regime on one corporation.

In addition to the policy to insure the integrity of the corporation it deals with, the government is furthering corporate social responsibility.

EVERYDAY ETHICS 10.1

SNC-Lavalin and the Integrity Regime

SNC-Lavalin one of the leading engineering and construction groups in the world operating in over 50 countries. Founded in 1911, it is headquartered in Montreal, PQ, has 40,000 employees, and revenues of about $7 billion with about two-thirds from Canadian projects.

Since 2012, SNC-Lavalin has faced corruption scandals including fraud, bribery and money laundering in Algeria, Bangladesh, Libya, and Montreal. Former managers face criminal charges relating to corruption of Libyan officials. The perpetrators and SNC-Lavalin's CEO were fired as a result.

In February 2015, criminal fraud and bribery charges were laid against the company under the *Corruption of Foreign Public Officials Act*. If convicted, the company would not be able to bid on Canadian government projects for five years. SNC-Lavalin executives say this is too harsh and warned that the company might be broken-up or cease to exist. If convicted and disbarred, innocent employees and investors would be harmed. Needless to say the company's reputation has been severely damaged.

SNC-Lavalin argues that charges should be laid against individuals, not the company. Moreover, since 2012 the company has gone through a rehabilitation process including: establishing an ethics hotline, forming an Ethics and Compliance Committee, making key leadership and structural changes, appointing a new Chief Compliance Officer, holding Ethics and Compliance Awareness Sessions, and updating the Code of Ethics and Business Conduct.

SNC-Lavalin is facing a very uncertain future and the well-being of many stakeholders will be impacted.

Sources: Adapted from "Ethics & Compliance Timeline," SNC-Lavalin, accessed July 24, 2016, http://www.snclavalin.com/en/ethics-compliance-timeline; *Corruption of Foreign Public Officials Act* (S.C. 1998, c. 34), http://laws-lois.justice.gc.ca/eng/acts/c-45.2/index.html; Jeff Gray and Bertrand Marotte "SNC-Lavalin Charged with Fraud, Bribery after Settlement Talks Fall," *The Globe and Mail,* Feb. 20, 2015, A1; Theresa Tedesco, "SNC Vows to Fight Charges," *National Post,* Feb. 20, 2015, A1, A3; and Drew Hasselback, "SNC-Lavalin Charges Reveal the Teeth in Canada's New Anti-bribery Law," *National Post,* Feb. 19, 2015, Online edition at http://business.financialpost.com/legal-post/snc-lavalin-charges-reveal-the-teeth-in-canadas-new-anti-bribery-law.

LO 10.4 Government Involvement in Corporate Social Responsibility

Governments have become involved in CSR through legislation, regulations, or simply by encouraging CSR or sustainability practices.

Demands to legislate CSR and accountability have occurred at various times. Some morality has been legislated through the legal system. For example, there are laws against dishonest business practices, laws to prevent monopolistic behaviour, laws relating to the health and safety of employees, and laws that prohibit conducting business with corrupt foreign regimes. This type of legislation has provided safeguards to various stakeholders, including investors, consumers, and employees. The demands increase after a corporate scandal. For example, the Enron failure led to American corporations being held more accountable, the BP oil disaster in the Gulf of Mexico led to demands for greater regulation in the petroleum industry, and recent Ponzi schemes have prompted calls for more protection of individual investors.

More directly, the federal government has been involved in several initiatives that have influenced the corporate social responsibility of Canadian corporations, including:

- Whitehorse Mining Initiative [1993]—The Mining Association of Canada initiated the process bringing together business, government, environmental NGOs, and Aboriginal groups to ensure social and environmental goals were considered in mining development.

- The Kimberley Process [2000]—The Canadian government was involved in labelling diamonds to prevent the sale of those used to finance conflicts or produced by slave or child labour.

- Voluntary Principles on Security and Human Rights [2000]—These principles provide a broad framework that helps companies operate in ways that provide security to their facilities while respecting human rights and fundamental freedoms. Canada committed to the Principles in 2009.

- Extractive Industries Transparency Initiative [2003]—This initiative was to address corruption in resource-dependent countries. Canada did not join until 2007. This eventually led to Building the Canadian Advantage: A Corporate Social Responsibility Strategy for the Canadian International Extractive Sector, which includes a CSR Counsellor and CSR Centre of Excellence [2009]. This was revised as the Doing Business the Canadian Way: A Strategy to Advance CSR in Canada's Extractive Sector Abroad [2014]

EVERYDAY ETHICS 10.2

Public–Private CSR Partnership

The Government of Canada's Global Affairs Department is partnering with IAMGOLD Corporation and Plan Canada, a private, non-profit aid NGO, to implement a social responsibility project in Burkina Faso. The government developed a CSR strategy for the Canadian mining corporations operating in developing countries. The strategy is to better prepare corporations to manage social and environmental risks and is being administered by Global Affairs Canada. The project involves job training in 13 communities for 13- to 18-year-old youths so that they develop skills suitable for employment in the mining and other industries. Global Affairs provides $5.6 million of the funding with IAMGOLD contributing $1 million and Canada Plan $900,000.

This partnership is a change in government foreign aid policy and there are several projects of this type. They are criticized as a taxpayer subsidy to profitable corporations that could afford to finance the projects themselves. There are benefits for the corporations including the reduction of conflict between the mining companies and local communities. It is alleged that the strategy allows corporations to put a positive spin on operations that often involve adverse impacts on the environment and abuses of human rights.

Source: Adapted from IAMGOLD Corporation, accessed August 16, 2015, http://hss.iamgold.com/default.aspx?SectionId=8072b0bc-cf69-4a6d-a201-e58239067fa3&LanguageId=1; Plan Canada, "Plan in Burkina Faso," http://plancanada.ca/Burkina-faso, accessed September 7, 2012; and Canadian International Development Agency, "Capacity-Building of Youth to Grow the Economy: A Public-Private Partnership," accessed August 16, 2015, http://www.acdi-cida.gc.ca/cidaweb%5Ccpo.nsf/projEn/S065292002.

- National Roundtables on Corporate Social Responsibility and the Canadian Extractive Sector in Developing Countries [2006]—These were established to encourage Canadian corporations operating overseas to conduct their activities in a socially and environmentally responsible manner and in conformity with international human rights standards.

- Several federal government departments have extensive websites dealing with CSR, including Industry Canada, Foreign Affairs and International Trade Canada, and Natural Resources Canada.

A recent development has been the federal government's public–private CSR partnership described in Everyday Ethics 10.2. This new initiative is controversial but is also a trend with other governments. It appears that all the government's initiatives are designed to increase the economic success of corporations, particularly those operating in foreign countries, while accepting social and environmental responsibilities for their operations.

Another area where there are ethical and responsibility issues for corporations relates to the political system under which they operate.

LO 10.5   The Ethics of Business and Involvement in Politics

Many issues are associated with the involvement of business in politics either as corporations or businesspersons, and there are pros and cons to such involvement. It is a pluralistic right for business to be involved, as corporations are an institution in society and thus have a moral responsibility to take part in the political system. Business influences society and, in addition, corporations pay taxes. Businesspersons are very knowledgeable of economics and finances, and have the information and skills to make a contribution to the political process. Participation by business is necessary to counterbalance the anti-business activity of other groups, for example of unions.

On the other hand, some downsides to business involvement exist. It is argued that politics should be left to politicians, and business should be publicly neutral. Politicians have to address issues across a wide spectrum, and businesspersons are not necessarily qualified to deal with many of the social issues the government must address. Business is already accused of exerting too much power in society, and the involvement of businesspersons in politics could upset the pluralistic balance in society. Business involvement might also be interpreted as being biased, thus having an adverse effect on customers or shareholders, or conflicts of interest might exist. There is a risk of alienating a particular government that could result in legislation or regulation not desirable to business. It is difficult to find a satisfactory position on many of the emotional and highly political issues such as abortion, gun control, and human rights.

Nevertheless, business is involved in politics in several ways. The following is a discussion of this involvement.

- The financing of political parties—Corporations are a source of funds, but recent election laws limit the amounts. Corporations can also contribute "in kind"; for example, providing a party with free office space, or providing legal and other services to politicians during an election campaign. Also, corporations contribute to political leadership campaigns, where the money involved can be as great as for an election campaign.

- Publicly expressed support for a candidate or party—Support for a candidate or party can be expressed in several ways; for example, inviting campaigning politicians to address employees on company property, allowing the circulation of political materials to employees, endorsing a candidate in a newspaper advertisement with his/her affiliation mentioned, or allowing time off work to a particular candidate.

- Publicly expressed views on political issues—Business expresses views on political issues by purchasing advertisements, usually via contributions to industry or trade associations that support or oppose some political issues.

- Executives running for public office—Executives have management skills to bring to government, presumably as much as the occupational groups that are most common in elected positions now: lawyers, teachers, university professors, journalists, and engineers.

- Management's position on employee participation—Management must formulate policies relating to employee participation in the political process; for example, leave policy.

It is argued that Canadian business is very involved and influential in politics and is portrayed as having powerful influences on public policy without much accountability. Businesspersons must concern themselves with how they are perceived as influencing government policy and whether their positions are in the best interests of not only the corporation but also other stakeholders, including owners and society at large. Everyday Ethics 10.3 gives two illustrations of how corporations address the issue of business and politics.

EVERYDAY ETHICS 10.3

Addressing Political Involvement

Canadian corporations address the issue of involvement in politics in their codes of conduct or ethics. The following are two examples of company policies:

Political Activity

As a Bombardier employee, you may, subject to applicable laws, engage in legitimate political activity, as long as it is carried out on your own time and without using Bombardier property. You may seek election or other political office, but you must notify your supervisor or the Compliance Officer to discuss the impact your involvement may have on your duties at Bombardier. You may express your views on public or community issues of importance but it must be clear at all times that the views expressed are not those of Bombardier. Bombardier and its employees abide by all laws and regulations governing political contributions in every jurisdiction where the Corporation does business.

Political Contributions

We have the right to be politically active, but this activity should be on our own behalf and not as a representative of Agrium. We must not contribute any Agrium funds or assets to any political party or organization, nor to any individual who holds or is seeking public office, except where such contribution has been authorized by the Board of Directors or by a committee of the Board or is in accordance with Agrium's Political Donations Policy and budget.

Sources: Adapted from "Code of Ethics and Business Conduct," Bombardier, accessed August 17, 2016, http://www.bombardier.com/content/dam/Websites/bombardiercom/supporting-documents/BInc/Bombardier-code-of-ethics-currentversion-en.pdf, p. 19; and "Code of Conduct," Agrium Inc., accessed August 17, 2016, http://www.agrium.com/system/files/2016_revised_code_of_business_conduct_and_ethics_revised_v2_7462339_1.pdf, p. 4.

The types of involvement in politics by business and businesspersons are one way to influence politics, and thus public policy. An even more direct approach to influencing government is through lobbying activities, which also involve ethical and responsibility issues.

LO 10.6 The Ethics of Business Lobbying

Lobbying is defined as all attempts to influence directly or indirectly any government activity, and includes any attempt to influence legislators, their staff members, public administrators, and members of regulatory agencies. Specifically, the practice of lobbying government can be defined as including attempts to influence:

- the making or amending of legislation and regulations;
- the making or changing of government policies or programs;
- government decisions in the awarding of grants, contracts, contributions, or any similar benefits; and
- government appointments to boards, commissions, and any other public office.[6]

There are several types of business lobbyists. The first is business corporations that attempt to influence government through lobbying performed by business interest groups or associations. Examples of business interest groups that act as lobbies include the Business Council of Canada (an organization comprising the chief executives of the largest corporations); the Canadian Federation of Independent Business; the Canadian Bankers' Association; the Electrical Association; and the Automobile Parts Manufacturers Association of Canada. It is estimated that there are hundreds of such associations that regularly lobby government by distributing literature and information; appearing before parliamentary committees, royal commissions, inquiries, and other bodies; and interviewing politicians and civil servants.

The second type of lobbyist is the consultant who specializes in government–business relations and is paid by a corporation, a group of corporations, or a business association to make contact with government, or to tell business how to influence government. Government relations consultants monitor government activities for clients, and help them develop strategies and actively lobby for their clients. Independent consultants are often former politicians, civil servants, and political staff, sometimes with industry experience, who operate as individuals or in small partnerships.

A third type of business lobbyist exists where corporations develop lobbying capability "in-house," often referred to as government relations or public affairs staff. Such departments usually report to top management and constantly monitor the political environment for developments that will impact the corporation and industry. They prepare positions for management and may be involved directly in lobbying, or in making presentations to government departments or agencies and civil servants. These departments are discussed in a following section.

There are pros and cons to business lobbying. It is argued that business must lobby to offset the influence of other groups. It should be pointed out that business groups are not the only lobbyists. Consumers, farmers, labour organizations, environmentalists, and religious groups, to name a few, all lobby governments. In fact, such interest group lobbying is part of a capitalist system in a democratic society. It is believed that with each group presenting its point of view, government is better prepared to formulate public policies satisfactory to Canadians. Business argues that its opinion or perspective must be made known to governments if informed decisions are to be made about public policies affecting business.

Lobbying is criticized for several reasons. In the past, some of the practices of lobbying groups were unethical, as seen, for example, by the use of bribes, the offering of gifts, the making of improper political contributions, and even blackmail. As a result, many view lobbying as a distasteful, undesirable activity. It is also argued that the business lobby is far too powerful and presents a view that is too one-sided. Other groups in society claim there is unequal access to government and that business is over represented while other stakeholders are underrepresented. The cost of business lobbying can be passed on to consumers through the prices paid for goods and services, while other groups, such as consumers and environmentalists, do not have the financial and human resources to lobby effectively.

Business lobbying activities have grown and there is continuing involvement of government in the business system. This has necessitated greater lobbying to ensure that business interests are protected. Also, once one corporation or group starts to lobby, others follow out of necessity. It should be remembered that business groups often lobby against one another in an attempt to influence a government decision. For example, Canadian bicycle manufacturers might lobby for increased tariff protection, but retailers that import bicycles might lobby for lower tariffs. This point illustrates that business lobbying is not just business against other groups in society.

RESPONSIBILITY FOR ETHICS 10.3

The Lobbying Act

The *Lobbying Act* and its related Regulations came into force simultaneously on July 2, 2008. See below for key events in the history of the Canadian lobbyists registration regime.

The *Lobbying Act* is based on four key principles.

- Free and open access to government is an important matter of public interest.
- Lobbying public office holders is a legitimate activity.
- It is desirable that public office holders and the general public be able to know who is engaged in lobbying activities.
- The system of registration of paid lobbyists should not impede free and open access to government.

The Act applies to individuals who are paid to lobby. People who lobby on a voluntary basis are not required to register.

The Office has developed a Lobbyists' Code of Conduct available at https://ocl-cal.gc.ca/eic/site/012.nsf/eng/h_00014.html and lobbying activity can be searched at Lobbyists' Code of Conduct.

Source: Adapted from Office of the Commissioner of Lobbying of Canada, accessed January 14, 2016, https://ocl-cal.gc.ca/eic/site/012.nsf/eng/h_00008.html.

Nevertheless, increasing concern was being expressed about business lobbying, and in 1988 the federal government passed an act respecting the registration of lobbyists. In this act, the definition of lobbyist referred to "paid lobbyists" and included those who lobby on behalf of clients and employees of enterprises and organizations that function as lobbyists. According to the government, the purpose of the legislation is not to regulate lobbying, but to make the lobbying process better understood by identifying who is doing it and on what issues. Responsibility of Ethics 10.3 describes some aspects of this legislation.

The government is a major stakeholder in the business system influencing business operations, and as discussed in this section business influences government policies, legislation, and regulation through involvement in politics and lobbying.

Taxation is an area to which business devotes a lot of attention through lobbying. Also, it is an area involving ethical and responsibility issues.

connect   Want to learn more about **lobbying government?**

LO 10.7   Ethics and Responsibilities of Taxation

There are several ethical issues and responsibilities relating to the Canadian taxation of corporations and individuals. Society, as represented by government, has to decide what portion of taxation revenue is to be raised from business, both large and small, and individuals. Many Canadians believe that large corporations and high income individuals do not pay enough taxes. The ethics of avoiding taxes is questioned by many Canadians as they believe that corporations and high income earners have a responsibility to pay their share. In any taxation system, how the harms and benefits to be allocated is an issue.

Corporate Taxation

The corporate tax rate for corporations has been lowered and is now perceived to be lower than the rate paid by individuals. The percentage to federal government revenue paid by corporate income tax has been declining while the percentage acquired from individuals has been increasing. In addition to lower rates, there are other factors that are reducing the taxes paid by corporations. Corporations have more possibilities for reducing taxes through legal tax loopholes, various tax credits, and tax loss carry-forwards. A *Canadian Business* article in March 2014 identified several corporations paying almost no taxes and explained how they were able to do so legally. Canadian corporations studied included Canadian Pacific Railway Ltd., BCE Inc., Gildan Activeware Inc., Enbridge Inc., Laurentian Bank of Canada, and Sun Life Financial Inc.[7]

A controversial area is the transferring of profits on taxes to jurisdictions with lower taxation, in particular, taxation havens or as they are now referred to as taxation efficient jurisdictions. The issue is where Canadian multinational corporations should pay income taxes on profits made on operations in other countries where taxation is lower. This is done through **transfer pricing**, the price set for goods and services sold between legal entities of the corporation. This practice is described in Everyday Ethics 10.4 involving Cameco Corp.

A federal government policy has facilitated tax avoidance through its signing of tax information exchange agreements (TIERs) which enabled countries to exchange information about taxpayers. According to the government, these agreements will combat international tax evasion and ensure tax fairness by implementing standards developed by the Organisation for Economic Co-operation and Development (OECD). These agreements allow Canadian multinational corporations to pay the lower taxes in other countries and bring back profits and pay no taxes in Canada. Taxation experts claim that Canada has little choice but to sign those agreements as other developing countries are participating and are granting their multinational corporations tax breaks and exemptions. In 2015, TIERs existed with 23 countries with seven more being negotiated.[8]

There are some arguments for lower corporate taxation. It is argued that corporate taxation in Canada must be comparable to that in other countries. If not, Canadian operations will be transferred to other countries. The reverse is happening on a limited basis as American corporations acquire a Canadian corporation and transfer their head offices to Canada where corporate taxes are lower. Also, it is claimed that lower corporate taxation enables corporations to boost investments in their Canadian operations creating jobs. A counter argument is that corporate taxation should be low as ultimately consumers pay for them when purchasing goods and services. Some corporations are unable to take advantage of the lower taxation opportunities as they lack the resources to arrange them or their operations are not sufficiently mobile to allow the transfer of operations.

EVERYDAY ETHICS 10.4

Cameco Ltd. and Its Taxes

Cameco Ltd., with headquarters in Saskatoon, Saskatchewan, is one of the world's largest uranium producers with mines in Canada, U.S., and Kazakhstan. In 1999, it set up a subsidiary company, Cameco Europe Ltd., in Zug, Switzerland, a low-tax haven. This subsidiary purchases uranium produced by Cameco at US$10/lb and sells to customers around the world. Over the years, the price has been as high as US$140 and is now about US$40. Cameco generates few profits in Canada thus paying few taxes. By locating the subsidiary in a tax haven, it has avoided paying tax on billions of income saving about $1.5 billion in federal and provincial income tax.

Cameco states that having the marketing subsidiary in Europe is logical as it is closer to most customers. Cameco Europe has its own Board of Directors and one employee, the CEO, and operates out of an office rented from its law firm. Some paper work is done in Zug but all other functions are done by Cameco employees in Canada. Uranium never goes to Zug as it is shipped directly from Canada to customers.

The Canada Revenue Agency (CRA) is disputing the corporate structure saying it was only set up to avoid taxes. Also, CRA questions the transfer pricing arrangement. The U.S. Internal Revenue Service has also taken action against Cameco to recover avoided taxes. CRA won its court case against the company but the decision has been appealed by Cameco. It is estimated the Cameco might have to pay over $800 million in back taxes and penalties if it loses in court. Cameco claims that it is acting within the law.

Sources: Adapted from John W. Warnock, "Cameco Uses Dummy Corporation to Avoid Taxes," Saturday, 1 June 2013, accessed January 19, 2016, http://johnwwarnock.blogspot.ca/2013/06/cameco-uses-dummy-corporation-to-avoid.html; CBC News Saskatchewan,"Ottawa Accuses Cameco of Multi-Million Dollar Tax Dodge," September 19, 2013, accessed January 19, 2016, http://www.cbc.ca/news/canada/saskatchewan/ottawa-accuses-cameco-of-multi-million-dollar-tax-dodge-1.1860079; David Milstead, "Cameco's Tax Pit is Getting Deeper," *The Globe and Mail*, June 5, 2014, B11; and Cameco Corp., accessed August 17, 2016, http://www.cameco.com/.

Small Business Taxation

A special case is made for lower taxation on small business enterprises. Governments believe that small businesses are a major creator of jobs in the economy and should receive a preferential tax rate. Studies have not proven this conventional wisdom and it has been pointed out that while many small businesses are created, few grow. The preferential rate applies to small businesses with less than $15 million in taxable capital and the first $500,000 per year of qualifying active business income. Almost 700,000 small businesses benefit annually from this lower rate.[9] Other arguments supporting a preferential tax are that small businesses should be compensated for their limited access to capital, the high costs of compliance to various laws and regulations, and cash flow concerns facing smaller businesses.

A study at the University of Calgary contradicted the view that small business tax concessions encouraged growth. It could result in corporations being broken into smaller, less efficient units merely to take advantage of the tax concession. Some individuals might create small businesses in order to reduce their personal tax liabilities rather than grow corporations. Lastly, a threshold effect might exist that holds back small businesses from growth beyond the size limits to qualify for the concession.[10] Another study by the C.D. Howe Institute also found that the tax rate concession had only a minor impact on investment by small businesses and came with a social cost. This cost is that the government must recoup the foregone tax revenue by cutting spending or imposing higher taxes on other business corporations or individuals. Furthermore, encouraging the expansion of small businesses at the expense of larger ones may not result in the most productive businesses reducing the overall economic performance of the country.[11]

Individual Taxation

The Federal Government has increased the proportion of total income tax revenue that is received from individuals. This increases the tax burden on individuals. As with corporate taxation, the issue of fairness arises as many Canadians believe that wealthy individuals are able to avoid paying taxes. Legal schemes or loopholes are used by lawyers and tax experts to reduce the amount of taxes paid.

The Canadians for Tax Fairness is "a not-for-profit, non-partisan organization advocating for fair and progressive tax policies aimed at building a strong and sustainable economy, reducing inequalities and funding quality public services."[12] It receives most of its financial support from Canada's labour union organizations and is criticized by many economists for its misleading presentations. The organization advocates for closing of tax loopholes that are unfair and result in an ineffective tax system enabling some to avoid paying taxes. It wants a Financial Transaction Tax (also known as the Robin Hood Tax) imposed on international financial transactions as is being done by some countries. The money collected under this system would help address global poverty and climate change, and be used to deal with the debt and deficit crisis. Also, the organization wants the Canada Revenue Agency (CRA) to clamp down on **tax havens** defined by CRA as a jurisdiction with one or more of the following characteristics: no tax, or very low rates of taxation; strict bank secrecy provisions; a lack of transparency in the operation of its tax system; and a lack of effective exchange of information with other countries.[13] It is estimated that Canada's federal governments are losing tens of billions each year. Canadian businesses and individuals who are paying income tax question the fairness of the system that allows some to legally avoid paying taxes.

Increasing the taxation of the rich is advocated by many Canadians. It is claimed that the rich do not spend all their income. Reducing taxes on lower income earners, who do spend all their income, sparks economic growth. An argument opposing this view is that rich Canadians deserve their good fortune as they are providing goods and services that consumers want. They have played by the rules and should be encouraged and not penalized for their success. Higher taxation of the rich has not been successful in other countries as it does not raise more revenue. Instead, it increases the legal avoidance of taxes by accountants and lawyers searching for ways to avoid taxes through tax shelter arrangements. Nevertheless, many perceive that taxing the rich is a matter of fairness.

The taxation system is complex and the issues not easy to resolve. Moreover, this discussion only dealt with income taxes at the Federal Government level. Taxes are also imposed by provincial and municipal governments and there are many different types of taxes levied. Canadians believe that corporations should behave ethically and accept their responsibilities by contributing to the financing of public services.

In order to monitor government and formulate plans to lobby and otherwise influence government policies, corporations have established public affairs departments.

 Want to learn more **Canadian taxation policies?**

LO 10.8   Corporate Public Affairs Departments

Corporate public affairs is the management function responsible for monitoring and interpreting the governmental environment of the corporation or industry, and for managing the responses necessary to protect the interests of the corporation or industry. Public affairs or government relations departments have been established in many large corporations and managers of such departments should have knowledge of governmental decision-making processes and have credibility with relevant government officials or departments.

Although public affairs initially focused on the relationship between business and government, its role in some corporations has been expanded to include community relations, media relations, environmental monitoring, issues management, lobbying, and public relations. As a result, the corporate public affairs function is found in corporations under a variety of names. Also, corporate public affairs departments have expanded in response to the growing impact of government involvement in the business system, for example in the areas of diversity, environmental protection, occupational health and safety, and consumer protection. It has also been necessary to counteract the lobbying of other stakeholders in society promoting their interests, for example NGOs.

Corporate public affairs has evolved into an occupational profession represented by the Public Affairs Association of Canada (PAAC), a national, not-for-profit organization founded in 1984. Its principal objective is to help public affairs professionals succeed in their work by providing them with forums for professional development, the exchange of new ideas, and networking.[14] The PAAC has an extensive Statement of Ethical Principles, a portion of which is reproduced in Responsibility for Ethics 10.4.

Public affairs or government relations units continue to play a role when the corporation is attempting to influence government and in interpreting government's influence upon the corporation. Through the three approaches of involvement in politics, lobbying, and public affairs departments, business does influence government policy-making and regulation. These approaches raise the issues of corporate agenda and corporate welfare.

Those individuals and groups in society who question the increasing role of business frequently use the phrase **corporate agenda**, the real or imagined domination of public policy or government programs by corporations or business organizations in their own best interests. The concern is that corporations have too much influence over governments and the lives of individuals. Social activists and union leaders are prominent in their criticism of the alleged corporate agenda.

There is some consensus on the components of such an agenda. The corporate agenda usually includes some or all of the following:

- The reduction of government involvement in the economy through privatization, downsizing, and outsourcing.
- The deregulation of business and industry.
- Reduced corporate taxation and personal income taxation of higher-income earners along with an overall shifting of tax burdens to working individuals.

RESPONSIBILITY FOR ETHICS 10.4

PAAC Statement of Principles

The Public Affairs Association of Canada (PAAC) is a gathering place for the interchange of ideas and ideologies, professional development, and practical networking. As the established national organization of public affairs professionals, the PAAC helps define appropriate conduct.

Public affairs professionals work with corporate, charitable, and political clients to engage various audiences. The public affairs profession is recognized increasingly for its high standard of practice and expertise, as well as the impact practitioners have on the development and debate of issues. It is acknowledged for the value and diversity of its contributions to Canadian society.

Public affairs practitioners will:

1. Avoid acting in such a way as to bring harm or disrepute to the profession, colleague, employer, or client.
2. Respect regulatory statutes and meet in full their obligations for disclosure in particular the Charter of Rights, the federal and provincial Lobbyist Registration Acts, Privacy Legislation, and municipal codes as they apply to the jurisdiction of practice.
3. Provide advice, guidance, and an informed opinion as to the nature of the business, policy, or legislative issue in a manner that is forthright and credibly reasoned.
4. Avoid personal and professional conflicts of interest and inform clients and employers as soon as the potential for conflict arises.
5. Ensure that any new engagement is subject to full disclosure with respect to regulatory requirements, the firm, and the client.
6. Be transparent in the management of financial accounts, contractual matters, obligations, and client/organizational interest.
7. Respect interpersonal confidences and confidential information.

Source: Based on "Statement of Principles," Public Affairs Association of Canada, http://www.publicaffairs.ca/who-we-are/ethical-principles/. Used with permission of PAAC.

- Advocacy of deficit and debt reduction.

- Reduction in government expenditures on social services to low- and middle-income individuals.

- The enactment of free trade agreements and support for globalization.

- The weakening of unions and workers' right to organize.

- Increasing lobbying and involvement in the political process by business including the formation of partnerships between business and government.

Despite this alleged corporate agenda, corporations and industries appear increasingly willing to advocate for and accept government assistance referred to as **corporate welfare**—any action by municipal, provincial, or federal governments that gives a specific corporation or an entire industry a benefit not offered to others. It is a pejorative term attributed to Ralph Nader, who first used the term in 1956 to describe the special treatment received by business. The term "corporate welfare bums" was used by NDP leader David Lewis in the 1972 federal election campaign to emphasize the preferential treatment received by business.[15] The term contrasts with social welfare and suggests receiving a benefit without doing anything. All forms of government assistance are included, for example grants, loans, loan guarantees, tax breaks, trade barriers, and legislated monopolies. The practice is criticized as it is considered unfair to other corporations and to taxpayers and consumers. The term constantly appears in media stories relating to the subsidies received by business.

The hypocrisy of business lobbying for and accepting government assistance is not lost on many stakeholders. The corporate agenda advocates less government regulation and a reduction in social programs—that is, social welfare—while advocating for benefits to business.

Finally, the third type of regulation is described and some of the consequences of this trend to self-regulation identified.

LO 10.9   Business Regulating Itself

Corporate self-discipline is a form of regulation where norms or standards are developed, used, and enforced by the corporation itself. This is accomplished through mission and values statements, codes of conduct or ethics, ethics programs, or adherence to social and environmental reporting guidelines. The acceptance and practice of corporate social responsibility (CSR) is the most general form of self-regulation (refer to Chapters 7, 8, and 9). Even though it has received substantial attention recently, CSR is still criticized. It has failed to live up to its promise, and some corporations have been accused of participating only for appearances or on a token basis. The desire for profit maximization still exists, and the corporation's behaviour is a function of market imperatives rather than management's values or corporate structures. There is no assurance that all corporations will participate, and enforcement is a problem. On the other hand, measures of CSR are being increasingly used and pressures are being applied by various stakeholders advocating socially responsible behaviour.

Business also regulates itself at an industry level. Members of an industry can attempt to influence corporate behaviour and even enforce standards. Industry or trade associations often facilitate this type of regulation, and initiatives are undertaken to address industry issues that, if not addressed, may lead to government regulation. Advertising Standards Canada is an industry organization committed to the integrity of advertising through industry self-regulation with the Canadian Code of Advertising Standards. The Retail Council of Canada attempts to influence its members' behaviour in various ways, one of which is the Code Practice: Scanner Price Accuracy Voluntary Code. Another example is given in Responsibility for Ethics 10.5.

The power to prevent abuses is usually limited as the potential for anti-competitive behaviour limits the effectiveness of this type of regulation. In most industries participation is voluntary, and even when a member violates the standards, enforcement and remedial action is limited.

Business' ethics and responsibilities are influenced by various factors all related to market forces, government initiatives, and the behaviour of corporations. The result is a varied and dynamic environment of regulation.

RESPONSIBILITY FOR ETHICS 10.5

The Realtor® Code

The Canadian Real Estate Association promotes professionalism in the industry through its code of ethics called the REALTOR® Code. The Code includes a Standard of Conduct statement to protect the rights and interests of consumers. The Code may establish obligations higher than required by law.

The REALTOR® Code has been in existence in Canada since 1959 and has been amended many times over the years to reflect the changing needs of the public, the values of society, and to act as an assurance of higher professional standards. The current REALTOR® Code booklet is 24-page document. The Code of Ethics states that realtors are committed to:

- Professional, competent service
- Absolute honesty and integrity in business dealings
- Utmost civility
- Co-operation with and fairness to all
- Personal accountability through compliance with CREA's Standards of Business Practice

To meet their obligations, REALTORS® pledge to observe the spirit of the Code in all of their activities and conduct their business whether personally or through employees, associates or others in accordance with the Standards of Business Practice and the Golden Rule —

"Do unto others as you would have them do unto you."

Source: Used with the express permission of www.crea.ca, www.REALTOR.ca, www.REALTORSCare.ca. The trademarks REALTOR®, REALTORS® and the REALTOR® logo are controlled by The Canadian Real Estate Association (CREA) and identify real estate professionals who are members of CREA.

Your advice to Luke . . .

You advise Luke that you understand he may be somewhat quick in criticizing corporations for receiving government assistance; however, most citizens receive benefits from governments, including students. Hopefully, if loans are involved, they are repaid—unlike the practice with government assistance to business. Everyone should be cautious in accusing others of being social or corporate "welfare bums."

Summary

- Business is regulated by market forces, government, or self-regulation by business itself. Many in society believe that only government regulates business. Most economies rely on a combination of the three forms, with only a few communist countries relying on almost complete government oversight. (LO 10.1)
- The scope of government regulation of business is extensive. There are four areas where government has a major influence on business' ethics and responsibilities: by prescribing legal rules of conduct, by protecting the interests of business, by protecting the interests of various stakeholders, and by using regulation to manage large areas of business activity. Two trends have had a reduced the influence of government: deregulation and privatization. (LO 10.2)
- Through legislation and the Integrity Framework regime, the government is attempting to discourage corruption of public officials in Canada and abroad. (LO 10.3)
- The federal government has recognized the importance of corporate social responsibility and has been involved with several initiatives to ensure Canadian corporations behave in ways that are socially and environmentally responsible. (LO 10.4)

- Business is involved in Canadian politics through financing political parties, supporting particular candidates, expressing views on public issues, allowing employees to participate in the political process, and through businesspersons seeking public office. (LO 10.5)

- Lobbying is any attempt to influence directly or indirectly any government activity, and includes any attempt to influence legislators, their staff, public administrators, and members of regulatory agencies. Corporations or industry organizations can have their own employees as lobbyists or can hire consultants to perform the function. Lobbying is controversial and is being increasingly regulated. Even though business devotes considerable resources to lobbying, its efforts are not always successful. (LO 10.6)

- Government's taxation of corporate and personal income raises issues relating to the fairness of the taxation system and how some corporations and individuals can legally avoid paying taxes. This is accomplished by shifting operations to low-tax havens or finding loopholes in the system. (LO 10.7)

- Corporate public affairs departments perform the management function responsible for monitoring and interpreting the governmental environment of the corporation or industry and for managing the responses necessary to protect the interests of the corporation or industry. Some claim that business' capability to influence government has resulted in a corporate agenda where it dominates government actions. While business advocates the reduction of government involvement in the economy, it also seeks government assistance and protection—a practice known as corporate welfare. (LO 10.8)

- There has been an ideological shift away from relying on government to solve society's problems. This decline in government involvement and increased emphasis on business self-regulation has implications for corporations and their stakeholders. (LO 10.9)

Key Terms

Self-regulation

Deregulation

Privatization

Lobbying

Transfer pricing

Tax haven

Corporate public affairs

Corporate agenda

Corporate welfare

Critical Thinking and Discussion Questions

1. Why do most Canadians believe that only the government regulates business?
2. Why are there continuing demands for the regulation of some business activities despite the trend towards a reduction of government influence?
3. What are the controversies associated with the government dealing with corporate corruption?
4. Why should government be encouraging corporations to be socially and environmentally responsible?
5. Should corporations and businesspersons be involved in the political process at all?
6. How can business lobbying of government be justified?
7. What are some of the dangers of business lobbying?
8. Why do corporations and individuals attempt to avoid responsibility for paying the taxes they owe?
9. Why is it necessary for corporations to have a corporate public affairs department?
10. What evidence is there that governments operate with a corporate agenda?
11. Should corporate welfare be stopped?
12. What the dangers or downsides to business self-regulation?

Cases

10.1 REGULATING TIPS

Eammon O'Dwyer owned a successful upscale restaurant in Toronto. Many challenges were involved in operating this type of business, including the collection and distribution of tips or gratuities. In the past few years, proposals to regulate tips had been introduced in the Ontario Legislature.

Bill 81, the "Elimination of Automatic Tips Act, 2010," proposed that "No person who owns or operates an eating establishment shall charge any customer an automatic service charge, regardless of whether notice of the service charge is provided in advance." An exception was made for private functions and banquets. Often automatic tips were added to larger parties of six or more. The proposal raised the issue of whether tips should be given only in recognition of exemplary service, or imposed even if the service was poor. Eammon was of the view that his wait staff had to work harder with larger groups and they deserved a specified tip. Some patrons objected to the automatic aspect.

A second proposed regulation was Bill 107, "Protecting Employees' Tips Act, 2012," which would amend the Employment Standards Act, 2000, by adding the clause "An employer shall not take any portion of an employee's tips or other gratuities." The regulation was to prevent employers from "tipping out," that is, taking a cut of the tips received by employees. It was not intended to prevent tip pooling or tip sharing, where all employees, including host and kitchen staff, received a portion of the wait staff gratuities. Eammon knew that some restaurateurs were involved in the "tipping out" practice whereby they took a portion for themselves. He felt that this was not being fair to employees.

The proposed regulations created a lively discussion in the media both for and against regulation. Some staff believed that "tipping out," if properly done, would reduce the income inequity among staff. Many wait staff felt they deserved most of the tips as they worked the hardest. Others said they had no problems with tip pooling and received their share. Unfortunately, some unscrupulous operators took advantage of the "tipping out" practice according to some wait staff. Complaints about these operators had prompted the proposed regulations.

This type of regulation had a substantial impact on the Ontario restaurant industry, which had revenues of $24 billion and employed 30,000 people. The Canadian Restaurant & Foodservices Association (CRFA) stated that tips were a complex issue and that restaurant operators understood their significance to employees and their importance to customer service. The CRFA felt that the regulation was unwarranted and would be difficult to enforce.

Eammon thought that the proposed regulations extended the hand of government too deeply into his business and were not necessary. He felt that there must be better things for government to be doing.

Questions

1. What are the ethical issues involved with the proposed regulations?
2. Who are the stakeholders influenced and/or who can influence the issue?
3. Should government regulate business operations to this extent?
4. Should the regulations be put in place by the government?
5. What would be your view if you were Eammon, a wait staff, or kitchen staff?

Sources: "Elimination of Automatic Tips Act, 2010," Government of Ontario, Bill 81, accessed July 22, 2016, http://www.ontla.on.ca/web/bills/bills_detail.do?locale=en&BillID=2375&isCurrent=false&ParlSessionID=39%3A2; "Protecting Employees' Tips Act, 2012," Government of Ontario, Bill 107, accessed July 22, 2016, http://www.ontla.on.ca/web/bills/bills_detail.do?locale=en&BillID=2657; and "CRFA Tackles Tipping in Ontario," Canadian Restaurant and Foodservices Association, page 37, accessed July 26, 2016, https://issuu.com/riccardo11/docs/crfn_september_final.

10.2 THE ETHICS OF ASBESTOS

Canadians were aware of the dangers of asbestos and it had been removed from many public buildings, including the Parliament Buildings in Ottawa. Exposure to asbestos endangered health through asbestosis, lung cancer, and a more serious cancer referred to as mesothelioma, cancer of the lung's protective lining. Most countries had banned all forms of asbestos as it was considered a health risk. The Canadian government has supported the production and export of asbestos and still has not banned its use in Canada as have other developed countries including Australia, Japan, and all the countries in the European Union. It did not agree that asbestos be added to the Rotterdam Convention list of hazardous substances until 2012. No effort is being made by the government to ending asbestos use worldwide.

Asbestos was first mined in Canada in 1879 and continued until 2011 when the last mine closed and asbestos is no longer exported. The mining and use of asbestos in Canada has left two issues. First, the use of asbestos in construction has exposed workers in the past. As asbestos is present in many buildings throughout the country, exposure to asbestos-related diseases are still occurring as these buildings are renovated or demolished. The asbestos-related diseases have a long latency period 20 to 50 year and many affected cases may not show up for years.

The second issue relates to the importation and use of chrysotile asbestos products. Each year Canadian business is allowed by the government to import about $6 million worth of products containing asbestos including brake linings and pads, various construction materials, and clothing. Brake linings and pans make up about 60 percent of the imports and are used as they are less expensive than alternatives. Mechanics, construction workers and even do-it-yourself home renovators may be exposed and suffer asbestos related diseases.

Today, it is estimated that 152,000 workers are exposed to asbestos. In the past 20 years, 5,000 deaths have occurred from asbestos-related diseases making it the most common cause of workplace deaths.

In July 2015, Health Canada revised its website about asbestos by deleting a statement that chrysotile asbestos is less potent doing less damage and changed the statement that only breathing significant quantities of asbestos fibre would be dangerous to "breathing asbestos fibres can cause cancer and other diseases." The changes to the website were not publicly announced.

Still, the government refuses to ban the use of asbestos products.

Questions

1. Why is the government continuing to allow the use of asbestos and so reluctant to ban its use?
2. What are the ethical issues associated with the government's policies?
3. What are the ethical issues associated with Canadian businesses' continued use of asbestos products?
4. Who should take responsibility for the continuing use of asbestos?

Sources: "Health Risks of Asbestos," Health Canada accessed January 14, 2016, http://healthycanadians.gc.ca/healthy-living-vie-saine/environment-environnement/air/contaminants/asbestos-amiante-eng.php; "Health Canada Revises Its Position on the Health Risks of Asbestos," Occupational Cancer Research Centre, University of Toronto, accessed January 14, 2016, http://www.occupationalcancer.ca/2015/health-canada-revises-its-position-on-the-health-risks-of-asbestos/?gwcpp_catid=3; and Trevor Dummer and Carolyn Gotay, "Asbestos in Canada: Time to Change Our Legacy," *Canadian Medical Association Journal*, July 14, 2015, 187(10), E315-E316.

Used with the permission of Dennis Flynn

CHAPTER 11

Responsible Ownership and Governance

LEARNING OUTCOMES

After studying this chapter, you will be able to:

LO 11.1   Identify the owners of Canadian business.

LO 11.2   List and explain the ethical and responsibility issues of ownership.

LO 11.3   Define and understand the challenges of responsible investing.

LO 11.4   Describe approaches to protecting owners and investors.

LO 11.5   Define corporate governance and discuss the issues relating to corporate governance.

LO 11.6   Explain the relationships among ownership, corporate governance, and social responsibility and ethical conduct.

What would you do if...?

Felica Desterro was in the third year of a business program and recently had become interested in the role of responsible investing. Throughout her college years, she had also become interested in the environment including topics such as climate change, greenhouse gas, and CO_2 emissions. She regularly attended meetings of environmental groups held on campus and presentations by faculty or others on the damage occurring to the environment from our consumption of fossil fuels.

At one of the meetings, she was approached to become more active, and in particular, to organize a campaign to obtain a commitment from the College's Board of Governors to sell investments in fossil fuel corporations. College had an endowment fund of $75 million which provided student scholarships and an employee pension fund of $60 million. Over 40 colleges and universities in Canada, and hundreds around the world, had started such campaigns. In addition, municipal and religious institutions had become involved. Felica decided to do some research into these campaigns.

The divestment of the stocks held by colleges and universities is not a new initiative, for example, there was a divesting of tobacco stocks in the 1990s. The Canadian Youth Climate Coalition (CYCC) has been heading up the student environmental movement nationally. In January 2013 CCYC launched its Fossil Free Canada campaign calling for individuals and institutions to divest from fossil fuels. It is requesting that institutions immediately stop purchasing any new investments in fossil fuel corporations and to divest all investments within five years.

Felica would receive assistance from this group to prepare a campaign on campus. CCYC provided advice on how to launch a petition, build a team to assist, plan for the campaign, build support, press decision makers, and escalate the campaign with demonstrations. It provided posters, leaflets, buttons, toolkits, guides, and background materials. She learnt that most divestment campaigns were initiated by students, but faculty also participated in many cases. Any campaign would involve students, faculty, and the Board of Governors and would make a statement of the college's commitment to the environment.

During her research, Felica came across some counter arguments to divestment. First of all, it is a complicated process as investments are often in pooled funds (such as hedge, mutual, and venture funds) as opposed to individual stocks, and that there were few funds completely free of non-renewable energy corporations. Educational institutions had legal and financial obligations relating to the endowment funds that had to be respected. There are likely to be economic costs, that is, lower returns on investments. Resources for scholarships may be reduced or in the case of pension funds, payments had to be made to retirees.

Furthermore, energy corporations were major contributors to college campaigns for buildings and programs in addition to hiring many graduates. The fact that many energy corporations were involved with renewable energy sources was ignored. The divestment campaigns were criticized for being anti-business and were mainly symbolic rather than substantive. Some critics claimed that divestment campaigns had little economic effect on the targeted corporations. The campaigns had little impact on the consumption of fossil fuels as society, including students, relied on the products and services of these corporations every day. The alternatives suggested were to invest in researching cleaner energy technology, and to work with corporations to change their behaviour towards energy consumption. It was also pointed out that colleges could establish low-carbon endowment funds to which students and faculty could donate.

What is your advice to Felica?

Owners, also referred to as investors or shareholders, are key stakeholders in a capitalist system as they provide a major portion of the capital to finance corporations. Although many stakeholders influence the corporation, a corporation is for the shareholders; they own it, and should ultimately control it. The ownership patterns of Canadian business are changing, and owners have varying degrees of influence on corporate social responsibility and the moral behaviour of the corporation. Ownership will be the focus of the first four sections of this chapter.

The fifth and sixth sections will examine how the corporation is governed and discuss the main stakeholder involved, the members of the Board of Directors. A governing system includes the processes, structures, and relationships through which decisions are made. Corporate governance is defined and some aspects examined. The relationship between governance and performance is discussed along with the relationship to corporate social responsibility and the ethics of business.

LO 11.1   The Ownership of Canadian Business

Who owns Canadian business? A quick response would be "shareholders," but the answer is not as straightforward as this. Table 11.1 lists the main types of owners of Canadian businesses. Some owners personally own equity in the corporation either as investors, entrepreneurs, employees or managers, customers or consumers, or producers.

TABLE 11.1   Owners of Canadian Business

Investors—Investors are individuals who personally hold equity interests for investment purposes and who are not involved in the corporation as entrepreneurs or managers. Those individuals who have purchased shares in corporations listed on a stock exchange are an example of this type of owner.

Entrepreneurs—Ownership of business by individuals—that is, entrepreneurs—is a common form of ownership and has become increasingly so in recent years. Small businesses with fewer than 100 employees, are an important force in Canada, accounting for nearly 98 percent of all enterprises.

Employees and managers—Employees including managers may own all or parts of corporations. Employee ownership can take several forms, including participation in an employee stock purchase plan or employee share ownership plan (ESOP); cooperation with an entrepreneur to refinance a corporation and operate it as a going concern; and establishment of a worker cooperative.

Customers or consumers—The most common type of business organization owned by customers is the co-operative, and the most widely recognized among these are retail consumer co-operatives and financial institutions such as credit unions or caisses populaires. Co-operatives have been leaders in institutionalizing ethics and responsibilities.

Producers—Producer ownership is through co-operatives of various types. There are more than 150 agricultural marketing co-operatives in dairy, grain, poultry, and other endeavours. In addition there are farm supply, fisheries, and production co-operatives.

Ownership through mutual funds—A **mutual fund** is a pool of money from many individual investors that is invested on their behalf, usually in a specific kind of investment. Money contributed to equity mutual funds is invested by fund managers in a portfolio of shares in corporations. Ownership via mutual funds appeals to some investors as it allows them to participate in the stock market without having to make separate decisions about each purchase or sale of stocks.

Ownership interest through pension funds—A substantial portion of pension fund assets are invested in corporate stock. Thus, many Canadians are most likely unaware that they are investing in Canadian business.

Corporate ownership—Corporations often own shares in other enterprises. This inter-corporate ownership is widespread and is monitored by the government. The purpose of the monitoring is to ascertain whether monopoly behaviour occurs and to identify foreign ownership.

Private equity firms—**Private equity firms** manage large pools of money acquired from wealthy individuals or families and big institutions such as pension and mutual funds. The firms are private in the sense that they are not listed and traded on a stock exchange.

Venture capital companies—A **venture capital company** is a type of private equity firm that usually acquires part ownership of business enterprises for which they provide financial and management assistance.

Not-for-profit organization ownership—Examples of not-for-profit organizations are churches, non-governmental organizations (NGOs), foundations, and universities, and all are likely to be concerned with the integrity of business. Investment or endowment funds in these organizations sometimes own stock in corporations.

Government ownership—Canadian federal, provincial, and municipal governments all operate a large number of business enterprises, sometimes referred to as Crown corporations. Government-owned corporations have been used extensively as instruments of public policy implementation, and are considered by some to be part of the Canadian economic culture.

Challenges arise from any type of ownership but the issues facing investors are the most examined. In the situation when the ownership of the corporation is widely dispersed among thousands of shareholders, it is argued that management actually controls the corporation. Individual investors lack the means, and maybe the will, to unite and challenge management's decisions. At the other extreme, investors who are shareholders in corporations dominated by one or a few shareholders who have controlling interests are virtually powerless also. Their few votes make no difference, as sufficient votes are controlled by the dominating shareholder. Corporations with a dominant shareholder must be sensitive to treating minority shareholders with respect and fairness.

Traditionally, the ownership of one share meant one vote and, at least in principle, the owners of shares directed the affairs of the corporation by evaluating management's performance and deciding upon the acquisition and disposal of assets. In other words, shareholders had certain rights based upon their voting privileges. However, many corporations operate with **dual-class stock**, where more than one type of share or stock with different voting rights and dividend payments is issued by a single corporation. Also, **non-voting shares** or **restricted shares** (sometimes referred to as *uncommon shares*) are allowed on the Toronto Stock Exchange. Non-voting shares are common shares without voting privileges, while restricted shares involve some limit on voting, for example only one vote for every 10 or 100 shares owned. The creation of these types of shares allows management or majority owners to control the corporation by concentrating voting power in the hands of a few friendly shareholders. The result is ownership (or stake) without control (or influence), and the fundamental tenet that ownership entails control is contradicted. Such a circumstance is believed to represent a threat to economic democracy and might lead to a decay of a central feature of the free market system. Issues of fairness and rights of other shareholders arise when some shareholders have control through the use of non-voting shares. Often shareholders have no other recourse than to sell their shares if they disagree with the control exercised by the voting shares.

Investors or shareholders can be categorized as passive or active. **Passive shareholders** are those who do not attempt to influence the affairs of the corporation even though they have a legal right to do so. Many small shareholders simply cast their votes with management without considering alternatives. There may be a feeling of hopelessness, but nevertheless they have some responsibility for at least being informed about the corporation and exercising their voting privileges. **Active shareholders** are those who participate in the governance to the full extent allowed by the law. This can be an individual shareholder but also the individuals who manage pension and mutual funds. In the past, these shareholders were "passive"; that is, they did not exercise voting rights or otherwise attempt to influence the affairs of the corporation despite owning substantial numbers of shares. Active shareholders may take an interest in social responsibility issues as will be discussed later.

It is claimed that employee ownership increases morale and company loyalty, motivating employees to greater effort. Productivity rises, and higher profitability results. **Worker capitalism** is a term used to describe employee ownership as workers are turned into capitalists through stock ownership. If widespread, employee ownership could lead to a de-concentration of wealth. Employee ownership has been shown to be an important variable in reviving the fortunes of corporations that were not profitable enough to satisfy existing owners. Although not bankrupt, these corporations, or branch plants, were often abandoned by their owners and rescued by management, entrepreneurs, and employees. In this manner, jobs were saved.

Employee ownership is not without difficulties. Employees who invest in the corporation for which they work are in effect increasing their stake in the corporation. Their jobs, and often savings and pensions, depend now upon the fate of one corporation. Seldom do employees have majority ownership and control of the corporation. Management may still run the corporation as it wishes, not relinquishing control to employees. By not disclosing financial and operating results, employees are often kept unaware of how well the corporation is doing, and in some cases may be manipulated by management as needed information is not available. If employees own shares their participation in decision making may lead to nothing getting done, with the endless meetings, discussions, and votes being very time consuming. In some cases, only token democracy is practised in the workplace despite the employee involvement in ownership, and the prospects for job security are not enhanced.

Some issues directly related to ownership have been identified and the next section describes some issues related to corporate social responsibility.

LO 11.2   Ethical and Responsibility Issues of Ownership

There are ethical issues relating to how some owners are treated by others, and how owners treat other stakeholders. The actions of other stakeholders—for example governments, other corporations, and self-regulatory organizations—influence the owner stakeholder. Knowledge of how owners are influenced and/or influence is important to understanding the implications for corporate citizenship. The following are illustrations of the ethical issues relating to ownership and how they are acted upon.

RESPONSIBILITY FOR ETHICS 11.1

Social Responsibility Shareholder Resolutions

The *Canada Business Corporations Act* requires that shareholder proposals or resolutions be circulated to shareholders and voted upon at the corporation's annual meeting. Investor or shareholder resolutions are presented on a variety of topics, including those related to ethical and social responsibility, but they are seldom passed and sometimes withdrawn after discussions with corporate management. Examples of social responsibility–related proposals and corporation targeted are:

- Independent human rights assessment in Western Sahara (Potash Corporation of Saskatchewan)
- Provide ongoing reporting of how the corporation was working towards a low-carbon economy (Suncor Energy Inc.)
- Establish specific objectives to increase female representation on its senior management team (BCE Inc.)
- Paying one's fair share of taxes (several large banks)
- Report on Aboriginal claims to Crown lands (Teck Resources Limited)
- Feasibility of eliminating neonicotinoid pesticides (Canadian Tire Corporation)

Source: Compiled by the author from *The System for Electronic Document Analysis and Retrieval* (SEDAR), the electronic filing system for the disclosure documents of issuers across Canada, accessed July 27, 2016, http://www.sedar.com/homepage_en.htm.

 Want to learn more about **what shareholders are demanding of corporations?**

Investor owners have limited influence in making the corporation more socially responsible, but some do attempt it through presenting shareholder resolutions to annual meetings. Examples are provided in Responsibility for Ethics 11.1. Few of these resolutions are successful, but they alert management to social concerns and so do have an influence. These resolutions are proposed by a variety of stakeholders, including individual investors, mutual and pension funds, financial institutions such as credit unions, and non-governmental organizations. The resolution topics tend to vary over time with some relating to a variety of social responsibility issues.

Mutual funds can be purchased that invest in corporations considered to have a social, ethical and environmental focus or objective. Some pension plans have also revised their investment strategy to acquire the stock of socially responsible corporations. Some pension fund managers have endorsed the purchase of ethically and environmentally responsible investments of corporations with a good record of corporate social responsibility. Even the Canada Pension Plan (CPP) fund now invests in equities and has a responsible investing policy. This policy may satisfy Canadian citizens concerned about social responsibility and alerts managers to criteria used by the CPP when investing in corporations.

The investment or endowment funds of not-for-profit organizations sometimes own stock in corporations. The extent of this ownership is not great, and any one organization seldom owns a large portion of a particular enterprise. However, the influence of these owners may be greater than their small holdings indicate. In particular, church groups or NGOs have achieved a high profile by questioning aspects of a corporation's operations at annual meetings and other public forums. Some of these NGOs, for example Oxfam, may operate commercially oriented social enterprises. The portfolios of universities are carefully scrutinized by students and faculty for investments in corporations involved in unethical activities or irresponsible behaviour. This scrutiny has led to many universities divesting investments in some corporations as advocated by the Coalition of Universities for Responsible Investing. Its mission is to increase awareness of integrating social, environmental, and governance issues into investment decisions.

Employee, consumer, and producer owners have formed co-operatives through which to achieve ownership. Ownership in all co-operatives is based on the principle that one member has one vote, and each member contributes the same amount of equity. Profits are not the purpose of co-operatives, but some do distribute surplus funds equally to members. Employees, customers, and producers most likely become involved in business ownership for social purposes; that is, to preserve jobs, to provide particular goods or services that are socially acceptable, and to establish socially appropriate distribution systems. Co-operatives have been leaders in institutionalizing ethics and responsibilities, as the examples in Everyday Ethics 11.1 illustrate.

EVERYDAY ETHICS 11.1

Social Responsibility at Co-operatives and Credit Unions

Mountain Equipment Co-op (MEC) is Canada's largest retailer of quality outdoor equipment and has 4.5 million members, or owners, around the world. One MEC value is to operate ethically and with integrity. It fulfills this value by committing to the ethical sourcing of merchandise, constructing and operating "green" buildings, pursuing energy conservation and waste reduction, and supporting community conservation and outdoor recreation groups. In 2014 MEC had 18 stores with total sales of $336 million.

Vancouver City Savings Credit Union (Vancity) is a credit union providing banking, borrowing, lending, and insurance services. In 2014 it had 509,000 customers, or owners, in British Columbia and total assets of $18.6 billion. It has received many awards for its social responsibility and publishes an Accountability Report describing its social responsibility. It focuses on the environment by addressing climate change, practising green banking, indicating ways to grow the social economy, outlining socially responsible investing, and listing community initiatives.

Sources: Based on Mountain Equipment Co-op, http://www.mec.ca; and Vancouver City Savings Credit Union, https://www.vancity.com.

The accountability for economic, social, and environmental responsibilities has become common among publicly traded corporations. Other corporations are less, if at all, accountable, for example privately owned corporations and private equity firms. These corporations avoid much of the government regulation imposed on publicly traded corporations and can often ignore societal pressure. These companies do not have to disclose top management compensation and are not subject to the stock exchange disclosure requirements. This may change in the future as these corporations use capital provided by pension and mutual funds, which are more publicly accountable, often insisting on corporate social responsibility auditing and reporting.

The accountability, or control, of the corporations owned by the government has been a major public administration issue referred to as an "accountability dilemma." The trend to making Crown corporations operate in a more commercial manner has resulted in several accountability problems, including (1) the newly defined, commercially oriented objectives of many government-owned corporations that may be in conflict with social objectives in the national interest; (2) the consequences of evaluating performance based on commercial criteria (that is, profits); (3) the degree of autonomy that should be granted the corporations and their managements; and (4) the techniques for controlling and evaluating the commercial corporations. Just because government owns a corporation does not ensure it will practise appropriate corporate social and environmental responsibility.

Owners have an economic responsibility if they wish their corporation to survive while at the same time being concerned about the responsibility for the ethical or social impact of the business. Owners have varying influences over the operation of their businesses, including how the corporation responds to its social or ethical environment. Today, many owners are focusing on responsible investing, which is having an impact on how the corporation behaves.

LO 11.3   Responsible Investing

Responsible investment (RI) is the integration of environmental, social, and governance factors (ESG) into the selection and management of investments.[1] These investments are usually stocks of publicly traded corporations, but some funds comprise bonds and other investments that are "balanced" between equity and debt. RI is also referred to as socially responsible investing, ethical investing, sustainable investing, community investing, mission-based investing, impact investing, or social conscience investment, and, in the context of the environment, green investing or environmentally friendly investing. An organization promoting responsible investing in Canada is the Responsible Investment Association described in Responsibility for Ethics 11.2. This Association considers issues relating to climate change, water scarcity, supply chain ethics, Aboriginal and community relations, executive pay, and board diversity when examining its recommendations for investment. According to the Responsible Investment Association, over $1 billion of investments were made using some form of responsible investing strategies.[2]

RESPONSIBILITY FOR ETHICS 11.2

Responsible Investment Association of Canada (RIA)

The membership of the RIA includes "mutual fund companies, financial institutions, asset management firms, advisors, consultants, investment research firms, asset owners, individual investors and others interested in RI." Its members "believe that the integration of environmental, social and governance (ESG) factors into the selection and management of investments can provide superior risk adjusted returns and positive societal impact."

The Responsible Investment Association's purpose is to:

- Support the responsible investment activities of its members.
- Promote and support an integrated reporting framework in which there is standardized disclosure of material ESG information.
- Promote the integration of ESG factors into investment analysis and decision-making processes.
- Promote the practice of responsible investing in Canada.

The Association publishes an annual RIA Guide to Responsible Investment available at http://riacanada.ca/wp-content/uploads/2015/07/RIA_mag_v8.pdf.

Source: Adapted from "About," Responsible Investment Association, https://riacanada.ca/about/.

Awareness is growing surrounding the possibilities of achieving acceptable rates of return and social objectives at the same time. Individual investors have an appreciation of this, but the awareness has most likely been fuelled by the investment decisions of churches and other religious organizations, trade unions, women's organizations, co-operative systems, the environmental movement, universities and colleges, and pensions funds. The Canadian financial community has quickly responded to the growing awareness of and demand for socially responsive investments. One study found that responsible investing mutual funds financially outperformed all funds 63 percent and that they reduce risk in investment portfolios 55 percent of the time.[3]

Decisions on responsible investment usually use three possible approaches: positive screening, negative screening, or best-of-sector. Positive screening leads to investing in corporations with good social and environmental records and enlightened industrial and stakeholder relations. Negative screening identifies objectionable corporations; those, for example, involved in alcohol, tobacco, weapons, and nuclear power. Examples of investment criteria included in the screens are listed in Table 11.2. Not all funds apply all these criteria.

TABLE 11.2 Responsible Investment Criteria

The criteria or screens used in making responsible investments vary by fund and provide a method by which a prospective investment is judged to be socially acceptable. Activities that might be considered socially irresponsible or unethical include:

- poor employee/labour relations
- failure to promote racial and sexual equality and affirmative action programs
- the manufacture of weapons
- involvement in the nuclear industry
- the manufacture of "sin" products such as alcohol or tobacco
- the conducting of business in repressive regimes
- the violation of human rights
- environmentally damaging operations, for example, those that pollute
- unsafe goods and services, questionable marketing practices, and exploitive marketing in developing countries
- use of animals in product testing
- involvement in gambling and pornography
- factory farm production of animals
- genetically modified products

The best-of-sector approach compares and ranks corporations within an industry. As few corporations have perfect social responsibility records or performance, this approach identifies corporations best in an industry. It is believed that it preferable to invest in these corporations and attempt to influence them in improving their social responsibility. An acceptable target period or date should be established by which the corporations will improve. Not investing in a corporation with less than a perfect record does not give the investor a voice to influence corporation behaviour. This engagement with the corporation sends a signal from investors that social responsibility is important to investment decisions. Boycotting, or not buying a stock, seldom works in that the corporation is not influenced. Through ranking within an industry, the investor is trying to have some influence.

The motives of the financial community raise compelling thoughts. Does it really believe in socially responsible investing or is this simply a response to a market demand? Are the funds merely shrewd marketing? The motives of investors can also be questioned. For how long would they continue to invest in a socially responsible corporation or fund that lost money? There are several stock indices of corporate social responsibility performance listed in Responsibility for Ethics 11.3 for persons interested in making responsible investments.

Another dynamic of responsible investing is the role of mutual and pension funds. It is possible that the managers of such funds will come under pressure from fund contributors to invest in such a way that reflects their social values. The managers, in turn, might make an investment decision on social criteria that pressures corporation managers to behave in socially responsible ways. Also, some fund managers purchase shares in some corporations in the hopes of changing the corporation's behaviour. The influence of such pressure is not clear at this time. Even so, individuals making investments through funds may be prompting decisions that influence managers to improve their corporation's social performance.

There are challenges to ascertaining what a socially responsible investment is. In particular, one researcher claimed that social investing was a myth. His critique made the following points:

- The data relied upon are sketchy and the research is highly selective.
- The ratings are not completely objective and misrepresent the complexity of the modern corporation.
- The screenings are tainted by anachronistic, contradictory, idiosyncratic, and ideologically constructed notions of social responsibility.
- Claims of the growing financial impact are questionable.
- No coherent case has been made for why the criteria used for social responsibility are better at effecting social change.
- The researcher concludes that the general approach of social investment advocates is one of vindication of the true believer, not investigation.[4]

RESPONSIBILITY FOR ETHICS 11.3

Responsible Investment Stock Market Indices

Sustainalytics/Jantzi Social Index (JSI) (Canada)—A stock index of socially screened investments developed to create a benchmark against which investors can measure the performance of their responsible investments.

Domini 400 Social Index (U.S.)—A stock index comprising 400 socially responsible corporations selected on a screen developed by Domini Social Investments.

Dow Jones Sustainability Indexes (U.S.)—Dow Jones has developed indices that reflect the sustainability performance of corporations that create long-term shareholder value by embracing opportunities and managing risks deriving from economic, environmental, and social developments.

FTSE4Good Index Series (U.K.)—These indices provide investors with information on "globally recognized companies that meet globally recognized corporate responsibility standards. The indices are designed to identify and measure the performance of companies that are working towards environmental sustainability, developing positive relationships with stakeholders and upholding universal human rights."

Sources: Adapted from Jantzi Research, "What We Do," Sustainalytics, accessed August 16, 2016, http://www.sustainalytics.com/JSI; "The Domini 400 Social Index," Domini Social Investment, accessed February 12, 2016, http://www.domini.com/; Dow Jones Sustainability Indexes, accessed February 12, 2016, http://www.sustainability-index.com/; "FTSE4Good Index Series: Add Values to Your Investment," accessed February 12, 2016, http://www.ftse.com/Indices/FTSE4Good_Index_Series/index.jsp.

RESPONSIBILITY FOR ETHICS 11.4

Centre of Excellence in Responsible Business

York University's Schulich School of Business has established a centre in responsible business. The mission of the Centre is to be a global leader in:

- Creating and disseminating new knowledge about responsible business;
- Enabling and inspiring managers, policy makers, students, academics, and consumers to integrate ethics, social responsibility and sustainability into the core of their decision making processes;
- Fostering a new generation of business leaders who will be equipped to chart a course towards a more just and sustainable society through responsible business.

Its teaching, research, executive development, and outreach activities address two main themes: ethics, integrity and responsibility in business; and sustainable enterprise.

Source: Schulich School of Business - "Mission Statement", Centre of Excellence in Responsible Business, Schulich School of Business, York University accessed August 17, 2016, http://www.sustainableenterpriseacademy.org/client/schulich/schulich_lp4w_lnd_webstation.nsf/page/coerb-mission-statement?OpenDocument. Used with permission of Dr. Phil Wesley Cragg, CBERN

It is not always easy to be socially responsible, but corporations are making the efforts. Furthermore, the concept of responsible investing is being taught in universities and colleges and centres to study it are being established. One such centre is described in Responsibility for Ethics 11.4. Investors or shareholders own the corporation and many efforts are made to ensure they are responsible stakeholders. Their influence includes the corporation's approach to corporate social responsibility, and the most direct way to accomplish this is through responsible investing, a trend that is increasing. Whether investors are concerned about responsible investing or not, there is still a need to protect their interests.

LO 11.4   Protecting Owners and Investors

Protection of owners or investors is a primary issue and several stakeholders are involved, including directors, governments, self-regulatory agencies, financial industry institutions and associations, shareholder activists, and managers. A term used to describe the responsibilities towards owners is **shareholder democracy,** the exercise of power of owners to ensure that they are treated fairly and enjoy equally the privileges and duties of ownership. There is general agreement that shareholders have some of the same rights as owners, namely voting power on major decisions, the transfer to ownership when desired, the entitlement to dividends, and accessibility to accurate and timely financial information. These rights vary with the type of share owned.

  Want to learn more about **shareholder democracy**?

Several stakeholders attempt to ensure these rights; many of them are identified in Responsibility for Ethics 11.5. Given the numerous financial scandals, inappropriate market activity, and losses suffered by investors, governments and the financial industry are currently re-examining the adequacy of investor protection. Despite the numerous government initiatives, self-regulatory organizations, and industry associations, investors are still suffering losses due to illegal or unethical behaviour on the part of financial industry managers. Reliance on the government regulation does not appear sufficient to protect shareholders, and it is suggested that no one is guarding the guards—that is, the regulators, whether government or self-regulators.

RESPONSIBILITY FOR ETHICS 11.5

Stakeholders Protecting the Rights of Owners

Governments

- Incorporation and securities laws, for example the *Canada Business Corporations Act*, protect shareholder rights. Such laws exist at the provincial level also.

- The *Sarbanes-Oxley Act* of 2002, which is U.S. legislation passed to protect investors by improving the accuracy and reliability of corporate disclosures. Canadian corporations are affected if they obtain capital on U.S. markets; this Act established practices later included in Canadian legislation and regulations.

- The RCMP's Integrated Market Enforcement Teams, which are groups of highly specialized investigators dedicated to ensuring that those who commit serious capital market fraud offences will be detected, charged, and prosecuted.

Self-Regulatory Agencies and Organizations

- Stock exchanges—in particular the Toronto Stock Exchange, the largest in Canada—which provide markets for trading equity capital, and develop and enforce their own rules and regulations relating to corporate listings and the protection of investors.

- Securities Exchange Commissions in each province and territory, of which the Ontario Securities Commission is the most influential. The 13 securities commissions have formed the Canadian Securities Administrators organization to coordinate and harmonize regulation of the Canadian capital markets.

- Investment Industry Regulatory Organization of Canada (IIROC) is the national self-regulatory organization that oversees all investment dealers and trading activity on debt and equity marketplaces in Canada.

- The Canadian Investor Protection Fund is a not-for-profit organization that provides investor protection for investment dealer bankruptcy.

- The Mutual Fund Dealers Association of Canada, which oversees the sale of mutual funds. It regulates the activities of members and ensures they adhere to the rules, bylaws, and policies of the MFDA, as well as applicable securities legislation.

Shareholder Activists

- Individuals such as Robert Verdun and Yves Michaud, who for years have attempted to have the small investor's voice heard at bank annual meetings.

- Jarislowsky Fraser Limited, an investment counselling firm, which has for years advocated for the protection of investor interests.

- The Small Investor Protection Association, a volunteer member organization committed to fair practice in the investment industry.

- The Shareholder Association for Research and Education (SHARE), a non-profit organization created by the Canadian labour movement to improve institutional investment practices to protect investors.

- The Canadian Foundation for Advancement of Investor Rights (FAIR) is an independent national non-profit organization advocating for Canadian investors by providing information and education to the public, governments and regulators about investors' rights and protections.

connect   Want to learn more about **investment scams and frauds?**

Although government and other stakeholders are attempting to ensure that owners are treated fairly, the role of boards of directors and managers should not be ignored. Many corporations have investor relations departments. The managers of these departments strive to maintain the confidence of investors and are active in communicating information about the corporation to existing and potential investors.

There are challenges associated with the ownership and control of Canadian business corporations. But, the situation should not be viewed as one of hopelessness. The composition of ownership is always changing, and at the same time there is a shifting influence, or control, by various owners. Given the dynamic nature of the Canadian business system, there will always be owners and other stakeholders who care enough to challenge the existing centres of influence.

The governance of the corporation is a topic related to ownership and the trend to responsible investing. The following section defines corporate governance and the major stakeholder involved, the board of directors. A final section will link governance to corporate responsibility.

LO 11.5   Corporate Governance and the Board of Directors

How corporations are governed became an issue in the 1990s, when many corporations failed and it appeared that boards of directors were not performing their function well; that is, they were not protecting the interests of shareholders. In the 2000s, major scandals and bankruptcies reinforced the interest in governance. The board of directors has been the object of many suggestions for reform. The result has been the reform, or reorganization, of the board as the principal body involved with the processes, structures, and relationships through which decisions are made. Owners or shareholders have also been pressuring for change through the use of resolutions examples of which are given in Responsibility for Ethics 11.6.

The definition of corporate governance has evolved over time. One definition of **corporate governance** is the processes, structures, and relationships through which the shareholders, as represented by a board of directors, oversee the activities of the corporation. A second frequently used definition is from the literature: Governance is concerned with the intrinsic nature, purpose, integrity, and identity of the institution, with a primary focus on the entity's relevance, continuity, and fiduciary aspects. Governance involves monitoring and overseeing strategic direction, socioeconomic and cultural context, resources, externalities, and constituencies of the institution.[5]

In the first definition the owner and director stakeholders were mentioned, representing a more traditional view. In the second definition, the scope is much greater and the word *constituencies* is used in recognition of the numerous stakeholders that influence the governance of the corporation. A third definition is a more practical or applied one: "Corporate governance" means the process and structure used to direct and manage the business and affairs of the corporation with the objective of enhancing long-term value for shareholders and the financial viability of the business. The process and structure define the division of power and accountability among shareholders, the board of directors, and management, and can have an impact on other stakeholders such as employees, customers, suppliers, and communities.[6] Again the influence of stakeholders is identified. The definitions illustrate how corporate governance has changed. The changes have involved many issues, some of which will be examined.

RESPONSIBILITY FOR ETHICS 11.6

Governance Shareholder Resolutions

The *Canada Business Corporations Act* requires that shareholder proposals or resolutions be circulated to shareholders and voted upon at the corporation's annual meeting. Many investor or shareholder resolutions are related to governance, but they are seldom passed. Examples of governance proposals, including issue and corporation targeted are:

- Gender representation on Board (Dollarama Inc.)
- Director qualifications: Shortcomings in social and environmental responsibility (SNC-Lavalin Group Inc.)
- "Say-on-Pay" advisory vote (Quebecor Inc.)
- Executive pension plans (Bank of Nova Scotia)
- Adopt a policy setting a normal retirement age of 65 years for executives (North West Company Inc.)
- Unanimous board approval for material acquisitions (Sherritt International Corporation)

Source: Compiled by the author from The System for Electronic Document Analysis and Retrieval (SEDAR), the electronic filing system for the disclosure documents of issuers across Canada, accessed July 27, 2016, http://www.sedar.com/homepage_en.htm..

At an international level, the inclusion of stakeholders in the definition of corporate governance was an important step and has been endorsed by the OECD. The OECD Principles of Corporate Governance included a section on the role of stakeholders. This role includes the following points:

- The rights of stakeholders are respected when established by law or mutual agreements.

- Effective redress should be available to stakeholders when their legally established rights are violated.

- If stakeholders participate in the governance process, they should have access to all the information necessary to carry out their role.

- Stakeholders should be allowed to freely communicate concerns about illegal or unethical practices to the board without fear of retaliation.[7]

Members of a corporation's board of directors are the stakeholders directly involved with governance. A **board of directors** is a group of individuals elected by shareholders to govern or oversee the corporation's affairs. The role of the board is to monitor and evaluate the corporation's activities and performance. The board has the power to select, evaluate, and terminate the chief executive officer and top management. The directors are required to provide shareholders with financial statements and an auditor's statement, and other financial and operational information required by the articles, by-laws, or a shareholder agreement. This information is usually presented as an annual report. The board should be planning for the longer term by participating in a strategic planning process, and ensuring continuity and succession in the management team. Usually major transactions and ventures are evaluated and approved. The role described includes what are referred to as **fiduciary duties**, obligations owed by directors to shareholders that are prescribed by laws or regulations.

The board of directors selects chief executive officers, monitors their behaviour, evaluates their performance, and, if necessary, dismisses them. Some CEOs have not been sufficiently accountable to the board, and thus to the owners of the corporation. It is suggested that there has been an imbalance of power as some managers behaved like absolute monarchs or military dictators. Corporate governance reform has restored power to the board and taken it away from the all-powerful CEO. The board is now more independent; in particular, its audit committee is a much more independent body.

Corporate governance practices have changed substantially in the past few years. In the past, directors may have questioned management's decisions but rarely countermanded them even though they had ultimate authority over key policy decisions. They are now playing a bigger role in determining and assessing strategy, acquisition decisions, succession planning, crisis responses, financial reporting practices, relations with stakeholders, and ethical responsibilities. Boards are meeting more often; seeking more qualified directors, often with particular competencies; meeting without management present; and hiring their own experts on various matters including executive compensation, accounting policies, and legal issues.

Large institutional investors believe that good governance leads to better performance. Many of these investors have formed the Canadian Coalition for Good Governance (described in Responsibility for Ethics 11.7) to develop investor interest and promote changes in governance.

Five major issues relating to governance and boards of directors are the structure and members of the board, board diversity, executive compensation, disclosure and transparency, and board evaluation.

Board Structure and Membership

Most boards comprise 10 to 15 members who serve on various committees. The number of committees varies, as does the type. Common committees include audit, finance, human resources, pension, compensation, nominating, governance, and strategic planning. Often these areas are combined, usually resulting in three to six committees. A recent development has been the formation of social responsibility or environment committees.

The separation of the board chair and CEO positions has been controversial. Corporate governance experts and regulatory bodies recommend that different persons occupy the positions and that an independent director act as chair. The independence of the board is at issue and many boards have adopted the separation of the positions.

Becoming a board member was once a closed process with corporate executives dominating membership, acquaintances of executives appointed, and the existence of interlocking directorships; that is, directors serving on one another's boards. Corporate governance reform has altered this process in most publicly listed corporations. Director positions have job descriptions outlining what is expected. New members are sought through a nomination process, given an orientation to the corporation, and provided with a continuing education program. The qualifications of a director are varied. Financial acumen and the capability of identifying risk are essential. Operating experience is an asset, and knowledge of governance processes is expected.

RESPONSIBILITY FOR ETHICS 11.7

Canadian Coalition for Good Governance (CCGG)

Institutional investors such as pension funds, mutual funds, and third-party money managers have formed CCGG to represent their interests. This is accomplished by encouraging best corporate governance practices in the corporations in which they own shares, mostly corporations that are members of the S&P/TSX Composite Index. CCGG members manage about $3 trillion in assets on behalf of Canadian investors.

CCGG researches and publishes information on governance issues such as executive compensation, majority voting, director compensation, board shareholder engagement, and disclosure of financial and governance information. By making submissions on governance-related matters to stock exchanges, securities commissions, and governments, it attempts to influence the regulation of the securities industry.

Each year, it prepares a Best Practices for Proxy Circular Disclosure report to assist managers and board members. Also, it annually awards Governance Gavel Awards such as the "Best Disclosure of Board Governance Practices and Director Qualifications," recently won by Canadian Pacific Railway Limited, and "Best Disclosure of Approach to Executive Compensation," recently won by Pembina Pipeline Corporation.

CCGG members believe that good governance practices result in a greater return to investors who are participating in the financial market through indirect pension and mutual funds ownership.

Source: "About CCGG," Canadian Coalition for Good Governance, accessed July 27, 2016, http://www.ccgg.ca/index.cfm?pagepath=About_CCGG&id=17564.

A major issue on board memberships has been their independence from the operations and management of the corporation. A definition of an **independent (or unrelated) director** is "a director who is free from any interest and any business or other relationship which could, or could reasonably be perceived to, materially interfere with the director's ability to act in the best interests of the corporation."[8] Family members, current executives, recently departed members of management, and professional advisers such as lawyers are not considered independent. There must be a majority of independent board members or an appropriate explanation provided. Prospective directors must be interested in the quality and reputation of the existing board, the quality of governance processes, the board's independence, and the corporation's approach for integrity and social responsibility.

Board Diversity

The recruitment of women and, to a lesser extent, minorities is receiving attention. About 20 percent of the directors of Canada's largest corporations are women depending upon the corporations surveyed. Modest progress has been made in increasing the number of women. Many corporations say they want women directors, but few heed the advice and elect them. It is argued that the pool of qualified applicants is small and that women lack experience as chief financial officers and CEOs. A "critical mass" of three or more female directors is required before they influence the board. Responsibility for Ethics 11.8 describes organizations involved in enhancing the board membership diversity. Mandatory quotas have been suggested, but they are opposed by most advocates who want to of increase board diversity.

RESPONSIBILITY FOR ETHICS 11.8

Organizations Promoting Board Diversity

Several organizations are promoting diversity of membership on boards of directors. The Canadian Board Diversity Council is promotes a range of unrepresented communities while the 30% Club and Catalyst are concerned mainly with gender representation. DiverseCity OnBoard focuses on volunteer boards.

Canadian Board Diversity Council (CBDC)—The Council was set up to promote diversity on Canadian boards of directors by increasing the representation of women, visible minorities, Aboriginal peoples, and persons with disabilities. CBDC conducts research on the progress of the diversity and publishes an annual report card. It has an education program in governance to create a greater number of highly skilled diverse board candidates and maintains a database of qualified men and women from across Canada who have the competences to serve on boards.

30% Club Canada—This organization exists in many countries and is committed to increasing gender balance on board and in senior management to at least 30 percent. It cooperates with Catalyst Canada.

Catalyst Canada—This is another international non-profit research and advocacy organization dedicated to creating opportunities for women and business in Canada. The Catalyst Canada Honours annually recognizes individual champions of women in business. The Catalyst Accord is a call to action for the largest corporations to increase the representation of women on their boards.

DiverseCity OnBoard—This program connects qualified, pre-screened candidates from visible minority and underrepresented communities to volunteer board positions. It provides training in governance through an online learning campus supplemented by in-person discussions and events.

Source: Adapted from Canadian Board Diversity Council, accessed July 21, 2016, http://www.boarddiversity.ca; 30% Club Canada, accessed July 21, 2016, http://30percentclub.org/about/chapters/canada; Catalyst Canada, accessed July 21, 2016, http://www.catalyst.org/regions/canada; and "About DiverseCity OnBoard," DiverseCity OnBoard, accessed July 21, 2016, http://diversecityonboard.ca/about.

In December 2014, Canadian Securities Administrators issued the NI58-58-101 Disclosure of Corporate Governance Practices rule, which required corporations to disclose corporate governance practices including the number women on boards of directors and in executive officer positions, the policies relating to the identification and nomination of women directors, and targets for women on boards and in executive officer positions. This rule became known as "comply or explain."

In 2015, the Canadian Securities Administrators reviewed the corporations listed on the Toronto Stock Exchange to determine their compliance with corporate governance practices relating to women on boards of directors and in executive officer positions. The findings of this review included:

- 49 percent of corporations had at least one woman on their board.
- 60 percent had at least one woman in an executive position.
- Over 30 percent of large corporations (market capitalization of over $2 billion) had adopted a written policy for identifying and nomination women directors.
- 60 percent of large corporations had two or more female directors.[9]

Some progress has been made, but board diversity is still a significant issue for Canadian corporate governance and initiatives are underway to continue addressing it.

Executive and Director Compensation

A controversial item involving disclosure and transparency is the compensation of executives and directors. Securities regulation requires disclosure of executive compensation in publicly traded corporations, and many have detailed statements of compensation. The compensation received by executives has several components including salary, bonuses, incentive plans, share grants, and options in addition to various perks such as health and pension plans. Issues exist for all forms of payment and include the criteria used to determine salary, the magnitude of the compensation, the basis for bonus and incentive plans, the inverse relationship that sometimes exists between salary and corporate performance, the amount and pricing of options, and excessive severance and pension payments. Two recent developments had increased attention to the appropriateness of compensation.

Say-on-pay is the ability of shareholders to vote on the remuneration of executives. It is an annual shareholder advisory vote on the board's approach that provides shareholders with an opportunity to express their satisfaction with the board's approach to executive compensation. Many public corporations in Canada have adopted this policy, but it has been criticized as being ineffective. Most shareholder votes on compensation have been supportive, but there are exceptions where over 50 percent opposed the proposed compensation. There are instances when a majority or even a minority of shareholders opposed the compensation scheme, changes were made. Some shareholder democracy are advocating for mandatory requirement for say-on-pay as it increases the accountability of boards to shareholders.[10]

Another board accountability initiative is the disclosure of a **CEO pay ratio** that has been implemented by the U.S. Securities and Exchange Commission in August 2015. This is the ratio of the compensation of the corporation's chief executive officer (CEO) to the median compensation of the corporation's employees. It is an indication of income inequality in society and will provide shareholders more information when voting on "say on pay." This initiative has not been adopted in Canada.[11]

Director compensation has also become an issue recently as it has increased to reflect the demands being placed on directors. Directors can receive an annual retainer, board meeting fee, annual committee retainer, and committee meeting fee. Some directors receive options, considered appropriate because some boards require directors to own shares in the corporation to enhance their stake. A director's compensation for a Canadian corporation can now amount to hundreds of thousands of dollars.

The compensation of executives and boards is an issue that has received a lot of attention recently.

Disclosure and Transparency

Corporate governance reform has focused on disclosure and transparency of the corporation's operations, in particular financial reporting and disclosure, and how the board functions. This became an issue with the failure of many American and Canadian corporations in the 1990s and early 2000s, quite often due to inappropriate behaviour on the part of executives and directors.

In Canada, the regulations of the Canadian Securities Administrators, the stock exchange regulations, and the self-regulatory organizations have had some impact, but not nearly as extensive as in the United States. An example of the influence the securities administrators are attempting to gain is outlined in Responsibility for Ethics 11.9, where they argue for the improvement in the disclosure of governance practices. In order to more effectively regulate, it is proposed that a national securities regulator be formed instead of relying on the provincial ones now operating.

The document used to communicate with shareholders is the **management information circular** (also referred to as the management proxy circular or proxy circular disclosure report). The document is sent out to shareholders prior to the corporation's annual meeting and outlines the important matters to be discussed. It includes the information listed in Responsibility for Ethics 11.9. The Canadian Coalition for Good Governance recommends that the following matters also be included: board composition and succession planning, director continuing education, director attendance, director compensation and share ownership, strategic planning oversight, risk management oversight, shareholder engagement, and a Chair's Letter to Shareholders.[12] It also solicits proxy votes from shareholders who are not able to attend the annual meeting. The shareholder will vote to approve the slate of nominations for board of directors or have his/her vote withheld. There will also be voting for the selection of the auditor, any major decisions, shareholder resolutions, and sometimes other items such as say-on-pay.

In addition to these disclosure requirements, more responsibilities are being demanded of boards and their members. Corporations listed on Canadian stock exchanges are required to disclose the text of a board's written mandate. Such a mandate would include not only items mentioned above but also the following:

- The board's satisfaction with the integrity of the CEO and other executive members, and that they are creating a culture of integrity throughout the corporation.
- The board's approach to developing governance principles and guidelines specific to the corporation.
- Identification of measures for receiving feedback from stakeholders, including the possibility of them contacting independent directors directly.
- Listing expectations and responsibilities of directors to fulfill their duties, for example by attending meetings and reviewing materials prior to meetings.[13]

RESPONSIBILITY FOR ETHICS 11.9

Disclosure of Corporate Governance Practices

The Canadian Securities Administrators require that corporations listed on Canadian stock exchanges provide to shareholders information regarding their governance practices. Examples of the information required are:

- Board of directors—Identification of independent directors, other directorships held, and independence status of chair.
- Board mandate—Provide the text of the board's mandate.
- Position descriptions—For the board and committee chairs, CEO.
- Orientation and continuing education—Lists measures to familiarize board members with role of the board, its committees, and its directors, and the nature and operation of the corporation's business.
- Ethical business conduct—Disclose whether the board has adopted a written code of its directors, officers, and employees.
- Nomination of directors—Describe the process used to identify new candidates for board positions.
- Compensation—Describe how the compensation for the corporation's directors and officers is determined.
- Other board committees—List and describe functions of committees.
- Assessments—Indicate whether the board, its committees, and individual directors are regularly evaluated.

Source: Adapted from "Disclosure of Corporate Governance Practices," Canadian Securities Administrators, National Instrument 58-101, accessed August 17, 2016, https://www.osc.gov.on.ca/en/14198.htm.

The OECD promotes good corporate governance practices by issuing the OECD Principles of Corporate Governance, which includes some responsibilities in addition to those mentioned in the National Instrument:

- Treating all shareholders fairly where board decisions affect different shareholder groups differently.
- Applying high ethical standards and taking into account the interests of stakeholders.
- Monitoring and managing potential conflicts of interest among management, board members, and shareholders.
- Ensuring the integrity of the corporation's accounting and financial reporting systems.
- Overseeing the process of disclosure and communications.[14]

An important contributor to disclosure and transparency is the board's **audit committee.** An audit committee comprises members of the board of directors and oversees the internal and external accounting auditing function to ensure that financial statements accurately and appropriately represent the condition of the corporation and that regulated disclosures are made. The committee makes sure that the corporation is in compliance with all regulations and often oversees the corporation's codes of conduct and/or ethics. Today, corporations are expected to prepare a "charter" for the audit committee that discloses the names of committee members, indicates whether they are independent, and describes the experience and education of each member

Evaluation

The evaluation of board performance is one of the most challenging governance reforms to implement. The evaluation of board and director performance has not been common in the past despite the performance appraisal process being widely used in other levels of the corporation. There has been reluctance by many directors who do not believe evaluation is necessary, that the process may expose weaknesses in the governance process and be embarrassing, and that the collegial relationship among board members may be disrupted. Someone must initiate and champion the process, usually the chair or the board's governance committee. The criteria for assessing the board's performance must be established, but are usually based on regulatory requirements. Also, a process must be put in place to deal with the weaknesses uncovered in the evaluation.

RESPONSIBILITY FOR ETHICS 11.10

Best Corporate Governance Practices

Each year *The Globe and Mail* identifies the best corporate boards in Canada. The criteria used in assessing the Boards of Directors included:

- Board Composition—the percent of independent directors, board diversity, in particular, the number of women, and the approach to evaluation of directors.
- Shareholding and compensation—the number of shares owned by directors and the compensation of the CEO and directors.
- Shareholder rights—voting policies on various issues.
- Disclosure—details of disclosure relating to such things as directors background including age, attendance at meetings, retirement policy and existence of term limits.

The boards were assessed on 35 governance criteria.

In 2014, the five corporations with the best governance practices were: the Bank of Montreal, Sun Life Financial, Bank of Nova Scotia, Emera Inc., and Royal Bank of Canada.

Source: Adapted from "Board Games 2014 Methodology," *The Globe and Mail* online, accessed July 21, 2016, http://www.theglobeandmail.com/report-on-business/careers/management/board-games-2014/board-games-methodology-2014/article21538626/; and "Board Games 2014: The Best and Worst Governed Companies in Canada," *The Globe and Mail* online, November 23, 2014, accessed July 21, 2016, http://www.theglobeandmail.com/report-on-business/careers/management/board-games-2014/board-games-2014/article21525230/.

Directors must represent shareholder interests, give advice on how to increase shareholder value, challenge management of goals and results. In order to do this, they review the legal, financial, business and governance functions of the corporation. Today directors are expected to evaluate the social responsibility of the corporation. Included in this aspect of evaluation would be the monitoring of the external environment for social trends and stakeholder influences, overseeing ethics programs and the corporate social responsibility initiatives.

Various organizations recognize the best practices of boards or board members; an example is the Canadian Coalition for Corporate Governance's "Governance Gavel Awards" mentioned in Responsibility for Ethics 11.7. *The Globe and Mail* annually publishes "Board Games: Annual Corporate Governance Rankings." Some of the best governance practices of the five highest ranking corporations are given in Responsibility for Ethics 11.10.

Corporate governance has been reformed extensively and the new responsibilities for ethics and social responsibility have been added or enhanced.

LO 11.6 Ownership, Governance, and CSR

National Instrument 58-101 contains a clause relating to ethical business conduct that the Canadian Securities Administrators recommends is implemented. This clause is given in Responsibility for Ethics 11.11. Many corporate boards now have a code of ethical business conduct that applies to all, including directors.

RESPONSIBILITY FOR ETHICS 11.11

Disclosure of "Ethical Business Conduct"

National Instrument 58-101 requires that corporations disclose the following in relation to ethical business conduct:

1. (a) "Disclose whether or not the board has adopted a written code for the directors, officers and employees. If the board has adapted a written code:

   (i) disclose how a person or company may obtain a copy of the code;

   (ii) describe how the board monitors compliance with its code, or if the board does not monitor compliance, explain whether and how the board satisfies itself regarding compliance with its code;

   (iii) provide a cross-reference to any material change report filed since the beginning of the issuer's most recently completed financial year that pertains to any conduct of a director or executive officer that constitutes a departure from the code.

2. (b) Describe any steps the board takes to ensure directors exercise independent judgment in considering transactions and agreements in respect of which a director or executive officer has a material interest.

3. (c) Describe any other steps the board takes to encourage and promote a culture of ethical business conduct."

Source: Adapted from National Instrument 58–101, "Disclosure of Corporate Governance Practices, Clause 5," http://www.osc.gov.on.ca/en/14198.htm.

Owners are taking more responsibility for the social, ethical, and environmental impacts their corporations have on society. Corporate governance practices have come under increasing scrutiny and owners pressure the corporation's main governing body, the board of directors, to address corporate responsibility and sustainability challenges. Some owners are becoming more active, pressuring the board to implement governance improvements and to account for the corporation's social and environmental performance. In particular, institutional investors—that is, mutual and pension funds—have become more demanding of boards, directors, and management. The trend to responsible investing has also applied pressure to the board and management, but criticism continues.

Directors are the protectors of shareholders' interests and the overseers of strategy and financial responsibility. Recently, directors have also become overseers of CSR and ethical conduct—this is because they are ultimately responsible for everything that happens in the corporation. Pay systems, incentive plans, and performance goals can lead to misconduct on the part of executives and employees. Being responsible for ethical management practices is now another concern in looking after shareholders' interests. Colero recommends that directors ask the following five questions about the corporation's ethics management:

- What is our company's strategy to manage ethics?
- Who is responsible for ethics in our company?
- Are people in our firm equipped to recognize and resolve moral dilemmas?
- Are people in our organization provided with a safe opportunity to discuss ethical issues of concern?
- Do we reward or punish ethical integrity and moral courage if it has a negative impact on the bottom line?[15]

Another perspective on corporate governance, CSR, and ethical conduct relates to an appropriate response to external environment factors, trends, or events. Schacter argues that four factors have to come together requiring boards to pay attention to CSR: globalization, loss of trust, civil society activism, and investor interest in CSR.

Globalization has made it necessary for corporations to consider the economic, social, and environmental impacts on society, including those in developing countries. Corporations are also facing increasing demand to do something about these impacts. Several corporate scandals, excessive executive compensation, outsourcing of jobs, environmental disasters, and stock market declines have resulted in a loss of trust in business and the corporation.

Civil society organizations, including NGOs, are more active and effective in pointing out the mistakes and misdeeds of corporations. Finally, many investors, including mutual and pension funds, have become more interested in responsible investing. Added to this list is the growing pressure for improved corporate governance, more management accountability for the corporation's economic, social, and environmental issues, and increasing regulation.[16]

Directors are still responsible for the creation of wealth for shareholders, but there is a reputation risk involved in not responding to CSR and ensuring appropriate ethical conduct. Shareholder wealth may be adversely affected by boards of directors ignoring CSR and ethics management. The long-term interests of owners and stakeholders are interlinked, and through good governance practices boards must set an example for all the corporation's stakeholders and show that they are concerned about CSR and ethics management.

Your advice to Felica . . .

Felica's dilemma is not unusual. Just as it is often challenging to ascertain ethical versus unethical behaviour, responsible investing is often difficult to identify. Not everyone agrees on what is irresponsible corporate economic activity. Also, corporations that can appear responsible may lapse for some reason, sometimes beyond their control. The decision is further complicated by the expected dividends, or return, that the shareholder seeks. Which investment—or investments—to make is a judgment call involving pros and cons. Felica should obtain all the information she can about a particular investment to make an informed decision.

Summary

- Although other stakeholders have an influence on the corporation, it is owned by shareholders or investors. There are several types of owners including investors, entrepreneurs, managers, employees, producers, and mutual, pension, and investment funds. Issues arising from ownership include the appropriateness of widely held versus concentrated ownership, the treatment of minority shareholders, non-voting shares, dual-class shares, the pros and cons of employee ownership, the accountability of private corporations, and the accountability of government-owned corporations. (LO 11.1)

- Several issues relate to ownership with one in particular being of interest, the influence of owners on the corporation's social responsibility. One approach used by investors is to sponsor shareholder resolutions advocating that the board of directors and corporate executives take action on a particular economic, social, environmental, or governance issue. Co-operatives by definition are more socially sensitive and NGOs can use small share holdings to make corporations aware of social issues. (LO 11.2)

- Responsible investing is the screening of investments by corporations or mutual and pension funds for their response to social or ethical responsibilities as well as their financial or economic actions. This process is also referred to as ethical, green, environmental, and social conscience investing. Investments are examined by a screen comprising negative or positive criteria, and best-of-sector. Several stock market indices identify corporations that qualify for responsible investing. (LO 11.3)

- It is necessary to protect the rights of owners through government legislation, self-regulatory agencies, industry association, and individual and institutional activists. Corporations are mindful of owners and often have investor relations departments to maintain good relations. (LO 11.4)

- The definition of corporate governance has changed over the years to reflect developments in the area. Traditionally, the definition referred only to shareholders, but stakeholders are now included. The board of directors is elected by the shareholders and is mandated to represent shareholder interests. The board oversees all the affairs of the corporation and today this includes the ethical conduct and social responsibility of the corporation. Many corporations now have charters specifying the board's mandate. Several issues are related to corporate governance, including the board structure and membership, board diversity, executive and director compensation, disclosure and transparency, and evaluation. (LO 11.5)

- A connection exists between ownership, corporate governance, and ethical conduct and CSR. In fact, governance is now considered one influence on corporations to conduct their affairs appropriately in the interests of shareholders and other stakeholders, and as a part of the corporation's overall corporate social responsibility. (LO 11.6)

Key Terms

Mutual fund

Private equity firms

Venture capital company

Dual-class stock

Non-voting shares

Restricted shares

Passive shareholders

Active shareholders

Worker capitalism

Responsible investment

Shareholder democracy

Corporate governance

Board of directors

Fiduciary duties

Independent (or unrelated) director

Say-on-pay

CEO pay ratio

Management information circular

Audit committee

Critical Thinking and Discussion Questions

1. Why are owners an important stakeholder of the corporation? How does the corporation influence them, and how do owners influence the corporation?

2. Do owners always control the corporation?

3. How can owners influence the corporate social responsibility of the corporation?

4. How can an investor identify a responsible investment?

5. What can be done to protect the interests of owners or shareholders?

6. What are the responsibilities of the board of directors?

7. Why is diversity of the board of director's membership important?

8. Do the "say-on-pay" and "CEO ratio" initiatives make any difference to shareholders?

9. Why is disclosure and transparency important to shareholders and stakeholders?

10. What is the connection between corporate governance and the corporation's ethical conduct and social responsibility?

Cases

11.1 AUNT MABEL'S EXPERIENCE WITH OWNERSHIP

Karl Stillings' Aunt Mabel called him on a Saturday morning and wondered if he could drop in to visit her that afternoon. Aunt Mabel was a widow; Uncle Richard had passed away about 18 months ago. She was quite concerned about her investments and would appreciate Karl's advice since he had recently graduated from a business program.

During his visit Karl was not surprised to learn that his aunt had no investment experience—his uncle had looked after all financial matters. She had become a widow at 62 and found she had cash assets of about $200,000 from an insurance policy and savings. She approached a financial institution and was assigned an adviser. The adviser had Aunt Mabel sign an account agreement, which she admitted to Karl she did not read in detail as it was several pages and in small print. Besides, she trusted the financial institution and the young and very personable adviser.

The adviser initially invested the money in low-risk money market funds. A few months later he moved the money into higher risk equity or stock funds with higher fees and commissions. He then arranged a $100,000 loan secured against her existing equity, which he invested in very high-risk equity. Aunt Mabel questioned this, but was told it was allowed in the agreement she'd signed. While visiting the adviser recently, Aunt Mabel was told, after she had insisted, that she had lost $40,000 on her investments. She told the adviser she wanted out, but the adviser said there would be expensive redemption fees. Also, he advised waiting a while as markets turn around, and there was a possibility for making a lot of money. Aunt Mabel became very upset and did not know what to do. She decided to seek someone else's advice and that is why she contacted her nephew.

Over a cup of tea and biscuits, Aunt Mabel asked Karl what she should do now.

Questions

1. What type of ownership was involved? What can be assumed about this type of ownership? Was it appropriate for Aunt Mabel?

2. What stakeholders are involved?

3. What are the ethical issues or implications involved?

4. What ethical responsibilities do the adviser and the financial institution have toward any type of investor, and in particular toward an inexperienced and naïve one?

5. What advice should Karl give?

Sources: Adapted from Stuart Weinberg, "In Advisors We Trust, Though Not Always Wisely," *The Globe and Mail*, October 21, 2006, B13; Gordon Pape, "Wanted: One Impartial Financial Planner," *CARP Magazine*, June 2007, 52; Jonathan Cheveau, "Giving CFPs More Respect," *National Post*, June 10, 2008, FP15; Doug Steiner, "A Moral Gauge," *Report on Business*, January 2009, 23; and Hugh Anderson, "Investors Need Better Information," *National Post*, October 30, 2007, FP6.

11.2 WHAT SHAREHOLDER DEMOCRACY?

John Hurrell had recently become a shareholder in a large Canadian corporation. He felt good about being an owner and hoped to make some money from his investment. He was taking his ownership responsibilities seriously and thought that shareholder democracy was important. John's understanding of shareholder democracy was that owners should have power to ensure that they are treated fairly and enjoy equally the privileges and duties of ownership.

He was monitoring the media for business news, and kept coming across articles about shareholder democracy. This lead him to identifying some organizations interested in shareholder democracy including the Canadian Coalition for Good Governance, Shareholder Association for Research and Education (SHARE), the Small Shareholder Protection Association, and Canadian Foundation for Advancement of Investor Rights (FAIR). He visited the websites of these organizations and found them very useful. There were several issues relating to shareholder democracy and John found three to be particularly interesting: voting for board of directors' members, the "say-on-pay" motion, and shareholder resolutions.

On the Management Proxy Circular he received, John only had two choices, to vote for the persons nominated by the corporation to be directors, or to withhold his vote. This meant that he could not vote against any of the nominated directors he opposed. There had been suggestions that shareholders who held more than 3 percent should be able to propose nominations up to 20 percent of the board. There also a suggestion that when a majority of shares withheld their votes for a particular nomination, the person should withdraw. Neither of these suggestions had been legislated and John was left feeling powerless.

Say-on-pay votes had been included on many proxy statements, but their effectiveness was questionable. Only a few corporations had adjusted their compensations plans when a large percentage of shares voted against the motion, that is, did not support the compensation scheme proposed. John voted against the say-on-pay motion but he was not convinced it would do any good.

Shareholders were allowed to submit resolutions to be voted upon at the annual meeting. The resolutions addressed various issues such as board diversity, the requirement to publish a sustainability report, executive compensation schemes, and director qualifications. Management always recommended that shareholders vote against shareholder resolutions and very few received many votes. John voted for the shareholder resolutions but he was not hopeful that it would do any good.

John also read a couple of editorials that were critical of shareholder democracy. The editorials stated that corporations and management should focus on maximizing shareholder profits instead of being concerned about some populist and moralistic fads. Besides, owners can always sell their shares if they are unhappy. The critics said that the focus on shareholder democracy was not relevant in the capitalist system.

John was disillusioned and his enthusiasm for being an owner of a Canadian corporation diminished.

Questions

1. Who controls the corporation?
2. Is democracy needed in the governance of the corporation?
3. Should the government pass laws to improve shareholder democracy?
4. What should John do?

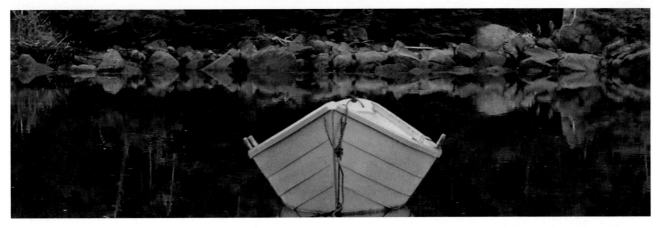

Used with the permission of Dennis Flynn

CHAPTER 12

Ethics and Responsibilities in the Workplace and Marketplace

LEARNING OUTCOMES

After studying this chapter, you will be able to:

LO 12.1 Explore the ethics and responsibility issues associated with the employee, consumer, competitor, and supplier stakeholders.

LO 12.2 Elaborate on key issues relating to employees and the workplace.

LO 12.3 Learn about the influence the consumer stakeholder has on the marketplace and the influence the marketplace has on the consumer.

LO 12.4 Describe the dynamics and desirability of competition in the marketplace.

LO 12.5 Understand the changing influences on suppliers in a product's supply chain.

LO 12.6 Explain the progression of the supply chain and the influence of factors including sustainability purchasing and fair trade.

What would you do if...?

Phyllis Cramer enjoyed her job as an assistant manager at a large discount department store. It was a demanding job, but she liked the quick pace and the dynamic atmosphere. Among her duties was responsibility for implementing the store's loss prevention, or shoplifting, policy. The policy had recently changed, and Phyllis was concerned about the consequences.

Between 1.5 and 2.5 percent of retail sales are stolen or lost in some way depending on the type of merchandise. About 40 percent of the loss is due to shoplifting by customers, about 35 percent is due to employee theft, about 20 percent is due to administrative and paper errors, and the remaining loss is due to vendor mistakes or theft. Because preventing any loss contributes directly to the store's profitability, the reinforcement of a loss prevention policy is important to the store's financial success.

Of most concern to Phyllis is the loss experienced through customer shoplifting. The store had been very strict about shoplifting and prosecuted everyone regardless of the dollar amount stolen. She realized that this zero-tolerance policy was expensive to enforce. Lawyers' fees and court costs were substantial. Not only was her time involved, but employees had to testify in court on company time. In addition, sometimes the local police force expressed concern at the resources it had to devote to petty thefts.

The new policy would excuse first-time thieves when the value of shoplifted merchandise was less than $25. The store manager said this would allow Phyllis to focus on the professional shoplifters rather than teenagers, and to devote more time to preventing employee theft. The manager also indicated that the new policy would be less costly to implement.

Phyllis was concerned about the difference in treatment of shoplifters based upon dollar amounts. To her, stealing was stealing no matter how small the amount. She agreed with employees who felt the policy undermined their efforts and might even encourage more shoplifting. She believed the policy really avoided the problem rather than solving it.

Phyllis worried about the ethical implications of such a policy for the store, its employees, and customers who did not steal. Most importantly, she agonized in her own conscience about the policy, in particular letting some thieves get away without any punishment. She did have some sympathy with first-time teenage shoplifters and their parents, but to let them off scot-free was not appropriate either. Phyllis knew that implementing the new policy was not going to be easy.

What is your advice to Phyllis?

LO 12.1 The Corporation's Key Stakeholder Relationships

The purpose of this chapter is to examine the influence of four stakeholders on the corporation and how the corporation influences them. The four stakeholders to be discussed are employees, consumers, competitors, and suppliers. Employees are stakeholders internal to the corporation and their relationship gives rise to many ethical issues, one of which is illustrated in the scenario at the beginning of this chapter. Consumers are obviously important, because without them the corporation has no reason to exist. Competitors and suppliers are business-to-business stakeholders primarily involving economic or commercial relationships, but ethical issues also are evident. A corporation's relationship with suppliers becomes particularly complex because of the supply chain links. For most corporations, all four are significant stakeholders in that numerous ethics and responsibilities are associated with them.

Issues relating to the ethics and responsibilities will be identified for each stakeholder and will serve as the basis for discussing them. The purpose of this chapter is not to provide readers with a comprehensive examination of each issue, but instead to provide an appreciation of a wide range, multiplicity, and complexity of issues existing in this area.

LO 12.2 Employees in the Workplace

Employees are almost always identified by corporations as critical or key stakeholders. The relationship with this stakeholder group has always been a challenge, and given the downsizing, retrenchment, and technological changes of the recent past it will be even more so. There are many issues relating to ethics and responsibilities between employees and employers, including working conditions, workforce reduction, workplace privacy, fair compensation, employee loyalty and duties, diversity management, right to due process, and employee engagement. This list illustrates a range of issues in the relationship between the corporation and the employee stakeholder. Not all of the issues will be examined, but the following sections will focus on the work ethic, employee loyalty, and diversity and discrimination.

There are several competitions to identify the best employers in Canada through nomination or survey processes. Corporations that make the list publicize the achievement on letterhead, advertisements, and reports. The presence of these competitions promotes good employee relationships. Responsibility for Ethics 12.1 gives examples of the competitions and winners. These surveys provide insights into what makes a good employer or place to work.

RESPONSIBILITY FOR ETHICS 12.1

Canada's Best Employers

"Best Workplaces in Canada 2015"—A list of best workplaces is compiled by Great Place to Work® Canada and published in *The Globe and Mail*. Four corporations were recognizing as leaders in sustaining best workplaces: TD Bank Group, Softchoice, Carswell (a division of Thomson Reuters Canada Limited), and Urban Systems.

"Best Employers in Canada 2016"—List prepared by Aon Hewitt Associates, a human resources firm, and published in *Maclean's*. The survey has found that employee engagement leads to: greater business results and organizational performance; greater employee retention and morale; better customer service; lower absenteeism; improved personal health; and less job stress.

Canada's Best Employers 2016—Employees in 236 Canadian employers were surveyed on how they felt about being motivated to work, whether success is rewarded, leadership attitudes, and whether they are proud to work for their employer. The listing is prepared by Aon Hewitt and published in *Canadian Business*.

Sources: Adapted from Great Place to Work® Institute, accessed January 8, 2016, http://www.greatplacetowork.ca/; Best Employers in Canada 2016, accessed January 8, 2016, http://www.aon.com/canada/products-services/human-capital-consulting/consulting/best_employers/index.html; Canada's Top 100 Employers, accessed January 8, 2016, http://www.canadastop100.com/national/; and Canada's Best Employers 2016, accessed January 8, 2016, http://www.canadianbusiness.com/lists-and-rankings/best-jobs/best-employers-ranking-2016/.

Many employees are seeking greater participation in decisions affecting the work environment. Moreover, many businesspeople are also committed to greater employee involvement as an approach to improving working conditions and performance. Many aspects of how employees are treated are legislated by governments, but the status of employees is influenced by voluntary actions of employers or advocated by employees seeking greater participation. The result might be viewed as employee claims to certain conditions in the workplace, or employee rights.

The concept of the work ethic has been used to establish the different positions employees and employers find themselves in today. Work has changed, and so has the approach to employees. Although employees may be still considered a critical resource, many issues confront human resource management.

The Work Ethic

The work ethic is a set of values that holds that work is important to members of society insofar as work influences the qualities or character of individuals; that work is a purposeful activity requiring an expenditure of energy with some sacrifice of leisure; that some gain, usually monetary, is involved; and that through work a person not only contributes to society but becomes a better individual. The work ethic as a concept had some origins in religion as labour was believed to be the worthy way to serve God, a calling through which one proved one's worthiness of redemption. Leisure or hedonistic activities were not considered appropriate.

Working hard and accumulating wealth were seen as outward signs of a person's morality. They also provided some assurance of a good life on Earth as well as a good afterlife. The basis for the work ethic is not clear, for while religion is involved so is economics. Although the work ethic was considered as divine dignity, the concept lost some of its piety because the accumulation of wealth countered the religious basis of the ethic, and consumption, much of it conspicuous and made possible by the earnings of work, was inconsistent with saving and investment, or frugality.

Today there are often calls for a return to the work ethic of the past. Arguments can be made for both positions. Many people consider work as only a part of life and instead want time to spend with family, satisfaction from what they do, and a sense of purpose from their job and life. This phenomenon is also described as "backing off the fast track" and focusing more on the quality of life. Work, by itself, is no longer as sufficiently fulfilling as it was in the past. This is manifested in several ways, for example:

- opting out of the labour force; for example, early retirement
- collecting employment insurance or welfare payments rather than accepting low-paying or unattractive jobs
- changing careers

- refusing to perform overtime work
- feeling alienation caused by pressure in the workplace
- questioning traditional authority.

One counterargument for this is that employees are working harder than ever and that more is expected of them in terms of productivity and improved quality, with comparisons made to Japanese workers. Evidence of the work ethic includes the long hours that management and professional persons spend at their jobs or places of business. Work has become an obsession to many, as people have to work harder to keep up with inflation or to make ends meet, and more work is expected from the same or fewer number of employees. Workers fear job loss, and fewer people are available for backup.

Canadians were surveyed about whether or not they still believe in the work ethic. Canadian attitudes toward work ethic include the following, suggesting that the work ethic still exists.

- Canadians are, in principle, committed to work.
- Canadians choose work over most leisure activities when they have to make that kind of choice.
- Canadians would rather work than collect employment insurance.

Other studies have found that Canadians are both strongly motivated to work and that most express overall satisfaction with their jobs.

Table 12.1 lists some issues associated with the work ethic today. It is not known how all these issues affect the work ethic. There is evidence that employees are working longer and harder, yet employers are willing to lay off workers even when skills shortages exist in many occupations.

TABLE 12.1	Contemporary Implications on the Work Ethic

- Workplace stress has increased, according to recent studies. The stress is created by a variety of factors, including many of the items mentioned below.
- Increasing use of part-time or temporary workers has raised concerns about how they are treated.
- Fringe benefits are changing in response to employee demands and efforts by some employers to retain highly qualified workers; for example, elder care, working from home, job sharing, child care, discount programs, and recreational facilities. On the other hand, benefits received from health care and pension plans are declining as employers find them too costly.
- The makeup of compensation is changing, with greater emphasis on pay for performance through cash bonuses, stock purchase, and grant plans.
- Employees are more concerned about being able to balance work and personal life.
- Moonlighting has increased.
- Job insecurity has increased as employers are willing to lay off employees on short notice.
- There is a consensus that Canada is suffering a labour skills shortage and that the shortage will become worse.

Many issues exist with employees in the workplace. Only three will be discussed: loyalty of employers to employees and vice-versa, diversity in the workplace, and employee privacy.

Employee Loyalty

Loyalty creates that extra effort and extra drive in employees to perform. It encourages self-motivated behaviour, and reflects employees' confidence in management, their vision, and the corporation's purpose. Loyalty means commitment by employees to the organization they work for. In turn, employers are loyal to employees by providing career-long employment, good salaries, and other benefits. But has this relationship changed with the new employment environment?

Most managers probably believe that employees should be loyal. Signs of a lack of commitment are easy to detect (turnover, early retirements), but measuring loyalty is much more difficult. Low turnover is not necessarily a sign of loyalty, but instead may mean that employees are tied through benefit plans (particularly pensions), or that no other job opportunities exist. Managers should also be cautious of extreme loyalty; overzealous behaviour by an employee does not necessarily mean that the employee is performing in the best interests of the enterprise. But, given the pressures of change, it may not be possible for management to provide some of the things that in the past encouraged loyalty—for example, job security and good compensation packages.

Employees in today's society often want to be entities unto themselves and are seeking challenging opportunities. Some consider loyalty to self more important than to the corporation. Such employees might be seen to be loyal and dedicated to the job itself, rather than to the corporation they are employed by to do that job. On the other hand, many employees wonder why they should be loyal when corporations may lay them off. It is management's responsibility to provide the environment that engenders loyalty. Intelligent human resource management goes a long way toward doing this. Employees must first be trusted and managers must be loyal to employees. It is critical for managers to give trust and loyalty before expecting it. Managers often assume that they cannot expect loyalty, but loyalty and the commitment it involves can be generated by management initiatives.

In order to improve loyalty, managers must communicate a persuasive corporate image to employees. Employees who demonstrate loyalty must be appropriately rewarded—not only by monetary compensation. In pursuit of loyalty, management should bear in mind the following: loyalty must be a corporate priority and it must start at the top with the CEO; persons at all levels in the organization must be involved; the process takes a long time; and token, one-shot efforts must be avoided. Managers must be careful to distinguish between employee loyalty to individuals and to the corporation. Loyalty to individuals represents personal loyalty and is not as beneficial as loyalty to the organization, which is more enduring.

The blind loyalty of employees that may have existed in the past is unlikely today. On the other hand, managers are finding it more difficult to demonstrate that employees owe them loyalty. Corporate loyalty might need to be redefined in the context of the current situation, where jobs are less secure. It is unreasonable to expect dedicated efforts from employees whose future is insecure. But employees still basically want to think well of the company they work for, as it means thinking well about themselves. Employers will have to honestly explain the need for retrenchment, technological change, and heavier individual workloads. Another issue related to employee loyalty is whistleblowing, which was described in Chapter 6. Management may view it as an indication of disloyalty, and employees may be reluctant to engage in it for the same reason. Nevertheless, many corporations are establishing whistleblowing policies and procedures.

Managing Employment Diversity

Despite the improvements in labour and human rights legislation, some individuals or groups in the workforce still claim that they are being treated unfairly by employers. **Discrimination** is the preferential (or less than preferential) treatment on bases not directly related to qualifications of the job or performance on the job. The discrimination occurring is often prejudice against certain persons that could be based on such grounds as race (including Aboriginal), gender, nationality, age (young and old), disability, marital status, physical appearance, sexual orientation, and health (for example, HIV/AIDS). Sometimes discrimination is obvious, but it also can be based on habit, custom, and tradition and be barely noticeable.

Most discrimination is addressed by employment equity legislation and corporate policy. **Employment equity** is the fair and equal treatment of employees. Federal and provincial/territorial governments have legislation to implement employment equity. An example of federal government legislation is the *Employment Equity Act,* whose purpose is to:

> *achieve equality in the workplace so that no person shall be denied employment opportunities or benefits for reasons unrelated to ability and, in the fulfillment of that goal, to correct the conditions of disadvantage in employment experienced by women, aboriginal peoples, persons with disabilities and members of visible minorities by giving effect to the principle that employment equity means more than treating persons in the same way but also requires special measures and the accommodation of differences.[1]*

Accompanying legislation is the *Canadian Human Rights Act* (R.S., 1985, c. H-6); its purpose is to:

> *extend the laws in Canada to give effect . . . to the principle that all individuals should have an opportunity equal with other individuals to make for themselves the lives that they are able and wish to have and to have their needs accommodated, consistent with their duties and obligations as members of society, without being hindered in or prevented from doing so by discriminatory practices based on race, national or ethnic origin, colour, religion, age, sex, sexual orientation, marital status, family status, disability or conviction for an offence for which a pardon has been granted.[2]*

The Canadian Human Rights Commission administers the *Canadian Human Rights Act* and is responsible for ensuring compliance with the *Employment Equity Act*. Both laws ensure that the principles of equal opportunity and non-discrimination are followed in all areas of federal jurisdiction.

Provincial governments have passed anti-discrimination laws to ensure fair employment practices. Most provinces prohibit discrimination on the grounds of race, religion, national origin, colour, sex, age, and marital status, and in selected cases the prohibited grounds include political beliefs, ethnic origin, physical handicap, creed, and sexual orientation.

Laws themselves do not prevent discrimination and enforcement is a problem. Some employees are still discriminated against and have little recourse through which to seek remedial action. To a large extent, the individual employer must be relied upon to treat employees and possible employees fairly. The corporation has a major role to play in reducing employment discrimination.

Most corporations comply with legislation and many are involved with **diversity management,** a voluntary initiative that goes beyond what is required by law to eliminate workplace discrimination. The following section examines feminist ethics as it relates to gender equality and its relationship to business ethics and CSR.

Influence of Feminist Ethics on Business Ethics and CSR

Feminist ethics is defined as "a diverse set of gender-focused approaches to ethical theory and practice."[3] The objective is to develop non-sexist ethical principles, policies, and practices in society. With regard to business organizations, women have not advanced as owners, managers, professionals, and members of boards of directors relative to men, creating a demand for gender equality and dignity for women. In addition, it is argued that feminist ethics can improve a corporation's overall approach to business ethics and CSR.

It was argued that traditional ethical theories did not consider or value women's moral experience. The theories were more concerned with men's issues, and ignored the nurturing and caring characteristics of women. Masculine traits like independence, autonomy, hierarchy, and domination were overemphasized in comparison to feminine traits of interdependence, community, sharing, joy, and peace. Moral reasoning favoured male ways of thinking based on rules, rights, justice, and universality, which leads to fair, objective, and consistent treatment or outcomes. Female ways emphasized empathy, harmony, responsibilities, care for one another, and healthy relationships.

There were many gender-centred approaches to ethics, but they can be categorized as either care- or power-focused. Care-focused ethics highlight the differences between men and women and the inferior status of women. Women are more likely to consider the views of others and assess situations differently. Also, women have a more nurturing and mentoring approach, and place more consideration to relationships through attachment, networks, and connections. The power- or status-focused approach emphasized issues related to domination and subordination of women. Power and how power was used to oppress women was described. Gender equality would be achieved through changes in systems, structures, institutions, and practices that differentiate between the roles and status of men and women in organizations.[4]

Borgerson discussed why feminist ethics should be harmonized with business ethics and CSR. She argued that feminist ethics placed emphasis on three concepts that provided better approaches to recognizing, evaluating, and addressing ethical concerns: relationships, responsibility, and experience. The focus of feminist ethics on these concepts resulted in a superior appreciation of business ethics than that of the traditional theories discussed in Chapter 5.

Greater attention was given to the role of relationships. In traditional theories, individual or group autonomy when considering ethical action and decisions was viewed as appropriate. But more reflection on relationships advocated by feminist ethics increased the stakeholders considered or consulted. A distinction was made between taking and having responsibility. Active willingness was necessary when taking responsibility. There were implications for those not included or chosen in the responsibility taken, and this applied whether women and others were involved. Feminist ethics supported having responsibility, which was beyond the choice of deciding whether or not to take responsibility. Finally, experience involved taking an interest in understanding marginalized individuals or groups. Feminist ethics advocated listening to other voices, which resulted in a broader acknowledgment of human involvement or interaction. Thus, there was a sensitivity to the lives of others that encouraged a more critical reflection on a social or ethical issue or dilemma.[5]

The approaches of feminist ethics allow for deeper insight into decisions relating to business ethics and corporate social responsibility than do traditional ethical theories. Not only is the status of women in business considered, but the status of all stakeholders. The concepts of relationships, responsibility, and experience are critical in stakeholder relationships, assessing ethical issues, and formulating social responsibility programs.

Workplace Privacy

Workplace privacy is a sensitive issue with many legal and ethical challenges, only some of which will be discussed. A fundamental component of privacy is use of an employee's personal information. Employees have the right to control access to personal information, but employers have some rights to obtain information. Privacy of personal information is regulated by the federal government's *Personal Information Protection and Electronic Documents Act (PIPEDA)* and other provincial legislation. PIPEDA requires that organizations hold personal information in a responsible manner, permit individuals to access and correct personal information, and allow individuals to have control over information about themselves. Responsibility for Ethics 12.2 summarizes the Act's "Fair Information Principles."

RESPONSIBILITY FOR ETHICS 12.2

Personal Information Protection and Electronic Documents Act (PIPEDA)

The Act requires that businesses and organizations manage personal information according to the following "Fair Information Principles."

- *Accountability*—put systems and people in place to manage information
- *Identifying purposes*—understand the uses to which the information will be put
- *Consent*—obtain permission to use personal information
- *Limiting collection*—collect only information that is appropriate and necessary
- *Limiting use, disclosure, and retention*—restrict the use of personal information
- *Accuracy*—minimize the collection of incorrect information
- *Safeguards*—make sure the information is stored and accessed appropriately
- *Openness*—inform stakeholders of the use by personal information
- *Individual access*—allow individuals to see their personal information
- *Provide recourse*—arrange for individuals to have a course of action if they have an issue with their personal information

---

Source: Adapted from Personal Information Protection and Electronic Documents Act—A Guide for Businesses and Organizations, The Office of the Privacy Commissioner of Canada 2010. Minister of Public Works and Government Services Canada, 2013, accessed June 8, 2016, http://www.priv.gc.ca/information/guide_e.pdf.

Employers have a responsibility for workplace privacy, but they also have a right to some personal information. When hiring, employers need to know the applicant's qualifications and previous work experience. On the other hand, they have no right to personal information such as weight, age, medical records, race, blood type, fingerprints, or marital status. Employers are challenged to justify what aspects of an employee's personal life are relevant to the job—for example whether that applicant has AIDS/HIV, or uses illegal drugs. Testing for substance abuse is a controversial issue for both employees and employers, especially where a stakeholder's safety may be at risk.

Workplace privacy has been challenged by the emergence of electronic technology and social media. Employees have access to email systems, the Internet, and wireless telephones and other devices that may be used inappropriately. One issue is the appropriate use of electronic technology particularly in relation to social media. A related issue is the surveillance or monitoring of email and Internet usage; another is the use of cameras. Employers claim that such monitoring is necessary to avoid liability, to improve productivity and avoid excessive use, and to maintain network security. Employees claim that the employers are violating their personal privacy. As future employees, managers, or entrepreneurs, students will no doubt be exposed to the issues surrounding workplace privacy.

connect   Want to learn more about **privacy in the workplace?**

Employees and CSR

Research has found that a connection exists between corporate social responsibility and sustainability and **employee engagement**, defined as the emotional and intellectual commitment of an individual or group to an organization that supports building and sustaining business performance.[6] A study by Hewitt Associates and CBSR (Canadian Business for Social Responsibility) found a strong correlation between employee engagement and employees' views of the employer's record on CSR. Corporations with a "high employee engagement have a higher degree of readiness to focus on CSR as a strategy to improve overall organizational performance and better meet the needs of employees and external stakeholders." The most frequent CSR activities were community investment, waste reduction, business travel reduction, and responsible purchasing.[7] A later Hewitt Associates study found that when employees had a positive view of their employer's CSR there was greater employee engagement, which corporate managers stated was important to long-term success.[8]

When employees believed that supervisors acted ethically, they also were likely to behave ethically. In other words, a direct correlation exists between the ethical behaviour of supervisors and that of employees.[9] Similarly, it was found that when employees believed their company was adhering to high ethical standards, the employees were more committed to the company.[10] Employers effectively communicating CSR within the corporation are more likely to attract and retain employees. Satisfied employees need to link work to personal life through CSR, feel connected to the corporation, and take opportunities for self-enhancement—all of which increase loyalty, productivity, and commitment.[11] Another study found that employees who gave money or time to social causes felt more committed to their employers. Through helping colleagues, employees considered themselves and their employers to be more caring.[12]

Related to this, research has found that students are searching for meaningful work as demonstrated by a prospective employer's involvement in social issues. Students want their work to align with social and environmental causes such as climate change, renewable energy, and innovative products and processes. In other words, employers are expected to incorporate sustainability and social responsibility into the design of jobs.[13] A Network for Business Sustainability study identified the sustainable practices that are being demanded by future employees. It was found that students wanted employers to promote environmental efficiency through reduced waste and to encourage carbon regulation. Independent evaluation that employers were meeting their social licence was expected along with increased CSR transparency. Students wanted increased involvement in business and increased community engagement by corporations.[14]

LO 12.3   Consumers and Consumption

While employees are internal workplace stakeholders, consumers are external marketplace stakeholders. Their role is critical to corporations: without their participation through purchases, corporations cannot succeed. Fundamental to understanding the consumer stakeholder in the marketplace is knowledge of the consumer sovereignty concept.

Defining Consumer Sovereignty

A review of the literature does not disclose a definitive definition of "consumer sovereignty," but several essential characteristics of a definition are included in the following:

- Consumers, not producers or governments, dictate the type, quality, and quantity of goods and services to be provided.
- Elements of democracy are present, including the idea of voting through purchase decisions, and that these decisions are made based upon the preferences of a majority.
- Consumers are free to make their own choices and are not unduly influenced by producers or governments.
- An economic system operates more efficiently when consumers determine production.[15]

As demonstrated the concept is imperfectly defined, as its objective could be considered impossible and its realization in the market far from perfect. Government has become involved and is making many decisions that, in theory, should be made by consumers. Economists say consumers should be protected from those who are convinced they know better than consumers what is best.

The distinction between consumer and producer (any corporation, for example a manufacturer or farmer) is an important one to make. It is argued that consumers have relinquished their sovereignty to producers. Producers and consumers may have conflicting interests and the producers' notions of what satisfies consumers may be influenced by what satisfies them as producers. As a result, consumers become impotent as influencers in the economic system.

The principle of consumer sovereignty is unlikely to be observed unless consumers have freedom of choice and are actually allowed to register their preferences in a market. In this respect, consumer sovereignty is really a front for the individualistic ethic, which holds that freedom is valuable in itself. If this ethic is accepted, one must accept the freedom to offer choices as well as the freedom to choose. Businesspersons often argue the former, but forget the latter. It might be argued that governments forget that consumers should have the freedom to choose.

Consumers and the Marketplace

The conditions of consumer sovereignty are seldom fulfilled in the marketplace, as buyers face high information costs, offensive and often misleading advertising, and shoddy and unsafe goods. Consumers may be manipulated by persuasive, at times misleading, advertising. It is also argued that as a small number of large firms dominate the market for some goods and services, consumers are being forced to purchase what producers provide. Consumer preferences are manipulated by large corporations in which market power has become concentrated. Also, in product development, there may be a difference between what consumers think the alternatives are and what producers think they are, meaning that the actual market choices may not reveal what consumers really want.

On the other hand, consumers do have some influence on the corporation and the marketplace. The most obvious way is of course their decision whether or not to purchase a corporation's products or services, but there are other influences. Consumer sovereignty exerts influence through **consumerism**, a social movement seeking to protect and augment the rights and powers of buyers in relation to sellers. An objective of the consumer movement is to make consumers aware of their place or role in the marketplace. Consumerism is considered necessary because some goods and services supplied by corporations fail to meet acceptable standards relating to product safety, information, performance, and pricing. Consumers may experience poor after-purchase service and might be the victims of retail misbehaviour, such as high-pressure sales tactics and misleading advertisements.

Consumers have formed organizations to promote their interests. One example is the Consumers' Association of Canada, formed in 1947, which is a voluntary, non-profit organization committed to the improvement of the standard of living in Canadian homes. It studies consumer problems and issues and brings the views of consumers to corporations and governments. The most well-known consumer advocate is the American Ralph Nader. In Canada, Phil Edmonston formed the Nader-style Automobile Protection Association to represent car owners. In addition, dozens of small consumer organizations exist across Canada. Being informed also enhances the influence of consumers in the marketplace. Print and broadcast information informs consumers, as does access to the Internet. From consumerism, a set of consumer rights have emerged. These rights, with accompanying responsibilities, are presented in Responsibility for Ethics 12.3.

RESPONSIBILITY FOR ETHICS 12.3

Consumer Rights and Responsibilities

Rights illustrate a source of influence for consumer stakeholders, but with rights come responsibilities. The first four rights were outlined in a speech in 1962 by U.S. President John Kennedy. U.S. President Gerald Ford added the fifth right in 1970, and over time other rights have been added by consensus.

Consumer Rights	Consumer Responsibilities
To safety	To follow instructions and take precautions
To choose	To make independent, informed consumption choices
To be heard	To make opinions known and to complain in a constructive manner
To be informed	To search out and use available information
To consumer education	To take advantage of education opportunities

Consumer Rights	Consumer Responsibilities
To redress	To fight for the quality and service expected
To a healthy environment	To minimize environmental damage by careful choice and use of goods and services

The consumer influence may also be exerted by government. Governments have enacted legislation and regulations to protect the consumer, and one example is the federal government's *Competition Act.* The Act is intended to promote and maintain fair competition so that Canadian consumers can benefit from competitive prices, product choice, and quality services. Responsibility for Ethics 12.4 summarizes legislation to protect consumers in the area of advertising and deceptive market practices.

maintain fair competition

RESPONSIBILITY FOR ETHICS 12.4

Protecting the Consumer

Federal law
most business conduct   *deceptive*

The Competition Bureau promotes truth in advertising in the marketplace by discouraging deceptive business practices and by encouraging the provision of sufficient information to enable informed consumer choice. The *Competition Act* is a federal law governing most business conduct in Canada. It contains both criminal and civil provisions aimed at preventing anti-competitive practices in the marketplace.

False or misleading ordinary selling price representations—The ordinary selling price provisions of the *Competition Act* are designed to ensure that when products are promoted at sale prices, consumers are not misled by reference to inflated regular prices.

Performance representation not based on adequate and proper tests—Businesses should not make any performance claims unless they can back them up. The *Competition Act* prohibits any representation in the form of a statement, warranty, or guarantee of the performance, efficacy, or length of life of any given product that is not based on adequate and proper testing. The *Competition Act* prohibits:

- the sale or rent of a product at a price higher than its advertised price

- "bait-and-switch" selling, which occurs when a product is advertised at a bargain price but is not available for sale in reasonable quantities

- the supply of a product at a price that exceeds the lowest of two or more prices clearly expressed in respect to the product

- any promotional contest that does not disclose the number and approximate value of prizes and the odds of winning

  misleading warranties guarantees

- misleading warranties and guarantees

- the unauthorized use of tests and testimonials, or the distortion of authorized tests and testimonials

Pyramid selling

Pyramid selling—Pyramid selling is illegal in Canada. It is a multi-level marketing plan that includes either compensation for recruitment, required purchases as a condition of participation, inventory loading, or the lack of a buy-back guarantee on reasonable commercial terms.

Source: Adapted from Competition Bureau of Canada, Competition Bureau of Canada, 2012. The Minister of Public Works and Government Services Canada, 2013, accessed January 8, 2016, http://www.competitionbureau.gc.ca/eic/site/cb-bc.nsf/eng/h_00125.html. Used with permission.

Consumer sovereignty can be excessive and is reflected in the antagonism toward materialism, selfishness, greed, and the destruction of mankind's natural virtue. It is an expression of individualism as opposed to collectivism. There is no doubt that the concept concentrates on the individual instead of society as a whole, and largely ignores the higher purposes to which the narrow interest of individuals should be subservient. But this is true of any economic system based upon individualism and competitive markets. The assumption is that individual decision making is preferable to centralized, unitary decision making. If individualism and self-interest are acceptable as motivators in a business system, it seems logical that they should also be motivators for consumers. Everyday Ethics 12.1 discusses whether or not this means "the customer is always right."

EVERYDAY ETHICS 12.1

"The Customer Is Always Right"

The meaning of consumer sovereignty would suggest that the customer, or consumer, is always right. Although consumers have rights, they also have responsibilities and are expected to behave in an ethical manner.

Sometimes consumers are wrong. Consumers are sometimes ill-informed or overwhelmed by information and thus may not make a decision in their best interests. Some consumers behave badly, for example, requesting a refund for an item not sold by the retailer, making abusive remarks to employees or treating them badly, or returning failed products after misusing them.

There are situations when customer demands involve morals. There may be commercial reasons for accommodating consumers but moral reasons for not, for example, selling pornographic materials, consulting one service provider and then having another perform work, or demanding unjustified returns.

On the other hand, there may be moral reasons for accommodating consumers but stronger commercial reasons for not doing so, for example, overbooking aircraft or costly product recalls.

The cliché "The customer is always right" illustrates the challenges of attempting to accommodate all stakeholders. There are other stakeholders—for example, employees—and consumers have to be reasonable in their expectations.

Sources: Adapted from Dawn Iacobucci, Kent Grayson and Amy Ostrom, "Customer Satisfaction Fables," *Sloan Management Review,* Summer 1994, 93–96; Tom Sorell, "The Customer Is Not Always Right," *Journal of Business Ethics,* Volume 13, 1994, 913–914.

Consumers and CSR

Consumers are demanding a wide range of ethical or socially responsible products, goods, and services, and business is responding. According to research, about 20 percent of consumers based purchase decisions on ethical or socially responsible considerations. Three factors motivate consumers to make these purchases: CSR information must be available; there must be a moral alignment of CSR practices with the consumer on moral values; and the products must be considered affordable.[16]

Table 12.2 lists the types of ethical products available in the marketplace. Many issues are associated with this list. Consumers are often conflicted; for example, they are critical of big-box stores (such as Walmart), but still patronize them. Corporations, in particular retailers, are able to charge higher prices for ethical products and increase profits. Retailers such as Whole Foods Market and The Body Shop have built profitable corporate strategies based upon ethical products. Government policies or non-governmental organization (NGO) pressures may restrict consumer choice, for example banning eggs from caged birds on university campuses.

Corporations promoting socially and environmentally friendly products are accused of greenwashing—that is, making token efforts, or saying one thing and doing another. It is questionable that some products are actually ethical. The meaning of *organic* is not clearly established and the term is used inappropriately sometimes. Certification standards and systems have not been established in some areas, and labelling can be misleading.

In the case of food, the calculation of "food miles" is difficult and misleading. The calculation of benefits must take into account all factor costs in the food production life-cycle and not just transportation miles or costs. Furthermore, consumers in developed countries demand more than can be produced locally and must rely on imported items. Locally produced food is often more expensive and the benefits to the environment are not certain.

TABLE 12.2 **Examples of Ethical Products**

Food: • Organic • Local • Fair trade **Housing:** • Energy efficient **Clothing:** • Eco-chic—fashionable clothes from organic cotton, hemp, bamboo, flax, soy • Slow fashion—eco-friendly design • Recycled (Value Village, etc) • Fair trade fashions (Fair Indigo, etc) • Organic sneakers **Cosmetics:** • Natural ingredients • No animal testing **Green weddings:** • Efforts made to use particular clothing, special catering requirements; not using expensive limousines	**Financial Products:** • Ethical and green mutual funds • Ethical and SR stock (sustainability) indices • Green mortgages **Travel:** • Eco-travel • Carbon offsets (e.g., Air Canada) • Eco-resorts **Jewellery:** • Gold and diamonds—certification of source **Energy:** • Fluorescent light bulbs • Energy-saving devices • Clean sources of energy • Biofuel (ethanol and bio-diesel) **Transportation:** • "Terror-Free Gas"—gasoline sourced in nations that do not support terrorism • Hybrid vehicles • Carbon offsets

 Want to learn more about **ethical products and services?**

A major issue with ethical products is whether socially conscious consumers are willing to pay for these types of products. Two researchers undertook a study to review 30 years of literature to ascertain the following: "Are consumers willing to reward firms for their sustainability actions with price premiums or increased purchases?" Many influences, impediments, and enhancements affected three consumer behaviour intentions—willingness to change behaviour, willingness to pay a premium, and willingness to punish. The main finding of the study was that ". . .the average premium for socially conscious products and services is 10%. Some consumers will demand a discount for 'unsustainability', even greater than the premium for sustainability."[17]

Other research studied the trade-offs consumers are willing to make when paying more for products with ethical features. Socially conscious features are definitely more important to some consumers and social features will make a difference when functional and price features are satisfied. It was found that some social features were more important than others; for example, avoiding child labour was more important than working conditions and animal testing more important than the use of animal by-products.[18]

There are many issues relating to ethical or sustainable products and services. Some consumers are willing to pay a higher price for these products and corporations are responding, but the ethical claims must be legitimate.

LO 12.4   Competitors and Competition

Competition is necessary, even crucial, for an effective market economy. It encourages innovation, productivity, entrepreneurship, and efficiency. The principal beneficiary when competitive forces exist is the consumer, who is provided with quality products, choice, and the best possible price.

Competition, as one of the fundamentals of the business system, was discussed in Chapter 2. In the context of business, competition is a struggle or rivalry for supremacy, often expressed among corporations as *market share*. Two or more corporations offer the same or similar product or service in many ways—for example, by offering a better product, through use of advertising, or by superior distribution or service. Competition might result in the defeat or destruction of one of the corporations. Business failures do result from competition, and if only one corporate structure survives a monopoly situation exists. Although competition does result in the failure of some corporations, the usual result is that some survive and new businesses enter the industry. Thus, competitors are a stakeholder group that most managers must recognize and respond to in some way.

Competition: Ethics and Responsibilities

Implications for social responsibility are associated with the degree of competitive rivalry existing in a business system. One position is that increased competition and pressure to be competitive has resulted in an increase in unethical or questionable practices. Industrial spying, espionage, and sabotage are now of such concern that industrial or economic security has replaced national security as a major national issue. Practices range from eavesdropping and theft of research and development technology, to hiring the competitor's key employees. It is argued that the practices are much more widespread than reported and that many remain undisclosed either because companies are unaware of them or are too embarrassed to report them.

Several causes of this trend have been identified, including the cutthroat global economy, aggressive competitive tactics, and shorter product cycles necessitating faster responses to competitor initiatives. The copying or counterfeiting of products appears more common and increasingly difficult to control, as there appears to be little reluctance to steal ideas from others.

Society is concerned about the concentration of corporate power in a few corporations or a few groupings of interconnected corporations. There is a concern that a few large corporations may have too much influence over the economy and possibly too much influence over government. Concentration of corporate power can also be measured within a single industry by providing the percentage of sales controlled by the four or eight largest firms.

There are two concerns about industrial concentration—the possibilities for collaboration and higher profitability. In highly concentrated industries, corporations often behave in a similar fashion. For example, packaging changes are copied and prices matched. In less concentrated industries, it is much more difficult to keep track of all competitors and to predict their behaviour. Economists have been concerned that corporations in highly concentrated industries tend to be more profitable.

The high degree of market concentration in some industries plus the high degree of concentrated ownership constitutes a centre of power in society. When this concentration is combined with a capability to influence other stakeholders, especially governments, a controlling power structure is set in place. Many Canadians are fearful of this.

Government Influence to Encourage Competition

Competitive behaviour or the conduct of business in Canada is regulated by the *Competition Act* (R.S.C. 1985, c. C-34). This Act establishes the basic principles for the conduct of business in Canada so that competition is encouraged and maintained. The purpose of the Act is to promote the efficiency and adaptability of the Canadian economy; ensure that small and medium-sized corporations have an equitable opportunity to participate in the Canadian economy; and provide consumers with competitive prices and product choices. If it could be accomplished, this purpose would result in an ideal marketplace. Responsibility for Ethics 12.5 lists clauses in the *Competition Act* that apply to how competitors should behave.

RESPONSIBILITY FOR ETHICS 12.5

Regulation of Competitors

The *Competition Act* governs business conduct among competitors. Some of the Act's features are as follows:

Conspiracy—This is any agreement, arrangements, or combination designed to lessen competition unduly in relation to supply, manufacture, or production of a product and includes fixing prices, or preventing competitors from entering the market.

Bid-Rigging—Any arrangement between two or more persons or corporations where one party will refrain from bidding in a call for tenders, or where there was collusion in the submission of bids.

Predatory Pricing—There are two types of predatory pricing: (i) selling products in one region of Canada at prices lower than in another region for the purpose of lessening competition; and (ii) selling products at unreasonably low prices where the intent is to lessen competition.

Review of Mergers—When a merger occurs, the Competition Bureau may decide to examine it and recommend whether or not actions should be taken to preserve competition.

Abuse of Dominant Position—The *Competition Act* provides for remedies where dominant corporations in a market engage in anti-competitive behaviours, such as acquisition of a customer who would otherwise be available to a competitor to impede a competitor's entry into the market; purchase of products to prevent the reduction of existing price levels; and selling articles at a price lower than the acquisition cost to discipline or eliminate a competitor.

Source: Adapted from "Our Organization," Competition Bureau of Canada, The Minister of Public Works and Government Services Canada, 2013, accessed June 8, 2016, http://www.competitionbureau.gc.ca/eic/site/cb-bc.nsf/eng/h_00125.html; and *The Competition Act*, accessed June 8, 2016, http://www.cb-bc.gc.ca/eic/site/cb-bc.nsf/eng/h_00148.html.

Although the role of government in encouraging competition in the Canadian economy is important, it is only one of several factors determining competitive behaviour. The following is a selected list of such factors:

Entrepreneurship—It should be remembered that the business system involves a life-cycle process in which corporations are formed, grow, and dissolve. There is a constant supply (or birth) of new small businesses, many of which grow in stature and provide competition for large, well-established firms.

Deregulation and privatization—Government initiatives to deregulate some sectors of the economy have influenced the growth of businesses, and efforts to sell off the business corporations it owns have increased opportunities for entrepreneurs (discussed in Chapter 10).

Technology—A multitude of technological developments have encouraged competitive rivalry. New technology has led to new business corporations, for example in electronics and various computer-related industries, and has changed how other industries operate.

Decline of natural monopoly—Utility-type companies often operated as natural monopolies, for example in telephone and cable television. With deregulation and new technologies, neither of these industries can now be considered a natural monopoly. Competition exists in the telephone industry and cable television is under pressure from wireless and new providers.

Global trends in trade—The reduction of some barriers to trade is increasing competition in Canada. This is accomplished through trade agreements such as the World Trade Organization (WTO), the North American Free Trade Agreement (NAFTA), and the most recently negotiated Trans-Pacific Partnership (TPP) an agreement among twelve Pacific Rim countries. Despite free trade agreements, many barriers to trade exist, especially non-tariff barriers.

Mergers/takeovers—Mergers or takeovers tend to occur in cycles, with the later 1970s and 1980s being two periods of high acquisition activity. Such acquisitions can reduce competition, especially if they are acquisitions in the same industry.

LO 12.5   Suppliers and the Supply Chain

In **Business-to-business** commercial activity, one corporation (a supplier) sells goods or services to another corporation rather than to consumers. Traditionally, the relationship between suppliers and their customers was an adversarial one. Today the relationship is more likely to be one of mutual interdependence based on trust and collaboration. Everyday Ethics 12.2 is an example of a customer attempting to influence the behaviour of suppliers. Purchasers or buyers are recognizing suppliers who cooperate with them and are committed to considering social and environmental responsibilities.

EVERYDAY ETHICS 12.2

Influencing Suppliers

An example of how a corporation influences its suppliers is the use of "supplier codes of business conduct." A good example is the *Canadian Tire Principles of Business Conduct,* which includes a section on "Expectations of Suppliers."

- Compliance with laws
- Employment standards
- Wages and benefits
- Working hours
- Child labour
- Forced or slave labour
- Discrimination/human rights
- Disciplinary practices
- Workplace environment
- Environmental protection
- Confidentiality and privacy
- Unlawful payments
- Dealing with the company's employees
- Sub-suppliers

Also included are descriptions of supplier certification, supplier assessment and monitoring, enforcement of the code, and reporting and addressing code violations. The reason for selecting this code is that it appears comprehensive. Other retailers and manufacturers have similar codes.

Source: Adapted from "Supplier Code of Business Conduct," Canadian Tire Corporation, Limited, accessed July 8, 2016, http://corp.canadiantire.ca/EN/AboutUs/Documents/CTC%20Supplier%20Code%20of%20Conduct%20July%204%202012.pdf.

The relationship between customers and suppliers is governed informally by several rights. The supplier expects to have the right to supply goods and services to a customer. Preferential treatment is not expected from the customer or received by the supplier. A fair deal is expected, which is negotiated ethically without lies, deception, non-disclosure, or threats. Conflicts of interest are expected to be disclosed. Loyalty by both sides may exist, but not to imply automatic acceptance of terms or conditions offered.

The influence of suppliers varies. Where the customer has several sources of goods and services, the customer will exert more influence over the supplier. If the supplier is the sole source of particular goods or services, the supplier will have greater influence over the transaction.

The buyer's purchasing staff and the supplier's sales staff are sometimes confronted with ethical dilemmas when bribes, kickbacks, gifts, and hospitality are offered. Suppliers and their customers have formed professional associations, such as the Supply Chain Management Association (SCMA), to guide the behaviour of these employees. Responsibility for Ethics 12.6 provides an outline of the Code of Ethics formulated by SCMA.

RESPONSIBILITY FOR ETHICS 12.6

Supply Chain Management Association (SCMA)

Supply Chain Management Association (SCMA) is a professional association of supply management managers and provides training, education, and professional development. Its professional designation is SCMP—Supply Chain Management Professional. The association embraces all aspects of strategic supply chain management, including: purchasing/procurement, strategic sourcing, contract management, materials/inventory management and logistics and transportation.

A condition of membership is adherence to its Code of Ethics. Components of the code include:

- Standards of conduct: Avoidance of conflicts of interest; protection of confidential or sensitive information; maintenance of business relationships; acceptance of gifts, gratuities, and hospitality; and promotion of environmental and social responsibilities.

- Professional principles: Professional competency; professionalism; honesty and integrity, responsible management, serving the public good; and compliance with legal obligations.

Enforcement procedures outlined are compliant process, conduct of investigations, and nature of sanctions.

Source: Adapted from "SCMA Code of Ethics for Professionals in the Field of Supply Chain Management," Supply Chain Management Association (SCMA), accessed August 4, 2016, http://scma.com/en/about-scma/join-scma/code-of-ethics.

RESPONSIBILITY FOR ETHICS 12.7

Regulation of Suppliers

The *Competition Act* contains the following provisions to ensure suppliers do not take advantage of their customers:

Exclusive dealing, tied selling, and market restrictions—These practices generally occur when a supplier places conditions on the supply of a product that constrain the customer in terms of, for example, what else the customer must buy to obtain supply, where the customer may subsequently market the product, or what other product lines the customer may or may not carry. Although not illegal in themselves, they will be investigated if they are found to have caused, or to be likely to cause, a substantial lessening of competition in a market.

Price discrimination—This exists when a supplier charges different prices to competitors who purchase similar volumes of an article.

Price maintenance—This involves attempts to influence upward or to discourage the reduction of price at which another corporation supplies or advertises a product, or refusing to supply anyone because of that corporation's low pricing policy.

Refusal to deal—Refusal to deal involves situations where a buyer cannot obtain supplies of an available product on usual trade terms and, as a result, is substantially affected in her or his ability to conduct business, resulting in an adverse effect on competition.

Source: Adapted from Competition Bureau of Canada, Competition Bureau of Canada, 2012, The Minister of Public Works and Government Services Canada, 2013, accessed July 14, 2016, http://www.competitionbureau.gc.ca/eic/site/cb-bc.nsf/eng/h_00125.html.

Government legislation governs the relationship between buyers and suppliers. Responsibility for Ethics 12.7 lists clauses in the *Competition Act* that apply to this relationship. As discussed in this section and the one that follows, suppliers are now regulated more by other stakeholders, such as consumers, their business customers, and NGOs.

The next section looks at the supply chain in more detail to reveal how complex the relationship is between a corporation and its suppliers.

LO 12.6 The Supply Chain

A **supply chain**, or value chain, is the route that a product travels from the procurement of raw materials, the transformation into intermediate goods and then final products, and the delivery to consumers through a distribution system to its ultimate disposal by the consumer. Planning, scheduling, and controlling the supply chain appropriately means that the corporation has the right product, in the right place, at the right time, and in the right condition. Figure 12.1 is a basic supply chain applicable to most products.

FIGURE 12.1 *Stages in a Supply Chain* Value chain

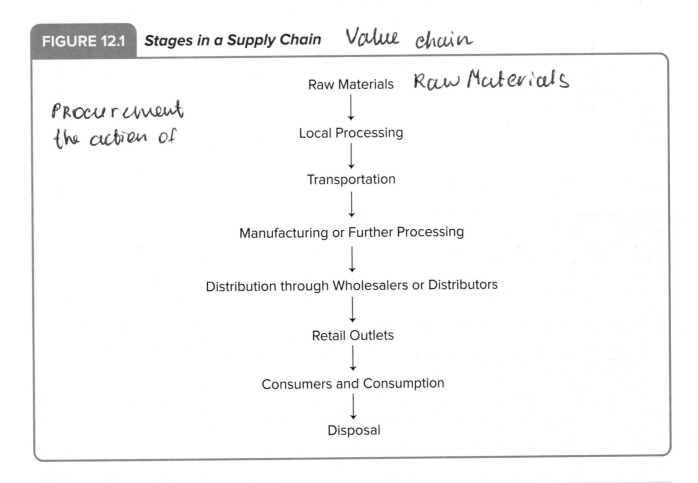

Raw Materials — Raw Materials

PROcurement the action of

Raw Materials
↓
Local Processing
↓
Transportation
↓
Manufacturing or Further Processing
↓
Distribution through Wholesalers or Distributors
↓
Retail Outlets
↓
Consumers and Consumption
↓
Disposal

connect — Want to learn more about **sustainability in supply chains?**

Today supply chain management includes paying attention to ethical, social, and environmental issues along with the accompanying responsibilities. When this is done, the supply chain is referred as being ethical or sustainable.

Raw materials may come from several sources and are often from developing countries. Materials such as wood, minerals, and petroleum have many associated environmental issues. Materials from developing countries frequently involve issues such as human rights, child labour, low wages, and dangerous working conditions. Sometimes the raw materials are shipped out of the country for processing, depriving local workers of employment.

Not all products follow the same chain; some may involve additional stages and some fewer. Retailers may purchase directly from manufacturers, bypassing wholesalers, or consumers may buy directly from manufacturers. Although a single chain is shown, branches may exist as by-products are produced, or the product at some stage may be sold to another corporation as ingredients for another product. Waste may be produced at different stages, which must be disposed of or sold to be used in other products. Profitability varies along the chain and with the type of product. Different issues impacting different stakeholders exist along the chain. NGOs often play major roles in improving conditions for workers in raw material production facilities. Governments tend to be more influential in downstream sections of the chain.

More attention has been focused on product disposal and who is responsible. **Extended producer responsibility** is "an environmental policy approach in which a producer's responsibility, physical and/or financial, for a product is extended to the post-consumer stage of a product's life cycle."[19] "Producer" in this definition refers to manufacturers or distributors. The responsibility for disposal is being shifted upstream to producers and away from consumers and local governments responsible for waste management. The policy is to provide incentives to producers to take environmental considerations into the design of the product.

Supply chains can be extended in another sense; that is, geographically or globally. Global supply chains add another dimension for management and often these chains are more complicated. The Network for Business Sustainability published a study that provided guidance and listed best practices. The first step is to list all stakeholders that influence a corporation's approach to sustainable supply chains. The study found that the following stakeholders want sustainable supply chains: consumers, government, general public, activists (NGOs), media, industry peers, employees, and investors. The key sustainability issues in supply chains included working conditions, the environment, CSR, low wages, human rights, child labour, health and safety, forced labour, and sweatshops. According to the study's authors, there are three steps to developing a sustainable global supply chain:

- Identify Motivators: What is motivating change in the industry? What does the corporation stand to gain and lose? The key motivators were found to be customers, compliance, costs, competitive advantage, and conscience.

- Assess Levers: Seven key levers can facilitate or inhibit efforts to build a sustainable supply chain. Internal levers are purpose—that is, alignment of sustainability with organizational strategy; clear policy statements/codes of conduct; and people—that is, leadership/management support. External levers are industry collaboration; partnerships, including trust in supplier engagement; supportive government regulation; and power as represented by organizational size or influence over suppliers.

- Improve Practices: The four most prevalent practices were found to be a code of conduct that set expectations throughout the supply chain, certification as a screening device in selecting suppliers, rigorous selection process to reduce supply risks, and monitoring or auditing to ensure compliance with expectations.[20]

Global supply chains are now influenced by industry codes of conduct established by socially responsible corporations in collaboration with NGOs, trade unions, universities, and sometimes governments. The Fair Labour Association (FLA) is an example which has a Workplace Code of Conduct.[21] Another example is the toy industry's International Council of Toy Industries' code called ICTI Care (Caring, Awareness, Responsible, Ethical), a program to promote ethical manufacturing, in the form of fair labor treatment, as well as employee health and safety.[22]

These codes and others vary in their success as implementation depends on how rigorously compliance is enforced and what remedial action is imposed. The existence of reliable auditing processes is key especially when the audits are verified by a third party. In developing countries, the extent of corruption and the influence of governments are factors in determining how successful such codes are. In some cases, the codes are not delivering improvements. When adequate investments of time and money are made other codes have resulted in improvements.

The following section elaborates on sustainability purchasing, whether local or global.

Sustainability Purchasing

The focus on ethics and responsibility in purchasing has been referred to as *sustainability purchasing*. Other terms associated with this approach to purchasing are responsible purchasing, fair trade, ethical sourcing, and ethical trade.

Sustainability purchasing is defined as

...the acquisition of goods and services ("products") in a way that gives preference to suppliers that generate positive social and environmental outcomes. It integrates sustainability considerations into product selection so that impacts on society and the environment are minimized throughout the full life cycle of the product. Sustainability purchasing entails looking at what products are made of, where they have come from, who has made them, how they will be ultimately disposed—even considering whether the purchase needs to be made at all. It encompasses environmental, social and ethical dimensions and brings benefit to the environment and local and global communities and workers.[23]

This definition makes it clear that sustainability purchasing applies to the complete product chain, which could also be equated with the life cycle of the product. Sustainability purchasing is a form of regulation imposed on the corporation or industry by stakeholders other than government. Consumers, usually with the help of or prompting by NGOs, apply pressure to change purchasing practices. Retailers often prompt action after being influenced by consumers or NGOs.

Corporations recognize this influence and in turn respond through professional or trade associations (as illustrated by SCMA), or by participating in networks promoting sustainable purchasing, an example of which is given in Responsibility for Ethics 12.8. This type of network enables corporations to find suppliers who endorse sustainability practices.

RESPONSIBILITY FOR ETHICS 12.8

BuySmart Network

The BuySmart Network was established in 2005 in Vancouver as the Sustainability Purchasing Network. It is a non-profit organization supported by partners and sponsors interested in sustainability purchasing that will forge healthier, greener, and socially beneficial supply chains in Canada.

Some of the features of the Network as identified on their website are:

- The goals of the BuySmart Network are to: encourage the demand for and use of products and services that support positive social, economic and environmental impacts; and help organizations meet their strategic goals through sustainable procurement.
- Explaining the programs and services offered, including being a resource centre, a learning hub, and a place for learning.
- Including a "Resources" page that includes lists of purchasing organizations, case studies, topics in sustainability purchasing, supplier directories, and tools and tips.

Source: Adapted from BuySmart Network, accessed January 13, 2016, http://web.buysmartbc.com.

Fair Trade

Another influence on sustainability purchasing is the fair trade movement. **Fair trade** is commonly used to identify products that are involved with sustainability purchasing but usually focuses on the beginning of the product chain. The Fairtrade Foundation's definition is as follows:

Fairtrade is about better prices, decent working conditions, local sustainability, and fair terms of trade for farmers and workers in the developing world. By requiring companies to pay sustainable prices (which must never fall lower than the market price), Fairtrade addresses the injustices of conventional trade, which traditionally discriminates against the poorest, weakest producers. It enables them to improve their position and have more control over their lives.[24]

The fair trade movement is not anti-capitalist, but instead intends to use the market system to enhance the influence of the supplier stakeholder. The best known fair trade products are coffee, spices, tea, cocoa, and fruit, but today retailers carry many fair trade products including wine, flowers, and beauty products. In Canada, Fairtrade Canada is the coordinator of fair trade initiatives and performs three functions: (1) it is responsible for certifying that Canadian products bearing the Fairtrade certification marks meet international Fairtrade standards; (2) it licenses Canadian companies to use the Fairtrade certification marks and attempts to ensure that licensed companies abide by the standards required of the marks; and (3) it promotes the use of Fairtrade certification marks and certified products. It is a member of Fairtrade International, which is responsible for the international coordination of Fairtrade standards, organizing support for producers around the world, developing fair trade strategy, and promoting global trade justice.[25]

Controversy arose in early 2013 related to the certification of fair trade products in Canada. Competition in labelling has emerged between Fairtrade International and Fair Trade USA. Fairtrade Canada is a branch of Fairtrade International, which uses a circle symbol with the image of a producer against a blue and green roundel with a black background. Fair Trade USA uses a green/white/black label with a farmer holding a bowl. Fair Trade USA has started to certify products in Canada.

Fairtrade International/Fairtrade Canada allows only democratically organized groups of farmers in a cooperative to be certified and does not allow privately operated farms. It signs up farmers who must meet specified labour, environmental, and social standards and secures buyers in developed countries who pay more for the products. Farmers are guaranteed a minimum wage or return. Twenty percent of the product's ingredients must be fair trade to obtain the certification.

Fair Trade USA split from Fairtrade International because it felt that the latter's certification was too strict and not able to provide the volume of products needed in the market. It certifies non-cooperative farms that are privately owned estates or plantations. The certification label is applied to ingredients within a product; that is, the whole product does not have to contain a specified amount of fair trade ingredients. The existence of two fair trade labels in the Canadian market will likely cause some confusion for consumers. This is another illustration of buyer beware, depending upon which specifications a consumer believes are appropriate.[26]

The entrepreneurs promoting fair trade products claim that the local suppliers in developing countries are now receiving a higher price for their product. Initially fair trade was sponsored by NGOs such as Oxfam, Rainforest Alliance, and Traidcraft, but corporations are now developing their own sources in countries where the products are produced; this often occurs in partnership with NGOs. An example of an international organization promoting fair trade is given in Responsibility for Ethics 12.9.

RESPONSIBILITY FOR ETHICS 12.9

The Ethical Trading Initiative (ETI)

The Ethical Trading Initiative (ETI) is an alliance of companies, trade unions, and voluntary organizations that work together to improve the lives of workers in developing countries that make or grow consumer goods. Its vision is ". . . a world where all workers are free from exploitation and discrimination, and work in conditions of freedom, security and equity." The alliance enables ETI to tackle many of the issues that cannot be addressed by individual corporations.

One of ETI's projects focuses on purchasing practices, which involves investigating how the buying practices of corporations can undermine their progress in ethical trading. Practices hindering ethical trading include last-minute changes to orders and shorter lead times, which contribute to excessive overtime, and pressure to reduce prices, which makes it difficult to pay living wages.

Nearly 70 corporations are members, including Gap Inc. and The Body Shop International.

Source: Adapted from Ethical Trading Initiative, accessed January 14, 2016, http://www.ethicaltrade.org/about-eti.

Fair trade has been criticized for several reasons, and some critics claim that the fair trade movement has failed. It is claimed that little of the extra paid by consumers for fair trade products actually reaches the producers or farmers, and a positive impact is difficult to prove.[27] Further, a criticism is that not only is the lot of poor farmers not improved, but fair trade also may actually help to impoverish them because problems exist with certification. The poorest farmers may not be able to afford the fees for certification. It is claimed that the certification process is lax and almost impossible to monitor, as farmers and middlemen can get around the system.[28]

Other criticism includes the claim that exploitation of labour still exists. Even with the focus on labour practices, the cocoa industry still has slavery, poor working conditions, and illegal farming on protected land. Some critics argue that the focus on labour practices has resulted in neglecting farming techniques and pesticide use. There are challenges for the users of fair trade commodities in developed countries. The proliferation of labels and organizations licensing and certifying commodities is confusing and unreliable. The use of fair trade ingredients by Canadian businesses is more expensive, supply is not always available, and quality can be inconsistent. Overall, critics claim that fair trade is more about easing the consciences of consumers in developed countries than reducing poverty in developing countries.[29]

Employees, consumers, competitors, and supplier stakeholders are among the most influential for any corporation. The economic, social, and environmental issues are numerous, and this chapter has provided an introduction to them. The following chapter examines other stakeholders that might be influential: non-governmental organizations (NGOs), the media, policy development institutions (think tanks), and religious and educational institutions.

Your advice to Phyllis . . .

You understand that Phyllis faces a dilemma with the contradictions that confront managers. As an employee, she is faced with the task of implementing a policy with which she may not totally agree. What is involved are different approaches to ethical reasoning. A caring ethic would suggest that exceptions should be made. A justice ethic would attempt to treat all so that equitable outcomes occur. A utilitarian ethic would attempt to identify stakeholders and the benefits and harms to each. It appears that Phyllis's concern is that not all shoplifters should be treated the same and maybe they have rights. Her dilemma is not an uncommon occurrence in the retail workplace.

Summary

- Numerous ethics and responsibility issues arise in the relationship between the corporation and employees, consumers, competitors, and suppliers. (LO 12.1)

- Canadian employers and employees face many challenges in their relationship and three topics were discussed. Most Canadians still believe in the work ethic; several factors affect the loyalty of the employee to the employer; and employment diversity is a matter that employers must manage in today's workplace. (LO 12.2)

- According to consumer sovereignty, consumers should be determining what goods and services are available in the marketplace. In reality, this does not occur and consumers must also rely on rights and government legislation and regulation. Corporations are placing numerous "ethical" products in the marketplace. (LO 12.3)

- It is desirable that competitive rivalry exists in the marketplace, but many ethical and responsibility issues arise. Government has enacted legislation to encourage honest, fair, and open competition in the marketplace. Several factors in the economy determine competitive behaviour. (LO 12.4)

- Pressure on suppliers and the supply chain to consider ethics and responsibilities in the marketplace has increased. In general, the relationship between suppliers and their customers has changed from an adversarial one to a co-operative one. (LO 12.5)

- The supply chain identifies the progress of a product from raw material sources through to the consumer and ultimately disposal. Sustainability purchasing takes into consideration ethical, social, and environmental factors in acquiring materials and products. Fair trade is a version of this type of purchasing that attempts to improve the economic well-being of people working in the upstream component of the supply chain. (LO 12.6)

Key Terms

Discrimination

Employment equity

Diversity management

Feminist ethics

Employee engagement

Consumerism

Business-to-business

Supply (or value) chain

Extended producer responsibility

Sustainability purchasing

Fair trade

Critical Thinking and Discussion Questions

1. Is the work ethic concept relevant in today's workplace?
2. Why should employees be loyal to the corporation? How does the corporation express its loyalty to employees?
3. What does the corporation gain from workplace diversity?
4. To what extent does the consumer sovereignty concept apply in today's marketplace?
5. Are consumers adequately protected in the marketplace?
6. What are the pros and cons when competition results in the failure of a business?
7. Can the government encourage competition? If so, how does the government do it?
8. Which stakeholders are influencing the commercial activities along the supply chain?
9. Who should be responsible for the disposal of a product after it is used by the consumer?
10. What are the benefits of sustainability purchasing to corporations?
11. Why are fair trade products popular with consumers?

Cases

12.1 LOBLAW'S TREATMENT OF ITS SUPPLIERS

The Canadian food retailing industry is hyper-competitive with corporations aggressively seeking market share and attempting to maintain profits. Loblaw is the largest grocery industry retailer followed by Sobeys and Metro Inc. Recently Loblaw acquired Shoppers Drug Mart and Sobeys took over Safeway Canada. Other retailers in the industry included Walmart, Costco, smaller regional chains, convenience stores and independent grocers.

In the past few years, there have been growing tensions over competition in the industry and between retailers and suppliers. In particular, Loblaw was accused of unfair practices towards its suppliers such as:

- Charging fees for flyer promotions, prominent shelf space, stocking of store shelves, and late deliveries
- Seeking volume rebates
- "Ad matching" that involves demanding compensation from suppliers when a rival retailer offers a lower price than Loblaw on the supplier's product

- "Ad collisions" where the supplier is expected to pay the difference between a competitor's flyer price and Loblaw's advertised price
- Retroactively charging price breaks back to suppliers
- Refusing to accept price increases by imposing price freezes on suppliers

Such practices were not unique to Loblaw but it appeared to be more aggressive, for example, a "three strikes and out" policy existed if a supplier violated Loblaw's policy repeatedly.

Suppliers attempted to counter such practices. They wanted minimum pricing to protect their brands' images and not have brands become loss leaders. They wanted a level playing field and resisted the increasing number of fees they were being charged. They sought a code of conduct governing practices between suppliers and the retailers as exists in the United Kingdom and the Australia.

Loblaw claimed that its policies benefited consumers as they were attempting to keep prices low. Smaller, independent retailers were likely being charged more by the suppliers to protect their profits after pay outs to Loblaw. This likely resulted in higher prices for consumers in the smaller retailers.

The Competition Bureau has been following the practices in the industry as it considered some of the practices might be anti-competitive. In May 2015 it applied for a court order seeking information from Loblaw about the practices. It obtained the order and the industry was waiting for a response from the Bureau.

Questions

1. What are the economic, social and ethical issues involved?
2. How are Loblaw's stakeholders influenced and how is Loblaw influenced by stakeholders?
3. Should the government, through the Competition Bureau, regulate the industry?

Sources: Adapted from "Competition Bureau Reviewing Documents from Loblaw Over Pricing Practices," Canadian Hardware and Housewares Manufacturers Association accessed January 15, 2016, http://www.chhma.ca/Public/Newsletter-Articles-June-03-2015; "Competition Watchdog Continues Probe into Loblaw's Pricing Practices," *The Globe and Mail* online, accessed January 15, 2016 http://www.theglobeandmail.com/report-on-business/competition-watchdog-continues-probe-into-loblaws-pricing-practices/article26674211/; "Affidavit Reveals Glimpse into Loblaw Pricing Practices." RegulatorWatch.com, accessed January 15, 2016, https://regulatorwatch.com/reported_elsewhere/affidavit-reveals-glimpse-into-loblaw-pricing-practices; and "Loblaw's Pricing Practices Continue to be Under Scrutiny," Canadian Federation of Independent Grocers, accessed January 15, 2016, http://cfig.ca/2015/10/08/loblaws-pricing-practices-continue-to-be-under-scrutiny.

12.2 SODIUM AND ETHICS

Sodium, a mineral, is found in table salt, which is 40 percent sodium and 60 percent chloride. It is found in meat, fish, poultry, eggs, milk, and cheese, and is highest in processed foods. In addition, consumers season their food with salt. The daily requirement for sodium is 1,500 mg and is supplied by natural, unprocessed foods. Canadians consume about 3,000 mg per day.

High consumption of sodium might cause high blood pressure, from which about 20 percent of Canadians suffer. High blood pressure and related diseases are the world's leading cause of deaths. About 80 percent of salt intake by Canadians is from fast food and processed foods.

The World Action on Salt and Health surveyed food products around the world and gathered statistics on sodium content from food manufacturer websites. One of its findings was the high sodium in fast food and processed foods in Canada in comparison to levels in other countries. Some examples include the following:

- Burger King onion rings: In Canada, 0.681 mg sodium per 100 mg compared to 0.159 mg in the U.K.
- Kelloggs All Bran cereal: In Canada, 0.861 mg sodium per 100 mg compared to 0.258 in the U.S.
- KFC Popcorn chicken: In Canada, 0.908 mg sodium per 100 mg compared to 0.560 in Malaysia.
- McDonald's Sausage McMuffin with egg or equivalent: 0.980 mg sodium per 100 mg compared to 0.400 mg in France.

Sodium content was not high or the highest in all the Canadian products surveyed.

Manufacturers point out that ingredients of their products are listed publicly and that they are responding to consumer taste preferences. Yet the Canadian Medical Association is concerned and the issue is receiving considerable media coverage. Salt intake is a serious societal issue and business has some responsibility to address it.

Questions

1. Whose responsibility is it to control salt in Canadian diets?
2. Is it desirable to allow consumers to take personal responsibility for their sodium intake?
3. Should governments regulate? How could this be accomplished?
4. What can/should fast-food and processed-food industries do to address this issue?

Sources: Adapted from "New Research Reveals Huge Differences in Salt Contents in Global Foods," World Action on Salt and Health, http://www.worldactiononsalt.com/media/recent_press_releases.htm; Carly Weeks, "The Cereal Killer: From All-Bran to Burgers, Study Finds Food has More Salt in Canada," *The Globe and Mail*, July 23, 2009, A1, A5; and Carly Weeks, "Ottawa Must Act on Salt Crisis, Doctors Say," *The Globe and Mail*, September 15, 2009, A1, A11.

Used with the permission of Dennis Flynn

CHAPTER 13

Civil Society Stakeholders

LEARNING OUTCOMES

After studying this chapter, you will be able to:

LO 13.1 Define non-governmental organization (NGO) and describe NGO issues and tactics.

LO 13.2 State arguments for and against NGOs.

LO 13.3 Identify strategies business can use to build relationships with NGOs.

LO 13.4 Outline how partnerships between business and NGOs work.

LO 13.5 Describe the media as a stakeholder of the corporation.

LO 13.6 Explain the influence of the media on the corporation and the corporation on the media.

LO 13.7 Understand the implications of business ownership of the media.

LO 13.8 Appreciate the media's approach to CSR.

LO 13.9 Define policy development institutions (think tanks) and their influence.

LO 13.10 Describe the influence of religious organizations on business.

LO 13.11 Understand the relationship between education institutions, and business and society.

What would you do if...?

Debbie Belbin is crazy about animals! She and her boyfriend have two dogs and three cats all living together in a third floor one bedroom apartment. They spend much of their spare time caring for the pets including extensive walks and runs with the dogs.

Debbie has always loved animals and grew up in the household with various pets. She was aware of several organizations, or NGOs, that advocated for the fair treatment of animals. She supported the local branches of the Humane Society of Canada and the Society of the Prevention of Cruelty to Animals and volunteered at shelters for abused and abandoned animals. Over the years, she had made donations to NGOs dedicated to animal welfare and rights including: People for the Ethical Treatment of Animals (PETA), Vegetarians International Voice for Animals, the Sea Shepherd Conservation Society, and the Animal Alliance of Canada.

However, she was becoming increasingly concerned about the operations and tactics used by some of the NGOs. Her concerns included:

- The use of misleading advertisements, in particular billboards, by some groups.
- The inappropriate expenditure of funds raised, and the alleged large salaries and perks paid to some animal organization management.
- The threats made against corporate executives, including the picketing of their homes and families.
- The destruction of property during protests.
- Blockages of access to properties for unreasonable periods of time and sometimes causing harm to employees.
- The illegal entry into business properties, for example, breaking into barns and releasing chickens.
- Campaigns against the consumption of some food, in particular, PETA's campaign against children drinking milk.

Debbie acquired a business degree three years ago and now worked for a computer company. She did not believe that everything done by corporations was evil or unethical. She was concerned that some of the tactics used by these NGOs not only harmed business but other stakeholders as well. There appears to be moderate NGOs concerned about animal welfare, that is, how animals are treated, but extremist ones exist advocating animal rights, that is, animals should be treated as humans. She wondered how she could sort out the "good" from the "bad" animal protection NGOs to ascertain which she should support.

What is your advice for Debbie?

Civil society comprises the voluntary, community, and social organizations or institutions that contribute to the functioning of society but are usually not related to or supported by government. Civil society institutions are corporation stakeholders; examples include non-governmental organizations, the media, community-based organizations, civic clubs, trade unions, charities, social and sports clubs, cooperatives, environmental groups, professional associations, policy development institutions, educational institutions, and organized religion.

In this chapter, two civil institutions that have substantial influence on business will be discussed in detail: non-governmental organizations (NGOs) and the media. Corporations and their managers must develop a relationship with these institutions in which managers not only learn about these stakeholders but also recognize their role in society and develop mechanisms for interacting with them. This focus is not one-way but instead is a proactive relationship in which managers understand and respect the roles of these civil society stakeholders. In addition to NGOs and the media, other civil society stakeholders influence business and/or are influenced by business; three are described briefly: policy development institutions (think tanks), religious institutions, and educational organizations.

LO 13.1 The Non-Governmental Organization (NGO) Stakeholder

The definition of this stakeholder is problematic because different terminology can be used—for example, "public interest," "special interest," or just "interest" groups. Such groups are usually discussed in the context of their influence on public policy formulation, thus the *public interest group* terminology. *Special interest group* is used to describe an association that seeks the advancements of financial interests of its members, for example doctors or lawyers. Although both groups indirectly influence business, the focus of this section is on interest groups that interact with or influence business more directly. Current practice is to refer to these groups as non-governmental organizations (NGOs). A well-known example of such an organization is Mothers Against Drunk Driving (MADD); see Everyday Ethics 13.1.

EVERYDAY ETHICS 13.1

Mothers Against Drunk Driving (MADD)

Mothers Against Drunk Driving (MADD Canada) is a non-profit, grassroots organization that is committed to stopping impaired driving and supporting the victims of this violent crime. At the heart of MADD Canada are volunteers who include not only mothers, but also fathers, friends, business professionals, experts in the anti-impaired driving field, and concerned citizens who want to make a difference in the fight against impaired driving. There are 100 branches and 7,500 volunteers across Canada to deliver its programs.

MADD Canada's aim is to offer support services to victims, heighten awareness about the dangers of drinking and driving, and to save lives and prevent injuries on our roads. Driving while under the influence of alcohol or other drugs is a terrible crime that touches all of our lives and it is an irresponsible, dangerous, and intolerable act.

Source: Adapted from Mothers Against Drunk Driving, "MADD Canada: Learn More," http://www.madd.ca.

A **non-governmental organization (NGO)** is any group that holds shared values or attitudes about an issue confronting society and advocates for changes relating to the issue. NGOs make claims or demands that business take actions that will be consistent with the group's attitudes or principles. It should be noted that these groups are part of the private sector, not part of government, and are usually but not always non-profit organizations supported by volunteer members and activists. The distinction from government is an important one to make, but there are exceptions. NGOs are able to do things that governments will not or cannot do. NGOs operating in developing countries are sometimes supported by governments, for example those involved with the distribution of foreign aid as contractors acting on behalf of governments unable or unwilling to perform the necessary functions.

TABLE 13.1	Examples of NGO Societal Issues Relevant to Business

Numerous societal issues are addressed by NGOs, and this list identifies some of those relevant to business organizations. Some issues may overlap, and particular NGOs may be involved in more than one. The issues are at both the domestic and international or global levels.

Animal welfare versus rights—Some advocate for the entitlements of animals as humans. Others are concerned about animal welfare, that is, the care given animals. Extreme groups oppose consumption of any meat products and promote vegetarianism.

Technology—Opposed to biotechnology developments; for example, genetic modification of foods. Also concerned about reproduction of life forms.

Economic—Often oppose capitalism and advocate for forms of collectivist enterprise or government ownership. Concerned about concentration of ownership and domination of the economy by the "corporate agenda" or the corporate elite.

Social development—Concerned with the gap between the rich and poor in Canada but particularly in developing countries. Promote community development, cultural and social activities, and social services such as housing and health care.

Workers'/human rights—Identify the working conditions of labour especially in developing countries. Advocate for union organization and codes of practice. Also concerned with human rights.

Environment—One of the most common causes of NGO activity. Covers all aspects of the environment in Canada and around the world.

Religious activism—Form of activism that is more common recently, especially in the U.S. Local churches and alliances of evangelical churches pressure corporations on their support of social issues such as gay rights and abortion.

NGOs are not new to society; they have existed for hundreds of years. For example, NGOs have opposed slavery in various parts of the world and foot binding in China, advocated for women's voting rights, demanded better working conditions for children, and supported minimum wage laws. In recent times their numbers have proliferated; they can be locally based in a community or operate around the world. There are many economic, ethical, and environmental issues that form the basis or belief for an NGO; some of the most common issues that influence business are listed in Table 13.1 on the previous page.

Managers must be aware of the variety of approaches or tactics used in an attempt to influence the corporation or its stakeholders. Understanding the possible tactics is important because of a shift in the focus of influence. At one time, NGOs concentrated their efforts on lobbying or otherwise influencing government policies or regulation toward business. Some NGOs attack or attempt to influence corporations by taking actions directly against them. There has been a shift in recent years to indirectly influencing corporations through other stakeholders, for example shareholders, consumers, or suppliers. Responsibility for Ethics 13.1 lists some commonly used tactics to influence corporations.

RESPONSIBILITY FOR ETHICS 13.1

NGO Tactics

The following are examples of tactics used by NGOs to influence the ethical conduct of corporations:

- Putting pressure on governments and politicians to change policies or regulations
- Generating damaging publicity on the corporation in the media
- Disrupting annual meetings
- Developing shareholder social policy resolutions (after purchasing a few shares)
- Damaging physical property or sabotaging activities
- Occupying corporate premises
- Sponsoring demonstrations or picketing corporate locations
- Picketing managers' homes
- Sponsoring demonstrations or picketing corporate locations
- Organizing boycotts to prevent purchases
- Organizing buycotts (that is, campaigning to buy the products or services of a particular company or country) to recommend purchases from preferred sellers
- Launching letter-writing campaigns, including letters-to-the-editors of newspapers
- Participating in digital protest movements
- Holding public meetings
- Using social media to initiate campaigns on social or environmental issues
- Initiating legal proceedings
- Participating in hacktivism, the non-violent use of the Internet for activist protests
- Developing anti-business or anti-corporate websites and "Watch"–type sites—for example Walmart Watch
- Supporting the development of anti-business documentaries and facilitating their distribution
- Providing support for alternative sources of goods and services (e.g., fair trade products, credit unions, employee-owned enterprises)

connect   Want to learn more about **digital protest movements**?

LO 13.2 The Case For and Against NGOs

Corporations and their managers should not dismiss NGOs as a nuisance or useless stakeholder. Their members are very dedicated to their cause or issue and their existence in society supports structures that allow for a wider cross-section of society to influence events. NGOs facilitated the preparation of the agreements on global warming, and they made available lower-cost drugs in developing countries. They generate ideas, knowledge, and solutions, disseminate information on issues, and, of course, pressure for results. Some NGOs have developed product certification systems that corporations have used in their marketing. NGOs can be agents for change, and can confer legitimacy when governments cannot act alone.

Governments and business will listen to NGOs when they operate in a transparent manner, are accountable for their actions, and are accurate in their claims or information.[1] In a report prepared by Canadian Business for Social Responsibility (CBSR), the benefits from partnerships with NGOs include identifying opportunities and risks, influencing public opinion, developing possibilities for innovation, enhancing reputation and trust by the public, creating expertise with in-depth knowledge of specific issues, facilitating employee engagement, and building large networks with other stakeholders.[2]

NGOs may advocate diverse views about the same issue. An example is provided by free trade, to which many NGO groups are opposed. Yet the Global Freedom to Trade campaign advocates for global trade freedom. Other NGOs such as Oxfam Canada support freer trade under certain conditions, and many forms of fair trade practices exist. Managers not only must identify the NGOs related to industry-relevant issues, but also must understand the positions held about these issues because some may be supportive.

Many NGOs do represent a threat to business. Many of the tactics listed in Responsibility for Ethics 13.1 can disrupt business operations. Many are clearly anti-business and anti–free trade or globalization, reducing the support for business in society. Their beliefs in redistribution of wealth and equality of results are inconsistent with business beliefs in economic markets and efficiency measures. Some NGOs are simply "anti" everything associated with business and constantly criticize while offering few if any alternatives.[3]

LO 13.3 Strategies for Relationships with NGOs

NGOs pressure corporations directly and indirectly through other stakeholders. If an indirect approach is the case, Spar and LaMure state that there are three key turning points for the corporation: (1) the NGO must be able to threaten the corporation with significant harm; (2) the corporation must respond to the threat by changing business practice; and (3) the change must serve to advance the NGO's goals. They argue that the corporation becomes the conduit by which outside stakeholders—that is, NGOs—attempt to achieve non-market objectives.[4]

Corporations cannot ignore the influence of NGOs and should not underestimate their power or tenacity. Many corporations do take NGO activism seriously and respond in different ways depending on the corporation's particular position or the type of industry. Spar and LaMure propose that the corporation's response to NGO activism is influenced by three variables: transaction costs, brand impact, and competitive position. There are also three possibilities when corporations are faced with NGO tactics. Resistance is possible, but not recommended in most situations. Capitulation may be the most advantageous in some cases, and pre-emption in others.

Transaction costs relate to capital and sourcing, and if substantial expenses are involved to meet the NGO's demands, the corporation is more likely to resist the demands. This is usually the case in natural resource industries where capital investments are high, or in industries where no other source of supply exists. In consumer goods industries, capitulation to NGO demands is usually less expensive and alternate sources of supply are available.

The greater the value a corporation places on its brand, the more susceptible it is to pressure from the NGO. In this situation, capitulation to the demands is a more logical response. Brand-name footwear and apparel companies can easily switch their sourcing and few, if any, capital costs are involved. By doing so, the corporation is more likely to gain a reputation as a socially responsible citizen.

In very competitive industries, being the first to meet or capitulate to NGO demands might provide a competitive advantage. This is particularly the case where brand recognition is high. Such action would be a pre-emptive strategy to gain on competitors.[5] Table 13.2 summarizes the strategies and the responses.

TABLE 13.2 Strategies for Relationships With NGOs			
Three Variables Influencing Response	**Transaction costs**	**Brand impact**	**Competitive position**
	↓	↓	↓
Responses	Resistance (resource industries)	Capitulation (consumer goods)	Pre-emption (competitive industries)

Managers do not always reply based on resistance, capitulation, and pre-emption. They may have personal motives and beliefs that can also motivate their decisions. Managers have values and ethical beliefs as a result of their upbringing or education that provide guidance in moral issues. It should not be assumed that managers always make decisions relating to NGO demands based on cost–benefit analysis or competitive positioning.[6]

A more aggressive response toward NGOs is possible but not recommended. An effort could be made to discredit NGOs with negative attacks, or to launch legal action. Both responses could backfire and complicate the relationship. However, it may be feasible to demand more accountability from NGOs, just as they are demanding the accountability of corporations. Some NGOs do not account appropriately to donors, or they spend funds on questionable activities. It can be pointed out that unrepresentative activists undermine the effectiveness of credible NGOs, and the corporation can provide evidence of its serious efforts at dialogue with some NGOs.

Some of the anti-business tactics used by NGOs are difficult to tolerate, but at times corporations find that ignoring their extreme positions may be preferable to attempts at countering. Business organizations have countered NGO-sponsored websites with NGOWATCH.org, a site that compiles factual data about NGOs, including analysis of relevant issues, treaties, and international organizations where NGOs are active. Lastly, business can suggest that NGOs also need a code of ethics and/or conduct to guide their operations.

  Want to learn more about **"watch" sites**?

Based upon Spar and LaMure's article and from the discussion of NGOs, some observations are possible about how corporations can view and build their relationship with NGOs.

- A preferable strategy is to proactively engage the NGOs and expect to interact with them.
- Do not underestimate the influence of NGOs on the corporation directly or indirectly through other stakeholders.
- Reversing a decision or withdrawing from a project should not be viewed as a defeat.
- Sometimes selective concessions are sufficient to address opposition from NGOs.
- Sometimes it is appropriate to establish a dialogue with "realist" NGOs and ignore the "radical" and "idealist" ones.
- A pre-emptive strategy may be feasible.

Several questions that managers should pose to learn about an NGO's approach include, Who are they? What do they want? What will they do to achieve their objectives? and What is the best way to deal with them?

LO 13.4   Partnership Relationships with NGOs

A Canadian Business for Social Responsibility (CBSR) report presents another view being advocated regarding relationships with NGOs; that is, one of partnership. The report explores a different type of partnership between business and NGOs: domestic partnerships that build business leadership through social, environmental, and economic success. It is pointed out that philanthropic partnerships have supported and empowered NGOs; for example, Microsoft Canada's partnership with the Royal Canadian Mounted Police and the Toronto Police Service to establish the Child Exploitation Tracking System. However, another form of partnership drives social success and innovation in business by involving all three sectors: business, government, and civil society.[7]

This type of partnership brings together business and NGO resources to address an issue including human, technical, financial, and knowledge interests. The process is not without risks to all involved—damage to reputations, high start-up costs, conflicts of interest, and alienation of stakeholders may be concerns. CBSR identifies four key ingredients to defining the success of a partnership:

- Corporate and NGO leaders must show leadership;
- The corporation must be open to change;
- There must be a commitment to being committed;
- Partners must have a shared goal.[8]

An article at Network for Business Sustainability identified the key lessons for collaboration with NGOs differently. It must be recognized that different perspectives exist; this can be challenging but also valuable as each partner's knowledge, expertise, and capabilities complement the others'. Secondly, it is important to assign a person responsible for the project and give that person authority and decision-making ability. This champion is necessary to overcome resistance and to indicate to the NGO that the corporation is taking the relationship seriously. Also, the NGO engagement must be part of the corporation's core business; that is, integrated into the operations of business units and not maintained as a separate, standalone operation. Lastly, the relationship must be allowed to evolve over time and accommodate changing circumstances as they arise. Corporate and NGO partnerships are challenging to management, but they can be beneficial to both partners.[9]

Examples of successful partnerships are described in Everyday Ethics 13.2. A more detailed example is the completion of the Canadian Boreal Forest Agreement (CBFA) described in Responsibility for Ethics 13.2; this was a significant accomplishment because of the number of NGOs and corporations involved, and its span across a whole industry. The agreement has been criticized on the grounds that NGOs have no right to determine public policy, especially through the use of intimidations and threats based on unproven claims. Some argue that the boreal forest was not under threat of destruction, and that the agreement would result in higher prices, fewer jobs, zero impact on climate, and reduced profits. CBFA believes that these are only the beginnings of many future innovative partnerships.

EVERYDAY ETHICS 13.2

Corporate–NGO Partnerships

Fairmont Hotels & Resorts and WWF-Canada—In partnership with World Wildlife Fund, Fairmont has made a world-class CO_2 emission reduction commitment that enables CO_2 footprint reductions from operations for both existing and new properties, and includes engaging suppliers, employees, and guests to promote the benefits and need to reduce emissions.

Gordon Food Service®—The company's Canada Home Office partners with Hope Network to prepare persons with cognitive and physical disabilities for permanent employment opportunities as they pursue career possibilities.

Potash Corp and Free the Children—These two organizations have announced a multi-year partnership to help address international food security and encourage youth in Saskatchewan and across Canada to take on this challenge locally and globally.

The Home Depot Canada Foundation—Home Depot supports the HireUp hiring portal for youth who have experienced homelessness. HireUp connects employers with youth-serving organizations to create meaningful employment opportunities.

Sources: "Fairmont Hotels & Resorts Achieves WWF's Climate Savers Program CO2 Reduction Targets," World Wildlife Fund (WWF), accessed January 20, 2016, http://www.wwf.ca/newsroom/?17062/fairmont-hotels--resorts-achieves-wwfs-climate-savers-program-co2-reduction-targets; Gordon Food Service® Canadian Stewardship Report 2014, accessed January 20, 2016, https://www.gfs.ca/sites/gfscanada.com/files/Canada_Stewardship_Report.pdf; Community Investment, Potash Corp., accessed January 20, 2016, http://www.potashcorp.com/sustainability/key_focus_areas/community_investment/topics/; and Hireup, accessed January 20, 2016, https://hireupyouth.ca/.

RESPONSIBILITY FOR ETHICS 13.2

Canadian Boreal Forest Agreement (CBFA)

In May 2010, an agreement was reached among nine environmental non-governmental organizations (ENGOs) and twenty-one forestry corporations on the management of the Canadian boreal forest. It is a significant agreement illustrating cooperation between ENGOs and the forestry industry. It was considered a historic event and was a model of ENGO/business cooperation.

The ENGOs participating are Canadian Boreal Initiative, Canadian Parks and Wilderness Society, Canopy, David Suzuki Foundation, ForestEthics, Greenpeace, The Nature Conservancy, Pew Environment Group International Boreal Conservation Campaign, and Ivey Foundation. They agreed to stop boycott campaigns against Canadian forest products. Also, they would endorse the purchase of Canadian products if the industry met performance standards specified in the Agreement.

There has been some disagreements among the original signatories and in 2016 the signatories participating were the Forest Products Association of Canada (FPAC), its 18 member-companies, Kruger Inc., and six leading Canadian environmental non-government organizations. The commitments made by the industry included not undertaking any environmentally unfriendly actions; becoming carbon neutral; establishing a caribou habitat; and matching global standards for forest product sustainability. The CBFA covers more than 73 million hectares of public forests licensed to FPAC member companies across Canada.

Sources: The Canadian Boreal Forest Agreement, accessed January 20, 2016, http://cbfa-efbc.ca/agreement/.

This section has described NGOs and some of the relationships that exist between NGOs and business. Although NGOs have been an increasingly influential stakeholder, another civil society stakeholder, the media, plays an important role in influencing the corporation.

LO 13.5 The Media Stakeholder

This section explores the relationship between business and the media—newspapers, periodicals, television, radio, and the Internet. The media is a stakeholder that can influence the views held by the public about business and cannot be ignored. In turn, business has some influence over the media. Most media operations are owned by private-sector enterprises, and advertising is a main source of revenue for them. In recent years business has taken on improved respectability in the media and this has led to increased coverage, especially for international business and personal finance.

Managers should realize that dealing with the media is a part of their responsibility and that the media are important in earning and keeping public trust and acceptance. Some managers see the media as intrusive, prying, and prejudicial, an unwelcome and necessary evil. But business needs to communicate with all stakeholders, and the media serve as a vehicle that may reflect owner, employee, consumer, community, and other stakeholder expectations about the ethics of business and its social and environmental responsibilities. The media are entitled to gather, digest, and regurgitate information on business as they do for any other institution in society, and media coverage of business activities can improve economic literacy and attitudes toward business.

Business is a major institution in society, and like any other major institution people have an intrinsic curiosity about it. People have developed the belief that they have a right to know about things that affect them, and this belief has been reinforced by access-to- information law. Thus, over the years, veils of secrecy that sheltered many institutions and organizations have been removed, or at least lifted. People now want to take a closer look at business and are asking tougher, more pointed questions.[10]

The Influence of Popular Media

Books, television, film documentaries, movies, and the Internet portray the operations of business and its relationship to society. Some of the portrayals are positive, but many are negative and receive a lot of attention. The extent to which the popular media influence attitudes toward business is not known for certain.

Many Canadian corporate histories and business biographies have been written, along with general books about the business system. Examples of books with a negative view of business are *Greed, Inc.: Why Corporations Rule Our World and How We Let It Happen*,[11] *The Corporation: The Pathological Pursuit of Profit and Power*,[12] and *Wealth by Stealth: Corporate Crime, Corporate Law, and the Perversion of Democracy*.[13]

Popular television programs also have mixed views of business. Business is often portrayed unfavourably as, on *The Simpsons* for example. In addition, television investigative reporting programs uncover corporate wrongdoing or questionable practices. Documentaries made for television and movie theatres have become popular recently, for example *Super Size Me, Roger & Me, Walmart: The High Cost of Low Price,* and *Capitalism: A Love Story*.

Although some crossover occurs between documentaries and movies, movies often focus on the ethics of business and corporate social responsibility. Some movies that have not portrayed capitalism in a good light are *Wall Street, Erin Brockovich, A Civil Action, The Constant Gardener, Blood Diamond, In Good Company,* and *Up in the Air.* Finally, the Internet is a source of information that is critical about business. Many large companies are the subject of "watch" sites, such as *Walmart Watch,* as are industries, such as *MiningWatch.* Some websites are critical of business in general, for example *CorporateWatch.*

Numerous newspapers and periodicals cater to business audiences, or those interested in the ethics of business and its responsibilities. Daily newspapers have some business coverage, even if it is simply an abbreviated stock market listing. *The Globe and Mail* (Toronto) has a "Report on Business" section daily. *National Post* offers daily coverage of finance and business in its *Financial Post* section. *The Globe and Mail* and *National Post* publish monthly business magazines, *Report on Business* and *National Post Business.* Other monthly magazines include *Inside Guide, En Route, Small Business Magazine,* and *Canadian Business.* There also are several regional business magazines, for example *Atlantic Canada Business* and *Alberta Business.*

Coverage of business has changed from domination by print to domination by live television and social media. Television and radio have extensive and immediate coverage of business topics. CBC-TV has a business-related program called *Marketplace,* and the cable television channel *Report on Business* devotes all programming to business and related topics. However, even newspapers respond to events quickly, with lengthy analyses of major business-related events. Their online editions are updated constantly. This trend to instant news has also resulted in the instant expert opinion. If a company produces an unsafe product or pollutes a waterway, experts are available to offer their analysis or comment, although sometimes biased or peripheral.

Finally, the technology of the media stakeholder is changing. The term **social media** describes the online technologies and practices that people use to share opinions, insights, experiences, and perspectives.[14] The ways that information from and about business is received by society are being transformed by new technologies, and discussions of the ethics of business and its responsibilities in these media will occur as well. It is not clear what influence this change will have on the relationships among business, the media, and society.

connect Want to learn more about **the efforts of OpenMedia.ca to keep the Internet affordable?**

The influence of the media, as measured by society's trust in it, has been declining along with trust in business. In 2015, the Edelman Trust Barometer for Canada found that 47 percent of respondents trusted the media, down from 58 percent in 2014. The comparable figures for business were 47 and 62 percent. Traditional media were trusted the most at 62 percent, online search engines at 55 percent, and social media at 35 percent.[15]

LO 13.6   The Interaction Between Business and the Media

Businesspersons have complained about what they consider to be inappropriate coverage in the media. On the other hand, the media complain about attitudes held by most businesspersons about their reporting practices. Table 13.3 summarizes complaints from both perspectives.

TABLE 13.3   Business–Media Relations

Business Complaints about the Media

- Reporters are not sufficiently knowledgeable about business and economics and fail to do their homework.
- The media are interested only in "bad" news that can be sensationalized.
- The media are unable to place the information they are provided into the correct context.
- The media have an inherent bias against business and are dominated by leftist journalists who neither support nor understand a market economy.
- Business reporting is not only biased, but also oversimplified and lacking in insight.
- Reporters do not respect "off-the-record" comments.

Media Complaints about Business

- Businesspersons confuse issues by waffling on details, stonewalling, attempting to hide negative information, or by lying.
- Businesspersons use the excuse that they are accountable only to shareholders, not the media.
- Businesspersons overreact to the process of reporting events and covering issues.

Some managers have attempted to manage the relationship to suit their purposes; press releases are an example. The media are viewed as a tap that can be turned on or off depending on what managers think stakeholders should know. Some corporations fear the damage that can be done by a reporter to a manager's or a corporation's image. But the consequence of not responding to requests from the media is also dangerous. If the media are rebuffed they will turn to more cooperative sources of information—which may not be sympathetic to the business view. For their part, businesspersons and managers have threatened to cancel subscriptions when (or if) negative stories are carried. Advertising has been withdrawn by some businesses as retaliation for an editorial view or certain news coverage.

Another phenomenon influencing media coverage, in particular the publication of books, is "libel chill." **Libel chill** occurs when a business threatens legal action if a particular article or book is published. With this threat present, writers, editors, and publishers impose on themselves a form of self-censorship, holding back on potentially controversial stories. This situation has an impact on the freedom of speech and the public's right to know. Publishers often back down for fear of a long and expensive court case and the possibility that they might lose.

Another challenge in business coverage is "media spin." Corporations have access to the services of public relations experts who are frequently able to put a particular "spin," or interpretation, on corporate events or information. This spin is incorporated into corporate press releases supplied to the media, often with supporting materials. Reporters, facing looming deadlines, have been accused of simply repackaging corporate press releases without further input. In turn, reporters may put their own spin on corporate news, particularly news that is not favourable to the corporation. The result is that some business news should be interpreted carefully.[16]

The issue is one of balance. The media should not get away with irresponsible, inaccurate, or scandalous reporting, but neither should businesspersons be allowed to unduly influence reporters and publishers. This discussion of the relationship between business and the media leads to a discussion of unfairness and biased reporting.

Whether media have a left-leaning, anti-business, big-government bias that tends to favour politically correct welfare-state solutions and downplay market realities, or a right-wing, corporate-agenda bias that tends to favour solutions that benefit the wealthy and powerful elite to the exclusion of marginalized and ordinary working people, is difficult to prove. According to Saunders, both positions are strongly supported in Canada; he uses content analysis to prove that reporters and editors are putting a particular ideological spin on the news. He states that although the process appears to be rigorous and to use scientific methods, the results of such analyses are questionable and a waste of time.[17]

A question arising from this discussion of fairness and bias in the media is whether it makes a difference. Corporations certainly think so. Managers worry about the type and tone of information that appears in the media and the influence this has on a company. Research into the relationship between media exposure and change in corporate reputation has for the most part been inconclusive. A study on the relationship between intensive media exposure and changes in corporate reputation concluded that media are a pervasive element in society and appear to be an important influence on the performance of modern companies.[18] Despite some positive findings, the author concluded that much remains to be done before the relationship is fully understood.

Wartick defined media exposure as "the aggregated news reports relating to a specific company within a prescribed period," and for corporate response used the definition "the aggregation of a single stakeholder's perception of how well organizational responses are meeting the demands and expectations of many organizational stakeholders."[19] He based his study on *Fortune*'s "Most Admired Corporations" and related the magnitude, direction, and total movement of change in corporate reputation with the amount, tone, and recency of media exposure. The tone of media exposure is a key factor associated with both the direction of the change in corporate reputation and the total movement of the change in corporate reputation. Recency is significantly associated with the magnitude of the changes in corporate reputation.[20]

LO 13.7   Media Ownership

Another dimension in the relationship between business and the media comes about because business enterprises own and operate media outlets. Ownership of the broadcast, telecommunications, and print media is now concentrated in multimedia business enterprises such as CTVglobemedia Inc., Postmedia Network Inc., Shaw Communications Inc., Rogers Media, the K.C. Irving Group, Torstar Corp., and Quebecor Media. At one time, the concern was for concentration of ownership within broadcast or print, but today most of these corporations own a variety of media.

Several issues emerge as a result of this ownership, including those surrounding (1) the newspaper monopolies held in some cities by large corporations; (2) the interlocking ownership between print and broadcasting media; (3) the licensing process in broadcasting where some corporations are allegedly favoured over others; and (4) the operation of newspaper chains that are concerned more with financial performance than professional journalism.

The power associated with media ownership is one issue. A related issue is the centralization of the media. This involves the concern that there may be too few voices in the media. Newspapers are suffering declining readership, especially with some age groups, and some have failed. But the availability of magazines has increased, as have alternatives available on television and radio. A problem with control arises when all media are concentrated with one or a few owners; this is not yet the case. However, although the independence of the media is an aspect of free privilege, this is countered by the professionalism of journalists and managers in the media. Some in society do challenge the influence of the media, as illustrated in Responsibility for Ethics 13.3.

RESPONSIBILITY FOR ETHICS 13.3

Adbusters and the "Media Carta"

The Adbusters Media Foundation describes itself as a social activist movement dedicated to reforming the media. Based in Vancouver, the Foundation publishes *Adbusters Magazine* (circulation of 101,000), maintains the Adbusters.org website, and operates an advocacy advertising agency.

One Adbusters project is focused on the way information flows and the way meaning is produced in society. Adbusters believes that people must launch a movement that enshrines "the Right to Communications in the constitutions of all free nations, and in the Universal Declaration of Human Rights." They are requesting that people sign their *Media Carta*, which states that citizens have:

- lost confidence in the commercial information system as it distorts the view of the world;
- lost faith in the institutions of mass media;
- lost hope in the national media regulators to act in the public interest, and lost patience waiting for reform.

Adbusters imagines a different system—a media democracy.

Sources: Adapted from "About Adbusters," Adbusters, accessed February 2008, http://www.adbusters.org/network/about_us.php; and "Sign the Media Carta," Adbusters, accessed February 2008, http://www.adbusters.org/campaigns/mediacarta/sign.

There is increasing specialization and fragmentation in the media. Mindszenthy listed the following types of media: trade journals; specialized consumer publications; all-news networks; cable TV stations; and the dedicated religious, lifestyle, business, weather, and sports networks. In addition, there are household or free-distribution newspapers, call-in and call-out radio and TV programs, and interview programs.[21] At the time same, the circulation of many magazines and most newspapers is declining.[22]

LO 13.8   The Media and CSR

Business topics and issues appear to have gained a new respectability in the media in recent years. In particular, there is increased coverage of the ethics of business and corporate social responsibility (CSR) in the media. Business' ethical, social, and environmental responsibilities are of increasing interest to the public. This seems to have led to increasing coverage of business topics and issues by the media. Businesspersons have responded by complaining less about biased reporting and by preparing themselves better for interacting with media representatives.

The corporations that own the media have recognized the importance of CSR or sustainability, and this is illustrated in the newspaper industry. *The Guardian,* a newspaper published in the United Kingdom, is recognized for its comprehensive annual sustainability report. A recent report is summarized in Everyday Ethics 13.3. Although the media make efforts to be responsible, failings have occurred. The News Corporation in the United Kingdom was accused of hacking telephone services and other corrupt practices. In Canada, a columnist at *The Globe and Mail* was accused of plagiarism. The managers and employees of media corporations must be as sensitive to the ethical implications of their behaviour as would those in other corporations.

EVERYDAY ETHICS 13.3

A Newspaper and Sustainability

Sustainability practice at a media corporation is illustrated by Guardian News and Media, a United Kingdom corporation best known as the publisher of *The Guardian* newspaper. It has been issuing sustainability reports for over 15 years, and its 48-page *Living Our Values: Sustainability Report 2015* covers operations, environmental impact, community initiatives, editorial approach, readers, and employees. The values that the corporation is following are: honesty, cleanness (integrity), courage, fairness, and a sense of duty to the reader and the community.

Another report, *Living Our Values 2015 Performance,* outlines how well the corporation performed. Its goals in four areas are identified and what the corporation did and how well it did it. The areas were:

- People and community: ethical culture, developing people, and duty to the community.
- Open and independent: courageous and independent, open access, and open reporting.
- Climate responsibility: operational efficiency, resource and pollution, and carbon management.
- Good business: championing sustainability, net positive revenue, and commercial security.

A concluding section outlined the targets for the next year.

Sources: Adapted from "Living our Values: Guardian News & Media Sustainability Report 2015," accessed January 20, 2016, http://image.guardian.co.uk/sys-files/Guardian/documents/2012/11/22/Sustainabilityreport2012.pdf.; "Living Our Values 2015, Printable Report," accessed January 20, 2016, http://www.theguardian.com/sustainability/2015/nov/04/living-our-values-2015-printable-report; and "Living Our Values 2015 Performance" accessed January 20, 2016, http://static.guim.co.uk/ni/1443171202420/LivingOurValuesReport2015.pdf.

Two civil society stakeholders—NGOs and the media—have been discussed in detail, but many other institutions can influence business or can be influenced by business. The following discussion briefly describes three others: policy development institutions or think tanks, religious organizations, and educational institutions.

LO 13.9 | Policy Development Institutions (Think Tanks)

A **policy development institution** or think tank is an organization that researches and analyzes various important social, economic, and political issues confronting business and society. Responsibility for Ethics 13.4 lists some examples the better known think tanks. They attempt to influence society's, in particular government's, position on various business and social issues. They try to bring fresh thinking to an issue and mould government public policy. Although they claim to be non-partisan and independent, the brief descriptions in Everyday Ethics 13.4 suggest that various ideological views are represented. Think tanks are not directly affiliated with political parties, but some do have a political agenda and are supportive of some ideological movements. Many think tanks have charity status for taxation purposes if no more than ten percent of their resources are devoted to political advocacy.

RESPONSIBILITY FOR ETHICS 13.4

Policy Development Institutions or "Think Tanks"

Most of these institutions are non-profit, non-partisan, and charitable organizations claiming to be independent.

- *C.D. Howe Institute*—Aims to improve Canadians' standard of living by fostering sound economic and social policy through independent research and analysis.
- *Caledon Institute of Social Policy*—Does research and analysis; seeks to inform and influence public opinion and to foster public discussion on poverty and social policy; and develops and promotes concrete, practicable proposals for the reform of social programs.
- *Canadian Centre for Policy Alternatives*—Conducts research and analysis concerned with issues of social and economic justice, and develops workable solutions to the policy questions facing Canadians today.
- *Canadian Labour and Business Centre*—Acts as a centre for business–labour dialogue and consensus building to develop effective public policy in labour market and skills issues.
- *Conference Board of Canada*—Builds leadership capacity for a better Canada by creating and sharing insights on economic trends, public policy, and organizational performance.
- *Fraser Institute*—Has as its objective the redirection of public attention through economic and social research to the role of competitive markets in providing for the well-being of Canadians.
- *Institute for Research on Public Policy*—Conducts research that aims to enhance the quality of the debate on the issues that matter most to Canadians by focusing on the strategic choices they must make to promote economic performance, social progress, and sound democratic governance.

Lists of think tanks can be obtained from Canajun Guide, "Think Tanks and Policy Research," http://canajun.com/canada/politics/think.htm; and Hillwatch.com, "Think Tanks: A Directory of Canadian and International Think Tanks," http://www.hillwatch.com/PPRC/Think_Tanks.aspx.

Usually think tanks are not connected to government, although government may provide funding. Most funding is provided by business corporations and trade unions. Wealthy individuals, foundations, member contributors, universities, and the sale of services (e.g., consulting, publications, etc.) finance others. Most Canadian think tanks were established in the 1970s and 1980s; they exist in most democracies, with some being international in scope.

Critics claim that think tanks lack transparency. Quite often who funds them is not identified on websites and if it is, the amount of their financial contribution is not. Foreign funding is allowed but is criticized. Some think tanks are merely public relations fronts and advocates for industry or labour sponsors. The research publications are often one sided and others are the result of research that is ideologically driven by member interests.

EVERYDAY ETHICS 13.4

Think Tank Views on Business and Society Issues

The following are examples of recent reports or studies produced by various think tanks. Note the variety of topics. The think tanks are good sources of views on many business and society issues.

- Fraser Institute: *Income Mobility, The Rich and Poor in Canada* finds that the notion that the rich are gaining at the expense of low income Canadians is false and contradicted by data on income mobility—the fact that people's incomes change over time.
- Canadian Centre for Policy Alternatives: *How Government Support for Social Enterprise can Reduce Poverty and Green House Gases* explains how a combination of governmental policies and initiatives in Manitoba allows social enterprises to reduce Manitoba's greenhouse gas (GHG) emissions while training and employing Inner City workers.
- Conference Board of Canada: *A Long, Hard Road: Reducing GHG Emissions in Canada's Road Transportation Sector by 2050* provides an evidence-based view of the contribution that road transportation might practically make to achieve the "80 by 50" greenhouse gas emissions reduction target in Canada.
- Public Policy Forum: *Retirement Security for Everyone: Enhancing Canada's Pension System* discusses how Canada's retirement savings can provide greater security and coverage to more Canadians, while ensuring pension plans stay financially healthy into the future. cial participation.

Sources: Adapted from Fraser Institute report "Income Mobility: The Rich and Poor in Canada," accessed January 20, 2016, https://www.fraserinstitute.org/sites/default/files/income-mobility-the-rich-and-poor-in-canada.pdf; Canadian Centre for Policy Alternatives report "How Government Support for Social Enterprise can Reduce Poverty and Greenhouse Gases," https://www.policyalternatives.ca/publications/reports/how-government-support-social-enterprise-can-reduce-poverty-and-green-house; Conference Board of Canada report "A Long Hard Road: Reducing GHG Emissions in Canada's Road Transportation Sector by 2050," accessed January 20, 2016, http://www.conferenceboard.ca/e-library/abstract.aspx?did=7491; and Public Policy Forum report "Retirement Security for Everyone: Enhancing Canada's Pension System," accessed January 20, 2016, http://www.ppforum.ca/publications/retirement-security-everyone-enhancing-canadas-pension-system.

A question for business and managers is whether the think tanks have much influence. Some argue that they have little influence, while others claim they can change the language of public debate. At the least, the think tanks most relevant to a corporation's industry, or that examine an issue of importance to the industry, should be monitored.

LO 13.10   Religious Institutions

Four topics discuss the influence of religion in business: the impact on managerial decision making, the existence of businesses supplying religious goods and services, spirituality in the workplace, and corporate response to religious activism.

The influence of religion on managerial decision making has been discussed extensively. Many argue that religious beliefs or practices have an influence on a manager's perceptions of what is ethical versus unethical, and can play a role in management education. Romar advocates Confucianism as a compelling managerial ethic because it is compatible with accepted managerial practices, it requires individuals and organizations to make a positive contribution to society, it recognizes hierarchy as an important organizational principle and demands managerial moral leadership, and its virtues provide a moral basis for hierarchical and cooperative relationships.[23] The Metanexus Institute is involved in an interdisciplinary social scientific research initiative on the economic and social consequences of religion and spirituality, referred to as "spiritual capital."[24] The Roman Catholic Church has commented on the relationship between business and society over the years. Responsibility for Ethics 13.5 summarizes a recent church publication that addresses business leadership in society and proposes six practical principles for business.

RESPONSIBILITY FOR ETHICS 13.5

The Church's Reflection on Business Leadership

The Roman Catholic Pontifical Council for Justice and Peace studied the role of business in society and concluded that the vocation of the businessperson was a genuine human and Christian calling. But, in dealing with the complex issues facing society and business, a need existed for businesspersons to base decisions on the foundational principles of human dignity and the common good. These principles should provide direction for business in organizing the labour and capital employed in a market system, and the processes of innovation.

The following summarizes a portion of the findings:

SIX PRACTICAL PRINCIPLES FOR BUSINESS

The principles of respect for human dignity and pursuit of the common good are the foundations of the Church's social teaching. Joined with the six practical principles of business, they can offer more specific guidance on the three broad business objectives.

Meeting the Needs of the World through the Creation and Development of Goods and Services

1. Businesses that produce goods which are truly good and services which truly serve *contribute to the common good.*
2. Businesses maintain *solidarity* with the poor by being alert for opportunities to serve deprived and underserved populations and people in need.

Organizing Good and Productive Work

3. Businesses make a contribution to the community by fostering the special *dignity of human work.*
4. Businesses provide, through *subsidiarity,* opportunities for employees to exercise appropriate authority as they contribute to the mission of the organization.

Creating Sustainable Wealth and Distributing It Justly

5. Businesses model *stewardship of the resources*—whether capital, human, or environmental—they have received.
6. Businesses are *just* in the allocation of resources to all stakeholders: employees, customers, investors, suppliers, and the community.

The study also recommended that the Reflection be discussed by faculty and students to: "see the Challenges and opportunities in the world of work; judge them according to the social principles of the Church; and act as leaders who serve God." The study provided a checklist for following the six principles.

Source: Adapted from "Vocation of the Business Leader: A Reflection," Pontifical Council for Justice and Peace, The Vatican, March 30, 2012, accessed August 9, 2016, http://www.pcgp.it/dati/2012-05/04-999999/Vocation%20ENG2.pdf.

Religion is generating many commercial opportunities in the economy; a religion-based theme park called Holy Land Experience in Florida; Christian literature publishers; retailers, including Walmart, selling religious items, music, and video games; and faith-based mutual funds.[25] A *BusinessWeek* article described how organized religion is even learning to operate like a business. Huge churches are being constructed, seating thousands, with large orchestras and choirs and state-of-the-art electronic communications.[26]

Effort by some businesses to integrate religion into the workplace is also discussed extensively in the literature.[27] The types of activities carried out in the workplace include spiritual, faith-based, and Bible study sessions; devotional prayer services; and the hiring of corporate chaplains to counsel employees. The introduction of religion into the secular corporation makes some feel uneasy. Although most activities are voluntary, employees may still feel pressure from religious employers. Customers have been subjected to open evangelizing by Christian-dominated corporations. Such activities are not necessarily associated with organized religion. Instead, they are referred to as **spirituality**, an individual's sense of peace or purpose with him/herself and the connection to others and even nature that provides meaning to life and a sense of one's self. Responsibility for Ethics 13.6 describes two initiatives relating to spirituality in the workplace. Even if discussed only briefly, it is possible to recognize that the relationship between business and religious institution stakeholders gives rise to many issues.

RESPONSIBILITY FOR ETHICS 13.6

Spirituality in the Workplace

Two organizations that are promoting and facilitating spirituality in the workplace are described below.

- Corporate Chaplains Canada's (CCC) mission is "to support business owners by helping their management and employees experience relational, emotional and spiritual growth, resulting in healthy individuals serving their companies, families and communities." It ministers to employees, management, and company owners in manufacturing plants, showrooms, hotels, restaurants, service facilities, offices, and stores focusing on non-religious counselling services. Today, CCC cares for over 1000 employees at corporations in B.C., Alberta, and Ontario. They promote the overall relational health of employees, stress caring for extended family needs, and provide moral and spiritual support when requested. The intended result is a work environment that is a better, more profitable place for employees and employer alike.

- The mission of the Workplace Centre for Spiritual and Ethical Development is "to serve the business community by advancing spirituality and ethics in the workplace." It "promotes the benefits of individual spiritual well-being; supports the study and practice of business ethics; and organizes programs and events which advance the understanding of spiritual values and ethical standards at work." Its values are listed as spiritual wholeness, cultural diversity, ethical business practices, wisdom of all communities of faith, individual dignity, and environmental sensitivity. The Centre is located in Vancouver, B.C.

Sources: Adapted from Corporate Chaplains Canada, accessed January 20, 2016, http://chaplains.ca/; and "About Workplace Centre," Workplace Centre for Spiritual and Ethical Development accessed January 20, 2016, http://workplacecentre.org/about-us.

Business must be careful in responding to religious activism or it might get caught in crossfire, particularly with conservative groups. *BusinessWeek* referred to this possibility as "culture wars" and posed the question, "When should companies take public positions on social issues?" Some of the social issues of concern identified in the article included support for gay rights, advertising on unacceptable television programs, and the pursuit of embryonic stem-cell research. The article concluded that the only way for a company to respond is to return to its core values. Companies should consider themselves the ultimate judge of what is socially acceptable and not be driven by the dogma of particular religious activism.[28]

LO 13.11   Educational Institutions

The appropriateness of business involvement in the education system has been controversial. The issue has become more prominent recently as various educational institutions seek assistance from business after government support has declined. Business is now involved in education from the kindergarten to post-secondary levels. The extent of involvement can be illustrated at the university level, where the following are of concern: the establishment of private, for-profit colleges; funding for buildings or centres from private sources with some conditions attached; conflicts of interest in the funding of research; the commercialization of research; and exclusivity agreements to provide goods and services.[29]

There are two views regarding the issue. The modern, pragmatic view looks at education and corporate money, or involvement in any form, as a mutually beneficial partnership. An example occurs when a business donates money to a school's athletic program and is allowed to advertise on team uniforms. The other view is that educational institutions should be places of unencumbered thought and considered a custodian of rights of the liberated human spirit. This view is strongly held in universities by many students and faculty. There are many variations between these extreme views, and the circumstances vary depending on the type of institution.

Many businesspeople sincerely believe in the partnership and that it helps the economy. The demands of the global marketplace and information age require skills that are best provided in the educational system. Thus, business has a role in improving the quality of education, and it is in its own interest to become involved. Partnerships have appeal for educators, from kindergarten teachers to university presidents, as resources formerly provided by governments have been reduced. As educators are financially squeezed, they overlook the ethical implications that might accompany the acceptance of assistance from business.

Many students and faculty oppose partnerships as they fear "market-driven" learning, leading to students being taught only topics of interest to them, universities dropping areas that are not currently popular, job "relevance" being the main criterion for what is taught, and efficiency being emphasized at the expense of social concerns. It is believed that the results would be greater social and economic disparities and loss of competitiveness in technology. There would be negative effects from this narrow focus as it alters the way society invests in higher education as a fundamental social institution. The economic needs of business are met, while the broader and more basic social and cultural needs are ignored.

There is a fear of losing control over what is taught and that the traditional role of the university would be changed. The university was traditionally viewed as a community of free and independent scholars, as an open forum for ideas, and as an institution that could be critical in its assessment of other societal institutions. Many fear that this traditional, and desirable, role would be reduced and possibly eliminated.[30]

Another perspective relates to the social responsibility and sustainability of colleges and universities. In other words, they have economic, social, and environmental responsibilities to society in a way similar to that of business corporations. The University of Guelph's recent fundraising campaign where it raised funds from individuals and corporations focused on social responsibility, as described in Everyday Ethics 13.5.

EVERYDAY ETHICS 13.5

The University of Guelph and Social Responsibility

The University of Guelph's recent fundraising campaign, The Better Planet Project, focused on what the university could do to make the planet better by addressing the world's challenges. A quotation from the Project's website states:

Leading the way in environmental and social responsibility, our exceptionally talented people blend caring and collaboration, turning scientific discoveries into meaningful change that will improve the quality of life for people around the world.

Although fundraising was involved, the University wanted to emphasize its responsibility to the sustainability of the community and society. The University stated it had the expertise and leadership to work on the changes necessary to improve life on the planet. It planned to raise $200 million by 2014 to fund faculty and staff activities that would lead to breakthroughs in four essential areas of life: food, environment, health, and community.

The Better Planet Project surpassed its goal.

Source: Adapted from The Better Planet Project, University of Guelph, accessed January 20, 2016, http://thebetterplanetproject.ca.

Educational institutions are addressing environmental issues through a variety of initiatives including supply management sustainability. An example of one university's program is provided in Everyday Ethics 13.6. The Association for the Advancement of Sustainability in Higher Education's (AASHE) mission is to empower higher education to lead the sustainability transformation. Sixty-four Canadian universities and colleges are members.[31] These examples are illustrations of how seriously education institutions take their responsibility to the environment.

EVERYDAY ETHICS 13.6

University of British Columbia's Sustainable Supply Management

The University of British Columbia (UBC) has a comprehensive sustainable supply management program. It contains information on supply management plus practical examples to illustrate sustainable purchasing. The overall benefits of sustainable purchasing for society are listed; a table summarizing the business case for sustainable purchasing is presented; a description of extended producer responsibility (EPR) is given; and a link to UBC's Supplier Code of Conduct is provided.

UBC's website outlines its supply management sustainability initiatives, lists the Principles of Sustainability for Supply Management, defines responsible sourcing, and identifies its partners—that is, suppliers in sustainability. Access is also given to *Buying into the Future: The UBC Sustainable Purchasing Guide*, which defines sustainable purchasing and extended producer responsibility, lists UBC's Sustainable Purchasing Guidelines, and discusses why UBC is involved with sustainable purchasing and the costs/savings. Information is provided on implementing the guidelines for a variety of goods and services.

Sources: Adapted from University of British Columbia,"Principles of Sustainability," accessed January 20, 2016, http://www.supplymanagement.ubc.ca/about-us/principles-sustainability-supply-management; "Sustainable Purchasing," accessed January 20, 2016, http://www.supplymanagement.ubc.ca/about-us/sustainable-purchasing; "Sustainability," accessed January 20, 2016, http://www.sustain.ubc.ca; and "Buying into the Future: The UBC Sustainable Purchasing Guide," accessed January 20, 2016, https://www.supplymanagement.ubc.ca/ubcbuysmart/sustainable-purchasing-guide.

Educational institutions are under pressure to seek a balance between the opportunities and challenges of accepting funding from corporations. At the same time, they are expected to be involved in sustainability practices as a responsibility to society.

NGOS, the media, policy development institutions, religious organizations, and educational institution stakeholders all influence business, and business influences them in return. Today's managers require the skills and talents to engage all these stakeholders.

Your Advice to Debbie . . .

As an animal lover, Debbie believes in supporting organizations taking care and protecting animals, but she will have to research these NGOs. Most publish reports including financial statements and from these she should be able to identify responsible NGOs. She may wish distinguish between NGOs that advocate animal rights versus animal welfare. Animal rights supporters believe that animals should have the same rights as humane treatment and protection from exploitation and abuse accorded humans. Animal welfare groups are more concerned with the animal care and whether or not their mental and physical needs are being met. If any of the NGOs are registered charities, she can check and Canada revenue agency (CRA) website. CRA examines the purpose of the charity and how their funds are spent.

Summary

- Civil society stakeholders are voluntary, community, and social organizations that represent society's views on business and society issues. They can influence the behaviour of corporations through advocacy. A full description and example of an NGO is given, providing a full picture of issues around which they form, and a list of their tactics for influence is provided. (LO 13.1)
- Non-governmental organizations are numerous, use a variety of tactics, and are varied in their positions on issues and influence on business. NGOs serve a beneficial role in society and their views should be identified and analyzed by corporations. A variety of strategies are possible in responding to NGO initiatives and the strategy selected depends on the issue involved and the influence of the NGO. (LO 13.2)

- Strategies for working with NGOs are provided, including the costs and benefits of each, and questions for managers to understand NGOs better. (LO 13.3)
- Partnerships between business and NGOs can work as long as key lessons for collaboration, which were listed, are followed. Successful partnerships were listed as examples. (LO 13.4)
- The media stakeholder is one that can influence society's attitudes toward business and one that business can influence. (LO 13.5)
- The media can pose challenges for business that can sometimes be exacerbated by business' dealings with them through public relations. (LO 13.6)
- With news services monopolized by a few media companies, information can come from too few voices; journalistic professionalism can pose a problem. (LO 13.7)
- Recently, there is increased coverage of the ethics of business and corporate social responsibility (CSR) in the media, leading to increased public interest in business. Media themselves have recognized the importance of their own CSR. (LO 13.8)
- Policy development institutions or think tanks are numerous and advocate various points of view on business and society issues. They influence government's—and society in general's—attitudes toward business. Many of these think tanks are supported by trade unions, universities, and corporations and views consistent with capitalism are promoted. (LO 13.9)
- Some businesspersons are influenced by organized religions or by spirituality. Corporate values can be determined by religious beliefs and reflected in business operations. Business must be careful when responding to religious activism. (LO 13.10)
- Considerable controversy surrounds the relationship between business and the educational institution stakeholder. Businesses are increasing their presence on campus by supporting research, financing buildings and programs, and operating services. Some students and faculty members believe that the presence of business has an adverse influence on the educational institution, in particular reducing its academic independence. (LO 13.11)

Key Terms

Civil society
Non-governmental organization (NGO)
Social media
Libel chill

Policy development institution (think tank)
Spirituality

Critical Thinking and Discussion Questions

1. What roles do NGO stakeholders play in business and society?
2. Are all the tactics used by NGOs appropriate—that is, ethical?
3. What strategies should corporations use in dealing with NGOs?
4. What are the benefits and dangers of forming partnerships with NGOs?
5. What influence does the media stakeholder have on business and what influence does business have on the media?
6. Does business manipulate the media?
7. What challenges do the new forms of participatory media present to business?
8. What roles do the policy development institutions (think tanks) play in business and society?
9. Should religion—organized or spiritual—be associated with business? How can you integrate your faith into your work?
10. What are the benefits and dangers of business' involvement with the educational institutions stakeholder?

Cases

13.1 A UNION STRIKES AND A SMALL BUSINESS IS CHALLENGED

Nick Bartiromo operated a restaurant and takeout service next to a Toronto subway station. Nick had started the business 10 years ago; the business had done quite well, and had a steady clientele for its breakfast and lunch meals. The business had five full-time and fifteen part-time employees even though it was only open five days a week, 6:00 a.m. to 3:00 p.m. Nick believed in paying his employees a decent salary, which was above the average rate for the hospitality industry.

In summer 2009, the 24,000 City of Toronto inside and outside workers represented by the Canadian Union of Public Employees went on strike. Nick had some understanding of industrial relations and knew that the workers had the right to strike and to picket their workplaces. The strike created a major inconvenience for Nick; the garbage from his restaurant was no longer picked up. The garbage was mostly food leftovers, which began to rot in the heat. The City had established several sites where citizens could drop off garbage, but they were some distance away and he had to hire a truck to haul the garbage. A bigger problem arose when he got to the site—the picketers delayed each person making a delivery and it took him hours to complete the task. The picketers were illegally stopping each person for 15 minutes and the City did not stop them. As he was restricted to three bags, he had to make the trip daily. Also, the stench of rotting food was almost unbearable and the sites were bound to attract pests such as rats and mice.

As the strike went on, his resentment for the municipal workers grew. The 1,100 garbage workers were paid well, an average of $25.00 per hour. Furthermore, their benefits were generous—they received six weeks of vacation and were allowed to bank 18 sick days per year and cash in six months' worth at retirement. This created an unfunded liability of over $150 million for the City. They had the right of permanent employment and their contract imposed strict work rules that increased costs of garbage collection. Nick read in the newspaper that it cost the City of Toronto $317 per dwelling to collect garbage, about 65 percent higher than the average for Canadian cities.

Nick was not impressed with the City politicians. They agreed to generous employee contracts to obtain labour peace, appearing unwilling to stand up to the unions. Between 2003 and 2008, City employee salaries had increased 32 percent. At the same time, taxes were increasing. The union had a monopoly on garbage collection, and knew how to use it. Some of Nick's customers complained that the strikers were fortunate to have such well-paying jobs especially during a period of higher unemployment.

Nick got to thinking about what could be done to reduce this imbalance in influence that some unions had in society. Two solutions were evident: declare garbage collection an essential service, and introduce competition. If made an essential service, the workers would lose the right to strike, a fundamental feature of industrial contracts. It was unlikely that the City could introduce this without a prolonged labour conflict.

The newspapers and his customers talked about outsourcing, or contracting out, the collection of garbage, as was done in Etobicoke. That municipality had been absorbed into Toronto but its private garbage collection contract remained in force. The Canadian Taxpayers Federation advocated the privatization of waste management to introduce competition in awarding contracts for providing the service. It estimated that Winnipeg had saved $5.7 million per year when it privatized collection.

If a monopoly exists in a particular industry, it either is ruled illegal under the *Competition Act* or other legislation, or is tightly regulated. Garbage collection in most cities is a monopoly of local governments and they lacked the incentives to reduce costs and introduce innovations as aggressively as private business. In effect, taxpayers were held hostage by a system with rigid work rules that prohibited rewarding superior performance. Furthermore, there was no threat to driving the City out of business. The usual result was higher taxes, and Toronto was no exception. In fact, taxes had increased so much that the Canadian Federation of Independent Business claimed that many businesses had already left the city due to high taxation.

Nick paid a lot in taxes, and expected good service in return. For the most part, he felt that the City was providing many services for these taxes. But, he felt that garbage collection was an exception. He believed that he was being held hostage by greedy municipal workers and politicians who were unable to confront the monopoly power of unions. He believed that it was time to do something about the union's monopoly.

Questions

1. Who are the stakeholders and what is their influence?

2. What issues associated with the business fundamentals as described in Chapter 2 are illustrated in the case?

3. What can or should Nick do?

4. What should be done about the union's monopoly?

Sources: Adapted from Charlie Gillis and Fate Lunau, "Toronto Stinks," *Maclean's*, July 27, 2009, 22–25; Gwyn Morgan, "Enough with This Union Monopoly of the Public Sector: Time to Contract Out," *The Globe and Mail*, July 20, 2009, B2; Katherine Laidlaw, "Councillor Backs Bid to Hire Waste Haulers," *National Post*, July 23, 2009, A1, A10; and Howard Levitt, "It is Up to Employers to Thwart Strikes," *National Post*, July 22, 2009, FP11.

13.2 SLAPPING GREENPEACE CANADA

SLAPP is an acronym for Strategic Lawsuits Against Public Participation. "SLAPPs are legal actions (usually defamation actions such as libel and slander) launched for the primary purpose of shutting down criticism, and without a strong cause of action. The plaintiff's goal in a SLAPP is not to win the lawsuit, but is rather to silence a critic by instilling fear of large legal costs and the spectre of large damage awards." Despite their right to free speech, critics or defendants may be frightened into silence. They may be required to take down websites, remove comments made online, remove printed materials, withdraw statements, and issue apologies.

Resolute Forest Products was accused of using a SLAPP against Greenpeace in 2013. The company took legal action against Greenpeace claiming $5 million in damages plus $2 million for punitive damages. It claimed that Greenpeace was using threats, intimidation, false accusations and harassing Resolute's customers to disrupt operations at the company's pulp and paper mills. Greenpeace was accused of spreading defamatory malicious falsehoods and intentionally interfering with the company's business. The NGO circulated defamatory articles about Resolute's forestry and corporate practices, and threatened and intimidated customers. As a result, jobs were lost in Northern Ontario and the economic well-being of communities threatened.

In addition, Resolute launched a campaign against Greenpeace and ForestEthics to counter what it said were inaccurate allegations. The campaign included full page advertisements in national and regional publications, direct mail, digital advertising, and social media campaigns. Five hundred municipalities, unions, and many First Nations in Ontario and Quebec have expressed concern about the NGO actions. In newspaper advertisements, Resolute urged readers to email the NGOs telling them to stop the campaign against the company which was harming the lives and livelihoods of many Canadians.

Resolute has received recognition for its sustainability practices. It was ranked as one of Canada's Best 50 Corporate Citizens for 2014 by Corporate Knights, is among leaders who have made the greatest contributions to clean capitalism in Canada, was selected as one of Canada's top 100 corporate R&D spenders, and was inner of The New Economy's Clean Tech award for best forestry and paper solutions.

Questions

1. Should SLAPPs be used against NGOs or even individuals who criticize a corporation or industry?

2. What stakeholders are involved in this issue?

3. What are the ethical implications of the use of SLAPPs and media campaigns?

4. What the ethical implications of the NGOs actions?

Sources: Adapted from SLAPP "Defamation and SLAPPs," Canadian Internet Policy and Public Interest Clinic, University of Ottawa, http://www.cippic.ca/en/defamation-and-slapps; Resolute Forest Products, http://www.resoluteforestproducts.com/en/?langtype=4105; the Resolute Blog, http://blog.resolutefp.com/; and Terence Corcoran, "SLAPP setback for Greenpeace," *National Post*, July 16, 2014, FP9.

PART V *The Environment, Globalization, and Changing Capitalism*

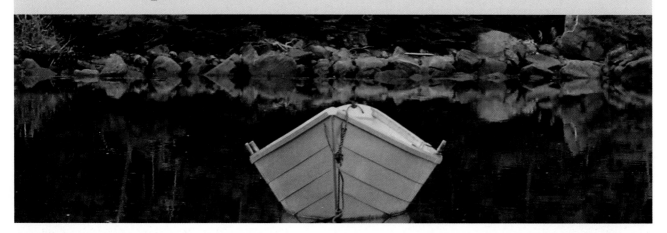

Used with the permission of Dennis Flynn

CHAPTER 14

The Environment and Business Responsibilities

LEARNING OUTCOMES

After studying this chapter, you will be able to:

LO 14.1 Understand the extensiveness of business' responsibilities toward the environment.

LO 14.2 Define two key terms: the environmental ethic and sustainable development.

LO 14.3 Identify and define the main environmental concerns confronting business and society.

LO 14.4 Describe the influence of government in addressing environmental concerns.

LO 14.5 Define environmental non-governmental organization (ENGO) and appreciate its influence on the corporation.

LO 14.6 Explain how market-driven environmentalism would work.

LO 14.7 Describe a corporation's structural and strategic responses to environmental concerns.

LO 14.8 Understand how the main functions of a corporation are influenced by environmental concerns and how to identify the responses necessary.

LO 14.9 List the sustainability measures and standards that exist and become aware of corporate and industry initiatives to report on their environmental responsibilities.

LO 14.10 Appreciate that there are dissenting views on the environment and consider how business should respond.

LO 14.11 Identify the opportunities and challenges for a corporation's response to environmental concerns.

What would you do if...?

Vivian Duveen was standing by the fish counter in her local supermarket. She planned to purchase salmon for her family's dinner but hesitated. Fresh salmon had become very popular; it was a healthy meal, and her family enjoyed it. Today she noted that she could choose between fresh wild or farmed salmon, which was a little less expensive.

Vivian had been researching salmon as a food and the pros and cons of wild versus farmed sources. She found that it was a complicated issue with contradictions in articles and lots of unsubstantiated claims on both sides. There were numerous issues including nutritional value, the operation of farms, and the impact on the environment.

Many sources claimed that wild salmon was nutritionally superior to farmed salmon. Wild salmon was firmer, 20 percent less fatty, and contained 20 percent more protein. Other sources disagreed with these figures. Because it was fattier, farmed salmon contained more omega-3 acids, a desirable characteristic. Dietitians recommended eating two servings of salmon a week whether it was wild or farmed as it was one of the healthiest foods.

Farmed salmon were confined to crowded pens where they were fed daily to saturation, resulting in their growing faster and producing an oilier product. The fish were fed pellets of concentrated nutrients that included plant-based proteins, fish meal, and antibiotics as necessary. It was alleged that the farms produced excessive waste from uneaten food and that some fish escaped to interbreed with wild stocks threatening to weaken the wild salmon's gene pool. Critics of farms claimed that toxins, including PCBs and pesticides, in the fish produced were up to ten times greater than in wild stocks. The farm operators denied these claims.

In contrast, wild salmon lived in natural surroundings, but were subject to many stressors as they did not feed regularly and had many predators. They were carriers of furunculosis, a devastating bacterial disease that farmed salmon were vaccinated against. Sea lice were a problem with salmon but an antibiotic could be included in the food for farms to eliminate them. Some toxins were found in wild salmon depending on their habitat.

In Canada, fish farming was regulated by government to prevent abusive practices. The harvesting of farmed salmon followed strict regulations. The fish were starved for seven days to clear the alimentary tract to ensure a quality product. Also, the process of harvesting farmed fish was monitored, while harvesting practices for wild fish were unclear. The farm economies of scale resulted in lower prices for consumers, but it was alleged that these lower prices threatened small wild fishing operations.

Fish farms supplied about 50 percent of the fish consumed worldwide. The existence of farms for popular fish such as salmon has taken the pressure off wild stocks and prevented their depletion. The industry has been talking with ENGOs about ways to improve their practices. The farm operators argued that farming was more sustainable and socially responsible than wild catches. The industry claimed that wild fish cannot supply the world's demand for fish.

Vivian reached into the refrigerated display case and picked up a package of salmon.

What is your advice to Vivian?

Sources: Lisa Gosselin, "Which Salmon Should I Buy?" accessed March 15, 2012, https://ca.news.yahoo.com/which-salmon-should-i-buy-.html; "Farmed vs. Wild Salmon—Which is Better?" ctvbc.ca, March 4, 2010, accessed March 21, 2012, http://www.ctvbc.ctv.ca/servlet/an/local/CTVNews/20100219/bc_ctv_investigates_food_fish_100219/20100304; David Cox, "Farmed vs Wild Salmon? A Comparison," Fish Vet Group, accessed March 30, 2012, http://www.thefishsite.com/articles/107/farmed-vs-wild-salmon-a-comparison; Wild Salmon vs. Farmed Raised: Which is Better?" Pays to Live Green, accessed March 30, 2012, http://www.paystolivegreen.com/2009/02/wild-salmon-vs-farmed-raised-which-is-better; Joseph Schwartz, "Wild versus Farmed Salmon: The Pros and Cons," *Medical News Today*, December 26, 2005, accessed March 30, 2012, http://www.medicalnewstoday.com/releases/35370.php; and "What's New and Beneficial about Salmon" The World's Healthiest Foods, accessed August 26, http://www.whfoods.com/genpage.php?tname=foodspice&dbid=104

There is increasing concern for the natural environment in Canada and around the world. The need to preserve and protect the environment is now so compelling that there is no question of its relevance for business—the natural environment is an issue that must be addressed. In other words, business has responsibilities toward achieving a sustainable environment.

Concern for the environment has been intensified by disasters such as Chernobyl and Three Mile Island (nuclear plant meltdowns), the Love Canal (pollution in New York), the *Exxon Valdez* (oil spill in Alaska), the BP oil disaster in the Gulf of Mexico, and the tsunami in Japan (and resulting nuclear power plant disaster). In addition, the depletion of the ozone layer, the greenhouse effect, acid rain, deforestation, pollution, energy depletion, and waste management are steadfast reminders of how compelling an issue our natural environment is.

This chapter describes how environmental concerns affect corporations and the many issues that arise with stakeholders. All stakeholders have an obligation to the environment and the key stakeholders influencing it are identified. The various ways that business is responding to its obligation to the environment are identified, as are the challenges involved for management.

LO 14.1 Business, Its Stakeholders, and the Natural Environment

Environmental issues confront virtually all aspects of the corporation, from the input of resources to the manufacturing process, and from workplace conditions through to the way products are packaged and sold. Managers must cope with planning, organizing, leading, and controlling all the aspects of the environmental issue. The ethical and responsibility issues identified in Table 14.1 are diverse; thus, a comprehensive environmental management approach is necessary. The following sections identify how corporations deal with the environment.

TABLE 14.1	Principal Stakeholders and Issues Involved in Business' Response to the Environment
Stakeholder	**Ethical Issues and Responsibilities for Managers**
Shareholders	Investment decisions influenced by the handling of the environment Risk associated with environment problems or disasters Establishment of "green" investment criteria
Directors	Getting environment issues on the board agenda Liability for environmental contamination Challenge of motivating management to address the issue
Employees	Workplace exposures to environmental problems (e.g., indoor air pollution) Refusal to perform tasks causing environmental problems Whistleblowing on employer
Customers/Consumers	Inconsistencies between concerns expressed about the environment and the consumption of environmentally unfriendly products Unwillingness to pay higher prices for environmentally friendly products/services if necessary The viability of "green" products
Lenders/Creditors	Need to assess increased financial risk
Suppliers	Must respond to demands for more environmentally friendly products Reassessing most appropriate transportation and packaging of supplies

Stakeholder	Ethical Issues and Responsibilities for Managers
Service Professionals	Familiarity with laws and regulations Design of appropriate audits Identification of full environmental cost accounting methods
Competitors	Consequence of competitive edge being obtained by making products more environmentally friendly
NGOs	How to respond to groups based upon environmental concerns
Media	How to respond to media coverage of environmental problems
Government	Complying with laws and regulations Influencing public policy

Although most business and society scholars do not consider the natural environment to be a stakeholder of business, there is agreement that it is influenced by stakeholders and/or has an influence on stakeholders. As a result, the natural environment can be viewed as a **commons**, or a resource used as though it belongs to all. Business has been able to use shared resources such as the environment simply because it wanted or needed to. In the past, for example, pollution was put into the environment without thinking about the damage and little regulation existed to prevent it. Through uncontrolled use, many in society believed that the environment as a commons was being destroyed. Often this destruction was occurring even though it was not the intent of the user—that is, business—and ownership was not an issue.

The concept of the commons was popularized by an article published in 1968 by Garrett Hardin.[1] Hardin described what would happen to a commons as illustrated by an unregulated pasture where all sheep herders added more sheep at no cost to them but their actions might lead to the destruction of the pasture for everyone. This behaviour can be explained, in part, by the individualism and economic freedom fundamental of capitalism described in Chapter 2 and the self-interest ethic described in Chapter 5.

 connect   Want to learn more about **the "tragedy of the commons"**?

Fortunately, most corporations and their stakeholders have recognized the real and potential damage to the environment of their actions. The remainder of the chapter examines this issue from various perspectives.

LO 14.2 Defining the Environmental Ethic and Sustainable Development

Business' responsibilities to the environment are exemplified by the environmental ethic corporations achieve and by management's understanding of sustainable development.

An **environmental ethic** is the set of values or principles that govern a corporation's practices relating to the environment. Concern for the environment has existed for some time, and an environmental ethic is evolving from this focus on ecology. Society and many businesspersons now have some sense of obligation or moral responsibility to the environment that is expressed in different ways. For a business enterprise, the values or principles include the idea that new business development needs to take account of the environment from the design stage through to ultimate disposal; that environmental management should be the responsibility of staff at all levels as an integral part of their job; that environmental performance should be built into the reward structure of the organization; that product and process responsibility should occur from cradle to grave; and that agreed-upon values and beliefs should be used as the guiding principles for conducting all business.[2]

The concept of "sustainable development" has received attention from governments, international agencies, and some business quarters. **Sustainable development** is defined as development ensuring that the use of resources and the impact on the environment today does not damage prospects for the use of resources or the environment by future generations. This was a theme in the report of the United Nations World Commission on Environment and Development (1987), which concluded that continued economic growth not only is possible, but also is necessary to reduce poverty and to sustain future generations.[3] Sustainable development has been endorsed by many businesspersons as an approach that allows environmental and economic concerns to coincide and makes economic progress possible.

Business sustainable development means "adopting business strategies and activities that meet the needs of the enterprise and its stakeholders today while protecting, sustaining, and enhancing the human and natural resources that will be needed in the future."[4] This definition was developed by the International Institute for Sustainable Development (IISD), a non-profit, private corporation established and supported by the governments of Canada and Manitoba to promote sustainable development in government, business, and individual decision making. This definition captures the sense of the concept as presented in the World Commission's report, but focuses on areas of specific interest and concern to business. It recognizes that economic development must meet the needs of the corporation and its stakeholders. The definition also highlights the dependence of the corporation's economic activities on human and natural resources as well as to physical and financial capital.

LO 14.3 Environmental Concerns in Business and Society

In order to illustrate the extensiveness of the environment issue in society and the challenges that confront business, the following discussion lists the major concerns. Some terms overlap or are interrelated, but all are frequently used and should be understood.

- *Acid rain*—**Acid rain** is a generic term used for precipitation that contains an abnormally high concentration of sulphuric and nitric acid. Industrial activities create general gas emissions that combine with water to form the acids.[5]

- *Air pollution*—Air quality is affected by various pollutants caused from the burning of fuels, emissions from industrial sites, and emissions from transportation vehicles. Smog is one form of air pollution.

- *Ecosystems*—An **ecosystem** is a biological community of interacting organisms and their physical environment. It is recommended that industry take an ecosystem approach to the environment; that is, recognizing the interrelationships among land, air, water, wildlife, and human activities.[6]

- *Energy production and consumption*—The generation of energy is usually damaging to the environment, as are the pollutants released when the energy fuel is used. Industry is responsible for many of the problems created, but so are consumers. Business has been emphasizing the efficient use of energy through the development of new technologies for itself and consumers.

- *Nature and wildlife*—There is concern for the harm caused to birds, mammals, fish, and plants by the operations of business. Endangered species are of particular concern.

- *Ozone*—**Ozone** is a naturally occurring gas, formed from normal oxygen, that protects Earth by filtering out ultraviolet (UV) radiation from the Sun. The thinning of the ozone layer in the upper atmosphere has resulted in increased UV radiation.[7]

- *Pollution*—Pollution involves any form of contamination in the environment. Business is under pressure to reduce its polluting of the environment.

- *Waste management*—**Waste management** is "disposal, processing, controlling, recycling and reusing the solid, liquid, and gaseous wastes of plants, animals, humans and other organisms."[8] Wastes often are hazardous, making the process more challenging. Recycling is described by the four Rs: reduce, reuse, recycle, and recover.

- *Water quality*—Water quality is determined by the presence of contaminants affecting its chemical and bacterial composition. Supply of safe drinking water is a concern in Canada. Corporations take on different environmental projects, as illustrated by the Royal Bank's decision to focus on water as described in Everyday Ethics 14.1.

EVERYDAY ETHICS 14.1

The RBC Blue Water Project

RBC's Blue Water Project is dedicated to protecting the world's most precious natural resource: fresh water. The main focus is a ten-year donations program supporting projects that help protect and preserve water. RBC has made a $50 million charitable commitment to support initiatives to protect water in towns and cities. The Project also supports conferences, economic reports, and events that help increase awareness about the importance of water.

RBC's Environmental Blueprint commits to reducing the use of landscape irrigation, reducing consumption by incorporating water-efficient technologies, and using environmentally responsible cleaning products to help protect water quality.

Source: Adapted from RBC Blue Water Project™, Royal Bank of Canada, accessed January 20, 2016, http://www.rbc.com/community-sustainability/environment/rbc-blue-water/about/index.html.

A term that captures the effects of the concerns listed above and that is frequently used today is *climate change*. **Climate change**, also referred to as *global warming*, is "the result of human activities altering the chemical composition of the atmosphere through the build-up of greenhouse gases that trap heat and reflect it back to the Earth's surface." This process has resulted in an increase in global temperatures and more frequent weather events. Note that greenhouse gases are "those that absorb and trap heat in the atmosphere," and that the greenhouse effect is "the phenomenon whereby certain gases that absorb and trap heat in the atmosphere cause a warming effect on the Earth."[9] Climate change is a major issue for society, as highlighted in Responsibility for Ethics 14.1.

RESPONSIBILITY FOR ETHICS 14.1

Al Gore and An Inconvenient Truth

Al Gore is a former U.S. vice-president, and *An Inconvenient Truth* is a documentary film about climate change, or global warming, in which he starred. Gore tells about his interest in the environment since college, reviews scientific evidence about climate change, and identifies the consequences of not taking action. He views the threat of climate change as the biggest moral challenge facing our global civilization, but he also states that there is time to do something about it. The film was released in May 2006 and did very well at the box office. It was widely reviewed and received a "two thumbs up" rating from film critics Roger Ebert and Richard Roeper. Gore has also authored a book by the same name.

There has been substantial criticism of Gore's thesis. Critics have pointed out several perceived inaccuracies, for example the suggestion that the melting of snow on Mount Kilimanjaro, Hurricane Katrina, the drying up of Lake Chad in Africa, and the drowning of polar bears were due to global warming. Critics claim that many sources have proven these claims incorrect. Others point out that the film is one-sided and ignores studies and facts.

Sources: Based on "About the Film *An Inconvenient Truth,*"; Marlo Lewis, Jr., "Al Gore's *An Inconvenient Truth:* One-Sided, Misleading, Exaggerated, Speculative, Wrong," Competitive Enterprise Institute, *CEInPoint* No. 108, September 28, 2006, accessed February 5, 2013, http://www.cei.org/pdf5539.pdf; "Criticisms of Al Gore's *An Inconvenient Truth,*" ClimateSanity, accessed February 5, 2013, https://climatesanity.wordpress.com/criticisms-or-al-gores-an-inconvenient-truth/; and Jan Lundberg, "The Inconvenient Truth about *An Inconvenient Truth:* Why Al Gore is Part Dangerous Politician," Culture Change Letter #138, August 3, 2006, accessed February 5, 2013, http://www.culturechange.org/cms/content/view/66/1/.

connect   Want to learn about **calculating your carbon footprint?**

LO 14.4   Government's Influence

Extensive government involvement exists through public policy formulation and the regulation of all aspects of the natural environment. The federal and provincial governments have passed environmental legislation, and are considering further legislation. Governments have announced various programs to create cleaner air, land, and water; to encourage sustainable resources; to develop parks and wildlife areas; to protect the Arctic regions; and to reduce global warming, ozone depletion, and acid rain. This section does not examine government initiatives in detail, but instead discusses the coordination of public and corporate policies on environment and identifies a range of policies that will impact on business.

Corporations should engage in a dialogue with government agencies so that their interests are protected and to contribute to the resolution of environmental problems. Governments may directly regulate activities of the corporation or introduce policy changes through taxation rates, the elimination or establishment of subsidies, international trade agreements, or the creation of markets in tradeable pollution permits. Business enterprises must establish mechanisms so that they can "listen" to what government is considering, and mechanisms so that they can "talk" to government.

Government departments and agencies have been established not only to regulate the activities of corporations, but also to assist them in meeting environmental performance targets. Governments have passed legislation to protect the environment that places obligations and responsibilities on business. An example of such legislation is the federal government's *Canadian Environmental Protection Act.*[10] It is not uncommon for the legislation to require that an environmental audit be undertaken by corporations or governments involved in environmentally sensitive projects.

Government legislation often stipulates that an environmental assessment document, or report, be submitted to relevant departments of the environment for review and approval. Although legislation varies among the federal and provincial governments, the report usually has to contain a description of the project, a list of reasons for the project, alternatives to the project, an outline of how the project and its alternatives will affect the environment directly or indirectly, an identification of the actions necessary to prevent those effects, and an evaluation of the advantages and disadvantages of the project to the environment and alternative ways to carry it out. The report is submitted for evaluation to an environmental assessment agency and often is followed by public hearings. Most corporations are now familiar with the environmental process and incorporate it into their decision making. Corporations also conduct audits and assessments even when not required by governments. Such audits often are of the whole organization and not restricted to particular projects or plants, and are designed to provide a "total picture" of the environmental circumstances of the corporation.

RESPONSIBILITY FOR ETHICS 14.2

UN Framework Convention on Climate Change (UNFCCC)

In December 2015, 195 nations met in Paris, France, to negotiate an agreement to combat climate change that will unleash actions and investment towards a low-carbon, resilient, and sustainable future. The main aspects of the agreement are:

- Limiting the raise in temperature to 1.5 degrees Celsius above pre-industrial levels in this century.
- Accounting for climate action through a transparency system and global stock-take. This requires for nations to submit action plans (nationally determined contributions) that detail their future objectives to address climate change.
- Strengthen the ability of countries to deal with climate impacts.
- Strengthen the ability to recover from climate impacts.
- Provide financial support for nations to build clean, resilient futures.

Climate finance will be increased to US$100 billion by 2020 and a further financing goal established by 2025. The increased financing will assist in accomplishing the last three aspects and in particular in developing countries.

The agreement is available at: http://unfccc.int/resource/docs/2015/cop21/eng/l09.pdf.

Source: "Historic Paris Agreement on Climate Change," United Nations Framework Convention on Climate Change (UNFCCC), accessed December 20, 2016, http://newsroom.unfccc.int/unfccc-newsroom/finale-cop21/.

The Canadian government has been involved in international agreements to control climate change, most of which failed. Reports stated that expected reductions in emissions were nowhere near projected goals and forecasts indicate that the government's targets under various plans will not be met. The most recent attempt at influencing climate change is the UN Framework Convention on Climate Change (UNFCCC) described in Responsibility for Ethics 14.2.

LO 14.5   Environmental NGO Influence

Environmental non-governmental organizations (ENGOs) are groups that hold shared values or attitudes about the challenges confronting the natural environment and advocate for changes to improve the condition of the environment. Dozens of these groups exist in Canada; some are described in Responsibility for Ethics 14.3. The activities, policies, and initiatives of these groups should be monitored to assess the potential impact on the corporation. This monitoring function may be performed by the environmental affairs department, by the managers responsible for environmental matters, or by consultants.

RESPONSIBILITY FOR ETHICS 14.3

Examples of Environmental Non-Governmental Organizations (ENGOs)

- *Greenpeace Canada*—Greenpeace is an independently funded organization that works to protect the environment. We challenge government and industry to halt harmful practices by negotiating solutions, conducting scientific research, introducing clean alternatives, carrying out peaceful acts of civil disobedience and educating and engaging the public. Its focus is: creating an energy revolution, that is, to address climate change; protecting the world's ancient forests; defending the world's oceans; campaigning for sustainable agriculture; and creating a toxic-free future.

- *Energy Probe*—"Energy Probe is a consumer and environmental research team, active in the fight against nuclear power, and dedicated to resource conservation, economic efficiency, and effective utility regulation." Current priorities include restoring strong regulation of energy markets, promoting competition in naturally competitive market; promoting clean energy sources, stopping nuclear energy, and protect consumer interests when considering energy options.

- *Friends of the Earth Canada*—Friends of the Earth (FOE) Canada is a charitable, non-profit environmental organization. Its mission is to be "a voice for the environment, nationally and internationally, working with others to inspire the renewal of our communities and the earth, through research, education and advocacy." It takes action to confront polluters, holding governments to account for their promises and insisting they enforce laws.

- *Pollution Probe*—Pollution Probe is a Canadian charitable environmental organization whose mission is "to improve the health and well-being of Canadians by advancing policy that achieves positive, tangible environmental change." Some of its main areas of interest are: human health, climate, energy, technology, waste, and water.

- *World Wildlife Fund Canada (WWF-Canada)*—WWF-Canada is a conservation organization supported by more than 150,000 Canadians. Its mission is to "stop the degradation of the planet's natural environment and to build a future in which humans live in harmony with nature." This mission is accomplished by "ensuring that the use of renewable natural resources is sustainable, promoting the reduction of pollution and wasteful consumption, and conserving the world's biological diversity."

Sources: Based on Greenpeace Canada, "About Us," accessed August 26, 2016, http://www.greenpeace.org/canada/en/About-us/; "About," Energy Probe, accessed August 26, 2016, https://ep.probeinternational.org/about/; Friends of the Earth Canada, accessed August 26, 2016, http://www.foecanada.org/; "About Pollution Probe," Pollution Probe, accessed August 26, 2016, http://www.pollutionprobe.org/about/; and "About WWF," WWF-Canada, accessed August 26, 2016, http://www.wwf.ca/about_us/.

The list in Responsibility for Ethics 14.3 illustrates the ENGOs' diversity of interests covering the concerns listed above. Environment groups are not always easy to deal with and use a variety of tactics. They can be involved in protests, blockades, boycotts, and sometimes make use of annual shareholders' meetings as platforms for protest. Canadian environmental groups are also often part of a global network of organizations. Protests about logging the Clayoquot Sound forests in British Columbia, as an example, are an alliance effort and have received impressive international attention.

A study identified the factors that lead ENGOs to target particular corporations. Hendry reviewed existing research on the environmental movement, stakeholder theory, and corporate social performance from which he formulated eight propositions that might explain how target corporations are selected. Five case studies of ENGOs were used to examine the validity of the propositions. Hendry found that the factors ranked as follows, from most influential to least:

- The greater the certainty among ENGOs that the firm is the source of an environmental impact, the more likely ENGOs are to target the firm.
- The more consequential the firm's actions are for the natural environment, the more likely ENGOs are to target the firm.
- The denser the relationships among the firm's ENGO stakeholders, the better able those ENGOs are to monitor the firm and share information about the firm, and the more likely those ENGOs are to target the firm collectively.
- The larger the firm, the more likely ENGOs will target the firm.
- To maximize the effects of mimetic isomorphism, ENGOs target corporations that are influential in their organizational fields and therefore likely to be imitated.
- The more previous interactions between the firm and a particular ENGO, the more likely the ENGO will target the firm.
- The closer the firm is to consumers in the supply chain, the more likely ENGOs will target the firm.
- The more well-known the firm's brands are, the more likely ENGOs will target the firm.[11]

Although this discussion has focused on ENGOs targeting corporations, an increasing amount of cooperation or partnership is occurring between business and ENGOs. Many corporations recognize the contributions of individuals and organizations in their efforts to protect the environment, and examples have been used throughout the book. Nonetheless, some ENGOs are reluctant to cooperate with corporations as they do not trust them and view such cooperation as a "sell-out" to business.

LO 14.6   Market-Driven Environmentalism

In addition to environmental initiatives being driven by government or pressures from ENGOs, there is a market-driven response to the environment. **Standard environmentalism** occurs when government regulation is a necessary remedy for the market's failure to provide enough environmental amenities. On the other hand, **market environmentalism** exists where economic incentives created by the market are more effective at protecting the environment than is government intervention.[12] Not everyone agrees with the market approach and argues that regulation and new technologies are more effective.[13] Nevertheless, market approaches are being considered and to some extent implemented.

The market factors influencing environmentalism are economic growth, free trade, and property rights. The differences among these approaches are summarized in Table 14.2, and highlight why free-market environmentalism is a possible approach.

The debate on a market orientation to environmentalism is only beginning, and standard environmentalism dominates at this time. However, examples of market-driven environmentalism are **carbon pricing**, a financial instrument that businesses and governments are using to reduce carbon emissions, which can be done in one of two ways:

- **Cap-and-Trade** where governments cap total carbon emissions and then give or sell companies carbon permits that add up to the cap. Companies can then trade permits with each other, with those who can reduce emissions cheaply and easily selling permits to those who cannot. The price of the permits is variable depending on the market. But generally, the lower the cap, the higher the price. Also referred to as *emissions trading*.
- **Carbon Tax**: governments impose a fee on carbon: the more a company emits, the more they pay. The price determines how effective the policy will be at lowering emissions—the higher the price, the greater the reductions.[14]

Both these approaches price carbon and create economic incentives to reduce emissions and increase green technology. They both generate revenue and can reduce emissions more effectively than regulations.

TABLE 14.2	Differences between Standard and Market Environmentalism	
Factors	Standard	Free-Market
Economic Growth	Viewed as destructive, because producing more creates more environmental harm	World is dynamic and two forces counteract harm: (1) increased income drives a demand for more environmental quality, and (2) stimulation of innovation that improves environmental quality
Free Trade	Considered part of the problem: prevents countries from following own higher levels of protection; and belief that rich countries exploit poor	Forces industries to be more competitive, accelerating adoption of newer, cleaner technologies; trade restrictions possible to protect environment under WTO; countries open to trade grow faster
Property Rights versus Regulation	Faith in government to solve problem for the public good	Powerful tool for protecting because ownership incentive creates stewardship incentive and gives individuals power to protect the environment.

Source: Summarized from Laura Jones, "A Different Kind of Environmentalist," *Fraser Forum*, April 2001, 4–6.

Another approach is to offset carbon emissions by promoting clean-energy projects—for example, wind generation, solar installations, geothermal plants, or biomass energy generation—that replace emissions from polluting sources. Another possibility is to finance carbon removal activities, for example reforestation. **Offsets**, or **emissions-reduction credits**, are credits purchased from other corporations or organizations to mitigate greenhouse gases released into the environment. The funds generated are used to finance undertakings that will result in the reduction of emissions. Everyday Ethics 14.2 describes two corporations involved in the provision of offsets.

EVERYDAY ETHICS 14.2

Offset Providers

There are many offset providers operating and two examples are:

- *Zerofootprint*—Zerofootprint holds a diverse portfolio of offsets that are registered on the CSA Clean Projects and reduction registries. All offsets are in compliance with ISO 14064 and have been verified by a third party. Offsetting is an interim measure used to deal with the ecological impact that is difficult to avoid. For example, if a business requires travel and travel is not yet "green," it can offset the impact with real, tangible, additional benefits to the environment. Using offsets in this way sets a price for the services the environment provides and that our economy doesn't reward.

- *Bullfrog Power*—By purchasing from wind and low-impact hydro generators, Bullfrog Power considers itself a completely green electricity retailer. These sources are viewed as producing clean, renewable electricity that is non-polluting and non–CO_2 emitting. Corporations or consumers access their electricity supply from Ontario's electricity grid but are actually purchasing it from Bullfrog.

Sources: "What are Carbon Offsets," Zerofootprint, accessed January 23, 2016, http://zerofootprintcarbon.com/corporate-ghg-accounting/offsets/; and "About us," Bullfrog Power, accessed January 23, 2016, https://www.bullfrogpower.com/our-story/.

Corporations are examining the possibility of storing their carbon emissions through **carbon capture and storage (CCS)**. With CCS, carbon dioxide emissions are captured and injected into underground formations. The practice is sometimes referred to as carbon sequestration or geosequestration. Downsides are that it is expensive, because the infrastructures do not exist, the underground storage may weaken, it requires a large amount of energy to implement, and it needs a 1,000-year monitoring program. Alberta's Energy Resources and Conservation Board has approved Shell Canada Limited's CSS carbon capture and storage project north of Edmonton, but imposed 23 conditions regarding additional data collection, analysis, and reporting.[15]

Recently, a policy development institution, or think tank, has been established to promote market-driven environmentalism, Canada's Ecofiscal Commission. Its aim is to increase awareness of practical options on the protecting the environment. Responsibility for Ethics 14.4 describes the Commission. It is funded by corporations and foundations.

RESPONSIBILITY FOR ETHICS 14.4

Canada's Ecofiscal Commission

The Ecofiscal Commission was formed by economists from across the country who wanted to broaden the discussion of ecofiscal policy reform. An ecofiscal policy corrects market price signals to encourage the economic activities such as job creation, investment, and innovation while reducing greenhouse gas emissions and the pollution of land, air, and water.

Ecofiscal policies put a price on pollution. When this is done there are incentives for investment in innovative technologies. This enables society to benefit economically from the country's natural resources while also providing better protection to the environment. The revenue generated from ecofiscal policies can create further economic benefits; for example, by reducing income and payroll taxes or investing in new technologies or critical infrastructure.

The Ecofiscal Commission and its Commissioners are fully independent and aim to serve policy-makers across the political spectrum, at all levels of government. The website contains case studies of how ecofiscal policies are implemented and gives reasons why Canada needs ecofiscal solutions.

Source: Adapted from "What is Ecofiscal," Canada's Ecofiscal Commission accessed January 21, 2016, http://ecofiscal.ca/the-commission/about-canadas-ecofiscal-commission/.

Controversy surrounds market-driven environmentalism. Its effectiveness is questioned, that is, whether there is an actual reduction of emissions. It is viewed as image polishing with no real commitment to the environment. Corporations are able to continue damaging the environment by avoiding addressing their environmental problems. Effective trading systems are being developed, but to be successful there supported by business and government.

LO 14.7 Managing Responses to Environmental Concerns

Whether corporations are forced by governments, pressured by environmental non-governmental organizations, or involved in market-environmentalism, managers must adapt the corporation by making changes to its organizational structure and by identifying its strategic approach.

Management positions and committees should be created to deal with the environment issue. Structural arrangements are put in place to ensure environmental matters are addressed starting at the top with the board of directors; some boards have environmental committees. It is key to have top management commitment so that there are practical principles to guide the corporation's environmental efforts, to integrate environmental affairs with operations, and to encourage environmental professionals to meet mounting environmental requirements.

Some business enterprises are hiring senior managers and other staff to focus on environmental matters alone. Senior managers' positions carry titles such as vice-president, environment; environmental director; corporate manager of environmental affairs; and environmental coordinator. In addition to senior managers there are numerous titles for staff with various specialties in the environment, for example vegetation management biologist, hydrogeologist, and site remediation engineer. One of the challenges is to find individuals with the appropriate environmental expertise and knowledge and adequate managerial capabilities, as a combination of managerial and technical expertise is necessary.

The issue of centralization versus decentralization of authority is also a challenge. In large, diversified corporations it is necessary to have top management commitment, but at the same time environmental matters are usually addressed at the unit or divisional levels. Often committees are formed to provide interlocks between the top and bottom of the organization, and to coordinate efforts across functions or divisions. Such a coordinating environmental group forms policies, establishes standards, and carries out planning strategies.

From a strategic perspective, corporations can choose among the following strategies in their approach to environmental concerns:

- *Token response*—The focus here is on damage control as problems arise and attempts are made to fix them. This is a reactive strategy still adopted by some corporations, but given the increased attention to the environment by many stakeholders, it is not recommended. Another token response is **greenwashing**, a form of advertising or public relations that deceptively provides the perception that a corporation's policies or practices are socially responsible. According to an environmental marketing agency, there are seven sins of greenwashing: hidden trade-offs, no proof, vagueness, worshipping false labels, irrelevance, lesser of two evils, and fibbing.[16] Today, greenwashing is usually disclosed quickly by consumers, regulators, or competitors.

- *Compliance with laws and regulations*—Concern about exposure to lawsuits and prosecution has motivated many directors and senior executives to adopt strategies of compliance. Some enterprises continue to ignore legislative and regulatory requirements, but those companies that do follow policies of compliance establish programs and organizational structures to implement and monitor their compliance with the legislation and regulations. Legal requirements or the government requirements ethic are the bases for the corporation's strategy.

- *Comprehensive environmental management*—Under this strategy, management seeks to gain a competitive advantage by taking an active stance on environmental issues. Simple compliance with legislation and regulation is not sufficient. In these companies, everyone becomes involved in environmental management. Environmental issues are integrated into all aspects of corporate management. Environmental objectives are set for key operating activities; they are not left to just the "environmental services department." There is internal and external corporate reporting and the development of environmental policies and codes of conduct. This strategy has been widely adopted within certain industries in some industrialized countries.

- *Sustainable development*—Businesses that follow this strategy integrate the concepts of sustainable development into their business strategies and environmental policies. Sustainable development is a natural extension of many corporate environmental policies. It requires that management consider the effect of its activities on the environment and on the long-term interests and needs of stakeholders. These enterprises engage in a different type of dialogue and consultation with their stakeholders. Their business strategies and activities are designed to balance the need for financial returns with the needs of the environment and various stakeholder groups. Mechanisms such as advisory panels and committees are established to facilitate communication with stakeholders. Corporate reporting expands in relation to the needs of stakeholders. They may also engage independent auditors to attest to their report's accuracy and reliability.[17]

Corporations need comprehensive environmental policies and programs, referred to as environmental management systems (EMS). These plans ensure that environmental practices become an important component of the corporation's overall strategy. While an EMS has an internal focus, green supply chain management (GSCM) focuses on making sure suppliers share the same commitment to the environment (supply chains are discussed in Chapter 12). EMS and GSCM allow for instilling a culture of continuous improvement inside and beyond the corporation. It also is important to plan strategically for the long term by establishing long-term goals, identifying opportunities to further reduce the impact on the environment, and taking advantage of these opportunities.[18]

No matter which approach or management system is used, corporations must understand and plan for the impact they are having on the environment. Research suggests that environmental practices and performance are key elements to corporate success, including achieving market leadership and keeping ahead of competitors. A study found that environmental activities enabled corporations to stay ahead of competition.[19] In conclusion, according to research by the Network for Business Sustainability, a corporation should consider environmental impacts and develop policies for reasons that include reducing costs, responding to investor demands, facilitating regulatory approaches and mitigating operational risk, hiring the best employees, and meeting consumer demand for "green" products and services.[20] These are convincing reasons for responding to environmental concerns.

LO 14.8 The "Greening" of Business Functions

Another approach to viewing a corporation's response to environmental concerns is by functional areas; that is, finance, marketing, human resources, and production. Although this approach does not cover all areas of a corporation's activities, it does address the main ones.

Financial Management

Financial management now includes consideration of environmental factors and involves many aspects, for example:

- Accounting guidelines require companies to unequivocally state on their balance sheets the estimated liability for restoring capital assets to environmentally sound conditions.
- "Eco-insurance" products are now available in response to the liability associated with environmental problems.
- The banking industry has also been affected by the environmental issue. Environmental assessments are necessary to determine the influence on financial performance and liability.
- Investments are being screened for environmental performance. Individual investors usually seek out environmentally friendly mutual funds. To obtain information on this aspect of performance, institutional investors use sustainability indices such as the Dow Jones Sustainability Indices (DJSI) or from the Toronto Stock Exchange including the Carbon Efficient Index, Fossil Fuel Free Index, and Renewable Energy and Clean Technology Index. An example of how seriously institutional investors are viewing climate change is given in Everyday Ethics 14.3.
- Shareholders unhappy with a corporation's environmental policy may hurt its financial performance, maybe more than the actions of ENGOs. A concerned shareholder can submit a resolution at the annual meeting arguing that the corporation is increasing its environmental risk and thus the financial risk to shareholders. Investment analysts are more influenced by such resolutions than by the actions of ENGOs such as boycotts, protests, lawsuits, demonstrations, or sit-ins to raise awareness of a corporation's poor environmental record.[21]

EVERYDAY ETHICS 14.3

The Carbon Disclosure Project (CDP)

Several Canadian financial institutions are among the 822 institutional investors who collaborate in the Carbon Disclosure Project (CDP), an independent not-for-profit organization holding the largest database of primary corporate climate change information in the world. Its goals are to tackle climate change through the reduction of greenhouse emissions, to promote sustainable water use by business and cities, and to mitigate environmental risk in corporate supply chains. The largest corporations in the world are sent questionnaires requesting disclosure of information on their greenhouse gas emissions. The investors view the information as critical in helping them decide how to allocate capital. The data are also made available to corporations, public-sector organizations, government bodies, academics, and the public.

Two hundred of Canada's largest corporations were surveyed each year and a separate report prepared, *The Carbon Disclosure Project Canada 200 Report*. Although emissions are growing in Canada, corporations have invested in carbon reduction projects that have reduced the growth rate of emissions. Canadian companies with ambitious carbon reduction targets include Bank of Montreal, BCE Inc., TD Bank, Air Canada, and TransAlta Corp.

Sources: Adapted from *Carbon Disclosure Project*, accessed August 8, 2016, www.cdproject.net/en-US/Pages/HomePage.aspx and www.cdp.net/en-US/WhatWeDo/Pages/Canada.aspx; *CDP Canada 200 Climate Change Report 2014*, accessed August 8, 2016, www.cdp.net/CDPResults/CDP-Canada-200-Climate-Change-Report-2014.pdf.

Financial regulators also recommend greater disclosure of environmental information. The Ontario Securities Commission (OSC) issued National Instrument 51–102, *Continuous Disclosure Obligations*, which requires public corporations to disclose information about environmental matters. The following summarizes the OSC's findings:

1. *Environmental liabilities*—Corporations should quantify the accounting estimate where quantitative information is reasonably available and would provide useful information to investors. Corporations should also disclose potential environmental liabilities not reflected in financial statements.

2. *Asset retirement obligations*—Corporations are required to identify asset retirement obligations in their financial statements. Environmental examples would be the remediation costs for a mining operation or the disposal of hazardous waste.

3. *Financial and operational effects of environmental protection requirements*—The costs of these requirements should be quantified and the impact of these costs on financial statements identified.

4. *Environmental policies fundamental to operations*—Corporations are required to describe the policies and the steps taken to implement them.

5. *Environmental risks*—These must be identified so that investors can assess the impact on operational and financial performance.

The OSC concluded that a meaningful discussion of material environmental matters is important to achieve fair presentation of the corporation's financial condition. The risks and liabilities associated with the environment must now receive more attention by boards of directors and audit committees. Critics point out that quantifying the risks will be difficult as there are no agreed-upon standards of measurement.[22]

Marketing

Green seems to be the most popular colour with business today, since it expresses society's concern for the environment. **Green marketing** involves selling environmentally friendly goods and services to consumers. Providing such products is necessary for many corporations if they are to survive, and doing so can provide a new opportunity to make money.

RESPONSIBILITY FOR ETHICS 14.5

Common Environmental Labels in Canada

Common green labels and claims are:

- Eco-Logo™: The Canadian EcoLogo (also known as Environmental Choice) helps you identify products and services that have been independently certified to meet strict environmental standards that reflect their entire life cycle—from manufacturing to disposal.
- ENERGY STAR: The international ENERGY STAR symbol marks products that are among the most energy efficient on the market.
- EnerGuide: The Canadian EnerGuide label lists a product's estimated annual energy consumption and compares it to the energy performance of similar products.
- Watersense®: The US Environmental Protection Agency developed this label to identify and promote products that help reduce water consumption.
- Green Seal™: Products with this label have less impact on people's health and the environment.
- Marine Stewardship Council Certification Logo: Products bearing the Marine Stewardship Council (MSC) label come from fisheries certified to have met the MSC standard for sustainable fishing
- Fairtrade Canada Logo: Fair trade schemes, such as Fairtrade Canada, set standards to ensure that certified products are produced in a socially and economically fair, and environmentally responsible manner.
- Canada Organic Logo: Food products that meet the Canadian standard for organic production (at all stages, from growing to marketing) and contain at least 95 percent organic ingredients and no GMOs (genetically modified organisms) may display the Canada Organic label.
- Möbius loop: The recycling symbol (or Möbius loop) indicates that a product or packaging is recyclable, contains recycled content, or both.

Source: Adapted from *Common Environmental Labels and Claims in Canada*, Office of Consumer Affairs (OCA), Government of Canada, accessed January 22, 2016, https://www.ic.gc.ca/eic/site/oca-bc.nsf/eng/ca02523.html.

Dozens of so-called "green" products are on the market: liquid soap products that offer plastic refill pouches to reduce packaging waste; coffee filters made without bleach; recyclable or degradable trash bags; dishwasher detergent that is phosphate-free; and foam plates and cups without chlorofluorocarbons. Packaging is an obvious area where the four Rs—reduce, reuse, recycle, and recover—can be practised, and is getting considerable attention.

Consumers have access to substantial information on the environmental friendliness of products. One way that consumers can increase their awareness of environment issues is by purchasing products displaying eco-labels. Some common eco-labels are listed in Responsibility for Ethics 14.5 on the previous page.

The issue remains as to whether consumers are willing to pay the increased prices often necessary for many green products. Research has found that the attributes of the sustainable products influence these purchase decisions. Attributes like "safe and gentle" were valued for products like baby shampoo; attributes like "strong and tough" were preferred when purchasing car shampoo. Also, consumers were more likely to use green products when being watched.[23] The latter point was found to also be the case in other studies. Although consumers expected corporations to address environmental issues, they liked to give the impression that they are environmentally conscious when this may not be so. Consumers responded more positively to advertisements informing them how they can save money than to those advertisements promoting the benefits to the environment.[24] Despite consumers expressing the desire to use green products, sometimes they have to be forced into doing so as Everyday Ethics 14.4 illustrates. It is difficult for business to anticipate how consumers will respond to environmentally friendly products.

EVERYDAY ETHICS 14.4

Plastic Bottled Water

In 2015, Wilfrid Laurier University completed the phasing out the use of single-use plastic water bottles on campus. Refillable bottles would be encouraged and more access to bottle fill stations would be available. The impact on the environment would be reduced as fewer bottles would go into landfills. There were several reasons for this initiative. The cost of tap water was less and according to a survey the banning of plastic bottles was supported by 75.6% of students responding. The banning of plastic bottles was also considered a human rights issue in that people should have access to free water. It was claimed that water bottle companies were extracting water large quantities of water and damaging underground sources.

An American university found that the implementation of such a policy had unintended consequences. At the University of Vermont, Burlington, VT, a ban on bottled water did not reduce number of bottles in the waste system as hoped. Students did not use the water fountains installed to refill bottles, and the consumption of other bottled, less healthy beverages increased. As these bottles were often thicker than the flimsy water bottles, the volume of waste increased. The share of the healthy beverages sold on campus declined. The environment and student health both suffered as a result of the ban.

Source: Adapted from "Laurier's Plastic Water Bottle Phaseout," Wilfrid Laurier University, accessed January 20, 2016, https://legacy.wlu.ca/page.php?grp_id=12304&p=27320; and Elizabeth R. Berman and Rachel K. Johnson, "The Unintended Consequences of Changes in Beverage Options and the Removal of Bottled Water on a University Campus," *American Journal of Public Health*, July, 2015, Vol. 105, No. 7, 1404-1408.

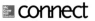 Want to learn more about **an environmental folk song?**

Human Resources

Eco-friendly policies and practices are influencing the recruitment and retention of employees. Such policies are emphasized in recruitment when prospective employees ask recruiters about the employer's environmental practices.[25] Students in particular are searching for environmentally friendly workplaces.

TABLE 14.3   Practices and Policies to Create the Green Workplace

- Offering a recycling program for office products, including donating and discounting used office furniture to employees or charities, and banning disposables such as plastic utensils and paper cups and plates.
- Conserving energy by using energy-efficient lighting systems and equipment, and installing automatic shutoffs of idle equipment.
- Reducing consumption of paper, packaging, and other office supplies, including not printing electronic documents.
- Encouraging employees to be more environmentally friendly by promoting walking, biking, and using public transport to work or car-pooling. Providing bike stands, showers, and fare subsidies.
- Creating a pesticide-free green landscape with trees, lawns, and gardens.
- Reducing emissions through less travel and climate control, and striving for carbon neutrality.
- Purchasing renewable energy credits.
- Conducting virtual meetings through video and teleconferencing thus reducing travel.
- Using natural lighting, with windows and skylights.
- Investing in community environmental initiatives.
- Requiring suppliers to be green.
- Publicly disclosing sustainability initiatives through reports that identify objectives and detail the progress made in achieving them.
- Convincing employees of program benefits and top management support.
- Providing incentives for environmentally friendly behaviour.
- Organizing employee committees to provide advice on practices.

A green workplace is even more important in retention of employees especially in tight employment markets. Employees satisfied with their employer's environment policies are proud of working for the company. Those employees not satisfied are likely to leave if they can find a green workplace.[26] Some of the practices that create an environmentally friendly workplace are listed in Table 14.3.

The benefits to employers of a green workplace include improved employee morale, a stronger public image, increased consumer confidence, a positive bottom line, and healthier employees. Barriers to a green workplace are implementation and maintenance costs, lack of top management support, lack of employee commitment, and concern for lower employee productivity. One study found that one-half of corporations surveyed had environmentally friendly workplace policies and believed that they benefited from them.[27] Another study found that when employees believe their employer is committed to the environment, they are more likely to become involved in eco-initiatives such as recycling and saving energy. In order to encourage such initiatives, management should develop environmental policies and communicate them to employees.[28] There appears to be a trend toward green workplace policies and practices.

There is increasing coverage in the media about environmentally friendly employment and Aon-Hewitt, a human resources consulting firm, annually identifies "Canada's Greenest Employers."[29] Of interest to students is the high demand for individuals with skills and experience in the green or environmental sectors.[30] An indication of the interest in "green" jobs is a job site that specializes in environment-related employment.[31]

Operations

Business is trying to implement environmentally friendly processes and technologies into all aspects of operations or the production function. Environmental issues have added complexity to supply chains, with pressure coming from consumers, competitors, employees, NGOs, and governments. Three areas of activity have been briefly mentioned: pollution reduction, waste management and recycling, and energy conservation. Everyday Ethics 14.5 describes one standard of certification for environmentally friendly practices in the construction industry.

EVERYDAY ETHICS 14.5

"Green" Construction

The Canada Green Building Council's (CaGBC) mission is to lead and accelerate the transformation to high-performing, healthy green buildings, homes, and communities throughout Canada. It works to change industry standards, develop best design practices and guidelines, and advocate for green buildings.

CaGBC's mission is accomplished through the Leadership in Energy and Environmental Design (LEED) Green Building Rating System™. This system encourages and accelerates global adoption of sustainable green building and development practices through the creation and implementation of universally understood and accepted tools and performance criteria. A whole-building approach to sustainability is promoted in five key areas of human and environmental health: sustainable site development; water efficiency; energy efficiency; materials selection; and indoor environmental quality.

LEED is a third-party certification program and an internationally accepted benchmark for the design, construction, and operation of high-performance green buildings. It provides building owners and operators the tools they need to have an immediate and measurable impact on their building's performance.

Source: Adapted from Canada Green Building Council, http://www.cagbc.org.

All Canadians pollute the environment, and the volume of garbage is growing faster than the Canadian population. Pollution comes from many sources, including aerosols, hydrocarbons, automobile exhaust, untreated sewage, and pesticides. Even packaging is a form of pollution; for example, many convenience goods are packaged in throwaway containers. Often pollution is attributed to large business enterprises that dump wastes into the water, air, or landfills. But consumers also create pollution. Thus, corporations are concerned with reducing not only their own pollution activities but also those of consumers.

Waste management is the handling and disposal of unwanted materials left after industrial production or individual consumption. The traditional method of getting rid of our garbage has been to bury it in landfills. These are easy to operate and are relatively inexpensive. But the problem exists of finding locations for new landfill sites: no one wants to live near a dump. As a result, many governments and businesses are developing methods to reuse or manage waste. Research and development and design take the impact of particular materials on the environment into account. Waste from the manufacturing process can be recycled as an input in the production of another product. The reduction of waste is sought, but there is also emphasis on recycling, the retrieval and reuse of suitable waste material such as paper, glass, metal, and plastics. An example of effective use of material that might go to waste but instead saves trees in given in Everyday Ethics 14.6.

EVERYDAY ETHICS 14.6

Jeff Golfman + Woody Harrelson = Tree-Free Paper

Jeff Golfman is a Manitoba entrepreneur who has started and sold several businesses. For the last 15 years he has been interested in producing paper from non-wood fibre, and in particular, agricultural fibre such as wheat straw. He noticed that Prairie farmers had to dispose of straw after harvesting their fields. This straw was sometimes burnt which produced carbon and proposed a health risk. Producing paper from wheat straw was difficult as long fibres were necessary to give paper its strength and straw fibres were short.

Woody Harrelson, actor and environmental activist, was interested in green manufacturing and the production of tree-paper caught his attention. Harrelson became aware of Golfman's efforts, met with Jeff, and together they became the co-founders of Prairie Paper Inc. Harrelson has invested in the project, promoted the product, and attracted other investors. Prairie Paper manufactures Step Forward Paper™, a revolutionary copy paper made up of 80 percent wheat straw waste and 20 percent Wood-Fibre, which is FSC ® certified.

Prairie Paper started selling photocopier paper in 2012 and later professional grade paper at several retailers including Staples and Basics. The paper is produced in India as there was no paper mill in Canada capable of producing it. Plans to construct a mill in Canada are underway but there are financing and raw material supply challenges.

Sources: Adapted from Jake MacDonald, "Field of Dreams," *Canadian Geographic Magazine*, April 2014, 44-48; "The First Straw: Why Print on Wheat Paper," "Little Startup on the Prairie," and "Woody's Paper Trail," *Corporate Knights*, November 2013, 6, 54-58 and 60-62; and Step Forward Paper™ Prairie Paper Inc., accessed August 8, 2016, stepforwardpaper.com.

Once a good has been used by the consumer, it can be disposed of as waste in a landfill or it can become a recyclable product. As a recyclable product, two alternative means of disposal exist: incineration or reuse. Incineration can be used to generate energy, which in turn can be utilized by consumers or manufacturers, although the process discharges some pollution to the environment.

Reuse involves collecting and sorting items, and is often performed by corporations. New technology for processing recycled materials and the availability of markets for recycled materials are making recycling businesses more viable. But problems still exist. The public has been so enthusiastic about recycling materials that the capacity of recycling facilities has been overtaxed. Markets for recycled materials have not grown fast enough to keep pace with the collection of recyclable materials. Once processing of the materials has occurred, they are recycled as raw materials in the manufacturing process.

Canadians are great users and abusers of energy, and growth in energy consumption has been levelling off only recently. As consumption rises, additional sources of energy must be found, placing demands on the environment. Hydro sites and petroleum production areas must be established. Furthermore, preserving the environment adds costs to energy that consumers may not be aware of.

Business is taking many actions to conserve energy. Companies are reducing their consumption in producing and marketing goods and services as well as in the construction of energy-efficient buildings. Also, corporations are introducing products that will enable consumers to conserve energy.

LO 14.9 Measuring and Reporting on Environmental Sustainability

Business can use several measures of sustainability to audit, monitor, and evaluate its environmental performance. These measures have been developed by business organizations, non-governmental organizations, and government agencies; some of these are described in Responsibility for Ethics 14.6 on the next page.

The indicators used to evaluate environmental performance are extensive. Examples include the following:

- Type and amount of materials used to provide the good or service, and cooperation with suppliers
- Source of energy and efficiency of use
- Source and quality of water
- Impact on biodiversity; that is, impact on location of operations, land use, nature, and species
- Reduction of emissions, effluents, and waste including hazardous materials
- Design of products and services to minimize impact on the environment
- Compliance with environmental regulations
- Use of efficient transportation mode[32]

RESPONSIBILITY FOR ETHICS 14.6

Environmental Sustainability Measures and Standards

- *Coalition for Environmentally Responsible Economies (Ceres)*—Ceres is a non-profit organization comprising investors and environmental organizations who work with corporations to address sustainability challenges such as climate change. (As a matter of interest, Ceres is the Roman goddess of fertility and agriculture.) Its network of investors, companies and public interest groups to accelerate and expand the adoption of sustainable business practices and solutions to build a healthy global economy.

- *International Organization for Standardization (ISO) Relating to the Environment*—ISO is an international non-governmental organization comprising standards institutions in 162 countries. It provides standards for environmental management with its ISO 14000 family of International Standards including ISO 14064 and ISO 14065 to help organizations to quantify their greenhouse gas emissions and communicate on them, and ISO 14001 and ISO 50001 promote good practice in environmental and energy management.

- *International Institute for Sustainable Development (IISD)*—IISD is a Canadian-based, not-for-profit organization promoting change toward sustainable development. It is working to develop, enhance, and apply measurement and assessment tools to assist business in better managing environmental issues.

- *Canadian Sustainability Indicators Network (CSIN)*—The purpose of this organization is to enhance the progress toward sustainability development by encouraging the development and use of sustainability indicators. CSIN is supported by various governments and foundations.

Sources: Based on Ceres, "About Us," http://www.ceres.org/about-us; "About ISO," International Organization for Standardization, http://www.iso.org/iso/home/about.htm; "About IISD," International Institute for Sustainable Development, http://www.iisd.org/about/; and "Welcome to CSIN," Canadian Sustainability Indicators Network (CSIN), http://www.csin-rcid.ca/.

Chapter 9 discussed the approaches to measuring and reporting corporate social responsibility and sustainability. Most of the measures discussed there apply to environmental sustainability reporting. An example is the Network for Business Sustainability's guide for measuring environmental impacts. The guide comprises four steps: Step 1 defines success by identifying pressures and establishing goals for addressing them; Step 2 decides what to measure for materials, energy, water, biodiversity, emissions, products and services, compliance, and transport; and Step 3 determines how to measure impacts, for example through life cycle analysis or environmental footprint, and to value them through ecosystem service valuation, or environmental input–output modelling. Finally, Step 4 incorporates the environmental measures into management decision making.[33]

Many corporations have prepared environmental policy statements or codes. The purpose of environmental codes is much the same as it is for codes of ethics: to increase awareness of the issue throughout the organization and to signal to other stakeholders that the enterprise is active in this area. Corporations are being recognized for their efforts at minimizing their impact on the environment. Responsibility for Ethics 14.7 describes one such Canadian award; several international ones also exist.

RESPONSIBILITY FOR ETHICS 14.7

Awards for Environmental Practices and Reporting

GLOBE Foundation of Canada is a private, non-profit organization created to promote the business case for sustainable development. Its guiding principles are:

- Environmental problems are business opportunities.
- Companies that can provide clean technologies and solutions will prosper.
- Proactive organizations that embrace environmental sustainability will be more competitive.

It gives awards for environmental excellence in several categories; the 2014 winners are listed below.

- The Corporate Award for Environmental Excellence—Teck Resources Limited
- The Award for Excellence in Emerging Technology—Solegear Bioplastics Inc.
- The Award for Technology Innovation and Application—Electronics Recycling Service (ERS) International
- The Award for Excellence in Urban Sustainability—Perkins + Will Canada Architects Co.
- The Association Award for Sustainable Leadership-Chemistry Industry Association of Canada (CIAC)

Sources: Adapted from *Awards for Environmental Practices and Reporting*; "Our Story," GLOBE Foundation of Canada, accessed January 22, 2016, http://globe.ca/home/about/our-story/; "GLOBE Awards," GLOBE Foundation of Canada, accessed January 22, 2016, http://www.theglobeawards.ca/; and "GLOBE Winners," GLOBE Foundation of Canada, accessed January 22, 2016, http://theglobeawards.ca/home/winners/.

Many corporations are assisted in practising environmental ethics and sustainability using standards or codes established by industry associations.

LO 14.10 Dissenting Views on the Environment

Not everyone agrees that business should be playing a leading role in protecting the environment. Some business journalists are particularly critical of sustainability for a variety of reasons:

- The concept is difficult to define and understand.
- It means stopping, or constraining, economic development.
- It implies that capitalism is unsustainable and morally lacking.
- It lacks understanding of markets and the moralistic system of markets.
- Executives are being misled into responding to it as a social issue, and the interest many have is merely as a public relations exercise.[34]

Many researchers have challenged environmentalism and sustainability; a prominent critic's view is described in Responsibility for Ethics 14.8.

RESPONSIBILITY FOR ETHICS 14.8

Bjørn Lomborg and The Skeptical Environmentalist

Dissenting views on the state of the environment exist. A controversial one was presented by Bjørn Lomborg, a Danish statistician, in his book *The Skeptical Environmentalist: Measuring the Real State of the World.* He challenged widely held beliefs that the global climate was getting worse, and even claimed that it was actually improving. The main points of his argument were that green activists and the media are overstating the environmental problems, technology that can reduce the damage is improving, Western lifestyles are environmentally sustainable, and the Kyoto Protocol was bad policy and too costly. He used statistics to support his position and was accused of misleading research; these charges were later dismissed. In 2004, he and others organized the Copenhagen Consensus Center, a think tank that increases awareness of the best ways to spend development money on addressing the major challenges facing the planet. In 2012, these challenges were as follows: armed conflict, biodiversity, chronic disease, climate change, education, hunger and malnutrition, infectious diseases, natural disasters, population growth, and water and sanitation. A second book, *Cool It: The Skeptical Environmentalist's Guide to Global Warming,* is also a film documentary and makes the case that many of the expensive and elaborate solutions to climate change will have little impact on the environment. Lomborg believes most solutions are based on emotional rather than strictly scientific assumptions.

Source: Adapted from Bjørn Lomborg website, accessed August 8, 2016, http://lomborg.com; and Copenhagen Consensus Center website, accessed August 8, 2016, http://www.copenhagenconsensus.com/Default.aspx?ID=1626.

Adding to these dissenting views are the mixed reactions received from consumers. It is not easy to interpret public opinion, as illustrated by consumption patterns, concern for jobs, and the reluctance to pay for improvements.

- Despite polls that confirm the concern Canadians have for the environment, consumers still purchase environmentally unfriendly products. Canadians still lead the world in energy consumption and generate the most household garbage.

- Canadians express strong views about conserving forests, reducing pollution, and halting hydroelectric projects. But if job losses result, their concerns about the environment are reduced.

- As most actions to improve environmental quality cost money, the issue becomes one of who will pay—that is, government, business, or consumers. Ultimately, the consumer and/or taxpayer pays, and many are unwilling to assume the costs. Most direct charges to consumers are resented.

Public opinion may express concern for the environment, but this concern is not always reflected in consumption patterns, the desire for jobs at the expense of the environment, and the reluctance to pay. These dissenting views leave corporations and managers uncertain about the course of action to follow.

A poll of Canadian business leaders also indicated that they are not serious about the environment. Only 12 percent had a policy for auditing the impact of greenhouse gases from their operations. While 83 percent thought a corporation's responsibility was to earn a return for shareholders, 56 percent did indicate that corporations had an obligation to adopt low-emission environmental practices. Many of the respondents doubted the reliability of the science behind climate change, and some thought Kyoto was a scam.[35]

The contradictions are illustrated further by what appears to be a paradox. Everyday Ethics 14.7 gives some common inconsistencies in various initiatives that are promoted as being good for the environment but also have unintended consequences. Some researchers have argued that a greater environmental paradox exists. The Millennium Ecosystem Assessment concluded that the capacity of ecosystems to provide services is low, which should mean that human well-being is declining. The Human Development Index, which measures literacy, life expectancy, and income, is improving in both rich and poor countries. The researchers are questioning why this is the case and what the implications are for society.[36]

EVERYDAY ETHICS 14.7

Paradoxical Environmentalism

Various stakeholders, governments, NGOs, or consumers often advocate for initiatives they claim will reduce damage to the environment. Many of these initiatives have unintended consequences that do not lead to the results expected. In some, there are trade-offs that reduce the benefits alleged to be gained. These contradictions challenge the course of action for business. The following are some examples that may be labelled "showcase environmentalism" in that they do not result in the environmental benefits claimed:

- *Fluorescent (CF) versus incandescent light bulbs*—Incandescent bulbs may use less energy but they contain mercury and the disposal of these bulbs has not yet been resolved.

- *Electric versus gasoline cars*—Electric cars reduce petroleum emissions but require a lot of energy to make the necessary batteries, not to mention the copper and aluminum needed to build them.

- *Plastic versus other bags*—Single-use plastic bags are environmentally unfriendly. However, decomposable plastic is available. Reusable cloth bags can become contaminated with repeated use.

- *Organic versus regular milk*—Fewer hormones and antibiotics are used in organic milk production but the low yields results in more cows being needed, which requires more feed and produces more methane.

- *Local versus global food*—It is claimed that local food is safer and reduces transportation costs. However, consumer choice is reduced and prices are higher with less competition.

LO 14.11 The Environment: Corporate Opportunities and Challenges

Corporations face many challenges as they attempt to develop an environmental ethic and practise sustainable development. These challenges are both opportunities and threats.

The reputations of corporations that make an effort to address the environmental issue are most likely enhanced, and they gain greater prominence in the marketplace. Customers are attracted, as investors might be, after a positive investment screening for environmental matters. Costs are reduced through recycling of materials, better control of pollution, energy conservation, and lower insurance. More competent staff might be attracted, and the enterprise becomes better integrated with the local community.

Business opportunities emerge from the development of new technologies or expertise to address environmental concerns. More efficient ways of producing products are found and better products are marketed. There is increasing evidence that responding to environmental concerns need not be costly, and that profitability can even be improved. The environment itself is an opportunity for some who provide the technology or expertise to address the concerns. Environmental product manufacturers include those that provide equipment for water pollution control, air pollution control, solid waste management, measuring instruments, chemicals for pollution control, and noise control. Examples of environmental services include waste handling, consultation services, assessment and control functions, laboratory services, and environmental research.

Several challenges for corporations exist if the environment is ignored. The corporate image deteriorates, and revenues may suffer as customers prefer products and services less damaging to the environment. Investors become more difficult to attract as the enterprises cannot meet the criteria for environmental and ethical screening. Material and production costs may increase faster than for corporations practising reduction and recycling. The financial penalties are becoming higher and directors and managers are being held legally responsible for pollution. Insurance premiums are high for corporations that do not reduce their pollution risk. Alienation may occur from the local community, and failure to act may provoke stricter legislation and regulation.

The management of the natural environment is a challenge for managers. Business must take on some of the responsibility for the environment, and many have already. For others, it is a matter of what type of response is appropriate and when. As an ideal, corporations should be evolving an environmental ethic to enhance sustainable development in society.

Your advice to Vivian . . .

This vignette illustrated how an everyday purchase decision can involve several economic, social, and environmental issues. The decision also illustrates a dilemma, and is a paradox for a consumer facing complex and contradictory information. It is difficult for consumers to be aware of all the issues, much less to research them extensively; this is but one decision among many on any given trip to the grocery store. The ultimate decision is up to the consumer because there is no authority to provide a definitive answer.

Summary

- Concern for the natural environment is widespread in society and business has a responsibility to respond. Responding to this concern is challenging as many stakeholders and issues influence corporations. (LO 14.1)

- Corporations must develop an environmental ethic or set of values relating to their practices toward sustainable development in the economy. Each corporation must develop strategies and practices to meet its own and its stakeholders' needs today while ensuring that future resources will be available. (LO 14.2)

- Environmental concerns are summarized in the descriptions of several topics: acid rain, air pollution, ecosystems, energy production and consumption, nature and wildlife, ozone, pollution, waste management, and water quality. Together these topics influence climate change or global warming. (LO 14.3)

- Governments have implemented environmental policies through legislation and regulations and the establishment of various agencies. Environmental assessments by businesses are now commonplace. However, the federal government is reducing its regulation of environmental impacts. (LO 14.4)

- Influence of a different type comes from environmental non-governmental organizations (ENGOs). Hundreds of such organizations exist and corporations are learning how to respond to or cooperate with them. (LO 14.5)

- Another possibility is to leave solutions to environmental concerns to market-driven initiatives. Instead of being required by governments to respond, it is argued that relying on market forces is more effective. Emissions trading and offsets are two examples. (LO 14.6)

- When corporations act on environmental concerns, the responses must be managed with appropriate organizational structures, environment management systems, and corporate strategies. (LO 14.7)

- As corporations attempt to respond to environmental concerns, there are implications for all the major functions of business: financial management, marketing, human resources, and operations/production. (LO 14.8)

- Many sustainability measures and standards have been developed by ENGOs, business organizations, and industry associations. Indicators that measure a corporation's environmental performance are used. Many corporations issue elaborate environmental reports. (LO 14.9)

- Dissenting views on the environment are held in the business community and by other stakeholders. Not all businesspersons believe that climate change is a problem. Even public attitudes are mixed in that surveys indicate consumers are concerned, but this concern is not always reflected in purchasing decisions. This inconsistency complicates business decision making. (LO 14.10)

- The environment presents corporations with opportunities and threats. But, many corporations are developing an environmental ethic that achieves sustainable development. (LO 14.11)

Key Terms

Commons

Environmental ethic

Sustainable development

Business sustainable development

Acid rain

Ecosystem

Ozone

Waste management

Climate change (global warming)

Environmental non-governmental organizations (ENGOs)

Standard environmentalism

Market environmentalism

Carbon pricing

Cap-and-trade

Carbon tax

Offsets (emissions-reduction credits)

Carbon capture and storage (CCS)

Greenwashing

Green marketing

Critical Thinking and Discussion Questions

1. Why is business' approach to environmental concerns so challenging for managers?
2. Is the concept of the commons applicable today? Give examples.
3. What is the relationship between sustainable development and climate change?
4. What should be government's role in influencing business' response to environmental concerns?
5. What should be the relationship between corporations and ENGOs?
6. How can market forces help achieve sustainable development?
7. What strategic approach should a corporation implement regarding society's concerns about the environment?
8. How does the environment impact business functions, financial management, marketing, human resources, and operations/production?
9. What purposes do sustainability measures and standards serve?
10. Why do dissenting views exist on the seriousness of the danger of business activities to the environment?
11. Do the opportunities presented by sustainable development outweigh the threats?

Cases

14.1 A DOG'S "ECO-PAWPRINT"

Geraldine Churchill had graduated from her business program and had accepted a job with an accounting firm. This meant she was leaving home and moving to another city where she would be living alone. For company and security, she planned to get a pet, most likely a dog adopted from an animal shelter.

She had given this move some thought and had done some research. Thirty-five percent of Canadian households had a dog as a pet. Articles on pets identified some benefits of dog ownership. They enhanced the owner's health by increasing physical activity, for example, dog owners walked farther than others. There were psychological benefits as a dog provided companionship and there was trend with young persons to have pets for this reason.

There were also challenges. There was a risk of the dog contracting an infection, so hand hygiene was important. The food would have to be carefully selected to insure the appropriate and adequate nutrition. Health care was critical and veterinary and drug expenses could run into thousands of dollars. Grooming was necessary and would have to be done by Geraldine or at a pet grooming shop. Dogs required some training and lessons would be necessary. It may be necessary to find a dog daycare, and if she travelled, it would be necessary to board the dog somewhere. It was estimated that owned a dog could cost $2,500 and more per year. Owning a dog meant assuming responsibilities and considerable expenses.

A big surprise for Geraldine was the "eco-pawprint" of a dog on the environment. First of all, there was the amount of food a dog eats. The environmental imprint for food was substantial including the land, fertilizers, pesticides, water, energy, production equipment, packaging and transportation. Much of the dog food sold contains more protein than necessary and can be as much as humans consume. This adds a burden to the environment and takes resources that could be used to feed under nourished persons in the world. Also, she read that dogs in Canada produced over 600,000 tonnes of solid waste per year most of which goes to landfills. One article claimed that owning a dog was more environmentally unfriendly than operating a vehicle.

Geraldine was rethinking her plans for a pet.

Questions

1. What are the issue(s) and stakeholders involved?

2. Are pets a burden on the environment?

3. What should Geraldine do?

Sources: "Consumer Corner: Canadian Pet Market Outlook, 2014," Alberta Agriculture and Forestry, accessed January 2, 2016, http://www1.agric.gov.ab.ca/$department/deptdocs.nsf/all/sis14914; "Latest Canadian Pet Population Figures Released," Released February 12, 2015, Canadian Animal Health Institute, accessed January 2, 2016, https://www.canadianveterinarians.net/documents/canadian-pet-population-figures-cahi-2014; The Pet Industry Joint Advisory Council - Canada, accessed January 2, 2016, http://www.pijaccanada.com/en/default.aspx; Canadian Animal Health Institute accessed January 2, 2016, http://www.cahi-icsa.ca/; Katrina Clarke, "Animal Magnetism: Young Professionals Looking for Companionship Aren't Getting Hitched – They're Getting Pets," *National Post*, July 19, 2014, A9; Garry Marr, "Doing the Math on Your Cute, but Costly, Best Friend," *National Post*, Sept. 11, 2013, FP6; E. Paul Cherniack and Ariella R. Cherniack, *Canadian Medical Association Journal*, July 14, 2015, 187 (10), 715-716; and "Dog-Dazed," CBC/Radio Canada, accessed January 2, 2016, http://www.cbc.ca/doczone/episodes/dog-dazed. "Dog-Dazed" also is available on YouTube at https://www.youtube.com/watch?v=E-F9Co_oFZc.

14.2 IS DR. SEUSS MISLEADING CHILDREN?

For generations, books by Dr. Seuss have been read to and by children. His books were often commentaries on social and political issues; for example, *Yertle the Turtle* had a theme based on totalitarianism, *The Sneetches* dealt with discrimination, and *How The Grinch Stole Christmas* criticized the commercialization of holidays. *The Lorax* discusses the threat to the environment.

The principal character in *The Lorax* is the Once-ler, who represents business. He cuts down the beautiful Truffula Trees to make a Thneed, which could be used for many things including shirts, hats, or gloves. The Lorax, a small, "mossy" creature who spoke for the trees and animals in the forest, asked the Once-ler to stop cutting down the Truffula Trees. But the Once-ler recognized the market potential of the Thneed and he set up a factory to manufacture even more of them.

The business grew bigger and the Once-ler cut down more and more trees to meet the demand. Animals that depended on the Truffula Trees lost their source of food. Smog and water pollution were created by the factories. The Once-ler said he had rights and was going to continue his business expansion. Eventually the last Truffula Tree was down, ending the production of Thneeds. The Once-ler realized his mistake and asked the readers to take the last Truffula Tree seed and plant it, take care of it, and protect it from those who want to chop it down.

Dr. Seuss wanted to make several points: the planet faces environmental problems such as pollution and the depletion of resources; these problems have serious implications for society; and there is some urgency necessary to address them. The story delivers a message that business is rapidly destroying the environment and that things will not change until people start to care and do something to stop the destruction.

In March 2012 the animated movie *The Lorax* was released to theatres in 2-D and 3-D. Most reviewers felt that it followed the book's pro-environmentalism and anti-capitalism themes. The movie stressed the dangers of overconsumption and corporate greed, and the virtue of conservation. There was a consensus that the movie was very colourful, the musical numbers were mediocre, and the voices of the characters were excellent. Many reviewers felt that young audiences might be influenced by the warnings against rampant capitalism which led to deforestation.

The story both in print and on-screen is very pessimistic and treats the business system harshly, and may be giving children an overly negative view of business. The positive aspects of the business system are not discussed; for example, explaining how business is essential to ensuring a high standard of living, how it creates employment, and how it provides innovative products and services. The story does not suggest that the environment and business activity can coexist.

Questions

1. Is it appropriate that children's stories contain anti-business messages? What are the ethical implications of this practice?

2. Today, who performs the role of the Lorax?

3. How would Dr. Seuss view sustainable development?

4. What other media contain messages that are critical of business?

5. Will you read *The Lorax* to children (including your own)?

Sources: Adapted from MovieReviewIntelligence, "Dr. Seuss's The Lorax Movie Reviews," http://moviereviewintelligence.com/movie-reviews/dr_seuss_the_lorax/, accessed December 12, 2012; and Rotten Tomatoes, "The Lorax Movie Reviews," http://rottentomatoes.com/m/the_lorax/reviews, accessed December 12, 2012.

Used with the permission of Dennis Flynn

CHAPTER 15

Globalization and Business Responsibilities

LEARNING OUTCOMES

After studying this chapter, you will be able to:

LO 15.1 Recognize that global business brings new business responsibilities.

LO 15.2 Define globalization, identify related issues, and list the pros and cons.

LO 15.3 Describe the role international non-governmental organizations play in influencing business.

LO 15.4 Name the main supranational institutions influencing globalization.

LO 15.5 Understand the connection between globalization and Canadian business and society.

LO 15.6 Become familiar with the international standards that are guiding and influencing the behaviour of multinational corporations.

LO 15.7 Appreciate the special challenges confronting business as a result of globalization.

LO 15.8 Link the reduction of poverty in developing countries to aspects of capitalism.

What would you do if...?

Claudia Merchant was viewing a website that offered for sale an Hermès Birkin handbag that was exactly what she had been looking for. She had always wanted a bag of this type and this one was being sold for a fraction of the price. Claudia began filling out the order form, and then paused.

Her Business Law professor had devoted a whole class lecture to discuss the counterfeiting and pirating of intellectual property, which was a major issue in the globalization of business. Claudia recalled her referring to an intellectual property crime statistics report by the RCMP. The main types of products involved were footwear, clothing and accessories, copyrighted works, consumer electronics, and pharmaceuticals. In one year, the RCMP had seized more than $38 million in counterfeit and pirated goods with China being the primary source.

The professor emphasized the seriousness of the problem, explaining why it even threatened Canada's economic integrity. Local merchants were unable to compete and sometimes failed as a result. Because the products were produced overseas, jobs in Canada were lost. These products were not produced to Canadian standards and often threatened the health and safety of consumers. Real dangers were associated with purchasing counterfeit medications, electrical and electronic devices, alcohol and food products, toys, cosmetics, condoms, and sporting equipment. In a report, the Canadian Anti-Counterfeiting Network stated there were some troubling ethics about the culture of piracy in Canada and that more had to be done to change the view that it was ethically acceptable to purchase these goods.

According to Claudia's professor, counterfeiting and piracy were big business globally and were very profitable for those involved. Another aspect of the problem, according to the RCMP report, was that organized crime, criminal gangs, and even terrorist organizations increasingly were involved. Consumers were often attracted to luxury products, such as the Hermès handbag Claudia was interested in, by prices that saved them a lot of money. Many of these street vendors and Internet sites appeared quite legitimate and induced consumers to make innocent purchases.

The picture of the handbag was very clear and there were close-ups of the stitching and finish. The handbag looked legitimate, but the price was very low. Claudia started wondering about the website, and realized she did not recognize the name of the corporation. She wondered whether or not she should go ahead and purchase. The handbag would really go well with several of her outfits.

What is your advice to Claudia?

Sources: "2011 Intellectual Property (IP) Crime Statistics," Royal Canadian Mounted Police, accessed August 9, 2016, http://www.rcmp-grc.gc.ca/fep-pelf/ipr-dpi/report-rapport-2012-eng.htm; and *Report on Counterfeiting and Piracy in Canada: A Road Map for Change*, Canadian Anti-Counterfeiting Network, accessed August 9, 2016, http://cacn.ca/wp-content/uploads/2013/09/Roadmap_for_Change.pdf and http://cacn.ca/wp-content/uploads/2013/09/CACN-Report-on-counterfeiting-Executive-Update-nov-2011.pdf.

LO 15.1   Global Business Responsibilities

Globalization is placing challenges on Canadian business, including new economic, ethical, and environmental responsibilities. Canadian corporations have no choice but to face the challenges presented by the more complex world economy that is evolving. Many believe that international business activities have the potential for distributing goods and services more equitably and for improving the standard of living for all people. Corporations subject to market forces and managed by private rather than government employees are believed to be more efficient at supplying the goods and services needed by the citizens of any country.

Globalization is not a new phenomenon. Historians have recorded trade in goods between regions since ancient times. Civilizations around the Mediterranean Sea traded among each other over land and by sea. As transportation and communications technologies improved, traders ventured farther to the Far East and the Americas. At times freer trade flourished, but over the centuries there have been periods of protectionism when countries believed it was in their best interests to restrict international commerce. The most recent occurrence of this was in the twentieth century until about 1980; after two World Wars and the Great Depression of the 1930s, governments became very protectionist and began to perform more of the economic functions in society. Gradually this view changed, and in the last two decades of the century attitudes toward trade and market systems evolved. Today, this new view toward trade and markets is referred to as *globalization.*

This chapter describes globalization, its impact on corporations, the challenges associated with it, the standards of conduct that are influencing it, and the emergence of capitalism as the predominant economic system in the world. Throughout the chapter, the increasing complexity of the corporation's economic, ethical, social, and environmental responsibilities in the global marketplace is identified.

LO 15.2 Defining Globalization and the Implications for Business

A general definition of **globalization** is a process of decreasing constraints on the interactions among the nations and peoples of the world. There are several dimensions to globalization; three important ones for business are economic, political, and social or cultural.

Economic globalization involves the integration of fragmented markets into a global economy. The markets for goods and services, information, capital, and labour become worldwide, leading to free trade among nations; although progress has been made, the world has a long way to go before this is fully implemented. Barriers still exist to free trade among nations even through developing nations are now the producers of many goods and services consumed in industrialized economies. This could eventually mean worldwide standards or practices for product quality, pricing, service, and design. This is the type of globalization that is most commonly being referred to when the term is used.[1]

Political globalization is the process by which world power relationships change and there is a loss of sovereignty by the state. The reduced role of the state is replaced by power being assumed by multinational corporations, religious organizations, non-governmental organizations, social movements, and transnational terrorism. New forms of governance emerge, for example United Nations organizations (such as the Global Compact described in Responsibility for Ethics 15.1), the Organisation for Economic Co-operation and Development (OECD), the European Union (EU), and the World Trade Organization (WTO). Thus, economic activity is less hindered by political boundaries.[2]

RESPONSIBILITY FOR ETHICS 15.1

The United Nations Global Compact

The Global Compact asks corporations to embrace, support, and enact, within their sphere of influence, a set of core values in the areas of human rights, labour standards, the environment, and anti-corruption. More than 6,000 corporations have signed on to the Compact, but only 62 are Canadian. The following are the Compact's "Principles of Responsible Investing."

Human Rights

- *Principle 1:* businesses should support and respect the protection of internationally proclaimed human rights; and
- *Principle 2:* make sure that they are not complicit in human rights abuses.

Labour Standards

- *Principle 3:* businesses should uphold the freedom of association and the effective recognition of the right to collective bargaining;
- *Principle 4:* the elimination of all forms of forced and compulsory labour;
- *Principle 5:* the effective abolition of child labour; and
- *Principle 6:* the elimination of discrimination in respect of employment and occupation.

Environment

- *Principle 7:* businesses should support a precautionary approach to environmental challenges;
- *Principle 8:* undertake initiatives to promote greater environmental responsibility; and
- *Principle 9:* encourage the development and diffusion of environmentally friendly technologies.

Anti-Corruption

- *Principle 10:* businesses should work against all forms of corruption, including extortion and bribery.

Source: "The Ten Principles," *The United Nations Global Compact*, http://www.unglobalcompact.org/AboutTheGC/TheTenPrinciples/index.html. © 2016 United Nations. Reprinted with the permission of the United Nations.

Social or cultural globalization is the emergence of a worldwide cultural system. This system emerges due to a variety of social and cultural activities, including common patterns of consumption, such as demand for American entertainment and brand-name clothing; worldwide sporting events, such as football competitions and the Olympic Games; increasing tourism travel; movements common around the world, such as environmentalism and the trend toward holding business accountable for social and environmental responsibilities; and health problems affecting most of the world, such as AIDS and flu pandemics. As a result, the world is thought of more as a single place.[3]

Globalization increases business' economic, social, and environmental responsibilities, including issues arising from the following:

- Damage to the environment occurring as a result of using natural resources, including pollution and depletion.
- Business' alleged support for oppressive governments.
- Criticism of the marketing practices of many industries and corporations, for example tobacco, pharmaceutical, and baby formula products.
- Businesses associated with the arms trade are blamed for facilitating violence and warfare in various parts of the world.
- The treatment of employees in developing countries, the existence of sweatshops in industrialized as well as developing countries, and the attempts to prevent union formation.
- In many parts of the world, including Canada, indigenous peoples are attempting to regain control over ancestral lands.
- Genetic modification of plants and animals has aroused concern, as has the patenting of life forms in the production of food.
- Corruption, bribery, and questionable payments are involved with doing business in some countries.

TABLE 15.1 The Pros and Cons of Globalization	
Globalists' Arguments	**Anti-globalists' Arguments**
• Trade is encouraged as it leads to the most efficient production of goods and services from which all gain. • Private corporations and open markets provide better goods and services to society. • Opportunities for employment and higher incomes are enhanced in developing countries. • The standard of living has increased in most developing countries. • The transfer of capital, technology, intellectual property, and even skilled labour occurs. • Several stakeholders benefit, including owners, consumers, suppliers, and employees.	• The expansion of global corporations is undesirable as decisions are based on profit-making or greed. • Conspiracies exist between corporations and governments resulting in any benefits being received by a few. • Unemployment is created in developed economies. • Poverty and inequality increases in the developing economies. • Periodic financial crises are caused disrupting the economies of many countries. • There is destruction of local environments as standards are lowered to attract developments. • The cultures of societies are lost or changed. • Human rights are violated, in particular in relation to sweatshops. • Questionable payments are made to governments or their officials to facilitate business. • Intellectual property is not respected. • The sovereignty of nations is undermined. • Worldwide organizations such as the World Bank, the International Monetary Fund, and the World Trade Organization have too much influence.

As a result of these issues and others, the desirability of globalization is open to debate.

Globalization has generated considerable controversy. The pros and cons of globalization have been discussed extensively and the main arguments on each side are summarized in Table 15.1 on the previous page. **Globalists**, individuals and organizations that support globalization, make the arguments for globalization; **anti-globalists** are individuals and organizations that oppose globalization or are critical of it.

It is unlikely that globalization can be halted, but its pace might be slowed. Businesspersons, as well as governments, should devise approaches to overcoming some of the downsides of globalization so that even more stakeholders benefit from the process. The existence of international non-governmental organizations, many of which oppose globalization, must be recognized and appropriate responses formulated.

LO 15.3 Globalization and International Non-governmental Organizations (INGOs)

Business is being made aware of its responsibilities arising from globalization. **International non-governmental organizations (INGOs)** are groups that hold shared values and attitudes about the issues relating to globalization and advocate for changes to improve the conditions in developing countries. Many issues arise in addition to those listed, and INGOs are putting pressure on corporations and governments. Many INGOs are opposed to globalization and attempt to counterbalance what they consider the excessive influence of multinational corporations. Some address all issues of globalization, while others focus on human rights or the environment. Sometimes INGOs are referred to as transnational non-government actors (TNGAs), or transnational social movement organizations (TSMOs). Responsibility for Ethics 15.2 gives examples of INGOs.

RESPONSIBILITY FOR ETHICS 15.2

Examples of INGOs

- *Corporate Watch*—This is an INGO whose purpose is to hold corporations accountable for their actions. It investigates and exposes corporate violations of human rights, environmental crimes, and fraud and corruption around the world. It works to foster global justice, to promote independent media activism, and to gain democratic control over corporations.

- *Oxfam International*—"Oxfam International is a confederation of 17 organizations working together with partners and communities in more than 90 countries to find lasting solutions to poverty, suffering and injustice." Its vision is "a just world without poverty" by helping to create lasting solutions to the injustice of poverty.

- *Amnesty International*—Amnesty International (AI) is a worldwide organization with 7 million members, supporters, and subscribers in 150 countries and territories. It campaigns for internationally recognized human rights; one current campaign is "Corporate Accountability." In this campaign, AI maintains that globalization through the existence of multinational corporations has changed the world we live in and presents new and complex challenges for the protection of human rights.

- *Greenpeace International*—Greenpeace is an independent global organization focusing on worldwide threats to the planet's biodiversity and environment. Issues addressed include climate change, the well-being of forests and oceans, food, toxic chemicals, and nuclear energy.

Sources: Adapted from "About CorpWatch," http://www.corpwatch.org/article.php?id=11314; accessed August 8, 2016, Oxfam International, "About us," accessed August 8, 2016, http://www.oxfam.org/en/about/; Amnesty International, "Who We Are," accessed August 8, 2016, https://www.amnesty.org/en/who-we-are/, accessed August 8, 2016; and Greenpeace International, "About Greenpeace," http://www.greenpeace.org/international/en/about/.

Such organizations have received considerable attention, particularly with demonstrations at world economic gatherings. A coalition of civil society and environmental INGOs plus labour organizations disrupted the WTO meetings in Seattle in fall 1999, World Bank meetings in spring and fall 2000, the G8 Summit in Genoa, Italy, in 2001, and the G8 and G20 Summits in Ontario in 2010. In addition, their publications, media events, and websites are influential.

INGOs believe that they have a role to play in globalization by representing those with the little or no voice, including the poor, sick, and uneducated; the victims of civil wars; and indigenous peoples. This role is an important contribution in civil society and cannot be ignored by governments or corporations. Not all INGOs are alike or hold the same views, and not all are opposed to globalization. However, they do believe that poverty and inequality must be addressed. They are concerned that rich countries are becoming better off and that rich persons within countries are becoming richer at the expense of the poor. It is believed that corporate influence is dominating government decision making and that corporate ownership of the media prevents alternative views from being aired.

On the other hand there is increasing cooperation between corporations and INGOs, as described in Chapter 13 where the pros and cons of partnerships with NGOs are discussed. Everyday Ethics 15.1 describes a partnership between an INGO and a corporation in the forestry industry.

EVERYDAY ETHICS 15.1

Domtar Corporation and the Rainforest Alliance

Domtar is a large Canadian manufacturer of fibre-based products including communication papers, specialty and packaging papers and absorbent hygiene products. The Rainforest Alliance is an international non-profit organization that works to conserve biodiversity and ensure sustainable livelihoods.

Domtar and Rainforest Alliance have collaborated on the certification of Domtar's EarthChoice® Office Papers products to Forest Stewardship Council (FSC) standards by the Rainforest Alliance. They are also endorsed by the World Wildlife Fund. In order to obtain this certification, Domtar must maintain forests according to FSC standards relating to biodiversity, protection of water sheds, and support the rights of those whose livelihoods depends on the forest. Rainforest Alliance certification assesses Domtar's operations through audits that include species inventories, forest inspections, management plan reviews, and with input from interested parties. Domtar is allowed to display the Rainforest Alliance Certified™ seal (a green frog) along with the FSC® trademark on qualifying products.

Source: Adapted from Domtar Corporations, "The Rainforest Alliance: Protecting Our Planet," accessed January 25, 2016, http://www.domtar.com/files/sustainability/The_Rainforest_Alliance_Protecting_Our_Planet.pdf; "A Successful Collaboration: Working with the Rainforest Alliance," accessed January 25, 2016, http://www.domtar.com/files/sustainability/ECAS_Final_Oct_2012_Rainforest_Alliance.pdf#search=%22Rainforest Alliance %22; and Rainforest Alliance, "Shop the Frog," accessed January 25, 2016, http://www.rainforest-alliance.org/shopthefrog/domtar.

LO 15.4   Institutions of Globalization

No one global governance institution exists as such, but several organizations have an influence on the global economy beyond that of a particular nation. This type of organization is known as a **supranational institution**, an international organization that transcends national boundaries where the member states share in decision making on particular issues pertaining to the members. They are usually viewed as economic agencies, but they can also have an impact on the ethical, social, and environmental responsibilities of the corporation. INGOs are often critical of such institutions as they promote globalization. Four supranational institutions are described: the World Bank, the International Monetary Fund, the International Labour Organization, and the World Trade Organization.

The World Bank was established with the objective of providing financing to enhance the economic development of countries after the Second World War. Today it focuses its financial and technical assistance to developing countries in Africa, Asia, Latin America, and the Middle East. The bank is owned by the 184 member countries and aims to reduce poverty and improve living conditions in developing countries. Low-interest loans, interest-free credit, and grants are given for education, health, infrastructure, communications, and other purposes.[4]

The International Monetary Fund (IMF) is "an organization of 188 countries, working to foster global monetary cooperation, secure financial stability, facilitate international trade, promote high employment and sustainable economic growth, and reduce poverty."[5] Although monetary and financial policies are a focus for the organization, it is also concerned with the social impacts of these policies.

The International Labour Organization (ILO) is the United Nations agency that "seeks the promotion of social justice and internationally recognized human and labour rights." It formulates standards of basic labour rights including the freedom of association, the right to organize, collective bargaining, abolition of forced labour, and equality of opportunity and treatment. This organization has been influential in the area of accountability for sweatshops in developing countries. It also established the World Commission on the Social Dimension of Globalization to assist people coping with changes brought about by globalization. The Commission is searching for innovative ways to combine economic, social, and environmental objectives.[6]

The World Trade Organization (WTO), which came into force on January 1, 1995, is an international body that oversees and coordinates agreements reducing trade barriers. There have been many NGO demonstrations at WTO meetings, mostly opposing the liberalization of trade. The issues identified include the unfairness to developing nations, the abuse of workers, the low prices received by producers, the arbitrary practices of multinational corporations, and the loss of jobs.

These institutions are viewed as being focused on economic matters, but as outlined above they are also influential in social, ethical, and environmental issues confronting the countries they are attempting to assist.

LO 15.5 Globalization and Canadian Business and Society

Canadian business is influenced by globalization and must respond; there are several implications. With global markets emerging, Canadian business is under pressure to forge international links as there will be less distinction between domestic and foreign enterprises. Ownership and control of business will be less important than performance at supplying goods and services. Canada, and Canadian business, has no choice but to meet the challenges of global market restructuring as new trading agreements are completed by governments. Several developing nations are becoming major economies—for example India, Brazil, Russia, and China—and Canadian business must prepare for the opportunities and threats that are emerging.

Canada must attract more investment in plants that further process our natural resources. Such investment will lead to productivity growth, increased competitiveness, and greater employment opportunities. On the other hand, Canadian direct investment abroad is a critical element in globalization. Businesspeople must be willing to invest money in operations outside of Canada. Governments must "think globally" when developing programs and policies, and be aware of the trend to globalization and encourage business to react appropriately.

In this global economy, Canadian corporations must be competitive with those from other countries in order to also behave as responsible corporate citizens. One measure of this ability to compete is the "Competitiveness Scoreboard" published annually by the International Institute for Management Development, which surveys the competitiveness of most national economies. Four factors are measured: economic performance, government efficiency, business efficiency, and infrastructure. In 2015 Canada ranked 5th out of 61 and on the four factors its rankings were 10th, 8th, 3rd, and 6th. Canada's ranking will face challenges in the future because of low productivity growth, lack of business scale, skilled labour shortages, and aging infrastructure.[7]

A second measure of competitiveness is provided by the "Global Competitiveness Report" published by the World Economic Forum, an independent international organization committed to improving the state of the world by engaging leaders in partnerships to shape global, regional, and industry agendas. A Global Competitiveness Index provides an overview of a country's productivity and competitiveness based on nine factors. On this Index, Canada ranked 13th but Canada's score is being dragged down by weak innovation, insufficient access to financing, and inefficient government bureaucracy.[8]

How well Canadian business is able to compete in the global market influences how well Canadian corporations can respond to social, ethical, and environmental responsibilities associated with globalization. Many Canadian corporations with global operations willingly accept, or are being pressured to accept, these additional responsibilities. The International Code of Ethics for Canadian Business provides assistance in this area. This Code was developed especially for Canadian businesses by a joint effort among an academic institution, business leaders, and public administrators. It comprises four parts: a vision statement, a list of beliefs, a list of values, and a set of principles. The Code includes a vision statement:

Canadian business has a global presence that is recognized by all stakeholders as economically rewarding to all parties, acknowledged as being ethically, socially, and environmentally responsible, welcomed by the communities in which we operate, and that facilitates economic, human resource, and community development within a stable operating environment.[9]

The principles of the Code are given in Responsibility for Ethics 15.3.

RESPONSIBILITY FOR ETHICS 15.3

The International Code of Ethics for Canadian Business Principles

The Code is based on the following principles:

A. Concerning Community Participation and Environmental Protection, we will:

- strive within our sphere of influence to ensure a fair share of benefits to stakeholders impacted by our activities
- ensure meaningful and transparent consultation with all stakeholders and attempt to integrate our corporate activities with local communities as good corporate citizens
- ensure our activities are consistent with sound environmental management and conservation practices
- provide meaningful opportunities for technology, training and capacity building within the host nation

B. Concerning Human Rights, we will:

- support and promote the protection of international human rights within our sphere of influence
- not be complicit in human rights abuses

C. Concerning Business Conduct, we will:

- not make illegal and improper payments and bribes and will refrain from participating in any corrupt business practices
- comply with all application laws and conduct business activities in a transparent fashion
- ensure contractor's, supplier's and agent's activities are consistent with these principles

D. Concerning Employees Rights and Health & Safety, we will:

- ensure health and safety of workers is protected
- strive for social justice and promote freedom of association and expression in the workplace
- ensure consistency with universally accepted labour standards, including those related to exploitation of child labour

Source: Schulich School of Business, *Compendium of Ethics Codes and Instruments of Corporate Responsibility*, York University, Toronto, http://www.yorku.ca/csr/_files/file.php?fileid=fileCDOICwJiei&filename=file_Codes_Compendium_Jan_2007.pdf. Used with permission of Dr. Phil Wesley Cragg, CBERN.

Many Canadian corporations are attempting to behave as responsible corporate citizens in the countries where they operate. Some of these corporations are identified by the Global 100 ranking described in Everyday Ethics 15.2.

EVERYDAY ETHICS 15.2

Corporate Knights' Global 100

Each year *Corporate Nights: The Magazine for Clean Capitalism* compiles a list of the 100 most sustainable corporations in the world. The indicators used in the selection are:

- Energy Productivity: $ Revenue per gigajoule of energy consumption
- Carbon Productivity: $ Revenue per tonne of direct/indirect GHG emissions
- Water Productivity: $ Revenue per cubic metre of water used
- Waste Productivity: $ Revenue per tonne of waste produced net of waste recycled/reused
- Board Diversity: Percentage of women who sit on company board
- Management Diversity: Percentage of women who work in senior executive positions
- CEO-TO-Average Worker Pay: How much more CEO gets paid, expressed as multiple compared to average worker
- Sustainability Pay Link: at least one senior executive's compensation tied to sustainability-themed performance targets

The nine Canadian corporations in the 2016 rankings were: Cameco (32nd), Teck Resources (37th), Enbridge (46th), Telus (53rd), Toronto-Dominion Bank (54th), WSP Global (63rd), Sun Life Financial (66th), Celestica (85th), and Bank of Montreal (86th).

Source: Adapted from "Global 2100," *Corporate Nights: The Magazine for Clean Capitalism*, Winter 2016, Volume 16, Issue 1, 32-38.

The Canadian mining industry operates around the world and responsible corporate citizenship is particularly important. An example of this citizenship is provided by Teck Resources, one of the Global 100 corporations, and described in Everyday Ethics 15.3.

EVERYDAY ETHICS 15.3

Teck Resources as a Corporate Citizen in Chile

Teck Resources is Canada's largest diversified resource company with main products being copper, zinc, and coal. It operates mines in Canada, Chile, Peru, and the United States. Its exploration efforts are worldwide and are focused on four commodities: copper, zinc, steelmaking coal, and gold. Teck's "Vision for Community" is "We build strong relationships and create lasting mutual benefits based on respect for what communities value."

Examples of Teck's efforts at developing relationships with the community at its operations in Andacollo, Chile, are:

- Teck along with local government and community organizations increased the use of solar power. They taught local citizens how to make and use solar ovens. This reduced by 60 percent the reliance on gas.
- Teck developed a Human Relations Assessment tool to identify and analyze how their activities were infringing upon or enhancing human relations with employees and communities.
- Dust levels were high in the community because of tailings left by other operators. The dust was a potential health risk as it contained particles of heavy metals and mercury. Teck worked with NGOs to remove and process the tailings.

Source: Adapted from "Our Sustainability Strategy: Community," Teck Resources Limited, accessed January 25, 2016, http://www.teck.com/responsibility/our-sustainability-strategy/community/.

All Canadians have been affected by globalization. The two most common ways are through the availability of lower-priced goods in greater variety, and the employment adjustments that occur from outsourcing goods and services. The well-being of Canadian society is increasingly influenced by the performance of Canada's corporations in the global environment both within and outside Canada. As well, societies and stakeholders in developing countries are being affected; some benefit, while others are harmed. The following section reviews the standards of conduct and accountability of corporations involved in global business.

LO 15.6 Standards of Conduct and Accountability for Global Business

Numerous codes, guidelines, or principles provide direction to corporations operating in the global economy. These measures are developed by various INGOs, some in cooperation with business, supranational institutions, business associations, or other civil society organizations. Corporations can use the standards to assess their response to social and environmental responsibilities relating to international business.

Standards of conduct apply to the worldwide operations of a multinational corporation (MNC) and are applicable to all, although compliance is voluntary. Responsibility for Ethics 15.4 lists some of the common standards, but many others exist.

RESPONSIBILITY FOR ETHICS 15.4

Global Standards of Conduct Developed by International Organizations

- *Caux Round Table: Caux Principles*—The "Caux Principles of Business" were developed by a network of senior business leaders from both industrialized and developing nations. The principles cover responsibilities to all stakeholders, economic and social impact of business, business behaviour, respect for rules, support for multilateral trade, respect for the environment, and avoidance of illicit operations.

- *OECD "Guidelines for Multinational Enterprises"*—This is one of the oldest guidelines and has influenced corporate behaviour around the world. Clauses include disclosure, employment and industrial relations, environment, combating bribery, consumer interests, science and technology, competition, and taxation.

- *Principles for Global Corporate Responsibility: Benchmarks for Measuring Business Performance*—This is a comprehensive set of more than 100 principles, 129 criteria, and 118 benchmarks to measure business' social and environmental performance. It was developed by interfaith organizations from several countries including the Taskforce on the Churches and Corporate Responsibility of Canada (TCCR, now KAIROS-Canada).

- *The Equator Principles (EPs)*—The Equator Principles is system for determining, assessing, and managing environmental and social risk in projects; it is primarily intended to provide a minimum standard for due diligence to support responsible risk decision-making. The EPs have been adopted by 82 financial institutions in 36 countries.

- *The United Nations' Principles for Responsible Investment (PRI)*—The Principles were formulated in partnership with the UNEP Finance Initiative and the UN Global Compact and developed by an international group of institution investors. The initiative has prompted as environmental, social, and corporate governance (ESG) issues can affect the performance of investment portfolios.

- *United Nations Global Compact Network*—In 1999, the World Economic Forum developed a set of principles referred to as the Global Compact, covering human rights, labour, and environment.

- *Global Reporting Initiative (GRI)*—GRI guidelines cover all aspects of economic, social, and environmental reporting and apply to multinational corporations. Refer to Chapter 9 for a description.

Sources: Adapted from "Principles of Business," Caux Round Table, accessed January 25, 2016, http://www.cauxroundtable.org/index.cfm?&menuid=8; "Guidelines for Multinational Enterprises," Organisation for Economic Co-operation and Development (OECD), accessed January 25, 2016, http://www.oecd.org/corporate/mne/; "Principles for Global Corporate Responsibility: Benchmarks for Measuring Business Performance," accessed January 25, 2016, http://www.benchmarks.org/; "About The Equator Principles," The Equator Principles Association, accessed January 25, 2016, http://www.equator-principles.com/index.php/about-ep/about-ep; and UNEP and the UN Global Compact, The Principles for Responsible Investment, accessed January 25, 2016, https://www.unpri.org/about/the-six-principles.

connect   Want to learn about **the International Principles of Responsible Investment?**

The following topics are covered in standards of conduct, but vary from one standard to another:

- *Political factors*—MNCs must respect national sovereignty and observe domestic laws, regulations, and administrative procedures. Corporations must not interfere (illegally) in the internal affairs of the countries in which they operate and adhere to taxation policies.

- *Sociocultural objectives and values*—MNCs should respect the social and cultural objectives, values, and traditions of the countries in which they operate.

- *Disclosure of information*—Information about operations should be available, but not to the extent that business confidentiality is violated. MNCs will issue CSR and environmental reports.

- *Competition*—Activities should not be undertaken that adversely affect competition by abusing a dominant position of market power.

- *Financing*—Corporate financing should be arranged to consider the impact on national balances of payments and credit policies.

- *Employment and human resources*—MNCs should respect the right of their employees to join trade unions, observe standards of employment and industrial relations, train persons from the local labour force, and be sensitive to the impacts of layoffs and closures. MNCs should respect human rights, not be involved in child or forced labour, and provide safe and healthy workplaces.

- *Science and technology*—MNCs must cooperate with the scientific and technological policies of the countries in which they operate and grant licences for the use of industrial property rights under reasonable terms.

- *Corrupt practices*—MNCs shall refrain from offering, promising, or giving any payment, gift, or other advantage to the benefit of a public official or politician.

- *Environmental protection*—MNCs shall carry out their activities in accordance with national laws, regulations, administrative practices, and policies relating to the preservation of the environment of the countries in which they operate and with due regard to international standards of sustainability.

- *Stakeholder consideration*—MNCs shall consider the interests of all stakeholders. Consumers must be dealt with fairly, marketing and advertising practices must be honest, privacy must be respected, and products sold must be safe and of good quality. The views of INGOs should be taken into consideration. Local supplier capacity should be developed.

- *Corporate governance*—The MNC shall follow appropriate governance practices.

Most of the standards cover a range of economic, ethical, and environmental measures. Human rights are included in most, but corporate governance practices in only some. They are a valuable resource for corporations and can be modified by industry. They provide a basis for reporting and guidelines for establishing policies. If used, there is need for annual auditing of compliance, preferably by an independent body or consultant. If not used or followed, any benefits from the standards will be lost.

LO 15.7   Special Challenges of Global Business

Some special challenges confront Canadian business as it participates increasingly in the global economy: the presence of corruption, respect for human rights, the use of sweatshop production, and the reduction of poverty.

Corruption

When operating in a global economy, Canadian corporations must be aware of the legal and ethical circumstances existing in various countries. Transparency International (TI) has developed an index of corruption, the Corruption Perception Index (CPI), to assist corporations in coping with particular countries. TI defines **corruption** as "the abuse of entrusted power for private gain" and their "Corruption Perception Index measures the perceived level of public sector corruption in countries and territories around the world."[10] Table 15.2 lists the CPI scores for the five least corrupt countries and the five most corrupt according to TI. Out of the 174 countries surveyed, Canada ranks 10th with a score of 81, and the United States 17th with a score of 74.

TABLE 15.2 **Corruption Perceptions Index Scores 2015 (score out of 100)**

Least Corrupt Countries	CPI Score	Most Corrupt Countries	CPI Score
Denmark	91	South Sudan	15
Finland	90	Sudan	12
Sweden	89	Afghanistan	11
New Zealand	88	North Korea	8
Netherlands	87	Somalia	8

Source: Compiled from Corruption Perceptions Index 2015. Transparency International: *The Global Coalition against Corruption.* For more information, visit https://www.transparency.org/cpi2015/#results-table.

connect   Want to learn more about **Transparency International?**

Bribery is a type of corruption that is widespread and insidious in some parts of the world. When managers of Canadian corporations operating overseas are confronted with this practice, ethical dilemmas arise. **Bribery** involves making questionable payments, or bribes, to government officials to influence their decisions. Sometimes bribes are referred to as *facilitation payments,* and involve smaller payments to expedite something an official should be doing by encouraging him or her to do it faster and more efficiently. Such payments may be justified as necessary to do business in a particular country and often are rationalized since everyone does it; bribery is an accepted practice and considered akin to a commission, tax, or compensation. On the other hand, there are numerous arguments against making such payments: it is viewed as being simply wrong, unacceptable, and illegal. The practice compromises a manager's ethical standards when honesty and fairness should be practised all the time. Some corporations simply refuse to deal with corrupt governments, because in the long term limited benefits exist and once started the practice is unlikely to stop. Bribery illustrates *ethical relativism,* described in Chapter 5. In some cultures and national environments bribery is an acceptable practice, and it is argued that foreigners accept it. Thus, managers can justify acting according to the circumstances in which they find themselves.

Several organizations monitor and measure bribery practices. TI conducts a Bribe Payers Survey, which allows it to evaluate foreign bribery by corporations in more than 20 countries by exploring the frequency of different types of foreign bribery. The three types of bribery assessed included:

- Bribery of high-ranking politicians or political parties.
- Bribery of low-level public officials to "speed things up."
- Use of personal or familiar relationships to win public contracts.

In the survey, Switzerland and the Netherlands practised the least bribery, with a score of 8.8 out of 10. Canada was 6th, with a score of 8.5. American corporations placed tenth, with a score of 8.1. At the other end of the spectrum, Russia ranked last with a score of 6.1, just below China (6.5), Mexico (7.0), and Indonesia (7.1).[11] Another effort at disclosing bribery, "Publish What You Pay," has been undertaken by a coalition of more than 680 NGOs and calls for the mandatory disclosure of all payments to governments made by companies in extractive industries such as oil, gas, and mining.[12]

Canadian corporations and managers must adhere to the *Corruption of Foreign Public Officials Act* when doing business globally. This Act features three offences: bribing of a foreign public official; laundering of property and proceeds; and possession of property and proceeds. In addition to this act, the federal government is participating in anti-corruption initiatives through organizations such as the Organisation for Economic Co-operation and Development (OECD), the Organization of American States, the Council of Europe, the Commonwealth of Nations, and the United Nations.[13]

In March 2011, the OECD released a report pointing out that Canada is doing a poor job at enforcing bribery practices. Canada has prosecuted and convicted only one case, in 2005, and has one ongoing prosecution and more than twenty cases under investigation. The report made the following recommendations to the Canadian government:

- Provide more resources to its lawyers to prosecute more cases.
- Clarify the Act to apply to all conduct, not just "for profit" business.

- Make sanctions more effective.

- Make sure to prosecute Canadian businesspersons for bribery.

- Eliminate factors such as national economic interests and relations with a foreign state from consideration in making a decision to prosecute.[14]

In early 2013, OECD's concern appeared to be confirmed when several Canadian corporations were highlighted in the media for their corrupt behaviour. Several allegations of corruption were facing SNC-Lavalin Inc., a Montreal engineering firm, including alleged ties with the deposed regime of Moammar Gadhafi in Libya, and alleged bribery involving a bridge project in Bangladesh. Griffiths Energy International Inc., a Calgary oil and gas company, was fined $10.5 million for bribing government officials in Chad. The federal government stated that it would be cracking down on the corrupt practices of Canadian corporations.[15]

Corporations operating in the global economy are increasingly disclosing information or being transparent about their activities and behaviour in the countries where they do business. Responsibility for Ethics 15.5 describes one organization's efforts to increase disclosure in the petroleum and mining industries. As Canadian corporations in resource industries operate around the world, Canadian managers are aware of the efforts to avoid corruption. An indicator of an increased effort against corruption and bribery, TRACE International, a non-profit anti-bribery group, argues that anti-bribery enforcement maybe gaining ground.[16] More countries are enacting legislation and taking more enforcement actions.[17]

connect   Want to learn more about **global corporate corruption?**

RESPONSIBILITY FOR ETHICS 15.5

Extractive Industries Transparency Initiative (EITI)

The Extractive Industries Transparency Initiative (EITI) is a global standard that promotes revenue transparency by monitoring and reconciling corporation payments and government revenues at the country level. It believes that in countries that are rich in oil, gas, and minerals, the revenues received from the extraction of these resources should be used to foster economic growth and reduce poverty. When the government systems are inadequate, the revenues may be lost through corruption or used to finance conflicts. EITI aims to strengthen governance by improving transparency and accountability in the extractives sector. The process is overseen by participants from the government, corporations, industry associations, INGOs, institutional investors, and supranational institutions. More than 90 of the world's largest oil, gas, and mining corporations support and actively participate in the EITI process including the Canadian corporations Barrick Gold, Goldcorp, Kinross, and Teck Resources.

Source: Adapted from Extractive Industries Transparency Initiative, accessed January 24, 2016, www.eiti.org.

Human Rights

Human rights are the fundamental rights and freedoms to which all individuals, groups, and societies are entitled. The list of rights involved is large and has been expanded over the years, but one reference point is the United Nations' *Universal Declaration of Human Rights*, adopted in 1948.[18] Canadian corporations operating on a global scale need proactive human rights policies and practices both globally and within Canada. Financing and human talent may be harder to obtain without attention being given to human rights. Respect for human rights is a key to establishing market footholds in developing countries—which is important as they are the largest untapped market, estimated at 3 billion.

Sweatshop Production

The sourcing of products from sweatshops in developing countries—and to a lesser extent within Canada—is an issue with most retailers. Goods are supplied at low costs, but the plants where they are produced violate many human rights through the abuse of workers. The abuses include child labour, low pay, poor working conditions, poor health and safety, and overall mistreatment of workers. This has become a major issue to which retailers have responded; one example is given in Everyday Ethics 15.4.

EVERYDAY ETHICS 15.4

Reitmans (Canada) Limited's Code of Conduct for Suppliers

Most retailers relying upon global sources for merchandise now have supplier codes and require suppliers to follow them. Reitmans, a Canadian clothing retailer, provides an example of such a code. The components of their Code of Conduct for Suppliers include:

- *Child labour*—Workers must be at least 15 years of age. The only exceptions are where 14 years old is allowed by law in a country, or younger if the compulsory school requirement is completed.

- *Forced labour*—Not allowed.

- *Discrimination*—Workers must be hired on the basis of ability and not subjected to discrimination in any aspect of employment.

- *Freedom of Association/Collective Bargaining*—Suppliers will not restrict workers from joining organizations protecting their well-being.

- *Wages & Benefits; Working Hours*—These will be in compliance with all applicable laws and regulations

- *Environment*—Suppliers must comply with all applicable environmental laws and regulations in the country in which they are located.

- *Working conditions*—Workers are to be treated with respect and dignity, and must work in a safe and healthy environment. They must not be subject to corporal punishment or any form of harassment. The required working conditions are listed, as are standards for dormitories if applicable.

Reitmans specifies a monitoring program for all suppliers, and their representatives must be allowed to inspect plants. To enforce the Code, Reitmans has the right to terminate its contract with the supplier if the Code is violated.

Source: Compiled from "Code of Conduct for Suppliers," Reitmans (Canada) Limited, accessed January 24, 2016, http://content.reitmanscanadalimited.com/pdf/code_of_conduct.pdf?_ga=1.180105892.1677103185.1453659477.

In addition to corporations developing policies and codes, many industries also have done so. Many INGOs monitor production facilities, often on behalf of the corporations. Consultants have specialized in the area of verifying the conditions and practices of these plants. Despite all these efforts, some suppliers in developing countries are avoiding labour rules and inspections.[19] Others argue that sweatshops are a stage in the industrial development of a country; they provide employment where there would be little or none and the developing economy is better off, which eventually leads to further economic development.[20]

Global Poverty

Human rights and sweatshop labour abuses are related to the reduction of global poverty. This issue has been receiving more attention in part because of the United Nations' Millennium Development Goals MDG), which identify the needs of the world's poorest. The private corporation will have to be involved if the goals are to be met, and some Canadian corporations have initiated projects to address various goals. Although governments shoulder much of the responsibility for human development, it is in business' interests to participate. An opportunity exists to capture future markets, corporations benefit from the stability of enhanced human development, and the risks of doing business are reduced. Business brings inherent skills to meet the goals, including providing leadership through partnerships and cooperative undertakings.[21] Much progress has been made in accomplishing the MDG and in 2016 they have been replaced by the Sustainable Development Goal listed in Responsibility for Ethics 15.6.

Globalization has increased the reliance on markets and corporations to provide goods and services around the world. The accomplishment of the Millennium Goals requires use of these features of a capitalist economic system.

RESPONSIBILITY FOR ETHICS 15.6

United Nations Sustainable Development Goals

The United Nations is working on a new set of goals, the Sustainable Development Goals (SDG). The SDG are still being developed and an initial proposal is listed below.

2016 presents an unprecedented opportunity to bring the countries and citizens of the world together to embark on a new path to improve the lives of people everywhere.

Countries have adopted a new sustainable development agenda and global agreement on climate change. Explore this site to find out more about the efforts of the UN and its partners to build a better world with no one left behind.

Goal 1: End poverty in all its forms everywhere.

Goal 2: End hunger, achieve food security and improved nutrition and promote sustainable agriculture.

Goal 3: Ensure healthy lives and promote well-being for all at all ages.

Goal 4: Ensure inclusive and equitable quality education and promote lifelong learning opportunities for all,

Goal 5: Achieve gender equality and empower all women and girls.

Goal 6: Ensure availability and sustainable management of water and sanitation for all.

Goal 7: Ensure access to affordable, reliable, sustainable and modern energy for all.

Goal 8: Promote sustained, inclusive and sustainable economic growth, full and productive employment and decent work for all.

Goal 9: Build resilient infrastructure, promote inclusive and sustainable industrialization and foster innovation.

Goal 10: Reduce inequality within and among countries.

Goal 11: Make cities and human settlements inclusive, safe, resilient and sustainable.

Goal 12: Ensure sustainable consumption and production patterns.

Goal 13: Take urgent action to combat climate change and its impacts.

Goal 14: Conserve and sustainably use the oceans, seas and marine resources for sustainable development.

Goal 15: Protect, restore and promote sustainable use of terrestrial ecosystems, sustainably manage forests, combat desertification, and halt and reverse land degradation and halt biodiversity loss.

Goal 16: Promote peaceful and inclusive societies for sustainable development, provide access to justice for all and build effective, accountable and inclusive institutions at all levels.

Goal 17: Strengthen the means of implementation and revitalize the global partnership for sustainable development.

Source: United Nations Sustainable Development Goals, accessed January 24, 2016, http://www.un.org/sustainabledevelopment/ and https://sustainabledevelopment.un.org/sdgs. © (2016) United Nations. Reprinted with the permission of the United Nations.

LO 15.8 The Acceptance of Global Capitalism

The emergence of globalization has occurred with the increasing acceptance of capitalism around the world. The trend to greater reliance on market systems rather than government initiatives is illustrated by some recent initiatives: the "Bottom of the Pyramid" concept, fair trade, microfinance, and increasing entrepreneurship in developing countries.

Business corporations may appropriately play a greater role in alleviating poverty in the world by applying the concept of the Bottom of the Pyramid (BOP). This concept was popularized by an article by C.K. Prahalad and Stuart L. Hart in 2002,[22] and by a book Prahalad wrote on the concept in 2005.[23]

The concept is that corporations should not ignore—as potential customers—the segment of the world's population living in poverty. An estimated 4 billion persons are in this segment, living on less than $2 per day. Individually they do not have much purchasing power, but collectively they do. The market potential for these people is often overlooked as corporations focus on the few wealthy customers or the emerging middle-income people in a developing economy.

If corporations are innovative enough, they can profitably market goods and services to those living in poverty. If corporations succeed in this, they will experience growth and profits while at the same time improving the living conditions of those persons and aiding regional development. This approach empowers those at the bottom by providing new options for improving their state. It allows corporations to make money and at the same time be socially responsible. Thus, the concept appeals to businesses that are pressured by various stakeholders to be more socially responsible.

Prahalad and Hart outlined the commercial infrastructure necessary at the bottom of the pyramid:

- Creating Buying Power: Giving persons in poverty access to credit that can be used to establish economic activity to generate income.
- Shaping Aspirations: This can be accomplished through consumer education and sustainable development of developing countries' resources.
- Tailoring Local Solutions: The solutions include targeted product development appropriate to developing economies and bottom-up innovation.
- Improving Access: Developing distribution systems and communication links within countries to facilitate economic activity and trade.

For success at the bottom of the pyramid, all aspects of this infrastructure must be put together in an appropriate way to facilitate the commercial efforts.

In June 2007, the Aspen Institute's Business and Society Program issued a bulletin on the Bottom of the Pyramid concept. It identified how the concept is being incorporated into the curricula for business programs and the university centres interested in the concept. Teaching materials were also identified. The bulletin asked some interesting questions about the BOP concept:

- Is the concept merely an academic fad, or will the trends of increasing curricular exposure to the topic continue?
- Why is a discussion of the concept noticeably absent from most top academic journals?
- Will corporations address the felt needs of the poor when providing goods and services or rather exploit marketing tactics to promote any potentially profitable product?[24]

Another example of a business approach to addressing the globalization issue relating to the low prices received by producers in developing countries has been fair trade. The Fairtrade Foundation, Oxfam, and Traidcraft have agreed on the following common definition of fair trade: "an alternative approach to conventional international trade. It is a trading partnership which aims at sustainable development for excluded and disadvantaged producers. It seeks to do this by providing better trading conditions, by awareness raising and by campaigning."[25] The fair trade movement is not anti-capitalist, but instead intends to use the market system to enhance the influence of the supplier stakeholder. The best known fair trade product is coffee, and today most retailers carry a fair trade product. Other fair trade products are flowers, spices, and cocoa. The entrepreneurs promoting fair trade products claim that the local suppliers in developing countries are now receiving a higher price for their product. Fair trade was also discussed in Chapter 12.

Microfinance is the provision of financial products, such as micro-credit, micro-insurance, and savings accounts, to persons living in areas of poverty without access to banking services. Organizations providing these services are often referred to as microfinancial institutions (MFIS). Micro-credit has received the most attention and involves making small loans to poor persons to start or expand small businesses. Women are often the entrepreneurs who borrow money. The practice started about 30 years ago; the pioneer in this approach was Muhammad Yunus and the Grameen Bank in Bangladesh (see Everyday Ethics 15.5). Today, as many as 10,000 other institutions are involved in the practice, including government, business foundations, and aid agencies as well as commercial banks.[26]

EVERYDAY ETHICS 15.5

Muhammad Yunus and the Nobel Peace Prize

The 2006 Nobel Peace Prize was won by Muhammad Yunus and the Grameen Bank for initiating the microfinance approach with the poor in Bangladesh. Small loans are made mainly to women to start or expand businesses, with no collateral but with significant interest rates. The loans are for business activity, not for consumption purposes. Yunus formed the Grameen Bank, which is more than 90 percent owned co-operatively by its customers.

Sources: Adapted from "Face Value: Macro Credit," *The Economist*, October 21, 2006, 78; Nobel Prize.org, "The Nobel Peace Prize 2006," http://nobelprize.org/nobel_prizes/peace/laureates/2006/index.html; and Grameen Bank, http://www.grameen-info.org.

Although promoted as an approach to alleviating poverty, microfinancial institutions have been criticized. The primary criticism is the high rates of interest charged, which is at 20 to 30 percent. The rates are justified on the higher costs of administering, making, and collecting the loans and administering small savings accounts. Some MFIS have been accused of pursuing growth by ignoring the ability to pay and using coercive collection tactics. Overlending is another problem, where multiple loans are made to the same person. There has been consideration of regulating the MFIS, for example by limiting the interest rates, but this may discourage lenders and force borrowers to less scrupulous lenders. Other initiatives to improve the industry include the establishment of credit bureaus, requirement of more transparency, and stronger ethical and regulatory framework. These actions are similar to the regulation of the payday loan industry in Canada. Finally, an issue is the morality of profiting by providing services that are intended to alleviate poverty.

The role of small business in improving the circumstances in developing countries has increased. This is illustrated by the Grameen Bank, which is a commercial, profit-making operation. One view of reducing poverty is to rely more on business models and less on aid or charity, which have failed in many cases to reduce poverty. The assumption is that the poor are assisted more by unleashing their energy, creativity, and entrepreneurial spirit. Corporations must realize that doing business with the poor benefits the poor *and* themselves. It will be necessary for some governments to eliminate the barriers to private enterprise or capitalism. Challenges are involved, including poor infrastructure, illiteracy, religious/racial/tribal tensions, crime, corruption, and excessive government regulation.

The trends and drivers behind implementing this new thinking and creating a favourable environment to start engaging the poor include the following:

- Many corporations see a need to break out of mature market sectors.
- Framework conditions in many developing countries are improving.
- Communications are faster and cheaper, making the world a smaller place.
- Public expectations of corporations are changing.
- New and better partners are available.
- Aid and investment are beginning to reinforce one another.[27]

Thousands of examples exist where corporations are cooperating with governments and INGOs in programs to enhance entrepreneurial capability as an approach to reducing poverty. Society benefits from more employment and the corporation increases its business. Despite these developments, the issue of global poverty remains as highlighted by an Oxfam report summarized in Everyday Ethics 15.6

EVERYDAY ETHICS 15.6

Poverty and Oxfam

Oxfam's vision is "a just world without poverty" and its mission is "to build lasting solutions to poverty and injustice with a focus on improving the lives and promoting the rights of women and girls."

In 2016, Oxfam International released a report on the world inequality crisis, that is, the gap between the rich and the poor, which found that it was getting worse. Oxfam concludes that this growing economic inequality is bad for society as it undermines growth and social cohesion. Among the findings of the report were:

- The richest individuals—the 1%—have more wealth than the rest of the world's population. Sixty-two individuals have the same wealth as the 3.6 billion poorest in the world
- The wealth of the richest has grown while the wealth of the bottom half the world's population has fallen.
- A global network of tax havens enables the richest individuals to hide $7.6 trillion.
- The average annual income of the poorest 10 percent of the world's population has risen by less than $3 in the last 25 years.

The report proposed several policy actions that could be taken to address the issue including: pay workers a living wage, promote women's economic equality, share the tax burden fairly, make medicines affordable, and end the era of tax havens.

Source: Adapted from "An Economy for the 1%," Oxfam Canada, accessed January 25, 2016, http://www.oxfam.ca/our-work/publications/an-economy-for-the-1.

Globalization has resulted in a reduction of government involvement in most economies and an increase in the reliance on markets and capitalism to provide society's goods and services. This trend reinforces the definition of globalization stated at the beginning of the chapter. It involves more than economic activities and is interwoven with the social and environmental responsibilities of business. Some question exists as to whether globalization will be influenced by the economic downturn beginning in 2015. It appears that the trend may be slowing, but there is little evidence that it is being reversed.

The current crisis of global capitalism—first in financial markets and now in a recessionary downturn in consumption and production —reveals the dependency of business on an underlying social culture of trust and responsibility

Your advice to Claudia . . .

Many Canadians do not realize that globalization is impacting them in many ways every day. The ethics involved with selling counterfeit and pirated products is one example. Persons purchasing these products will benefit by allowing self-interest to influence their purchase decision. But other stakeholders are harmed, for example Canadian business retailers and their employees. It could be argued that the workers in China benefit, but they are likely working for low wages and in poor working conditions. You advise Claudia that you know her personal ethics and responsibilities are being challenged in this situation and it is important that she is aware of the ethical issues. Globalization impacts everyone in society, often in unexpected ways.

Summary

- The globalization of business has brought numerous issues relating to business' economic, social, and environmental responsibilities. The impact of globalization on the Canadian corporation has been, and will continue to be, extensive. (LO 15.1)

- A general definition of globalization is a process of decreasing constraints on the interactions among the nations and peoples of the world. The three global dimensions important to business are economic, political, and social. Those in favour of globalization (globalists) and those opposed (anti-globalists) continue to debate the pros and cons. (LO 15.2)

- Many non-governmental organizations focus on globalization. They have exerted considerable influence on international corporations and in some cases are partnering with business on projects to reduce poverty in developing countries. (LO 15.3)

- Supranational institutions are influencing globalization economically, socially, and environmentally. Four prominent supranational institutions described are the World Bank, the International Monetary Fund, the International Labour Organization, and the World Trade Organization. (LO 15.4)

- Globalization affects Canadian business and society in several ways. Canadian business must remain competitive with corporations from other countries. The International Code of Ethics for Canadian Business provides guidelines for corporate behaviour. Many Canadian corporations are setting an example for corporate citizenship in developing countries. (LO 15.5)

- Several international standards of conduct have been developed that provide guidelines for corporate activities in developing countries. These standards can also be used as frameworks for reporting of their global responsibilities. (LO 15.6)

- Along with globalization comes the trend to rely on market systems and corporations more than requesting government involvement. This trend presents some special challenges for business, including responding to corruption, accommodating human rights in all operations and in particular in sweatshops, and contributing to the accomplishment of the UN's Millennium Development Goals. (LO 15.7)

- Globalization has embraced capitalism. Today, corporations are more likely to be privatized than nationalized. Microfinance and fair trade are examples of initiatives based more on business models than government ones. Entrepreneurship is increasingly taking hold in developing countries. (LO 15.8)

Key Terms

Globalization

Economic globalization

Political globalization

Social or cultural globalization

Globalists

Anti-globalists

International non-governmental organizations (INGOs)

Supranational institution

Corruption

Bribery

Human rights

Microfinance

Critical Thinking and Discussion Questions

1. Why has globalization occurred at this time?
2. Why is globalization so difficult to define?
3. Do the benefits of globalization offset the drawbacks?
4. Do INGOs play a significant role in business' response to globalization?
5. How do supranational institutions influence globalization?
6. Why is the competitiveness of Canadian business important?
7. What function do the various standards of conduct have?
8. What happens when corporations do not adhere to the standards or guidelines of conduct?
9. How do corporations deal with corruption?
10. Why should business support the UN's Millennium Development Goals?
11. What is the relationship between capitalism and globalization?

Cases

15.1 THE ETHICS OF BIOPROSPECTING

Bioprospecting, or biodiversity prospecting, is the "examination of biological resources for features that may be of value for commercial development." It involves collecting and testing plants, animals, and microorganisms to find the features as well as collecting knowledge of the resource from indigenous peoples. Bioprospecting results in the development of drugs, improvements to crop yields and features, and various industrial products.

Companies, in particular pharmaceutical firms, search the globe for biological resources that can be commercially exploited. Many of the products developed are beneficial; for example, more than 60 percent of all cancer drugs have been created from bioprospecting discoveries. However, there are few regulations governing the use of the biological resources, and indigenous peoples in developing countries seldom benefit financially from the discoveries.

An attempt to correct this situation was the Convention of Biological Diversity, produced in 1992 and ratified by 188 countries—but not the United States, which argues that it stifles innovation and undermines the patent system. Peru and Brazil have attempted to challenge the American position but they have been unsuccessful in overturning U.S. patents on several bioprospecting-discovered products.

The maca plant, grown by the Quechua Indians of Peru for hundreds of years, illustrates the issue. A concoction is made from its tuber roots that is said to boost stamina and sex drive. The Indians believe that the plant is a part of nature's bounty and belongs to no one in particular.

In 2001, an American company, PureWorld Botanicals, received a U.S. patent for "MacaPure," an extract of the maca's active libido-enhancing compounds. The Peruvians view this as "biopiracy" and plan to make it a test case. The companies that develop products from biological resources argue that it takes millions of dollars and extensive research to develop them. Several maca-based products—from powders and pills to jams and jellies—are in existence and the export of the plant helps Peru's economy.

Questions

1. Who owns the maca plant?
2. What stakeholders are involved?
3. What are the ethical, social, and environmental issues?
4. What can, or should, be done to resolve the controversy surrounding bioprospecting and, in particular, the maca plant?

Sources: Based on Government of New Zealand, Ministry of Economic Development, "What is Bioprospecting?" accessed August 9, 2016, https://www.beehive.govt.nz/release/bioprospecting-questions-and-answers; and Rick Vecchio, "Who Owns the Maca Plant?" *The Telegram* (St. John's, NL), January 8, 2007, B1.

15.2 FOOD RETAILING IN INDIA: REVOLUTION OR EVOLUTION?

Modern retailing approaches are evolving in India, especially in the food sector. It is common practice to shop for groceries in *kirana* stores, small neighbourhood shops and produce markets operated by entrepreneurs. In these retail outlets, the fruits and vegetables often are not good quality or in good condition, and the shops are not attractive or comfortable for shoppers. The owners are known for being wasteful, buying in small quantities, selling at high prices, lacking storage capability, and having no expertise in inventory control. There are about 12 million of these small family-operated outlets. In addition, there are 200 million pushcart vendors and hawkers who depend on the highly fragmented retail market for their livelihood.

Large Indian corporations have entered the market, such as Reliance Retail Ltd., with 300 stores in 30 cities across India. Some are opening modern North American–style supermarkets and hypermarkets while others are operating chains of produce shops. These stores are air-conditioned, brightly lit and clean, with trained workers. A greater variety of higher quality fruits and vegetables are available. Goods are neatly packaged, accurately weighed, and refrigerated. Most importantly, prices are lower. Modern retailing supply chain practices are being introduced, including distribution efficiency, high technology farming, and waste reduction. Some suggest that the farmers will receive more for their products as middlemen will be eliminated from the supply chain.

Another dimension of this issue is the restriction on foreign retailers' entry into the Indian market. Foreign retailers cannot sell directly to consumers. To circumvent this regulation, foreign corporations are entering at the wholesale level or in joint ventures or partnerships with Indian corporations. For example, Walmart has a joint venture with Bharti Enterprises, an Indian conglomerate. Other foreign retailers are attempting to enter the Indian market, including the U.K.'s Tesco PLC, and France's Carrefour SA.

The operators of the smaller stores have protested this trend and have called upon government to stop the large corporations from entering the market. They feel that they cannot compete with the new retailers and would become unemployed with no other form of work available to them. The Indian government is monitoring this retail revolution closely and is under political pressure from the small shopkeepers, opposition parties, and socialist groups. There is concern that the arrival of modern retailing reduces the opportunities for self-employment, especially among the poor. The state of Uttar Pradesh even ordered the closing of ten Reliance supermarkets to placate protestors.

Economists argue that the retail market, estimated at US$328 billion, is large enough for both traditional and modern retailers. The liberalization of retail trade in India is not yet a revolution, and barely an evolutionary trend. In November 2012, the Indian government announced that it would allow foreign investments in supermarkets and department stores.

Questions

1. Who are the stakeholders involved and what are their positions?
2. What are the issues relating to business and society? What dilemmas arise for Indian business and society?
3. How are the harms and benefits of the retail trade liberalization distributed?
4. Should foreign corporations be allowed to operate freely in India?

Sources: Adapted from Steve Hamm and Nandini Lakshman, "Widening Aisles for Indian Shoppers," *BusinessWeek*, April 30, 2007, 44; Rajesh Mahapatra, "Wal-Mart Taps into Booming Indian Market," *The Globe and Mail*, August 7, 2007, B8; Anuj Choppa, "Retail Giants Push India's Shopkeepers to the Brink," *The Globe and Mail*, October 30, 2007, B17, and "India Retreats on Retail Reform," *The Globe and Mail*, December 8, 2011, p. B8.

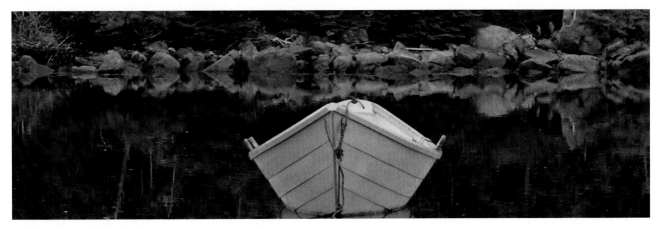

Used with the permission of Dennis Flynn

CHAPTER 16

The Socialization of Capitalism

LEARNING OUTCOMES

After studying this chapter, you will be able to:

LO 16.1   Define and learn about the Fourth Sector of the economy.

LO 16.2   Recognize that the socialization of capitalism can be achieved through a corporate sustainability strategy.

LO 16.3   Identify new corporate structures involved with socialization.

LO 16.4   Become aware of concepts associated with socialization and how it is expressed in the economy.

LO 16.5   Link the socialization of capitalism to business school programs and activities.

What would you do if...?

As Leah Bromberger was leaving to catch the subway to work in downtown Toronto, she picked up a bag of clothing she no longer wanted. She planned to drop off the bag at the Goodwill store located on the way to the subway. To her surprise when she got to the store there was a sign saying it had closed. The donation box was overflowing and many bags of clothing were stacked up against the store front.

Goodwill Industries is a non-profit social enterprise that retrained people for new jobs, by helping people develop job skills. Its vision was "Everyone is WORKING in sustainable communities" and its mission "Changing lives and communities through the power of WORK." The local store is a part of Goodwill Industries International, a network of 165 community-based agencies in the United States and Canada with affiliates in 13 other countries operating 2,700 stores and an online shopping site.

Goodwill is well known for operating stores selling recycled clothing. Goodwill Canada is also involved with several initiatives including: a Goodwill Career Centre to assist persons to obtain employment; Goodwill Pivotal Services providing warehousing and production space; a food operation known as Edgar and Joe's Café; Impact Loan to assist entrepreneurs financially; an information sharing initiative through Bridges Out of Poverty | Circles®; Goodwill Commercial Solutions, which provides commercial and light industrial services; and electronics recycling. Its operations rely on volunteers and donations from citizens. Goodwill is a registered charity and donations may qualify for a tax deductible receipt.

When Leah got to work she saw newspaper stories about the closing of 16 Goodwill stores and 10 donation locations in the Toronto area. Immediately affected were about 430 employees, many of whom had disabilities or criminal records and earned on the average $14 per hour. The store had sales of $28.1 million in 2014 but had a deficit of $1.4 million even with the $4 million in assistance from the Government of Ontario. Another challenge was the high rents for the stores especially since it was a low-margin business. The employees were unionized and recently there was a disagreement about staffing during winter months. Goodwill proposed decreasing hours but the union wanted full-time employees kept at regular hours and part-time staff laid off. This reduced Goodwill's staffing flexibility and created labour unrest.

The clothing recycling industry had become more competitive with Salvation Army Stores and operations like Value Village. Rather than donating clothing, some consumers were using Internet sites such as Kijiji to sell unwanted clothing. The Goodwill management was exploring options in an attempt to put together a recovery plan. It was talking with the union and other stakeholders.

Leah wondered about the viability of non-profit organizations to operate businesses as a failure of these organizations had similar consequences to what occurs when a private sector corporation failed. Maybe it was time to rethink her support for this type of organization.

What is your advice to Leah?

Sources: Adapted from "Goodwill Toronto Region Closes Locations Temporarily," Goodwill Industries Media Release, January 18, 2016, accessed February 5, 2016, http://goodwillindustries.ca/goodwill-toronto-region-closes-locations-temporarily/; Goodwill Canada, accessed February 5, 2016, http://goodwillindustries.ca/; and "16 Ontario Goodwill Stores Shut Down," *The Star* (Toronto), January 17, 2016, accessed February 5, 2016, http://www.thestar.com/news/gta/2016/01/17/16-ontario-goodwill-stores-shut-down.html.

The title of this chapter requires some explanation as the "Socialization of Capitalism" is not a commonly used term. The **socialization of capitalism** is the process through which the business system conforms to the expectations of society resulting in desired, socially responsible outcomes. The process recognizes society's consensus about the role of capitalism and establishes norms, customs, and values that will enable capitalism to adjust to the society's desires or expectations relating to social purpose.

There is increasing emphasis on the social purpose of capitalism in addition to its traditional financial focus. Throughout this text, there have been many examples of this emphasis:

- Chapters 1 and 2: The discussion of various forms of capitalism including responsible, stakeholder, clean, conscious and creative.
- Chapters 3 and 4: The development whereby corporations now consider a greater variety of stakeholders when making decisions. This has led to the development of engagement practices and a greater effort at issue identification and analysis.
- Chapters 7, 8, and 9: All the forms of corporate social responsibility and the accountability of corporations for their ethical, social and environmental responsibilities in addition to financial ones.
- Chapter 10: Through regulation, government and other stakeholders have been involved in encouraging corporations to be more socially responsible.
- Chapter 11: Ownership of corporations is now influenced by owners preferring responsible investing.
- Chapter 12: Stakeholders in the marketplace, consumers, employees, competitors, and suppliers, influence the corporation in a matter that increases its social purpose.
- Chapter 13: Civil society stakeholders, NGOs, the media, think tanks, and religious and educational institutions, are also increasing corporate social awareness.
- Chapters 14 and 15: Today, business corporations can seldom ignore their social, environmental and economic responsibilities as they relate to the environment and globalization.

Thus, there is a movement toward making capitalism more aware of the impact of its actions on society. At the same time, social organizations such as charities are using economic or commercial methods to finance their social goals. This chapter will describe various approaches to socialization that is occurring in Canadian capitalism. The first section describes the concept of the Fourth Sector, that is, a sector of the economy in addition to the traditional private, social, and public sectors. The Fourth Sector illustrates the interrelations between these sectors for social purposes.

The socialization of capitalism is illustrated by a sustainability approach to strategic management that is occurring in many corporations. Several sections discuss aspects of socialization that are occurring in Canadian capitalism: new corporate structures, different approaches to social undertakings in society, and the approaches to social integration. The final section describes the impact of socialization on educational programs in business schools.

LO 16.1   Socialization of Capitalism and the Fourth Sector[1]

■ connect   Want to learn more about **the types of capitalism?**

One approach to illustrating the extent of socialization of capitalism is to look at the traditional sectors in the economy, private, social, and public. The **private sector** is that part of economy not controlled and operated by government. It is run by individuals and corporations whose intention is to make profits. It is sometimes referred to as the citizen or free market sector. The **social sector** includes charities and non-profit organizations and is also referred to as the non-profit or voluntary sector. Technically this sector operates privately but a distinction is made from the private sector as it operates for social purposes with no intention to make profits. The **public sector** is operated by government departments, agencies, and organizations usually not to operate businesses or make profits. Governments function to provide such things as a legal system, policing and prison services, defense organizations, transportation infrastructure, and educational and health institutions.

In the economy, organizations in the three sectors are changing because of pressures from society. With its entrepreneurial incentive and efficient organizational skills, capitalism has influenced the social and public sectors. In the social sector, non-profit or charitable organizations are using business approaches to commercialize some of their activities. Likewise, the public sector uses business approaches to commercialize some of its operations and has even privatized, or sold off, operating units to the private sector.

There are reasons for this in each sector. The private sector is under pressure from stakeholders to be socially and environmentally responsible. The social sector, with its limited access to resources, has resorted to using business practices to enable them to fulfil their missions. The public sector partners with the private sector or utilizes business practices to provide the goods and services for which it is responsible. An example is the **public–private partnership (PPP)** defined as a cooperative venture between the public and private sectors, built on the expertise of each partner, that best meets clearly defined public needs through the appropriate allocation of resources, risks, and rewards. These partnerships among the sectors increase the involvement of the private sector, for-profit, and non-profit in the provision of government infrastructure and services. All this is necessary as society's stakeholders are demanding that inequity, poverty, short-term thinking, and greed be addressed.

In order to address society's concerns, new ways of thinking leading to changes in the design of organizational structures. Existing forms of organizations in private, social, and public sectors are not sufficient to generate the economic, social, and environmental benefits being demanded. The result is a **fourth sector** of the economy where new organizational forms integrate business or private, social and public methods, sometimes referred to as *hybrid organizations*. The result is illustrated in Figure 16.1 in which examples of fourth sector organizations are given.

While the mission and method of many new organizations in the business (private), social, and government (public) sectors are becoming steadily more similar, something more than simple blurring of the boundaries is occurring. Pioneering organizations in the three sectors are in fact converging toward a blending of economic, social, and environmental aims using business approaches. Not everyone agrees that a fourth sector exists but rather that organizations in the three sectors are merely working together to address society's concerns.[2]

The following sections describe some of the initiatives that are in some way addressing the integration of economic, social, and environmental purposes in today's organizations.

FIGURE 16.1 *Sectors of the Economy*

Private Sector	Social Sector	Public Sector
↓	↓	↓
Social Initiatives or Trends	**Commercialization of Activities**	**Commercialization and Privatization of Activities**
↓	↓	↓
	Fourth Sector Examples	
Corporate Social Responsibility	Social Entrepreneurship	Government-Owned Corporations
Social Auditing	Microfinance	Sale of Corporations and Other Assets
Sustainability Reporting	Co-operatives	Public–Private Partnerships
Stakeholder Engagement	Faith-Based Enterprises	Privatizing Goods and Services
Environmental Management	Fair Trade	
Volunteerism	For-benefit Corporations	
Employee Ownership	B-corporations	
Philanthropy		
Community Investment		
Social Impact Management		
Corporate Sponsorship		
Green Marketing		
Social License		
Social Venture Philanthropy		

LO 16.2 Socialization of Capitalism Through Corporate Sustainability Strategy

Social, ethical, and environmental responsibilities are increasingly being integrated into the strategic management process. This widely practised planning approach has traditionally focused on the economic responsibilities and the financial performance of the corporation, but this approach is changing. The result is a **sustainability strategy**, a plan that views economic, ethical, social, and environmental responsibilities more intensively and integrates corporate social responsibility (CSR) into all facets of the corporation's operations. A sustainability strategy is also referred to as a CSR strategy by some corporations.

There is no one approach to developing a sustainability or CSR strategy, and the strategies developed vary with management preferences, how well managers understand CSR, and industry environments. In order to understand the different variations of a sustainability strategy, a corporation's approach can be assessed using a four-stage continuum:

Amoral sustainability strategy

↓

Compliance-based sustainability strategy

↓

Emerging sustainability strategy

↓

Comprehensive sustainability strategy

The purpose of this continuum is to assess the extent of a corporation's sustainability strategy. It also provides guidance to the development of plans and to make improvements in an existing strategy. Although four stages are identified, it is unlikely corporations will fit perfectly in one stage. Table 16.1 identifies some of the characteristics of each strategy. This book provides illustrations of CSR being practised by Canadian corporations in many different ways.

With an amoral sustainability strategy, the corporation ignores sustainability but cannot be viewed necessarily as deliberately doing so. It simply does not address economic, social, and environmental issues in a deliberate or explicit manner. Also, some corporations may consciously avoid or resist the consideration of sustainability practices. Corporations adopting this strategy are vulnerable to sustainability issues as their lack of attention to them reduces their preparedness if problems or issues arise.

Some consideration is given to sustainability in a compliance-based strategy, but it is motivated by legal requirements and the possibility of public backlash or disapproval of corporate behaviour. Thus, sustainability is accepted because of the possible economic consequences of doing nothing and the fear of negative publicity. The strategy is legalistic, focusing on what should not be done, what is within the law, and what is required by government.

Strategy extends beyond what is legally required and the corporation voluntarily considers its economic, ethical, and environmental responsibilities in an emerging sustainability strategy. Many more aspects of ethics and corporate social responsibility are taken into account.

The comprehensive sustainability strategy becomes a key component of the corporate strategy in corporations that fully understand and embrace their economic, social, and environmental responsibilities. Implementation requires integration with all aspects of the corporation's planning and operations. This process needs managers who understand sustainability, and corporations are establishing management positions to oversee sustainability or corporate social responsibility. The positions have a variety of names, and can be as high-level as a vice-president. The Network for Business Sustainability identified "10 Things New Sustainability Managers Need to Know":

1. Whether there is payback on investments in sustainability, for example in cost savings or customer loyalty.
2. How to make sustainability a part of corporate culture.
3. How to make the supply chain competitive and sustainable.
4. Whether customers will pay more for sustainable products or services.
5. How to best engage stakeholders.
6. How to identify the best measurements of a corporation's environmental impact.
7. Whether corporate sustainability attracts and retains employees.
8. How a corporation can mitigate and adapt to climate change.
9. The meaning of business sustainability.
10. How to identify resources, including research, about sustainability and related issues.[3]

In addition, corporations and managers must be aware of the challenges and opportunities presented by the trend towards thinking in sustainable terms. Each year the Network for Business Sustainability prepares a list of the opportunities, and in 2015 the list was:

- Collaborating for sustainability
- Addressing climate change
- Building stakeholder trust

- Designing effective sustainability communications
- Turning sustainability into strategic priority
- Transitioning to green products and services
- Respecting free, prior and informed consent (consultation and accommodation with impacted stakeholders)[4]

TABLE 16.1 Main Characteristics of Sustainability Strategies

	Amoral	Compliance-based	Emerging	Comprehensive
Awareness	Little or none; avoids sustainability practices	Motivated by legal requirements and public disapproval; some written policies	Beyond legal requirements; voluntarily accepts 3E responsibilities	Full acceptance and understanding; key element in economic strategy
Stakeholder focus	Owners	Most likely customers, lenders, employees, suppliers, and government	All identified and consciously considered	Stakeholder engagement
Management/staff involvement	No training or rewards	Negative sanctions; some rewards Enforcement by HR and legal departments	Responsibility of senior manager or compliance officer Support resources provided Stronger focus on rewards and recognition	High-level management responsibility Integrated with compensation and performance appraisal systems
Board involvement	Unlikely	Restricted to that legally required and to maintain corporate reputation; no committee	Receive regular reports; possibility of CSR committee	Board committee oversees
Ethics program	None explicit Reflects management views	Rules-based Possible code of conduct	Codes of conduct and ethics Deliberate program	Complete, explicit program
CSR program	Ad hoc donations	Donations, sponsorships, voluntarism Public relations focus	More comprehensive, with community investment	Complete, explicit program
Reporting	None	Possible mention in annual reports	More extensive; possible separate report	Separate report with evaluation such as Global Reporting Initiative (GRI)

RESPONSIBILITY FOR ETHICS 16.1

The Transformational Company

A guide that managers can use to achieve comprehensive corporate sustainability is "The Transformational Company Qualities." The guide provides a benchmark for managers who wish to improve their corporation's social and environmental impact. The benchmark was developed by the Canadian Business for Social Responsibility (CBSR), "a non-profit member organization with a mission to accelerate and scale corporate social and environmental sustainability in Canada and challenge the 'business as usual' model." CBSR researched a new approach to corporate social responsibility and identified 19 qualities of a transformational company that could be used as a guideline for corporations.

The list of the qualities is available at http://cbsr.ca/transformationalcompany/, which the CBSR is willing to share so that corporations can improve their CSR and sustainability efforts in order to systematically address society risks, challenges, and opportunities.

To provide examples of the qualities, CBSR published case studies from across a variety of industry sectors and companies. CBSR believes that the "Transformational Company Qualities foster innovation, enhance a company's social license to grow, foster customer and supplier loyalty and help to attract, retain and engage employees."

Source: Adapted from Canadian Business for Social Responsibility (CBSR) website at http://www.cbsr.ca/.

An approach to achieving a comprehensive sustainability strategy is through the use of **strategic management**, the process through which a corporation establishes its mission and objectives, analyzes the environment and resource capabilities in order to formulate strategy, creates the organizational systems and processes needed to implement the strategy, and devises mechanisms for evaluating performance. Managers are increasingly recognizing the potentially positive relationship between sustainability and financial return. Many corporations are consciously using the strategic management model to improve their performance economically, ethically, and environmentally. Another model of corporate sustainability strategy to accomplish the same is described in Responsibility for Ethics 16.1, The Transformational Company.

Some managers are using sustainability concepts as rhetoric to maximize profits, or appear to be formulating and implementing a sustainability strategy when in reality it is superficial or done without commitment. However, many corporations today are taking sustainability seriously, viewing it as critical to their success or longevity.

LO 16.3 Socialization of Capitalism and New Corporate Structures

Some new forms of corporate structures have emerged that facilitate the integration of social and economic purposes.

Social Enterprise

There are many definitions of social enterprise and the one given in Chapter 8 was "a model of business operation where some or all profits are deliberately used to further social aims." One reason for several definitions might be because there are several types, as outlined in Table 16.2.

The type used is determined by the need for operational flexibility, financing and funding sources, preferential taxation treatment, and public perception. The use of social enterprises reduces reliance on donations from the public or corporations, foundations, or governments. In all cases, a feature of social enterprises is that they use business structures to accomplish a social purpose.[5] More information on social enterprise in Canada is available at The Social Enterprise Council of Canada (SECC), "an alliance of social enterprise leaders who leverage their networks, knowledge and experience in order to build a strong and enabling environment for social enterprise."[6]

TABLE 16.2   Types of Social Enterprise

Type	Characteristic
Non-profit organization	Have charitable status. Organized only for charitable purposes. Must meet Canada Revenue rules. Can issue donation receipts.
Non-profit organization	Without charitable status. Exempt from taxation. Operated only for charitable purposes.
Co-operative	Member controlled and operates for their social benefit. If profits occur, returned to members.
Hybrid corporation	With caps on dividends and asset distribution. Examples: Community Contribution Company in B.C. and Community Interest Company in NS. No tax advantages.
For-profit corporation	Owned by non-profit organization and can operate as subsidiary earning profits
For-profit corporation	Owned by investors. Can involve private returns to owners as well as committing a portion of profits to social purposes.

☐ connect   Want to learn more about **Canadian social enterprises**?

For-benefit and B-Corporations

A social enterprise can operate as is a **for-benefit (or benefit) corporation** that aims to make profits but also has a strong commitment to addressing social and environmental problems. For-benefit corporations are expected to have a material impact on society and to consider how their actions affect stakeholders. Accountability and transparency are requirements, and they are expected to publicly report their social and environmental performance using recognized third-party standards.[7] In the United States, several states have passed legislation allowing for the incorporation of for-benefit corporations, giving them legal status. No for-benefit incorporation legislation has been passed in Canada as it is considered unnecessary.[8]

A variation on the for-benefit corporation is the **B Corporation (or B Corp)**. A B-Corp also operates to make profits but has a strong commitment to addressing social and environmental problems. A certification process is required in order to be eligible to receive the designation of B Corp. The requirements for certification are making amendments to corporate documents—for example, bylaws—to permit boards of directors to consider other stakeholders, and meeting rigorous and independent standards of social and environmental accountability and transparency.

In Canada the certification is performed by the non-profit MaRS Centre for Impact Investing, Toronto. There are over 1,200 Certified B Corporations in 38 countries across 121 different industries. There are 110 in Canada in 7 provinces and one territory. B Corporations are a diverse community with a unifying goal to redefine success in business.[9] Everyday Ethics 16.1 lists examples of Canadian B Corporations.

One organization could operate as several types of organizations; for example, a new corporate form organization, a charitable organization, and a profit-making enterprise. The result is several organizational entities under one umbrella organization forming a portfolio. The following section describes an approach to managing this portfolio or organizations.

EVERYDAY ETHICS 16.1

Examples of Canadian B Corporations

Bullfrog Power, Toronto, ON—A green energy provider to homes and businesses through renewable energy solutions that reduce the impact on the environment.

Salt Spring Coffee, Richmond, B.C.—Coffee roasters that have formed farmer partnerships with a vision to be at the leading edge of coffee in quality, sustainability, pioneering, and origin.

PeaceWorks Technology Solutions, Waterloo, ON—Provides technology solutions that enable organizations to achieve their mission with increased ease and efficiency.

Enviro-Stewards, Elmira, ON—A company of engineers and scientists helping clients conserve their resources and effectively address their environmental liabilities.

Impakt—This B Corp believes corporations and civil society organizations should have a compelling social purpose and promotes various projects to accomplish this.

Sources: Compiled from Bullfrog Power, accessed August 9, 2016, www.bullfrogpower.com/our-story/; Salt Spring Coffee, accessed February 3, 2016, www.saltspringcoffee.com; PeaceWorks, accessed February 3, 2016, peaceworks.ca/about-us; Enviro-Stewards, accessed February 3, 2016, www.enviro-stewards.com/; and Impakt, accessed February 3, 2016, http://impaktcorp.com/#about.

Social Enterprise/Non-profit Sustainability Matrix

Social enterprises and non-profit organizations must consider their sustainability in terms of how well they accomplish their social aims or objectives and how they are able to maintain themselves financially. As with for-profit corporations, they must think strategically to survive. One approach to assessing strategic sustainability is to evaluate the organization on two dimensions: its purpose, that is, the social impact on society intended in the organization's mission, and whether or not the organization is financially viable.[10]

The assessment of the social impact depends on the mission of the organization. Some general criteria could be: the contribution to the intended mission, for example, jobs created or clients serviced; how well the services were performed; evidence that an unmet need was addressed; contributions to the community; and cooperation with other organizations. Financial viability would be assessed against the level of expenses and availability of funding, the meeting of budgets, the success of revenue generating enterprises, and the diversity of funding sources. The matrix in Figure 16.2 illustrates the four strategic sustainability possibilities created by degree of social impact versus financial viability.

Cell 1 indicates that the organization is making a substantial social impact but may have inadequate funding to sustain this level of activity. Cell 2 is a *status quo* situation where a modest impact is being made but at the same time, finances are sufficient. In Cell 3 the situation is one where there is sufficient funding for the social impact being made, and the enterprise could reassess its social impact, or reallocate funding. The best situation is illustrated in Cell 4 there substantial funding is available for the social impact being made.

The Matrix can be used to assess the strategic sustainability on an organization in two situations. A social enterprise or non-profit organization could assess itself to ascertain where it is on the matrix and then take the appropriate action. For example, if the enterprise assesses themselves in Cell 1, it will seek more funding. The second situation is where a social enterprise or non-profit organization has several programs or operating units. The programs should be balanced against one another. For example, it may be appropriate that programs in cells 3 and 4 could support or subsidize programs in Cell 1.

Social enterprises and non-profit organizations should think and operate in strategic sustainable approaches the same manner as commercial enterprises.

FIGURE 16.2 *Sustainability Matrix*

LO 16.4   Socialization of Capitalism Concepts and Expressions

There are many concepts and expressions of the socialization of capitalism in the academic literature, the business media, and in practice. This section describes several of the most common ones.

Social Licence

In Chapter 1, social licence is defined as the privilege of operating in society with minimal formalized restrictions—that is, legislation, regulation, or market requirements—based on maintaining public trust by doing what is acceptable to stakeholders in the business and society relationship. Social licence is a term that is increasingly appearing in media stories.

In a general sense, social licence involves society's trust that the activities of business are legitimate and consistent with social expectations and the values of stakeholders. Social licence is based on ethics, values, expectations, and self-regulation and is considered preferable to social or government control, which is based on regulation, legislation, litigation, and compliance. In practice, a balance exists between social licence and control, where the former is a proactive approach and the latter reactive. The balance can be shifted with intervention in the marketplace by government or the actions or demands of stakeholders—for example, through consumer boycotts.

In recent years, social licence has been a concept applied to individual projects. This is significant in Canada as a major portion of the economy is based on the resource industries where development projects involve social and environmental issues or risks. As a result, the application of social licence has become a concept increasingly discussed. Today, most new projects require the approval of the local community and other stakeholders, in particular NGOs. A social licence is based upon the beliefs, perceptions, and opinions held by the stakeholders, and is in effect granted by those harmed or benefiting from the project. The life cycle of the project is involved, including a properly conducted environmental assessment, careful design of the project, effective operation practices, and a closure strategy.

Some business persons are questioning the need for such a licence. They claim that the harms of development projects should be balanced with the creation of jobs, generation of business activity, and encouragement of investment. The rules, procedures, and processes for obtaining a social licence are vague making it difficult to obtain. Besides, there is already in existence a regulatory system, such as exemplified by the National Energy Board and environmental assessment agencies, that have been set up by government to oversee most development projects. The social licence is in addition to these formal requirements meaning that not only government must be satisfied but also another stakeholder, that is, society. The requirements for obtaining the social licence are too open-ended, undefined, and biased with unaccountable tests. According to the critics, this should not be the basis for decision making and the stakeholders involved, in effect, have too much power. There is uncertainty concerning which stakeholders should be consulted, for example, NGOs, business, courts, and public opinion. Also, there is an issue relating to how the feedback should be measured and evaluated for its significance. Perfect consensus is doubtful, especially for controversial projects. Thus, two licences are necessary, the first from the regulatory agency or government, and a second one from society. Some business persons wonder if the public interest has been ignored in this complicated process.

The existence of the social license is another indication of the need to integrate economic, social, and environment issues between business and society. Corporations and their managers must develop the skills and competences to deal with this development.

Social Innovation

In a general sense, social innovations are new ideas, products, services, institutions and relationships that offer a new way of addressing economic, social and environmental challenges. Examples include: emissions trading, fair trade, the emergence of cooperatives, and umbrella fundraising organizations. Social innovations occur at the edges of the private, social and public sectors of the economy and might be considered a part of the fourth sector. One definition of **social innovation** is "a novel solution to a social problem that is more effective, efficient, sustainable, or just than current solutions" where the "value created accrues primarily to society rather than to private individuals."[11]

Advocates of social innovation believe that society's most difficult and important problems cannot be understood and solved without involving the private, social, and public sectors of the economy. This involves an exchange of ideas and values, shifts in roles and values, and the integration of private capital with public and philanthropic support. Some social innovations permanently alter the perceptions, behaviours, and structures in society. An example of the changes in corporate structures is given in the previous section where social enterprise and for-benefits corporations were discussed. Social innovation is another expression of the socialization of capitalism and two examples of Canadian organizations involved with social innovation are described in Everyday Ethics 16.2.

EVERYDAY ETHICS 16.2

Two Canadian Social Innovation Organizations

There are many organizations involved with social innovation and the following represent different approaches.

The Centre for Social Innovation (CSI)—This is a social enterprise with a mission to increase the presence of social innovation in Toronto and around the world. CSI believes that society is facing unprecedented economic, environmental, social, and cultural challenges, and that new innovations are the key to turning these challenges into opportunities to improve communities and the planet. Its members include non-profits, charities, and social ventures employing over 2,500 people and generating annual revenues of $250 million. It partners across sectors to run programs such as the Ontario Catapult Microloan Fund and the Agents of Change programs. It has published a guide on innovation in social finance, *The Community Bond*. Community bonds have been used to purchase two buildings in downtown Toronto to support social innovation.

The McConnell Foundation—The Foundation's purpose is to enhance Canada's ability to address complex social, environmental and economic challenges and one program is the Social Innovation Fund. The Fund is to support work that will result in breakthrough ideas and approaches, game changing strategies and collaborations, and continuous innovation. The Fund supports work on early stage innovations, scaling up successful innovations, and multi-sector collaborations.

Source: Adapted from "About the Centre for Social Innovation" and "Social Innovation," Centre for Social Innovation, accessed February 9, 2016, http://socialinnovation.ca/about and http://socialinnovation.ca/about/social-innovation; and "About" and "The McConnell Social Innovation Fund," The McConnell Foundation, accessed February 9, 2016, http://www.mcconnellfoundation.ca/en/about and http://mcconnellfoundation.ca/en/programs/social-innovation-fund.

Social Impact Investing

Social impact investing is the financing of initiatives to address social and environmental challenges and that generates a financial return and measurable benefits to society. The new forms of capital and investment vehicles used include microfinance, various types of bonds including social impact, green and community, venture philanthropy, social enterprises, B Corps, and socially focused mutual funds. These new forms act as a bridge between the private, social, and public sectors with regard to the financing of initiatives. The initiatives can relate to a wide range of investments including in clean technology, green construction, renewable energy, water, microfinance, sustainable agriculture and food, and community economic development, for example, affordable housing, and health and educational facilities.

Impact investment is different from traditional investment in three ways: (1) Investors expect to receive a financial return with a defined societal impact. These investors include: high net worth individuals, foundations, community finance organizations (Aboriginal financial institutions and community loan funds), financial institutions (credit unions and chartered banks), pension funds, and governments. (2) Investees' business models are constructed to seek both financial and social value. (3) Both investors and investees expect to be able to measure social impact. The financing tools used include social impact bonds, community bonds, and green bonds.

There are several impact measurement frameworks:

- Impact Reporting and Investment Standards (IRIS) and the Global Impact Investment Rating System (GIIRS). These frameworks allow investors to compare across sectors, regions, and organizational sizes.
- Social Return on Investment (SROI). This framework is used to assign monetary value to the social value created by the initiatives financed.
- Environmental, Social and Governance (ESG) metrics. These are commonly used in conventional financing.
- Demonstrating Value. This is a measurement tool that combines business performance monitoring with social impact evaluation.

Governments are also involved in building the capacity for impact investment. They provide the investment rules and requirements and sometimes co-invest. Taxes, subsidies, reporting requirements and intermediation are established by governments. They also enable the corporate structures such as the Community Contribution Company (CCC) in British Columbia and the Community Interest Company (CIC) in Nova Scotia.[12]

A related concept is social finance, an approach to managing money to solve societal challenges. This approach would include socially responsible investing (SRI) which is different from social impact investing. The intent of social impact investing is made in organizations whose core mandate is to do social or environmental good. With SRI the economic, social, and governance risks are integrated into an analysis of all investments. SRI uses screens to avoid investing in corporations with poor economic, social, and governance practices. Negative screens use factors to disqualify investments, while positive screens use factors that identify corporations as the best or leading in their industry.[13]

The Shared Economy

Some consumers are interested in the social purpose of business and one expression of this is referred to as the **shared economy**, and sometimes as *peer-to-peer e-commerce* and defined as a sustainable social and economic system involving the sharing of human and physical resources. Examples of the trend include: swapping, exchanging, bartering, collective purchasing, shared ownership, renting or borrowing, and trading of used goods. Also associated with the trend are microfinancing, micro-entrepreneurship, social enterprises, and cooperatives. The trend is consistent with the philosophy of reducing, reusing, and recycling.

There is a greater desire in society to share rather than own as many believe that fewer resources should be used in the production and consumption of goods and services not only by individual consumers but also by business corporations. Technology, in particular the Internet, has enabled this trend to increase its presence in the economy. There are many areas where the shared economy is appearing. Airbnb allows individuals to rent accommodations in their homes without having to establish a bed and breakfast operation. By using Eatwith and Feastly, individuals with a talent for cooking can share their skills with others in their homes. In transportation, Uber enables private operators to provide taxi services for others without belonging to a taxi company. CarShare, AutoShare, and Student Car Share enable individuals to rent vehicles on short terms. The borrowing or exchange of goods is made possible by eBay, and Swapsity facilitates bartering. Swap Working Holidays finds jobs for those interested in working abroad.

The trend illustrates how individuals and corporations are taking responsibility for the demands they make on the environment and how they are seeking more social acceptable or ethical approaches to consumption. Most shared economy enterprises operate outside a government regulatory system, which can be problematic for consumers as there is less accountability for the quality and reliability of the services or goods provided.

connect   Want to learn more about **the sharing economy?**

Philanthrocapitalism

The Economist referred to the new approaches such as social venture philanthropy and social enterprise as *philanthrocapitalism*. **Philanthrocapitalism** draws upon modern business practices, that is, the philosophy of capitalist style objectives and criteria with an entrepreneurial spirit to get more from non-profit or social organizations.[14] It is a new approach for the philanthropy of the world's wealthiest "one percent." These philanthropists, or philanthrocapitalists, want to bring new ideas to social initiatives and to be more involved with the operations. Their donations can be used where others have not been or to take advantage of opportunities others have missed. One initiative to encourage the world's wealthiest persons to share more of their wealth to address the needs of the world is the Giving Pledge described in Everyday Ethics 16.3.

EVERYDAY ETHICS 16.3

The Giving Pledge

Bill Gates and Warren Buffett issued a "Giving Pledge" challenge to billionaires in June 2010, urging them to give away more than half of their fortunes. By January 2016, 141 billionaires from 14 countries had pledged. The Giving Pledge website states:

> *The Giving Pledge is an effort to invite the wealthiest individuals and families in America to commit to giving the majority of their wealth to the philanthropic causes and charitable organizations of their choice either during their lifetime or after their death.*

A list of current pledgers is available on Givingpledge.org. Canadians who have participated include Jeff Skoll (born in Montreal and the first president of eBay) and Charles and Edgar Bronfman (whose family established Seagrams).

Both domestic and international causes will receive funding. Each donor decides how his or her money is to be allocated and there is no central agency to distribute the funds. The process will work on an honour system; that is, the pledge is non-binding and represents a moral commitment rather than a legal one. The donors will meet once a year to review progress. The approach has been criticized as the lack of collaboration and coordination may result in duplication of effort. This is countered by the view that individual decision making is preferred over a groupthink approach that may result from a centralized process. A concern has been expressed that most of the funds will go to universities, colleges, medical centres, and arts and culture organizations instead of focusing on the poor or minorities.

Source: Adapted from "FAQ," The Giving Pledge, accessed January 4, 2016, http://givingpledge.org/faq.aspx. © 2010–2013 Giving Pledge LLC and its licensors and suppliers.

This philanthropy by the world's elite has become a new charitable paradigm in international development. Its goals are to address social issues in the developing world including improving human well-being, reducing poverty, and promoting equality. Attention was drawn to philanthrocapitalism when Facebook's Mark Zuckerberg and his wife Priscilla Chan announced that they were contributing 99 percent of their shares, valued at $45 million, to better the lives of millions.

Despite the generosity of the givers, there are several criticisms. The legal structure that Zuckerberg used was questioned when he contributed the shares to a limited liability company (LLC) instead of a foundation. Using the LLC allowed him to retain control and influence the operations. Also, there were fewer restrictions on his oversight than if a charitable foundation had been used. He can stay involved, gets a charitable deduction on this tax return, and does not pay capital gains on the shares.

Other criticisms are that they are undermining the work of NGOs and that the good causes pursued are dependent on the whims of a few. Avoiding taxation reduces the revenues that the government would have to address the same causes. Some critics say that the initiatives are undertaken merely to ease the social consciences of the donors and rarely tackle fundamental political and economic inequity. One critic referred to the approach as philanthropic colonialism providing band aid solutions that fail to find and address the underlying causes of the complex problems being addressed.[15]

Social Capital

The concept of social capital is used by a growing number of sociologists, political scientists, economists, and organizational theorists to improve the understanding of social relationships among individuals, organizations, and within and between societies.[16] Stakeholder concept researchers are beginning to use social capital as another approach to understanding the relationships between the corporation and its stakeholders.

As social capital is a broad concept and can be used in understanding many different types of relationships, many definitions and perspectives of the concept exist. This discussion examines social capital as it applies to understanding corporate stakeholder relationships.

Social capital is any aspect of a corporation's organizational arrangements that creates value and facilitates the actions of stakeholders within and external to the corporation. Social capital is created when the relations between stakeholders and the corporation change in ways that facilitate increased understanding, cooperation, and coordination. In effect, the corporation's stakeholders are a network; that is, a pattern of ties linking the corporation with those it influences and those that can influence it.[17]

Another perspective views social capital as the trust or goodwill existing between the corporation and its stakeholders. This is a valuable resource to the corporation and its source is in the relationships established with stakeholders and the nature of these relationships. The more trust and goodwill the better off the corporation is because it works more efficiently with stakeholders. Corporations benefit from social capital because it facilitates cooperation and coordination that minimizes transaction costs, such as boycotts, legal actions, negotiations, and disruptions in production. More effective and efficient relations with stakeholders may provide a competitive edge over corporations that possess less social capital.

A research report prepared for the Canadian Institute of Chartered Accountants outlined how value is created through social capital obtained from stakeholder relationships.[18] The report identified three levels of organizational culture that explain how corporations orient themselves toward stakeholders. Level 1 is a compliance culture that preserves the value of stakeholder relationships as established by laws and norms and seeks to avoid unacceptable destruction of value. Level 2 is referred to as a relationship management culture where value is created but often is traded off, usually after the demands of the shareholders are satisfied. Maximum value is created at Level 3, a sustainable organizational culture. This culture maximizes the creation of value simultaneously in economic, ethical, and environmental terms.[19] The research focused on corporations at Levels 2 and 3.

From the research, a model of social capital and business value creation was developed; it is shown in Figure 16.3.

Svendsen, Boutilier, and Wheeler summarize the source of social capital as three dimensions or attributes: structural, represented by the networks in which the relationships are embedded; relational, referring to trust and reciprocity; and cognitive, involving mutual understanding. Three manifest benefits of social capital were identified:

- Willingness to share information.
- Willingness to exert one's influence or power to benefit the other where influence also means control and power.
- Solidarity/norm adherence referring to group cohesiveness.[20]

The researchers identified the potential business value created by the benefits of social capital. The following are some examples:

- Information allows employees to access new ideas from external networks.
- Information and norm adherence enables employees to share information and work collaboratively.
- Norm adherence establishes a strong emotional connection between the corporation and its customers.
- Influence can be obtained by making a valuable contribution to the community.
- Influence and norm adherence allows the corporation and union to have reciprocal debts to each other that merge their interests in each other's success.[21]

FIGURE 16.3 *Model of Social Capital and Business Value Creation*

Source: Ann Svendsen, Robert G. Boutilier, and David Wheeler (2003). *Stakeholder Relationships, Social Capital, and Business Value Creation* (Toronto: The Canadian Institute of Chartered Accountants, 12. Reprinted with permission of Chartered Professional Accountants Canada, copyright 2003. Any changes to the original material are the sole responsibility of the author (and/or publisher) and have not been reviewed or endorsed by the Chartered Professional Accountants of Canada.

The concept of social capital is an additional approach to understanding stakeholder relationships and illustrates the sophistication possible in the analysis of stakeholder relationships. The argument that business value is created will most likely encourage other corporations to become involved with methodologies to increase their understanding of stakeholders.

Sustainable Capitalism

Al Gore, former U.S. vice-president, and David Blood, financial industry executive, have developed a document on an appropriate economy system for the future, *A Manifesto for Sustainable Capitalism: How businesses can embrace environmental, social and governance metrics.* They argue that it is time to move from short economic thinking to a longer-term version that they call **sustainable capitalism** which they define as an "economic system within which business and trade seek to maximise long-term value creation, accounting for all material ESG (environmental, social and governance) metrics."

Business must mobilize the financial resources to address challenges facing society such as climate change, water scarcity, poverty, disease, growing income inequality, urbanization, and massive economic volatility. This more responsible form of capitalism is a "framework that seeks to maximize long term economic value by reforming markets to address real needs while integrating environmental, social and governance (ESG) metrics throughout the decision-making process." Embracing sustainable capitalism will result in benefits for corporations:

- Sustainable products and services can increase a corporation's profits, enhance its brand, and improve its competitive positioning.
- Money will be saved by reducing waste and increasing energy efficiency in the supply chain, and by improving human-capital practices.
- Environmental, social, and governance metrics enable corporations to achieve higher compliance standards and better manage risk.
- Financial benefits such as lower cost of debt and lower capital constraints will result.

Investors should focus on the long-term value and potential of corporations when they make investment decisions. In order to respond to the urgency of the present threats, they recommend five key actions:

- Identify and incorporate risk from stranded assets, that is, those whose value would dramatically change, either positively or negatively, when large externalities are taken into account, for example, attributing a reasonable price to carbon or water.
- Mandate integrated financial and ESG performance reporting, which will enable corporations and investors to make better resource allocation decisions.
- End the practice of issuing quarterly earnings guidance which causes executives to manage and investors think in the short term instead of the longer term.
- Align compensation structures with long-term sustainable performance.
- Encourage long-term investing in securities that investors are loyal to in the long term.[22]

Corporate Social Integration

Porter and Kramer argue that corporations have not analyzed CSR initiatives using the same frameworks that guide their core business choices. CSR should not be thought of as a cost, constraint, or charitable deed, but instead as an opportunity, innovation, and competitive advantage. The authors viewed most CSR initiatives as being reactive and many as being merely cosmetic; that is, public relations, media campaigns, and glossy reports. According to Porter and Kramer, reports seldom offer a coherent framework for CSR activities.

The authors identified the prevailing justifications for CSR and their limitations. The moral obligation for corporations to do the right thing does not always provide guidance. Sustainability that involves environmental and community stewardship is subject to self-interest and trade-offs. The license to operate means that outside stakeholders have control over the social agenda. The emphasis on reputation as a justification focuses on external stakeholders. All these prevailing justifications focus on tensions between business and society, and that to improve CSR there must be a better understanding of the interrelationship between the corporation and society.[23]

The authors proposed that the CSR model should become a corporate social integration model approach, which would integrate social perspective with business strategy. This would be accomplished by identifying the points of intersection between business and society, choosing which social issues to address, creating a corporate social agenda, and integrating inside-out and outside-in linkages.

The interdependence between business and society takes two forms: inside-out linkages, which represent the corporation's positive and negative influence on society through its operations, and outside-in linkages, which represent society's positive and negative influences on the corporation.[24]

Social issues must be prioritized into three types: generic, value chain, and social dimensions of competitive context. Generic social issues are those that do not significantly affect the corporation but are important to society. Value-chain social issues are significantly affected by the corporation as it carries out business. Lastly, social dimensions of competitive context are "factors in the external environment that significantly affect the underlying drivers of competitiveness in those places where the company operates."[25]

Porter and Kramer categorize a corporation's involvement in society into two approaches, responsive and strategic. Responsive CSR includes the generic social impacts and efforts to mitigate harm from value-chain activities. More importantly, strategic CSR includes transforming "value-chain activities to benefit society while reinforcing strategy," and "strategic philanthropy that leverages capabilities to improve salient areas of competitive context."[26]

Strategic CSR is beyond best practices and will identify a competitive position advantageous to the corporation. Inside-out and outside-in dimensions must work together to produce shared value opportunities. In this way the social dimension is enhanced while at the same time reducing the constraints on the corporation's value chain. Several examples are given, including Marriott's training program for hospitality industry employees; Nestlé's efforts to purchase from small producers in developing countries; and Whole Foods's value proposition of selling organic, natural, and healthy food products.[27]

Porter and Kramer conclude that CSR should be viewed more appropriately as corporate social integration. Instead of thinking in the short term, viewing CSR as correcting something business has done wrong or merely corporate giving, think of it as creating shared value for all stakeholders involved, in particular governments, NGOs, and corporations themselves.[28]

This section has identified and described several concepts along with some expressions of the socialization of capitalism. When considered together, these concepts and expressions are evidence of a trend in capitalism towards greater attention being given to integrating social purpose with a corporation's economic purpose.

The programs in Canada's business schools must incorporate sustainability concepts, frameworks, and theories into course work and research. The schools themselves might have sustainability reports, and students can be involved in sustainability initiatives.

LO 16.5 Socialization of Capitalism and Business School Programs

Business programs in colleges and universities are responding to the increasing awareness of the ethics and responsibilities of business. The response takes various forms and business education programs are feeling the impact. More important is the benefit for students. When they enter the workplace, they will be confronted by ethical dilemmas and a requirement to respond to social and environmental issues. When they become managers they will encounter various aspects of ethical business practice and be confronted by numerous business and society issues that will affect their corporations.

This section highlights some of initiatives to increase the awareness of the socialization of capitalism undertaken in business schools through the curriculum redesign and other activities.

Teaching Sustainability in Business Schools

This chapter has been describing various initiatives to transforming the approach to business through the socialization capitalism. However, it is important to educate and train future leaders on the integration of economic and social factors. Business schools are ideal places to provide new ways of thinking about business and society and to challenge the established precepts.

Corporations have ethics or social responsibilities programs and there is increasing discussion of similar programs at business schools. Such programs might have several components:

- There could be a statement of values or philosophy.
- The curriculum could include core and elective courses on ethics and related areas such as social enterprise and sustainability. Degree programs could be offered that focus on ethics and corporate responsibilities.
- The faculty could follow codes of ethics or conduct relating to teaching and research. Teaching materials, such as cases, could be developed in addition to publications in academic journals.
- Students could have their own code of ethics or conduct, and form and support organizations related to social responsibility. Students could be involved in volunteer activities and take pledges or oaths committing themselves to ethical and socially responsible behaviour.

The Association to Advance Collegiate Schools of Business (AACSB) has joined the Aspen Institute's Business and Society Program, the European Foundation for Management Development (EFMD), and several other leading associations as co-conveners of the United Nations Global Compact to craft the first iteration of a global set of principles that acknowledge business schools' critical role in advancing socially responsible business leadership. These principles are listed in Responsibility for Ethics 16.2. Business schools take pride in being identified with these principles of responsible management education as corporations do with the various awards that exist for practicing sustainability.

RESPONSIBILITY FOR ETHICS 16.2

The Six Principles of Responsible Management Education

Principle 1

Purpose: We will develop the capabilities of students to be future generators of sustainable value for business and society at large and to work for an inclusive and sustainable global economy.

Principle 2

Values: We will incorporate into our academic activities and curricula the values of global social responsibility as portrayed in international initiatives such as the United Nations Global Compact.

Principle 3

Method: We will create educational frameworks, materials, processes and environments that enable effective learning experiences for responsible leadership.

Principle 4

Research: We will engage in conceptual and empirical research that advances our understanding about the role, dynamics, and impact of corporations in the creation of sustainable social, environmental and economic value.

Principle 5

Partnership: We will interact with managers of business corporations to extend our knowledge of their challenges in meeting social and environmental responsibilities and to explore jointly effective approaches to meeting these challenges.

Principle 6

Dialogue: We will facilitate and support dialogue and debate among educators, business, government, consumers, media, civil society organizations and other interested groups and stakeholders on critical issues related to global social responsibility and sustainability.

We understand that our own organizational practices should serve as examples of the values and attitudes we convey to our students.

Source: Adapted from "About," Principles for Responsible Management Education (PRME), http://www.unprme.org/.

Many business schools are going a step further and establishing sustainability centres to help create a more sustainable business model that integrates economic and social purposes. This is done by enhancing research and teaching programs as well as working with industry to make social and environmental change. The Network for Business Sustainability maintains a directory of more than 120 sustainability centres from around the world.[29] An example of one centre is described in Responsibility for Ethics 16.3.

It is believed that the initiatives of business to expose students to the concepts and expressions of the socialization of capitalism will change the ways students think about the relationships between business and society. For example, Wiek et al. identified the competences that students acquire when exposed to business programs that focus on sustainability. These competences were: systems thinking necessary to understand the complex economic, social and environmental issues; capability to consider long- and short-term implications of actions; consideration of the moral implications of actions; strategic thinking relating to stakeholder engagement and issues; and the importance of collaboration. The authors also identified the approaches used to develop these diverse competences in students: embedding sustainability into existing business programs; creating new courses and programs; and insuring that students were exposed to real-world problems.[30]

The various exposures to sustainability in business schools through courses and programs, providing sustainability-focused exchange and service learning opportunities, empowering students to make real-world impact through supervised projects, and engaging students to co-organize educational events will hopefully result in the development of future responsible managers. Some of the students initiatives to described in the following section.

RESPONSIBILITY FOR ETHICS 16.3

McGill's Social Economy Initiative

The Social Economy Initiative (SEI) is a "vehicle through which the Desautels Faculty of Management integrates social entrepreneurship and social innovation more formally into its teaching, research and outreach activities. Social entrepreneurs are applying innovative approaches to addressing social problems that have not been satisfactorily addressed by the public or private sectors. The outcome is social value creation, social impact and social change."

SEI's goals are:

1. To prepare a dynamic workforce to lead and serve organizations within the social economy by providing a world-class education.
2. To conduct leading-edge research into the social economy for the purpose of actionable knowledge.
3. To provide catalyzing experiential learning opportunities outside the classroom for our students by engaging with individuals and organizations active in the social economy.

The initiative is funded by Peter and Joan Monk (Barrick Gold Corporation) Endowment for Entrepreneurship and the KPMG Social Economy Fund.

Source: Adapted from "The Social Economy Initiative" (SEI), Desautels Faculty of Management, McGill University accessed February 10, 2016, http://www.mcgill.ca/desautels/integrated-management/mdiim-initiatives/social-economy-initiative.

Students and Sustainability

Stakeholders in society expect business to adopt and practise sustainability. It must be remembered that sustainability is the responsibility of all stakeholders, including students. Students support sustainability in several ways; examples of ways students can become involved with sustainability initiatives are given in Everyday Ethics 16.4.

Students should check out their college or university's sustainability policy or strategy. Some have comprehensive policies, for example the University of British Columbia and University of Northern British Columbia.[31] At some colleges, the Student Union will also have a sustainability program. Many universities have investments in endowment funds used to support scholarships or research. Students can lobby officials to follow socially responsible investing as described in Chapter 11. Some universities already belong to the Coalition of Universities for Responsible Investing (CURI), a forum for dialogue, collaborative action, and education on socially and environmentally responsible investing among Canadian universities.[32]

Students can also become directly involved in sustainability initiatives. Volunteering for campus or community projects and in support of social causes is possible, or local issues could be studied. Community-Based Research Canada (CBRC) is a network of people and organizations engaged in research to meet the needs of people and communities. Several Canadian universities are involved with CBRC.[33]

International volunteer service in a developing country is another possibility. This could involve travel with the purpose of studying an issue or aspect of life in a particular country. There is the possibility of living in a country for some time by seeking out a semester internship or a volunteer position. Some well-known organizations involved in this type of learning are Engineers Without Borders, Students Without Borders, Cuso International, and Projects Abroad.

Service-learning is a method of teaching, learning, and reflecting combining classroom learning with service to the community either locally or in developing countries. It can be done for credit and involves a service activity to fulfill a community need and provides a way to gain further understanding of course content. More can be learned about service-learning at the Canadian Alliance for Community Service-Learning (CSL) website.[34]

EVERYDAY ETHICS 16.4

Examples of Students and Sustainability

Centre for Social Innovation & Impact Investing (Sauder S3i), University of British Columbia—This centre is "focused on leveraging business tools to advance social innovation and sustainability, through research, incubation, and application. Sauder S3i defines social innovation as a new approach which fosters initiatives that contribute to solving existing social, cultural, economic, political, and environmental challenges."

Ivey Connects, Richard Ivey School of Business, Western University—Ivey Connects is a student-led organization working to inspire students to contribute in the societies in which they operate.

Students Without Borders (SWB), World University Service of Canada—SWB is a partner-driven program where qualified students spend a semester or more in Africa, Asia, or Latin America.

The Graduation Pledge of Social and Environmental Responsibility—"I pledge to explore and take into account the social and environmental consequences of any job I consider and will try to improve these aspects of any organizations for which I work." This pledge is widely used in the United States.

The Canadian MBA Oath, Telfer School of Management, University of Ottawa—In 2009, the graduating MBA class developed the Oath, and planned to have other universities in Canada participate.

Sources: Compiled from "About," Centre for Social Innovation & Impact Investing (Sauder S3i), Sauder Business School, University of British Columbia, accessed February 7, 2016, http://webcontent.sauder.ubc.ca/Faculty/Research_Centres/Centre_for_Social_Innovation_and_Impact_Investing/About; "Ivey Connects," Richard Ivey School of Business, Western University, accessed February 7, 2016, http://www.ivey.uwo.ca/iveyconnects/; "Students Without Borders (SWB)," World University Service of Canada, http://wusc.ca/en/swb; Graduation Pledge Alliance, accessed February 7, 2016, http://www.graduationpledge.org/; and "About the MBA Oath," The Canadian MBA Oath, Telfer School of Management, University of Ottawa, accessed February 7, 2016 http://sites.telfer.uottawa.ca/mbaoath.

Pledges or oaths to engage in ethical behaviour have been formulated. A pledge is proposed for first-year students that will increase their awareness of ethics and responsibilities, as described in Chapter 1. Another is taken upon graduation to emphasize consideration of the social and environmental consequences of the jobs students may accept. Finally, in recent years, students in MBA programs are taking oaths similar to the one described in Everyday Ethics 16.4. Considerable controversy surrounds these pledges and oaths, with critics pointing out that they are window dressing or greenwashing and that they cannot be enforced.

Concluding Comment

Evidence exists that the Canadian capitalism system through its corporations is becoming more aware of society's social needs. This chapter has outlined the paradigm shift that has occurred in the relationship between business and society during recent decades referred to as the socialization of capitalism. The business system is constantly changing along with the relationship between business and society.

The characteristics of the business system or capitalism are influenced by the fundamentals described in Chapter 2. The fundamentals are the same, but vary in influence over time. In turn, this impacts the ethics in Canadian business and society. Stakeholder influence changes over time, as do the issues that have an impact on the corporation. This leads to changes in the ethics of business and how corporate social responsibility or corporate sustainability is defined, practised, and reported.

Some stakeholders are more influential than others, and/or are influenced more by the corporation. The regulation of business is always present but it varies, as illustrated by the increase in self-regulatory mechanisms including CSR. Recently, the role of owners has changed and corporate governance has been reformed. Civil society stakeholders, in particular non-governmental organizations, are increasing their influence, but corporations also are making their efforts to influence them. Two areas of focus today are the natural environment and globalization. Managers cannot ignore these areas and must attempt to understand the consequences for their corporations.

Lastly, ethics of business, corporate social responsibility, or corporate sustainability now represents a strategic competence of management. This trend is unlikely to change in the near future.

Your advice to Leah . . .

Non-profit organizations in the social sector the economy are applying business or commercial approaches to operating and financing their initiatives. Along with these approaches comes the need to understand business practices and the ability to respond to the dynamics of the marketplace. This will be a challenge to some of these new organizations and, like private sector corporations, they may fail at times. Failure should not discourage this approach and like a corporation, the social sector organization will need to assess the realities of their situation and restructure their organization if feasible.

Summary

- The fourth sector is an illustration of the socialization of capitalism, or our business system today. The blurring of the boundaries among the private, social, and public sectors of the economy has created another sector where new organizational forms integrate private, social, and public approaches to providing goods and services in society. (LO 16.1)
- Corporate sustainability is a more comprehensive form of corporate social responsibility (CSR) that integrates social/ethical, environmental, and governance issues into the corporation's planning through strategic management. Corporations are at different stages on the sustainability continuum: amoral, compliance-based, emerging, and sustainability. There is no definitive description of a sustainable corporation, but the socialization of capitalism is occurring through corporate sustainability (LO 16.2)
- The socialization of capitalism has been facilitated by the creation of new organizational forms, in particular, social enterprises, for-benefit corporations, and b-corporations. (LO 16.3)
- There are numerous expressions of the socialization of capitalism and the concepts associated with it. These are: social licence, social innovation, social impact investing, the shared economy, philanthrocapitalism, social capital, sustainable capitalism, and corporate social integration. (LO 16.4)
- Business school programs are emphasizing the ethics of business and sustainability. Students are being prepared for confronting ethical dilemmas in the workplace and for understanding corporate responsibilities to society. Students can contribute to sustainability while attending colleges or universities. (LO 16.5)

Key Terms

Socialization of capitalism	B Corporation
Private sector	Social innovation
Social sector	Social impact investing
Public sector	Social finance
Public–private partnership	Shared economy
Fourth sector	Philanthrocapitalism
Sustainability strategy	Social capital
Strategic management	Sustainable capitalism
For-benefit corporation	Service-learning

Critical Thinking and Discussion Questions

1. Why has the fourth sector of the economy emerged in recent years?
2. Why are there different stages of sustainability strategies?
3. What is the relationship between strategic management and sustainability strategy?
4. What should be included in a job description for a "sustainability manager"?
5. What role do profits have in the social enterprise type of corporate form?
6. Should a social licence be difficult to obtain? Is the need for a social license for projects preventing the economic development of the country?
7. What is the difference between social impact investing and socially responsible investing (also discussed in Chapter 11)?
8. Are the giving initiatives of the "one percent" (philantrocapitalists) improving social well-being in the world?
9. Is "sustainable capitalism" practical or feasible?
10. What approach should business programs take toward the socialization of capitalism?
11. How can students participate in the socialization of capitalism?

Cases

16.1 STADIUMS, TAXPAYERS, AND SPORTS MILLIONAIRES

Calgary Mayor Naheed Nemshi and City Council were considering a proposal by the owner of the Calgary Flames to build a new arena and recreation complex. Calgary Sports and Recreation Corporation, which includes the NHL's Calgary Flames and the Canadian Football League's Calgary Stampeders, proposed a $890 million arena plus a combination stadium/field house for the downtown area. The complex would be financed with the corporation putting in $200 million, the City of Calgary $200 million, $250 million raised by a ticket tax, and $240 million by a community development levy where the taxpayers would be repaid by increased economic activity. In effect, Calgary taxpayers would be providing $440 million plus the land.

Similar schemes have been proposed by the owners of professional sports teams in other Canadian and American cities. Most involve wealthy franchise owners expecting taxpayers to subsidize the construction of new facilities. Sometimes pressure is applied by suggesting that the team will relocate to another city unless the new subsidized venue is not forthcoming. Often the new facilities are promoted as a stimulant to renewal of downtown areas and creating economic spinoffs thus having a multiplier effect.

Critics argue that the cities are victims and saying that taxpayers are giving money to the owners and well-paid players. Numerous studies, including those by academics, have found that subsidizing new stadiums does not generate new jobs, growth, or tax revenue. The wealthy owners of the sports franchises get a new facility and new revenue streams thereby increasing their profits. The subsidization is referred to as another form of corporate welfare. These critics state that if the new facility is not economically viable, then it should not be built.

Yet many cities do get involved in the schemes. Some believe that economic benefits are generated. Others simply get involved for emotional reasons: civic pride, the thrill of the game, and cheering for the "home" team.

The mayor and councillors are still considering the proposal.

Questions

1. Who are the stakeholders involved in the construction of new sports facilities?

2. What are the issues involved? How do these issues relate to the Fourth Sector approach to economic activity?

3. Can the building of these sports facilities be justified, and if so, on what rationale?

4. Should cities become involved in this type of private–public partnership?

Source: Adapted from Jason Markusoff, "If You Build It, He Will Come," *Maclean's Magazine*, October 19, 2015, 56-57; "Spinning Spinoffs," *The Telegram* (St. John's, NL), September 24, 2014, A6; "No Public Money for Saddledome 2.0," *National Post*, November 14, 2014, A16; and "A Monument to Government Waste," *National Post*, January 29, 2015, A8.

16.2 A UNIVERSITY'S CENTRE FOR CORPORATE SUSTAINABILITY

The Haskayne School of Business, University of Calgary, established the Centre for Corporate Sustainability which was "dedicated to finding a balance among economic development, social well-being and environmental protection." Its mission "is to enable partnership among research, industry, government and community to jointly generate dialogue, create best practices and disseminate knowledge." The Centre was announced in 2012 as a partnership with Enbridge Inc., which pledged support of $2.25 million over a ten-year period.

The Centre's activities included: encouragement of academic research; support for student projects on sustainable development; holding seminars on sustainability; a mentoring program for students; awarding of undergraduate scholarships; and offering of a doctoral scholarship and a post-doctoral fellowship. The Centre's activities were guided by an Academic Advisory Group and an External Advisory Board, comprised of scholars and practitioners of corporate sustainability from across North America.

In Fall 2015, CBC News featured a story about the relationship between Enbridge and the University of Calgary that the CBC suggested challenged academic integrity. The issues identified included: the circumstance surrounding the departure of the first director; Enbridge's hands-on approach to influencing board membership, staffing, and student awards; and the alleged use of the Centre to publicize the Enbridge's initiatives. Some stated that the Centre was being an apologist for the fossil fuel industry rather than an independent research centre.

A further complication was the involvement of the university president, Elizabeth Cannon. It was suggested that she did not do enough to address the issues surrounding the Centre. She had encouraged the Enbridge funding but also had a potential conflict of interest as she was a director of Enbridge Income Fund Holdings for which she received compensation.

The Canadian Association of University Teachers (CAUT) decided to launch an investigation into the allegations of conflict of interest, violations of academic freedom, the management of donations, and external interference in the establishment and operation of the Centre.

Enbridge issued a News Release stating that it was committed to the principles of academic freedom and that its support of the Centre came with no strings attached.

Questions

1. What are the issues involved and which stakeholders are associated with each issue?

2. Should business schools accept financing from business?

3. What is the best way to resolve the incident?

Source: Adapted from "Disseminating Knowledge in Environmental, Social and Economic Approaches in Energy," Centre for Corporate Sustainability, Haskayne School of Business, University of Calgary, accessed December 17, 2016 http://haskayne.ucalgary.ca/files/haskayne/CCSReport2015.pdf; "Enbridge's Partnership with the University of Calgary and the Centre for Corporate Sustainability," News Release November 2, 2015, accessed December 17, 2015, http://www.enbridge.com/MediaCentre/News/Enbridges-partnership-with-the-University-of-Calgary-and-the-Centre-for-Corporate-Sustainability.aspx; "Investigation Launched into U of Calgary Academic Freedom Controversy," Canadian Association of University Teachers (CAUT), News Release November 2, 2015 accessed December 17, 2015, http://www.caut.ca/news/2015/11/19/investigation-launched-into-u-of-calgary-academic-freedom-controversy.

Ethics, Responsibilities, and Sustainability Cases

 ## Energy Drinks at Prairie Pharmacy[1]

Victor Lukasik has just taken over the operation of the family drug store, Prairie Pharmacy. The pharmacy was started by his grandfather and carried on by his father, who now is semi-retired working as a relief or part-time pharmacist. The pharmacy was located in a Western Canada community of about 5,200 that was also served by a large retail drugstore chain. Despite the competition, Prairie Pharmacy continued to prosper because the loyalty of long-time customers and its personalized service. The pharmacy had started as a prescription filling outlet and sold a few over the counter mediations. Over the years, the pharmacy had grown and now sold a large variety of over-the-counter medications, snack food, candies and soft drinks, cosmetics, greeting cards, magazines, and personal care products. It had a Canada Post franchise outlet.

Victor completed a pharmacy degree and then went to work as a sales representative for a pharmaceutical company for five years. During that time, he completed an MBA part time and through distance education courses. He now felt that he had sufficient education and experience to take on the management of the family pharmacy. Besides, it was good to return to his hometown.

Victor had several ideas about operating the pharmacy and about how it would compete against the larger chain store. One area that particularly interested him was the social responsibility of the retail pharmacy industry. An issue of concern to him was the unhealthy products that were sold in the store. One such product was energy drinks, and he had done some primarily research.

What is an Energy Drink?

An energy drink is a beverage that is supposed to make a person more alert and give more energy. Common brands are Full Throttle, Monster, Tab Energy, Rockstar, Red Rain, Go Fast!, Rip It, and Red Bull. Most of these drinks contain caffeine, sugar, taurine, vitamins and herbs. Caffeine is a main ingredient and can be found in coffee, tea, chocolate, cola and certain medications. The range of caffeine in energy drinks ranges from 50 mg per can to above 200 mg per can, above the recommended daily intake for most children and teens. Too much caffeine can cause irritability, nausea, heart palpitations, feelings of hyper-energy, nervousness and loss of sleep, and is not recommended for children or young teenagers.[2]

Many energy drinks sold in large can sizes have lots of sugar, which provides energy in the form of calories. Although calories are added to a person's diet, sugar on its own adds no nutritional value. It is claimed that adding taurine, an amino acid associated with building protein, to energy drinks makes the consumer more alert. There is no scientific evidence to support this claim. Some vitamins, for example B and glucuronolactone, are added to increase energy levels, but there is no scientific evidence to support this practice. Medicinal herbs like ginseng and gingko biloba are added to some energy drinks as it is claimed that they improve performance, but again, there is no evidence to support this.

Energy drinks are widely available and found anywhere consumers purchase beverages including drug, grocery, and convenience stores and gas stations. They are packaged with flashy labels and often placed near juices and sports drinks.

Information Found

Victor found lots of information on energy drinks in the print and broadcast media, on the Internet, and in academic literature. Professional and trade associations had information energy drinks as well as numerous government sources. Many research organizations were involved in investigating the effects of consuming energy drinks. The following is some of the information found.

His industry trade associations did not provide much guidance. The websites for the Canadian Pharmacists Association (CPhA) and Neighbourhood Pharmacy Association of Canada contained no information on energy drinks that was accessible by the public.

A study of Atlantic Canadian high school students by the Propel Centre for Population Health Impact, University of Waterloo, found: the more students consumed energy drinks, the more they will suffer from depression or become addicted to alcohol or marijuana; the drinks appeal to young people because of temporary benefits, including increased alertness, improved mood, and enhanced mental and physical energy; younger teens were more likely to consume energy drinks than older teens possibly as the result of advertising designed to appeal to this age group.[3] The Canadian Beverage Association was critical of the study claiming that the findings reflect only an association and not causality.[4]

There was frequent mention of other research results including:

- Research has found that mixing alcohol and energy drinks increases the usage of alcohol alone.

- Research presented at an American Heart Association showed how energy drinks impacted cardiovascular health including causing irregular heartbeats that might contribute to heart attacks and sudden death. Energy drinks might also be associated with high blood pressure.

- The *Canadian Medical Association Journal* often warned of the dangers of caffeine in energy drinks and that they can pose a serious health risk to children and adolescents.

- The boost received from energy drinks is short-lived and often accompanied with other problems.

- Regular consumption increases the possibility of eroding tooth enamel.

- Consumption of six or more energy drinks per month increases the risk of smoking cigarettes, abusing prescription drugs, and engaging in physical fights.

- Excessive levels of caffeine in drinks impair cognition.

- Energy drinks are safe if consumed in moderation along with a good diet.

The sale of energy drinks was regulated in Canada under the *Food and Drugs Act* and *Food and Drug Regulations.* On the issue of caffeine, Health Canada limited the amount to 400 mg per litre in an energy drink. Most small energy drinks containers (less than 250 ml) would have between 80 to 100 mg of caffeine and larger containers could not have more than 180 mg. Health Canada deemed that energy drinks were safe for consumption as long as no more than 400 mg of caffeine was consumed per day.

Health Canada requires caffeinated energy drink labels are include: a nutrition facts table, statement of the total caffeine content from all sources, cautionary consumption statements, warnings to children, pregnant and breastfeeding women and others sensitive to caffeine, and a statement "Do not mix with alcohol." Consumption incidents reports from industry and consumers identifying health or safety concerns related to energy drinks are to be filed with the Canadian Food Inspection Agency.

In November 2010, a Health Canada Expert Panel on Caffeinated Energy Drinks made extensive recommendations about the regulation of energy drinks. Recommendations included: energy drinks should be referred to as "stimulant drug containing drinks;" the drinks should be sold under the supervision of a pharmacist and not sold to those under 18 years; extensive labeling changes including listing of ingredients and warnings of dangers; and there should be investigations into approaches to reducing the risks from energy drink consumption.[5] For the most part, the recommendations of the Panel have not been implemented.

The Canadian Beverage Association, a trade association for non-alcoholic drink manufactures, supported the consumption of energy drinks within limits and under conditions recommended by Health Canada. The Association pointed out that coffee, tea, chocolate, caffeinated soft drinks and over the counter medications contained caffeine. In fact, a 237 ml serving (8 ounces) of coffee contained about 180 mg of caffeine. Consumers were advised to be aware of their caffeine intake and not mix energy drinks with alcohol. The Association also recommended that its members adhere to "Energy Drinks Marketing Code." The Code stated that marketing and promotional practices should be consistent with the *Food and Drug Act* and regulations. The Code specified practices relating to advertising, the sponsorship of events, and not selling energy drinks in schools. Members were to provide consumers with information of energy drinks and not promote them to children.[6]

Victor found some pharmacists had taken action on the issue. In September 2014, Graham MacKenzie, owner of Stone's Drug Store in Baddeck, N.S., announced that the store would no longer by selling soft drinks and other sugary beverages. A year later he stated that sales of his store had been hardly affected and that consumer reaction was positive.[7] In 2010, Murphy's Pharmacies in P.E.I. stopped selling energy drinks to persons under the age of 18 years. Murphy's sales and marketing manager stated that it was the responsible thing to do.

Possible Actions

Victor concluded that had four alternatives to addressing the issue energy drinks: do nothing, attempt to educate his customers, sell only to adults, and not to sell energy drinks at all.

He felt in all conscience that he had to do something and should not ignore the issue especially since he was a health professional. If the consumption of energy drinks became a prominent issue, he could be accused of not taking action.

Educating customers about the issue was a possibility. He could post signs advising of the dangers of consuming energy drinks especially among young people. Also, he could make available brochures or pamphlets on the issue.

Any ban on selling energy drinks to young people would be challenging to implement. It is not clear at what age individuals can consume the drinks with less risk. A ban on the sale of the drinks children below the age of 12 years may be possible. There would be some administrative costs as identification would have to be checked. It might be appropriate to shelve the drinks behind the counter.

Lastly, Victor could decide not to sell energy drinks. There may be some financial consequences, that is, lower sales and profits. Banning the sale would bring attention to the issue in the community which may be appreciated. If he banned the sale of energy drinks, he would have to considering banning other unhealthy products containing excessive salt, fat, and sugar.

Victor wondered what he should do.

Gabriel Resources Ltd. and the Rosia Montana Saga[8]

A saga is any very long story or history describing dramatic events or parts involving a group, place, industry, or corporation. A saga exists relating to the mining of gold and other minerals in the Rosia Montana area of Transylvania, Romania. The mine is located the scenic Apuseni Mountains in the northwestern part of Romania, 400 kilometres from the capital, Bucharest. It is Europe's largest deposit of gold and other minerals and has been mined since the second century. The Romans mined the rich gold seams and used the gold to finance their expansion. Since then, many governments in the region mined the site, including communist regimes. The government-funded mine closed in 2006 as required for Romania's entry into the European Union.[9] The gold remaining is in low grade ore that would have to be processed with cyanide. Two thousand years of mining activity have has left environmental devastation and resulted in the region's economic decline as evidenced by an 80 percent unemployment rate in the area.

Canadian mining interests became involved in the late 1990s and Gabriel Resources Ltd. (Gabriel) was launched at that time and has been involved since then. In 1999, Gabriel received a licence from the Romanian government to go ahead with a new project to mine gold and silver from the area. For over 15 years, Gabriel has been attempting to start a new mining venture but has not been successful because of lack of government cooperation and opposition from Romanian and international NGOs. Gabriel's involvement may be the last stage in the Rosia Montana mineral deposit saga.

The Company and the Project

Gabriel is a Canadian resource company listed on the Toronto Stock Exchange (GBU.TSX) and obtaining permission to develop the gold and silver project has been its focus. The project is owned through Rosia Montana Gold Corporation S.A. (RMGC) in which Gabriel holds an 80.69 percent interest. The remaining 19.31 is owned the Romanian government-owned Minvest Roşia Montană S.A. The project was estimated to cost US$1.5 billion to develop.[10]

The project is one of the largest gold deposits in Europe with an estimated 10.1 million ounces of gold and 47.6 ounces of silver. Estimates vary, but the project could contribute US$24 billion to Romanian GDP depending on mineral prices. The project would provide jobs and stimulate other economic initiatives in the area reducing poverty. It is estimated that over 7,000 direct and indirect jobs would be created, with 2,300 jobs during construction and over 880 during the life of the mine.

Gabriel planned to use state of the art technology to build the open pit mine covering 300 hectares and requiring the relocation of about 2,000 residents. The waste rock and cyanide laced sludge would be deposited in nearby valley that would serve as a tailings pond contained by a dam over 100 metres in height. The workings of the historical mines would be cleaned up and the company indicated that it would remediate the polluted regions. It also had detailed environmental plans that included the replanting of trees, the treatment of run-off water, and the re-contouring of slopes with topsail and vegetation.

Gabriel was sensitive to safeguarding Rosia Montana cultural heritage and had spent over $30 million on various efforts including the establishment of a museum. Some areas of the community would be protected zones to preserve historic structures. Archaeological finds would be preserved and protected including the several miles of the Roman mining tunnels.

The company's intention was to achieve economic, environmental, social and heritage sustainability. Gabriel's sustainability policies included commitment to the United Nations Global Compact, the OECD's Guidelines for Multinational Enterprises, and the International Cyanide Management Code.

Gabriel management believed that its plans for the Rosia Montana were supported by many local residents although a minority were opposed. The project was a major undertaking as the old operations and the surrounding environment had to be rehabilitated, a community accommodated, and a new mine built that would minimize any adverse effects of a mining operation. There were many challenges in getting approval for the project from many sources.

Chronology of Challenging Events

Unfortunately in 2000, a tailing dam at a gold recovery mine in Northern Romania collapsed and 100,000 cubic metres of cyanide laced water was released and polluted the Somes, Tisza, and Danube rivers affecting 2.5 million persons in Hungary and Romania. This ecological accident alerted many Romanians and others of the potential dangers of mining and the tailings ponds used. Various environmental NGOs became involved and pressured the Romanian government not to allow any new mines. In 2005 a documentary, *New El Dorado,* produced by a Hungarian film maker was released portraying mining projects as a curse and not an asset to the country. The documentary generated considerable interest particularly among the NGOs and financial support for opposed the project poured in from Romania and internationally.[11]

Nevertheless, Gabriel operations continued with some support from the Romanian government while the World Bank rejected a request for funding. Gabriel ran newspaper advertisements promoting the project and partly financed—but did not have editorial control over—a countering documentary, *Mine Your Own Business.* Released in 2006 and subtitled "A Documentary about the Dark Side of Environmentalism," the film interviews some of the world's poorest people about how environmental NGOs are campaigning to keep them in poverty because their way of life is thought to be quaint. It examines campaigns against large mining projects in the developing world including Rosia Montana. The documentary claims that environmentalists distort and exaggerate the risks of mining projects and in doing so prevents poor people and communities from improving their well-being.[12]

Activity continued at the mine site and three-quarters of the properties on the site were purchased. Historical restoration of some properties was completed and a museum developed. In September 2007, the Romanian government's Ministry of the Environment suspended Gabriel's environmental review or assessment. There was opposition to the review from NGOs who claimed that the company had provided false documentation. Supporters of the mine claimed this move would discourage investment and that suspending the review was an arbitrary and illegal move. There was also a court challenge by Alburnus Maior, the local NGO, and the Open Society Institute. In November 2007, the court annulled the project's archeological discharge certificate and in December workers were laid off and the land acquisition program cancelled.

In 2009, a new Romanian government was attempting to encourage foreign investment after years of Communist regimes, in particular that of dictator Nicolae Ceausescu. There was renewed hope for the project, and the new government reopened the environmental review process in 2010. In August 2011, the Romanian president supported the project and an archeological discharge permit was awarded. The historical structures were protected, but an environmental assessment would need to be done.

These initiatives were criticized by environmentalists, archaeologists, historians, and various international organizations. They believed that the mine still threatened the environment and that priceless Roman era mining galleries were being destroyed. In December 2013, MiningWatch Canada, Greenpeace, Friends of the Earth, the Council of Canadians, and Earthworks requested in an open letter that the Canadian Minister of Foreign Affairs and Members of Parliament withdraw any Canadian government support for Gabriel's Romania project.

However, the government requested a revised share of the profits through higher taxation, royalties, and dividends. It was speculated that achieving these concessions would convince more Romanians of the financial benefits of the project. It also requested that the amount of cyanide laced materials to be dumped in the tailing pond be reduced. In April 2012 the archeological zoning permit was invalidated by the Romanian court. Protests against the project continued into 2013. By September of that year, Gabriel had spent $583 million and 15 years on the project.

Some positive news did occur. The Romanian government approved the draft law relating to the concessions but this would have to receive parliamentary approval. It was speculated that parliament may reject the draft because of protests being held across country, including in Rosia Montana. About this time, parliament voted to create a special commission to review the project which would report in a few months. Meanwhile, thirty-three miners occupied the mine demanding that the project go ahead.

In November 2013, the parliamentary commission opposed the draft bill stating that such a bill should apply to all mining operations and not specifically to Gabriel. As a result of these events, Gabriel began winding down the operations of RNGC and 400 employees were suspended with three-quarters pay.

Gabriel's Challenge

In January 2015, Gabriel filed a Notice requesting that the Romanian government engage formally in a process of consultation as contemplated by bilateral investment treaties. Investment treaties are agreements regarding a country's treatment, in this case Romania, of individuals or companies from another country, in this case Gabriel from Canada. Canada has two such treaties with Romania dating from 1997 and 2011. With this Notice, Gabriel sought to initiate positive dialogue and engage formally in the process of consultation leading to an amiable resolution of the problems associated with the project. There was no response from the Romanian government.

In a press release dated July 2015, Gabriel announced that it had filed a request for arbitration before the World Bank's International Centre for Settlement of Investment Disputes (ICSID) against Romania. The ICSID is an institution established for the resolution of investment disputes and it provides facilities and services to support conciliation and arbitration. Participation is voluntary and it is not a court of law. Canada had been a member of ICSID since 2011 and Romania had been a member since 1975.[13] Gabriel claimed that Romania had breached the bilateral investment treaty obligations. The company claimed that Romania had blocked and prevented the project without due process and without compensating Gabriel for the value of its investment in the project.

The saga continues.

 ## Corporate Social Responsibility to Food Banks[14]

Phillip Veldhuis was president of Savalot Enterprises, a small, family-owned wholesale food business. The company operated in a medium-sized Canadian city and its customers included health and educational institutions, restaurants, catering groups, and service clubs. Savalot's main social responsibility initiative was supporting the local food banks. Surplus edible food items were forwarded weekly to the food banks and the company made a substantial monetary donation each year.

Phillip fully understood the need for the food banks as outlined by Food Banks Canada, a national charitable organization of Canadian food banks. Located in Toronto, its mission was "to reduce hunger in Canada by enabling an effective food bank community that addresses both the short-term need for food and longer-term solutions." Its vision was "to be the voice for the hungry in Canada," and it embraced the values of Teamwork, Transparency, and Integrity.

Every year Food Banks Canada published statistics on hunger and the usage of the food banks, and recommended solutions to hunger. Statistical highlights from a recent publication were the following:

- Each month, about 850,000 Canadians turn up a food banks, one-third of them children and youth, and 1,700,000 will be helped during a year.
- The number using food banks was 26 percent higher than in 2008, before the start of the global financial crisis that year.
- Food bank use in March 2015 was 1.3 percent higher compared to the same period in 2014
- In Canada, 54 percent of food banks reported an increase in the number of people requesting food assistance.
- 7 percent of households helped by food banks live primarily on income from a pension.[15]

Corporations contribute about 6,400,000 kilograms of food a year, and about 80 percent of Food Bank Canada's revenues come from corporate donors. It acts as a clearing house mostly for food, sending it out to food banks across the country. Community food banks have their own local sources of food and funding.

The economy had taken a downturn in the area where Savalot operated, and Phillip believed that this might be part of the reason why food bank usage had also increased in his community. It seemed that each year the local food bank was faced with an increasing demand for food.

Despite the frequency of usage and the apparent need for food banks, Phillip had been reading about the problems associated with them. Some critics argued that food banks may provide some relief but they did not really address the problems causing hunger. Even Food Banks Canada indicated that high rents and lack of affordable housing, the high rates for early learning and child care, and an inadequate Employment Insurance system forced Canadians to use food banks.

Phillip also noticed that there had been considerable criticism of the food bank approach to alleviating hunger. Letters to the editor of various newspapers claimed that some users abused the food banks and that many were too lazy to find work. Other critics claimed that hunger will never be eliminated, and to suggest that it could be if more were donated was misleading. Many experiencing hunger did not use the food banks as they were reluctant or too embarrassed to accept charity. Those who do use food banks often felt that the experience was stigmatizing, humiliating, and degrading.

Furthermore, food banks alone were not providing all the food needed and some users were still hungry. Most food banks had to ration food offerings to once a week or month, and the best that could be done was to ensure that users experienced less hunger. Food banks were criticized for not giving out the most nutritious food given the focus on canned fruits and vegetables, staples such as flour and coffee, and boxed dried food like instant soups, macaroni and cheese dinners, and dry cereals. These foods contained salt and trans-fats or other ingredients not desirable in the diets of some people.

Others pointed out that food banks had been operating for over 35 years, having been established during the recession in the 1980s in Alberta. They suggested that the problem of hunger was too big for charities alone to solve and governments would have to help out. In fact, it was suggested that the operation of food banks by charities was enabling governments to avoid their responsibility to this social issue.

Phillip was shocked when he read the comments by Elaine Power, associate professor in the School of Kinesiology and Health Studies at Queen's University about food banks and the role of corporations. In reality, food banks are somewhere to dispose of their surplus edible food they cannot sell. Furthermore, corporate-sponsored food drives are good for employee morale but do not result in alleviating hunger as much as claimed. Power emphasized that the problem of hunger is a complicated one not addressed solely by food banks, and that all are complicit in ignoring the problem. This includes corporations that benefit from their donations by displaying to society that they are good corporate citizens, and by not having to pay to dispose of the food in a landfill.[16]

Phillip felt a little guilty, because in effect his business was using food banks to dispose of food products it could not sell for one reason or another. He wondered if, despite his company's best intentions, it may not be contributing much to address the underlying causes of the problem and to providing sufficient assistance to those in need.

Caterpillar Shuts Down Its Canadian Locomotive Plant[17]

The headline read "Caterpillar closes Electro-Motive plant in London."[18] On February 3, 2102, Caterpillar Inc. announced the closing of its subsidiary Electro-Motive Diesel (EMD) located in London, Ontario. With globalization, the closing of manufacturing plants in Canada by foreign corporations had become more frequent as exemplified in the closing of plants by Navistar International and Ford Motor. The EMD plant had operated in London for over 60 years and employed about 700 persons producing several products, in particular railway locomotives. The plant's history and its closing illustrated several economic, political, and social issues associated with plant closures.

History of Electro-Motive Diesel Inc.

The Electro-Motive Engineering Company was founded in 1922 by two Americans in Cleveland, Ohio, with the name later shortened to Electro-Motive Company. General Motors purchased the company in 1930 and operated it as a part of its Diesel Division. In 1950, a branch plant was opened in London, Ontario. The plant was established to avoid tariffs on manufactured goods and to become eligible for Government of Canada contracts. General Motors sold the division in 2005 to a private equity fund which operated the business as Electro-Motive Diesel Inc. In 2010, Caterpillar Inc., a large U.S. manufacturer of construction and mining equipment, bought the company and operated it under its wholly owned subsidiary Progress Rail Services Corp. Throughout its existence, the London plant was always American owned.

EMD used the London plant for the assembly, painting, and testing of locomotives. Over the years, the London plant also produced a variety of other products including transit buses and military vehicles, and manufactured locomotive underframes, traction motors, truck assemblies, and locomotive equipment racks. The plant was on a 100-acre site and included two main and several ancillary buildings totalling over 500,000 square feet. There was also a locomotive test track. The plant was ISO 9001 Certified for Quality and ISO 14001 Certified for Environmental Management.

In 2011, the plant had about 700 employees, of which 465 were members of the Canadian Auto Workers Union (CAW) who earned up to $34 per hour. Businesses dependent on the plant were estimated to employ about 1,000 more persons. The company and CAW began negotiating a new collective agreement the same year.

The Negotiations, Lockout, and Shutdown

During late 2011, a new labour contract was being negotiated and the union was faced with several demands by the company. The company sought pay cuts of 50 percent in many job categories, the elimination of the defined benefit pension plan, reductions in dental and other benefits, and the end of the cost of living adjustment to wages. The negotiations were difficult for the union, but it had been assured that the plant would not be closed during negotiations.

On January 1, 2012, EMD employees were locked out after their union refused to accept a 50 percent reduction in wages for most workers and the union immediately set up picket lines. EMD had recently announced that it would refurbish an old plant to manufacture locomotives at Muncie, Indiana, where employees received about one-half the wages of the London plant employees. This opening put subtle pressure on the London union and its members to accept the wage reduction if they wished to keep their jobs.

Caterpillar's Progress Rail Services announced the closure of the London plant on February 3, 2012.[19] The announcement stated that it was regrettable, but the cost structure of the London plant was not sustainable and it had not been possible to negotiate a new, competitive collective agreement. The high Canadian dollar made manufacturing in Ontario more costly, and the weak U.S. labour market made labour available. There were weaker labour laws in several states, and the union agreement at London imposed antiquated work rules causing quality problems.

Issues Surrounding the Closing

Several interrelated economic, social, and political issues were evident in the closing of the Electro-Motive plant: the impact of globalization, role of governments, the decline of union influence, and corporate strategies.

Challenges of Globalization

Changes were occurring in the global economy that influenced corporate decision makers. Multinational corporations shifted manufacturing to areas with cost advantages, in particular lower-wage areas. In the past, this involved outsourcing production or building plants in Asia, for example. Recently there had been a change in direction for some American multinationals that were now moving production back to the United States. There were several reasons for this. Unemployment levels in the United States were higher than in the past and labour was available. Some re-established production in the United States to take advantage of the government's "Buy America" purchase policies introduced to counter the 2008 economic downturn. Exchange rates had an influence as the value of the U.S. dollar had declined, a factor particularly affecting Canadian plants. There were more favourable labour laws in several states that reduced the influence of unions. In addition, many states were offering comprehensive assistance programs to entice investment.

Influence of Governments

Governments played a role in the establishment or closure of manufacturing plants. The Canadian government's high tariff policy contributed to the original establishment of the plant in London. If foreign corporations wanted to compete in Canada, it was necessary for them to build a plant in the country. These tariffs were reduced or eliminated with the free trade agreement between the United States and Canada. Similarly, the U.S. government's "Buy America" was a contributing factor in its closure in that products had to be produced in the country to take advantage of that government policy.

Canadian politicians had attempted to influence the London plant. In 2008, Prime Minister Harper visited the plant and promised $5 million in tax credit breaks to the purchasers of locomotives produced at the plant. The 2008 Budget allowed purchasers to double the cost allowance deduction on locomotive purchases. No direct government assistance was proposed for Electro-Motive Diesel Inc. itself.

On February 6, 2012, Ontario Premier Dalton McGuinty claimed that the federal government's foreign investment laws were outdated as they allowed a Canadian plant to be purchased and stripped within 18 months after the approval to take it over was given. The federal government responded, stating that what was happening fell under the province's industrial relations laws.[20]

Programs of some American states were also a factor; an example was those of Indiana. In order to attract the plant to Muncie, the Indiana state government provided $3.5 million in performance-based tax credits, $1 million in cash for employee training, and $1 million in infrastructure assistance. The state also agreed to assist the company in applying for U.S. federal government grants. Tax abatements of $22.5 million were obtained and some financing was available from the local county government.

Union's Influence

Globalization led to more volatile economic times and there had been an adverse impact on Canadian unions. Canadian private-sector union members were largely based in manufacturing industries and had been adversely impacted as manufacturing jobs disappeared. Also, automation in manufacturing had increased productivity and reduced the numbers of workers necessary. Overall, there were strong industrial relations laws in Canada but this did not prevent a decline in union membership. Only about 15 percent of the private-sector work force was unionized as newer service-type industries are more difficult to organize.

In addition, there were those in Canada who were critical of organized labour. Union leadership were accused of being more interested in their personal well-being than the interests of members. Restrictive work rules negotiated over years made improving productivity and product quality more difficult. It was alleged that unions fomented mistrust between workers and management. Critics stated that unions should be more transparent and accountable to members, for example by disclosing financial information which they were not required to do under Canadian law.

A trend in the United States toward right-to-work laws had been enacted in several U.S. states to encourage corporate investment and create jobs. Such laws allowed for a unionized workplace but gave workers an option of whether or not to join the union. As a result, many workers freeloaded off of those who agreed to join and pay the voluntary dues. This trend led to underfunded unions with less clout when negotiating contracts. As a result, some plants employing CAW members were attracted to the United States.

Nevertheless, the CAW attempted to protect the interests of its members at EMD. As early as December 21, 2011, Ken Lewenza, CAW president, sensed that EMD may leave. He called upon the federal government to conduct a review of Caterpillar's takeover of Canada's only locomotive manufacturer.[21] The federal government had not formally reviewed the takeover under the foreign investment regulations as the takeover was not large enough to be considered.[22] In a press release and letter to Industry Minister Christian Paradis on February 10, 2012, the CAW president demanded that the federal government provide details of the purchase of EMD by Caterpillar's Progress Rail Services in 2010. He requested that the government strengthen the regulations over foreign investment by:

- Improving transparency of the ultra-secretive Investment Canada process;
- Allowing broader stakeholder input to reviews;
- Closing loopholes that exempt most takeovers from scrutiny (including takeovers that are "too small" or reflect "indirect purchases" of companies);
- Strengthening and more clearly defining the "net benefit" test;
- Ensuring that government can enforce commitments attached to approved takeovers.[23]

With regard to the EMD closure, Lewenza stated that Caterpillar was exhibiting a "greedy, and frankly immoral, behaviour coming from a profitable company."[24] A large rally was held in London in support of the laid-off workers. Information picketing of Caterpillar outlets in various cities was organized and radio ads were broadcast.

Support from unions in Caterpillar plants in Belgium, France, and Italy stated that the EMD workers were "victims of a revolting blackmail."[25] The unions gave their full support to the London workers and stated that they would intervene before the local works councils in Europe. These initiatives had little impact on the decision.

Corporate Behaviour

Caterpillar was impacted by globalization and adjusted its corporate strategies. Instead of establishing plants overseas or outsourcing, new plants were being built in the United States. An example was its recent building of a new plant in Georgia where production was shifted from Japan as the market for some products had changed to North and South America. Also, several U.S. states had become friendlier to investment with less restrictive industrial-relations legislation, lower taxation, and their willingness to provide infrastructure and other incentives. Caterpillar was taking advantage of initiatives by some states that were becoming more aggressive in attracting investment and jobs.[26]

A factor in closing the London plant related to Caterpillar's strategy to become a major competitor in the train locomotive business. It recognized the increasing demand for freight and passenger train locomotives. New technologies had made the operation of locomotives more cost-effective, especially with regard to fuel consumption. Caterpillar was positioning itself in the locomotive business, and it needed to become efficient to compete with General Electric Co., its major competitor. As a part of this strategy, Caterpillar was refurnishing a plant in Muncie and thus closing the older, less efficient plant in London.

The profits of Caterpillar Inc. were an issue with the closure. The company achieved a profit of $4.9 billion in 2010, an 83 percent increase over the previous year, on sales of $60.1 billion.[27] A related issue was CEO Douglas Oberhelman's 2011 compensation of $10,550,300.[28] CAW's President Ken Lewenza said that the wage concessions were not necessary given Caterpillar's profits. He said: "What we're experiencing in London is a total injustice. It's shameful. It's completely hypocritical."[29]

Trends in the global economy presented challenges for Canadian stakeholders influenced by, or who could influence, the shutdown of the EMD plant. The union and governments appeared to have little influence on the decision. The corporation was implementing a global strategy in the best interests of its shareholders. As a result, another several hundred Canadians lost their jobs and many jobs were created in the United States.

The social responsibility toward workers after the closure of any plant was complicated. A component of social responsibility was the corporation's concern to employees and their well-being, present and past. The social obligation or legal requirement Caterpillar had to the displaced workers was an issue that still had to be addressed.

 # 500 Birds On a Pond[30]

The Alberta Oil Sands

Early explorers were aware of oil type substances, or bitumen, for over 200 years in areas now known as northern Alberta. It is believed that Aboriginal peoples repaired and sealed canoes with the oily materials. It was not until the twentieth century that research and development of these oily materials occurred. The first development in the early part of the century was the drilling of wells north of Fort McMurray, but no oil, in a liquid form, was discovered. Other ventures attempted to find commercially viable extraction methods, but failed technically and commercially. It was not until the 1960s that serious development occurred. Alberta government publications stated that oil production from the oil sands was commercially feasible and announced an oil sands policy designed to encourage the orderly development of the oil sands in an area known as the Athabasca Oil Sands Region. The first two major commercial developments were by Great Canadian Oil Sands (GCOS) Project (later Suncor Energy), which produced oil in 1967, and the Syncrude consortium formed in 1964, which started building a facility in 1973 and producing oil in 1978.

The production of oil from the sands was controversial from the beginning. Petroleum companies, industry organizations, and governments favoured developing the sands and producing oil while environmentalists, NGOs, some Aboriginal groups, and some think tanks opposed it. The media coverage of the controversy was extensive and attempted balance, although negative news stories dominated at times. Society at large, or the general public, had a mixed opinion of the development. Many agreed with the development for the economic growth and employment generated, while others became increasingly concerned over the environmental impact of other major projects being built to extract the oil.

Many of the arguments supporting oil production from the oil sands and those critical are summarized in Table 1.

TABLE 1	Arguments Supporting and Critical of Oil Sands
Arguments in Support of Production from the Oil Sands	**Arguments Critical of Production from the Oil Sands**
• Government policy allows for responsible development enabling economic growth and protection of the environment. Oil sands development is regulated.	• Oil sands development is out of control with new projects starting. NGOs are concerned about carbon dioxide emissions, destruction of the boreal forest, and tailing ponds that might contaminate local rivers. Government cannot monitor all aspects of developments.
• Only 4 percent of Canada's GHG emissions and less than one-tenth of one percent of global emissions are from oil sands production.	• Total emissions are up over 37 percent since 1990. The oil sands are the fastest growing source of Canada's emissions increase.

Arguments in Support of Production from the Oil Sands	Arguments Critical of Production from the Oil Sands
• Carbon dioxide emissions have decreased by 45 percent per barrel since 1990.	• Intensity targets reduce per barrel emissions but let overall emissions increase.
• By 2050, emissions will be 14 percent below 2005 levels.	• The new technology to capture carbon is not available until 2018.
• Ninety percent of water is recycled.	• Two to four barrels of water are required to produce each barrel of oil, and the Athabasca River flow is reduced in the winter.
• Disturbed lands are restored as required by law.	• The landscape is difficult to restore and it takes 50 years.
• Regulators inspect ponds for seepage, and there are rules requiring that birds be kept away.	• Fifty square kilometres of ponds exist with no plan for remediation.
• The Alberta government requires waterfowl protection plans to deter birds from ponds.	• Society cannot trust companies to report spills and harms to animals.
• Testing has found no downstream risks to communities.	• First Nations at Fort Chipewyan are worried about wildlife, water supply, and health, in particular bile-duct cancer.
• Only 20 percent of oil is from mined sands. Most of it is from "in-situ" process; that is, injecting steam into the ground and heating the heavy oil so it can be pumped to the surface.	• "In-situ" is a better way of extracting but it is still disruptive to the environment and requires a lot of energy.
• The Alberta oil industry is the most environmentally conscious in the world with higher standards.	• This may be so, but the industry can do better.
• Corporations operating in the oil sands are the most socially responsible.	• There is the possibility that greenwashing is taking place.
• Supporting publication: *Alberta's Oil Sands: Opportunity. Balance*, Government of Alberta, March 2008, http://www.assembly.ab.ca/lao/library/egovdocs/2008/alen/165630.pdf.	• Supporting publication: *The Most Destructive Project on Earth*, Environmental Defence, February 2008, http://www.environmentaldefence.ca/report/report-canadas-toxic- tar-sands-the-most-destructive-project-on-earth.

Sources: Compiled from numerous government and industry publications and media coverage.

Syncrude Canada Ltd.

Syncrude Canada is a joint venture owned by Canadian Oil Sands Limited (36.74 percent), ConocoPhillips Oil Sands Partnership II (9.03 percent), Imperial Oil Resources (25 percent), Mocal Energy Limited (5 percent), Murphy Oil Company Ltd. (5 percent), Nexen Inc. (7.23 percent), and Petro-Canada (12 percent). It is the largest producer of crude oil from the oil sands with a production capacity equivalent to over 15 percent of Canada's crude oil requirements. It employs more than 5,000 persons and is the largest industrial employer of Aboriginal peoples in Canada.[31]

Syncrude's 2007 Sustainability Report described its economic, social, and environmental obligations and achievements. The corporation's contribution to the economy included employment, materials purchasing, and royalty payments of $1.6 billion. It produced 111.3 million barrels of oil, and contributed $4.9 billion to the Canadian economy.[32]

Social sustainability included Syncrude's stakeholder engagement approach to Aboriginal communities, advocacy groups, contractors, educators, governments, industry groups, local community groups, NGOs, suppliers, and employees. The company supported various community investment initiatives by contributing $4.2 million. Its safety record improved substantially over previous years.

Syncrude was involved in several environmental initiatives: air quality, involving reducing odours and emissions; reclaiming mined land; resource conservation through energy use reduction and recycling waste water; projects addressing climate change; and waste management.

Ducks Land on a Pond

Some of the oil production facilities required large quantities of water in their processes. After use, the water was recycled if feasible but some was mixed with other materials and stored in large constructed ponds estimated to cover 50 square kilometres. The ponds—referred to as tailings, waste, toxic or tar ponds—were a mixture of clay, water, sand, hydrocarbons, and heavy metals. Syncrude's Aurora North mine north of Fort McMurray contained such a pond.

The oil sands are on the migratory routes of several bird species and the oil companies are required to have plans to keep the birds off the ponds. The ponds do not freeze over as quickly as fresh water and may thaw sooner in the spring. One method used to frighten the birds from landing is using propane-fired cannons. On April 28, 2008 at 9:30 a.m., an estimated 500 ducks, including mallards, buffleheads, and goldeneyes, were discovered on the Aurora North pond by a Syncrude employee. The birds were heavily soaked from the residual oil on the pond's surface and could not fly. Although regulations required immediate notification, the Alberta Government's Fish and Wildlife Office was not called until noon.[33]

Alberta Energy Company and the Ethics of Operation Kabriole[34]

It is September 1998. Gwyn Morgan, President and CEO of the Alberta Energy Company (AEC), has a difficult decision to make that could affect his company immensely. He was approached by the Alberta RCMP with a proposal that may finally put an end to the industrial sabotage that had plagued not only his company, but also the entire oil and gas industry. The terrorism had been costly and had intimidated company staff.

AEC's operations were focused on two aspects of the petroleum business: four upstream operations in natural gas and oil exploration and production, and two midstream operations in natural gas storage, pipelines, and natural gas liquids processing. Its 1997 revenues were over $1.2 billion, with net earnings of $21.7 million.

The production and processing of natural gas and oil involved substantial risk for the environment. The potential for adverse impact of their operations on the environment was a major challenge for the company. One challenge was the use of flare stacks at well sites. Flaring was routinely used in the energy industry worldwide. A typical use was when oil was being produced and the solution gas (gas that bubbles out of the oil as it is brought to surface pressure) was uneconomical to recover and is flared (burned) near the well site. In 1996, Alberta alone had more than 5,200 solution gas flares operating. The theory was that through flaring, substances in the gas were converted to their safest form possible even though it released some 250 compounds. Referred to as *sour gas*, farmers believed it was these toxins that caused health problems in their families, livestock, and crops.

Farmers were increasingly vocal and active regarding the effects of pollution on their families and farms. Health problems alleged to be associated with flaring included asthma, coughing, headaches, aching muscles, shortness of breath, and memory loss. Illness in cattle and poor crops were also attributed to the pollution. There was a growing perception among farmers that their concerns were not being taken seriously. Many reports of these problems appeared in newspapers and other media. The stories claimed that farmers could not get help from government or through the legal channels such as the Alberta Energy and Utilities Board's Environmental Appeals Board set up to deal with farmers' concerns.

The situation became volatile, with acts of terrorism occurring against the oil and gas industry. In February 1998, a particularly violent event occurred near Bowden, Alberta, when a beef farmer shot and killed an oil and gas company vice-president supervising the cleanup of a well site on his farm. Another petroleum company that had operated the site had caused the pollution. The farmer had been trying to get the well cleaned up for two and a half years and apparently broke down over all the frustrations at getting the cleanup done.

The eco-terrorism took place in AEC's operations in northwest Alberta, especially in the Peace River area. In the mid-1990s, the vandalism of petroleum installations began and continued during 1997 and into 1998. Over 100 acts of terrorism had occurred since mid-1996; the major acts are listed in Table 1. Property damage was running into the millions of dollars, and there was concern for the safety of field workers and neighbours. Some employees received threats of harm, but the RMCP had not charged anyone with responsibility for the acts. The police force was experiencing a staff shortage and had limited resources to devote to the terrorism. The petroleum industry's concern for its property and for employees and neighbours, plus the inability of the police to address the problem, resulted in cooperative efforts between the industry and the police.

TABLE 1	Chronology of Selected Terrorist Activities
Date	Event
1996	Nails are thrown on remote roads on land leased by oil companies. Power lines are cut down. Shots are fired through offices of two gas plants near Hythe, AB.
December 1997	A fire occurs at a Norcen Energy well site south of Hythe, AB, and cement studded with shotgun shells is found.
April 25, 1998	Three shots are fired at AEC well site building.
June 16, 1998	An AEC pipeline is hit with homemade projectile bomb.
July 31, 1998	An AEC sweet gas well at Goodfare, AB, is bombed.
August 2, 1998	A sour gas well near Demmitt, AB, is bombed.
August 24, 1998	A Suncor Energy oil well south of Hinton, AB, is bombed.

"Operation Kabriole" and the Sting

The petroleum industry, the police, and the communities in the area were increasingly concerned about the vandalism. In late summer 1998, the RCMP put together a special initiative labelled "Operation Kabriole"[35] to focus on the petroleum vandalism problem, and asked the industry for assistance. The operation was targeted at Wiebo Ludwig, leader of the Church of the Shepherd King sect of the Christian Reform Church who, along with his friend, Richard Boonstra, felt strongly that flaring was responsible for a range of human and animal birth deformities and stillbirths. Ludwig was widely known as an outspoken critic of the petroleum industry and flaring in particular, and he and his supporters were to be under 24-hour ground and airplane surveillance. The operation's budget was $354,750, but before it was over the operation would cost $750,000.

Ed McGillivary, AEC's director of environment, health, and safety, received a call from Robert Wraight, a friend of Ludwig's. Wraight offered his services as an undercover agent if AEC purchased his land for $109,000. AEC flew Wraight, at their expense, to Calgary and set up a meeting with the RCMP.

After discussions with the RCMP, Wraight agreed to become a paid agent and attempted to gather evidence for a case against Ludwig. The evidence-gathering included wearing a concealed tape recorder while visiting the Ludwig farm. As an informant, Wraight was given a $10,000 signing bonus and placed on the payroll at $475 per week. Later the police picked up $14,000 in other expenses that he incurred. AEC did not purchase Wraight's farm.

The RCMP approached AEC for their cooperation and the company agreed to provide resources if it would help solve the vandalism problem. The company offered to supply high-tech night vision equipment from its private security firm. This offer was refused, as it was not consistent with RCMP policy. The security firm was to provide tips to the RCMP on Ludwig's movements, something that many other organizations and individuals were doing.

In order to enhance Wraight's credibility, the RCMP proposed that a petroleum installation be deliberately vandalized. The RCMP proposed blowing up an old vehicle that they were willing to purchase from AEC for $8,000. Gwyn Morgan objected to this as he felt that it would cause stress among employees who feared that their vehicles might be vandalized. Instead, it was agreed that an abandoned, remote petroleum site building would be bombed. No date was set for the bombing but all agreed—the sooner the better.

Gwyn Morgan's Moral Dilemma

Gwyn Morgan was being asked to approve an act of vandalism and the company would not be able to disclose its involvement in the near future. All through the planning of the sting, he expressed that he wanted a complete disclosure of the context for AEC's cooperation. He knew that this might be difficult, given the process through which charges are laid and the timing of court proceedings.

Morgan was concerned that the vandalism was escalating into life-threatening sabotage. The direct and indirect costs to AEC were now over two million dollars, but there were more serious concerns. Placing explosive devices on wellheads, pipelines, and gas production facilities was dangerous to employees, and potentially dangerous to surrounding residents. Employees had received anonymous death threats, creating stress for them and their families.

Morgan had much to think about as he considered the decision. He was concerned about how the public would react to being deceived. Although the RCMP had assured him that the explosion would be safely discharged, he still worried about the success of the clandestine operation. He agonized over the level of cooperation between AEC and the RCMP, even though the RCMP assured him that such cooperation would be helpful in preventing extremely serious crimes. Only four others at AEC knew of the operation, and he wondered how shareholders, directors, and other employees would react when the event was disclosed.

He was aware that injury or death could be avoided and thought that to do nothing by being a bystander was the easy way out. Furthermore, the company was cooperating with an organization that society relies upon for law and order. Despite this, he anticipated that it might be viewed differently in the future as the media and the public questioned the close relationship between the company and the RCMP. The public might perceive that the line between corporate interests of the oil industry and law enforcement had become blurred. Moreover, they may not appreciate the company having been less than forthcoming about the staged bombing.

He knew that he and the company would be held accountable in any judicial process if the eco-terrorists were caught and charged. The public may not consider it appropriate for business to supply money and other resources to a police force. Thinking back over the events of the preceding months, he wondered if cooperating with the RCMP had been wise or appropriate. He, AEC's security firm, and Ed McGillivary had been in contact with the police force.

The dilemma for Morgan meant agonizing over compliance with the RCMP sting or be a bystander resisting any further involvement with police attempts to catch those responsible. He had to balance the protection of individuals from harm and the inclination to cooperate with the police against the consequence to be less than forthcoming in corporate announcements. How would he explain his actions to the company's directors and shareholders after the fact? How would they react? How would the industry react? How would the media respond? How would the nearby residents and communities feel? He wondered how things had reached this point. He was President and CEO, and it was his decision to make.

Crisis at Maple Leaf Foods Inc.[36]

In the summer of 2008, Canada experienced a serious outbreak of listeriosis, which resulted in seriously ill and caused the deaths of 22 individuals. Listeriosis is one of about 250 food-borne illnesses *salmonella*, *E. coli,* and the Norwalk virus. It results from consuming food contaminated with a bacterium called *Listeria monocytogenes* and any form of disease or invasive infection that results is given the name listeriosis. Older persons, those with compromised immune systems, and some pregnant women have a higher risk of being affected. A significant characteristic of listeriosis is the time between eating contaminated food and the onset of illness, which can range from three to seventy days. In comparison, *salmonella* causes illness within 12 to 72 hours. The most common forms of listeriosis are sepsis (bloodstream infection), infection of the central nervous system (usually meningitis), and miscarriage, stillbirth, or premature birth. It usually is not identified until blood samples are diagnosed in a laboratory.[37]

A Chronology of Events

The *Report of the Independent Investigator into the 2008 Listeriosis Outbreak* gave a detailed chronology of the chain of events related to the outbreak from July through September 2008. The Report covered all sectors of Canada's health and safety systems, but the following chronology lists only some of the events, and in particular those relating to the source of the contamination, Maple Leaf Foods.

TABLE 1	Chronology of Selected Crisis Events
July 10	First listeriosis cases diagnosed in a Toronto-area long-term care home.
July 16	Toronto Public Health begins investigating the two cases.
July 18	Match confirmed on DNA fingerprinting from first two human samples.
July 21	Food samples picked up by Toronto Public Health from long-term care home.
July 23	Long-term care home removes high-risk foods such as cold cuts, cheeses, and ice cream.
July 25	More cases show up on provincial surveillance system.
August 4	Some of the samples from the long-term care home test positive for *Listeria monocytogenes*.
August 6	The Toronto-area long-term care home suspects Maple Leaf Foods (MLF) products as the cause of the listeriosis.
August 7	The Canadian Food Inspection Agency (CFIA) initiates a food safety investigation.
August 8	The CFIA requests deli meats distribution records from MLF Sales Office but it is closed for the weekend.
August 11	Distribution records are received from MLF. Sure Slice brand products sold to hospitals, long-term care homes, prisons, restaurants, and hotels are suspected. Search begins for unopened food packages to verify the source.
August 12	National outbreak indicated. Unopened packaged meat products located and sent for testing. Two other possible cases identified.
August 13	MLF advises distributers not to sell Sure Slice roast beef, corned beef, and Black Forest ham. Possible link to MLF's Bartor Road plant identified.
August 14	Confirmation of first listeriosis death in mid-June linked to deli meats.

ust 15	Ontario institutions advised to stop serving Sure Slice products.
August 16	CFIA confirms *Listeria monocytogenes* in unopened Sure Slice package.
August 17	Consumers warned not to eat two Sure Slice products and MLF voluntarily recalls two products.
August 19	Consumers warned not to eat 23 additional MLF deli meat products and company announces second recall.
August 20	MLF suspends all production at the Bartor Road plant and announces that it is voluntarily recalling 23 products.
August 21	It is confirmed that 18 products from the Bartor Road plant are contaminated.
August 23	The link between human illness and contaminated deli meats is confirmed and MLF issues third recall of products—recalling all products made at the Bartor Road plant.

Source: *Listeriosis Report*, Chapter 6, "How did events unfold," 47–60.

Maple Leaf Foods Inc.

The history of Maple Leaf Foods can be traced for over 100 years. It is the result of amalgamations and mergers of companies in the food industry, making it Canada's major food-processing corporation. In 2008, the controlling shareholders were the McCain Capital Corporation and the Ontario Teachers' Pension Plan Board, and the company was publicly traded on the Toronto Stock Exchange. Headquartered in Toronto, it employed 23,000 people in Canada, the United States, the United Kingdom, and Asia. Maple Leaf Foods comprised three major groups: Meat Products—fresh and packaged meat; Bakery Products—fresh, frozen, and specialty bakery foods; and Agribusiness Products—including hog, rendering, and biodiesel production. Its main product brands were *Maple Leaf*®, *Schneiders*®, and *Dempster's*®. The company's 2007 sales were over $5 billion with 76 percent in Canada, 12 percent in the United States, and 12 percent in the rest of the world. Its net earnings for 2007 were $195 million.[38]

In August 2008, Michael McCain, president and CEO, and other senior management were wondering what public action to take other than recalling products. The company's lawyers and public relations staff were advising caution, in particular about accepting responsibility because of the legal implications, which could lead to future legal expenses and costly settlements. Some managers were concerned about the cost of recalling products not proven to be contaminated, potentially in the tens of millions. Still others pointed out that the company met all government standards and regulations and that its food safety policies and procedures were as high as any other company in the food industry. Some felt that the company could wait for government agencies to take initiative, with Maple Leaf Foods reacting as necessary. Others argued that the company should be open, admit its mistakes, and take responsibility for what happened. On August 23, it was decided that Michael McCain, the CEO, should make a national statement about the crisis.

 ## Just Dump It in the Lake[39]

On February 21, 2009, a "Notice of a Proclamation Exempting the Waters of Sandy Pond from Section 22 of the Navigable Waters Protection Act" appeared in the *Canada Gazette*, the official newspaper of the Government of Canada.[40] The Notice stated that "interested parties may make representations concerning the proposed proclamation within 30 days after the date of publication of this notice."[41] Those opposing the project had until March 21 to respond.

The Environment and Mining

Mining has several impacts on the environment; a major one relates to disposing or storing of waste materials or tailings after a processing or refining process. In the past, the tailings were simply put in piles, dumped in bodies of water, including the ocean, or contained in human-made holding areas or ponds. All of these approaches threatened the environment and possibly the health of surrounding residents. As a result, the industry sought better ways to dispose of the waste materials. Research suggested an approach whereby waste materials would be deposited in natural lakes, which would contain the harmful chemicals. Ideal lakes for this approach would be near the plant, have limited watershed, and be deep. This approach was preferable to constructing open holding ponds that might leak and were expensive to build and maintain.

In order to do this, some way had to be found to get around existing legislation, in particular, the *Fisheries Act*, which made it illegal to pollute fish-bearing waters.[42] However, the "Metal Mining Effluent Regulations" of the Act allowed federal bureaucrats to redefine a lake as a tailing impoundment area. To date, 16 sites have been applied for and listed in Schedule 2 of the regulations.[43]

In order for a lake to be listed, a notice must be issued exempting the lake from Section 22 (see Table 1) of the *Navigable Waters Protection Act*. An Order in Council[44] is necessary under Section 23 (see Table 1) to place the lake on Schedule 2 and allow for the dumping of waste into the body of water.

TABLE 1	Sections 22 and 23 of the *Navigable Waters Protection Act*
22. No person shall throw or deposit or cause, suffer or permit to be thrown or deposited any stone, gravel, earth, cinders, ashes or other material or rubbish that is liable to sink to the bottom in any water, any part of which is navigable or that flows into any navigable water, where there are not at least twenty fathoms of water at all times, but nothing in this section shall be construed so as to permit the throwing or depositing of any substance in any part of a navigable water where that throwing or depositing is prohibited by or under any other Act.	
R.S., c. N-19, s. 20.	
23. The Governor in Council, when it is shown to the satisfaction of the Governor in Council that the public interest would not be injuriously affected thereby, may, by proclamation, declare any rivers, streams or waters in respect of which sections 21 and 22 apply, or any parts thereof, exempt in whole or in part from the operation of those sections, and may revoke the proclamation.	
R.S., c. N-19, s. 21.	

Source: Department of Justice, Government of Canada, Navigable Waters Protection Act, Chapter N-22, R.S., C. N19, s.1. Reproduced with the permission of the Minister of Public Works and Government Services Canada, 2010.

Vale's Sandy Pond Proposal

Vale planned construction of a hydromet nickel processing plant at Long Harbour, Newfoundland and Labrador, 100 kilometres west of St. John's. Plant construction was to begin in 2009, and completed by 2012 at an estimated cost of $2.17 billion. It would employ 1,600–2,000 persons in the construction stage and about 400–450 full-time employees when in operation. The plant was intended to process 50,000 tonnes of nickel, 3,270 tonnes of copper, and 2,460 tonnes of cobalt annually from ore mined at the company's Voisey Bay mine in NL.

The facility required a disposal of tailings plan and the company decided to use Sandy Pond. About 400,000 tonnes of effluent would be dumped in the lake annually. The pond was about 6 kilometres from the plant and covered about 38 hectares. Dams would be constructed to enlarge the holding area to about 78 hectares. Vale was a signatory to the Mining Association of Canada's "Towards Sustainable Mining (TSM)" initiative.[45] The company stated that it accepted responsibility for the environment and acted responsibly.[46]

Arguments Supporting the Use of Sandy Pond

Vale said that it had seriously studied the alternatives and their environmental impact. It claimed that using Sandy Pond was the most environmentally friendly approach and stated that the Department of Fisheries and Oceans agreed. Submerging the waste prevents oxidization, which releases toxic substances. Ponds do not leak and human-made holding ponds would be much larger, requiring 180 hectares. Economically the pond made sense as costs of using the pond were $62 million versus $490 million for a human-made holding pond. Overall, using Sandy Pond was the least threat to the environment and the health of the community. Furthermore, the economic development was needed in the area of high unemployment after a phosphorus plant closed about 20 years prior.

Arguments Opposing the Use of Sandy Pond

Using lakes as dumps is an emotional issue. Environmentalists stated that Sandy Pond was a pristine lake with trout, eels, and smelt and used for local recreation. Mining Watch complained that the government was making it too easy to use lakes as industrial waste dumps and disposal sites. Moreover, there was a "hidden subsidy" to the mining industry when it managed to get around the *Fisheries Act* enabling it to reduce costs.

The controversy over Sandy Pond generated substantial public comment. Opposition to the dumping of wastes came from stakeholders such as Centre for Long Term Environmental Action NL (CLEANf/Ld), the Sierra Club of Canada, the Council of Canadians, the New Democratic Party, the Canadian Union of Public Employees, the David Suzuki Foundation, and Maude Barlow, a senior adviser on water to the United Nations.

 ## Professor Murray's Ethical Dilemmas[47]

Everyone in their workplace, personal life, or society is confronted with ethical dilemmas from time to time. College instructors are no exception. Much has been written on teaching ethics, but little about the ethics of teaching. Yet all instructors have their personal integrity to consider and a responsibility to teach in an ethical manner. Also, they should consider the ethical implications of actions taken by colleagues, students, and themselves.

Below are incidents that present ethical dilemmas for college or university instructors. For each incident, identify what the dilemma is, the stakeholders involved, what the instructor should do, and who is harmed by or benefits from the decision. In addition, identify the ethical principle that formed the basis for the decision.

Incident #1

Professor Wayne Murray answered a knock at his door to find a young man whom he did not recognize. The young man explained that he represented a used-book company that gathered textbooks and then sold them to bookstores. These stores then resold them at prices lower than new copies, thus saving students money. He offered to purchase any "sample" or "inspection" copies of textbooks that Professor Murray had received from publishers that he did not need.

Professor Murray often received free textbooks from the publishers and had not recommended most of them for use in his courses. Such textbooks sat on his book shelves for years, were thrown out, or sometimes sent to educational institutions in developing countries. The young man was a student at the university for whom this part-time job would help him finance his education. Professor Murray was not sure what he should do.

Incident #2

Professor Murray had taught general management courses, such as strategy management, at a Canadian university for over 15 years. Despite his experience, he was still uneasy when students requested extensions to assignments or examination deferrals.

The assignments were described in detail on course outlines distributed at the first class. This was a requirement for all courses and all instructors complied with the policy. As a result, all students were aware of all assignment due dates and the dates of mid-term examinations well in advance.

Each semester, Professor Murray received several requests for extensions or deferrals. The reasons for the requests could be categorized into three types: (1) those based upon student illness or an illness or death in the student's family or close friends; (2) those based on work overload resulting from several assignments or examinations occurring at the same time; and (3) those based on the student's claim that he or she was busy with work and/or extracurricular activities.

The first category presented no difficulty for Professor Murray. He granted the request for extension usually without requiring documentation. But, the second and third reasons concerned him.

Professor Murray was particularly concerned about the ethical implications of the requests and of the actual granting of extensions. He was concerned about fairness and justice to students who worked to meet the deadlines. He worried about consistency in dealing with the requests and their legitimacy. He did not believe that students fully appreciated the awkward position in which these requests placed him.

Incident #3

As a professor of management, Professor Murray attempted to keep up-to-date on his area of specialization by reading selected academic journals. He felt this improved his teaching as students would be presented with recent research discoveries. He also tried to keep track of research developments so that he could use them to enhance his own research activity.

A colleague's research was in a related area and Professor Murray always read these articles out of interest and so that he could discuss the findings with his colleague. Last year, his colleague published an excellent article that tested a management theory. The article included a comprehensive six-page review of relevant literature and Professor Murray had used this review himself to prepare lecture materials. This year his colleague published another article in a different journal testing a similar theory. However, the literature review for this article included five pages from the previous article without any alterations. Furthermore, his colleague did not state that the review had been previously published.

Plagiarism was a serious problem with student assignments. Students had been warned of the seriousness of the practice and three students had been expelled for copying the writings of others without referencing them. Professor Murray was taken aback by the fact that his colleague had plagiarized, even if it was his own work.

Incident #4

Students were frequently used as subjects for professors' research projects. Such a practice was convenient for the professors as it reduced the need to recruit participants. Furthermore, students were contributing to the advancement of knowledge, which they may or may not have appreciated. Although occurring less frequently, the practice still occurred. There were college policies relating to the practice and agencies that funded research had strict policies about obtaining consent and making participation voluntary.

Professor Murray had colleagues who used students as research subjects. He had heard that some of his colleagues secretly conducted surveys in their classes without advising the administration. He thought that students should not be asked to participate in a study by their professor under any circumstances. It was difficult, if not impossible, to eliminate the real or perceived influence or power that the professor had with students. He was thinking of proposing a college policy that disallowed soliciting survey participation in the classroom setting. If faculty wanted to use students in their studies, they should advertise for them and perhaps offer incentives. The important point would be that the studies would not be associated with a particular course and classroom setting. Some of Professor Murray's colleagues felt that he was being too strict and limiting their ability to conduct research.

Incident #5

Professor Murray and his colleagues were alarmed at the reports of student cheating at colleges and universities. *Maclean's* magazine carried several stories on the subject with titles such as, "The great university cheating scandal" (Feb. 12, 2007, 32–36), "Cheating? Who us?" (Feb. 26, 2007, 41), and "Cheating on your exam? It's no big deal" (June 25, 2007, 25). There was considerable discussion of the issue and some codes of conduct were developed at his college. Students were advised of the college's policy regarding cheating and the fact that students could be expelled. From his experience and according to his colleagues, cheating continued.

One of the *Maclean's* articles stated that 44 percent of professors said that they didn't report students caught cheating. This statistic became more relevant when Professor Murray suspected a student of cheating in an examination. First of all, Professor Murray saw the student leaning over and reading the papers of students beside him. Secondly, the same student was seen removing a piece of paper from his shirt sleeve.

Professor Murray found it awkward to do anything at the time, as approaching the student would have disrupted the examination. He thought that it was not fair to other students that this student should get away with cheating. But, he concluded that it would be difficult to prove that the cheating occurred; it would be his word against the student's. Furthermore, he did not look forward to the numerous meetings and hearings that would be involved if he accused the student of cheating.

Incident #6

In one of his courses, Professor Murray assigned several case studies which the students could purchase online from the Harvard Business School. On the day when the first case was to be discussed, he asked how many had purchased the case. About half of the students held up their hands. He then asked if the others had the case and had read it. They informed him that they had obtained the case for free from an Internet site. He was able to access the Harvard site, which provided a count of the number of sales along with the names of the students who had bought the case. About half of the students had purchased the cases. Given this situation, Professor Murray discussed in class the appropriateness of obtaining the cases and that copyright issues were involved. However, he did not mention that he had access to sales data.

Before the next class, when another case was to be discussed, Professor Murray searched the Internet and could not find the case available. He then checked the Harvard site again. The number of sales had not changed. He wondered how he should deal with this in the class. Should he tell the students he could see who had purchased the case? Then again, he was unsure of whether he should have told the students upfront that he had access to this information. He wondered what to do, and whether he should do anything at all.

Fortis and the Chalillo Dam: Balancing Economic Development and Environmental Impact[48]

Fortis Corporation

Fortis Inc. is a diversified electric utility holding company headquartered in St. John's, NL. *Fortis* is a Latin word meaning strong, powerful, and firm. [Fortis Inc. is not associated with the Fortis international banking and insurance financial firm headquartered in The Netherlands and Belgium.]

In 2001, Fortis wholly owned Newfoundland Power Inc., the principal distributor of power in Newfoundland and Labrador, Maritime Electric Company Limited, the main distributor in Prince Edward Island, and Fortis Properties, a non-utility subsidiary with investments in commercial properties in Atlantic Canada. Other financial interests included electric utilities in Ontario, New York State, the Cayman Islands, and Belize. The Belizean interests were 67 percent of Belize Electricity Limited (BEL), the only distributor of electricity in Belize, and 100 percent of Belize Electric Company Limited (BECOL), which owned a hydroelectric plant on the Macal River at Mollejon, Belize.

The Fortis operations in Belize embroiled the company in an environmental responsibility issue that consumed substantial costs, time, and energy. BEL had been owned by the Government of Belize and was the main supplier of electricity in the country. In October and November 1999, Fortis Inc. acquired 67 percent of the company for $36 million in cash. It later acquired BECOL and a proposal by this company to develop a hydroelectric project in Belize received international attention and became a sensitive issue for management.[49]

The Chalillo Project

Fortis, through BECOL, proposed construction of a dam on the Macal River in the Cayo District of western Belize at cost of about US$27.3 million. The site was located in an unpopulated wilderness area, part of which was in the Mountain Pine Ridge Forest Reserve and Chaquibul National Park. These areas covered most of the southern half of Cayo district. It would produce 7.3 MW of electricity for the Belize network and regulate the river's flow. The control over the water flow would increase the productivity and reliably of the Mollejon hydro power station downstream.

The Chalillo project included:

- a 49.5 m high by 340 m wide dam on the river,
- a reservoir with a total surface area of 9.5 km^2,
- a powerhouse at the foot of the dam,
- an 18 km transmission line from the powerhouse to the Mollejon plant, and
- ancillary requirements including an access road and construction camp.[50]

There were benefits to the Belizean citizens and the country's economy. Most importantly, the project would increase electrical output and raise energy self-sufficiency. The second dam on the Macal River would increase the productivity of the existing electrical plant at Mollejon. The output from the two plants would reduce reliance on petroleum generation as diesel-fuelled generators could be closed. This would reduce greenhouse gas emissions and the possibility of oil spills.

A large portion of Belizean electrical energy was imported from Mexico under a contract that was to expire in 2008. The Mexican system experienced difficulties and it was not a stable source, resulting in power outages in Belize. The completion of the Chalillo project meant that Belize would have a more reliable and secure supply of electricity, stabilizing and possibly reducing prices. Alternative sources of energy were examined by the government and BEL including thermal options (diesel and gas turbines), biomass, Battery Energy Storage Systems, and solar and wind power. Studies by BEL determined that power generated from the hydro source was less expensive than any other. However, BEL was committed to purchasing power from a bagasse-fuelled generation facility planned by Belize Sugar Industries Limited (BSI). The facility would produce energy by burning crushed sugarcane and wood wastes from nearby sawmills.

There were other benefits to the project. The dam and reservoir would control flooding on the Macal River with significant economic, health, and safety benefits to downstream residents, many of whom lived in the river's floodplain. Also, there would be a steadier supply of water for residents especially during the dry season. Employment would be created during construction and there would be economic benefits from supplying goods and services to the project.[51]

Opposition to the Project

During 2001, criticisms and opposition were voluminous. Several Canadian print and broadcast media carried stories, there were letters to the editor in newspapers, and protest websites were established.

Numerous environmental non-governmental organizations (ENGOs) campaigned against the project, including:

- Probe International (PI)
- Natural Resources Defense Council (NRDC)
- Sierra Club of Canada
- Belize Alliance of Conservation Non-Governmental Organizations (BACONGO)
- Humber Environmental Action Group
- Humber Natural History Society
- Petitcodiac Riverkeeper
- Action Environment
- Defenders of Wildlife
- Environment Coalition of Prince Edward Island
- Falls Brook Centre

In particular, PI carried out an aggressive campaign and coordinated the protests of other ENGOs.[52] PI is an environmental advocacy group that fights to stop ill-conceived aid, trade projects, and foreign investments. It works to give citizens the tools they need to stop such projects using the rule of law, democratic processes, and honest and transparent accounting. It is a division of the Energy Probe Research Foundation, a well-known Canadian environmental and energy policy ENGO created in 1980. Its tactics include writing letters to public officials, preparing and publishing reports and articles, media releases, speech presentations, and public demonstrations.

The other main opposition came from NRDC, an environmental action group founded in 1970. Its mission is to safeguard the Earth: its people, plants, and animals, and the natural systems on which all life depends. It has offices in seven U.S. cities, staff of about 300 lawyers, scientists, and policy experts, and about 1 million members. Robert F. Kennedy, Jr., a lawyer, was the main spokesperson for NRDC on the Chalillo project.[53]

PI maintained an elaborate website in opposition to the project. Another website devoted exclusively to the Chalillo project was Stop Fortis! (no longer available), which contained extensive information on the project including photographs. Several environmental groups placed advertisements in Canadian newspapers.

The criticisms of Fortis's practices and the dam's construction are summarized in Exhibit 1. Fortis and Stanley Marshall, President and CEO, responded to this criticism. A news release was issued on November 1, 2001, "Decision to Build Hydroelectric Dam in Belize Should Reside with Belizeans." The main points made in the release were:

- Belizeans should decide on the construction of the dam.
- Contrary to information from ENGOs, the dam is economically feasible and will ensure a more stable energy supply.
- Information presented by ENGOs is misleading the media about the environmental impact of the project.
- Fortis is willing to review its business activities with stakeholders.

EXHIBIT 1   **Main Criticisms of the Chalillo Project**

- The threat to wildlife and plant life, especially endangered species.
- The dam would exacerbate the water quality problems downstream.
- The dam may flood Maya ruins destroying the cultural landscape.
- Limestone caves may drain the reservoir.
- The claim that the project was uneconomic and not the cheapest option. The only reason the project was viable was because BEL had a monopoly and could recover costs from captive customers.
- Fortis' unwillingness to consider alternative sources, denying consumers the right to better and cheaper electricity.
- The allegation that Fortis asked the Canadian government, through CIDA, to pay for a study justifying the project. It was claimed that the study was biased, involved too much secrecy, and failed to promote and ensure effective stakeholder consultation.
- According to environmental groups, Fortis denied them access to pertinent information and failed to consult them.
- Fortis wouldn't make its own geology studies and engineering plans public or agree to an independent panel review.
- There was insufficient information on the impact of the project.

Source: Used with permission of Probe International.

In a story in *The Telegram* on November 2, Marshall stated to a reporter, "This bombardment in the media of misleading information is putting enormous pressure on me, attacking me personally and inundating the media with lies." He also said, "Whatever we do as an electric company will impact the environment, but it's a question of how well we can manage our activities. On balance, this project is a good one. If I felt personally that we were going to threaten an endangered species and wipe it out—no. I would not propose going ahead with it."[54]

The project had consumed a lot of time, energy, and resources, and Fortis management wondered whether or not it was worth it. There might be less demanding projects that would add as much value to the company.

Endnotes

Preface

1. These environments are similar to those identified by the previous domain statement of the Social Issues in Management Division, Academy of Management.

2. Mark S. Schwartz and Archie B. Carroll, "Integrating and Unifying Competing and Complementary Frameworks: The Search for a Common Core in the Business and Society Field," *Business and Society* 47, no. 2 (June 2008): 148–186.

3. Academy of Management, Social Issues in Management Domain statement at http://aom.org/Divisions-and-Interest-Groups/Academy-of-Management-Division---Interest-Group-Domain-Statements.aspx#sim

Chapter 1

1. Based on Pete Engardio, "Beyond the Green Corporation," *BusinessWeek*, January 29, 2007, 50–64.

2. Richard T. De George, *Competing with Integrity in International Business* (Oxford: Oxford University Press, 1993).

3. DeGeorge, *Competing with Integrity in International Business*.

4. Tyler Hamilton, "Clean Capitalism Superheroes Lead Evolution of Free Enterprise," *Corporate Knights: The Magazine for Clean Capitalism,* Winter 2013, Vol. 11, Issue 4, 8.

5. "What is the Social License," On Common Ground Consultants Inc., and Robert Boutilier and Associates, accessed October 9, 2012, http://socialicense.com/definition.html.

6. Eric Beauchesne, "Canadians Reward Responsible Businesses: Poll," *The Telegram* (St. John's, NL), April 21, 2005, D3.

7. Janet McFarland, "Survey Finds Business View Does Not Match Public's," *The Globe and Mail*, October 31, 2006, B12.

8. John H. Tory, "Integrity Tops the List for Essential Qualities of Good CEO," *The Globe and Mail*, September 2, 2002, B5.

9. Martin Patriquin, "The Great University Cheating Scandal," *Maclean's,* February 12, 2007, 32–36.

10. Michael E. Porter and Mark R. Kramer, "Strategy and Society: The Link Between Competitive Advantage and Corporate Social Responsibility," *Harvard Business Review* 84, Issue 12 (December 2006): 83–84.

Chapter 2

1. Portions of this chapter are a revised and expanded version from Robert W. Sexty, "The Fundamentals of Canadian Capitalism: Theoretical and Practical Perspectives," in *Canadian Business and Society: Understanding Social and Ethical Challenges* (Scarborough, ON: Prentice-Hall Canada Inc., 1995), 37–46.

2. The forms listed are adapted from Christopher Farrell, "Faces of Capitalism," *BusinessWeek* (Special 1994 Bonus Issue), November 18, 1994, 19.

3. More information at the Conscious Capitalism website, at http://consciouscapitalism.org and the Conscious Capitalism Alliance website, at http://consciouscapitalismalliance.onefireplace.com. A recent book on the approach is John Mackey, Rajendra Sisodia, and Bill George, *Conscious Capitalism: Liberating the Heroic Spirit of Business* (Boston: Harvard Business Review Press, 2013).

4. Bill Gates, "Making Capitalism More Creative," *Time* (online), July 31, 2008, accessed January 2, 2016, http://www.time.com/time/printout/0,8816,1828069,00.html.

5. Ian Bremmer, "State Capitalism and The Crisis," *McKinsey Quarterly* (online), July 9, 2009, accessed January 2, 2016, http://www.mckinseyquarterly.com/home.aspx; and Pete Engardio, "State Capitalism," *BusinessWeek,* February 9, 2009, 39–43.

6. 2015 Edelman Trust Barometer: Canadian Results, Edelman, accessed January 2, 2016 http://www.slideshare.net/EdelmanInsights/2015- edelman-trust-barometer-canadian-findings.

7. These views can be found at: Robert W. Tracinski, "The Moral Basis of Capitalism," The Center for the Advancement of Capitalism accessed January 2, 2016, http://www.capitalismcenter.org/Philosophy/Essays/The_Moral_Basis_of_Capitalism.htm; Devin T. Stewart, "Is Ethical Capitalism Possible?", Policy Innovations, January 21, 2009, accessed January 2, 2016, http://www.policyinnovations.org/ideas/commentary/data/000105; and Joel F. Wade, "The Moral Defense of Capitalism," *The Daily Bell,* August 8, 2011, accessed January 2, 2016, http://www.policyinnovations.org/ideas/commentary/data/000105.

Chapter 3

1. This definition is based on the work of R. Edward Freeman in *Strategic Management: A Stakeholder Approach* (Boston: Pitman, 1984), 53.

2. Freeman, *Strategic Management,* 45.

3. Ibid, 45.

4. Jack Kapica, "Pope Warns of Profitability over People," *The Globe and Mail,* May 2, 1991, A6; and George Bragues, "The Capitalist Pope," *National Post,* April 5, 2005, FP23.

5. William C. Frederick, Keith Davis, and James E. Post, *Business and Society: Corporate Strategy, Public Policy, Ethics* (New York: McGraw-Hill, 1988), Chapter 4.

6. Henry Mintzberg, *Power In and Around Organizations* (Englewood Cliffs, NJ: Prentice-Hall, Inc., 1983), chapters 4 and 9.

7. Robert Phillips, "Some Key Questions about Stakeholder Theory," *Ivey Business Journal* (online), March/April 2004.

8. Coro Strandberg, "The Sustainability Pay Link," *Corporate Knights*, Summer 2014 Issue, accessed May 12, 2016, http://www.corporateknights.com/channels/workplace/the-sustainability-pay-link-14018967/

9. John Argenti, "Stakeholders: The Case Against," *Long Range Planning* 30 (1997): 442–445.

10. Andrew Campbell, "Stakeholders: The Case in Favour," *Long Range Planning* 30 (1997): 446–49.

11. Steven L. Wartick and John F. Mahon, "Toward a Substance Definition of the Corporate Issue Construct," *Business and Society,* Vol. 33, No. 3, December 1994, 308.

12. This definition is based upon one formulated by Jon Johnson, "Issues Management—What Are the Issues?" *Business Quarterly* 48 (Fall 1983): 1.

13. Steven L. Wartick and Robert E. Rude, "Issues Management: Corporate Fad or Corporate Function?" *California Management Review* 29 (1986): 132–36; and Joseph F. Coates et al., *Issues Management: How You Can Plan, Organize and Manage the Future* (Mt. Airy, MD: Lomond Publishers, Inc., 1986), 15–16.

14. Coates, *Issues Management,* 19–20.

15. Steven Fink, *Crisis Management: Planning for the Inevitable* (New York: AMACOM, 1986).

16. Ibid, 15–16.

17. Ibid, 15–16.

18. Christine M. Pearson and Ian I. Mitroff, "From Crisis Prone to Crisis Prepared: A Framework for Crisis Management," *Academy of Management Executive*, Vol. 7, No 1, 1993, 48-59.

19. Norman R. Augustine, "Managing the Crisis You Tried to Prevent," *Harvard Business Review*, November–December 1995, 147–158.

20. Ian I. Mitroff and Paul Shrivastava, "Effective Crisis Management," *The Academy of Management Executive*, Vol. 1, No. 3, 1987, 283-29; Jonathan L. Bernstein, "The Ten Steps of Crisis Communications," *Crisisnavigator*, Vol. 11, Issue 4 (April 2010), available at http://www.crisisnavigator.org/The-Ten- Steps-of-Crisis-Communications.490.0.html; and Daniel F. Muzyka, "Communicating in a Crisis: Act with Honesty and Empathy," *The Globe and Mail*, June 9, 2008, B8.

21. Linda Stamato, "Should Business Leaders Apologize? Why, When and How an Apology Matters," *Ivey Business Journal,* July-August 2008, 1–8.

Chapter 4

1. Archie B. Carroll, *Business and Society: Ethics and Stakeholder Management* (Cincinnati, OH: South-Western Publishing, 1989), 62.

2. Edward R. Freeman, *Strategic Management: A Stakeholder Approach* (Boston: Pitman, 1984).

3. Ibid, 53.

4. Ibid, 54–64.

5. Ibid, 64–69.

6. Ibid, 69–73.

7. John M. Bryson, *Strategic Planning for Public and Nonprofit Organizations: A Guide to Strengthening and Sustaining Organizational Achievement,* revised edition (San Francisco: Jossey-Bass Publishers, 1995), 284–286.

8. Paul C. Nutt and Robert W. Backoff, *Strategic Management of Public and Third Sector Organizations: A Handbook for Leaders* (San Francisco: Jossey-Bass Publishers, 1992), 196–98; and Bryson, *Strategic Planning for Public and Nonprofit Organizations,* 285–286.

9. Grant T. Savage, Timothy W. Nix, Carlton J. Whitehead, and John D. Blair, "Strategies for Assessing and Managing Organizational Stakeholders," *Academy of Management Executive* 5(2) (1991): 61–75.

10. Freeman, *Strategic Management,* 142–144.

11. Ronald K. Mitchell, Bradley R. Agle, and Donna J. Wood, "Toward a Theory of Stakeholder Identification and Salience: Defining the Principle of Who and What Really Counts," *Academy of Management Review,* Vol. 22, No. 4 (1997): 853–86.

12. Ibid, 289–293.

13. Jeff Frooman. "Stakeholder Influence Strategies," *Academy of Management Review,* Vol. 24, No. 2 (1999): 191–205.

14. Ibid, 196–197.

15. Ibid, 198.

16. Jeanne Liedtka, "Collaborating across Lines of Business for Competitive Advantage," *Academy of Management Executive Journal,* Volume 10, No. 2 (1996): 20–37.

17. Ann Svendsen, *The Stakeholder Strategy: Profiting from Collaborative Business Relationships* (San Francisco: Berrett-Koehler Publishers, 1998), 2–5.

18. Ibid, 71–184.

19. Archie B. Carroll, *Business and Society: Ethics and Stakeholder Management* (Cincinnati, OH: South-Western Publishing, 1989), 479–489; and John M. Bryson, *Strategic Planning for Public and Nonprofit Organizations* (San Francisco: Jossey-Bass Publishers, 1988).

20. Ronald K. Mitchell, Bradley R. Agle, and Donna J. Wood, "Toward a Theory of Stakeholder Identification and Salience: Defining the Principle of Who and What Really Counts*,"* *Academy of Management Review*, Vol. 22, No. 4 (1997): 853–86

21. Jonathan Bundy and Ann K. Buchholtz, "Strategic Cognition and Issue Salience: Toward An Explanation of Firm Responsiveness to Stakeholder Concerns," *Academy of Management Review*, Vol. 38, No. 3 (2013): 352-376

22. "Results of Stakeholder Analysis Conducted in 2014," Corporate Sustainability Report 2014 entitled *Citizens of the World*, Air Canada, August 15, 2015, page 13, accessed December 18, 2015, http://www.aircanada.com/en/about/documents/csr_2014_report_en.pdf?r=Friday, 21-Aug-15 19:48:31

Chapter 5

1. Philip V. Lewis, "Defining Business Ethics: Like Nailing Jello to a Wall," *Journal of Business Ethics* 4 (1985): 381.

2. Larue Tone Hosmer, "Strategic Planning as if Ethics Mattered," *Strategic Management Journal* 15 (1994): 23.

3. Larue Tone Hosmer, *The Ethics of Management* (Homewood, IL: Irwin, 1987), 96.

4. *An Inquiry into the Nature and Causes of the Wealth of Nations,* published in 1776. Online edition available at the Adam Smith Institute website, http://www.adamsmith.org.

5. Larue Tone Hosmer, *Moral Leadership in Business* (Burr Ridge, IL: Irwin, 1994).

6. Ian Maitland, "The Human Face of Self-Interest," *Journal of Business Ethics* 38 (2002): 3–17.

7. John Kaler, "Reasons to Be Ethical: Self-Interest and Ethical Business," *Journal of Business Ethics* 27 (2000): 161–173.

8. Ibid.

9. Anthony M. Pagano, "Criteria for Ethical Decision Making in Managerial Situations," *Proceedings* (New Orleans: National Academy of Management, 1987): 1–12.

10. Hosmer, "Strategic Planning As If Ethics Mattered," *Strategic Management Journal*, June 14, 2007.

11. Lawrence Kohlberg, "The Claim of Moral Adequacy of a Highest Stage of Moral Judgment," *The Journal of Philosophy* LXX (1973): 630–646; Lawrence Kohlberg, *Essays on Moral Development, Vol. 1: The Philosophy of Moral Development* (New York: Harper and Row, 1981); and Lawrence Kohlberg, "Stage and Sequence: The Cognitive Development Approach to Socialization," in *Handbook of Socialization Theory and Research,* D.A. Goslin, ed. (Chicago: Rand McNally, 1969), 347–480.

12. L. Kohlberg and R. Ryncarz, "Beyond Justice Reasoning: Moral Development and Consideration of a Seventh Stage," in C. Alexander and E. Langer, eds., *Higher Stages of Human Development: Perspectives on Adult Growth* (New York: Oxford University Press, 1990).

13. Linda Klebe Treviño and Michael E. Brown, "Managing to Be Ethical: Debunking Five Business Myths," *Academy of Management Executive,* Vol. 18, No. 2 (2004): 69–72, 77.

14. Mahzarin R. Banaji, Max H. Bazerman, and Dolly Chugh, "How (Un)ethical Are You?" *Harvard Business Review,* Vol. 81, Issue 12, December 2003, 56–64.

Chapter 6

1. Lisa Jones Christensen et al, "Taking Responsibility for Corporate Social Responsibility: The Role of Leaders in Creating, Implementing, Sustaining, or Avoiding Socially Responsible Behaviors," *The Academy of Management Perspectives,* 2014, Vol. 28, No. 2, 172-174.

2. Michel Dion, "Corporate Citizenship as an Ethic of Care: Corporate Values, Codes of Ethics, and Global Governance," in Jorg Andriof and Malcolm McIntosh, *Perspectives on Corporate Citizenship* (London: Greenleaf Publishing, 2002), 118–137.

3. Jack Kooten, *Strategic Management in the Public and Nonprofit Organization* (New York: Praeger, 1989), 125.

4. Lee Ginsberg and Neil Millier, "Value-Driven Management," *Business Horizons,* May/June (1992): 23–27.

5. Errol P. Mendes and Jeffrey A. Clark, "The Five Generations of Corporate Codes of Conduct and Their Impact on Corporate Social Responsibility," *Human Rights Research Centre*, University of Ottawa, accessed January 23, 2003, http://www.cdp-hrc.uottawa.ca/publicat/five.html.

6. Laura L. Nash, "Ethics without the Sermon," *Harvard Business Review,* November–December 1981, 79–89.

7. Ibid, 89.

8. Anthony M. Pagano, "Criteria for Ethical Decision Making in Managerial Situations," *Proceedings,* National Academy of Management, New Orleans (1987): 1–12.

9. This is a variation of a definition by Michael McDonald, "Ethics and Conflict of Interest," the W. Maurice Young Centre of Applied Ethics, University of British Columbia, http://www.ethics.ubc.ca/people/mcdonald/conflict.htm.

10. Kenneth Kernaghan and John W. Langford, "Conflict of Interest," chapter 6 in *The Responsible Public Servant* (Halifax: The Institute for Research on Public Policy and The Institute of Public Administration of Canada, 1990), 133–155.

11. Competition Bureau Canada, "Whistleblowing Study—Models of Whistleblowing Protection," http://www.competitionbureau.gc.ca/internet/index.cfm?itemid=1276&lg=e.

12. Ontario Securities Commission, OSC Policy 15-601 - Whistleblower Program, http://www.osc.gov.on.ca/en/SecuritiesLaw_rule_20151028_15-601_policy-whistleblower-program.htm.

13. Stephen M. Kohn, "The Sarbanes-Oxley Act ('Sox'): Legal Protections for Corporate Whistleblowers," National Whistleblowing Center, http://www.whistleblowers.org/html/sarbanes-oxley.htm.

14. Steven Bavaria, "Corporate Ethics Should Start in the Boardroom," *Business Horizons,* January–February (1991): 9–19.

15. James Gillies, *Boardroom Renaissance: Power, Morality and Performance in the Modern Corporation* (Toronto: McGraw-Hill Ryerson, 1992), Chapter 8.

16. Archie B. Carroll, "The Moral Leader: Essential for Successful Corporate Citizenship," in Jorg Andriof and Malcolm McIntosh, *Perspectives on Corporate Citizenship* (London: Greenleaf Publishing, 2002), 145–150.

17. André Nijhof, Olaf Fisscher, and Jan Kees Looise, "Coercion, Guidance and Mercifulness: The Different Influences of Ethics Programs on Decision Making," *Journal of Business Ethics* 27, 1–2 (September 2000): 33–42.

18. Ibid, 35.

19. Ibid, 38.

20. Ibid, 39.

21. *Management Ethics,* Summer 2008, 66–67.

22. Max B.E. Clarkson, "Ethics and Profit: The Changing Values of Business in Society." Unpublished presentation to the Faculty of Business Administration, Memorial University of Newfoundland, St. John's (March 3, 1993).

23. Ibid.

24. Gene Laczniak, "Business Ethics: A Manager's Primer," *Business* (Georgia State University, 1983): 23–29.

25. Free Management Library, *Business Ethics: Managing Ethics in the Workplace and Social Responsibility,* http://www.managementhelp.org/ethics/ethxgde.htm#anchor33077.

26. Linda Klebe Treviño and Michael E. Brown, "Managing to Be Ethical: Debunking Five Business Myths," *Academy of Management Executive* 18, no. 2 (May 2004): 69–81.

27. Literature reviewed for this section: Trevor Cole, "Why Good People Do Bad Things," *University of Toronto Magazine,* Winter 2005, 1927; Charles D. Kerns, "Why Good Leaders Do Bad Things," *Graziadio Business Review,* Vol. 6, Issue 4 (2003), available at http://gbr.pepperdine.edu/2010/08/why-good-leaders-do-bad-things; N. Craig Smith et al., "Why Managers Fail to Do the Right Thing: An Empirical Study of Unethical and Illegal Conduct," *Business Ethics Quarterly,* Vol. 17, Issue 4 (2007): 633–667; Sunday Samson Babalola, "Determinants of Unethical Business Behaviour among Owner–Managers," *Journal of Human Values,* Vol. 15, No. 1 (January/June 2009): 61–75; and Yuri Mishima, "Why Pressure Makes Good People Do Bad Things," Network for Business Sustainability, posted May 6, 2011, available at http://www.nbs.net/csr/8536/.

Chapter 7

1. *Guidance on Social Responsibility,* International Organization for Standardization, 2009, Section 2.1.18, http://isotc.iso.org/livelink/livelink/fetch/-8929321/8929339/8929348/3935837/3974907/ISO_DIS_26000_Guidance_on_Social_Responsibility.pdf?nodeid=8385026&vernum=-2, pp. 3–4. Additional information on ISO 26000 available at http://www.iso.org/iso/catalogue_detail?csnumber=42546.

2. Roger A. Buchholz, "Corporate Responsibility and the Good Society: From Economics to Ecology," *Business Horizons* (July/August 1991): 19.

3. Alexander Dahlsrud, "How Corporate Social Responsibility Is Defined: An Analysis of 37 Definitions," *Corporate Social Responsibility and Environmental Management* 15 (2008): 1–13.

4. Donna J. Wood, "Corporate Social Performance Revisited," *The Academy of Management Review,* Vol. 16, No. 4 (1991): 695.

5. Ibid, 695–700.

6. "The Good Company: A Survey of Corporate Responsibility," *The Economist,* 24-page special section and editorial, January 22, 2005: Special Section and 11.

7. "The World According to CSR: Good Corporate Citizens Believe That Capitalism Is Wicked But Redeemable," The Good Company: A Survey Of Corporate Social Responsibility, *The Economist,* January 22, 2005, 10–14.

8. "The Ethics of Business: Good Corporate Citizens, and Wise Governments, Should Be Wary of CSR," The Good Company: A Survey of Corporate Social Responsibility, *The Economist,* January 22, 2005, 20–22.

9. Ian Davis, "The Biggest Contract: By Building Social Issues into Strategy, Big Business Can Recast the Debate about Its Role," *The Economist,* May 28, 2005, 69–71.

10. "Analyze This! An Analysis of *The Economist* 's Analysis of CSR," *Corporate Knights,* Spring 2005, 30–33.

11. "Just Good Business: A Special Report on Corporate Social Responsibility," *The Economist,* January 19, 2008.

12. Ibid, 12–13.

13. Richard J. Klonoski, "Foundational Considerations in the Corporate Social Responsibility Debate," *Business Horizons* (1991, July/August): 16.

14. Ibid, 16.

15. Archie Carroll, "The Pyramid of Corporate Social Responsibility: Toward the Moral Management of Organizational Stakeholders," *Business Horizons* (July/August 1991): 39–48.

16. Ibid, 39–43.

17. Marcel van Marrewijk, "Concepts and Definitions of CSR and Corporate Sustainability: Between Agency and Communion," *Journal of Business Ethics* 44, No. 2 (2003): 102–103.

18. Peter W. Roberts and Grahame R. Dowling, "Corporate Reputation and Sustained Superior Financial Performance," *Strategic Management Journal* 23 (2002): 1077–1093.

19. The Aspen Institute, "Social Impact Management: A Definition," http://www.aspeninstitute.org/site/c.huLWJeMRKpH/b.729881/k.5FC2/Social_Impact_Management_A_Definition.htm.

20. Ibid.

21. Wayne Norman and Chris MacDonald, "Getting to the Bottom of 'Triple Bottom Line,'" *Business Ethics Quarterly*, Vol. 14, Issue 2 (2004): 243–262.

22. World Economic Forum—The Business Case for Corporate Citizenship, "Global Corporate Citizenship," http://web.worldbank.org/archive/website00818/WEB/OTHER/THE_BUSI.HTM.

23. Donna J. Wood and Jeanne M. Logsdon, "Theorising Business Citizenship," in Jörg Andriof and Malcolm McIntosh, *Perspectives on Corporate Citizenship* (London: Greenleaf Publishing, 2002), 87.

24. Dirk Matten and Andrew Crane, "Corporate Citizenship: Towards an Extended Theoretical Conceptualization," *Academy of Management Review* 30, No. 1 (2005): 166–179.

25. Ibid, 172–173.

26. Ibid, 174.

27. Ibid, 175.

28. Wood and Logsdon, 83–103.

29. Ibid, 87.

30. Ibid.

31. Mark S. Schwartz and Archie B. Carroll, "Integrating and Unifying Competing and Complementary Frameworks: The Search for a Common Core in the Business and Society Field," *Business and Society*, Vol. 47, No. 2 (June 2008): 148–186.

32. Ibid, 168.

33. Ibid, 169.

34. Ibid, 171.

35. Ibid, 173.

Chapter 8

1. Christian Aid, "Behind the Mask: The Real Face of Corporate Social Responsibility" (2004), http://www.christianaid.org.uk/indepth/0401csr/index.htm.

2. "Corporate Citizenship," Imagine Canada website, accessed November 2, 2012, http://www.imaginecanada.ca/node/33.

3. Minda Zetlin, "Companies Find Profit in Corporate Giving," *Management Review* (December 1990): 10.

4. Elizabeth Bihl, "Sponsorship Makes Good Business Sense," *Canada Export*, Vol. 10, No. 11 (1992): 2.

5. Ibid, 2, 7.

6. John Pepin, "Venture Capitalists and Entrepreneurs Become Venture Philanthropists," http://efc.issuelab.org/resources/16185/16185.pdf.

7. "Benefits of Caring and Sharing," *The Times* (London), Public Agenda Section, May 24, 2005, 11.

8. Randy Ray, "A Social Conscience, and Skills in Demand," *The Globe and Mail*, May 25, 2006, C1.

9. "Is Giving Back Worthwhile," *Profit Magazine*, May 2014, 22.

10. Lisa Princic et al., *Engaging Small Business in Corporate Social Responsibility* (Vancouver: Canadian Business for Social Responsibility, October 2003), 13.

11. Ibid, 16.

12. This list was generated from a student assignment, "Corporate Social Responsibility and Small Business," Business 7010—Business and Society, Faculty of Business Administration, Memorial University of Newfoundland, Winter 2006.

13. Heledd Jenkins, "A Critique of Conventional CSR Theory: An SME Perspective," *Journal of General Management,* Vol. 29, No 4 (Summer 2004): 37–57.

14. "Working with Community Groups: A Guide for Small Business," Network for Business Sustainability, November 5, 2012, http://nbs.net/wp-content/uploads/SME-Resource-Community-Engagement.pdf.

15. Robert Sexty, "Small Business/Entrepreneurship Biography of Social Responsibility & Ethics." Available from the author at rsexty@mun.ca.

16. Business for Social Responsibility, "Community Involvement," http://www.bsr.org/AdvisoryServices/CI.cfm.

17. Some of the report's findings are summarized. The report was published by the Conference Board of Canada on August 15, 2015 and authored by Alison Howard.

18. Terry Macalister, "Corporate Social Responsibility: A Change in the Climate: Credit Crunch Makes the Bottom Line the Top Issue," *The Guardian,* March 6, 2008, 28.

Chapter 9

1. The last three points are from the "Quality, Credibility and Communications" assessment criteria used in *Corporate Sustainability Reporting in Canada,* Ottawa: Stratos Inc., December 2005, 39, http://www.stratos-sts.com/wp-content/uploads/2013/04/2005_12_CSR-Gaining-Momentum.pdf.

2. C. J. Fombrun, *Reputation: Realizing Value from the Corporate Image* (Boston: Harvard Business School Press, 1996), 72.

3. Steven L. Wartick, "Measuring Reputation: Definition and Data," *Business and Society* 41, 4 (December 2002): 371–392.

4. Mary Choquette and Peri Turnbull, "How Corporate Social Responsibility Can Affect Your Reputation," Members' Briefing 302, Ottawa: The Conference Board of Canada, November 2000, 1–2.

5. John F. Mahon, "Corporate Reputation: A Research Agenda Using Strategy and Stakeholder Literature," *Business and Society* 41, 4 (December 2002): 428.

6. Dylan Minor and John Morgan, "CSR as Reputation Insurance: *Primum Non Nocere,* " *California Management Review,* Vol. 53, Issue 2 (Spring 2011): 40–59.

7. Jay Janney and Steve Gove, "Reputation and Corporate Responsibility Aberrations, Trends, and Hypocrisy: Reactions to Firm Choices in the Stock Option Backdating Scandal," *Journal of Management Studies,* Vol. 48, No. 7 (2011): 1562–1585.

8. Andrea Stanaland and Patrick Murray, "Consumer Perceptions of the Antecedents and Consequences of Corporate Social Responsibility," *Journal of Business Ethics,* Vol. 102 (2011): 47–55.

9. Jantzi Social Index, "About the JSI," http://www.jantzisocialindex.com.

10. Dow Jones Sustainability Indexes, "Welcome to the Dow Jones Sustainability Indexes," http://www.sustainability-index.com/.

11. Sandra E. Martin, "Staff Stay at Companies with Heart," *National Post,* August 16, 2004, FP10.

12. Arthur B. Laffer, Andrew Coors, and Wayne Winegarden, "Does Corporate Social Responsibility Enhance Business Profitability?" CSRWatch™/SRIWatch, http://www.csrwatch.com/Sub/Resources/csr_profitability.htm.

13. H.E. Bowman and W. Haire, "A Strategic Posture Towards Corporate Social Responsibility," *California Management Review* 18 (1975): 49–58.

14. Marc Orlitzky, Frank L. Schmidt, and Sara L. Rynes, "Corporate Social and Financial Performance: A Meta-Analysis," *Organizational Studies* 24 (2003): 403–441.

15. Joshua D. Margolis and James P. Walsh, "Misery Loves Companies: Rethinking Social Initiatives by Business," *Administrative Science Quarterly* 48 (2003): 273–278.

16. John Peloza, "Primer: Valuing Sustainability," Network for Business Sustainability accessed November 6, 2012, http://nbs.net/knowledge/business-case/valuing-sustainability/primer; and "Metrics for Valuing Business Sustainability: A Framework for Executives," Network for Business Sustainability, 2011, accessed November 6, 2012, http://nbs.net/wp-content/uploads/NBS-Executive-Report-Valuing.pdf.

17. Conference Board of Canada, "Corporate Responsibility Assessment Tool," http://www.conferenceboard.ca/GCSR/CR_AT/.

18. Canadian Centre for Ethics and Corporate Policy, "About Us," http://www.ethicscentre.ca/EN/about/.

19. "Welcome," The Accountability Project, http://www.theaccountabilityproject.ca.

20. "About GRI," Global Reporting Initiative, accessed January 12, 2016, https://www.globalreporting.org/information/about-gri/Pages/default.aspx.

21. "GRI Sustainability Reporting Guidelines," Global Reporting Initiative, accessed January 12, 2016, https://www.globalreporting.org/resourcelibrary/GRIG4-Part1-Reporting-Principles-and-Standard-Disclosures.pdf.

22. Aaron Chatterji and David Levine, "Breaking Down the Wall of Codes: Evaluating Non-Financial Performance Measurement," *California Management Review,* Vol. 48, No. 2 (2006): 29–30.

23. Ibid, 44–48.

24. Compiled from Diana McLaren, "Measuring the Good Global Citizen," *The Globe and Mail,* November 26, 2008, B18; and *CSR Trends: A Comprehensive Survey of Corporate Social Responsibility Report Trends, Benchmarks and Best Practices,* Craib Design & Communications and PricewaterhouseCoopers LLP study, http://www.craib.com/craib_public/pdf/ARTrends/CSR_TRENDS_3_LR.pdf.

25. Mary Choquette and Peri Turnbull, "How Corporate Social Responsibility Can Affect Your Reputation," Members' Briefing 302 (Ottawa: Conference Board of Canada, November 2000), 3–4.

26. "2015 Better World: MBA Ranking, " *Corporate Knights: The Magazine for Clean Capitalism,* Fall 2015, Vol. 14, Issue 4, 40-45

27. Coro Strandberg, *The Future of Corporate Social Responsibility* (Vancouver: VanCity Credit Union, 2002).

28. Ibid, 5.

29. Ibid, 7–16.

30. Ibid, 17.

31. White, Allen L. *Fade, Integrate or Transform? The Future of CSR* (San Francisco: Business for Social Responsibility, 2005).

Chapter 10

1. David Heald, "Privatization: Analysing Its Appeal and Limitations," *Fiscal Studies* 5:1 (1984): 36.

2. Jonathan N. Goodrich, "Privatization in America," *Business Horizons* (January–February 1988): 11–17.

3. Corruption of Foreign Public Officials Act (S.C. 1998, c. 34) at http://laws-lois.justice.gc.ca/eng/acts/c-45.2/index.html.

4. "Integrity Framework" Public Works and Government Services Canada, http://www.tpsgc-pwgsc.gc.ca/ci-if/ci-if-eng.html; and "Principles" at http://www.tpsgc-pwgsc.gc.ca/ci-if/principes-principles-eng.htm.

5. "Government of Canada's Integrity Regime," Public Works and Government Services Canada, http://www.tpsgc-pwgsc.gc.ca/ci-if/ci-if-eng.html; and "Government of Canada Announces Improvements to Integrity of Federal Procurement," Government of Canada, http://news.gc.ca/web/article-en.do?nid=995629.

6. Bruce Carson, Registration of Lobbyists, *Library of Parliament Current Issue Review* (Ottawa: Supply and Services Canada. Cat. No. YM32-1/86-18-1988-05E 1988), 8.

7. Joe Castaldo et al, "How to Pay No Taxes," *Canadian Business*, March 2014, 62–67.

8. Tax Treaties and Tax Information Exchange Agreements websites at http://actionplan.gc.ca/en/initiative/tax-treaties-and-tax-information-exchange#sthash.Xzki58QJ.dpuf and http://www.fin.gc.ca/treaties-conventions/tieaaerf-eng.asp.

9. "Economic Action Plan 2015," Department of Finance, Government of Canada at http://actionplan.gc.ca/en/initiative/reducing-taxes-small-businesses#sthash.GGBi5nv7.dpuf.

10. Duanjie Chen and Jack Mintz, "Small Business Taxation: Revamping Incentives to Encourage Growth," *The School of Public Policy, University of Calgary, SPP Research Papers*, Volume 4, Issue 7, May 2011.

11. Benjamin Dachis and John Lester, "Small Business Preferences as a Barrier to Growth: Not so Tall After All," C.D. Howe Institute, Commentary No. 26, May 2015.

12. "About Us," Canadians for Tax Fairness website at http://www.taxfairness.ca/

13. "Using Tax Havens to Avoid Paying Taxes Worth the Risk?," Canada Revenue Agency website at http://www.cra-arc.gc.ca/E/pub/tg/rc4507/rc4507-09e.pdf

14. "Profile," Public Affairs Association of Canada, http://www.publicaffairs.ca/whoweare/profile.shtml.

15. Based upon a definition in Donald L. Barlett and James B. Steele, "Corporate Welfare," *Time* Canadian Edition, November 9, 1998, 32.

Chapter 11

1. "About," Responsible Investment Association accessed at http://riacanada.ca/about/

2. "About CURI," Coalition of Universities for Responsible Investing website, https://ccuri.wordpress.com/who-we-are/about-curi/.

3. Tessa Hebb, *Canadian Responsible Investment Mutual Funds: Risk/Return Characteristics Study Findings,* Carleton Centre for Community Innovation, May 1, 2015.

4. Jon Entine, "The Myth of Social Investing: A Critique of Its Practices and Consequences for Corporate Social Performance Research," *Organization and Environment*, Vol. 16, No. 3 (September 2003): 352–368.

5. Robert K. Mueller, "Changes in the Wind in Corporate Governance," *Journal of Business Strategy* 1(4) (1981): 9.

6. *Report of the Toronto Stock Exchange, Committee on Corporate Governance in Canada* (Toronto: The Toronto Stock Exchange, 1994), 7.

7. *OECD Principles of Corporate Governance* (Paris: OECD Publications, 2004): 18–19, 32–39, http://www.oecd.org/topic/0,2686,en_2649_34813_1_1_1_1_37439,00.htm.

8. *Where Were the Directors: Guidelines for Improving Corporate Governance in Canada* (Toronto: Toronto Stock Exchange Committee on Corporate Governance in Canada, May 1994), 24. There are many definitions of independence and this one was not adopted in National Instrument 58–201.

9. Canadian Securities Administrators, CSA Multilateral Staff Notice 58-307, Staff Review of Women on Boards and in Executive Officer Positions – Compliance with NI58-58-101 Disclosure of Corporate Governance Practices, September 28, 2015.

10. Barbara Shector, "Canadian Shareholders Increasingly Aggressive on 'Say-on-Pay,' *The National Post,* May 1, 2015 accessed at http://business.financialpost.com/news/canadian-shareholders-increasingly-aggressive-on-say-on-pay; Katy Pitch, "Say-on-Pay": Back in the Spotlight this Proxy Season," Stikeman Elliot website accessed at http://www.canadiansecuritieslaw.com/2015/05/articles/corporate-governance/sayonpay-back-in-the-spotlight-this-proxy-season/; and Darren Henderson, "Why Canada Should Adopt Mandatory Say-on-Pay," *Ivey Business Journal* accessed at http://iveybusinessjournal.com/publication/why-canada-should-adopt-mandatory-say-on-pay/.

11. "SEC Adopts Rule for Pay Ratio Disclosure," Securities and Exchange Commission website at http://www.sec.gov/news/pressrelease/2015-160.html.

12. "2015 Best Practices for Proxy Circular Disclosure," Canadian Coalition for Good Governance at http://www.ccgg.ca/site/ccgg/assets/pdf/2015_bestpractices.pdf page 5

13. "Disclosure of Corporate Governance Practices," National Instrument 58–201, https://www.osc.gov.on.ca/documents/en/Securities-Category5/rule_20050617_58-201_corp-gov-guidelines.pdf.

14. OECD Principles of Corporate Governance: 24–25.

15. Larry Colero, Crossroads Programs, Inc., "Five Questions That Directors Should Ask," University of British Columbia, The W. Maurice Young Centre for Applied Ethics, accessed November 7, 2006, http://www.ethics.ubc.ca/papers/invited/5questions.html.

16. Mark Schacter, *What Directors Need to Know about Corporate Social Responsibility* (Ottawa: Mark Schacter Consulting, 2004), 4–5, 10.

Chapter 12

1. *Employment Equity Act,* 1995, C.44, s. 2.

2. *Canadian Human Rights Act,* 1986. c. 14, s. 1.

3. Rosemarie Tong, "Feminist Ethics," *Encyclopedia of Business Ethics and Society,* (ed.) Robert W. Kolb, (Thousand Islands, CA: Sage Publications Inc.) Online Edition 2007.

4. "Feminist Ethics: An Alternative Voice," Villanova University, MPA 8300 Leadership Ethics, accessed February 20, 2013, http://www83.homepage.villanova.edu/richard.jacobs/MPA%208300/theories/feminist.html; and Rosemarie Tong and Nancy Williams, "Feminist Ethics," *The Stanford Encyclopedia of Philosophy (Summer 2011 Edition),* (ed.) Edward N. Zalta, accessed January 21, 2013, http://plato.stanford.edu/entries/feminism-ethics.

5. Janet L. Borgerson, "On the Harmony of Feminist Ethics and Business Ethics," *Business and Society Review,* Vol. 112, No. 4 (December 2007): 477–509.

6. Hewitt & Associates, "CSR as a Driver of Employee Engagement," Canadian Business for Social Responsibility, accessed December 2012, http://cbsr.ca/blog/csr-driver-employee-engagement.

7. "Hewitt and CBSR Data Establishes Strong Relationship between Employee Engagement and Views on CSR," Press Release, Hewitt Associates, January 25, 2010.

8. Maria José Ramos, "CSR as a Driver of Employee Engagement," Canadian Business for Social Responsibility, accessed December 7, 2012, http://cbsr.ca/blog/csr-driver-employee-engagement.

9. D.M. Mayer et al., "Who Displays Ethical Leadership and Why Does It Matter? An Examination of Antecedents and Consequences of Ethical Leadership," *Academy of Management Journal,* Vol. 55, Issue 1 (February 2012): 151–171.

10. Jindeck Chun et al., "How Does Corporate Ethics Contribute to Firm Performance? The Mediating Role of Collective Organizational Commitment and Organizational Citizenship Behavior," *Journal of Management,* Vol. 20 (January 2011): 1–15.

11. C.B. Bhattacharya et al., "Listing Corporate Social Responsibility to Win the Way for Talent," *M.I.T Sloan Management Review,* Vol. 48, No. 2 (2008): 37–44.

12. Adam Grant et al., "Giving Commitment: Employee Support Programs and the Prosocial Sensemaking Process," *Academy of Management Journal* 51 (2008): 898–918.

13. Janice Obuchowski, "Searching for Meaningful Work," *National Post,* March 23, 2010, FP10.

14. "The New Normal: Sustainable Practices Your Future Employees Will Demand," Network for Business Sustainability, January 11, 2010, accessed December 7, 2012, http://nbs.net/knowledge/perspectives-from-students-on-how-organizations-can-be-more-sustainable.

15. Robert W. Sexty, "Defining Consumer Sovereignty," *Canadian Business and Society: Understanding Social and Ethical Challenges* (Scarborough, ON: Prentice-Hall Canada, 1995), 352–354.

16. Magdaiena Öberseder et al., "Why Don't Consumers Care About CSR? A Qualitative Study Exploring the Role of CSR in Consumption Decisions," *Journal of Business Ethics,* Vol. 104, No. 4 (2011): 449–460.

17. June Cotte and Remi Trudel, *Socially Conscious Consumerism: Executive Briefing on the Body of Knowledge,* Network for Business Sustainability, Richard Ivey School of Business, University of Western Ontario, 2009, accessed July 7, 2016, http://nbs.net/wp-content/uploads/NBS_Consumerism_Brief_2009.pdf.

18. Pat Augar et al., "Do Social Product Features Have Value to Consumers?" *International Journal of Research in Marketing,* Vol. 25, No. 3 (2008): 183–91.

19. "Extended Producer Responsibility," Environment Canada, https://www.ec.gc.ca/gdd-mw/default.asp?lang=En&n=FB8E9973-1.

20. Stephen Brammer et al., "Managing Sustainable Global Supply Chains: Frameworks and Practices," May 25, 2011, Network for Business Sustainability, http://nbs.net/wp-content/uploads/NBS-Executive-Report-Supply-Chains.pdf.

21. Fair Trade Association, accessed January 18, 2016, http://www.fairlabor.org/about-us.

22. International Council of Toy Industries, accessed January 18, 2016, http://www.toy-icti.org.

23. "Top 10 Sustainability Shopping List," Sustainability Purchasing Network, accessed January 13, 2016, http://www.buysmartbc.com/_Library/Resources/bsn_10_shopping_tips_web.pdf.

24. "What Is Fairtrade?" Fairtrade Foundation, accessed July 14, 2016, http://www.fairtrade.org.uk/en/what-is-fairtrade/faqs.

25. "About Fairtrade," Fairtrade Canada, accessed August 4, 2016, http://fairtrade.ca/sitecore/content/fairtrade/home/what-is-fairtrade?sc_lang=en.

26. Fairtrade International, accessed February 10, 2013, http://www.fairtrade.net; Fairtrade Canada, accessed February 10, 2013, http://www.fairtrade.ca; and Fair Trade U.S.A., accessed February 10, 2013, http://www.fairtradeusa.org.

27. Peter Griffiths, "Ethical Objections to Freetrade," *Journal of Business Ethics,* Vol. 105, No. 3 (2012): 357–373.

28. Tina D. Beuchelt and Manifred Zeller, "Profits and Poverty: Certification's Troubled Link for Nicaragua's Organic and Fair-Trade Coffee Producers," *Ecological Economics* 70 (2011): 1316–1324.

29. Fair Trade, Employment and Poverty Reduction Research, SOAS University of London, accessed January 20, 2016, http://ftepr.org/about/; Signe Langdford, "The Fair Trade Dilemma," *The Globe and Mail,* June 10, 2015, L5; and "Fair Trade: Good Thing, or Bad?," *The Economist,* July 5, 2014, 72.

Chapter 13

1. Michael Edwards, "Part 1: The Case for NGOs—The Mouse That Roared," *The Globe and Mail,* January 3, 2002, A15.

2. *Partnering for Innovation: Driving Change Through Business/NGO Partnerships* (Vancouver: Canadian Business for Social Responsibility, 2005), 7–8. Also available at http://www.cbsr.ca.

3. Alan Rugman and Karl Moore, "Part 2: Are NGOs a Threat? Biting the Hand That Feeds Us," *The Globe and Mail,* January 4, 2002, A13.

4. Debora L. Spar and Lane I. LaMure, "The Power of Activism: Assessing the Impact of NGOs on Global Business," *California Management Review,* Vol. 45, No. 3 (Spring 2003): 81.

5. Ibid, 84–85.

6. Ibid, 85.

7. *Partnering for Innovation: Driving Change Through Business/NGO Partnerships* (Vancouver: Canadian Business for Social Responsibility, 2005), 3–4. Also available at http://www.cbsr.ca.

8. Ibid, 10–12.

9. Jonathan Doh, "Partnering with NGOs: The 4 Keys to Success," Network for Business Sustainability, July 19, 2012, accessed December 10, 2012, http://nbs.net/partnering-with-ngos-the-4-keys-to-success/.

10. Bart J. Mindszenthy, "Issues and Media Relations," *Business Quarterly* (March 1987): 76–83.

11. Wade Rowland, *Greed, Inc.: Why Corporations Rule Our World and How We Let It Happen* (Toronto: Thomas Allen Publishers, 2005).

12. Joel Bakan, *The Corporation: The Pathological Pursuit of Profit and Power* (Toronto: Viking Canada, 2002).

13. Harry Glasbeek, *Wealth by Stealth: Corporate Crime, Corporate Law, and the Perversion of Democracy* (Toronto: Between the Lines, 2002).

14. "Social Media," Wikipedia, http://en.wikipedia.org/wiki/Social_media.

15. 2015 Edelman Trust Barometer: Canadian Results, accessed January 20, 2016, http://www.slideshare.net/EdelmanInsights/2015-edelman-trust-barometer-canadian-findings.

16. Bruce Livesey, "Rough Handling," *Financial Post,* May 10, 1987, 26–27; and Leisa Stangret, "Media Accept 'Spin' on So-Called News," *National Post,* December 9, 2000, 8.

17. Doug Saunders, "Manufacturing Media Bias," *The Globe and Mail,* March 22, 1997, D2.

18. Steven Wartick, "The Relationship Between Intense Media Exposure and Change in Corporate Reputation," *Business and Society* (Roosevelt University), Vol. 3, No. 1 (1992): 33–49.

19. Ibid, 34.

20. Ibid, 43.

21. Bart J. Mindszenthy, "Issues and Media Relations," *Business Quarterly* (March 1987): 76–83.

22. Grant Robertson, "Internet Takes Bite out of Canadian Magazine Readership," *The Globe and Mail,* March 30, 2007, B2.

23. Edward J. Romar, "Virtue Is Good Business: Confucianism as a Practical Business Ethic," *Journal of Business Ethics,* Vol. 38 (2002): 119–131.

24. "Spiritual Capital Research Program," Metanexus Institute, http://www.metanexus.net/spiritual%5Fcapital/.

25. Peter Goodspeed, "Faith in the Marketplace," *National Post,* June 17, 2005, A1, A12.

26. William C. Symonds, "Earthly Empires: How Evangelical Churches Are Borrowing from the Business Playbook," *BusinessWeek,* May 23, 2005, 78–88.

27. Michelle Conlin, "Religion in the Workplace: The Growing Presence of Spirituality in Corporate America," *BusinessWeek,* November 1, 1999, 151–158; Ian I. Mitroff and Elizabeth A. Denton, *A Spiritual Audit of Corporate America: A Hard Look at Spirituality, Religion and Values in the Workplace* (San Francisco: Jossey-Bass Publishers, 1999); Robert A. Giacalone and Carole L. Jurkiezicz, "Right from Wrong: The Influence of Spirituality on Perceptions of Unethical Business Activities," *Journal of Business Ethics* 46 (2003): 85–97.

28. Symonds, "Earthly Empires."

29. Robert W. Sexty, Business and Education. Working Paper #02–05. Faculty of Business Administration, Memorial University of Newfoundland, St. John's, NL, 2002.

30. Ibid.

31. The Association for the Advancement of Sustainability in Higher Education (AASHE), http://www.aashe.org/.

Chapter 14

1. Garrett Hardin, "The Tragedy of the Commons," *Science*, Vol. 162, December 13, 1968, 1243–1248.

2. Colin Hutchison, "Environmental Issues: The Challenge for the Chief Executive," *Long Range Planning* 25(3) (1992): 58.

3. United Nations, *The World Commission on Environment and Development: Our Common Future* (New York: Oxford University Press, 1987).

4. *Business Strategy for Sustainable Development: Leadership and Accountability for the '90s* (Winnipeg: International Institute for Sustainable Development, 1992), 11.

5. Environment Canada, "Glossary of Terms," http://www.ec.gc.ca/default.asp?lang=En&n=7EBE5C5A-1; and Environment Canada, "What Is Acid Rain?" http://www.msc.ec.gc.ca/cd/factsheets/acidrain/index_e.cfm.

6. Environment Canada, "Glossary of Terms."

7. Environment Canada, "Stratospheric Ozone," http://www.ec.gc.ca/indicateurs-indicators/.

8. Environment Canada, "Glossary of Terms."

9. Environment Canada, "Glossary of Terms."

10. *Canadian Environmental Protection Act, 1999*. Available at http://laws-lois.justice.gc.ca/eng/acts/c-15.31/.

11. Jamie R. Hendry, "Taking Aim at Business: What Factors Lead Environmental Non-Government Organizations to Target Particular Firms?" *Business and Society*, Vol. 45, No. 1 (March 2006): 47–86.

12. Laura Jones, "A Different Kind of Environmentalist," *Fraser Forum*, April 2001, 4.

13. "When Regulation Beats Market Mechanisms," *National Post*, March 27, 2007, FP15.

14. "How Companies Can Win with Carbon Pricing," Network for Business Sustainability, August 10, 2015, accessed January 23, 2016, http://nbs.net/how-companies-can-win-with-carbon-pricing/.

15. "Shell Quest CSS Project Approved with Conditions," News Release, Energy Resources and Conservation Board, Calgary, July 10, 2012.

16. "The Seven Sins of Greenwashing," TerraChoice Environmental Marketing at http://sinsofgreenwashing.org/findings/the-seven-sins/.

17. *Business Strategy for Sustainable Development: Leadership and Accountability for the '90s* (Winnipeg: International Institute for Sustainable Development, 1992), 21–24.

18. Nicole Darrnall et al., "Environmental Management Systems and Green Supply Chain Management: Complements for Sustainability," *Business Strategy and the Environment*, Vol. 17 (2008): 30–45.

19. Bruce Hofer et al., "The Competitive Determinants of a Firm's Environmental Management Activities: Evidence from US Manufacturing Industries," *Journal of Operations Management*, Vol. 30 (2012): 9–84.

20. "Measuring and Valuing Environmental Impacts: An Introductory Guide," Network for Business Sustainability, http://nbs.net/wp-content/uploads/NBS-Executive-Report-Impacts.pdf.

21. I.B. Vasi and B. King, "Social Movements, Risk Perceptions, and Economic Outcomes: The Effect of Primary and Secondary Stakeholder Activism on Firm's Perceived Environmental Risk and Financial Performance," *American Sociological Review*, Vol. 77, No. 4 (2012): 1–24.

22. OSC Staff Notice 51–716–Environmental Reporting, Ontario Securities Commission, February 29, 2008; Janet McFarland, "Clean Up Environmental Disclosure: OSC," *The Globe and Mail*, February 28, 2008, B4; and Sandra Rubin, "When OSC Goes Green, Lawyers See Red," *The Globe and Mail,* March 19, 2008, B7.

23. Michael Lucins et al., "The Sustainability Liability: Potential Negative Effects of Ethicality on Product Acceptance," *Journal of Marketing*, Vol. 74 (2010): 15–31.

24. John Peloza, "What Makes Your Consumers Go Green? It Depends on Who's Around," April 16, 2012, Network for Business Sustainability at http://nbs.net/what-makes-your-consumers-go-green-it-depends-on-whos-around/.

25. "Going Green Can Attract and Keep Employees," *The Globe and Mail*, January 19, 2008, B16.

26. Marjo Johne, "Show Us the Green, Workers Say," *The Globe and Mail*, October 10, 2007, C1, C6.

27. "SHRM Survey Asks How 'Green' Is the American Workplace," Society for Human Resource Management, Press Release, January 16, 2008.

28. Catherine Ramus and Ulrich Steger, "The Roles of Supervisory Support Behaviours and Environmental Policy in Employee 'Ecoinitiatives' at Leading-Edge European Companies," *Academy of Management Journal*, Vol. 43, No. 4 (2000): 605–626.

29. "Employees Identify Aon Hewitt's 'Green 30' Organizations Based on Eco-Friendly Programs and Practices," April 26, 2012, accessed August 8, 2016, http://www.newswire.ca/en/story/962169/employees-identify-aon-hewitt-s-green-30-organizations-based-on-eco-friendly-programs-and-practices. Also published by *Maclean's*; a recent example is Adrian Lee, "Canada's Green 30: Companies that Integrate Sustainability Programs into Their Workplace Culture Win Praise from Their Employees," May 12, 2014, accessed August 8, 2016, http://www.macleans.ca/economy/business/green-where-it-counts-the-green-30/.

30. Rebecca Walberg, "Green Careers Are Growing," *National Post*, March 23, 2010. FP9.

31. GoodWork Canada at http://www.goodworkcanada.ca/.

32. "Sustainability Reporting Guidelines—G3 Version for Public Comment," Global Reporting Initiative, Amsterdam, The Netherlands, 2006, 18–18; "Sustainability Reporting Guidelines," Global Reporting Initiative, Amsterdam, The Netherlands, 2002, 47–50.

33. "Measuring and Valuing Environmental Impacts: An Introductory Guide," Network for Business Sustainability Web site, at http://nbs.net/wp-content/uploads/NBS-Executive-Report-Impacts.pdf.

34. Mark Steyn, "'Sustainable' Development? There's No Such Thing," *National Post*, September 3, 2002, A12; and Peter Foster, "Sustainability Scam," *National Post*, April 8, 2006, FP19.

35. Peter Nowak, "Few Taking Leadership Role on Environment," *National Post*, September 25, 2006, FP2.

36. Anantha K. Duraiappsah, "Ecosystem Services and Human Well-Being: Do Global Findings Make Any Sense?" *BioScience*, Vol. 61, No. 1 (January 2011): 7–8; and Clara Raudsepp-Hearne et al., "The Paradox Persists: How to Resolve It," *BioScience*, Vol. 61, No. 1 (January 2011): 11–12.

Chapter 15

1. John Black, "Globalization," *A Dictionary of Economics* (Oxford University Press, 2002). Oxford Reference Online, Oxford University Press, Memorial University of Newfoundland, http://www.oxfordreference.com/views/ENTRY.html?subview=Main&entry=t19.e1359.

2. Andrew Hurrell, "Globalization," *The Concise Oxford Dictionary of Politics*. Ed. Iain McLean and Alistair McMillan (Oxford University Press, 2003). Oxford Reference Online, Oxford University Press, Memorial University of Newfoundland, http://www.oxfordreference.com/views/ENTRY.html?subview=Main&entry=t86.e554.

3. John Scott and Gordon Marshall, "Globalization," *A Dictionary of Sociology* (Oxford University Press, 2005). Oxford Reference Online, Oxford University Press, Memorial University of Newfoundland, http://www.oxfordreference.com/views/ENTRY.html?subview=Main&entry=t88.e937.

4. World Bank, http://www.worldbank.org/.

5. International Monetary Fund, http://www.imf.org/.

6. "About the ILO," International Labour Organization, http://www.ilo.org/public/english/about/index.htm.

7. Institute for Management Development, Country Profile-Canada https://worldcompetitiveness.imd.org/countryprofile/CA

8. "Global Competitiveness Report," World Economic Forum, http://www3.weforum.org/docs/gcr/2015-2016/Global_Competitiveness_Report_2015-2016.pdf.

9. *Compendium of Ethics Codes and Instruments of Corporate Responsibility*, Schulich School of Business, York University, Toronto, http://hrlibrary.umn.edu/business/canadianethics.html.

10. "Who We Are," and "Corruption Perceptions Index 2015," Transparency International, accessed August 9, 2016, http://www.transparency.org/whoweare/organisation/faqs_on_corruption and https://www.transparency.org/cpi2015/#results-table.

11. "2011 Bribe Payers Index Report," Transparency International, http://www.transparency.org/bpi2011/results.

12. Publish What You Pay, http://www.publishwhatyoupay.org/.

13. *The Corruption of Foreign Public Officials Act: A Guide,* May 1999, Justice Laws Website, http://laws-lois.justice.gc.ca/eng/acts/C-45.2/page-1.html.

14. "Canada's Enforcement of the Foreign Bribery Offence Is Lagging; Must Urgently Boost Efforts to Prosecute," OECD Newsroom at http://www.oecd.org/document/31/0,3746,en_21571361_44315115_47443999_1_1_1_1,00.html; "Canada: Phase 3—Report on the Application of the Convention on Combating Bribery of Foreign Public Officials in International Business Transactions," OECD, accessed August 9, 2016, https://www.oecd.org/canada/Canadaphase3reportEN.pdf; and "2009 Revised Recommendation on Combating Bribery in International Business Transactions," OECD, accessed August 9, 2016, https://www.oecd.org/daf/anti-bribery/44176910.pdf.

15. Theresa Tedesco, "Boards Must Step Up on Corporate Crime," *National Post*, January 24, 2013, FP2; and Terence Corcoran, "Rooted in Government," *National Post,* February 6, 2013, FP1, 3.

16. Information on TRACE International is available at http://www.traceinternational.org/.

17. Alexandra Wrage, "Corruption Interruption," *Corporate Knights,* Winter 2016, 68–69.

18. "Universal Declaration of Human Rights," United Nations, accessed August 9, 2016, http://www.un.org/en/universal-declaration-human-rights/index.html.

19. Dexter Roberts and Pete Engardio, "Secrets, Lies, and Sweatshops," *BusinessWeek*, November 27, 2006, 50–58.

20. Nicholas D. Kristof, "Fight Poverty: Build Sweatshops," *National Post*, June 7, 2006, A20; and Michael Walker, "Why the World Needs More Sweatshops," *Fraser Forum,* March 2006, 3–4.

21. *Canadian Business and the Millennium Development Goals* (Vancouver: Canadian Business for Social Responsibility, 2005).

22. C.K. Prahalad and Stuart L. Hart, "The Fortune at the Bottom of the Pyramid," *Strategy + Business,* Issue 26, 2002.

23. C.K. Prahalad, *The Fortune at the Bottom of the Pyramid: Eradicating Poverty Through Profits,* (Upper Saddle River, NJ: Pearson Education Inc. Wharton School Publishing 2005).

24. "Bottom of the Pyramid," Aspen Institute, www.CasePlace.org.

25. "A Common Definition of Fair Trade," Fairtrade Foundation, http://www.fairtrade.org.uk/.

26. Tavia Grant, "Major World Banks Join Microfinance Revolution," *The Globe and Mail*, November 23, 2006, B11.

27. *Doing Business with the Poor: A Field Guide* (Conches-Geneva: World Business Council for Sustainable Development, 2004), 10–14.

Chapter 16

1. Further discussion of the fourth sector is available at Fourth Sector, http://www.fourthsector.net/; and "The Emerging Fourth Sector," Aspen Institute, https://www.aspeninstitute.org/sites/default/files/content/docs/pubs/4th%20sector%20paper%20-%20exec%20summary%20FINAL.pdf.

2. Anadila Mahbub, "The Economy's Fourth Sector," Sustainability Law at Lewis and Clark Law School, accessed August 9, 2016, http://sustainabilityandlaw.com/2011/04/22/the-economyd-fourth-sector-by-anadila-mahbub/.

3. "10 Things New Sustainability Managers Need to Know," Network for Business Sustainability, http://nbs.net/wp-content/uploads/10-Things-for-Managers1.pdf.

4. "From Challenges to Opportunities: The 7 Sustainability Opportunities for Canadian Business," Network for Business Sustainability, accessed February 4, 2016, http://nbs.net/wp-content/uploads/NBS-2015-Opportunities-Report.pdf.

5. Andrew Valentine, "Social Enterprise: 20 Questions for Directors of Non-Profit Organizations," Chartered Professional Accountants Canada, Toronto, 2014.

6. The Social Enterprise Council of Canada (SECC) website at https://socialenterprisecouncilcanada.wordpress.com/

7. Heerad Sabeti, "The For-Benefit Enterprise," *Harvard Business Review*, November 2011, 99–104.

8. More information can be found at "What Are B Corps?" Certified B Corporation website, http://www.bcorporation.net/.

9. MaRS Centre for Impact Investing, accessed February 3, 2016, http://impactinvesting.marsdd.com/strategic-initiatives/benefit-corporation-b-corp-hub/.

10. Adapted from Steve Zimmerman and Jeanne Bell, *The Sustainability Mindset: Using the Matrix Map to Make Strategic Decisions* (San Francisco, CA: Jossey-Bass, 2015), chapters 1, 5, and 6.

11. "Defining Social Innovation," Graduate School of Business, Stanford University, accessed February 29, 2016, https://www.gsb.stanford.edu/faculty-research/centers-initiatives/csi/defining-social-innovation.

12. "Impact Investing in Canada: State of the Nation, March 2014," MaRS Centre for Impact Investing, accessed February 29, 2016, https://www.marsdd.com/mars-library/impact-investing-in-canada-state-of-the-nation/

13. "The Landscape for Social Impact Investing - a White Paper," Toronto Dominion Bank, March 31, 2013, accessed February 29, 2016, https://www.td.com/document/PDF/corporateresponsibility/publications/The-Landscape-for-Social-Impact-Investing-a-White-Paper-Links.pdf.

14. "The New Powers of Giving," *The Economist*, July 1, 2006, 64.

15. Naomi Buck, "Meddling Billionaires," *Corporate Knights*, accessed August 10, 2016, http://www.corporateknights.com/channels/social-enterprise/meddling-billionaires-14435064/; Joe Chidley, "The Price of Doing Good," *National Post,* December 3, 2015, FP11; and Adam Waldman, "Zuckerberg's LLC is Built for Highly Leveraged Social Change," *The Globe and Mail,* December 9, 2015, B4.

16. Paul Adler and Seok-Woo Kwon, "Social Capital: Prospects for a New Concept," *Academy of Management Review*, Vol. 27, No. 1 (2002): 17–40.

17. Scott E. Seibert, Maria L. Kraimer, and Robert C. Linden, "A Social Capital Theory of Career Success," *Academy of Management Journal*, Vol. 44, No. 2 (2001): 220.

18. Ann Svendsen, Robert G. Boutilier, and David Wheeler, *Stakeholder Relationships, Social Capital and Business Value Creation* (Toronto: The Canadian Institute of Chartered Accountants, 2003).

19. Ibid, 4

20. Ibid, 18.

21. Ibid, 19–20.

22. Al Gore and David Blood, *Manifesto for Sustainable Capitalism*, Generation Foundation, accessed February 4, 2016, https://www.genfound.org/media/pdf-wsj-manifesto-sustainable-capitalism-14-12-11.pdf and https://www.genfound.org/frameworks/.

23. Ibid, 78-92.

24. Ibid, 78-92.

25. Ibid, 85.

26. Ibid, 85.

27. Ibid, 89–91.

28. Ibid, 92.

29. "Sustainability Centres," Network for Business Sustainability, accessed February 9, 2016, http://nbs.net/sustainability-centres/.

30. A. Wiek, L. Withycombe, and C.L. Redman, "Key Competences in Sustainability: A Reference Framework for Academic Program Development," *Sustainability Development,* 6, 203–218.

31. UBC Sustainability at http://www.sustain.ubc.ca; Canada's Green University at http://www.unbc.ca/green.

32. Coalition of Universities for Responsible Investing, accessed August 10, 2016, http://www.curi.ca/.

33. Community Based Research Canada (CBRC), accessed August 10, 2016, http://communityresearchcanada.ca.

34. Canadian Alliance for Community Service-Learning, accessed August 10, 2016, http://www.communityservicelearning.ca.

Cases

1. This is a fabricated case and the names of persons and places are fictitious. This case was prepared from public sources to provide material for classroom discussion, and it is not intended to illustrate either effective or ineffective response to a business and society managerial situation.

2. EatRight Ontario website, http://www.eatrightontario.ca/en/default.aspx.

3. "Energy Drinks Linked to Teen Health Risks," Propel Centre for Population Health Impact, University of Waterloo, March 6, 2014, https://uwaterloo.ca/propel/news/energy-drinks-linked-teen-health-risks.

4. "Energy Drinks in Canada: Know the Facts," Canadian Beverage Association, http://www.canadianbeverage.ca/wp-content/uploads/2014/01/Energy-Drink-Brochure-Layout-English-layout-Sept-23-to-print.pdf.

5. Report of the Expert Panel on Caffeinated Energy Drinks, November 2010, Health Canada, http://www.hc-sc.gc.ca/dhp-mps/prodnatur/activit/groupe-expert-panel/report_rapport-eng.php; and "Questions and Answers: Caffeinated Energy Drinks," Health Canada, http://www.hc-sc.gc.ca/fn-an/prodnatur/questions-caf-eng.php and http://www.hc-sc.gc.ca/fn-an/prodnatur/questions-caf-eng.php#a1.

6. Energy Drinks Marketing Code, http://www.canadianbeverage.ca/wp-content/uploads/2013/12/CBA-Energy-drinks-Code-FINAL-English.pdf.

7. Stone's Drug Store, http://www.stonespharmasave.com/; "Press Release: Soft Drinks and Sugary Beverages," Graham's Blog, http://stonespharmasave.com/blog/?p=560; "Store Stops Selling Energy Drinks to Minors," CBC News – Prince Edward Island, http://www.cbc.ca/news/canada/prince-edward-island/store-stops-selling-energy-drinks-to-minors-1.932565.

8. This case was prepared from public sources to provide material for classroom discussion, and it is not intended to illustrate either effective or ineffective response to a business and society managerial situation.

9. Rosia Montana Gold Corporation (RMGC), accessed August 9, 2015, http://en.rmgc.ro/index.html; and Gabriel Resources Ltd., www.gabrielresources.com/.

10. Eric Regular, "The New Romans," *Report on Business*, November 2010, 57-67

11. *New El Dorado*, Institute of Documentary Film, accessed August 9, 2015, http://www.dokweb.net/cs/.

12. *Mine Your Own Business,* accessed August 9, 2015, www.mineyourownbusiness.org

13. "About ICSID," International Centre for Settlement of Investment Disputes, accessed August 9, 2015, https://icsid.worldbank.org/apps/ICSIDWEB/about/Pages/default.aspx.

14. This case was prepared from public sources to provide material for classroom discussion, and it is not intended to illustrate either effective or ineffective response to a business and society managerial situation. This is a fabricated case, and the names Phillip Veldhuis and Savalot Enterprises are fictitious.

15. Information on Food Banks Canada was from its website, accessed February 29, 2012, http://www.foodbankscanada.ca/.

16. Views attributed to Elaine Power were contained in personal correspondence and permission was granted to use. Other information was obtained from the following: Dietitians of Canada, "Food Banks," *Practice: Exploring Members' Practice Issues,* accessed February 29, 2012, http://www.practiceblog.dietitians.ca/2010/01/food-banks.html; Jeff Nield, "Will Closing Food Banks Help End Hunger?" Tree Hugger, accessed February 29, 2012, http://www.treehugger.com/green-food/will-closing-food-banks-help-end-hunger.html; Elaine Power, "Canadian Food Banks: Obscuring the Reality of Hunger and Poverty," *Food Ethics,* Winter 2011, Vol. 6, Issue 4, 18–20; and Elaine Power, "Time to Close Our Food Banks," *The Globe and Mail,* July 25, 2011, A11.

17. This case was prepared from public sources to provide material for classroom discussion, and it is not intended to illustrate either effective or ineffective response to a business and society managerial situation.

18. Rob Ferguson, Robert Benzie, and Tanya Talaga, accessed August 10, 2016, https://www.thestar.com/news/canada/2012/02/03/caterpillar_closes_electromotive_plant_in_london.html.

19. "Progress Rail to Close London (ON) Locomotive Production," Canada News Wire, accessed August 10, 2016, http://www.newswire.ca/en/story/915677/progress-rail-to-close-london-on-locomotive-production.

20. "McGuinty Blames Ottawa for Electro-Motive Closing," CTV News, accessed July 20, 2012, http://toronto.ctv.ca/servlet/an/local/CTVNews/20120206/mcguinty-blames-ottawa-electro-motive-120206/20120206?hub=TorontoNewHome.

21. "CAW Urges Harper to Review Caterpillar Purchase of London Locomotive Plant," CAW Press Release, accessed July 18, 2012, http://www.caw.ca/en/10812.htm.

22. Takeovers of less than $300 million did not require a formal review.

23. "CAW President Demands Ottawa Release Details of Caterpillar Purchase, Close Loopholes in Investment Canada Act," CAW Press Release, accessed July 19, 2012, http://www.caw.ca/en/10952.htm.

24. "Caterpillar Picketed Today in a Dozen Canadian Cities," CAW Press Release, accessed July 18, 2012, http://www.caw.ca/en/10889.htm.

25. "Caterpillar, Incorrigibly Antisocial!" Press Release, accessed July 19, 2012, http://www.caw.ca/assets/images/0216-lock_out_EMDC_(EN).pdf.

26. "Why Caterpillar Is Bringing Jobs Home," CNN Money video, accessed July 23, 2012, http://money.cnn.com/video/news/2012/02/17/n_caterpillar_ceo_georgia_plant.cnnmoney/.

27. "Caterpillar 2010 Year in Review," accessed August 10, 2016, http://s7d2.scene7.com/is/content/Caterpillar/C10005394

28. Proxy materials to shareholders, April 29, 2011, accessed August 10, 2016, http://s7d2.scene7.com/is/content/Caterpillar/C10477614.

29. "Caterpillar Demands for Cuts Prove Groundless in Wake of Record Profit Announcement, CAW President Says," CAW Press Release, accessed July 19, 2012, http://www.caw.ca/en/10890.htm.

30. This case was prepared from public sources to provide material for classroom discussion, and it is not intended to illustrate either effective or ineffective response to a business and society managerial situation.

31. "About Us," Syncrude Canada Ltd., accessed August 10, 2016, http://www.syncrude.ca/our-company/overview/.

32. "Sustainability Report 2007," Syncrude Canada Ltd., accessed August 11, 2016, http://www.syncrude.ca/assets/pdf/sustainability-reports/SyncrudeSD2007.pdf.

33. "Hundreds of Ducks Trapped on Toxic Alberta Oilsands Pond," CBC News online, April 29, 2008, accessed August 11, 2016, http://www.cbc.ca/news/canada/edmonton/hundreds-of-ducks-trapped-on-toxic-alberta-oilsands-pond-1.699019; Hanneke Brooymans and Jim Farrell, "Syncrude Faces Scrutiny after Ducks Land on Toxic Pond," *National Post* online edition, April 30, 2008, accessed August 10, 2016, http://www.nationalpost.com/news/canada/story.html?id=482931.

34. This case was prepared from public sources to provide material for classroom discussion, and it is not intended to illustrate either effective or ineffective response to a business and society managerial situation.

35. Note about Kabriole: If spelled with a "c" instead of a "k," the word refers to a curved, tapered leg, often with a decorative foot, characteristic of Chippendale and Queen Anne furniture and named after its resemblance to the leg of a leaping animal.

36. This case was prepared from public sources to provide material for classroom discussion, and it is not intended to illustrate either effective or ineffective response to a business and society managerial situation.

37. "What Is Listeriosis?" *Report of the Independent Investigator into the 2008 Listeriosis Outbreak,* Government of Canada, July 2009, 5–6. The report will be referred to as the *Listeriosis Report* and is available at http://www.cpha.ca/uploads/history/achievements/09-lirs-rpt_e.pdf.

38. "Corporate Information," Maple Leaf Foods Inc., accessed August 10, 2016, http://www.mapleleaffoods.com/news/maple-leaf-foods-reports-results-for-fourth-quarter-fiscal-2007/.

39. This case was prepared from public sources to provide material for classroom discussion, and it is not intended to illustrate either effective or ineffective response to a business and society managerial situation.

40. "About Us," *Canada Gazette,* Government of Canada, http://www.gazette.gc.ca/cg-gc/about-sujet-eng.html.

41. *Canada Gazette,* Vol. 143, No. 8, February 21, 2009, accessed August 10, 2016, http://publications.gc.ca/gazette/archives/p1/2009/2009-02-21/pdf/g1-14308.pdf.

42. *Fisheries Act.* Government of Canada. R.S., c. F-14, s. 1, http://laws-lois.justice.gc.ca/eng/acts/F-14/page-1.html#s-1.

43. "Metal Mining Effluent Regulations," Environment Canada, Government of Canada, http://gazette.gc.ca/rp-pr/p1/2010/2010-05-15/html/reg1-eng.html#REF10.

44. An order in council is a notice of an administrative decision originating with the Canadian federal cabinet and is approved by the Governor General. Orders in council can be notices of appointments or regulations or legislative orders in relation to and authorized by an existing act of parliament. Orders in council are published in the *Canada Gazette.*

45. "Towards Sustainable Mining Guiding Principles," Mining Association of Canada, http://mining.ca/towards-sustainable-mining/tsm-guiding-principles.

46. "Sustainability Management: Environment," Vale, accessed August 10, 2016, http://www.vale.com/canada/EN/aboutvale/communities/environment/Pages/Sustainable-Mining.aspx.

47. This case was prepared from public sources to provide material for classroom discussion, and it is not intended to illustrate either effective or ineffective response to a business and society managerial situation. Professor Wayne Murray is a fictional character.

48. This is a fabricated situation with background information obtained from the following. Certified General Accountants of Canada, CGA-Canada Code of Ethical Principles and Rules of Conduct, Version 2.12, June 2011, http://www.cga-canada.org/en-ca/StandardsLib/ca_ceproc.pdf. This case was prepared from public sources to provide material for classroom discussion, and it is not intended to illustrate either effective or ineffective response to a business and society managerial situation.

49. *Generating Growth 2001 Annual Report,* Fortis Inc., 10–24.

50. Information for this section was obtained from "Chalillo Hydropower Project Summary," a brochure published by Fortis Inc., Belize Electric Company Ltd., and Belize Electricity Limited, October 2001, 10.

51. Ibid, 7, 10, 15–17.

52. Probe International, accessed August 10, 2016, https://journal.probeinternational.org/2001/01/25/press-release-environmentalists-urge-newfoundland-based-fortis-corporation-abandon-hydro-scheme-belize/.

53. Natural Resources Defense Council, http://www.nrdc.org/about/.

54. Will Hilliard, "Dam Opponents Misled: Fortis," *The Telegram* (St. John's, NL), November 2, 2001, A3.

Glossary

Acid rain: A generic term used for precipitation that contains an abnormally high concentration of sulphuric and nitric acid.

Active shareholders: Those who participate in the governance to the full extent allowed by the law.

Anti-globalists: Individuals and organizations that oppose globalization or are critical of it.

Audit committee: Comprises members of the board of directors and oversees the internal and external accounting auditing function to ensure that financial statements accurately and appropriately represent the condition of the corporation and that regulated disclosures are made.

B Corporation (or B Corp): A social enterprise that operates to make profits but has a strong commitment to addressing social and environmental problems. A certification process is required in order to be eligible to receive the designation of B Corp.

Board of directors: A group of individuals elected by shareholders to govern or oversee the corporation's affairs.

Bribery: Making questionable payments, known as bribes, to government officials to influence their decisions.

Business citizenship: Includes the responsibilities of corporate citizenship on a local and national basis and extends it to a global or universal scope.

Business ethics: The rules, standards, codes, or principles that provide guidelines for morally right behaviour and truthfulness in specific situations.

Business sustainable development: According to the IISD, "adopting business strategies and activities that meet the needs of the enterprise and its stakeholders today while protecting, sustaining, and enhancing the human and natural resources that will be needed in the future."

Business-to-business: Commercial activity where one corporation sells goods or services to another corporation rather than to consumers.

Cap-and-Trade: A system whereby governments cap total carbon emissions and then give or sell companies carbon permits that add up to the cap. Also referred to as *emissions trading*.

Capitalism: An economic system that allows for private ownership of the means of production (land, labour, and capital) and assumes that economic decision making is in the hands of individuals or enterprises who make decisions expecting to earn a profit.

Carbon capture and storage (CCS): Carbon emissions are captured and injected into underground formations.

Carbon pricing: A financial instrument that businesses and governments use to reduce carbon emissions.

Carbon tax: When governments impose a fee on carbon: the more a company emits, the more they pay.

Cause-related marketing: The purchase of a particular product results in a donation being made by a corporation to a non-profit organization's program.

CEO pay ratio: The ratio of the compensation of the corporation's chief executive officer (CEO) to the median compensation of the its employees.

Charitable foundation: A corporation or trust that is constituted and operated exclusively for charitable purposes.

Civil society: The voluntary, community, and social organizations or institutions that contribute to the functioning of society but are usually not related to or supported by government.

Clean capitalism: Based on Corporate Knights' definition as "an economic system that incorporates the social, economic and ecological costs (and benefits) into our marketplace activities and the prices we pay."

Climate change (global warming): According to Environment Canada, it is "the result of human activities altering the chemical composition of the atmosphere through the build-up of greenhouse gases that trap heat and reflect it back to the Earth's surface." Also referred to as *global warming*.

Code of conduct: Explicitly states what appropriate behaviour is by identifying what is acceptable and unacceptable.

Code of ethics: A statement of principles or values that guide behaviour by describing the general value system within which a corporation attempts to operate in a given environment.

Collaboration: A meta-capability to establish and maintain relationships that allows the organization to tap into a powerful source of creative energy, a large pool of innovative ideas, and a wider network.

Commons: Any resource used as though it belongs to all.

Community investment: The efforts of a corporation to help develop a community and create economic opportunities through a variety of means, from donations to direct involvement in commercial undertakings.

Competition: The condition in a market system in which many rival sellers seek to provide goods and services to many buyers.

Conflict of interest: A situation in which an individual has a private or personal interest that is sufficient to appear to influence the objective exercise of that individual's duties.

Conscious capitalism: The reorientation of business from a single focus on profits to emphasizing integrity, higher standards of corporate behaviour, and inclusion of all stakeholders.

Consumer sovereignty: The assumption existing in an economy that consumers have and exercise power over producers through the decisions they make in purchasing the goods and services provided by corporations.

Consumerism: A social movement seeking to protect and augment the rights and powers of buyers in relation to sellers.

Corporate agenda: The real or imagined domination of public policy or government programs by corporations or business organizations in their own best interests.

Corporate citizenship: Occurs when a corporation demonstrates that it takes into account its complete impact on society and the environment as well as its economic influence.

Corporate ethics programs: Some combination of a statement of values, code of conduct and/or ethics, ethics training, ethics audits and consulting services, ethics officers and committees, and ethics reporting systems.

Corporate governance: The processes, structures, and relationships through which the shareholders, as represented by a board of directors, oversee the activities of the corporation.

Corporate philanthropy: The effort of business to contribute to society socially; manifested by donations of money or goods and services in kind, voluntarism (where corporate employees work for social causes), and sponsorship of events that contribute to society.

Corporate public affairs: The management function responsible for monitoring and interpreting the governmental environment of the corporation or industry, and for managing the responses necessary to protect the interests of the corporation or industry.

Corporate reputation: As defined by Fombrun, "a perceptual representation of a corporation's past actions and future prospects that describes the corporation's overall appeal to all of its key constituents [stakeholders] when compared with other leading rivals."

Corporate social responsibility (CSR): The way a corporation achieves a balance among its economic, social, and environmental responsibilities in its operations so as to address shareholder and other stakeholder expectations.

Corporate social responsibility (CSR) reporting: A management function that documents the corporation's economic, ethical/social, and environmental responsibilities and initiatives, and communicates this information to relevant stakeholders. Also known as *sustainability reporting*.

Corporate sponsorship: A partnership between a business sponsor and an event or a non-profit organization that is established for mutual benefit.

Corporate sustainability (CS): Corporate activities demonstrating the inclusion of social and environmental as well as economic responsibilities in business operations as they impact all stakeholders.

Corporate voluntarism: The time and talent employees commit to community organizations with support and/or consent from employers who recognize the value of such efforts to society.

Corporate welfare: Any action by municipal, provincial, or federal governments that gives a specific corporation or an entire industry a benefit not offered to others.

Corruption: According to Transparency International, "the abuse of entrusted power for private gain."

Creative capitalism: Places the resolution of social needs as primary instead of secondary to economic activity and performance.

Crisis: A turning point, a crucial time, and a situation that has reached a critical point.

Crisis management: An approach involving planning and removing much of the risk and uncertainty, allowing the corporation to achieve more control over events.

Deontological ethics: An approach to ethics that determines goodness or rightness from examining the acts rather than from the consequences of the acts.

Deregulation: The reduction of government influence or impact over the economy allowing for a freer and more efficient marketplace.

Discrimination: The preferential (or less than preferential) treatment on bases not directly related to qualifications of the job or performance on the job.

Diversity management: A voluntary initiative that goes beyond what is required by law to eliminate workplace discrimination.

Dual-class stock: More than one type of share or stock with different voting rights and dividend payments is issued by a single corporation.

Economic freedoms: Exist when the business system operates with few restrictions on its activities.

Economic globalization: The integration of fragmented markets into a global economy.

Economic system: An arrangement using land, labour, and capital to produce, distribute, and exchange goods and services to meet the needs and wants of people in society.

Ecosystem: A biological community of interacting organisms and their physical environment.

Employee engagement: The emotional and intellectual commitment of an individual or group to an organization that supports building and sustaining business performance.

Employment equity: The fair and equal treatment of employees.

Environmental ethic: The set of values or principles that govern a corporation's practices relating to the environment.

Environmental non-governmental organizations (ENGOs): Groups that hold shared values or attitudes about the challenges confronting the natural environment and advocate for changes to improve the condition of the environment.

Equality of opportunity: The assumption that all individuals or groups have an even chance at responding to some condition in society.

Ethic of caring: Gives attention to specific individuals or stakeholders harmed or disadvantaged and their particular circumstances.

Ethic of justice: Considers that moral decisions are based on the primacy of a single value: justice.

Ethical relativism: The belief that ethical answers depend on the situation and no universal standards or rules exist to guide or evaluate morality.

Ethics audit: A systematic effort to discover actual or potential unethical behaviour in an organization.

Ethics committee: A group, comprising directors, managers, or staff, formed to monitor ethical standards and behaviour.

Ethics of business: The rules, standards, codes, or principles that provide guidance for morally appropriate behaviour in managerial decision making relating to the operation of the business enterprise's and business' relationship with society.

Ethics officer: An independent manager, reporting to the board of directors or CEO, who reviews complaints or information from anyone in the organization or any stakeholder, studies the situation, and recommends action if necessary.

Extended producer responsibility: From Environment Canada, it is "an environmental policy approach in which a producer's responsibility, physical and/or financial, for a product is extended to the post-consumer stage of a product's life cycle."

Fair trade: A term commonly used to identify products that are involved with sustainability purchasing; usually focuses on the beginning of the product chain.

Feminist ethics: Diverse, gender-focused approaches to ethical theory and practice.

Fiduciary duties: Obligations owed by directors to shareholders that are prescribed by laws or regulations.

For-benefit corporation: A social enterprise that aims to make profits but also has a strong commitment to addressing social and environmental problems. Also called a *benefit corporation*.

Fourth sector: New organizational forms that integrate business or private, social, and public methods. Sometimes referred to as *hybrid organizations*.

Free enterprise system: An economic system characterized by ownership of private property by individuals and enterprises, the profit motive, a competitive market system, and a limited involvement by government.

Global Reporting Initiative (GRI): A non-profit organization that works toward a sustainable global economy by providing guidance in sustainability reporting.

Globalists: Individuals and organizations that support globalization.

Globalization: A process of decreasing constraints on the interactions among the nations and peoples of the world.

Greed: The excessive desire to acquire or possess more, especially more material wealth, than one needs or deserves.

Green marketing: Selling environmentally friendly goods and services to consumers.

Greenwashing: A form of advertising or public relations that deceptively provides the perception that a corporation's policies or practices are socially responsible.

Human rights: The fundamental rights and freedoms to which all individuals, groups, and societies are entitled.

Independent (or unrelated) director: "A director who is free from any interest and any business or other relationship which could, or could reasonably be perceived to, materially interfere with the director's ability to act in the best interests of the corporation."

Individual rights ethic: Relies on a list of agreed-upon rights for everyone that will be upheld by everyone and that becomes the basis for deciding what is right, just, or fair.

Individualism: The view that the individual, and not society or a collective, is the paramount decision maker in society; assumes that the individual is inherently decent and rational.

Influence pathway: Occurs where withholding and usage strategies could be performed by an ally of the stakeholder with whom the organization has a resource dependence.

Integrity management: An ethics program that combines a compliance-based and a values-based approach.

Integrity: The appropriateness of a corporation's behaviour and its adherence to moral guidelines acceptable to society such as honesty, fairness, and justice.

Intellectual property: An umbrella term for patents, copyrights, trademarks, industrial designs, integrated circuit topographies, and plant breeders' rights.

International non-governmental organizations (INGOs): Groups that hold shared values and attitudes about the issues relating to globalization and advocate for changes to improve the conditions in developing countries.

Issue: A point in question or a matter that is in dispute where different views are held of what is or what ought to be corporate performance–based management or stakeholder expectations.

Issue analysis: Any effort to understand the source, nature, and extent of a question or matter in dispute facing the corporation which will result in addressing or resolving the matter.

Issues management: A systematic process by which the corporation can identify, evaluate, and respond to those economic, social, and environmental issues that may impact significantly upon it.

Laissez-faire capitalism: An economic system operating with absolute minimum interference by the government in the affairs of business. Government involvement is strictly limited to providing essential services such as police and fire protection.

Legitimacy: A generalized perception or assumption that the actions of an entity are desirable, proper, or appropriate within some socially constructed system of norms, values, beliefs, and definition that is based on the individual, the organization, or society.

Legitimacy: The belief in the rightness of an institution, in this case the appropriateness of our business system to supply the goods and services wanted by Canadian society.

Libel chill: Occurs when a business threatens legal action if a particular article or book is published.

Lobbying: All attempts to influence directly or indirectly any government activity; includes any attempt to influence legislators, their staff members, public administrators, and members of regulatory agencies.

Management information circular: The document used to communicate with shareholders.

Market environmentalism: Exists where economic incentives created by the market are more effective at protecting the environment than is government intervention.

Matrix mapping: A technique of categorizing an organization's stakeholders by their influence according to two variables; usually involves plotting them on a two-by-two matrix.

Microfinance: The provision of financial products, such as micro-credit, micro-insurance, and savings accounts, to persons living in areas of poverty without access to banking services.

Moral reasoning: A systematic approach to thinking or reasoning through the implications of a moral problem or issue.

Moral standards: The means by which individuals judge their actions and the actions of others based upon accepted behaviour in society.

Mutual fund: A pool of money from many individual investors that is invested on their behalf, usually in a specific kind of investment.

Non-governmental organization (NGO): Any group outside of the public and private sectors that holds shared values or attitudes about an issue confronting society and advocates for change around that issue.

Non-voting shares: Common shares without voting privileges.

Offsets (emissions-reduction credits): Credits purchased from other corporations or organizations to mitigate greenhouse gases released into the environment.

Oligopoly: A type of competition where the few sellers in an industry behave similarly.

Owners: Those individuals or groups who have invested in a corporation in the form of equity or shares; usually referred to as shareholders.

Ozone: Naturally occurring gas, formed from normal oxygen, that protects Earth by filtering out ultraviolet (UV) radiation from the Sun.

Passive shareholders: Those who do not attempt to influence the affairs of the corporation even though they have a legal right to do so.

Personal virtues ethic: An individual's or corporation's behaviour is based upon being a good person or corporate citizen with traits such as courage, honesty, wisdom, temperance, courage, fidelity, integrity, and generosity.

Philanthrocapitalism: According to *The Economist*, draws upon the philosophy of capitalist style objectives and criteria with an entrepreneurial spirit to get more from non-profit or social organizations.

Pluralistic society: One where influence or power is decentralized by dispersing it among a variety of institutions.

Policy development institution (think tank): An organization that researches and analyzes various important social, economic, and political issues confronting society.

Political globalization: The process by which world power relationships change and there is a loss of sovereignty by the state.

Power: A relationship among social actors in which one social actor, A, can get another social actor, B, to do something that B would not otherwise do.

Private equity firms: Firms that manage large pools of money acquired from wealthy individuals or families and big institutions such as pension and mutual funds.

Private sector: That part of economy not controlled and operated by government but run by individuals and corporations to make a profit.

Privatization: According to Heald, the "strengthening of the market at the expense of the state."

Profits: The excess of revenues over expenses; closely associated with competition.

Public sector: The part of the economy operated by government departments, agencies and organizations usually not to operate businesses or make profits, but to provide such things as a legal system, policing and prison services, defense organizations, transportation infrastructure, and educational and health institutions.

Public–private partnership: A cooperative venture between the public and private sectors, built on the expertise of each partner, that best meets clearly defined public needs through the appropriate allocation of resources, risks, and rewards.

Reputation management: Any effort to enhance the corporation's image and good name; in the past, the focus of these efforts was on media and public relations and, to some extent, crisis management.

Resource dependence: Exists when a stakeholder is supplying a resource and can exert some form of control over it.

Responsible corporation: A business undertaking that responds to social, ethical, and environmental responsibilities in addition to its economic obligations.

Responsible enterprise system: An economic system operating as a free enterprise system but incorporating the element of accountability.

Responsible investing: Screening investments in corporations or mutual and pension funds for their response to social or ethical responsibilities as well as their financial or economic performance.

Restricted shares: Involve some limit on voting, for example only one vote for every 10 or 100 shares owned; sometimes called *uncommon shares*.

Right of private property: The legal right to own and use economic goods, for example land and buildings.

Salience: The degree to which managers give priority to competing stakeholder claims.

Say-on-pay: The ability of shareholders to vote on the remuneration of executives.

Self-interest ethic: Individuals or corporations set their own standards for judging the ethical implications of their actions; only the individual's values and standards are the basis for actions.

Self-regulation: Regulation imposed by the corporation or industry and not by the government or market forces.

Service-learning: A method of teaching, learning, and reflecting, combining classroom learning with service to the community either locally or in developing countries.

Shared economy: A sustainable social and economic system involving the sharing of human and physical resources. Sometimes referred to as *peer-to-peer e-commerce*.

Shareholder democracy: The exercise of power by owners to ensure they are treated fairly and enjoy equally the privileges and duties of ownership.

Social auditing: A systematic assessment that identifies, measures, evaluates, reports, and monitors the effects an enterprise has on society that are not covered in the traditional financial reports.

Social capital: Any aspect of a corporation's organizational arrangements that creates value and facilitates the actions of stakeholders within and external to the corporation.

Social enterprise: A model of business operation where some or all profits are deliberately used to further social aims.

Social entrepreneur: An innovative, visionary leader of a non-profit or for-profit business with real-world problem-solving creativity and a high awareness for ethical, social, and environmental considerations.

Social entrepreneurship: The activities undertaken to enhance social wealth in some innovative way.

Social impact investing: The financing of initiatives to address social and environmental challenges and that generates a financial return and measurable benefits to society

Social impact management: Defined by the Aspen Institute as "the field of inquiry at the intersection of business needs and wider societal concerns that reflects and respects the complex interdependency between the two."

Social innovation: According to Graduate School of Business, Stanford University, it is "a novel solution to a social problem that is more effective, efficient, sustainable, or just than current solutions" where the "value created accrues primarily to society rather than to private individuals."

Social licence: The privilege of operating in society with minimal formalized restrictions—that is, legislation, regulation, or market requirements—based on maintaining public trust by doing what is acceptable to stakeholders in the business and society relationship.

Social media: Online technologies and practices that people use to share opinions, insights, experiences, and perspectives.

Social or cultural globalization: The emergence of a worldwide cultural system.

Social sector: That part of the economy that operates privately but, unlike the private sector, operates for social purposes with no intention to make profits.

Social venture philanthropy: The investment of human and financial resources by corporations in non-profit community development agencies to generate a social return instead of only a financial one.

Socialization of capitalism: The process through which the business system conforms to the expectations of society resulting in desired socially responsible outcomes.

Spirituality: An individual's sense of peace or purpose with him/herself and the connection to others and even nature that provides meaning to life and a sense of one's self.

Stakeholder: An individual or group who can influence and/or is influenced by the achievement of an organization's purpose.

Stakeholder capitalism: An economic system in which corporations accept broader obligations beyond financial ones for shareholders.

Stakeholder engagement: Efforts by a corporation to understand and involve relevant individuals, groups, or organizations by considering their moral concerns in strategic and operational initiatives.

Stakeholder management capability: The ability of managers to identify stakeholders and their influence, to develop the organizational practices to understand stakeholders, and to undertake direct contact with stakeholders.

Standard environmentalism: Occurs when government regulation is a necessary remedy for the market's failure to provide enough environmental amenities.

State capitalism: An economic system in which governments manipulate market outcomes for political and social purposes.

Statement of values: A description of the beliefs, principles, and basic assumptions about what is desirable or worth striving for in an organization.

Strategic giving: An attempt to rationalize the shareholder interest with corporate philanthropy where the corporation benefits directly from the funds given.

Strategic management: The process through which a corporation establishes its mission and objectives, analyzes the environment and resource capabilities in order to formulate strategy, creates the organizational systems and processes needed to implement the strategy, and devises mechanisms for evaluating performance.

Supply (or value) chain: The route that a product travels from the procurement of raw materials, the transformation into intermediate goods and then final products, and the delivery to consumers through a distribution system to its ultimate disposal by the consumer.

Supranational institution: An international organization that transcends national boundaries, where the member states share in decision making on particular issues pertaining to the members.

Sustainability purchasing: According to BuysmartBC, it is "the acquisition of goods and services ('products') in a way that gives preference to suppliers that generate positive social and environmental outcomes. It integrates sustainability considerations into product selection so that impacts on society and the environment are minimized throughout the full life cycle of the product."

Sustainability strategy: A plan that views economic, ethical, social, and environmental responsibilities more intensively and integrates corporate social responsibility (CSR) into all facets of the corporation's operations.

Sustainable capitalism: As defined by Al Gore and David Blood, an "economic system within which business and trade seek to maximise long-term value creation, accounting for all material ESG (environmental, social and governance) metrics."

Sustainable development: Development ensuring that the use of resources and the impact on the environment today does not damage prospects for the use of resources or the environment by future generations.

Tax haven: Defined by CRA as a jurisdiction with one or more of the following characteristics: no tax, or very low rates of taxation; strict bank secrecy provisions; a lack of transparency in the operation of its tax system; and a lack of effective exchange of information with other countries.

Teleological ethics: An approach to ethics that focuses on outcomes or results of actions.

Transfer pricing: The price set for goods and services sold between legal entities of the corporation.

Triple-E (economic, ethical, and environmental) bottom line: Evaluates a corporation's performance according to a summary of the economic, social, and environmental value the corporation adds or destroys.

Universal rules ethic: Ensures that managers or corporations have the same moral obligations in morally similar situations.

Urgency: The degree to which the stakeholder's claim or relationship calls for immediate attention; exists when a claim or relationship is of a time-sensitive nature and when that claim or relationship is important or critical to the stakeholder.

Usage strategies: An approach in which the stakeholder continues to supply a resource but specifies how it will be used.

Utilitarian ethic: Focuses on the distribution of benefits and harms to all stakeholders with the view to maximizing benefits.

Value judgments: Subjective evaluations of what is considered important; based on how managers intuitively feel about the goodness or rightness of various goals.

Venture capital company: A type of private equity firm that usually acquires part ownership of business enterprises for which they provide financial and management assistance.

Virtue ethics: An approach to ethics that emphasizes the individual's character or identity and focuses on being instead of doing.

Waste management: According to Environment Canada, it is the "disposal, processing, controlling, recycling and reusing the solid, liquid, and gaseous wastes of plants, animals, humans and other organisms."

Whistleblowing: An act of voluntary disclosure of inappropriate behaviour or decisions to persons in positions of authority in an organization.

Withholding strategies: An approach where the stakeholder discontinues providing a resource to an organization with the intention of changing a certain behaviour.

Work ethic: A code of values, or a body of moral principles, claiming that work is desirable, a natural activity, and is good in and of itself.

Worker capitalism: Describes employee ownership as workers are turned into capitalists through stock ownership.

Index

30% Club Canada, 224

A Civil Action, 118
A Long, Hard Road: Reducing GHG Emissions in Canada's Road Transportation Sector by 2050, 270
A Manifesto for Sustainable Capitalism, 339
abuse of dominant position, 246
academic integrity, 16–17, 20
    ethics, and, 2
    plagiarism, 20, 268
acceptance of gifts or benefits, 114*tab*
accountability, 8, 101, 216
    corporate social responsibility, 143–144
    corporation, 9
    for-benefit corporation, 332
    global business, 313–314
    government-owned corporations, 214–216
    non-public corporations, 216
    private corporations and private equity firms, 214–216
    stakeholders' expectations of, 177–178
accountability audits, 185
accountability dilemma, 216
Accountability Project, The, 180
accounting fraud, 124
acid rain, 280, **282**
acquisitions, 246
Action Environment, 367
active shareholders, **214**
activism
    protection of rights of owners, 219–220
    religious, 272
    shareholders, 45–46
activist groups, 90
Adbusters Magazine, 267
Adbusters Media Foundation, 267
Advertising, self-regulation, 47
Advertising Standards Canada, 207
Advertising Standards Council, 47
advocacy groups, 90
Agents of Change, 335
agricultural marketing organizations, 32
Agrium Inc., 15, 174, 200
Air Canada, 81, 163, 244, 290

air pollution, 282, 294
AirMiles, 168
Alberta Business, 265
Alberta Energy Company (AEC), 358–360
Alberta Energy and Utilities Board 359
Alberta oil sands, 2, 356–358
Alberta School of Business, 185
Algo Centre Mall, 12
allocation of resources, 11
American Heart Association, 349
Amnesty International, 308
amoral model of social responsibility, 120*tab*, 136–137, 137*tab*, 154
amoral sustainability strategy, 328*fig*, 329
amoral view of social responsibility, 136–137, 137*tab*
An Inconvenient Truth, 283
Anheuser-Busch InBev, 39, 94
Animal Alliance of Canada, 258
antagonistic stakeholders, 68
    strategies for, 69
anti-dumping, 194
anti-globalists, 307*tab*, **308**
Aon Hewitt Associates, 235, 293
apparent conflict of interest, 115
arbitration, 98, 352
Aristotle, 6, 7*tab*
Armstrong, Lance, 94
artificial being, 9
Aspen Institute, 142, 319, 341
asset misappropriation, 11
asset retirement obligations, 291
Association for the Advancement of Sustainability in Higher Education (ASSHE), 273
Association of Chinese Canadian Entrepreneurs, 47
Association of Ukrainian Businessmen, 49
Association to Advance Collegiate Schools of Business (AACSB), 184, 341
Athabasca Oil Sands Region, 356–358
Atlantic Canada Business, 265
Atlantic Subway Ltd., 128
Atlas Shrugged, 93
attitudes
    media attitudes toward business, 266–267
    society's attitudes toward business, 10–14
    unemployment, and, 12

audit committee, 222, **226**
Augustine's six stages of crisis management, 59
automobile industry, 47
Automobile Parts Manufacturers Association of Canada, 200
Automobile Protection Association, 241
automobile recalls, 2
AutoShare, 336

B corporation, 328*tab*, **332**–333
B.C. Technology Social Venture Partners, 164
"backing off the fast track", 235
bait-and-switch selling, 242
balance of power, 228–229
Balsillie School of International Affairs, 189
Balsillie, Jim, 189
bank ATM fees, 71
Bank of Montreal, 31, 227, 290, 314
Bank of Nova Scotia, 31, 221, 227
banking industry, 31
banking industry profits, 31
bankruptcy, 11, 194
bankruptcy fraud, 11
banks/bankers and mismanagement, 2
Barlow, Maude, 364
Barrick Gold Corporation, 117, 142, 174, 316, 343
Battery Energy Storage Systems, 367
Bavaria, Steven, 119
BCE Inc., 202, 215, 290
Behind the Mask: The Real Face of Corporate Social Responsibility, 154
Belize Alliance of Conservation Non-Governmental Organizations (BACONGO)
Belize Electric Company Limited (BECOL), 366
Belize Electricity Limited (BEL), 366
Belize Sugar Industries Limited (BSI), 367
benefit-cost test, 114
Benefit plans and employee, 236
Bentham, Jeremy, 7*tab*
Best 50 Corporate Citizens 2016, 78
Best 50 Corporate Citizens in Canada (Corporate Knights), 169, 182

Best Employers in Canada 2016, 235
Best Workplaces in Canada 2015, 235
Better Business Bureau (BBB) Canada, 89, 157
Better Planet Project, The, 273
Bharti Enterprises, 323
bias in the media, 266
bid rigging, 11, 246
Big Brothers of Vancouver, 143
Big One, The, 12
biofuel, 244*tab*
biopiracy, 323
bioprospecting, 322–323
Birks Family Foundation, 159
black market, 26
BlackBerry Ltd., 53
blogs, 13
Blood Diamond, 265
Blood, David, 339
Blue Spruce RV Park, 61
Blue Water Projects, 283
blue-collar workers, 45
board committees, 222
Board governance in globalization, 228
Board of Trade, 47
boards of directors. *See also* directors
    audit committee, 222
    defined, **222**
    evaluation of performance, 226–227
    fiduciary duties, 222
    membership, 222–223
    purpose of, 44–45
    responsibilities and duties, 222
    responsibility for ethics, 119
    separation of board chair and CEO positions, 222
    structure of, 222
    tasks of, 14–15
Body Shop, The, 165, 243, 252
Boiler Room, 118
Bombardier Inc., 142, 200
"boondocking", 61
Bottom of the Pyramid, 318–319
boycotts, 46
Boys and Girls Clubs of Vancouver, 143
BP oil disaster, 198, 280
brand impact, 260, 262*tab*
Breast Cancer Research, 143
Bribe Payers Survey, 315
bribery, 112, 124, 196–197, **315**

Bronfman, Charles and Edgar, 337
Buffett, Warren, 152, 337
Building the Canadian Advantage, 198
Bullfrog Power, 287, 333
Burger King, 255
business
  academic integrity, 16–17
  attitudes, changing, 11–14
  Canadian business system, 7–9
  changing attitudes, 11
  church's reflection on leadership, 272
  complexity of business and society, 3–4
  economic responsibility, 23–24
  environmental issues. *See* environmental issues
  ethical implications, potential, 88*fig*
  government. *See* government
  integration of society and, 17
  integrity in business, 4–6, 5*tab*
  legitimacy, 17
  media portrayal of, 12
  media relationship, 264–265, 266*tab*
  patron saint of, 48
  politics. *See* politics
  society's attitudes toward, 11–14
  society's permissions for, 10
  stakeholder concept and, 43–44
business citizenship, **146**–147
  See also corporate citizenship
Business Council of Canada, 47, 200
business cycles, 11, 36
business enterprise system, 7–9, 23–24
  See also Canadian business system
business ethics, 4, **87**, 238
  See also ethics of business
Business Ethics Magazine, 183
business failures, 36
business interest groups, 200
business lobbying, 200–202
business organizations, 47, 90, 139
business schools, 184–185, 341–344
  ethics, 341–344
business sustainable development, **282**
business value creation, 81
business-government relationship. *See* government

business-to-business, **247**
BusinessWeek, 270, 272
"Buy America", 354
Buying into the Future: The UBC Sustainable Purchasing Guide, 274
BuySmart Network, 251

C.D. Howe Institute, 203, 269
Caledon Institute of Social Policy, 269
Calgary Youth Justice Society, 164
Cameco Corporation, 108, 156, 174, 203, 312
  Value Statements, 108
Canada, gender equality, 28
Canada Business Corporations Act, 14, 15, 215, 220, 221
Canada Green Building Council (CaGBC), 294
Canada Home Office, 263
Canada Organic, 291
Canada Pension Plan (CPP), 215
Canada Post, 348
Canada Revenue Agency (CRA), 41, 43, 203, 274
Canada Student Loan Program, 192
Canada's Best 50 Corporate Citizens for 2014, 277
Canada's Best Employers 2016, 235
Canada's Greenest Employers, 293
Canadian Alliance for Community Service Learning (CSL), 343
Canadian Anti-Counterfeiting Network, 305
Canadian Association of University Teachers (CAUT), 188, 347
Canadian Auto Workers Union (CAW), 353–356
Canadian Bankers' Association, 200
Canadian Beverage Association, 349
Canadian Board Diversity Council (CBDC), 224
Canadian Boreal Forest Agreement (CBFA), 263, 264
Canadian Boreal Initiative, 264
Canadian Business, 22, 23, 202, 235, 265
Canadian business
  diversity of business interests, 9
  factors influencing attitudes, 11–12
  factors influencing morality, 7–9

  globalization and, 310–313
  government presence, 8
  ownership of, 212–214
  people who run Canadian business, 14–16
  reputation and trust of, 176
  society's attitudes towards, 11–14
  stakeholders responsible for operation of, 14–16
Canadian Business Corporation Act. *See Canada Business Corporations Act*
Canadian Business for Social Responsibility (CBSR), 11, 139, 179, 240, 261, 262, 263, 331
Canadian business system
  corporation and, 9–10
  described, 3, 7–9
Canadian Cancer Society, 143
Canadian Centre for Ethics & Corporate Policy, 139, 180
Canadian Centre for Ethics in Public Affairs (CCEPA), 139
Canadian Centre for Philanthropy, The, 157
Canadian Centre for Policy Alternatives, 269, 270
Canadian Chamber of Commerce, 47, 196, 227*tab*
Canadian Charter of Rights and Freedoms, 96–97
Canadian Children's Book Centre (CCBC), 151
Canadian Coalition for Good Governance (CCGG), 222, 223, 225, 231
Canadian Code of Advertising Standards, 207
Canadian Corporate Community Investment: Emerging Trends and Impact Measurement, 168
Canadian Council of Chief Executives, 196, 227*tab*
Canadian economic system
  competition, 29–30
  consumer sovereignty, 32–33
  economic freedoms, 26–27
  equality of opportunity, 27–29
  government, role of, 33–34
  individualism, 26–27
  market system, 23–24
  private property rights, 24–25
  profits, 30–31
  work ethic, 31–32
Canadian Environmental Protection Act, 284
Canadian Federation of Independent Business, 47, 168, 200
Canadian Food Inspection Agency (CFIA), 58, 361–362

Canadian Foundation for Advancement of Investor Rights (FAIR), 220, 231
Canadian Human Rights Act, 237
Canadian Human Rights Commission, 238
Canadian Imperial Bank of Commerce (CIBC), 31, 142
Canadian Institute of Chartered Accountants (CICA), 178, 338
Canadian International Development Agency (CIDA), 162
Canadian International Extractive Sector, 198
Canadian Internet Policy and Public Interest Clinic (CIPPIC), 33
Canadian Investor Protection Fund, 220
Canadian Labour and Business Centre, 269
Canadian Manufacturers and Exporters, 47, 196
Canadian MBA Oath, 386
Canadian Medical Association, 256, 349
Canadian Medical Association Journal, 349
Canadian mining industry, 12, 76–77, 198
Canadian Motor Vehicle Arbitration Plan (CAMVAP), 98
Canadian National Railway Company (CNR), 4, 5, 30
  sustainability report, 5
Canadian Oil Sands Limited, 358
Canadian Pacific Railway Ltd. (CPR), 30, 53, 202, 223
Canadian Parks and Wilderness Society, 264
Canadian Payday Loan Association, 62
Canadian Pharmacists Association (CPhA), 348
Canadian Radio-television and Telecommunications Commission (CRTC), 50, 195
Canadian Real Estate Association (CREA), 207
Canadian Restaurant & Foodservices Association, 209
Canadian Securities Administrators, 224, 225, 226, 227
Canadian Sustainability Indicators Network (CSIN), 296
Canadian Tire Corp., 69, 215, 247
Principles of Business Conduct, 247

Canadian Transportation Commission, 50, 195

Canadian Union of Public Employees, 276, 364

Canadian Youth Climate Coalition (CYCC), 212

Canadians' legal rights and responsibilities, 96–97

Canajun Guide, 269

Canopy, 264

cap-and-trade, **286**

capitalism. *See also* capitalist fundamentals
Canadian business, in, 3
clean-capitalism, 8
Confucian capitalism, 34
conscious capitalism, 35
consumer capitalism, 34
creative capitalism, 35
defined, **7**, 34
democratic capitalism, 35
employee capitalism, 35
family capitalism, 34
father of capitalism (Adam Smith), 8
forms of, 34–35
frontier capitalism, 35
global capitalism, 318–351
laissez-faire capitalism, 8
liberal market capitalism, 34
new forms of, 37
people's capitalism, 35
producer capitalism, 34
regulation within, 193
stakeholder capitalism, 8, 35
state capitalism, 35
theory of, 24
worker capitalism, 214

Capitalism: A Love Story, 12, 265

capitalist fundamentals
Canadian capitalism, 34–35
challenges, 35–36
competition, 29–30
consumer sovereignty, 32–33
economic freedoms, 26–27
equality of opportunity, 27–29
ethics and responsibilities, 35–37
government, role of, 33–34
individualism, 26–27
private property rights, 24–25
profits, 30
various forms of capitalism, 34–35
work ethic, 31–32

carbon capture and storage (CCS), **288**

Carbon Disclosure Project (CDP), 290

Carbon Efficient Index, 290

carbon offsets, 244*tab*

carbon pricing, **286**

carbon tax, **286**

care-focused ethics, 238

caring, ethic of, **95**

caring corporate sustainability, 141

Carrefour SA, 323

Carroll's pyramid of corporate social responsibility, 139–141, 140*tab*

Carroll, Archie, 139, 140, 141

CarShare, 336

Carswell, 235

Cascades Inc., 174

cases
A Union Strikes and a Small Business is Challenged, 276
A University's Centre for Corporate Sustainability, 347
Accepting a Job in the Payday Loan Industry, 62
Alberta Energy Company and the Ethics of Operation Kabriole, 358–360
Aunt Mabel's Experience with Ownership, 230–231
Boondocking at Wal-Mart, 61–62
Campus Boycotts: Who Makes the Call?, 39–40
Caterpillar Shuts Down Its Canadian Locomotive Plant, 353–356
Citizen's Arrest: The Law and Ethics, 127
CSR and the Closure of a Neighbourhood Supermarket, 83–84
Corporate Social Responsibility to Food Banks, 352–353
Crisis at Maple Leaf Foods Inc., 361–362
Detecting Plagiarism and Academic Integrity, 20
Dog's "Eco-Pawprint", 301–302
Economics of Textbook Pricing, 84–85
Energy Drinks at Prairie Pharmacy, 348–350
Ethical Responsibility on Mount Everest, 104
Ethics of Asbestos, 210
Ethics of Bioprospecting, The, 322–323
500 Birds On a Pond, 356–358
Food Retailing in India: Revolution or Evolution?, 323–324

Fortis and the Chalillo Dam: Balancing Economic Development and Environmental Impact, 366–368
Gabriel Resources Ltd. and the Rosia Montana Saga, 350–352
Having to Give at the Office, 172
Heidi Heise, Sub Samaritan, 127–128
Is Dr. Suess Misleading Children?, 302–303
Just Dump It in the Lake, 362–364
Loblaw's Treatment of its Suppliers, 254–255
Philanthropy and Academic Freedom, 188
Professor Murray's Ethical Dilemmas, 364–366
Pillaging of Pension, The, 19–20
Responsible Alcohol Consumption, 171
SLAPPing Greenpeace Canada, 277
Sodium and Ethhics, 255–256
Sodium and Ethics, 255–256
stadiums, taxpayers and sports millionaires, 346–347
TD Grade One Book Giveaway, 151
The Economics of Textbook Pricing, 84–85
What Shareholder Democracy?, 231–232
Working Overtime, 104
Would You Like To Donate?, 150–151
Zapping Sales and Taxes, 40–41

Catalyst Canada, 133, 224

Catalyst Paper Corporation, 51, 174
Sustainability Report, 51

Catamaran Corp., 53

categorical imperative, 114

categorical imperative ethic, 96

Caterpillar Inc., 353–356

cause-related marketing, **158**

Caux Round Table Principles for Business, 181, 313

Celestica Inc., 78, 133, 314
Sustainability Report 2015, 79

cell phone towers, 80

Centre for Corporate Social Performance and Ethics, 122

Centre for Excellence in Responsible Business, 219

Centre for International Innovation (CIGI), 189

Centre for International Studies and Cooperation (CECI), 162

Centre for Long Term Environmental Action NL (CLEANf/Ld), 364

Centre for Social Innovation & Impact Investing, 344

Centre for Social Innovation (CSI), 335

CEO pay ratio, **225**

CEOs
essential qualities, 16
separation of board chair and CEO positions, 222

certification standards, 243

Certified Financial Planner (CFP), 110, 111

Chalillo Project, 366–368

Chamandy, Glenn J., 133

Chamber of Commerce, 47, 160

Chan, Priscilla, 337

Charitable Accountability Standards, 157

charitable foundation, **158**

charities, 49, 163, 178, 327

Charity Intelligence Canada, 157

Chartered Professional Accountants of Canada (CPA Canada), 40, 46, 47

cheating scandals, 365

Chemistry Industry Association of Canada (CIAC), 193, 194, 297

Chen, David, 127

Chen, John, 53

Chernobyl, 280

chief executive officer. *See* CEOs

child care, 236*tab*

Child Exploitation Tracking System, 262

child labour, 112

China, 34

Christian Aid, 154

Christian Reform Church, 359

Chronicle Herald, 128

Church of the Shepherd King, 359

Citigrow Inc., 168

citizen's arrest, 127

citizenship. *See* corporate citizenship

City of Toronto, 276

Civil Action, A, 265

civil society
defined, **258**
educational institutions, 272–274
media stakeholder, 264–265
non-governmental organizations (NGOs), 258–260

policy development institution (think tank), 269–270
religious institutions, 270–272
Clarkson, Max, 122
Clayoquot Sound, 286
clean capitalism, **8**
climate change, **283**
co-operatives, 215, 332*tab*
  consumer, 215
  employee, 215
  ethics, 215
  producer, 215
Coalition for Environmentally Responsible Economies (CERES), 296
Coalition of Universities for Responsible Investing (CURI), 215, 343
Code of Behaviour, 109
code of conduct
  code of ethics, vs., 110*tab*
  content, 112
  contributions of, 110
  criticism, 113
  defined, **109**
  example, 110–111
code of ethics
  code of conduct, vs., 110*tab*
  content, 112
  contributions of, 110
  criticism, 113
  defined, **109**
  example, 111–112
collaboration, 77–78
  strategies for, 71
colleagues, 90
collective ownership, 25
commercial expression, restricting freedom of, 34
commercialization of education, 48
Commitment to Responsible Care, 193
commons, **281**
Commonwealth of Nations, 315
communication activities, 183
Community Contribution Company (CCC), 332*tab*, 336
Community Interest Company (CIC), 332*tab*, 336
community investment, **168**
  See also corporate social responsibility (CSR)
Community-Based Research Canada (CBRC), 343
competition, 8, **29**–30, 194, 245–246, 314
  ethics, 245–246
  free market system, 8
  government influence, 245–246

multinational corporations, 314
regulation of, 246
responsibilities, 245
restricted, 29
Competition Act, 90, 242, 245, 246, 248, 249, 276
Competition Bureau, 119, 242, 255
competitive advantage, 261
competitive behaviour, 90
competitive position, 261, 262*tab*
Competitiveness Scorecard, 310
competitors, 47, 245–246, 281*tab*
complete egoism, 92
complexity of business and society, 3–4
compliance culture, 338
compliance-based ethics programs, 121–122, 122*tab*
compliance-based sustainability strategy, 329
compliance-driven corporate sustainability, 141
comprehensive environmental management, 289
comprehensive sustainability strategy, 329
concentrated ownership, 213–214
concession doctrine, 9
Conference Board of Canada, 23, 139, 168, 176, 180, 269, 270
confidential information, use of, 114*tab*
conflict of interest, 40, 101, 112, 113
  apparent conflict of interest, 115
  common conflicts of interest, 114*tab*
  defined, **114**
  example, 115
  potential conflict of interest, 115
  real conflict of interest, 115
  understanding, 114–115
Confucian capitalism, 34
Connections Counselling and Consulting, 164
ConocoPhillips Oil Sands Partnership II, 358
consequential theory of ethics, **6**, 7*tab*
conspiracy, 246
Constant Gardener, The, 265
constituencies, 221
constituency theory, 138*tab*
consultants, 116
consumer capitalism, 34
consumer interest groups as stakeholders, 52
consumer rights, 96

consumer rights and responsibilities, 241–242
consumer sovereignty, **32**–33, 241
  consumers, 240–241
consumerism, **241**
consumers
  concerned, 177
  consumer sovereignty, 240–241
  consumption, 240–241
  corporate social responsibility (CSR), 243–244
  corporate social responsibility (CSR) reporting, 177
  ethical consumers, 45–46
  ethical marketplace, 241–243
  green consumer, 292
  marketplace, 241–242
  owners as, 213*tab*
  protecting, 242
  rights and responsibilities, 241
  stakeholders, as, 45–46
Consumers' Association of Canada, 241
Consumption by consumers, 240–241
contract public agencies, 196
contracting out, 196
contracting out service delivery, 196
contracts, 194
control, share ownership, vs., 214
Convention of Biological Diversity, 322
conventional level, 100*tab*
Cool It: The Skeptical Environmentalist's Guide to Global Warming, 297
cooperatives, 27, 213*tab*, 252
  See also retail cooperatives
Copenhagen Consensus Center, 297
copyright, 25
corporate accountability, 130
corporate agenda, 201, **205**
Corporate Chaplains Canada, 272
corporate citizenship, 130
  business citizenship, 146–147
  defined, 5*tab*, **144**
  equivalent view, 145
  extended view, 145
  Imperial Oil Ltd., at, 144–145
  inappropriate view, 145
  limited view, 145
  new approach, 146–147
  social-view theory of social responsibility, 138*tab*
  views of, 144–147, 145*tab*
corporate crime, 36
corporate donations, 156

corporate ethics, 89, 130
corporate ethics programs
  approaches, 121–122
  benefits of, 122–124
  business schools, 341–342
  classification of programs, 121
  code of conduct, 109–113
  code of ethics, 109–113
  compliance-based, 121–122, 122*tab*
  defined, **108**
  dialogical approach, 121
  ethics audits, 116
  ethics committee, 116
  ethics consultants, 116
  ethics officers, 116
  ethics reporting system, 117–119
  ethics training, 113–115
  evaluation of, 122–124
  formal approach, 121
  integrity-based, 121, 122*tab*
  monological approach, 121
  statement of values, 108–109
  sustainability and, 339–341
  values-based, 121–122, 122*tab*
  whistleblowing, 117–119
corporate financing, 314
corporate giving. *See* corporate philanthropy
corporate governance, 212
  attention to, 225–226
  best practices and, 227
  board membership, 222–223
  board structure, 222
  corporate social responsibility (CSR), 228
  criticism of reform, 228–229
  defined, **221**
  disclosure, 225–226
  ethical conduct, 228
  evaluation of board and director performance, 226–227
  multinational corporations, and, 313–314
  performance, and, 227–229
  rebalancing power in the organization, 228–229
  responsibilities of board, 221–222
  shareholder rights, 221–222
  stakeholders, 228
  transparency, 225–226
Corporate Knights, 3–4, 8, 78, 135, 142, 169, 173, 185, 277, 312
Corporate Knights Inc., 139, 182
corporate misdeeds, 11–12
corporate ownership, 215
corporate philanthropy

arguments against, 156–157
arguments for, 156–157
Cameco Corporation, at, 156
cause-related marketing, 158–159
charitable foundation, 158–159
concerns, 158–159
corporate donations, 156
corporate giving decisions, 157–158
defined, **156**
organizations assisting in, 158–159
strategic giving, 159
trends, 158–159
corporate public affairs, 200–202
corporate reporting. *See* corporate social responsibility (CSR) reporting
corporate reputation, **176–177**
"Corporate Responsibility Assessment Tool", 180
corporate responsibility, 130
Corporate Responsibility Officer (CRO), 183
corporate self-discipline regulation, 194
corporate service corps, 162
corporate social integration, 340–341
corporate social responsibility (CSR), 15
See also corporate social responsibility practices
amoral view, *120tab*, 136–137, *137tab*, 154
approaches to, 153–155, *154tab*
arguments against, 132–134
arguments for, 132–134
challenges to, 154–155
consumers and, 243–244
contemporary concepts, 141–144
continuum of future commitment to, *186tab*
corporate governance, and, 228
corporate reputation and, 176–177
corporate social integration, to, 340–341
corporate sustainability, 141
criticism of, 134–136
debate over, 132–136
defined, *5tab*, **130**
describing, 130–132
economic responsibilities, 140
employees and, 240
ethical responsibilities, 140
feminist ethics and, 238

government involvement in, 198–199
importance of, 131–132
justification for, 340–341
key elements of, 130–132
legal responsibilities, 140
legislation, 198–199
measuring, 174–175
media, 268
organizations supporting CSR, 139
personal view, 137
philanthropic responsibilities, 140
planning for, 155
principles of, 132
profitability, and, 178–179
pyramid of, 139–141, *140fig*
quotations about, 131
rationale for, 130–131
reporting. *See* corporate social responsibility (CSR) reporting
reputation management, 142
responses to, 153–155, *154tab*
responsive, 338
risks of not practising, *155tab*
small business and, 166–168
social impact management, 142–143
social responsibility theories, 136–139
social view, 137–138, *138tab*
strategy. *See* CSR strategy
triple-E (economic, ethical, & environmental) bottom line, 143–144
VBA model, 147–148, *148tab*
Wood's principles, *132tab*
corporate social responsibility (CSR) practices. *See also* corporate social responsibility (CSR)
contemporary CSR, 168–169
corporate philanthropy, 156–159
corporate sponsorship, 162–164
corporate voluntarism, 160–162
planning for CSR, 155
responses for CSR, 153–155, *154tab*
small business, 166–168
social enterprise, 165–168
social entrepreneur, 165–168
social venture philanthropy, 164
corporate social responsibility (CSR) reporting
business schools and, 184–185
communication of results, 183

criteria, 179–181
defined, **175**
evaluation of Canadian CSR reporting, 181–182
future of, 185–186
Global Reporting Initiative (GRI), 180–181
social auditing, 174
stakeholders and, 177–178
surveys, 183
Wood's principles, *132tab*
corporate sponsorship, **162**–163
corporate sustainability (CS), *5tab*, **141**
corporate sustainability reports, 3
corporate taxation, 202
corporate voluntarism, **160**–162
corporate policies, 161–162
corporate service corps, 162
defined, **160**
employee voluntarism, *161tab*
forms of support, 160–161
organizations supported, 160–161
corporate volunteerism, 341
Corporate Watch, 265, 308
corporate welfare, **206**
corporate wrongdoing, 12
corporation
accountability, 9
"freedom of association" doctrine, 9
going concern principle, 9
responsibility, 10
"state within a state", 9
Corporation, The: Pathological Pursuit of Power and Profits, The, 12, 265
corporations
balance of power, 228–229
Canadian business system, and, 9–10
doctrines of incorporation, 9–10
environmental opportunities and challenges, 299
government-owned corporations, 9, 215–216
interactions with society, 50
media, ownership of, 267–268
mission, vision and values statements, 91
multinational corporations, 313–314
non-public, 216
owners, as, 215
politics and. *See* politics
stakeholder, and, 52
strategies for relationships with NGOs, 261–262, *262tab*

corrective justice, 97
corrupt practices, 314
corruption, 26, 197, 314
economic freedoms, 26
Corruption of Foreign Public Officials Act (CFPOA), 196, 197, 315
Corruption Perception Index (CPI), 314–315, *315tab*
cost approach, 175
cost-benefit analysis, 95–96
Costco, 254
Council of Canadians, 351, 364
Council of Europe, 315
creative capitalism, **35**
credit unions, *213tab*
creditors, 46
stakeholders, 52
Criminal Code of Canada, 127, 196
crisis, **57**
crisis management
Augustine's six stages of, 59
defined, **57**
Fink's anatomy of a crisis, 57–59, *58fig*
CRO Magazine, 183
crony capitalism, 34
Crown corporations, *213tab*, 216
See also government-owned corporations
CSA Clean Projects, 287
CSR. *See* corporate social responsibility (CSR)
CSR reporting. *See* corporate social responsibility (CSR) reporting
CSR strategy
approaches to social and environmental responsibilities, 328–331
beliefs, 334
business programs and sustainability, 339–341
corporate social integration, to, 340–341
defined, 328
environmental responsibilities, 328–331
financial view, 329
managerial preferences view, 329–331
mission, 334
social responsibilities, 328–331
stakeholder view, *330tab*
values, 334
vision, 334
working with communities, *167tab*
CTVglobemedia Inc., 267

cultural associations, 49
cultural globalization, **307**
Cuso International, 343
Customers. *See also* consumers
    owners, as, 213*tab*
    stakeholders, as, 45–46

David Suzuki Foundation (DSF), 264, 364
De George, Richard T., 4
dealers, 47
decentralized decision-making, 11
Defenders of Wildlife, 367
deferred prosecution agreement, 197
defined benefit plans, 19
defined contribution plans, 19
definitive stakeholders, 73–74*tab*
deforestation, 280
Deloitte, 142
democratic capitalism, 35
deontological theory of ethics, **6**, 7*tab*
Department of Fisheries and Oceans, 363
deregulation, **195**, 206, 246
derivative stakeholders, 52
Desautels Faculty of Management, 185, 343
Desjardins Group, 174
developing countries, 314, 318–321
Diageo plc, 171
diagnostic typology of organizational stakeholders, 70–72, 71*fig*
dialogical approach, 121
direct owners, 14, 213–214
directors. *See also* boards of directors
    compensation of, 224–225
    corporate governance, CSR, and, 227–229
    evaluation of performance, 226–227
    fiduciary duties, 222
    independent director, 223
    stakeholders, as, 44–45
    unrelated director, 223
    women directors, 223
disbarment, 196
disclosure, 225–226, 314
disclosure audience, 95
Disclosure of Corporate Governance Practices (CSA), 226
discrimination, **237**, 238
distributive justice, 97
distributors, 47
DiverseCity OnBoard, 224

diversity management, 234, **238**
diversity of business interests, 9
divestiture, 196
"do-gooder" funds, 220
doctrines of incorporation, 9–10
Dollarama Inc., 221
Domini 400 Social Index, 218
Domtar Corporation, 174, 309
donations, 150, 156
Donner Canadian Foundation, 159
Douglas, Michael, 36
Dow Corning Corporation, 162
Dow Jones Sustainability Indexes (DJSI), 142, 177, 218, 290
Dr. Seuss, 302
dual-class stock, **214**

early retirement, 235
EarthChoice Office Papers, 309
Earthworks, 351
Eatwith, 336
eBay, 336, 337
Ebert, Roger, 283
eco-chic, 244
eco-insurance, 290
Eco-Logo, 291
eco-resorts, 244*tab*
eco-travel, 244*tab*
Ecofiscal Commission, 288
Ecole des sciences de la gestion, 185
Ecologo, 291
economic black holes, 84
economic cycles, 36
economic downturn, 45
economic freedom and foreign investment, 26
Economic Freedom of the World project, 27
economic freedoms, **26**–27, 320
economic globalization, **306**
economic growth, 209, 286, 287*tab*
economic paradigm, 154
economic responsibilities, 140
economic system
    assumption, 23–24
    Canada, in. *See* Canadian economic system
    defined, **7**
Economist, The, 135, 136, 337
ecosystem, **282**
Edelman Trust Barometer, 36, 176, 265
Edmonston, Philip, 241
education
    commercialization of, 48
    influence on ethical behaviour, 90
    institutions, 48, 272–274

educational institutions, 48, 272–274
egoism, 92
elder care, 236*tab*
Electrical Association, 200
Electro-Motive Diesel (EMD), 353–356
Electronics Recycling Service (ERS) International, 297
Eligibility Procedures and Standards for Business Accreditation, 184
Elimination of Automatic Tips Act, 209
embed-and-integrate scenario, 186
embezzlement, 11
Emera Inc., 227
emerging sustainability strategy, 329
eminent domain, 24–25
emissions trading, 286
emissions-reduction credits, **287**
employee capitalism, 35
employee engagement, **240**
employee loyalty, 234, 236–237
    recession, 237
employee ownership, 214
employee rights, 112
employee share ownership plans, 213*tab*
employee stock purchase plan, 213*tab*
employees, 234–240
    benefit plans, 236
    corporate social responsibility (CSR) reporting, and, 177
    diversity management, 234
    employee loyalty, 234
    employee participation, 234
    employment insurance, 236
    engagement of, 240
    examples of issues in the workplace, 234
    fair compensation, 234
    feminist ethics, 238
    loyalty, 234, 236–237
    moonlighting, 236*tab*
    owners, as, 214
    ownership pros and cons, 214–215
    participants in politics, 199–200
    privacy, 234
    recession, 237
    right to due process, 234
    right to work, 234
    stakeholders, 52, 234–240
    stakeholders, as, 45
    stock purchase plan, 213*tab*
    turnover, 236

unions, 234
use of employer's property, 114*tab*
voluntarism, 160–162, 161*tab*
work ethic, 235–236
worker capitalism, 214
workforce reduction, 234
workplace conditions, 234
workplace privacy, 234, 239
employment, 12, 314
employment diversity, 234, 237–238
employment equity, **237**
Employment Equity Act, 237, 238
employment insurance, 235
    employee, 236
Employment Standards Act, 209
En Route, 265
Enactus, 165–166
Enbridge Inc., 174, 202, 314, 347
EnCana Corp., 174
Endowment for Entrepreneurship, 343
endowment funds, 215
EnerGuide, 291
energy depletion, 280
energy drinks, 348–350
Energy Probe, 285, 367
energy production and consumption, 282
Energy Resources and Conservation Board, 288
Energy Star, 291
Engineers Without Borders, 343
ENGOs. *See* environmental non-governmental organizations (ENGOs)
Enron, 198
Enterprising Non-profits Program Vancouver, 164
entrepreneurs, 213*tab*
entrepreneurship, 165–166, 246
Enviro-Stewards, 333
environment, 259*tab*, 280, 281
    asset retirement obligations, 291
    corporate policies, 291
    financial effects, 291
    liabilities, 291
    operational effects, 291
    paradox, 298
    risks, 291
Environment Coalition of Prince Edward Island, 367
Environmental Choice, 291
environmental ethic, **281**–282
environmental issues
    acid rain, 282
    air pollution, 282
    approaches to viewing, 328–331

business and stakeholders, and, 280–281

business sustainable development, 282

carbon capture and storage (CCS), 288

climate change, 283

compliance with laws and regulations, 289

comprehensive environmental management, 289

corporate opportunities and threats, 299

dissenting views, 297–298

ecosystem, 282

emissions trading, 286

emissions-reduction credits, 287

energy production and consumption, 282

environmental ethic, 281–282

environmental non-governmental organizations (ENGOs), 264, 279, 285–286, 367

financial management, 290–291

global warming, 2, 283

government departments and agencies, 284

government, influence of, 284–285

greening of business function, 290–295, 293*tab*

greenwashing, 289

human resources, 292–293

management of responses to, 288–289

market environmentalism, 286, 287*tab*

market-driven environmentalism, 286–288

marketing, 291–292

measurement of environmental sustainability, 295–297

mining, 362–364

multinational corporations, 314

nature and wildlife, 282

offsets, 287, 289

operations, 293–295

ozone, 282

pollution, 282

reporting on environmental sustainability, 295–297

standard environmentalism, 286, 287*tab*

sustainable development, 282, 289

terms, 282

token response, 289

waste management, 282

water quality, 282

environmental laws, 195

environmental liabilities, 291

environmental management systems (EMS), 289

environmental non-governmental organizations (ENGOs), 264, 279, **285**–286, 367

environmental policies, 291

environmental protection, 112
  multinational corporations, 314
  requirements, 291

environmental risks, 291

environmental sustainability measurement and reporting, 295–297

environmental sustainability reporting, 295–297

environmental, social and governance (ESG) factors/metrics, 216, 217, 336

environmentally friendly, 220

equality of opportunity, **27**–29

Erin Brockovich, 118, 265

espionage, 30

ethic of caring, **95**

ethic of justice, **97**–98

ethical behaviour
  corporate governance, and, 228
  corporate or organizational influences, 89
  economic efficiency influences, 90
  government and legal system influences, 90
  individual influences, 89
  influences on, 89–91
  societal influences, 90–91
  students, 16–17*tab*
  theoretical basis for, 92–98

Ethical Business Conduct, 228

ethical consumers, 45–46

ethical egoism, 92–93

ethical implications. *See also* business ethics
  approaches, 99*tab*
  assessment of, in business decisions, 88
  business-government relationship, 206
  compensation packages, 26
  competition, 29–30
  consumer sovereignty, 45
  economic freedoms, 27
  equality of opportunity, 27–29
  government, role of, 33–34
  individualism, 27
  intellectual property rights, 24–25
  moral standards, 88

potential, in business operations, 88*fig*

prevalence of, 2

private property, 24

profits, 30–31

right of private property, 24–25

value judgments, 88

work ethic, 31–32

ethical investment, 221

ethical leadership, 107–108, 124–125
  ethical form, 107
  forms of, 107–108
  responsible, 107
  servant, 108

ethical marketplace and consumers, 241–243

ethical mutual funds, 244*tab*

Ethical Oil: The Case for Canada's Oil Sands, 189

ethical principles
  ethic of caring, 95
  ethic of justice, 97–98
  ethical egoism, 92–93
  individual rights ethic, 96–97
  moral standards, vs., 91*tab*
  personal virtues ethic, 94–95
  self-interest ethic, 92–93
  universal rules ethic, **96**
  utilitarian ethic, 95–96
  value judgments, vs., 91*tab*

ethical products, examples, 244*tab*

ethical relativism, **91**, 315

ethical responsibilities, 104–105, 140

ethical thinking, main approaches to, 6–7, 7*tab*

Ethical Trading Initiative (ETI), 252

ethics
  business schools, 341–344
  co-operatives, 215
  robots, of, 102

ethics as taught in business schools, 341–344

ethics audits, **116**

ethics committees, **116**

ethics consultants, 116

ethics management
  codes of conduct and ethics, 109–112
  corporate ethics programs. *See* corporate ethics programs

ethics of business. *See also* ethical implications
  Aristotle and, 7*tab*
  assessment, in business decisions, 88

boards of directors, responsibility of, 119

capitalist fundamentals, and, 35–37

challenges, 101–102

corporate ethics programs. *See* corporate ethics programs

defined, 5*tab*, 87

ethical principles. *See* ethical principles

feminist ethics and, 238

influences on ethical behaviour, 89–91

introduction to, 87

levels of ethical assessment, 88*fig*

management, responsibility of, 119–120

moral reasoning, 98–101

myths, 101

prevalence of, 101–102

responsibility for, 119–120

theoretical basis for ethical conduct, 92–98

ethics officers, **116**

Ethics Practitioners' Association of Canada (EPAC), 107, 116

ethics programs. *See* corporate ethics programs

ethics reporting systems, 117–119

ethics training
  checklists, 113–114
  conflict of interest, 113–115
  described, 113
  online exercises, 113
  tests, 113–114

EthicsCentre.ca, 139, 180

ethnic association, 49

ethnic culture, 90

European Foundation for Management Development (EFMD), 341

European Union (EU), 306, 350

EvenStart for Children Foundation, 164

exclusive dealing, 248

executive compensation schemes, 2

expectant stakeholders, 73–74*tab*

Export Development Corporation, 67

expropriation, 25

extended producer responsibility, **250**, 274

external outcomes, 179

external stakeholder, 44, 52

externally verified social reports, 175

Extractive Industries Transparency Initiative (EITI), 198, 316

Exxon Valdez, 280

Facebook, 13, 33, 65, 337
facilitation payments, 315
fad-and-fade scenario, 185
fair compensation, 234
Fair Indigo, 244*tab*
Fair Labour Association (FLA),
   250
fair trade, 45, 165, 244*tab*, **251**,
   319
   certification mark, 252
fair trade products, 45
Fair Trade USA, 252
Fairmont Hotels & Resorts, 263
Fairtrade Canada, 252, 291
Fairtrade Foundation, 251, 319
Fairtrade International, 252
faith-based principles and
   business, 270–272
Falls Brook Centre, 367
family capitalism, 34
Farrell, Dawn, 133
favouritism, 101
Feastly, 336
FedEx, 162
feminist ethics, 238
fiduciary duties, **222**
financial crisis, 36, 45
financial institutions, 177, 213*tab*
financial management and
   greening of business functions,
   290–291
Financial Planners Standards
   Council, 111
financing, 314
Fink's anatomy of a crisis, 57–59,
   58*tab*
Finkelstein, Harvey, 33
firm outcomes, 179
firm processes, 179
First Nations, 25
   property rights, 25
"First Year Pledge of Social
   Justice, Economic Strength,
   and Environmental
   Responsibility, The", 2
fish farming, 279
Fisheries Act, 363, 364
flaring, 358–360
Food and Drugs Act, 349
Food banks, 352, 353
Food Banks Canada, 352
"food miles", 243
for-benefit corporation, 332–333
Ford Motor, 353
Foreign Affairs and International
   Trade Canada, 199
Foreign Corrupt Practices Act,
   197

foreign investment and economic
   freedom, 26
Forest Products Association of
   Canada (FPAC), 47, 264
Forest Stewardship Council, 309
ForestEthics, 264, 277
formal approach, 121
Fort Chipewyan First Nations,
   357
Fortis Inc., 366–368
Fortune, 267
Fossil Fuel Free Index, 290
Fountainhead, The, 93
fourth sector, **327**
franchisees, 47
   regulation, 47
Fraser Institute, The, 23, 26, 27,
   269, 270
fraternal associations, 49
fraud, 2, 11, 124, 197
   bankruptcy fraud, 11*tab*
free enterprise system, **8**
free market system and
   competition, 8
Free the Children, 263
free trade, 195, 196, 286, 287*tab*
freedom of association, 9
   doctrine for the corporation, 9
freedom of the press, 266
Freeman's stakeholder
   management capability, 66–67
Friedman, Milton, 134
Friends of Music, 166
Friends of the Earth Canada
   (FOE), 285, 351
frontier capitalism, 35
FTSE4Good Index Series, 218
fundamentalism, 137*tab*

Gabriel Resources Ltd., 350–352
Gap Inc., 252
Gates, Bill, 35, 337
Gekko, Gordon, 36
gender equality, 27, 28
Gender Parity Score, 28
General Electric Co., 355
General Motors, 353
Generation Y, 31
generic social issues, 258–260
Germany, 35
gifts, 114*tab*
Gildan Activewear Inc., 133,
   142, 202
Gilead Sciences Inc., 67
Girling, Ross, 133
Giving Pledge, The, 337
Global 100 Most Sustainable
   Corporations, 169
Global Competitiveness Index,
   310

"Global Competitiveness Report"
   (World Economic Forum), 310
global corporate reporting
   guidelines, 180–181
Global Freedom to Trade, 261
Global Fund, The, 46
Global Gender Gap Index, 28
Global Impact Investment Rating
   System (GIIRS), 336
Global Reporting Initiative
   (GRI), 180–181, 182, 313
global standards of conduct, 313
*Global Strategy to Reduce
   Harmful Use of Alcohol*, 171
global supply chains, 249–250,
   250
global warming, 283
globalists, **308**
globalization, 12
   acceptance of global
      capitalism, 318–321
   anti-globalists, 308
   board governance, 228
   "Buy America", 354
   Canadian business and society,
      310–313
   challenges of, 314–318, 354
   corporate citizenship and, 146,
      355, 356
   corruption, 314–316
   debate over, 307–308
   defined, **306**
   economic globalization, 306
   fair trade, 319
   globalists, 308
   government influence, 354
   human rights, 316
   implications for business,
      306–308
   institutions of, 309–310
   international
      non-governmental
      organizations (INGOs),
      308–309
   introduction, 305
   issues, 307
   microfinance, 319–320
   multinational corporations,
      313–314
   NGOs, and, 261
   political globalization, 306
   poverty reduction, 318
   pros and cons of, 307*tab*
   social or cultural globalization,
      307
   standards of conduct and
      accountability, 313–314
   supranational institution, **309**
   sweatshop labour abuses,
      316–317
   union influence, 355

Globe and Mail, The, 22, 23,
   142, 172, 227, 235, 265, 268
Globe Foundation of Canada,
   296–297
goals of stakeholders, 52
going concern principle, 9
   corporation, 9
gold, 350–352
Goldcorp, 316
Golden Rule, 95, 114
Golfman, Jeff, 294
"good puppy" theory, 114
Goodwill Industries, 154*tab*, 325,
   326
Google, 13, 14
Gordon Food Service, 263
Gore, Al, 283, 339
governance, 221, 225–226
governing system, 212, 221
   See also corporate governance
Government. *See also* public
   policy
   architects of economic growth,
      194–196
   attitudes towards business, 12
   corporate social responsibility
      (CSR) reporting, 178
   corporate welfare, 206
   decreasing government
      involvement, effect of, 206
   encouraging competition,
      245–246
   environmental issues,
      influence on, 284–285
   ethical implications in
      business-government
      relationship, 206
   ethics in, 90, 206
   interventions, 26
   legislation. *See* legislation
   mixed enterprises, 198
   owner of business enterprises,
      198
   ownership, 216
   partner with business,
      198–199
   politics. *See* politics
   prescriber of business rules,
      195
   presence of, 8
   private business activity,
      198–200
   private property, 24–25
   privatization, 206
   promoter and subsidizer of
      business, 198
   protecting rights of owners,
      220
   public-private partnership
      (PPP), 198, 199
   regulation and legislation. *See*
      government regulation

role of, 33–34
scope of government-business relationships, 198–202
stakeholder, as, 50, 178, 281*tab*
stakeholders, 52
government regulation
advertising, of, 32
arguments for, 193
business, of, 194–196
competitors, of, 246
corporate social responsibility, 198–199
described, 198
economic freedoms, and, 26
impact of changing involvement, 206
mandated self-regulation, 194
scope of, 198–202
whistle-blowing provisions, 119
government sector, 9
government-owned corporations, 9, 196, 215–216
Graduation Pledge of Social and Environmental Responsibility, The, 344
Grameen Bank, 319, 320
Great Canadian Oil Sands (GCOS), 356
greed, 11, **35**–36, 92
Greed Inc.: Why Corporations Rule Our World and How We Let It Happen, 265
Green Building Rating System, 294
green construction, 294
green consumer, 292
green marketing, **291**–292
green mutual funds, 244*tab*
Green Seal, 291
green supply chain management (GSCM), 289
green workplace, 293
greenhouse effect, 280, 283
greenhouse gases, 283
greening of business functions
described, 290
financial management, 290–291
green marketing, 291–292
human resources, 292–293
production, 293–295
Greenpeace Canada/International, 264, 277, 285, 308, 351
greenwashing, 154*tab*, **289**
Griffiths Energy International Inc., 316
Guardian News and Media, 268
Guardian, The, 169, 268

Guiding Principles for University Collaboration (CAUT), 188

Habitat for Humanity, 154*tab*
Harrelson, Woody, 294
Harrison, Hunter, 53
Haskayne School of Business, 185, 347
Health Canada, 210, 349
Heritage Foundation, The, 27
Heritage Institute, The, 26–27
Hermes Birkin, 304
Hewitt Associates, 240
Hewlett-Packard (Canada) Co., 11
Hillary, Sir Edmund, 105
Hillwatch.com, 269
HireUp, 263
historical example, 138*tab*
holistic corporate sustainability, 141
Holy Land Experience, 271
Home Depot Canada Foundation, 263
honesty, 59
Hope Network, 263
How Government Support for Social Enterprise can Reduce Poverty and Green House Gases, 270
How the Grinch Stole Christmas, 302
Hudson's Bay Company, 9
Human Development Index, 298
human resources
greening of business functions, 292–293
multinational corporations, 314
human rights, 96, 112, **316**
poverty, 317
Humane Society of Canada, 257
Humber Environmental Action Group, 367
Humber Natural History Society, 367
Husky Energy Inc., 174
Conflict of Interest Policy, 115
hybrid corporation/organization, 327, 332

IAMGOLD Corporation, 198
IBM Canada, 20
ideological example, 138*tab*
Imagine Canada, 95, 139, 156, 169
immoral model, 120*tab*
Impact Reporting and Investment Standards (IRIS), 336
Impakt, 333

Imperial Oil Ltd., 144–145, 157, 358
In Good Company, 265
incineration, 294
income inequality, 22, 23
Income Mobility: The Rich and Poor in Canada, 270
income tax, 195
corporate, 202
Inconvenient Truth, An, 283
incorporation, 9–10, 194
independent director, **223**
Indigo, 150
indirect owners, 14, 215–216
individual activists, 220
individual agreement, 137*tab*
individual morals, 89
individual rights ethic, **96**
individualism, **26**–27
industrial democracy, 27
industrial design, 25
industrial espionage, 30
industrial property, 194
industries
Canadian mining industry, 76–77, 198
environmental codes and standards, 296
main issues, selected industries, 55
petroleum, 198
self-regulatory organizations, 194
industry associations, 90, 220
Industry Canada, 199
industry organizations, 90, 220
industry self-regulation, 194
inequality, 27
inequities in society, 11
inflation rate, 26
influence pathway, **75**
influence peddling, 114*tab*
influence strategies, 75–77, 76*tab*
Information Technology Association, 196
innovation, 12
Inquiry into the Nature and Causes of the Wealth of Nations, An, 8, 90
Inside Guide, 265
insider trading, 11, 124
Institute for Management Development, 310
Institute for Research on Public Policy, 269
institutional activists, 220
integrated circuit topography, 25
Integrated Market Enforcement Team, 220
integrity, **4**–6, 5*tab*, 16–17

Integrity Framework, 196, 197
integrity management, 121
integrity-based ethics programs, 121, 122*tab*
intellectual property, **25**, 194
interest groups, 200, 258
internal stakeholders, 44, 52
International Centre for Settlement of Investment Disputes (ICSID), 352
International Code of Ethics for Canadian Business, 181, 310, 311
International Council of Toy Industries, 250
International Cyanide Management Code, 351
International Ethics Standards Board for Accountants (IESBA), 46
international exchange, 26
International Institute for Management Development, 310
International Institute for Sustainable Development (IISD), 282, 296
International Labour Organization (ILO), 309
International Monetary Fund (IMF), 307, 309, 310
international non-governmental organizations (INGOs), **308**–309
International Organization for Standardization (ISO), 130, 181, 296
Internet, social media, 265
internet forums, 13
inventory approach, 175
investing, responsible, 216–219, 217*tab*
investment funds, 215
Investment Industry Regulatory Organization of Canada (IIROC), 119, 220
investor activists, 214
investors, 213*tab*, 215, 219–221
invisible hand concept, 8
involvement. *See* corporate social responsibility (CSR)
Ipsos Reid, 142
ISO 9001, 353
ISO 14000, 296
ISO 14001, 143, 296, 353
ISO 14064, 287, 296
ISO 14065, 296
ISO 26000, 130, 181
ISO 50001, 296
ISO CSR Reporting Standards, 181
issue life cycles, 56–57, 57*fig*
issue salience matrix, 81*fig*

issues
  analysis of issues, 56
  approaches used by corporations, 58*tab*
  defined, **55**
  environmental issues. *See* environmental issues
  globalization, 307
  identification of issues, 56
  main issues, selected industries, 55
  non-governmental organizations (NGOs), 259*tab*
  ownership issues. *See* ownership issues
issues management
  analysis of issues, 56, 79
  approaches used by corporations, 58*tab*
  benefits of, 56
  defined, **56**
  evaluating response, 80
  formulating issue response, 56, 80
  identification of issues, 56, 79
  implementation of issue response, 57, 80
  issue life cycles, 56–57
  monitoring and evaluating issue response, 57, 80
  prioritizing of issue, 80
  process, 56–57, 79–80
  purposes of, 56
  ranking of issue, 80
  support for, 56
Ivey Business School, 139
Ivey Connects, 344
Ivey Foundation, 264

J. W. McConnell Family Foundation, 159
Jantzi Social Index, 177, 218
Jantzi-Sustainalytics Canada Social Investment Database, 177
Jarislowsky Fraser Ltd., 220
job sharing, 236*tab*
John Labatt Ltd., 157
John Molson School of Business, 185
Johnson & Johnson, 306
joint-venture participants, 47
Journal of Corporate Citizenship, 144
Junior Achievement, 2, 160
justice
  ethic of, 97–98
  principles of, 6
Juvenile Diabetes, 143

K.C. Irving Group, 267
KAIROS-Canada, 313
Kaler's gradations of self-interest and morality, 93*fig*
Kant, Immanuel, 7*tab*
Kelloggs, 255
Kennedy, Robert F., Jr., 367
Kentucky Fried Chicken, 255
KFC, 75, 255
kickbacks, 11, 112
Kijiji, 326
Kimberley Process, The, 198, 224
Kinross Gold Corporation, 174, 316
Kohlberg's stages of moral development, 100–101, 100*tab*
KPMG, 142
KPMG Social Economy Fund, 343
Kramer, Mark R., 17
Kruger Inc., 264
Kyoto Agreement/Protocol, 297

Labatt Brewery Company, 39–40
labour, 112
labour unions as stakeholders, 45
laissez-faire capitalism, **8**
laissez-faire market regulation, 33, 193
Lance Armstrong Foundation, The, 94
large retail development, 69
latent stakeholders, 73*tab*
Laurentian Bank of Canada, 202
Leadership in Energy and Environmental Design (LEED), 294
leadership models, 120*tab*
"Leave for Change" initiative, 162
legal creator, 138*tab*
legal recognition, 137*tab*
legal responsibilities, 140
legal system
  ethical behaviour and, 90
  government and, 50
legislation. *See also* government regulation; regulation; self-regulation
  competition, 29, 90
  corporate social responsibility, 198–199
  environmental issues, 284–285
  National Instrument 58–101, 224
  prescribed rules, 196
legitimacy, **10**, 72, 131
lenders, 46
level playing field, 34
Lewenza, Ken, 355, 356

Lewis, David, 206
Lewis, Phillip, 87
libel chill, **266**
liberal market capitalism, 34
light of day test, 114
LinkedIn, 13
Lions Club, 49
listeriosis, 361–362
Livestrong, 94
Living Our Values 2015 Performance, 268
Living Our Values: Sustainability Report 2015, 268
lobbying, 200–202
Lobbying Act, 201
Lobbyists' Code of Conduct, 201
Loblaw Companies Limited, 83–84, 150, 254
Locke, John, 7*tab*
Lomborg, Bjorn, 297
Lorax, The, 302
loss prevention, 233
Love Canal, 280
low priority stakeholders, 68
  strategies for, 69
loyalty, 234, 236–237

Maclean's, 16, 84, 169, 182, 235, 365
Magna International Inc., 53
Maior, Alburnus, 351
majority shareholders, 214
management and managers
  approach to stakeholders, 52–54
  employees' political involvement, on, 199
  management and leadership models, 120*tab*
  operation of business, and, 15–16
  owners as, 213*tab*
  response to NGOs, 261
  responses to environmental concerns, 288–289
  responsibility for ethics, 119–120
  stakeholders, as, 52–54
  understanding stakeholder relations. *See* stakeholder relations
  view of social and environmental responsibilities, 328–331
Management Ethics, 180
management information circular, **225**
management of ethics. *See* ethics management
management proxy circular, 225, 231

managerial discretion, 131, 132*tab*
managers
  employees, as, 45
  views on ethics, 11
  views on social responsibility, 11
Manulife Code of Conduct, 110–111
Manulife Financial, Code of Business Conduct and Ethics, 110–111
Maple Leaf Foods Inc., 361–362
marginal stakeholder, strategies for, 69, 70, 71
Marine Stewardship Council, 291
Maritime Electric Company Limited, 366
market-driven environmentalism, 286–288
market-driven learning, 273–274
market environmentalism, **286**, 287*tab*
market restrictions, 248
market share, 245
market system, 23
marketing
  cause-related marketing, 159
  charity, vs., 163
  green marketing, 291–292
Marketplace, 265
marketplace and consumers, 241–242
Marriott, 340
MaRS Centre for Impact Investing, 332
Marshall, Stanley, 367, 368
matrix mapping, **67**–70
McAfee, Ted, 61
McCain Capital Corporation, 362
McCain, Michael, 362
McConnell Foundation, 335
McDonald's, 150, 255
McGillivary, Ed, 360
McGuinty, Dalton, 354
McKinsey & Company, 135
McKinsey Global Institute, 28
media
  balance, 266
  bias, 266
  business-media relations, 264–265, 266*tab*
  centralization, 267
  changes in attitude toward business, 266–267
  corporate social responsibility (CSR), 268
  corporate social responsibility (CSR) reporting, 178
  fragmentation, 267
  freedom of the press, and corporate ownership, 267

influence of, 12, 265
influence on ethical behaviour, 90–91
information source, as, 185
libel chill, 266
ownership of, 267
social media, 265
specialization, 268
stakeholder, as, 49, 264–265
Media Carta, 267
media exposure, 266–267, 267
media spin, 266
membership rights, 25
Memorial University of Newfoundland Student Union, 39–40
mergers, 246
Metanexus Institute, The, 270
Metro Inc., 254
Michael Clayton, 118
Michaud, Yves, 220
microfinance, **319**
Microsoft Canada, 262
Mill, John Stuart, 7*tab*
Millenials, 31–32
   work ethic, 31–32
Millenium Ecosystem Assessment, 298
Mine Your Own Business, 351
minimum wages, 23
Mining Association of Canada, 198, 363
mining industry, 76–77, 350–352, 362–364
   Canadian, 12, 350–352, 362–364
MiningWatch, 265, 351
minority shareholders, 214
Mintzberg, Henry, 52
misleading advertising, 9, 195, 242
misleading financial statements, 11
misleading guarantees/ warranties, 242
misrepresentation, 9
mission, 90
mistrust, 36
misuse of shareholders' money, 11
mixed blessing stakeholder, strategies for, 69, 70, 71
Mobius loop, 291
Mocal Energy Limited, 358
Molson Coors Brewing Company, 171
monetary policy, 26
money laundering, 196, 197
MoneySense, 157
monological approach, 121
monopolistic competition, 9

monopoly, 195, 246, 276
   media ownership, 267
Montreal, Maine and Atlantic Railway, 12
moonlighting, 40, 114*tab*
   employee, 236*tab*
Moore, Michael, 12
moral awareness, 101
moral development stages, 100–101, 100*tab*
moral gratitude/reciprocity, 138*tab*
moral model, 120*tab*
moral reasoning, **98**–101
moral standards, **88**, 91*tab*
morality, 6
morality of Canadian business
   diversity of business interests, 9
   government presence, 8
   influencing factors, 7–9
   stakeholders influencing, 12–14
Morgan, Gwyn, 358–360
Mothers Against Drunk Driving (MADD Canada), 258–259
Mount Everest, 104–105
Mountain Equipment Co-op (MEC), 3, 173, 216
movies, 12, 118, 265
Muhlhauser, Craig, 133
multi-level marketing plan, 242
multinational corporations, 313–314
   See also globalization
Munk, Peter and Joan, 343
Murray, Wayne, 364–366
Murphy Oil Company Ltd., 358
Murphy's Pharmacies, 349
mutual company, 217
mutual funds, **213**, 215, 217
   defined, 213*tab*
   ethical, 244*tab*
   green, 244*tab*
   ownership through, 215
Mutual funds, responsible investment, 218
Mutual Funds Dealers Association of Canada (MFDA), 119, 220

Nader, Ralph, 206, 241
national culture, 90
National Energy Board, 195, 335
National Instrument 51–102, 290
National Instrument 58–101, 224, 227, 228
National Policy (1890s), 33
National Post, 22, 23, 136, 265
National Post Business, 265

National Roundtable on Corporate Social Responsibility, 199
Natural Resources Canada, 199
Natural Resources Defense Council (NRDC), 367
nature, 282
Nature Conservancy, The, 264
Navigable Waters Protection Act, 362, 363
Navistar International, 353
negotiated settlement, 197
Neighbourhood Pharmacy Association of Canada, 348
Nemeth, Jack, 133
Nestle, 340
Net Generation, 31
Network for Business Sustainability (NBS), 139, 167, 179, 240, 250, 263, 289, 296, 329, 342
New Democratic Party, 364
Newfoundland and Labrador Public and Private Employees, 39
Newfoundland Power Inc., 366
News Corporation, The, 268
New El Dorado, 351
newspapers, 268
Nexen Inc., 174, 358
NGOs. *See* non-governmental organizations (NGOs)
NGOWatch.org, 262
Nike, 94
Nobel Peace Prize, 319
non-governmental organizations (NGOs), 215
   activist or advocacy groups, 90
   case for and against NGOs, 261–262
   corporate social responsibility (CSR) reporting, 178
   defined, **48**, **259**
   describing, 258–260
   environmental non-governmental organizations (ENGOs), 285, 286
   evaluation of CSR programs, 155
   globalization, 261
   international non-governmental organizations (INGOs), 308–309
   issues relevant to business, 259*tab*
   owners, as, 215
   partnerships relationships with, 262–264
   societal influences on ethics, 90–91
   stakeholder map, on, 66

stakeholders, as, 48, 178, 281*tab*
   strategies for relationship with, 261–262, 262*tab*
   tactics, 260
   World Trade Organization (WTO), and, 306
non-profit corporation/ organization, 327, 332*tab*
non-profit sector, 9
non-public corporation, 216
non-supportive stakeholder, strategies for, 69, 70, 71
non-tariff barriers, 194
non-voting shares, **214**
nonstakeholder, 74*tab*
Norcen Energy, 359
normative stakeholder, 52
Nortel, 20
North American Free Trade Agreement (NAFTA), 196, 246
North West Company Inc., 221
not-for-profit organization ownership, 215
not-for-profit organizations, 215
Novartis Pharmaceuticals Corporation, 162
Novex Couriers, 143

oaths, 341
Obama, Barack, 23
Oberhelman, Douglas, 356
"objectionable" funds, 220
OECD Guidelines for Multinational Enterprises, 181, 313, 351
OECD Principles of Corporate Governance, 222, 223
Office of the Privacy Commissioner of Canada, 14
offsets, **287**, 289
oil sands, 2
oligopoly, **29**, 195
Olympic Games, 307
Onex Corporation, 53
online behavioural advertising, 14
Ontario Catapult Microloan Fund, 335
Ontario College of Trades, 67
Ontario Securities Commission (OSC), 119, 220, 290
Ontario Teachers' Pension Plan Board, 362
Open Society Institute, 351
"Operation Kabriole", 358–360
operations and greening of business functions, 293–295
Oprah Winfrey Network, 94
organic foods, 243

Organization for Economic Co-operation and Development (OECD), 110, 181, 202, 222, 306, 313, 315, 351
Organization of American States, 315
organizational ethics, 89–91
outlay approach, 175
outside employment, 114*tab*
overclaiming credit, 101
owners
  categories of, 14
  corporate ownership, 217
  customers as, 215
  defined, **44**
  direct owners, 14, 212–214
  employees as, 213*tab*, 214
  entrepreneurs, 213*tab*
  ethics and responsibility issues of ownership. *See* ownership
  government ownership, 216
  indirect owners, 14, 215–216
  individual, direct ownership, 213*tab*
  individual, indirect ownership, 215–216
  investors, 213*tab*
  managers, as, 213*tab*
  media, ownership of, 267
  mutual funds, through, 215
  non-profit organization ownership, 215
  ownership of Canadian business, 212
  pension funds, through, 215
  private equity firms, 213*tab*
  producers as, 215
  protection of, 219–221
  responsible investing, 216–219, 217*tab*
  stakeholders, 52
  stakeholders, as, 44
  venture capital companies, 213*tab*
ownership issues
  accountability, 214–216
  dual-class stock, 214
  employee ownership, 214
  minority vs majority shareholders, 214
  passive vs active shareholders, 214
  widely held vs concentrated ownership, 213–214
Oxfam Canada/International, 215, 252, 261, 308, 319, 320
ozone, **282**
ozone layer, 280

PAAC Statement of Ethical Principles, 205
Pagano model, 114
paradoxical environmentalism, 298
Parents For French, 49
partnerships, 9
passive shareholders, **214**
patents, 25
payday loans, 46
PeaceWorks Technology Solutions, 333
peer-to-peer e-commerce, 336
peers, 90
Pembina Pipeline Corporation, 223
pension funds, 213*tab*, 217
  responsible investment, 218
pension plans, 215, 236*tab*
People for the Ethical Treatment of Animals (PETA), 74, 258
people's capitalism, 35
performance representation, 242
Perkins + Will Canada Architects Co., 297
personal conduct, 115*tab*
Personal Information Protection and Electronic Documents Act (PIPEDA), 14, 33, 239
personal view of social responsibility, 137
personal virtues ethic, 94–95
PETA (People for the Ethical Treatment of Animals), 74, 258
Petitcodiac Riverkeeper, 367
Petro-Canada, 358
Pew Environmental Group International Boreal Conservation Campaign, 264
philanthrocapitalism, **337**
Philanthropic Foundations Canada (PFC), 159
philanthropic responsibilities, 140
plagiarism, 20, 268
Plagiarism.org, 20
Plan Canada, 198
planning for corporate social responsibilities, 155
plant breeders' rights, 25
plant closures, 2
Plato, 7*tab*
pledges, 341
Plener, Harley, 33
Plener, Jordan, 33
plural sector, 9
pluralistic society, **43**
policy development institution, **269**–270
political factors, 314
political globalization, **306**

political involvement, 199
political parties, 50, 199
politics
  business involvement in, 199–200
  executives running for public office, 199
  financing political parties, 199
  lobbying, 200–202
  management's position on employee participation, 199
  multinational corporations, and, 314
  publicly expressed support, 199
  publicly expressed views, 199
pollution, 280, 282, 294
Pollution Probe, 285
Ponzi schemes, 2, 12, 124, 198
Ponzi, Charles K., 12
popular media. *See* media
Porter, Michael E., 17
position-importance matrix, 68*fig*
post-employment, 115*tab*
Postmedia Network Inc., 267
Potash Corporation of Saskatchewan, 215, 263
potential conflict of interest, 115
poverty, 11, 317–318
  human rights, 317
power
  defined, 72
  stakeholders, of, 52
Power, Elaine, 353
power-focused ethics, 238
Prairie Paper Inc., 294
Prairie Pharmacy, 348–350
pre-conventional level, 100*tab*
predatory pricing, 246
prejudice, 101
prevalence of ethics in business, 101–102
price controls, 26
price discrimination, 248
price fixing, 9, 124
price maintenance, 248
primary interactions, 51
Principles for Global Corporate Responsibility, 313
principles of justice, 6
Principles of Responsible Management Education, 341
privacy, 234, 239
Privacy Act, 14
Privacy Commissioner of Canada, 33
private enterprise, 8
private equity firms, 214–216
private equity fund, 213
private property rights, 24–25

private sector, **327**
privatization, **196**, 206, 246
Probe International (PI), 367
problematic stakeholders, 68
  strategies for, 69
procedural justice, 97
process approach, 175
producer capitalism, 35
producer interest, 32
producer ownership, 215
producers, 213*tab*
Product Red Brand, 46
Production and greening of business functions, 293–295
professional associations, 90
profit-drive corporate sustainability, 141
profitability, CSR, and, 178–179
profits, **30**
  banking industry, 31
  motive, 7
  waste management, 294
program management, 175
Progress RailServices Corp., 353–356
Projects Abroad, 343
Propel Centre for Population Health Impact, 349
property rights, 26, 194, 260, 286, 287*tab*
  economic freedoms, 26
  first nations, 25
protection of owners and investors, 219–221
proxy circular disclosure report, 225
public affairs, 204–206
Public Affairs Association of Canada, 205
public interest, 32
public interest group, 258
public policy. *See also* government
  corporate agenda, 204–206
  corporate public affairs, 204–206
Public Policy Forum, 270
public policy implementation, 213*tab*
public-private partnership (PPP), 198, 199, **327**
public responsibility, 131
public sector, 9, **327**
PureWorld Botanicals, 323
pyramid selling, 242

quasi-egoism, 92
Quebecor Media Inc., 221, 267
Queen's School of Business, 142
Queen's University, 353
Quiznos, 128

quotas, 194

Rainforest Alliance, 252, 309
Rand, Ayn, 93
rationalization, 124
Rawls, John, 7*tab*
re-marketing, 14
real conflict of interest, 115
recession, 237
recycling, 244, 295
refusal to deal, 248
registered retirement savings plan (RRSP), 19
regulation
    advertising, self-regulation, 47
    compliance with environmental concerns, 289
    corporate self-discipline regulation, 194
    distributors, 47
    economic freedoms, and, 26
    forms of, 192–194
    franchisees, 47
    government regulation. *See* government regulation
    influence on ethical behaviour, 90
    laissez-faire market regulation, 193
    private business activity, of, 199–200
    producer interest, 32
    property rights vs., 287*tab*
    public interest, 32
    scope of, 199–200
    self-regulation. *See* self-regulation
    suppliers, 248
    taxi industry, 195
    types of regulation, 192–194
Reitmans (Canada) Limited, 232, 317
relationship management culture, 338
Reliance Retail Ltd., 323
religion, 90
religious activism, 272
religious groups, 48
religious institutions, 270–272
Renewable Energy and Clean Technology Index, 290
rent control, 195
Report on Business, 22, 265
Report on Business Magazine, 136
reputation management, 142, 144
Research in Motion (RIM), 189
Resolute Forest Products, 277
resource allocation, 11
resource dependence, **75**

responsibility of the corporation, 10
Responsible Care, 193, 194
responsible corporation, **4**
    defined, 4
responsible enterprise system, **8**
responsible investing, 216–219, 217*tab*
responsible investment, **216**, 217–219
    best-of-sector approach, 218
    criteria, 217
    motives, 218
    mutual funds, 218
    pension funds, 218
Responsible Investment Association, 216, 217
Responsible Management Education, 342, 343
responsive CSR, 338
restricted competition, 29
restricted shares, **214**
retail consumer cooperatives, 215
retail cooperatives, 215, 216
Retail Council of Canada, 207
retail sales tax, 195
Retirement Security for Everyone: Enhancing Canada's Pension System, 270
retributive justice, 97
reusing, 295
reusing materials, 295
Richard Ivey School of Business, 344
right of private property, **24**–25
right to due process, 234
risk-taking behaviour, 125
Roger & Me, 12, 265
Rogers Communications/Media/ Wireless, 95, 267
Roman Catholic Church, 270
Roman Catholic Pontifical Council for Justice and Peace, 271
Rosia Montana Gold Corporation S.A. (RMGC), 350–352
Rotary Club, 49
Rotary International, 49
    Guiding Principles, 49
Rotterdam Convention, 210
Rowe School of Business, 185
Royal Bank of Canada, 31, 180, 227, 282, 283
Royal Canadian Mounted Police, 220, 262, 304, 305, 358–360
rule of law, 112, 260
rule-based theory of ethics, **6**, 7*tab*

S&P/TSX Clean Technology Index, 290

Safeway Canada, 254
salience, 72–81, 81*fig*
Salt Spring Coffee, 333
Salvation Army, 326
SAM Group, 142
Sandy Pond, 363, 364
Sarbanes-Oxley Act, 119, 220
Savalot Enterprises, 352
say-on-pay, **225**, 231
Scanner Price Accuracy Voluntary Code, 207
Schulich School of Business, 185, 218
Schwartz, Gerald, 53
science, 314
Scotiabank, 221
Sea Shepherd Conservation Society, 258
Seagrams, 337
Securities Exchange Commission (SEC), 220
SEE-IT (Social-Environmental-Economic Integration Toolkit), 143
self-censorship, 266
self-dealing, 114*tab*
self-delusion, 124
self-interest, 11, 35, 92, 124
self-interest ethic, **92**–93
self-regulation, 112
    advertising, 47
    corporate self-discipline regulation, 194
    criticism of, 194
    defined, **194**
    industry self-regulation, 194
    involving stakeholders, 194
    mandated self regulation, 194
self-regulatory organizations (SROs), 220
service associations, 49
service learning, **343**
service professionals, 46–47, 178
share ownership vs control, 214
shared economy, **336**
shareholder activism, 45
Shareholder Association for Research and Education (SHARE), 220, 231
shareholder democracy, 45, **219**
shareholder resolution, 214
shareholders
    active shareholders, 214
    corporate social responsibility (CSR) reporting, 177
    dual-class stock, 214
    majority shareholders, 214
    minority shareholders, 214
    non-voting shares, 214
    owners of Canadian business, of, 212

protection of, 219–221
    restricted shares, 214
    rights, 214, 221–222
    stakeholders, 52
shares, 214
Sharp, David, 104–105
Shaw Communications Inc., 267
Shell Canada Limited, 288
Sherritt International Corporation, 221
shoplifting, 233, 234
Shoppers Drug Mart, 150, 254
showcase environmentalism, 298
Sierra Club of Canada, 364, 367
Silkwood, 118
Simpsons, The, 265
Skeptical Environmentalist, The (Lomberg), 297
Skoll, Jeff, 337
small business
    corporate social responsibility practices, 166–168
    developing countries, and, 320
    taxation, 203
Small Business Magazine, 265
Small Investor Protection Association, 220
Small Shareholder Protection Association, 231
Smith, Adam, 7, 8, 19, 90
SNC-Lavalin Group Inc., 12, 135, 197, 221, 316
Sneetches, The, 302
Sobey School of Business, 185
Sobeys, 254
social auditing
    approaches, 175
    corporate social responsibility (CSR) reporting. *See* corporate social responsibility
    criteria, 179–181
    defined, 174
    future of, 185–186
    Global Reporting Initiative (GRI), 180–181
    sustainability reporting, for, 175
social capital, **338**
Social Capital Partners, 164
social conscience investment, 217
social contract, 138*tab*
Social Dimension of Globalization, 310
social dimensions of competitive context, 338
Social Economy Initiative, 343
social enterprise, 27, 165–168, 331–332
    non-profit sustainability matrix, 333–334

types of, 332*tab*

Social Enterprise Council of Canada (SECC), 331

social entrepreneur, 165–168

social entrepreneurship, **165**

social globalization, **307**

social impact, 138*tab*

social impact investing, **336**

social impact management, **142**

social indicators, 175

social innovation, **335**

Social Innovation Fund, 335

social interpenetration, 138*tab*

social involvement. *See* corporate social responsibility (CSR)

social issues, 340–341

social licence, **10**, 334–335

social market, 54

social market economy, 34

social media, **13**–14, 239, 265

social networking, 31, 32

social objective setting, 175

social paradigm, 153, 154

social permission, 138*tab*

social responsibility, 2, 3, 130, 132, 273

  See also corporate social responsibility (CSR)

social responsibility accounting, 175

social responsibility theories
  amoral view, 136–137, 137*tab*
  personal view, 137
  social view, 137–138, 138*tab*

social responsible investing, 336

Social Return on Investment (SROI), 336

social sector, **327**

social spending transfers, 23

Social Venture Partners, 164, 165

social venture philanthropy, **164**

social view of social responsibility, 137–138, 138*tab*

socialization of capitalism, **326**, 327

socially responsible investment, 216

society
  approaches to viewing social responsibilities, 328–331
  attitudes toward business, 11–14
  civil society. *See* civil society
  complexities of business and society, 3–4
  corporate social responsibility (CSR) reporting, 178
  ethical behaviour, 90–91
  globalization, and, 310–313
  inequities, 11

integration of business and, 17

permission for business, 10

pluralistic society, 43

stakeholder, as, 48, 178

Society for the Prevention of Cruelty to Animals, 257

sociocultural objectives and values, 314

sodium, 255–256

Softchoice, 235

sole proprietors, 9

Solegear Bioplastics Inc., 297

Solomon, Robert, 7*tab*

sour gas, 358

special interest group, 255, 258

spiritual capital, 270

spirituality, **272**

sponsorship, 162–163

St. Anne-Nackawic Pulp Company, 20

St. John's Bakery, 165

stages of moral development, 100–101, 100*tab*

stakeholder analysis, 65–66
  approaches to, 66
  worksheet, 66*tab*

stakeholder capitalism, **8**, 35

stakeholder engagement, **65**, 78–79

stakeholder influence strategies, 75–77, 76*tab*

stakeholder management, 65
  See also stakeholder relations, understanding

stakeholder management capability, **66**, 67

stakeholder relations, understanding
  approaches to, 66
  basic stakeholder analysis, 65–66
  corporate-stakeholder relations, 78*tab*
  diagnostic typology of organizational stakeholders, 70–72
  Freeman's stakeholder management capability, 66–67
  jobs in, 67
  matrix mapping, 67–70
  salience, 72–75
  stakeholder collaboration, 77–79
  stakeholder identification, 72–75
  stakeholder influence strategies, 75–77, 76*tab*
  stakeholder typology, 72–75, 73*fig*

stakeholders, 2
  animals as, 50

antagonistic stakeholders, 68

argument for stakeholder concept, 54

bank ATM fees, 71

bankers, 36

boards of directors, 14–15

business organizations, 47

Canadian mining industry, 76–77

categorizing, 52, 68–70

cell phone towers and, 80

charities, 49

civil society. *See* civil society

collaboration, 77–79

competitors, 47

concept, 43–44

conflict, 52

consultation with, 175

consumer interest groups, 52

consumers, 36, 177, 240–244, 280*tab*

corporate governance, and, 228

corporate reputation, 44

corporate social responsibility (CSR) accountability, and, 177–178

corporate social responsibility (CSR) reporting, and, 176, 177–178

corporations, and, 52, 78*tab*

creditors, 46, 52, 280*tab*

customers or consumers, 45–46, 280*tab*

dangerous, 74*tab*

dealers, 46

defined, 5*tab*, 44

definitive, 74*tab*

demanding, 73*tab*

dependent, 74*tab*

derivative, 52

differing goals and power, 52

directors, 44–45

discretionary, 73*tab*

distributors, 46

dominant, 73*tab*

dormant, 73*tab*

educational institutions, 48, 272–274

employees, 45, 52, 177, 234–240, 280*tab*

environmental issues. *See* environmental issues

expectant stakeholders, 73–74*tab*

external, 44, 52

financial crisis, 36

financial institutions, 177

franchisees, 47

government, 29, 36, 50, 52, 178, 281*tab*

antagonistic stakeholders, 68

identification of, 44–50, 72–75

influence strategies, 75–77, 76*tab*

influence, dynamics of, 51–52

influence, variations in, 52, 177–178

internal, 44, 52

investment dealers, 36

joint-venture participants, 47

key relationships, 234

labour unions, 45

large retail development, and, 69

latent stakeholders, 73*tab*

lenders and creditors, 46

low priority stakeholders, 68

managers, 15–16, 52–54

marginal stakeholder and strategy, 70

media as information source, 194

media. *See* media

mixed blessing stakeholder and strategy, 70

monitoring responsible investment, 220

multinational corporations, 314

non-governmental organizations (NGOs). *See* non-governmental organizations

nonstakeholder, 74*tab*

nonsupportive stakeholder and strategy, 70

opposition to stakeholder concept, 54

owners, 52

pluralistic society, 51

policy development institution (think tank), 269–270

potential for threat or cooperation, 70–71, 71*fig*

problematic stakeholders, 68

protecting rights of owners, 220

regulators, 36

relations. *See* stakeholder relations, understanding

religious groups/institutions, 48, 270–272

responsible for operation of Canadian business, 14–16

self-regulation, 194

service professionals, 46–47, 178, 281*tab*

service/fraternal/cultural/ ethnic associations, 49

shareholders, 52, 177, 280*tab*

social responsibility function, 138*tab*

society at large, 48, 178

suppliers, 46, 52, 247–249, 280*tab*

supply chains, 250

supporter stakeholders, 68

supportive stakeholder and strategy, 70

types of, 73–74*tab*

typology, 72–75, 73–74*tab*

standard environmentalism, **286**, 287*tab*

standard of living, 11

Standards for Professional Responsibility, 112

Standards of Practice, 109

Standards of Professional Conduct, 109

state capitalism, **35**

statement of values, 108–109

stereotyping, 101

stewardship, 130

stock exchanges, 220

stock manipulation, 9, 11

Stone's Drug Store, 349

strategic giving, **159**

Strategic Lawsuits Against Public Participation (SLAPP), 277

strategic management, **331**

    See also CSR strategy

Student Car Share, 336

student volunteerism, 343

students and sustainability, 343–344

Students Without Borders, 343, 344

Subway Restaurants Canada, 127–128

Sun Life Financial Inc., 202, 227, 314

Suncor Energy Inc., 67, 174, 215, 356–358

Super Size Me, 265

supplier discrimination, 9

suppliers, 247–249

    influencing, 247

    regulation, 248

    socially responsible, 46

    stakeholders, 52

    stakeholders, as, 46, 280*tab*

    supply chain and, 247–249

supply chain, **249–252**

    defined, 249

    fair trade, 251–252

    global, 249–250

    green, 289

    stages in, 249*fig*

    stakeholders, 250

    suppliers and, 247–249

    sustainability purchasing, 251

Supply Chain Management Association (SCMA), 248

supporter stakeholders, 68

strategies for, 69

supportive stakeholder, strategies for, 69, 70, 71

supranational institution, **309**

sustainability, 130

    business programs and, 341–344

    corporate, 141–142

    indices, 290

    justification for CSR, 339*fig*

    measures, 295–297

    newspaper and, 268

    purchasing, 251

    reporting. *See* corporate social responsibility reporting

    students and, 343–344

sustainability indices, 290

sustainability measures, 295–297

sustainability purchasing, **251**

Sustainability Purchasing Network, 251

sustainability reporting. *See* corporate social responsibility (CSR) reporting

Sustainability Reporting Guidelines, 180–181

sustainability stewardship, 130

sustainability strategy

    amoral, 328*fig*, 330*tab*

    business programs and, 341–344

    characteristics of, 328*fig*, 330*tab*

    compliance-based, 329*fig*, 330*tab*

    comprehensive, 329*fig*, 330*tab*

    defined, **328–331**

    emerging, 329*fig*, 330*tab*

    establishment of objectives, 334–335

    ethics programs for business schools, 341–342

    evaluation of, 339–340

    implementation of, 339–340

    purpose of, 329

    strategic management, 331

    students and, 343–344

    teaching ethics in business schools, 341–342

sustainable capitalism, **339**

sustainable development, **282**, 289

Sustainable Development Goals, 317, 318

sustainable guidelines, 175

sustainable organizational culture, 338

sustainable pay, 53

sustainable supply management, 274

Sustainalytics/Jantzi Social Index, 218

Swap Working Holidays, 336

Swapsity, 336

sweatshop labour abuses, 316–317

Syncrude Canada, 358

synergistic corporate sustainability, 141

takeovers, 246

Talisman Energy Inc., 90, 174

tariffs, 194

Taskforce on the Churches and Corporate Responsibility of Canada, 313

tax credits, 202

tax information exchange agreements, 202

tax loss carry forward, 202

taxation, 25

    economic freedoms, 26

    personal, 204

    small business enterprises, 203

taxation evasion, 26

taxi industry, regulation, 195

TD Bank Group, 23, 31, 151, 235, 290, 314

TD Grade One Book Giveaway, 151

technology, 239, 246, 314

Teck Resources Limited, 3, 174, 215, 297, 314, 316

Telegram, The, 368

teleological theory of ethics, **6**, 7*tab*

television programs, 12

Telfer School of Management, 344

Telus Corporation, 3, 160

terror-free gas, 244*tab*

Tesco PLC, 323

The Big One, 12

The Coffeepot, 64–65

The Corporation: The Pathological Pursuit of Profit and Power, 265

The Informant, 118

The Insider, 118

The Rainmaker, 118

Theory of Moral Sentiments (Smith), 8

Thierer, Mark, 53

think tank, 269–270

Third Sector, 9

Thomson Reuters Canada Limited, 235

Three Mile island, 280

Tides Foundation, 164

tied selling, 248

Tim Hortons, 3

tipping, 209

token response, 289

tokenism, 154*tab*

Top 50 Socially Responsible Corporations, 84, 169, 182

Toronto Police Services, 262

Toronto Public Health, 361–362

Toronto Stock Exchange (TSX), 214, 220, 290, 350, 362

    Toronto-Dominion Bank, 314

    See also TD Bank

Torstar Corp., 267

Toyota, 2

"Towards Sustainable Mining (TSM)", 363

TRACE International, 316

trade barriers, 261

trade-offs, 3

trade trends, 251–252

trademarks, 25

traditional shareholders model, 137*tab*

tragedy of the commons, 281

Traidcraft, 252, 319

Training. *See* ethics training

Trans-Pacific Partnership (TPP), 246

transaction costs, 261

TransAlta Corp., 133, 290

TransCanada, 133

transfer pricing, **202**

transfer pricing arrangement, 203

"Transformational CSR Framework and Approach" (CBSR), 179

transition-and-transformation, 186

transnational non-government organizations (TNGOs), 308

transnational social movement organizations (TSMOs), 308

transparency, 10, 225–226

    for-benefit corporation, 332

Transparency International (TI), 314

transportation industry, 33

Trek, 94

triple-E (economic, ethical and environmental) bottom line, 5*tab*, 130

    defined, 5*tab*, **143**

    reporting, 175

triple-P bottom line (profits, people, and planet), 5*tab*, 143

trust, 36, 81

tsunami in Japan, 280

Tucingo, Homobonus, 48

Turnitin.com, 20

turnover, 236

    employee, 236

Twitter, 13, 65

U.S. Internal Revenue Service, 203
U.S. -Canada Free Trade Agreement, 196
Uber, 195
UN Global Compact, 181, 306, 313, 341
uncommon shares, 214
understanding stakeholder relations. *See* stakeholder relations, understanding
unemployment
    attitudes and, 12
    defined, 12
    Employment Insurance payments, 31
unemployment insurance, 31
union contracts, 90
unions, 27, 234
United Nations, 315
United Nations Convention on Climate Change (UNFCC), 284, 285
United Nations Global Compact, 181, 306, 313, 341, 351
United Nations Millennium Development Goals, 317, 318
United Nations World Commission on Environment and Development, 282
United States Anti-Doping Agency (USADA), 94
United Way, 143, 160
United Way of Saskatoon and Area, 67
Uniterra Program, 162
Universal Declaration of Human Rights, 96, 267, 316
universal rules ethic, **96**
University of British Columbia, 274, 343, 344
University of Calgary, 203
University of Guelph, 273
University of Northern British Columbia, 343
University of Ottawa, 344
University of Vermont, 292
University of Waterloo, 349
unrelated director, **223**
Up in the Air, 265

Urban Food, 168
Urban Systems, 235
urgency, 72
US Environmental Protection Agency, 291
usage strategies, **75**
usage strategy, **75**
use of employer's property, 114*tab*
utilitarian ethic, **95**–96, 138*tab*
utilitarian social-view theory, 95–96, 138*tab*
utilitarianism, 6
utility boards, 195

Vae, 363, 364
value chain, 249
    See also supply chain
value chain social issues, 340
value judgments, **88**, 91*tab*
Value Village, 154tab, 244*tab*, 326
values, 147
    defined, 334
    statement of, 108–109, 334
values statements, 90
values-based approaches, 121–122, 122*tab*
Vancouver City Savings Credit Union (Vancity), 3, 173–174, 216
VBA model, 147–148, 148tab
Vegetarians International Voice for Animals, 258
veil of ignorance test, 6
ventilation test, 114
venture capital company, **213**
venture capitalists, 164
Verdun, Robert, 220
virtue ethics, **6**, 7*tab*
virtue-based social-view theory, 138*tab*
vision, 90, 334
Volkswagen (VW), 12, 129–130, 135
voluntarism, 160–162
Voluntary Principles on Security and Human Rights, 198

voluntary sector, 327
volunteering, 343

wage controls, 26
Wal-Mart Canada, 69, 271, 323
Wal-Mart: The High Cost of Low Prices, 265
Walker, Donald, 53
Wall Street, 36, 265
Wall Street: Money Never Sleeps, 36
Walmart, 150, 254
Walmart Watch, 260, 265
waste management, 280, **282**, 294
water quality, 282
Watersense, 291
Wealth by Stealth: Crime, Corporate Law, and the Perversion of Democracy, 265
Wealth of Nations, 8, 90
webcasts, 13
websites, 13
welfare payments, 235
West Virginia University, 12
Western University, 139, 344
Whistleblower Protection Act, 119
whistleblowing, 117–119
white-collar workers, 45
Whitehorse Mining Initiative, 198
Whole Food Markets Inc., 45, 154*tab*, 243, 340
Whole Foods Supermarkets, 340
widely held ownership, 213–214
wildlife, 282
Wiebe, Ludwig, 359, 360
Wilfrid Laurier University, 292
withholding strategy, **75**
women directors, 223
Wood's principles of corporate social responsibility, 132*tab*
work ethic, **31**–32, 235–236
    Canadian, 236
    contemporary implications, 236*tab*
    Millenials, 31–32

worker capitalism, **214**
workforce reduction, 234
working conditions, 234
Workplace Centre for Spiritual and Ethical Development, 272
Workplace Code of Conduct, 250
workplace privacy, 234, 239
World Action on Salt and Health, 255
World Bank, 307, 309, 351, 352
World Commission on the Social Dimension of Globalization, 310
World Economic Forum, 23, 28, 144, 310–311, 313
World Health Organization (WHO), 171
World Trade Organization (WTO), 196, 246, 306, 307, 309, 310, 311
World University Service of Canada (WUSC), 162, 344
World Wildlife Fund, 263, 309
World Wildlife Fund Canada (WWF-Canada), 285
Wraight, Robert, 360
WSP Global, 314
WWF-Canada, 263

XL Foods Inc., 58

Yamana Gold, 174
Yertle the Turtle, 302
York and Smith Limited, 152, 153
York Construction, 152, 153
YouTube, 13
Yunus, Muhammad, 319

zero-tolerance policy, 234
Zerofootprint, 287
Zuckerberg, Mark, 337